ANTHROPOLOGY OF WEAKER SECTIONS

About the Editors

Dr. S.C. Sinha was director of Anthropological Survey of India. Later, he became vice-chancellor of Vishwabharati University. This project was conceived and implemented by him.

Dr. Ranjit Bhattacharya, the associate editor, is acting director of Anthropological Survey of India.

Dr. N.K. Das, Anthropologist, was associated with the analysis of the data.

ANTHROPOLOGY OF WEAKER SECTIONS

Editor
SURAJIT CHANDRA SINHA

Associate Editors
RANJIT BHATTACHARYA
N.K. DAS

Introduction by
K.S. SINGH

CONCEPT PUBLISHING COMPANY, NEW DELHI 110059

ISBN 81-7022-491-8

First Published 1993

Published and Printed by
Ashok Kumar Mittal
Concept Publishing Company
A/15-16, Commercial Block, Mohan Garden
NEW DELHI 110059 (India)

Lasertypeset by
Printing Express
H-13, Bali Nagar,
NEW DELHI 110015

INTRODUCTION

I

In the early 1970s the Anthropological Survey of India launched a national survey of the weaker sections of the populations in villages to (i) determine the social disabilities suffered by the weaker sections, (ii) spell out socio-economic and political constraints faced by them, (iii) assess the level of their access to the socio-political control institutions including control over land, and (iv) to find out why there has been only marginal improvement in the socio-economic conditions of these sections.

This study could be seen at two levels. First, it is a continuation of the village studies which have been undertaken since the 1950s. Such studies revolved around the studies of caste organisation, ranking of castes and their inter-relationship, the dominant caste etc. The present study has generated data on caste-wise ownership of land, distribution of landholding, population composition, occupational pattern, level of education, per capita annual income, indebtedness etc. At another level, the present study could be seen as the first anthropological study of the weaker sections, of their world view and ideology, their weak resource base, their deprivation and exploitation.

The survey was restricted to 24 villages, four of them in West Bengal, three in Uttar Pradesh, and one each from other states of "caste" India."Tribal" India and the Union Territories were left our for good reason, because the focus was on the weaker sections in caste society.

These studies tell us about the dominant caste in the village, its control over resources, its power base, its linkages. Earlier studies had identified dominant communities in various parts of the country. In large parts of peninsular Gujarat which fell outside the sway of "Brahmanical Hinduism" the Gujarat Vanias (Vaishyas including Jains) overshadowed the Brahmans in economic and political arenas for several centuries. In Punjab and its neighbouring regions the Jats have been the politically and economically dominant group. The Rajputs in several north Indian states remain the dominant communities in rural areas; the Thakurs, in the eastern regions of Uttar Pradesh, particularly constituted the most dominant group, politically and economically. There were a few regions which were the strongholds of Brahmans, the Maithili speaking region around Darbanga in Bihar, Brahman villages around Puri in Orissa and the settlement of the Desastha Brahmans of Maharashtra. A Brahman community, Maithi, could enjoy absolute political control by virtue of owning the largest proportion of land in Darbanga region.

The dominant communities consisting of the higher castes or higher middle castes control the resources in different parts of India. It was mainly through control over resources, particularly land that they derive their political power. The present study also identifies dominant castes but less in terms of the traditional higher castes and more in terms of the richer and more powerful sections of the intermediate castes.

We fed the data generated under this project into computer for analysis (See concluding remarks). In all 386 communities were covered under this study. Of them, 176 communities were identified as constituting the weaker sections. Almost all of these weaker communities belong to the lower and lower-middle strata of caste hierarchy in their respective regions/villages. There are backward classes and the other backward classes (134). Fortytwo communities among them are identified as what were formerly known as Harijan and now as the Scheduled Castes. They form the decisively weak segment of our rural population.

The distribution of the Scheduled Castes in India is rather uneven. Some of them are small in numbers. Others, like the Chamar, are very large with numerous sub-castes. The largest concentration of this caste was and is found in the irrigated wheat and rice regions of the Indo-Gangetic plains and in the coastal belts. In terms of physical setting villages all over India have clusters of 'Harijan' houses located in the remote corners. The physical and social divide based on 'clean' and 'unclean' castes remains relatively valid even today. These village studies reveal that the members of higher castes have their own drinking water wells, whereas lower castes depend on ponds, or on public wells which are available in a limited number of villages. The Harijans are invariably landless and suffer social disabilities including segregation. Percentage of literacy among the "lower caste" people, except in Kerala and Maharashtra, was lowest. The wages paid to "low caste" agricultural labourers were low. There was hardly any effort to mobilise politically the "low caste" labourers, except in Kerala.

A good deal of the social and economic conditions of the weaker sections as observed by our investigators two decades ago remain to some extent unchanged. The picture of rural poverty, drawn in these reports, reveals association of low caste status with landlessness, illiteracy, lack of opportunities, and indebtedness. Poverty as portrayed in this book is manifestation of a much deeper malaise. It is the control of economic resources on part of the affluent sections that keeps the weaker sections below the line of divide. Various progressive legislations like Untouchability Act, Land Reforms Acts have made only a little dent on their living conditions. Much of what is reported here about rural areas of 16 states is not without relevance today.

These studies also suggest that caste differentiation and hierarchy fairly correspond to levels of economic differentiation and socio-economic inequality. Caste system is primarily based on the principle of economic dominance, which questions somewhat the other view that caste system is based on religious values only. Thus viewed from economic perspective and from the perspective of the weaker sections themselves caste system is a system of economic exploitation.

Though much of stigma and many of the disabilities associated with being a 'lower caste' have been removed, and democratic institutions have minimised inequalities, equality of opportunities remains somewhat elusive. Hence between the 1970s and 1990s, there remains a substantial number of poor even though during the last three decades (particularly after the writing of these reports) positive changes are reported towards equalisation of opportunities and reduction in poverty levels.

II

From early 1970s substantial economic development has taken place and the social and economic conditions of the weaker sections have relatively improved. A summary of such developments extracted from the excellent studies of Rao, Ray, Subbarao and others is given below.

The implementation of land reforms has been tardy. In large areas of the country except West Bengal the share croppers have yet to be given the security of tenancy. The landless labourers are yet to receive remunerative wages everywhere. There no doubt has been large scale re-distribution of land by the Government among the weaker sections, but the goal of land ceiling as an instrument of land re-distribution has remained elusive particularly in areas like Bihar where former Zamidars still own illegally large chunks of land.

There has been decline in poverty levels from 50 to 28 per cent of population over the last twenty years. The long term growth of GNP until 1970s which was no more than 3.5 per cent per annum, adding up to a meager growth of about 1 per cent per annum in per capita income, increased to about 5 per cent per annum during the 1980s. It was during this period for the first time that there was evidence of decline in the proportion of people below the poverty line, a process which according to some economists started towards the end of 1970s. In fact, rural poverty which oscillated around 50 per cent of rural population through the sixties and seventies for the first time showed a decline of 10 percentage points between the late seventies and mid-eighties when there was some acceleration in the overall rate of growth. The latest estimates from the Planning Commission point to a further decline in rural poverty to around 28 per cent in 1989-90, in spite of the stagnation of agricultural output during the eighties.

The regions experiencing a high rate of agricultural growth have shown a steeper reduction in rural poverty than the regions experiencing slow growth. The incidence of poverty is much higher among the economically and socially disadvantaged sections like the Scheduled Castes and Scheduled Tribes than among those of the other populations. The rate of reduction in poverty over a period of time was also lower among these disadvantaged sections than among the general population. It may be noted in this context that in the eastern region of India, the districts accounting for higher proportion of the Scheduled Tribes recorded negative or slow growth in agricultural output. Tribal agriculture is characterised by slow growth in productivity. On the other hand, the Scheduled Caste population, which is basically landless and migration prone, was more widespread in districts recording higher growth where the demand for labour and wage could be high. In India, the proportion of rural population below the poverty line is highest for unirrigated or dry areas and declines with the increase in irrigation.

A reason for the alleviation of poverty has been the rise in income of the weaker section through the implementation of a number of programmes for employment generation and elimination of rural poverty launched as part the strategy of 'direct attack' on poverty. These programmes made a positive impact on rural society by way of generating employment and reducing poverty. The contribution of poverty alleviation programmes such as Integrated Rural Development Programmes (IRDP) and National Rural Employment Programmes and Rural Landless Employment Guarantee Programme (now merged into Jawahar Rozgar Yojana) to the reduction in poverty has been substantial. Under the IRDP, about 30 million families were assisted for self-employment during the Sixth and Seventh Plan periods. About 5 million households were given a second dose of assistance for enabling them to carry on their enterprises. Under wage-employment schemes, from about 20 million mandays of employment generated annually in the mid-sixties, the employment generated in 1989-90 under the Centrally Sponsored Schemes as well as those undertaken by Maharashtra, amounted to about 1,000 million mandays under Employment Guarantee Scheme.

The area development programmes such as the Drought-Prone Areas Programme, the programmes for the development of Hill and Tribal Areas, have also contributed to augmenting the incomes of the rural poor. The performance of IRDP was found to be distinctly better in the infrastructurally developed regions where the awareness levels and bargaining power of the beneficiaries are also higher. However, the new strategy showed little concern for labour-absorption in the process of agricultural development itself and was not sufficiently integrated with the objective of agricultural growth through the development of infrastructure for increasing agricultural productivity.

Agricultural output has been growing at the rate of about 2.7 per cent per annum both in the pre and post green revolution periods. In the case of food grains, there is evidence of mild improvement in the annual growth rate 2.3 per cent during the first decade of green revolution (1967-68 to 1977-78) to 2.7 per cent between 1977-78 to 1988-89.

In the recent period, the eastern states e.g., Assam, Bihar, Orissa,

Madhya Pradesh and West Bengal, where labour is abundant and poverty is widespread have emerged as a dynamic growth region, with agricultural growth picking up. Their performance in respect of food grains, in the last decade of green revolution (1977-78 to 1988-89) is nearer or even higher than the all-India average. All these States have experienced a step-up in the growth of rice during the last decade and some of them have recorded higher growth than the national average . Labour-use per unit of land for major crops like wheat and rice in these regions is at least 50 per cent higher than in the western States like Punjab and Haryana (Planning Commission, 1990). In view of the recent pick-up in agricultural growth in the eastern States, the demand for labour has been increasing. This may explain why inter-State disparities in real wages for agricultural labour have started declining in the eighties.

There is clear inter-relationship between the levels of agricultural developments and rural poverty on the one hand, and ecological degradation on the other (Mellor, 1988). As mentioned earlier, while the direct contribution of agricultural growth to poverty reduction through additional employment generation has been modest, its indirect contribution through the augmentation of food grains surpluses and through the decline in their relative prices seems to have become relatively more important.

There are also disturbing trends. There is evidence of deceleration in the growth of employment in agriculture as well as in the rural sector. The annual growth of employment in agriculture declined from 2.3 per cent during 1973-78 to mere 0.7 per cent during 1983-88. The growth in rural employment showed a decline from 2.5 per cent to about 1 per cent over the corresponding period. The large farmers have been able to re-arrange the cropping pattern and input mix in such a way that labour cost per unit of output is minimised. Large farmers have also resumed land for self-cultivation from share-cropper because of the profitability of new technology. It has led to lower labour absorption and reduced incomes for erstwhile tenants. Therefore recent trends in employment indicate a discernible decline in the proportion of workforce engaged in agriculture and a significant increase in employment in the informal rural (non-agricultural) sector, comprising, services and construction etc. These activities are highly income-elastic and it appears that green revolution, improvement in the growth of GNP and urbanisation in the last decade have started making an impact in terms of the diversification of rural occupations.

The higher rate of urbanisation in the recent period, and the increased migration of the rural poor in search of livelihood in the informal urban sector have, among other factors contributed to a reduction in the proportion of workers dependent on agriculture. The rural-urban disparities in per capita income have been increasing which also accounts for the increase in rural-to-urban migration. Thus part of the rural poverty and inequalities are shifted to the more dynamic urban sector where the proportion of the population below the poverty line is smaller, even though inequalities in income and wealth are greater. However, the social inequalities and discrimination based on caste are more severe in the traditional rural environment which also explains, to some extent, the out-migration of the rural poor belonging to depressed classes.

The disparity between male-female wage rate has started declining in several states. These recent developments in India agriculture point to the possibility of a significant rise in employment and wage for labour in the poverty stricken states, if appropriate strategies are adopted for stepping up agricultural growth.

The causes of deforestation and degradation of dry lands, apart from population growth and poverty are the pressure of demand for fuel-wood, timber, meat and wool from high income segments including urban areas has been a major cause of denudation of environment. However, the rural poor have been the prime victims of this ecological degradation. This is because, the rural poor derive a significant part of their income from village commons and forests in the dry regions (Jodha, 1986). Even through the proportion of income derived from such sources is greater for the rural poor than for the non-poor, the later are responsible for the greater share of denudation of forests than the rural poor. As a result of environmental degradation, the rural poor, particularly women and children, have to walk much longer distances to collect fuel wood and fodder, and drinking water has become scarcer owing to the decline in water table.

III

As the present study shows, a substantial part of the weaker sections consist of the backward classes and the other backward classes. On 16 November 1992 the Supreme Court by a majority decision, upheld the core of the Mandal Commission's report that caste is central to Indian society. A backward caste now is identified with a backward class. Caste, together with other factors like poverty and occupation has hence forth to be taken into account while identifying backwardness. It is a recognition of the social reality that a caste could be, and it is often, a social class. If it is socially backward, it would be a backward class for the purpose of Article 16 (4). A backward class cannot be identified only with reference to the economic criteria. In this sense the Mandal Commission's argument that the backwardness of any group or class is not due to economic backwardness but it is due to social backwardness, which in turn may be directly related to class, has been upheld. By recognising caste as class the Supreme Court has rejected the argument that the Constitution of India envisaged a cohesive unified casteless society in which there was no room for casteism. However, the Supreme Court, in its majority judgment, has not accepted the criterion of caste as the sole determinant of backwardness. While upholding the provision for 27 per cent reservation for the benefit of the backward, the court has made a distinction between the backward and the more backward sections and introduced the economic criterion in determining severe backwardness. In doing so the court has not accepted the Mandal Commission's recommendation that all backward classes should be treated equally for the purpose of their share in 27 per cent reservation, that the well off among the backward class consist of only a negligible minority, and that even if their financial position has improved their social status or standing has not. The Supreme Court has now directed the Union Government to set up a commission "to siphon off the creamy layer" of the backward classes and to specify the basis and identify the relevant and requisite socio-economic criteria to exclude socially advanced persons. The Court has also limited the quantum of reservations to 50 per cent. There will be no reservation in promotion. The socially backward class will include non-Hindu like Christian and Sikhs who will get reservation benefit.

The reason for mentioning the judgement at some length is that it is supported by the findings on social and economic conditions of the weaker section of own study conducted in the 1970s.

IV

The project was conceived, designed and implemented by Dr. Surajit Chandra Sinha, the then Director. We are happy that he wrote a

Foreword to it. Dr. Ranjit Bhattacharya and Dr. N.K. Das were brought in as associate editors to update the material and put it in the theoretical and contemporary foci.

The manuscript remained unpublished for almost 20 years, for reasons beyond our control. We are publishing the material now for three reasons. First, such data do not become out of date. Secondly, caste has again come to the centre-stage, where it always was, with the recent order of the Supreme Court, upholding 27 per cent reservation for backward classes, as mentioned above. Thirdly, the socio-economic problems of the weaker sections are still with us, in spite of improvement in some areas.

This work will be found relevant for yet another reason, as a set of baseline data for 24 villages, as a profile of the village and caste structure, as a descriptive account of the weaker sections. The modern researcher will miss in them discussions of such issues as the gender question, but a few of such and other lacunae are offset by the richness of data.

K.S. SINGH

REFERENCES

Jodha, N.S. 1986. 'Common Property Resources and Rural poor in Dry Regions of India' *Economic and Political Weekly*. July 5

Jose, A.V. 1988 'Agricultural Wages in India' *Economic and Political Weekly*. June 25

Mellor, John W 1988 'The Intertwining of Environmental Problems and Poverty'. *Environment*. November

Nadkarni, M.V., Syed Ajmal Pasha and L.S. Prabhakar, 1989, *Political Economy of Forest Use and Management*, Sage Publications, New Delhi.

Nayyar, Rohini, 1987, 'Famine Participation Rates in Rural India', *Economic and Political Weekly*, December 19

Planning Commission, 1990, 'Employment : Past Trend and Prospects for 1990s', Working Paper, New Delhi.

Rao, C.H. Hanumantha, 1975, *Technological Change and the Distribution of Gains in Indian Agriculture*, The Macmillan Company of India, Delhi

Rao, C.H. Hanumantha, 1991, Rural Society and Agricultural Development in course of Industrialisation, case of India. *Economic and Political Weekly*, Annual number, March, 1991

Rao, C.H. Hanumantha, D.B. Gupta and P.S. Sharma, 1986, 'Infrastructural Development and Rural Poverty in India: A Cross-Sectional Analysis' in John W Mellor an Gunvant M Desai (Ed), *Agricultural Change and Rural Poverty : Variations on a Theme* by Dharm Narain, Oxford University Press, Delhi.

Rao, C.H. Hanumantha, Susanta K Ray and K Subbarao, 1988, *Unstable Agriculture and Droughts : Implications for Policy*, Vikas Publishing House, New Delhi

Subbarao, K., 1985, 'Regional Variations in Impact of Anti-Poverty Programme: A Review of Evidence', *Economic and Political Weekly*, October 26

PREFACE

Following the example of the British administrator scholars, who introduced the discipline of anthropology for knowing the life styles and customs of the people of India, Indian anthropologists and sociologists have also been interested in persuing the intricacies of caste based socio-ritual stratification into many layers.

It has increasingly come to our notice that such multi-layer patterns of inter-caste socio-ritual hierarchy in the varna-jati system are often rearranged into simple workable binary hierarchies which facilitate day-to-day interaction among the people living in villages. In rural West Bengal, for example, the endogamous categories Bhadralok and Chhotolak or Chhoto Jat essentially divides the non-manual and manual workers into two groups. Such binary divisions are essentially the products of practical compromise between the long-range historical stream of varna-based caste hierarchy and the concrete situational context of distribution of wealth and power.

In Anthropological Survey of India we became interested in finding out, on the basis of anthropological field survey of purposively selected villages in different States of India how far, since Independence, the weaker landless, or virtually landless, people in the selected villages have been able to cross the boundary of deprivation in economy, social status and power and to re-arrange their life situation.

I congratulate all the members of the research team of the A.S.I. who have made it possible to present reports on 24 villages covering 16 States of India. I thank the Anthropological Survey of India for taking responsibility of overall editing of the reports which have been submitted by the different field researchers.

I do hope that the substantive information covered by this extensive survey will be of considerable use to the leaders in public affairs in coming to grips with the reality of the position of the weaker section of India's rural population who have still a long way to go to cross the threshold of all round deprivation. We also hope that this report will also be made available for further problem-oriented research on the factors that continue to stand in the way of the weaker groups crossing the threshold of comprehensive socio-cultural backwardness.

SURAJIT SINHA

EDITORIAL NOTE

The project owes its emergence to two factors, viz. (a) an expansion of the Survey during 1971-74 and thus making available a number of technical manpower for undertaking All India surveys in connection with relevant major projects; and (b) the Planning Commission's interest in the welfare of backward classes evident in their endeavour of setting up a Steering Group for the purpose. The Ministry under the auspices of which the Survey operates as the premier anthropological research organization, takes care of the charge of social welfare as well. This commitment involved the Survey to play an active and decisive role in the welfare of backward classes. Consequently, this plan-oriented project was designed and taken up in 1972 (c.f. *Newsletter*, Anthropological Survey of India, March-April, 1972).

The research staff of the Head Office along with the Heads of four Regional Stations participated in Workshop Seminars at Calcutta in July, 1972 in order to prepare comprehensive guidelines for the Project. The draft guidelines thus formulated were circulated among the entire scientific staff of the Survey for scrutiny and comments. Soon the Project guidelines were finalized incorporating relevant suggestions from the research staff. These guidelines clearly spelled out objectives of the study; had a brief note on the "methodology" to be utilized in the study; and delineated itemwise the area of coverage.

Objectives of the Study

1. "To identify the weaker section of the Indian population in terms of access to the socio-political control over institutions and control over the means of production".
2. "to find out the social disabilities and stigma suffered by the weaker sections and also the socio-cultural implications of being weak".
3. "to spell out the constraints – social, economic, political and others – on account of which the opportunities by which they

can cross the line of divide, either do not reach them or even when they reach, they are not able to use them in the fullest sense".

4. "conversely, to see if there is a discernible trend suggesting increase in the number of weaker sections and their conditions becoming more acute, and if so, what are the compelling reasons for such a situation".
5. "even it is assumed that there has been an improvement in the general economic and social conditions of the weaker sections during the last 25 years or so we may find out why the improvement has been only marginal" (*Newsletter*, 1Anthropological Survey of India, July – August, 1972).

On the basis of the guidelines and objectives mentioned therein village-based field studies were undertaken on the rural folk in the following States of the country :

1. Andhra Pradesh (in Telengana region only),
2. Assam (work was limited only to a study of the operation of caste system in a valley. Shillong Station of the Survey conducted the study),
3. Bihar (South and North),
4. Gujarat,
5. Haryana,
6. Karnataka (Northern),
7. Kerala,
8. Madhya Pradesh,
9. Maharashtra (three studies, viz. Marathwada, Vidarbha and Western Maharashtra),
10. Orissa,
11. Punjab,
12. Rajasthan,
13. Tripura,
14. Uttar Pradesh (Western and two studies in Eastern region only) and
15. West Bengal (four studies, viz. Burdwan, North Bengal, Purulia and South Bengal (24 Parganas).

Kashmir and the tribal dominated states, namely, Arunachal Pradesh the Himachal Pradesh and Meghalaya could not be covered.

The survey was confined to twenty-two villages of approximately six million Indian villages. Meanwhile all the twenty-two reports which had already been submitted to this office, were formally discussed in Workshop Seminars organized at Calcutta from July 3 to 10, 1975 and thereafter.

Although to start with no pan Indian model was incorporated in the guidelines, the available reports broadly record a differential mode of participation of the rural population in the national, political, economic, social and cultural resources roughly dividing it into *comparatively* "weak" and "strong" sections. Furthermore, the reports reveal a general pattern of the social situation of the weak sections in terms of their economic, political, communicational and other constraints hindering them from deriving benefit in order to uplift them from abject poverty. The reports also reveal a general pattern manifested mainly in terms of well known *varna-jati* order of Indian social system. *Varna* based *jati* stratification comprising upper and lower caste groups conforms to the socio-economic categories of "strong" and "weak" of the Indian population. Weaker sections as identified by our field research mostly belong to the lower caste population of the *jati* hierarchy and have a characteristic disadvantage both in terms of their control over the means of production (in the agrarian economy of the peasantry it has been especially delineated in relation to landholding) and in terms of their access to the socio-political control over institutions (such as club, school committee, Puja committee, etc., if any, and village panchayat, district board committee mainly in terms of numerical representation of members from weaker sections). Thus the social situation of the decisively weak section and their social, economic, political, communicational and other constraints hinder them from deriving benefit from various developmental programmes launched in order to uplift them from abject poverty and the situation roughly corresponds to the age-old condition of the members of the lowest *varna* (Sudra) and low castes of *jati* stratification.

Variations in the pattern of *varna-jati* order have no doubt been observed and noted in different regions of India (such as absence of one to one correlation between the poorer sections and the lower *jat* or absence of such evidence as upper *jat* holding proportionately larger shares of land). These variations while taken *emically* are found to be local and seem to be restricted within the system and not outside the threshold of it. However, we felt it necessary to precisely define our terms for comparison of these regional variations that have so far been observed and recorded. In such an attempt a pan Indian model of *varna-jati* which contains certain basic assumptions needed for comprehending the rural class structure (especially in terms of mode of agrarian production as evident in the reports of our field studies) was found suitable as a common denominator for comparison.

Although an understanding of the fundamental problem of the genesis of "poverty" is not so crucial within the immediate purview of our survey, yet we cannot deny the fact that the state of poverty is directly dependent on unequal possession of wealth by members within a society. Here it may be mentioned that so far we have not devised any standard of measure that could help estimate the nature of inequality by drawing a sharp line of divide between observable categories of the "haves" and the "have nots". However, for an understanding of the situation we have tried to single out the *portion* of ownership of cultivable land as the foremost observable criterion of inequality. Once this division has thus been made, we have next included a number of concomitantly noticeable criteria (such as level of education mainly in terms of literacy and illiteracy, intensity of control over political institution like panchayat in terms of proportion of numerical representation and manual and non-manual orientation in the involvement of agricultural operations) for a better comprehension of the line of divide. This analysis helped us in categorizing the landless and others with proportionately meagre landholding, falling within the fold of poverty and as such these sections of the Indian population were labelled as weaker sections. We have, thus, identified the weaker sections of the Indian agrarian society mainly in terms of inequal access to ownership of land or in other words their actual " relation of production" as observed from outside. One might wonder why we are suggesting a *varna-jati* model in course of understanding such basic economic relationships. In our endeavour to answer aptly this self-posed question we have to understand the mode of production prevalent in India at present.

From our finding it is evident that in most cases the landless and nearly landless people are agricultural labourers, whereas the landowning sections are supervisors of agricultural production. As such, paradoxically, the actual orientation of involvement in production never depends on the basis of access to land : the upper castes, especially Brahmans usually avoid manual involvement in certain agricultural operations (there are, however, exceptions, see Topno 1974). Poor individuals from these castes are seldom found to be engaged as *agricultural* labourers. However, it has been observed that in most cases, they take up manual work in factories, business houses and in non-traditional walks of life as well. Otherwise, they mostly go for non-manual jobs such as petty business. This shows us clearly that the relation of production after all is manifested and functions in the "limited" bounds of the social system. Even in the organization of production, services of specialist castes like Kamar (blacksmith), carpenter in the secular sphere and Brahmans in the sacred realm are still in vogue. The relation between those who serve and those who enjoy the services is not "class" styled. The Brahman in all instances and the carpenter (caste) in certain cases enjoy higher status even after serving clients of lower social position in the local hierarchy.

The only explanation of this kind of relation, we find lies in the ideology or the "conscious model" (Levi-Strauss 1963) of the organization of production which dictates reciprocity of services. Here, we do not want to be too "romantic" like Dumont (1972) in dealing with such an "epic view", but at the same time we feel that it would not be worthwhile to underestimate the view (see Misra 1974), especially in the Indian context where on the whole, the organization and ideology of production dictates a status hierarchy rather than a class structure (see Weber 1958). The former is mediated through the *grand* social system of India, namely, *varna-jati* model. This all pervasive model of Indian social system thus becomes inevitably important while considering the relation of production in rural India. It is needless to mention here that our present venture would give us a unique opportunity to delineate the perpetuating condition of poverty and its corollary, "exploitation" (which may be conceived of as typical phenomena of civilized societies at large), as manifested in a status oriented (in the Weberian sense) ideologically reciprocative social system.

Jajmani, the economic transactional pattern based on hereditary division of labour of the *varna-jati* model is essentially a pre-market one. A look into our findings and those of our predecessors (Bose 1958) shows that this kind of transaction has nearly stopped functioning. The prevalent mode of economic transaction among the rural Indians of today is market economy. From a "functionalist's point of view the existence of the pre-market *varna-jati* social structural phenomenon in the present Indian scene would seem utterly anomalous. From this theoretical comprehension of a social anomaly, we feel that we need to be scrupulous in our attempt to apply the model in this research project on the weaker sections.

There is a general feeling that India has not undergone a genuine *Great Transformation* (see Polanyi 1957) from pre-market to market economy. The market economy has however flourished. On the other hand, the pre-market economy could not sustain itself because of the very exigencies of the situation and at the same time it got no political support as such.

R.K. BHATTACHARYA

CONTENTS

LIST OF TABLES

1

BAMUNA : A VILLAGE IN ASSAM

S.K. MUKHERJEE

Introducing the District

The district of Kamrup with an area of 3,811.2 square miles lies between 25°43′ and 26°53 N and 90°39′ and 92°11′ E. The district is divided into two parts by the mighty Brahmaputra river. The northern portion is twice as big as the southern. The southern portion consists of plains broken up by hills. North of the Brahmaputra falls roughly into three natural divisions, namely, the tracts near the river, the central plains, and the Kachari Duars. The marshy portions of the district, particularly in the Barpeta sub-division, have been cleared by the immigrants who produce jute and rice there.

According to the 1961 Census, the population of Kamrup is 2,062,572. Since 1931, Kamrup has been the most populous district of Assam although in point of area it stands third among the plains districts and sixth among the districts of Assam.

The total number of villages in the district is 2,971. The district is populated by a number of ethnic groups viz., Brahman, Ganak, Kayastha, Kalita, Keot, Shau, Saloi, Napit, Jugi, Koch, Hira, Dom, Namasudra and so on. The Kachari or Bodo, with their kin the Rabha, are strongly represented in this district and there is a large number of Koch, the caste into which the Kachari is received on conversion. The district also has a good number of Muslim population.

The Village

Bamuna is situated at a distance of about 8 kilometres from Barpeta town. It is the centre of *mahapurusia dharma* promulgated by

Srimanta Sankardev in the fifteenth century. An all-weather gravelled road connects the village with Barpeta, the nearest market centre and town. The nearest Railway station, Barpeta Road, is situated about 35 km from the village.

There is no available written account of the village. Following the genealogical tree of the Kayastha, it is, however, learnt that they first migrated here from a nearby village eight generations ago. They built the Bamuna *satra* (monastery) and for this purpose received a good amount of land from the Ahom King. Subsequently from the neighbouring areas and districts the Keot, Kalita, Napit, and Hira came and settled here. At present the village consists of six castes with a total population of 702 persons.

TABLE 1: Distribution of families and population by caste

Sl.no.	Caste	Total families	Percentage of total families	Population	Percentage of total population.
1.	Kayastha	4	3.51	22	3.13
2.	Kalita	2	1.75	10	1.42
3.	Keot	41	35.96	290	41.31
4.	Napit	8	7.02	58	8.26
5.	Hira	58	50.88	316	45.01
6.	Namasudra	1	0.09	6	0.09
	Total	114 (100.00%)	99.21 (100.00%)	702	99.22

General Layout

Each caste is clustered in separate neighbourhoods of the village. The village is broadly divided into two *paras* (wards), which are known as *bhakatpara* and *rayatpara*. The *bhakatpara*, which is in the eastern side of the village, is inhabited by members of clean castes like the Kayastha, Kalita, Keot, and Napit. The *rayatpara*, which is in the western side, is occupied the Hira and Namasudra. These two *paras* are again divided into smaller paras (sub-localities) like Thakoorpara, Pathakpara, Bezpara, Hirapara and so on.

Differences are observed in residential styles among the different communities of this village. The houses of the Kayastha, Keot and Kalita are better than the houses of Napit and Hira. The houses of the former are spacious and having large compounds. The houses of the Hira are small and stuffy. Their locality is also crowded. There are a dozen wells in the village five of which are in Hirapara. They are not allowed to draw water from wells of the high castes.

Land distribution

Land is unequally distributed among different castes. It is found that 8.80 per cent of the village land is owned by the Kayastha. The Keot, who are numerically the second biggest group in the village, possess 52.72 per cent of the village land. The Kalita own 1.81 per cent village land. The Napit have 6.28 per cent of land. The Hira, who are numerically the largest group in the village have 29.89 per cent of the land.

The Kayastha own 20.25 *bigha* (3 bigha make one acre) of land per family. The Keot own 11.83 *bigha* of land per family. The Napit own 7.80 bigha of cultivable land per family. In terms of land per family it is found that the Hira have only 4.74 bigha of land per family. In terms of landlessness it is found that among the Kayastha and Kalita there is no landless family. Among the Keot 14.65 per cent are landless and among the Napit 37.5 per cent are landless. Comparatively the Hira have the highest percentage of landless families (43.1%). The high castes like Kayastha and Keot are able to acquire land in neighbouring villages whereas the Napit and Hira had to sell their land to the high caste people due to poverty.

The method of cultivation in the plains district of Assam is similar to the all-India pattern, more particularly to the system prevailing in the Bengal delta. The main crops of rice and jute are cultivated in the rainy season. As there is very little rainfall during winter, crops requiring less moisture, e.g., rope mustard, sugarcane, pulses, tobacco, potato, and other vegetables are grown during this period. The main occupation of the rural people, who constitute 95 per cent of the total population of the state, is agriculture. It is observed that more than half of Assam's national income comes from agriculture alone. (Goswami, P.C. 1963:66).

As in other areas, the power used in agriculture is derived from bullocks and human labour. The main implements for cultivation are wooden plough and steel hoe. There are three varieties of rice grown viz., autumn rice, winter rice, and spring rice, named according to the time of harvest. The autumn rice (*ahu*) is mainly grown by the broadcast method. The sowing time of autumn rice is March, April, any May and the harvesting time is July and August. Winter rice is grown by transplantation system. The transplantation from nursery beds (where it is sown in May and June) is done in June, July, and August. The crop is harvested in November and December. Another variety of winter rice (*bao*) is specially grown in areas which remain submerged throughout the year. This variety of rice grows when the rain water accumulates in shallow paddy fields. '*Bao*' rice is sown during March-April and is harvested in November-December. Spring rice is sown in October-November and is harvested in February-March. Spring rice is grown in marshy land during dry season.

The basic livelihood of the people of Bamuna is agriculture. The common mode of livelihood based on agriculture has led to a considerable amount of inter-dependence between the various ethnic groups of the area. There are some instances of share cropping across the community line. It is pertinent to note that many of the Hira households have share-cropping ties with the Muslim and Kachari tribals from neighbouring villages.

Two sets of people are involved in management of land and its production. They are owner cultivators and superior land owners of various categories at the one hand and sharecroppers and agricultural labourers on the other. Irrespective of caste affiliation those who have sufficient cultivable land usually do the supervisory work of cultivation. Those who do not possess land or possess a small amount of land, work as sharecroppers or as agricultural labourers. In the economic life of the village big land-holders have maximum control over economic resources.

The land-holders generally engage two types of labourers:casual labourer and permanent labourers. Generally the villagers prefer to employ landless Muslim of the neighbouring villages as agricultural labourer for they have good reputation as sincere workers and are available at cheaper rate. Except the Kayastha, the other caste groups who work as share-cropper or agricultural labourer are Kalita, Keot, Napit, Hira, and Namasudra. It may be noted that usually people of higher castes like the Brahman, Kayastha do not takeup the job of agricultural labourer.

The relationship of a landlord or *malik* with the permanent labourer is different from that of the seasonal labourers. At the time of distress, a permanent labourer gets help from his master. He can borrow money from him with a nominal rate of interest or free of interest. With the seasonal labourer the relationship of a land-owner is mostly contractual limited to the extent of getting the work done and paying the daily wages. "Agricultural workers get employment of the average of 208 days(all India-189 days) in agricultural operations. It would appear that agricultural workers are generally better employed in Assam than in India as a whole. But as agricultural workers form only 11 per cent of the rural population is Assam, these figures do not recollect condition of the rural population in general. The very low percentage of agricultural workers, on the other hand, implies the lack of employment opportunities in agricultural operations in Assam. In fact, the state surveys have shown that only 15 to 20 per cent of the agricultural families and half of the wholly agricultural families (who constitute about 60 per cent of the rural families) do not receive any income during the slack season. Because of the smallness of their holdings and lack of facilities for cultivation in the winter months, it has become difficult to employ the available labour forcefully". (Goswami P.C., 1963:49).

In the village two types of tenant cultivation are practised: on share cropping basis (*adhi*) and contract basis (*thika*). Most of the land-owners of high caste give their land to share tenants. In the first type of tenancy the tenant has to pay 50 per cent of the produce of the land. In the second type, the tenant has to pay a fixed amount per *bigha* of land to the land owner. It may be noted that the tenant has to pay his due even if the yield is insufficient.

Agricultural Innovations

It is observed that in the village mostly the big land-owners of high castes are utilizing modern technology, improved seeds and fertilizers. Except one or two Hira and Napit families most of them could not get fertilizers, insecticides etc., at the normal controlled rates. This is so, because many of the villagers do not have proper contact with the officials of the block. On the other hand, rich landowners manage to get them because of better contact. The rules for loans provided by the Block and Bank for agricultural purposes are reported to be complex for the poor rural peasantry, and hence the poor and uneducated small farmers do not go for them.

Live-stock

Apart from land, other economic resources at the disposal of the rural people is livestock. Cattle which includes cow, calves, and other draught animals are the most important among livestock. Goats and ducks are reared by all the castes. The villagers do not rear chicken as they are the followers of Vaishnavite faith.

Largest number of cows, oxen and calves are possessed by the Keot. They have 104 heads of cattle. Next comes the Kayastha (50), Hira (48) Napit 20 and Kalita 18 in order. Most of the families among the Hira do not have any livestock.

The total number of goats in the village is 30. Out of these the Keot have 14, Kalita have 4, Kayastha have 5, Napit have 3, and the Hira have got only 4.

Besides cultivation and livestock, the villagers, other than the Hira, practise handloom. Till recently, family handloom was the only source through which the family members used to get their apparels. This was particularly true of women folk who depended entirely on their family looms. Except the Hira women, who are always busy in pot-making, the women of other castes weave at leisure hours. The Assamese weavers not only produce their own apparels, but present such apparels to other members of the family, especially, towels with embroidery works during Bihu festivals. Women are also helpful to family in many ways. Except the Brahman and Kayastha women, women of other castes help in many ways in agricultural operations and they also catch fish in their leisure hours for domestic consumption.

Assets and Income

One's status is counted in terms of land holding (*mati*), household orchard (*bari*), living hut (*ghar-duar*), ornaments (*gahanagathari*) and utensils (*bachan-bartan*). Of the movable properties the metallic utensils and containers are highly prized possessions. Among the high caste people these are used for domestic as well as for ritual purposes. There are no such utensils in possession of the Hira and Napit of the village. The Kayastha, Kalita, and Keot women generally have ornaments of gold and silver whereas in case of Napit and Hira women (except three or four families) gold ornaments are rarely seen.

The Kayastha, Kalita, and Keot in general have comparatively better income than the Napit, Hira, and Namasudra. Much of their expenditure is on rice alone, leaving very little for vegetables, fish, meat, and milk. With the meagre income these groups find little scope for expenditure on education, medicine, repairs of homestead etc. Some of the families among these castes could not imagine of spending on washing and recreation.

Indebtedness

The burden of indebtedness is higher on the Hira and Napit than on other castes in the village. Although the households with higher income have incurred debts, the purpose of their indebtedness is quite different from those households with lower income. Most loan in village are taken for the purpose of consumption, marriage, and other ceremonies and for purchasing bullocks, seeds, medical care etc. Well to do cultivators of the village and neighbouring areas supply credit to debtors. In many such cases land is generally mortgaged. The debtor forfeits the right to cultivate the land as long as the loan remains outstanding. In some cases poor villagers borrow money from *mahajans* of the neighbouring areas. After harvesting the *mahajan* take grains form the farmers at a much cheaper rate than the market. Here it should be mentioned that the *mahajan* and well to do cultivators mostly belong to high castes.

Occupational Pattern

Among the caste occupations agricultural activities rank next to ritualistic activities of the Brahman, who, too, take to agricultural practices without degradation of their status. The artisans whose trade is customarily associated with a lower status, raise their status when they take to agriculture.

In the village the Kayastha, who are the *adhikara* of the *satra*, are mainly agriculturist. At present they are engaged as teachers, clerk and in other services (see table 3).

The table shows that alongwith the Kalita the Keot also practise agriculture. In the village 48.8 per cent of the Keot follow their traditional occupation (agriculture) as their primary occupation and 17.1 per cent as subsidiary occupation. A few educated Keot have taken to teaching. Three of them are primary school teachers. They sell stationery articles, food-stuffs, rice, and other grains. There are two contractors among them. A small percentage of them (9.8%) are those who have lost their lands and work as agricultural labourers or share-croppers. Nearly 12 per cent of them are engaged in different types of jobs in Government and semi-Government organizations.

All Napit families of the village have given up their traditional occupation of hair-cutting and taken to agriculture.

The Hira are traditional potters. In the village at present 69 per cent of them follow their traditional occupation. The percentage of agricultural labourer and daily labourer is the highest among them. They also do the jobs of peon, driver, chowkidar, carpenter etc. Some of them depend on agriculture (8.6%) as their primary occupation.

Occupational Mobility

The Kayastha who were originally *adhikara* of the *satra* have now taken up every type of white collar jobs like teaching, government service, and so on. Spread of education and economic pressure have forced them to give up their hereditary profession. Although their religious status deteriorated due to occupational change but their social and economic condition has improved.

The Kalita are by occupation agriculturists who follow their traditional occupation. The Keot of the village are now adopting almost every type of occupation. Along with Kalita they are less fastidious about the cleanliness of job than the Kayastha.

The Napit are not carrying their hereditary occupation. Most of them are now engaged in agriculture. Although occupational change did not help them to improve their economic condition but their social status has to some extent improved.

Most of the Hira are engaged in traditional occupation. The percentage of agricultural labourer and daily labourer when combined together is however the highest among the Hira. Some of them changed their occupation as it fetches little money now-a-days. Those who have got jobs in government and semi-government organizations are few in number but their social as well as economic positions are better than that of the other Hira families. It was observed that one each from the Kayastha and Kalita, three Keot who are educated and four Hira have left the village for taking up various jobs.

Pottery Industry of the Hira and its Present Condition

As indicated earlier the Hira are traditional potters. Their speciality is that they make pots by hands only., without making use of the wheel. The preparation of pots is exclusively a feminine task. The Hira women work almost all the time of the year except sometime during rainy season. Men collect earth from Goalpara by boat, sand and wood. Selling of earthenware in the market as well as in the Muslim and tribal villages are also man's job. In the village the earthen wares are generally bought from the Hira through barter. The *jonga* or big pots for brewing rice are made exclusively for the tribal folk.

With the increased tendency of giving up drinking among the Kachari tribe of the neighbouring areas, the demand for *jonga* is gradually diminishing. As a result, they are getting lower price for their products than earlier. Further, aluminium wares have made their appearance in the local market affecting their livelihood. At the time of author's fieldwork in the village some of the Hira potters told that, "*Babu, aaitu babasai kari ajikali knueo tiki thakiba no-ware. Sital Samayat saj bikri kari ami kuno-rakame dui-chari mah chalibi paru. Kjntu barisar samayat ami suksari thakibo lage. Tetiya ami mati aniba nowaroo, beleg kam powao tan hai pare. Kochari aru musalmanor goan-ot amar bastoobr besi salisil. Kintoo Bongaigoan-ot factori hai amar'saj ekebare na chala haise*". (With this pot making business as means of livelihood, it is difficult now-a-days for one to survive. In winter we can sell our products and with this we are just able to live for two or three months, but in rainy season we had to suffer a lot. At that time due to rain we could not make earthen ware or anything, nor we could get a substitute job to maintain our livelihood. Previously, we could sell our products to the Kachari tribe and Muslim but as there is one aluminium factory at Bongaigoan now nobody is purchasing our products).

Religion

All households of Bamuna are the followers of Hindu religion and belong to *mahapurushiya* sect. The term *mahapurushiya* is popularly believed to have derived from the epithet *mahapurusia*, generally applied to mean Srimanta Sankardev, the great Assamese Vaisnav saint and social reformer of 15th - 16th Century.

In the village there were two *namghars* (prayer hall), one was for the high castes like Kayastha, Kalita, Keot, and Napit, and another one is for the Hira and Namasudra. but at present due to quarrel with the Kayastha, the Keot alongwith Kalita and Napit have built another *namghar*. The *namghar* serves the purpose of a prayer hall as well as a hall for holding religious meetings and discussions. It also serves as a stage for dramatic performances and venue for village Panchayat meetings.

The Vaisnava festivals in the village mainly centre round the saints connected with the *mahapurusia* sect. The sacred as well as secular festivals like Bihu are observed by different castes. Although high caste people try to observe almost all the festivals and rituals, the Hira are able to observe only *thithis* of Sankardev and Madhabdev and Magh and Bahag Bihu separately in their own Namghar. A Pathak (one who reads Bhagwat) from their own caste reads Bhagwat and perform others rituals.

The offering of *naivedya* in all the ceremonies is considered to be of ritual importance. *Naivedya* usually consists of soaked gram, *Mug*, pulse, rice, banana, sugar-cane cut into pieces, betel nuts etc. The germinated gram (*gaji*) and pulses mixed with rice are considered the main elements of Naivedya. There is a separate religious fund for observing the rituals in the *namghar*. During important festivals villagers try to visit Barpeta and Sunderdia Satra.

Social Dimension

Caste hierarchy: Assam presents only two functional castes., viz. Brahman and the non-Brahman or Sudra. Under these categories are included all the castes and subcastes of the Hindu people.

The ranking of castes of the village as recognised by the informants are as follows : As there are no Brahman in the village, the Kayastha are at the top of the hierarchy. They are followed by the Kalita. Next to them are the Keot (Halwa or cultivator) and Napit, who occupy the same position. The majority of the informants place the Napit below the Keot. The Jaliya Keot (fishing subdivision of the caste), who are living in the neighbouring villages, occupy a very low position in social hierarchy.

The Hira and Namasudra belong to the lowest category in the caste hierarchy. They are considered to be ritually impure and nobody from the higher caste normally accepts water or food from their hand. They are also considered to be low because of their traditional occupation.

Social interaction Previously, untouchability was said to be practised very vigorously, but now this has slackened to a greater extent. Author observed that the young educated boys of higher castes were freely mixing with the educated boys of the Hira. They also participated together in picnics. At the time of Panchayat election the high caste candidates visited the Hira at their place and if offered tea accepted the same which they never did earlier. But in *namghar* of the high castes, the Hira are not welcome on formal occasions, like wedding. The educated well to do Hira are invited by the high caste people. In that case they have to sit apart and eat food separately. In towns no such distinction is observed and the Hira and other low castes are allowed to sit with high castes. No separate glasses are maintained for the low castes. During any community work and ritual occasions the Hira work as a separate group and other communities do not associate them in these activities.

The villagers while addressing one another, irrespective of caste use a few terms of address, for example, the high castes are addressed as *kaka, jeta* and so on by the low caste. The same type of generalised terms of addresses are used by the people of high caste to refer to members of low castes.

On numerical strength the Hira are the dominant group in the village (see table 1). Numerically, the next dominant people are the Keot. Some of them are quite influential and wealthy. The headman of the village is from their caste. In the affair of the village Namghar they have maximum control. The Kalita and Kayastha are economically dominant but their numerical strength is very poor. Although the Hira are numerically dominant, the majority of them are very poor. Some of the individuals among the Hira are educated and wealthy.

Social Organisation The most important social unit in the village is the *khel*. In the village there is a *khel* among the Keot, Kalita, and Napit. There is another *khel* among the Hira. Within the network of the *khel* system,however, the traditional caste rules of separate eating and endogamous marriage are maintained. A *khel* may, however, split into a number of factions due to certain internal disputes. One of the features of *khel* grouping is that in all the crises of a person's life such as birth, marriage, and death fellow members of the *khel* have to be entertained through a feast or prayer assembly. Whereas the caste system forms nearly water-tight compartments, the *khel* system cuts across this rigid compartmentalism by unifying different castes in one social group.

The number of nuclear family is the highest among the Hira. They get married early and prefer to set up their independent establishments. The marriage area of Kayastha, Kalita, and Keot are bigger than that of the Hira.

Literacy & Education While analysing the level of literacy among various castes it is found that the highest percentage of literacy in the village is among the Kayastha (100%) and Kalita (100%). Then it is followed by the Keot (60.98%) Napit (50%) and Hira (44.83%) The percentage of illiteracy is highest among the Hira (55.17%) (see table 2).

There are five graduates in the village of which two are from the Kayastha and one each from Kalita, Keot and Hira castes.

There is a primary school within the village. Both boys and girls attend it. But the poor representation of boys and girls from the Hira is well marked. As per the Hira informants, they do not send their boys and girls to school due to economic reasons. The little boys of seven and eight years have to go out and work and earn something to help the family.

Social Mobility Organised social movement was first started by the Hira in 1925. A few people among the Hira who were wealthy and educated took the lead. Those who took the lead mostly belonged to Sunderdia, a village close to Bamuna.

At Sunderdia, there was a well known *mahapurushiya satra*. The land of the *satra* was endowed by the old Assam *rajas* by a *pholi* (copper plate) (The *pholi* is still lying with the *adhikara* of the *sunderdia satra*). There was a big prayer hall (*kirtanghar*) in the *satra* where all the religious ceremonies were performed and daily prayer and worship were held.

Social Unrest

The Hira are untouchables. They had no permission of entry from the north gate of the *satra* which was meant for the high caste people. The Hira could use only the western gate. At the end of 1925 there started a quarrel between the *adhikara* (who belong to Kayastha) and the Kalita. The Kalita were the dominant group in the village. They have maximum control over the management of the *satra*. The

TABLE 2: Land and literacy: literacy of the head of the households

Sl. No.	Caste	No.of persons	No. of family	Residen-tial land	Cultivable land	Percent-age to total	Cultiva-ble land	Per family cultivable land	Per capita cultivable land	Percent-age dist-ribution of land-less families	Literate	Illite-rate
1	2	3	4	5	6	7	8	9	10	11	12	13
1.	Kayastha	22	4	16.0	81.0	21.56	8.80	20.25	3.68	0.0	4(100.00%)	-
2.	Kalita	10	2	2.0	16.6	2.70	1.81	8.30	1.66	0.0	2(100.00%)	-
3.	Keot	290	41	26.0	485.0	35.04	52.72	11.83	1.67	14.6	25(60.98%)	16(39.02)
4.	Napit	58	8	22.2	62.4	2.96	6.78	7.80	1.08	37.5	4(50.00%)	4(50.00)
5.	Hira	316	58	28.0	275.0	37.74	29.89	4.74	0.87	43.1	26(44.83%)	32(55.17%)
6.	Namasudra	6	1	-	-	-	-	-	-	100.0	-	1(100.00%)
	TOTAL	702	114	74.2	920.0	100.00	100.00	8.07	1.31	30.7	61(53.52%)	53(46.49%)

Note: Acre = 3.025 *bigha*

TABLE 3: Occupational distribution

Occupation	Kayastha		Kalita		Napit		Kewat		Hira		Namasudra	
	Main	Subsidi-ary	Main	Subsidi-ary	Main	Subsidi-ary	Main	Subsidi-ary	Main	Subsidi-ary	Main	Subsidi-ary
Cultivation	2	2	2	2	21	20	7	5	4	-		
	50.0%	50.0%	100%	25%	12.5%	48.8%	17.1%	8.6%	6.9%			
Agricultural Labour	1	-	4	1	6	1	1					
	12.5%	9.8%	2.4%	10.3%	1.7%	100%						
Teaching	1	-	3	-								
	25.0%	7.3%										
Service	1	-	1	-	5	-	4	-				
	25.0%	12.5%	12.2%	6.9%								
Business	1	-	3	4	2	2						
	12.5%	7.3%	9.8%	3.4%	3.4%							
Casual Labour	1	-	3	-	-	13						
	12.5%	7.3%	22.4%									
Pottery Making	40	10										
	69.0%	17.2%										
Carpenter	1											
	1.7%											
Contractor	3											
	7.3%											
Begging	1											
	12.5%											
Domestic Servant	1											
	12.5%											
TOTAL	4	2		2	8	1	41	12	58	30		1
	100%	50.0%		100%	100%	12.5%	100.0%	29.3%	99.00%	51.6%		100%

adhikara of the *satra* sold a plot of land to one Hira without prior permission of the *satra*. So the managing committee which is dominated by the Kalita decided to boycott the *adhikara*. They also requested all the villagers not to take initiation from him as he sold the *satra* land without consent of the managing committee. But the Hira of the village issued it and some of them took initiation from the *adhikara*. As a result, the Kalita were very much angry with the Hira and after sometimes the western gate of the Satra was closed. This prevented the Hira from going in to the Kirtanghar. Then the Hira appealed to the managing committee of the Satra for social justice. Sri Pushparam Das who led the movement appealed to all the Hira of the neighbouring areas to help them so that they can fight against this injustice. The Hira were inspired by the call given by him. Several meetings were held in different places and at last the Hira decided to file a case against the managing committee of the Satra and in the month of May, 1926 they filed a case in the Sub-divisional court claiming that they have been for several generations living in Satra land and they had also a right to enter up to the 7th room from the western gate. The Hira won the case and got the right to enter into Satra through the western gate.

As a result of this achievement, the Hira of other village were also greatly inspired. The Hira of Bamuna had a common Namghar with the Keot, Kalita, and Napit. But here too the Hira had no prevention to enter the *namghar*. In 1927 at the time of a festival the Hira of this village demanded that there will be one *deori* (one who distributes *prosad*) from their caste. But the other castes did not agree. The Hira were numerically dominant in the village and their pressure was such that the high caste people without finding any alternative built a separate *namghar* for their own.

After Independence also they made several attempts for social justice but failed. In 1955, when the 'Untouchability Act' was passed, they made an effort to enter from the north gate with the high caste people and appealed to the Court. The then S.D.O. helped them to enter into Satra with high caste people through the same gate.

The high caste people of the village were not very happy over the development though they do not protest or display any outward resentment.

Social Control Coming to the matter of the village socio-political organization, it should be noted that there is a government appointed *gaonbura* (headman) for Bamuna. The present Gaonbura is a Keot.

He has very limited formal duties to perform. The various problems and disputes arising within a caste or community are concerns of that caste. Yet one group may seek the help of *Samaj* belonging to other groups. The castes of the village meet as a common body. The Hira have no separate *Samaj* for their own. They seek the help of others in case of disputes. A person when proved guilty will be penalised or boycotted. Excommunication is also a method of punishment. A person can retrieve his position by paying fine imposed on him by the Samaj.

Emergence of Jati Sabha The Hira of Bamuna, Sunderdia, Budartup and Barpeta together formed a Jati Sabha which is known as Charigaon Hira Samaj. There is one member from each village. Every year all the Hira of these four villages meet together in a village and discuss their problems and, after that, through their General Secretary they contact the local M.L.A. and place their demand so that they can get economic help to better their condition.

During 1973-74 a joint Jati-Sabha was formed by the Hira and Namasudra of Assam which is known as All Assam Hira-Namsudra Jati Sangha.

Conclusion

In this report the author has tried to understand the problems of the weaker section by applying the tests such as economic potentialities of the people living in the village, social hierarchy, and the extent of political control they wield in the village. The economic test has been applied in more detail than the other criteria assuming that economy has a significant role in identifying the "weak". As mentioned earlier, numerically the Hira are the dominant group in the village, but socially as well as economically a large portion of them fall within the category of the weaker section. Economically the Kayastha and Kalita are dominant but numerically they are very small, while the political power is in the hands of the Keot, who are numerically the second largest group in the village. There are wealthy and influential families among the Keot but among them also a few families fall within the category of weaker section.

By and large, the Hira as a caste group have emerged as weak in relation to other castes of the village. Although some of them are educationally better off, yet the Hira as a whole faced more problems than the other castes. Their condition further deteriorated as the demand for their finished products, pottery, decreased on account of establishment of an aluminium factory in the area.

NOTES

1 Satra: An assembly of holy persons were the cult of devotion in all its aspects is practised.
2. Adhikara: Owner or possessor of Satra.
3. Khel: ". . . a body of the Hindus who eat and drink together and associate with each other". Report of Census of Assam 1891, Chapter 10:202 as quoted in Census of Assam, 1961 Vol. III, Part IV.

REFERENCES

Basu, N.G. *The Social History of Kamrup*. 1912.

Goswami, P.C. *The Economic Development of Assam*. 1963.

Goswami, M.C. *Bell Metal Workers of Sarthebari, Assam*. Bulletin of the Dept. of Anthropology, Gauhati University, Vol. II, 1973.

Sarma, S.N. *The Neo Vaishnavite Movement and The Satra Institution of Assam*. 1966.

Pakyntein, E.H. *Census of India, Assam*. 1961.

Acknowledgement

The study was undertaken in a village in Kamrup district during 1974-75 for two months. I am highly thankful to Dr. A.K. Danda, N.K. Syamchoudhuri, B.B. Goswami,R.Bhattacharjee and S.Chakraborty of the Anthropological survey of India, for necessary advice in the preparation of the paper.

2

OLD AGARTALA : A VILLAGE IN TRIPURA

BHABANANDA MUKHERJEE and PRANABJYOTI DE

Introduction

The paper is based on three months' field investigation in Old Agartala between December and February during 1972-73. The village is eight kilometers away from Agartala, the present capital of Tripura. The village was the third capital of Tripura (about 100 years ago). The dilapidated palace, other relics, big tanks, and ancient temple of *Chaturdash Devata* still bear the glory of the past.

Due to migration of 11 lakhs refugees from Bangladesh, it is difficult to find a traditional village without any recent immigrants there. Old Agartala, however, consists of a high percentage of non-immigrant Hindu and tribal population.

Old Agartala has considerable urban element though is by and large a traditional village. In the past, the villagers entirely depended on agriculture. At present 15 percent of them follow urban professions.

Many items of modernity like school, post office, club, library, panchayat office, charitable dispensary, co-operative societies, social education centre, and market have been added to Old Agartala after the independence.

The village has only homestead land. All agricultural lands owned by the villagers are in adjoining Meklipara East and West, Champamura, and Khairpur.

The old settlement pattern does not indicate segregation by caste. Members of certain landless lower castes used to live in a place, Tamal Tala. Residential areas of the Fisherman (Kaibarta) Washerman (Dhopa), and the Tripuri (a tribe) are separate.

Socio-political System

In the past, the social control and administration was controlled by the palace. When the capital was shifted to Agartala, the royal lineage, living in the village, continued to hold the reign of administration. Even the activities of priests was controlled by the state and the *Rajguru* (royal perceptor). All priests were engaged by the state and forced by the king to render ritual services to the Tripuri who were gradually absorbed within the local caste order.

The caste system in tribal Tripura did not have its natural growth. The tribal king did not allow the priestly caste a free choice in this matter. There was, thus, limited commensality across so-called castes and no jajmani system.

Most of the people had land and did cultivation. The Fisherman and Washerman had specific traditional occupation and caste councils. Inter-group relationships were contractual and non-hereditary.

Regardless the fact that four or five inter-community marriages have taken place within the village, principle of village endogamy is still in practice. Inter-dining is no bar. Most other people avoid washerman in this respect not because they are unclean but as they are poor and dirty in habits.

All except the priestly Brahmans do manual work. Discrimination on the basis of association with manual work is absent in the village.

Caste system did not seem to function in Tripura in regulating the day to day activity of the people but operated at the ideological plane, particularly in the employment of priestly services for ritual purpose. The priestly service rendered by *Rarhi Brahmans are restricted to Kayastha, Singh, and Tripuri. All other castes in old Agartala have their respective priests*.

The discussion of the caste system in the study of the weaker section appears relevant as caste differentiation and its hierarchy fairly corresponds with economic differentiation and socio-economic inequality.

Affiliation to a caste do not necessarily unite its members. Each caste has economically well off and poor sections who maintain intra-group social distance. For election or similar other purpose caste is politicized.

Of the Kayasthas living in the village, the Dey Kayastha consisting of indigenous and refugees tried to politicize caste by forming an association known as Dey Committee. It soon ceased to exist as the members fell out and all Dey Kayastha did not join.

Two concepts : *grihasti* and *muni* have secular connotation among the villagers. *Grihasti* indicates landownership but stands for gentleman and *muni* means landless labourers and the poor. These two concepts cut across caste lines. Any member of any caste having land belongs to the former and any labourer belonging to any caste belongs to the later category.

Ethnic Groups

Old Agartala consists of 282 families of which 163 (57.8%) are refugees settled during the last twenty five years. The people are divided into 17 ethnic groups and a sect. Prior to settlement of refugees Old Agartala had 12 ethnic groups. The Potter, Barber, Confectioner, Gandha Banik, Mahisya Das, and Natya are later immigrants.

The people of Old Agartala are not culturally homogeneous. The indigens, both non-tribals and tribals, claim to be the sons of the soil and consider the refugees intruders. Distribution of population in the village by ethnic groups is given in table 1.

TABLE 1: Distribution of population

Ethnic groups/sect	Family Settled/Old	Refugees/New	Total
Acharya Brahman	1	9	10
Brahman	1	11	12
Dhopa (Washerman)	6	1	7
Gandha Banik	-	1	1
Goala	1	1	2
Jugi-Debnath (Weaver)	9	16	25
Kaibarta (Fisherman)	23	17	40
Kayastha	44	32	76
Kshatriya	11	13	24
Kumbhakar (Potter)	-	33	33
Mahisya Das	-	2	2
Malakar	1	1	2
Modak (Confectioner)	-	3	3
Natya	-	1	1
Seal (Barber)	-	1	1
Sunri	1	16	17
Tripuri (Tribe)	17	-	17
Vaishnava (Sect)(*1)	4	5	9

(i) They are religious mendicants belonging to five different groups, namely Kshatriya, Kayastha, Jugi, Potter, and Mahisya Das.

Differential Positions of the Ethnic Groups

Ritual

All castes in Old Agartala do not have specific ritual status. The Brahmin, however, enjoy the highest position and the fisherman and washerman occupy low status. The Tripuri consider themselves the Kshatriya. Ritual ranking of other ethnic groups appears arbitrary. The villagers are generally indifferent about their caste status.

Numerical

Numerically the Kayasthas from the most dominant group in the village (520). They are followed by Kaibarta (179), Kumbhakar (172), Kshatriya (159), Jugi (141), and Sunri (119) in this respect. As they are internally divided into various factions, their numerical dominance has never been reflected in any social situation except in small scale at the time of election of settling inter-caste disputes.

Literary

Average literacy level (59%) is high in the village but the distribution by caste is not uniform. Table 2 gives the distribution of illiteracy by caste of major ethnic groups.

TABLE 2: Distribution of literacy

Ethnic group	Percentage of illiteracy
Dhopa	82.6
Kumbhakar	66.29
Kaibarta	58.01
Jugi	48.93
Priestly Brahmin	37.34
Tripuri	15.61
Acharya Brahmin	32.89
Kayastha	32.5
Kshatriya	27.38
Sunri	24.36

Level of illiteracy is high among scheduled and artisan castes. No perceptable difference has, however, been observed between refugees and old settlers regarding literacy distribution.

At the school level, the literacy position is satisfactory. At the college level there is a decline in this respect.

The Sunri among all communities are emerging as the most educated and well-off section in thc village. Among the scheduled castes, the Kaibartas are much ahead of the Dhopa. The Tripuri are next only to the Sunri in this regard.

Table 3 gives the distribution of levels of literacy of certain selected groups of Old Agartala.

TABLE 3: Levels of literacy of selected groups

Ethnic groups	Total population	School			College
		Junior Basic	Senior Basic	High	
Dhopa	46	4 (8.66%)	3 6.52%)	1 2.01%	-
Jugi	141	33 (23.4%)	31 (21.27%)	5 (3.54%)	3 (2.12%)
Kaibarta	179	26 (16.52%)	30 (16.75%)	16 (8.93%)	3 (1.67%)
Kayastha	520	153 (29.42%)	117 (22.5%)	61 (11.73%)	20 (3.84%)
Kshatriya	157	41 (26.11%)	51 (32.48%)	18 (11.46%)	4 (2.54%)
Kumbhakar	172	37 (21.51%)	14 (8.13%)	6 (3.48%)	1 (0.58%)
Priestly Brahman	83	20 (24%)	25 (30.12%)	5 (6%)	2 (2.4%)
Sunri	119	35 (29.41%)	30 (25.21%)	18 (15.12%)	7 (5.88%)
Tripuri	73	21 (28.76%)	15 (20.54%)	10 (13.69%)	1 (1.36%)

Economic

The indigens possess more agricultural land and the refugees own more homestead land. About 98 acres (244 Kani-II Ganda-I Kara) of agricultural lands and 47 acres (117 Kani-2 Ganda-2 Kara) of homestead lands are in the possession of the former an 61 acres (154 Kani-7 Ganda-1 Kara) of agricultural land and 67 acres (167 Kani-7 Ganda) of homestead lands are in the possession of the latter. Table

4 gives the distribution of agricultural land by ethnic group.

TABLE 4: Distribution of agricultural land by ethnic group

Ethnic group	Kani-Ganda-Kara(*)	Ethnic group	Kani-Ganda-Kara
Kayastha	114-6-1	Vaishnava	3-10-0
Kaibarta	91-0-0	Malakar	2-0-0
Sunri	40-10-0	Natya	1-0-0
Goala	40-0-0	Modak	0-12-0
Kshatriya	20-6-2	Seal	0-0-0
Acharya Brahmin	19-8-1	Mahisya Das	0-0-0
Taipuri	17-0-0		
Jugi	14-10-0		
Kumbhakar	12-15-0		
Priestly Brahmin	11-10-0		
Dhopa	5-0-2		
Gandha Banik	5-0-0		

* 16 *Kani* = 1 *Drone*; 20 *Ganda* = 1 *Kani*; 4 *Kara* = 1 *Ganda*; 2.5 *Kani* = 1 acre.

The total amount of agricultural land in the possession of the villagers is 159 acres of which nearly 50 per cent are in the possession of the Kayastha. Seal and Mahisya Das have no land. Average land per family in the village is 0.56 acres.

A Goala family has two *kani* per capita landholding which is highest in the village. Because of substantial control over economic resources, this family has a dominating role in the village. By virtue of his economic power the head of the family could occupy important village offices.

Political

The composition pattern of the *gaon-sabha* in Old Agartala is multi-ethnic. The members belong to seven ethnic groups, namely, Brahman, Kayastha, Kshatriya, Sunri, Kumbhakar, Kaibarta, and Tripuri. The head of the *sabha* is called *Pradhan* who is normally a Kshatriya.

No single ethnic group has absolute control over the *gaon-sabha*. No single factor, numerical strength, ritual status, or control over resources could enable any group or caste to have control over the *gaon-sabha*.

There are factions at all levels in Old Agartala. The old settlers do not see eye with the refugees. They irrespective of caste or community affiliations have respective stereotypes.

Every ethnic group has two or three leaders and factions. Due to internal quarrel and politics, the two co-operative credit societies in the village are in moribund state. The cooperative society of the Kumbhakar for manufacture and sale of pottery has been liquidated, the Krisak Samiti, an organization of the landless labourers, and the Dey Committee of the Kayasthas have become defunct.

The village factions are political groups controlled by members of the *gaon-sabha* and well-to-do and educated individuals.

During 1970-71, a serious conflict arose between the Bazar Party and Bani Sangha due to their involvement in local politics. The result was the suspension of community festivals, fighting, court case, and tension. This stood in the way of implementation of developmental programmes in the village.

The few individuals who are politically dominant have economic power, social position, education, and administrative and political linkage. All of them are connected with some institutions of the village, like library, club, school, social education centre, and co-operative credit society.

The agricultural land around which traditional social relations grew in Old Agartala has become inadequate with the influx of population. There are excess labourers for the same quantum of work. As a result, the villagers are moving towards urban centres. Thus, the degree of dependence on rural occupations and land has decreased. Non-ascribed professions and contractual relations are replacing the traditional semi-obligatory relations. The refugees did not care to uphold the traditional values of social relations prevailing in the village and this has accelerated the process of transformation.

The Weaker Sections

It has been observed that no caste or ethnic group is dominant in Old Agartala in terms of numerical strength, social control, and economic and political power. Therefore, classification of dominant and weak in terms of cultural categories is not satisfactory in view of the fact that dominance or weakness does not manifest in ethnicity. When social relations are contractual in nature and diversification of economy has become the norm of the day, the household may be an appropriate unit for such classification and secular criteria, namely, land holding, income, and education should be the basis for the determination of the dominant and weak.

The amount of viable agricultural landholding that can maintain five members in a family (average size of family being 5.88) is 2 acres (5 *kani*). People having no such land and annual income below Rs.600.00 may be considered as weak.

Caste affiliation of individuals does not seem to be very important in determining weakness in Old Agartala. As observed by Leach (1971 : 6) "The low castes suffer economically not because they are low castes but because present conditions have turned them into an unemployed working class".

TABLE 5: Distribution of land per family by ethnic group

Ethnic Group	Landless	1K-3 *kani*	+3K-(-) 5 *kani*	5 *kani*	+5k-10 *kani*	+10-16 *kani*	+16 *kani*
Kayastha	40	24	4	3	2	3	-
Kaibarta	22	9	3	2	2	2	-
Sunri	13	-	-	-	2	2	-
Kshatriya	16	7	-	-	-	1	-
Acharya Brahman	5	4	-	-	-	1	-
Jugi	16	8	1	-	-	-	-
Kumbhakar	24	9	-	-	-	-	-
Priestly Brahman	8	3	-	-	1	-	-
Goala	1	-	-	-	-	-	1
Dhopa	3	3	1	-	-	-	-
Gandha Banik	-	-	-	1	-	-	-
Vaishnab	6	3	-	-	-	-	-
Malakar	1	1	-	-	-	-	-
Natya	-	1	-	-	-	-	-
Modak	2	1	-	-	-	-	-
Seal	1	-	-	-	-	-	-
Mahishya Das	2	-	-	-	-	-	-
Tripuri	9	7	-	-	1	-	-
Total : 282	169	80	9	6	8	9	1

In view of possession of landholdings and per capital income the weak in Old Agartala may be categorised as below :

a. 61 landless families dependent solely on labour are the weakest. They constitute 21.63 percent.
b. 108 landless families dependent on service and business are weaker. They together form 31.29 percent.

c. 29 families of marginal peasants and small *rayats* dependent partly upon labour are weak. They form only 1.02 percent.

People belonging to category c, that is only 1.02 per cent have some chance to cross the threshold. For others the future appears bleak.

Out of the total population of 1,661 in the village, 383 are earners. Among the landless per family earner is 1.27, whereas average family size is 5.41. Per capita annual income derived from labour, service and business is Rs. 489.45 and the per capita expenditure is Rs. 604.21.

Out of 282 families of Old Agartala, 135 (47.87%) are indebted. Of this, 89 families (65.92%) comprising 15 caste belong to landless category.

Forty-nine landless families do not have homestead land which they had to sale out due to heavy pressure of indebtedness. All of them have sold out agricultural land also. Fifty-eight per cent of transferred agricultural land and 70.37 percent of sold out homestead land belonged to the present landless.

The highest amount of land lost since independence is by the landless category. Landlessness, poor income, want of work, and high cost of living create a vicious circle from which the weak can scarcely come out. Continuous pressure of poverty make people weak to fight out and cross the threshold.

Members of the weaker section, high or low in caste hierarchy, have their own social world. No organisation is visible among them beyond the household limit. Lack of patterned participation in important community affairs and their social disengagement are marked. Their only social identity is *muni* or labourer. Although they to some extent share the ideology of the dominant and high castes, they are guided by their own code of conduct.

General Discussion

Existing social relations between landowners and landless labourers or between the rich and the poor benefit the landowners and the rich. As there is conflict of interest between the two, the poor being weak cannot derive any benefit. This leads to strained sometimes antagonistic social relations.

The landowners and the well-to-do hold the view that 75 per cent of the poor are not sincere to their purpose. They are extravagant and do not take interest in education of their children. The poor lack initiative and want that everything should be done for them. Most of them are addicts and have no integrity. They quote the following proverb in support of their view :

> "Goddess of wealth does not stay with those who sleep more and eat more".

According to the weaker sections, the landowners and the well-to-do are deceitful, exploiters, and land-grabers. They engage themselves in all dirty works. They abuse the poor in filthy language do not trust them or give them their due share of benefit out of their labour.

Consequent to all these the weaker sections have developed an ideology and world view of their own. Their ideology and the world view are based on facts of deprivation. Unpleasant social experiences have made them rudely realistic. Their world view has thus a reference to immediate environment, hard life, starvation, exploitation, unemployment, and exploitation. They hold that the government is trying to improve their condition and social changes are taking place but the landowners, well-to-do social and political elites, and officials do not allow any benefit to trickle down to the poor. Their level of aspiration is low having reference only to want, work, and wages. Poverty has come upon some of them as a hangover from the past and who appear mentally prepared to pass it on to their next generation. They say : "Our ancestors lived on their toil, we do not aspire our children to become king". They complain but rationalize by attributing their misery to fate and *karma*.

The process of exploitation is regular and systematic in Old Agartala. Moneylenders, landowners, employers, shop keepers, religious preceptors, and political elites all exploit them alike,. This is perhaps the worst social mechanism which perpetuates impoverishment, pauperisation, and has set an imbalance in the social relations of the community.

The hope of the landless labourers has been frustrated as the abolition of zamindary did not give them ownership to land. In fact, according to them, big *rayats* still behave like zamindars.

Nothing has happened since independence which has given the poor and the landless the right of social assertion though some changes have taken place. The village factions could grow into a political force from caste and kinship base, but the numerically dominant weaker section can not unite and turn into a political force because the weaker section has no social and political base and the community relations and solidarity do not pull them up.

The existing social relations have not been able to affect any qualitative change in the social and economic standing of the poor. On the contrary, they are caught up in the process of steady impoverishment. They appear to constitute a sub-structure of the society having no effective communication with the super-structure that constantly exerts pressure on them.

REFERENCES

Dantwala, M.L. *Poverty in India*. Macmillan India, 1973.

Epstein, T.S. *Economic Development and Social change in South India*. Manchester University Press. 1962.

Fonseca, A.T. (ED.) *Challenge of Poverty in India*. New Delhi, 1971.

Leach.E.R. (ED.) *Aspects of Caste in South India, Ceylon and North West Pakistan*. Cambridge University Press. Cambridge, 1971.

Lewis, Oscar *Village Life In Northern India: Studies in a Delhi Village*. Urbana : University of Illinois Press, 1958.

Singh, K. *Raj Mala*. Tripura, 1283 (B.S.).

Warriner, Doreen *Land Reform in Principle and Practice*. Oxford, 1967.

3

BASILARDANGA : A VILLAGE IN NORTH BENGAL

GOPA BANERJEE

In this paper an attempt has been made to study the weaker sections in a villave named, Basilardanga, in the district of Jalpaiguri, West Bengal. Numerically Rajbanshi is the dominant ethnic group in this area. But after partition of Bengal a large number of refugees from then Pakistan came and settled here.

Field investigation was carried out for about three and half months during December '74 to middle of April '75. Besides applying traditional anthropological tools in collecting data, charts and schedules were also used. Interview with some old informants was particularly found very useful.

The Village

The name Basilardanga is derived from an agricultural implement *basila*. The village is situated on the bank of river Souli. The settlement pattern of the village is somewhat scattered and it does not follow any ethnic line. The village consisted of 196 households, distributed into twenty *tanribari* and one hundred scattered domiciles. Tanribari means the household of a Jotdar and a group of smaller houses of his share croppers or *adhiar* who are generally landless. But at present most of the *jotdar* of this village settled are in the town or in more advanced villages and occasionally visit their respective *tanribari*. Most of the *jotdar* are Rajbanshi. After inmigration of refugees some of them settled in the *khas* land of the government and several bought large landholdings.

In the village there is a primary school, a *Mahila Samiti (agency)*, a public sacred place *bhandanithan* where the worship of goddess *vandani* is observed mainly by the local Rajbanshi. In front of the temple there is an open space where the weekly market is held. There are fifteen wells used for fetching drinking water. Nine small ponds supply irrigation water.

There are two roads for separate population in this village, viz. the Rajbanshi (refugees as well as original settlers of the village) and Bengali Hindu refugees. There are of course, further divisions in each of these categories which have been shown in Table 1. The Badia although inhabit the village do not fall in either of the group.

There are altogether twelve ethnic groups in the village and their total population is 1029. The Rajbanshi alone comprise about 55.1 per cent of the total popultion. Considering all the ethinic groups of the Rajbanshi category, viz. Napit or barber, Tanti or weaver, Achikari or precepters together they have a total population of about 61.7 per cent. The inmigrant Bengali population including Brahman, Kayastha, Moira, Jele, Teli, Kumhar and Bania, form only 38.6 per cent of which Jele (30.3%) and Moira (10.9%) are the dominant. The Bedia community represents two per cent of total popultion. Numerically, thus there are three main clusters viz. Rajbanshi, Jele, and Moira.

Economic Dimension

The villagers largely depend on agriculture. The Rajbanshi did not know any improved methods of cultivation. They used to produce single crop viz. paddy. The refugees introduced both improved methods of cultivation and double cropping. Now-a-days, the Rajbanshi also have started it. In almost every plot of agricultural land there is a well. As most of the lands are high there is no adquate water and the irrigation facilities provided by the government are yet to reach this village. Naturally, the villagers depend on rain.

There are three types of land in this village, viz. 1) *danga* or high land, 2) *sahori* or medium, and 3) *dahola* or low land. *Dahola* produces *amon* or *heuti* paddy while *danga* produces *aus* or *bhaidoi* paddy. *Sahori* land gives better yield. Mainly three crops are cultivated, viz. Paddy-*heuti* and *bhadoi*, Jute or *pata*, and tobacco or *tamkku*. Wheat has been introduced in 1975 and that has been cultivated by the rich farmers only.

TABLE 1: Distribution of Population

	Name of ethnic groups	Traditional occupation	Total Family No.	%	Male No.	%	Female No.	%	Total Population No.	%
Rajbanshi										
	1.Rajbanshi	Agriculture	109	55.6	305	55.2	262	54.9	567	55.1
	2.Adhikari	Priesthood	10	5.1	24	4.3	26	5.4	50	4.9
	3.Napit	Shaving	1	0.05	5	.9	4	.8	9	.8
	4.Tanti	Weaving	1	.05	1	.1	-	-	1	.01
Bengali										
	1.Brahman	Priesthood	1	.05	4	.7	3	.6	7	.6
	2.Kayastha	Scribe	3	1.5	16	2.8	11	2.3	27	2.6
	3.Moira	Confectioneries	20	10.2	63	11.4	50	10.4	113	10.9
	4.Jele	Fishery	42	21.4	108	19.4	101	21.1	209	20.3
	5.Teli	Oilpressing	1	.05	2	.3	2	.4	4	.3
	6.Benia	Goldsmith	1	.05	3	.5	4	.8	7	.6
	7.Kumhar	Potter	3	1.5	7	1.2	7	1.4	14	1.3
	1.Badia	Drumbeater	4	2.0	14	2.5	7	1.4	21	2.0
			196		552		477		1029	

Average yield of *heuti* paddy in *dahola* land is six to seven maunds per *bigha*. In *danga* land different crops are grown. The average yield of Bhadoi paddy is four to five mds., Jute four mds., and in *sahori* land it's yield is about five mds. The yield of tobacco per bigha comes to about 2.5 mds. There are differential costs of production for various croups as shown in Table 2.

TABLE 2: Main agricultural yields and expenditure

Crops	Period	No.of labourer	Expenditure approximately	Approximate yield	Price(Just after harvesting
1. *Paddy*					
Bhadoi	April-May to August-September	14	Rs.126	4 mds	Rs.200
Heuti	June-July to November-December			6 mds	Rs.300
2. *Jute*					
Bhadia Nal	April to August	20	Rs.180	4 mds	Rs.260
Heutia Nal	April-May to September-October			5 mds	Rs.325
3. *Tobacco*	July-August February-March	8	Rs. 50	2 mds. to 2.5 mds.	Rs.120 to Rs.180

From the table it is seen that *Heuti* paddy and tobacco are more profitable than the other crops. Even though the ordinary cultivators are less interested in cultivating the same. The low land is more fabourabvle for *heuti* paddy cultivation. It also needs irrigation. Most of the oridinary farmers do not possess low land and can not spend money on irrigation.

In case of tobacco, it needs constant observation. Much water as well as scorching sunrays are harmful to this. Besides it needs longer period for a crop.

In agricultural organization four types of occupational categories are noticed. It may diagrametically be represented as below :

TABLE 3: Engagement of people in agricultural operation

Name of ethnic groups	No. of families	Labour Kamla	Labour Chokindar	Owner cultivator Cultivated by himself	Owner cultivator Cultivated by owner sh. cropper	Sharecropper Bhota Khaoa	Sharecropper Uttungkara Kara	Supervisor
1. Rajbanshi	109	23 (21.1%)	10 (9.1%)	24 (22.0%)	21 (19.2%)	15 (13.7%)	8 (7.3%)	5 (4.5%)
2. Adhikari	10	4 (40.0%)		4 (40.0%)			2 (20%)	
3. Napit	1					1 (100%)		
4. Tanti	1 (100%)							
5. Brahman	1 (100%)						1 (100%)	
6. Kayastha	3						2 (66.6%)	
7. Moira	20	6 (30%)		4 (20%)	4 (20%)		3 (15%)	3 (15%)
8. Bania	1			1 (100%)				
9. Teli	1			1 (100%)				
10. Jele	42	8 (19.0%)	2 (4.7%)	13 (13.9%)	8 (19.0%)		9 (21.4%)	
11. Kumhar	3			1 (33.3%)	2	(66.6%)		
12. Badia	4	4 (100%)						
	196	58-(29.5%)		81-(41.3%)		43-(21.4%)		8-(4.5%)

TABLE 3 *Contd.*

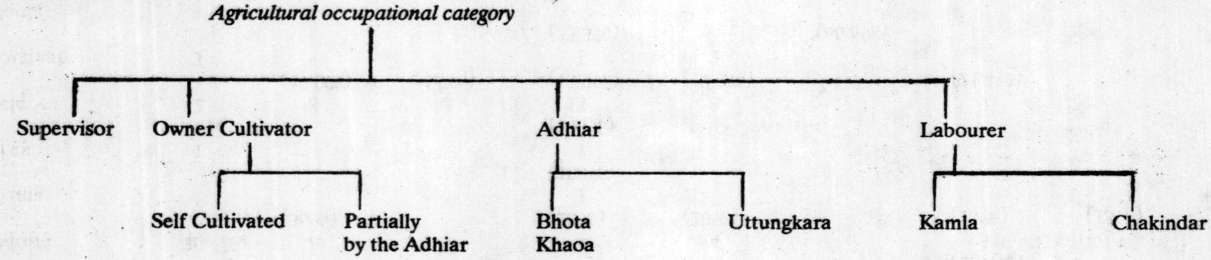

Table 3 details the number of families of different communities engaged in the agricultural operation.

1. *The Supervisor* They have more than 20 acres of land per family. The land is partly cultivated by the paid labourer and partly by sharecroppers. Alltogether eight families (Rajbanshi 5 and Moira 3) i.e. only four per cent belong to this group.
2. *Owner cultivator* They are of two types and comprise 41.3 per cent of families.

   a) Cultivator for self only who may also work in other fields.
   b) The land is partially cultivated by the owner as well as by the share-cropper.

3. *Adhiars or share-croppers* Nearly 21 per cent of families belong to this category. With respect to the terms and condition of share-cropping they are of two types, viz.

   a) *Bhota-khaoa Adhiar* : They are usually landless and live in the *Tanribari* of the landowner. As they are *Ni-Halua* i.e., have no bullock and plough, they usually take per *hal*, 15 bighas of land, 6 mds. of paddy in advance which they return back to the *deunia* or owner, after harvesting, with 50 per cent share of the produce. The owner bears the cost of the seed. Primarily Bhota - *khaoa adhiar* come from the Rajbansi community.
   b) *Uttung-hara Adhiar* They may have inadequate land or they are landless. The owner gives half of the share of the seed and fertilizer while the adhiar gives the other half and use his labour, own plough and bullocks. The produce is divided equally between them.

4. *Labourers*: 29.5 per cent of the families belong to this category. Most of them comes from Rajbansi and Badia group. According to the terms and condition labourers are of two types.

   a) *Kamla* or daily paid labourer are those who are appointed against cash payment @Rs. 2 to 2.50, one meal, breakfast and half seer of paddy per day. Sometimes they are paid

@Rs.3.50 to Rs.4 but are not provided with food.

b) *Chakindar* or contract labourer who are appointed on seasonal basis. They have to perform all the domestic as well as agricultural work. They are paid Rs.100 to Rs.120 annually and are provided with three meals, betel, biri, tea every day and a pair of dhoti and napkins annually.

Besides these four categories another category may be included which comprises of persons having no capital. So they give land to others for share-cropping. They may work in other's field as daily labourer.

Altogether 3.3 per cent of families belong to this group including two families of Jele and three families Rajbanshi.

The villagers perform many occupations other than their respective caste occupations. Distribution of different occupations has been given in table 4. A Bengali Brahman accepted goldsmithy and share-cropping as his profession. Rajbansi are weaver, Bengali Teli, Moira, Bania, and potter earn their livelihood from cultivation. There are two Rajbanshi teachers. A person from Moira community is working as tailor. Some are engaged in petty business. Some of the caste groups are still practicing their traditional occupation such as Adhikari (preceptors), Napit (barber), Badia (drum beater), Jele (fisherman). Beggars mostly come from the Adia community. Bhota-khaoa adhiar mostly come from the Rajbanshi community. The majority of the *uttungkara adhiar* belong to the Bengali Jele community. Most of the agricultural labourer come from the Rajbanshi, Badia, and Jele community.

The women are not allowed to work as daily labourer. They may help their men in the field. They earn only through husking paddy and their rate of payment is Rs.0.75 for husking 12 kg. of paddy. Four Rajbanshi women work as maidservant in the houses of Asamia Brahman and Bengali Baidya of Gartali Jalpesh village. There are two Rajbanshi and two Badia women beggars.

Altogether 337 males are earners and 215 are nonearners. Among the female 118 are earners and 359 are nonearners. The average family size is 5.2 and 2.3 of whom are earners.

The working days are spread approximately over eight months. They do not get jobs during the months of Asarh, Bhadra, Aswin, and Magh. So the poor villagers look for other means of livelihood some of which are given below :

TABLE 4: Different occupation of the ethnic groups

Name of Caste	MALE: Agriculture		Bhota		Uttung		D.L.		C.L.		Traditional occupation		Service		Business		Beggars		Total Earner		Total Non-Earner		FEMALE: Husking		Begging		Maid Servant		Total Labour		Total Non-Labour	
	No.	%	No.	%	No.	%	No.	%	No.	%	No.	%	No.	%	No.	%	No.	%	No.	%	No.	%	No.	%	No.	%	No.	%	No.	%	No.	%
Badia							3	25	1	8.3	4	33.3					4	33.3	12		2		3	6	2	40			5		2	
Moira	17	50			6	17.6	5	15	3	8.8			3	8.8					34		29		5						5		45	
Kayastha	4	57.1			2	28.5									1	14.3			7		9		2						2		9	
Bania	1	100																	1		2		1						1		3	
Teli	1	100																	1		1										2	
Kumhar	2	33.3			4	66.6													6		1		2						2		5	
Brahmin	3	72			1	25													4				1						1		2	
Jele	27	41.5			11	16.9	10	15.3	1	1.5	16	24.6							65		45		15						15		86	
Rajbanshi	70	31.8	15	8.1	13	7.02	53	28.6	26	14.0			2	2.02	3	10.6	2	1.08	185		120		73	92.3	2	2.5	4	5	79		187	
Napit			1	20			1	20	1	20	2	40							5				2						2		2	
Adhikari	7	43.7			2	12.5	3	18.7	4	25									16		8		6						6		20	
Tanti																	1		1													
																			337		217								118		363	

W.B. Bhota = Bhota khaoa Adhiar
Uttung = Uttung kara Adhiar
D.L. = Daily Labourer
C.L. = Contract Labourer

1. *Bahomara* It is a communal fishing. The owner of the pond first catches fish and then a day is fixed for communal fishing from his pond.
2. *Kurani* Once the harvest is over the poor collect the left over grains from the field.
3. During rainy season overflooded low lying area gives an opportunity for fishing.
4. During lean period the poor also collect roots, herbs, snails etc. for consumption.

Those who have some capital work as middlemen. Sometimes they receive money from big moneylenders or Jotdar and buy paddy, jute, etc. from weekly markets when the market price is low. They sell those items when the market price is high. They are given a commission at the rate of one kg. rice (cost is Rs.1.30) per md. Sometimes they buy tobacco from the villagers at cheaper rate and also get commission. They also collect eggs for wholeseller and get one egg per dozen as remuneration.

Sometimes well to do farmers give goats, fowl and pigeon on share basis to the poor who receive products equally. The rich farmers earn cash money through betelnut cultivation. Per acre they earn about Rs.1,500 to Rs.1,600.

There were four Jotdars in this village, three are Rajbanshi and one is a Bengali. With the abolition of *jotdary* system in 1953, most of the land was transferred to the Bengali refugees who came with cash money prior to 1947. Some of the land became *khas* land of the government.

Total land of the village is 3,469 *bigha* of which the Rajbanshi and Bengali community of this village possess 1246.5 *bigha* and 853.10 *bigha* respectively. Approximately 150 *bigha* are non-cultivable land or pond. The rest of the land is in possession of the Asamia Brahman, Khain, Bengali Brahman and Baidya, and Bihari and Marwari of Gartali village. Altogether 32.6 per cent families are landless.

Badia, Napit, Tanti are totally landless. Most of the communities possess 1-6 acres of land except three families of Moira community and five families from Rajbanshi community who possess 20 acres per family.

TABLE 5: Landholding pattern

Name of the ethnic family	Total groups	Total persons	Amount of land possess by the ethnic groups	Per Family holding	Per capita holding	Landless families Bigha Bigha	1-2 acres	3-6 acre	7-10 acre	11-15 acre	16-19 acre	20 and above	Total land holder
Badia	4	21	-	-	-	4(%)	-	-	-	-	-	-	-
Moira	20	113	400 *Bigha*	20.9	3.5	4(20%)	2(12.5%)	5(31.2%)	1(25%)	2(12.5)	1(6.2%)	3(12.5%)	16(80%)
Kayastha	3	27	24 *Bigha*	8	8	1(33.3%)	1(50%)	1(50%)	-	-	-	-	2(66.6%)
Jele	42	209	381 *Bigha* 13 *Kathas*	9	1.8	4(9.4%)	18(47.3%)	11(28.9%)	6(15.5%)	1(2.6%)	2(5.2%)	-	38(90.6%)
Bania	1	7	10 *Bigha* 10 *Kathas*	10	1.4	-	-	1(100%)	-	-	-	-	1(100%)
Teli	1	4	11 *Bigha*	11	2.5	-	-	1(100%)	-	-	-	-	1(100%)
Brahman	1	7	2 *Bigha*	21	0.28	-	1(100%)	-	-	-	-	-	1(100%)
Kumhar	3	14	17 *Bigha*	5.6	1.2	-	1(38.3%)	2(66.6%)	-	-	-	-	3(100%)
Rajbanshi	109	567	1192 *Bigha* 10 *Kathas*	10.9	2-1	45(41.3%)	13(11.9%)	25(22.9%)	15(13.7%)	5(5.6%)	1(.9%)	5(3.6%)	64(58.7%)
Napit	1	9	-	-	-	1(100%)	-	-	-	-	-	-	-
Adhikari	10	50	54 *Bigha*	5.4	1.0	4(40%)	4(66.6%)	2(33.3%)	-	-	-	-	6(60%)
Tanti	1	1	-	-	-	1(100%)	-	-	-	-	-	-	-
						64 (32.6%)	40 (30.3%)	48 (36.3%)	22 (16.6%)	8 (6.0%)	4 (30.3%	8 (6.0%)	132 (67.3%)

Note : One *Bigha* is equivalent to 1/3rd of an acre.

TABLE 6: Income per capita (monthly)

Name of the ethnic groups	Rs. 1 to Rs. 50 (Very poor)		Rs. 51-100 (poor)		Rs.101-150 (Marginal)		Rs.151 & above (Rich)	
	No. of families	%	No. of families	%	No. of families	%	No. of families	%
Badia	4	-	-	-	-	-	-	-
Napit	1	-	-	-	-	-	-	-
Tanti	1	-	-	-	-	-	-	-
Adhikari	6	60	4	40	-	-	-	-
Brahman	1	-	-	-	-	-	-	-
Kayastha	2	66.6	1	33.3	-	-	-	-
Moira	6	30	3	15	6	30	5	25
Kumar	3	-	-	-	-	-	-	-
Teli	-	-	1	-	-	-	-	-
Bania	1	-	-	-	-	-	-	-
Jele	22	51.7	14	33.4	4	9.8	2	4.9
Rajbansi	68	62.4	20	18.3	16	14.7	5	4.5
Total	115	58.7	43	21.9	26	13.2	12	6.1

Table 6 rather gives a very gloomy picture. The first category i.e., the very poor or weakest are either landless or have 1 to 6 *bigha* of land per family. They are mostly from labourer group and their per capita monthly income varies from Rs. 10 to Rs. 50. About 67 per cent of Kayastha, 62.4 per cent of Rajbanshi and 51.7 per cent of Jele families, and the total of Bedia, Tanti and Kumhar are economically the weakest. The second category includes those families which have land below 20 *bigha* per family. Their per capita monthly income varies from Rs. 51 to Rs. 110. They are mainly share-cropper and are landless, some of them have inadequate land. They may be grouped as the poor. Forty per cent of the Adhikari, 33.4 per cent of the Jele, 18.3 per cent of the Rajbanshi and 15 per cent of the Moira families belong to this group. Therefore the landless labourers, sharecroppers and small farmers may be identified as economically the weaker section. The third group i.e. marginal group are those who have land above 20 *bigha* per family. Their per capita monthly income varies from Rs.101 to Rs.150. They are mainly owner cultivators. Some of them, of course employ share-croppers. Thirty per cent of the Moira and 14.7 per cent of the Rajbanshi families are marginal. The fourth category are the rich or well off families. They are the Jotdar. They have at least 40 *bigha* of land per family. They also supplement their income through business and service. Their per capita monthly income is above Rs. 151. They have some savings also and give loans to others at high rates of interest. They are mainly the supervisor cultivators and some are also owner cultivators. Twentyfive per cent of the Moira, 4.9 per cent of the Jele and 4.5 per cent of the Rajbanshi families are rich.

Economic Interaction

Through various economic activities the villagers are tied-up with each other as share croppers, labourers, creditors, — Bahomara, Hauli etc. Inmigration of different ethnic groups to the area from different states of India has also enlarged the field of economic interaction beyond the village level.

All the *bhota khaoa* share-croppers are Rajbanshi who have taken land from the Khain, Assami Brahman, Baidya, Marwari, and Bihari of Gartali village and Moira and Rajbanshi of this village. The majority of the *uttungkara* share-croppers come from Bengali families. They cultivated about 69.6 acres of land last year as share-croppers.

The Rajbanshi Napit earns through *jajmani* relationship with the Rajbanshi and some other castes except the Bengali. Last year he earned a cash money of about Rs. 375 and about 31 mds. of paddy from Rajbanshi *jajman* at the rate of 12 kg. of paddy per family. Now-a-days some Rajbanshi also pay in cash. As payment in kind is insufficient, they prefer to give service to those who pay in cash. Rajbanshi agriculturists, Tanti, Napit are the *jajman* of the Adhikary.

The *mahajani* or money lending business is operating in this region. Three persons from Asamia Brahman, and a Baidya from the Bengali community of Gartali village and five Rajbanshi and a Moira of this village are the *mahajan*.

Only 32 cases of land transfer due to economic distress like social obligations and liabilities, for loan payment have been reported. Of these in five cases (2 Jele, 1 Teli, 1 Kayastha and 1 Kumhar) land has been transferred by the Bengali to the Rajbanshi. In the remaining 27 cases land has been transferred by the Rajbanshi to their own community, Bengali Moira and Jele of this village and the Asamia Brahman, Khain, and the Baidya of Gartali village. Money is given on loan on cent per cent interest basis. Sometimes the creditors do not charge any interest out of sympathy. It is interesting that sometimes it so happens especially among the poor Rajbanshi that when they are not able to repay their loan with interest, they go to the money lenders and touch their feet and appeal "you are my father and I am your son, excuse me, I can not return you loan". This system is locally known as *bapdai*. Those who have no bullock to plough land sometimes come to *jotdar* for a pair of bullocks on temporary basis to plough their own land or to work as share-croppers.

Sometimes the *jotdar* or creditors do not claim any interest as they get sure supply of labour during agricultural season. They may also get tobacco at a cheaper rate. At present the creditors do not generally give loan to the landless poor as they often fail to repay it. On the other hand they prefer to give loan to the share-croppers as they have some security.

Agricultural Innovation

Improved varieties of seeds and chemical fertilizers are used mostly by the rich Bengali farmers and two Rajbanshi. Marginal farmers of the Bengali community specially the Moira want to use improved varieties of seeds and chemical fertilizers, but due to lack of capital they can not afford to do so. They use the mixture of ash and cowdung and say that it serves the purpose of urea fertilizer. Some of the rich Rajbanshi farmers prefer their traditional methods. They say that the constant use of chemical fertilizer decreases the production. There are fourteen members who have taken group loans as well as individual loan for buying cattle, fertilizer, land improvement, betel nut cultivation etc. Among them twelve individuals belong to the Bengali community and two are Rajbanshi.

Landless labourers do not get any loan as they have no land for security. Sharecroppers say that if the *deunia* borrow loan for seeds and fertilizer they do not give them any share. Therefore the poorer section are not benefitted by these loans.

Food Habit and Material Culture

Usually the villagers take there meals a day. During lean period, however, the poor depend mainly on raw tea, betel leaves, boiled roots, and leaves of *kachcha*. Dried fish is a delicacy to the people. The Bedia eat flesh of dead animals.

A Rajbanshi house can easily be distinguished from those of the Bengali. There is, of course, no concrete or *pacca* house in this village. The roof of the house of Jotdar (three Rajbanshi and one Bengali) are made of tin. The walls are made of bamboo splits plastered with cowdung and mud. The houses of the poor are made of straws, hard stricks of jute and bamboo splits. A poor Rajbanshi house has one bedroom, one kitchen, one cattle shed, a courtyard and a space for *thakurthan* (sacred place) and a *kachcha kua* (well). A poor Bengali house has only a bedroom and a kitchen. Cattleshed and well may not be present. The house of a *jotdar* consists of a guest room in addition to the above.

Social Dimension

It is popularly believed that the Rajbanshi came from the Koch parenthood, and are descendants of a royal lineage. Several scholars like o'Danieal, Dalton, Risley, Gait have observed that the Rajbanshi are the converted Koch. Dr. Charu Chandra Sanyal says that Jelia Kaibarta, Namasudra, Bagdi, Malo, Koch, Mog, Dhimol, Pod, Rabha, Mech and Kantai broke away from their original caste or tribal fold and recorded themselves as Rajbanshi Khatriya Jati. From the past history of Koch it is found that a sort of ranking existed among themselves. In 1912, there was mass movement viz. khatro-movement in Rangpur under the leadership of Shri Panchanan Roy Burman. A mass acceptance of sacred thread had taken place. Since that time there were two distinct sections, one was clean and the other was unclean section.

The Rajbanshi of this village claim their Khatriya identity and also claim that their language and culture are more or less approximate to that of the upper Hindu castes. They have also the clean and unclean sections. For example the *adhikari* or the preceptors who offer food to the household deities. 2) The landed aristocrats and agriculturists use surnames as Roy, Burman, Basunia, Kongar, etc. The third group comprises of Napit and Tanti who strict to their traditional occupations. Their surnames are Seal and Basak respectively.

The Bengali community of this village is ritually stratified into three groups. 1) The first group includes the Brahman and Kayastha, 2) *Nabasakha* i.e. Moira, Kumbar, Teli, Bania or Swarnakar. 3) The third one is Namosudra i.e. Jele or fishermen. From social hierarchical point of view the immigrant Bengali and the local Rajbanshi have independent sets of hierarchy orders as shown in Table 7.

TABLE 7: Social hierarchy

Bengali	*Rajbanshi*
1. Brahman	1. Adhikary (Preceptors)
2. Kayastha	2. Landed Aristocrats and agriculturists
3. Moira	3. Napit (Barber)
4. Kumhar	4. Tanti (Weaver)
5. Teli	
6. Bania or Swarnakar	
7. Jele	

The Bengali consider the Rajbanshi lower than themselves and rank the Baida at the lowest position in the regional hierarchy. The Rajbanshi accept the higher status of the Bengali as a whole and regard the Basua lower than themselves.

Most of the Rajbanshi, including their barbers and weavers like the Adhikary, who is regarded as the *guru* or priest of their household deities wear sacred thread. The Rarhi Brahman serve the Bengali Brahman, Kayastha, Moira, Kumhar, and Teli. The *Swarnakar* or Bania are served by the degraded Brahman. The Namosudra or Jele have their own priest. The Bengali Napit who serves the high caste does not serve the Jele. As there is no Bengali Brahman or Napit in this village they come here from Jalpaiguri and Mainaguri towns. The Bengali upper castes do not accept cooked food from the Jele.

Some of the Bengali castes do not perform their traditional caste occupation and have accepted agriculture as their profession. To work in other's field or to plough land are considered low by both the Brahmin and Kayastha.

The Rajbanshi have no Brahman of their own. The Asamia Brahman serve them as their priest. The Adhikary serves all sections of the Rajbanshi. Though agriculturist, the Rajbanshi can not become the Adhikary as they are not allowed to worship the household deities although inter-marriage between these two sections is practised. A Napit cannot marry a Tanti. Marriage between the Rajbanshi having and without sacred thread is an usual practice. All belong to kasyapa *gotra*. So marriage within the same clan is the obvious result.

Both the Bengali and the Rajbanshi regard *Bedia* as low because they perform degraded avocations, like beating of drum, castration of goat and so on. The Bengali are termed *Dhakaia* or *Bhatia* by the Rajbanshi as they are the immigrants, while the former call the later the Bahe. The Bengali, including the lowest ranked Jele, do not accept cooked food from the Rajbanshi.

The Rajbanshi have no clear conception of *bhadrolok* and *chhotolok*. They distinguish *deunia* or landowner from *proja* or *adhiar* or sharecropper and *kamla* or daily wage labourer. A Rajbanshi kamla *kishan* or *adhiar* does not address his landowner as Babu but terms as *deunia*. On the other hand the Bengali landowner is always addressed as *Babu*. If a *adhiar* acquires land and becomes rich landowner he is not to be regarded as *deunia*.

The *chhotolok* — *bhadrolok* concept is more clear among the Bengali. The upper caste Bengali regard the Jele as *chhotolok*. But the Jele do not consider themselves so. According to the Bengali, the labour class in general is considered as the *chhotolok* and the landholder group is regarded as the *bhadrolok*. Even the poor high caste Bengali do not consider the Badia, Rajbanshi and the Jele as their equal. A rich Jele was always trying to keep contact with the rich high castes. But he is not in a position to reach their status. The member of high castes always try to avoid the poor section of their own castes. But if we consider the case of high castes a different picture is noticed. Thus, a well educated Kayastha who was once a rich farmer but had to dispose off all his land due to economic distress is still a member of the village Panchayat. He has also a good contact with the B.D.O. and other officials beyond the village level. Thus, he enjoys prestige in the village though he is not economically sound. His social constraints prevent him to move freely with the labourer class.

The Moira is accepted as a high caste. After the abolition of *jotdary* system they acquired some land through which they have achieved prestige and high status among all sections of the people. One of them also achieved membership of the panchayat.

A superordinate and subordinate relationship corresponds the labourer and master relationships. A *proja* or *adhiar* is not supposed to sit before his *deunia* or enter into the house of the latter. *Deunia* is often seen to be present in every social function of his *proja*. Some of the younger generation Rajbanshi landowner refer the sharecroppers by kin terms, such as *kaka*, *dada*, while the latter address the former as *Bapo*, *Khura*, *Ajo* and so on. Generally the Rajbanshi landowners address the share-croppers by their names.

A Bengali Brahman who works as *adhiar* and goldsmith claims that he was not a priest as he did not get any other opportunity to earn money he has accepted this job. According to the statement of the Adhikari, they are not the priest like the Bengali Brahman as they have nine knots in their sacred thread while the Brahman priest have six knots.

Elites, political leaders, musicians, educated and influential landowners get special prestige irrespective of their caste status. According to the villagers, there are five *Mani* or respected persons in the village, among whom three belong to the Rajbanshi and two belong to the Jotdar family. One Moira is considered a respected person because he is rich, maintains a good relationship with the Block Office as well as with the political leaders of Jalpaiguri. He is educated and a member of the panchayat. The Kayastha is respected as he is a rich farmer. He is also educated, a member of the panchayat, and maintains connections with high officials. All these factors led him to be a *Babu*.

The percentage of literacy in the village is very low. Table 8 shows the percentage of literacy among various ethnic-groups. Out of 552 male 164 are literates while among 477 females only 49 are literates. Literates mostly belong to the Bengali community. Sixty eight per cent of the Moira and 22.7 per cent of the Rajbansi are literates. Badia, Tanti, and Napit are all illiterate.

TABLE 8: Level of literacy by caste/community

	MALE										FEMALE					
Name of the Caste	Primary		Secondary		S.F.		Graduate		Total		Primary		Secondary		Total	
	No.	%	No.	%	No.	%	No.	%	No.	%	No.	%	No.	%	No.	%
Badia	-	-	-	-	-	-	-	-	-	-	-	-	-	-	-	-
Moira	25	39.6	16	25.3	2	3.1	-	-	43	68.2	13	26	-	-	13	26
Kayastha	3	18.7	4	25	1	6	-	-	8	50	1	9.9	5	45.4	6	45.4
Jele	14	12.9	16	14.8	3	2.7	-	-	33	3.5	7	6.9	2	1.9	9	8.9
Bania	1	33.3	-	-	-	-	-	-	1	33.3	2	50.0	1	25	3	75
Teli	1	50	-	-	1	50	-	-	2	100	-	-	-	-	-	-
Brahman	-	-	-	-	1	25	-	-	1	25	-	-	-	-	-	-
Kumar	2	28.5	-	-	-	-	-	-	2	28.5	-	-	-	-	-	-
Rajbanshi	37	12.1	32	10.4	1	0.32	1	0.32	71	23.2	12	2.5	4	0.83	16	3.3
Napit	-	-	-	-	-	-	-	-	-	-	-	-	-	-	-	-
Adhikari	3	12.5	1	4.1	-	-	-	-	4	16.6	2	7.6	-	-	2	7.6
Tanti	-	-	-	-	-	-	-	-	-	-	-	-	-	-	-	-

Religious Dimension

The Rajbanshi observe their traditional festivals and the rituals of their life cycle. The Bengali are found to participate in some of their festivals, such as *Mechhine Brato*. With their traditional gods and goddess, like *Bisohari*, *Mashan*, *Satyapirh*, *Vundani*, *Bisna*, *Gram Thakur* etc. they also worship some Hindu God - Goddess like *Durga*, *Saraswati*, *Kali*, *Satyanarayan*, etc.

Both the low and high caste people are found to participate in most of the festivals. But the Badia are not allowed to enter into the temple of vandani. They are allowed only to sweep and clean the courtyard and the space around the temple.

There are two types of Adhikari: (i) *Pat Tulsi* Adhikari are the *Guru*. They learn incantation from their ancestors. They can teach the sacred incantation to their followers who may not be a member of the Adhikari family. After completion of teaching the Adhikari gives a leaf of *tulsi* to his deciple and allows him to worship the deities. (ii) The second type of preceptors are termed as *kan tulsi*.

Magico-religious treatment of disease is very much in vogue, specially, among the Rajbanshi. But the present generation as well as educated elites do not want to put much weight on it. They prefer to consult physicians rather than to take the advice of the traditional *Ojha*.

Political Dimension

The power structure of the village rests on the two institutions like the Gram Sabha and Anchal Panchayat. Before Independence, the village was controlled by the Rajbanshi. After Independence, the refugees came with cash money. They were literate. Both the Bengali and the Rajbanshi were elected as members of the panchayat. An inter-ethnic cleavage is observed among them. In the Gram Panchayat out of 14 members only two belong to Bengali community. In the Anchal Panchayat out of 11 members six belong to the Bengali and five to the Rajbanshi. Generally the Gram Panchayat deals with cases like rape, theft, land dispute, quarrels between the neighbours, marital dispute, etc. The Anchal Panchayat mainly deals with the welfare of the village. The Chaukidar collects tax which is used for the village welfare such as construction of drinking water wells. Besides, the Panchayat also spends money for medicine, education, clothing, milk, etc. for the poor and needy persons or for the construction of village roads.

Anchal and village Panchayat distribute the governmental relief to the poor and needy sections through some middlemen. These middlemen are generally members of the village Panchayat. They belong to both the Bengali and Rajbanshi communities. The 15 wells which were built by the Block are mostly found in the courtyards of the Panchayat members and well-to-do Rajbanshi or Bengali. The benefits that are supposed to go to the needy persons do not reach them. The villagers argue that most of these meterials are consumed by the middlemen. The poorer section of the Bengali said that these goods are preserved by the Rajbanshi members while the poorer section of the latter say that these are preserved by the Bengali. Both the sections blame each other.

There are two classes of ration cards given to the poor i.e. (i) *Ni-Hatua* or those who have no plough and bullocks and (ii) *Hatua* or those who have plough and bullocks. The former get rice, wheat, oil, and sugar and the latter get only sugar and kerosene oil at controlled rates. But due to village faction it is found that some members of the former category get only sugar and kerosene oil instead of rice and wheat. Various types of loans like land development loan, cattle loan, seed and fertilizer loan etc., sanctioned for the villagers do not entirely reach the hands of the poor. Because of the lengthy and complicated process of getting such loans, and minimum contact with officials the poorer section can hardly avail themselves of such benefit.

There are three political parties with their followers in the village viz., (i) Pradesik Kisan Samiti (C.P.M.), (ii) Krisok Union (Congress), (iii) Sanjukta Krishok Sabha (R.S.P.). The leadership of these parties are vested in the hands of the well-to-do and influential villagers. The C.P.M. leaders and their followers mainly belong to the Bengali community, while R.S.P. and Congress followers are mostly the Rajbanshi. The poor and the socially weak by and large remain outside any party politics. They blindly follow the order of their *deunia*. The Bengali elites are mostly interested in the socio-political matter of their own community. But little concerted effort has yet been made for any welfare of the village as a whole.

Development Measures

Though government has taken up measures for the betterment of the poorer sections, yet fruits of the measures have not reached them. After Independence, construction of an *Ali Bandh* for irrigation was taken up under the C.R.S. scheme but could not be completed due to various reasons. A road has been constructed from Tekatoli to Cooch Bihar Border via this village under C.S.P.E. scheme. Only 1 km. is completed at the expenditure of Rs. 6187.

Discussion

In sum, it may be said that no great change has has taken place among the weaker sections since independence. Pressure from the high caste Hindu, abolition of *jotdary* system, over population, illiteracy, unemployment, extravagancy are some of the causes of poverty of the Rajbanshi. They are unable to compete with the Bengali in respect of education, occupations or social status.

It may be observed that weakness is not always determined in terms of caste or ethnic group. It is being perpetuated by both the high and low castes. Though the destitutes and the weaker groups believe that they are exploited by the dominant and the rich, yet they do not deny the fact that the creditors or the *mahajan* and the rich farmers help them during the lean period. Even the high rates of interest are not considered as channels of exploitation.

The Badia may be considered as the weakest of all the caste groups. They are landless and mainly depend on their low remunerative traditional occupation like drum-beating and begging. They have the lowest social position and no political control. They do not get any benefit from the government. Sometimes they do not even get the job of daily labourers. Thus with no other alternatives left for them to survive they are forced to resort to theft, collection of food materials from other's ponds or fields, and begging.

From economic point of view Bengali Kumhar, Teli, Bania, Kayastha, and Brahman are weak. It may be argued that social weakness is not necessarily connected with economic weakness. It is seen that although the Kayastha and the Brahman are economically weak, they still maintain a high social position. Inspite of their low economic position they can not adopt any socially degraded occupation like daily wage-earning. Their education, political position, greater contact with outsiders and high social position operate as constraints to have free choice to earn their livelihood.

The Bengali Jele community even after acquiring some land in recent time do not enjoy a high social position. Some of them are quite rich. But they can not mix freely with the high castes. They are considered as *chhotolok*. It is interesting to note that these rich Jele families avoid contact with the labourer class of their own community. Thus it is seen that inspite of numerical and economic strength they are not in a position to gain social prestige and to be a member of the Panchayat. A social pressure prevents them to cross the barrier of ther socio-political weakness.

The Moira are economically dominant, literate and have high social status in the village. They have also the political power, they are, therefore, regarded as respected men in the village. The poor Moira mix with the other poorer sections. But they, too, are aware that they have a high social position.

The Rajbanshi are numerically dominant. Those who were *jotdar* in the past are still regarded as *jotdar* even after the abolition of the *jotdary* system. Most of the *jotdar* families are literate and they have considerable political control. The *bhotakhaoa* share-cropper previously used to cultivate the superior equality of land of their *deunia* and used to get all expenditure of cultivation. But they are not provided with all these facilities any more. As a result their numbers are decreasing and they are gradually becoming daily wage earners. At present the share-croppers have to use their own plough and bullocks. But most of the share-croppers do not possess even the primary tools of production. So they have no other way but to be a *kamla-kishan*. In contrast to this most of the Bengali possess plough and bullock. They are more hardy than the Rajbanshi. So the Rajbanshi landowner prefer to have the Bengali as daily labourers or sharecroppers. Due to their illiteracy the Rajbanshi are also not able to compete with the Bengali in other fields.

With the process of Sanskritization and Khatriyaization the Rajbanshi elites, who are conscious about their past, have started to consider themselves as equivalent to other high castes. It may be said that neither the pressure of the economically dominant high castes nor the exploitation can be attributed to poverty of the Rajbanshi, their illiteracy, ignorance, idleness, indifference toward overcoming the distress etc. It is often seen that they are unwilling to work even if they get some job. A Rajbanshi labourer said that "*Rantar sukh o Bishram darkar ranta ke sukhi na koirle ranta paban hoey jabar parek. Imra Bhatia. Charuar jait mui chasigulal bebak khatai mare*" i.e. " The body also requires adequate rest otherwise it would break down.

These Bengali get us overworkcd". As they are the descendants of the Royal family, they are more conscious of it and do not allow their women to work in other's field. They are much interested to perform social functions and entertain guests.

A common Rajbanshi proverb is that "*Bachhoradhek t or thone sakai khaor asil tao mor konek khouit paril na*". i.c. "We come to your house only once a year and even then you could not entertain us satisfactorily". It is very insulting to them. So in order to rejuvenate their so-called royal prestige and status they do not even hesitate to sell their land and property to entertain their guests during social or religious occasions.

Conversely the Bengali do not want to sell their land. Author was told by a Jele labourer that "*Naran charah mejei maran. Jomi kono abasthate bechim na. Pater sange judha koira baincha thakum*". i.e.under no circumstances will we sell our land. We will continue our struggle for survival.

The poorer sections attribute their misfortune to the presence of the middlemen like the panchayat members through whom governmental relief meterials are supposed to trickle down to them. One of them said that, "*Sela nengti pindichl ilam ela dhuti pindi, khabar na hoiela. Ranta dhakte chal bikote hoi Giththnire photar thone shari pindai. Shari na pindile bairon jai na. Kharocher dam charait jaset din ba din ki kari bachin. Mui adibasi chasi dhuti pindi kamla hosi*". i.e. "When we used to wear loin clothes we had food and were quite happy. Now-a-days although we wear *dhoti* and our women use *shari*, the happiness has gone. For our clothing we have to sell our food. So, for wearing modern clothes we became *kamla kishan*.

From the above discussion it may be said that though there is a trend of upward mobility among certain castes and groups of people but socio-ritual as well as economic pressures prevent the weaker sections to cross the threshold of weakness.

REFERENCES

1. Beteille, A. "Ideas and Interest",*Journal of International Social Science*. 21(2) 219, 1969.
2. Burman, U. *Rajbanshi Khatriya Jatir Itihas*. 1370 B.C.
3. Das, K.K. and Sharma, D.R. "Governmental Resources and Scheduled Castes Communities". *Indian Journal of Social Research*. ed. Hallen, G.C., 12(1) April, 44-50. 1970.

4. Das, K.K. "Origin and Developmentof Rajbanshi Community" 11(4) January, 1970, 1973-75, 1969-70.
5. Dasgupta, B.K. "A Note on the Rajbansi of Eastern India with Special Reference to Social Movements". *Bulletin of the Anthropological Survey of India*. January, 1969.
6. De Costa, E.P.W. "A Portrait of Indian Poverty" *Challenge of Poverty in India*. ed., Fonseca A.J., 1971.
7. Hicks, John "Elemination of Poverty in India". *Challenge of Poverty in India*. ed., Fonseca, A.J., 1971.
8. Mukherjee, B. "Socio-economic and Religious Organization of the Rajbansi". *Bulletin of the Anthropological* Survey of India. 12(1&2) January and July, 1968.
9. Sanyal G.C. *The Rajbansis of North Bengal*.
10. Gruming, J.F. *East Bengal District Gazetters 11* Jalpaiguri. 1911.
11. Census of India *District Census Handbook*. 1961.

4

PITAMBARA : A VILLAGE IN SOUTH BENGAL

CHANDRIMA CHOWDHURY

The Village

The village Pitambara lies in Diamond Harbour Police Station area of 24-Paraganas district. It is situated on the western side of the Saresha *hat* (market) about two miles away from the main bus route of Diamond Harbour, Calcutta. The whole of this area falls under reclaimed Sundarban lands. The reclamation began as early as in 1765, and initially reclamated lands were leased out rent free until the leases made some progress in cultivation (O'Mally 1911). The clearance of jungle of south 24-Parganas was taken up about 200 years ago after the advent of the East India Company and the lands were subsequently brought under cultivation.

The present field investigation was carried out by the author residing in the village for about four months from December '74 to April '75. In collecting the data, besides applying traditional anthropological tool, government records of various nature were also consulted from Land Revenue Office and Block Development Office.

Ethnic Composition

There are nine ethnic groups in this village eight of which are Hindu and the remaining one is Muslim. The Hindu comprise several caste groups including the Kshatriya claiming to have migrated from the Punjab some six or seven generation back and settled in the adjacent villages. They claim to be Rajput. They settled in that village as Zamindar's employees, as Manager or supervisor, for supervising the Zamindar estate. They claim to be of royal lineage. Only one family that was living in one of the adjacent villages settled at Pitambara by purchasing the homestead land. The Karan (Kayastha of Orissa),

Mahishya, Gandhabanik, Pod (Pandra Kshatriya), Kolu, Dhopa, and the Keora are the other Hindu castes.

The social lay-out of village is significant. Each caste lives in separate settlement known as *para*. The *para* of different castes are arranged in a very scattered way. It will be seen from the table 1 that there are 12 *para* in this village and they are designated by the title of a particular caste or by the caste name or by the name of the place from where the occupant migrated.

TABLE 1: *Para* distribution of the village

Sl. No.	Name of the *para*	Caste or community living in the *para*	No.of *para*	Remarks
1.	Sardarpara	Keora	2	6 *Para* are named after the surname
2.	Maralpara	Mondal (Pod)	1	
3.	Mistripara	Dhoba	1	
4.	Barmanpara	Kshatriya	1	
5.	Bhandaripara	Mahisya	1	
6.	Mollapara	Muslim	2	5 *Para* are named after the name of the caste or community
7.	Kolupara	Kolu	1	
8.	Podpara	Pod	1	
9.	Benepara	Gandhabanik	1	
10.	Urepara	Oriya from Orissa	1	1 *Para* is named after the name from where they migrated

Except the Pod and Muslim all the castes were originally settled in this village by the local Zamindar, Sri Barada Prasad Roy Chowdhury, for performing different functions within the village to ensure economic self-sufficiency, as was the custom in the past. He settled only a few families initially and distributed some lands to them but in course of time migration of each community took place from surrounding areas due to marriage and kinship relationship and the population of the village increased gradually.

The Zamindar also built a famous Shiva Temple of Keshabeswar at Mandirbarar area in 1755. The Zamindar had his residence in village Khorda which is adjacent to Pitambara. It may be stated here that in the past such temples were immensely important, not only as the centre of religious life but the entire social structure of the village life moved round such institutions.

Population

The population of the village is shown according to various ethnic groups in table 2.

TABLE 2: Distribution of population

Sl. No. Caste/ Community	No. of House-holds	%	Male	%	Female	%	Total Popula-tion	%
1.Kshatriya	1	0.62	2	0.42	1	0.22	3	0.32
2.Karan	24	14.91	68	14.26	84	18.42	152	16.29
3.Mahishya	10	6.21	32	6.71	28	6.14	60	6.43
4.Gandhabanik	2	1.24	8	1.67	6	1.32	14	1.50
5.Pod	37	22.98	111	23.27	110	14.12	221	23.69
6.Kolu	6	3.73	20	4.19	16	3.51	36	3.85
7. Dhopa	27	16.77	75	15.72	63	13.82	138	14.79
8. Keora	28	17.39	75	15.72	77	16.88	152	16.29
9. Muslim	26	16.15	86	18.03	71	15.57	157	16.82
Total	161	100%	477	100%	456	100%	933	100%

Literacy and Education

Table 3 illustrates the distribution of literacy in the village by sex and community.

It is clear from the table that an overwhelming majority of population (among most of the ethnic groups) are illiterate (82.5%) and the condition of the female is even worse. The literacy among the Kshatriya, Karan, Gandhabanik, Pod, and Kolu is fairly good.

TABLE 3: Distribution of literacy

Caste/ Community	Total population	Literate persons			Percent
		Male	Female	Total	
Kshatriya	3	2	1	3	100%
Karan	152	46	18	64	42.1%
Mahishya	60	6	4	10	16.6%
Gandhabanik	14	5	1	6	42.8%
Pod	221	22	7	29	13.0%
Kolu	36	14	4	18	50.0%
Dhopa	138	18	6	24	17.3%
Keora	152	3	1	4	2.6%
Muslim	157	6	-	6	4.3%
Total	933	122	42	164	17.5%

TABLE 4: Level of education

Caste/ Community	Upto Class IV			Upto Class XI			Upto B.A.		
	Male	Fem-ale	To-tal	Male	Fem-ale	To-tal	Male	Fem-ale	To-tal
Kshatriya	1	2	2	1	x	1			
Karan	13	9	22	27	9	36	3	3	6
Mahishya	4	4	8	2	x	2			
Gandhabanik	3	1	4	2	x	2			
Pod	9	7	16	13	x	13			
Kolu	10	2	12	4	2	6			
Dhopa	13	5	18	5	1	6			
Keora	2	1	3	1	x	1			
Muslim	3	-	3	3	-	3			
Total	58	30	88	58	12	70	3	3	6
			53.6%			42.6%			3.6%

Considering the level of education, the picture appears still more gloomy. Out of a total of 164 literates, 88 (53.6%) have only a primary standard of education, 70 of them with Class X, and only six of them have passed B.A. The education above primary level is restricted to certain castes.

Economic Dimension

Agriculture is one of the main sources of livelihood of the people of this area. This is primarily a rice growing area and generally only one crop is grown. The lands being rainfed, the village is without any artificial irrigation system and as such the area is mono-cropped. Although the land of the village may be classified as high (*unchu*), medium (*majhari*) and low (*khala*) according to the topography of land, there is very little difference between any two of them from the production point of view. Average production is about 9 mds. or 333 kgs. of paddy per *bigha* or 0.47 acre of land. The main varieties of paddy which are grown in this locality are *Aus Punjati*, *678*, *Jaya*, *Dhule*, *Nonabakra*, *Chamarsal*, *Baktulsi*, *Dudher Sar*, *Chhilta*, *Kalam kantika*. The first three are high yielding variety but these were grown without proper irrigation; their yield is not upto the expectation. Another high yielding variety, '*Taichung*' is cultivated during December-April by those who have sufficient water source. The yield of *Taichung* is 1.5 mds. or about 56 kgs. per *katha* (1/20th of a bigha). For the other varieties no fertilizer is required as it does not affect the yield much. But the *Taichung* variety requires fertilizer and insecticides like Folidol and Endrine. This enhances the cost of production of this variety. It comes to about Rs. 600.00 - 700.00 per *bigha* as against about Rs. 150.00 in case of ordinary varieties.

Local-Rural-Industry

Preparation of molasses from palm juice is another main source of income of the villagers. They borrow money during the lean period and repay the loans as soon as they take up the seasonal industry of preparing molasses from palm juice. A man can collect upto 110 kgs. of palm juice per day and can prepare 22 kgs. of *patali_gur* (jaggery). The price of rich jaggery per kg. amounts to Rs. 2.50. To get about 22 kgs. of jaggery about 40 kgs. of fuel is required. Thus an average daily income from 22 kgs. of *Patali* comes to about Rs. 55.00. Now, if we deduct the cost of fuel (about Rs. 10.00) the net daily income comes to about Rs. 45.00. The earning from molasses could be made for about three months i.e. from March to middle of June.

A man collects juice from a maximum number of 28 palm trees per day. They take these trees on lease. The lease value of each tree varies from Rs. 10.00 to Rs. 20.00 according to the condition of the tree. The owners of these trees are the Karan and Pod. To start with, a small amount of money is required for buying earthen pot, bamboo and acid powder. They also use dry cow-dung, leaves, straw and dried *kachuri pana* from ponds as fuel.

Landholding

Agriculture being the main source of livelihood, it is necessary to scrutinise the pattern of landholding which is shown in Table 5.

Total area of the village is 230.67 acres. From table 5 it is found that total agricultural land possessed by the villagers is about 118.20 acres. Per capita land holding of the village is very poor i.e. 0.12 acre. Except Karan and Kshatriya (only one family in the village), all the villagers have very little amount of land in possession. The maximum number (36.73%) of landholding families belong to Karan caste and the Pod hold the second position (30.61%) among the 49 landowning families. Combining the Karan and Pod together we find that about 90.24 acres (76%) of land is in their hand. But when we consider per capita land holding, the Pod do not differ much from many of other castes. The Keora shows the highest proportion (22.3%) of landless families and minimum per capita holding of land (0.07 acre).

Occupation

The people of Pitambara have diverse occupations as their primary source of livelihood. They are shown in table 6.

From table 6 it is seen that out of a total population of 933 only 243 are engaged in different types of occupation. Non-working force are the children, old or aged persons, and most of the women of this village. Generally the women do not work outside their household. Out of 243 working individuals, only eight are women. It is further evident that the Karan are the most hard pressed and they virtually depend on day labour. About 5 per cent of the total working force of the village are engaged as wage labourer. There is a tendency for non-caste occupation among villagers, only a few cling to their traditional caste occupations.

Secondary Occupation

Some of the people pursue the secondary occupation such as cultivation, day-labour, sale of parched rice and vegetables, preparing and sale of *talgur* (Molasses), sale of fish, share-cropping, service, working in grocery-shops, rickshaw pulling, sale of country made liquor, drum-beating etc. as shown in table 7.

TABLE 5: Distribution of landholding

Caste/ Community	No. of house-	Population owning hold	No. of land land owning families	Percentage of land families families	Total land holding families	Per family land holding	Per capita land- less	No. of of land- less	Percentage
Kshatriya	1	3	1	2.04	4.23	4.23	1.41	-	-
Karan	24	152	18	36.73	65.80	2.74	0.43	6	5.36
Mahishya	10	60	2	4.08	6.58	0.65	0.11	8	-
Gandhabanik	2	14	2	4.08	1.41	0.70	0.10	-	-
Pod	37	221	15	30.61	24.44	0.66	0.11	22	19.64
Kolu	6	36	2	4.08	0.94	0.15	0.03	4	3.57
Dhopa	27	138	4	8.16	3.05	0.11	0.02	23	20.54
Keora	28	152	3	6.12	1.88	0.07	0.01	25	22.32
Muslim	26	157	2	4.08	9.87	0.37	0.06	24	21.43
Total	161	933	49	99.98	118.20	0.73	0.12	112	100.00

TABLE 6: Distribution by primary occupation

Caste/ Community	PO	OC	DL	PR	CA	TM	FB	BT	GC	MS	WM	TL	CH	WG	SS	RP	BM	OP	BG	Total
Kshatriya	3	1																		1
Karan	152	15	4	9	1	1			2				4	9						45
Mahishya	60	2	6	2									4		1				1	16
Gandha-banik	14	2											2							4
Pod	221	9	33		1	1	1						2	1	1	3		1	1	53
Kolu	36	2	1	2									4				1			10
Dhopa	138	1	19								1		2	3	9				1	36
Kaora	152		30				3			1		1		1	1				1	38
Muslim	157	1	22M/1F					7		1		2		3		1			1	40
Total	933	33	116	13	2	2	4	7	2	2	1	3	18	17	12	4	1	1	5	243

Abbreviation

PO -	Population	TM -	Telgur or Molusses	TL -	Tailoring	BM -	Bidi making
OC -	Owner Cultivator	FB -	Fish Business	CH -	Cattle herding	OP -	Oil pressing
DL -	Day labourer	BT -	Butcher	WG -	Work in grocery	BG -	Begging
PR -	Parched rice and vegetable seller	GC -	Green coconut seller	SS -	Service (Jute mill, school teacher etc.)		
		MS -	Maid Servant				
CA -	Carpenter	WM -	Washer woman	RP -	Rickshaw pulling		

TABLE 7: Secondary occupation

Caste/ Community	Cul.	D.L.	P.R.& V.S.	T.M.	F.S.	G.C.S.	S.C.	Ser	S.W.	R.P.	L.S.	D.B.	Tot.
Kshatriya	-	-	-	-	-	-	-	-	-	-	-	-	-
Karan	3	3					1		1				8
Mahishya	1	3	3	1									8
Gandhabanik	-	-	-	-	-	-	-	-	-	-	-	-	-
Pod	10	3	-	24	1		4	1			1		44
Kolu	2	1	1										4
Dhopa	2	4		1			1			7			15
Keora	1	2		2	12		9					5	31
Muslim		2		2		1							5
Total	19	18	4	30	13	1	15	1	1	7	1	5	115

Cul. - Cultivation
D.L. - Day labourer
P.R. & V.S. - Parched rice and vegetable seller
T.M. - Talgur making
F.S. - Fish seller
G.C.S. - Green coconut seller
S.C. - Share cropper
Ser. - Service
S.W. - Shop worker
R.P. - Rickshaw puller
L.S. - Liquor seller
D.B. - Drum beater
Tot. - Total

TABLE 8: Distribution of workers in agricultural and non-agricultural occupation

Caste/ Community	Total working individuals	Owner cultivator	%	Day labourer	%	Other occupation	%
Kshatriya	1	1	100	-	-	-	-
Karan	45	15	33.33	4	8.88	26	57.78
Mahishya	16	2	12.50	6	37.5	8	50.00
Gandhabanik	4	2	.50.00	-	-	2	50.00
Pod	53	9	16.98	33	62.27	11	20.75
Kolu	10	2	20.00	1	10.00	7	70.00
Dhopa	36	1	2.78	19	52.78	16	44.44
Keora	38	-	-	30	78.95	8	21.05
Muslim	40	1	2.5	23	57.5	16	40.90
Total	243	33	13.58	116	47.74	94	38.68

From table 8 it is seen that 13.58 per cent of villagers are engaged in cultivation of their own land, 47.74 per cent are day labourers and 38.68 per cent are engaged in non-agricultural occupation.

From the stand point of each ethnic group, the highest number of Kshatriya, Gandhabanik, and Karan belong to the owner cultivator category, whereas the percentage of land holding cultivators among the Keora is none, and among the Dhopa and Muslim it is 2.78 per cent and 2.5 per cent respectively. Most of the day labourers come from the Keora community. The Kshatriya and the Gandhabanik show none and the Karan and Kolu have very low percentage of day labourer.

Income

All sources of income of each individual in a family for the whole year has been considered for arranging them into different economic groups.

It was told to the author that about 10 *bigha* or 4.70 acres (or .94 per capita land) of land or a per capita monthly income between Rs. 100 and Rs. 150 can fairly maintain a family of five members. An approximate income from 10 *bigha* of land is above Rs. 6,500 and this gives a monthly per capita income of about Rs. 108.33. From the economic point of view those who are above this level of income may be termed as 'dominant'. There are of course several degrees of 'dominance' or 'weakness' like 'most dominant' or 'weakest'.

TABLE 9: Distribution of households by income

Caste/ Community	No. of house- hold	Per capita monthly income level							
		Rs.5-50		Rs.51-100		Rs.101-150		Rs.151-300	
		No.	%	No.	%	No.	%	No.	%
Kshatriya	1							1	100
Karan	24	10	41.6	6	25.0	4	16.7	4	16.7
Mahishya	10	7	70.0	1	10.0	1	10.0	1	10.0
Gandhabanik	2	2	100.00						
Pod	37	18	48.4	14	38.8	2	5.4	3	7.4
Kolu	6	5	83.3	1	16.3				
Dhopa	27	24	88.8	2	7.4	1	3.8		
Keora	28	23	82.1	4	14.2			1	3.7
Muslim	26	23	88.4	3	11.6				
Total	161	112		31		8		10	
Percentage	100%	69.57%		19.25%		4.97%		6.21%	

Taking all castes or communities together it is seen from table 9 that 69.57 per cent of the total households of village fall under the 'weakest' category and only 4.97 per cent are just at subsistence level. From table it is also seen that the only Kshatriya family is economically dominant. Among the Karan 41.6 per cent of their families fall in the weakest category, 25 per cent fall in the weaker category, 16.7 per cent fall within the subsistence level and 16.7 per cent fall on the dominant category. Among the Mahishya 70 per cent fall within the weakest category, 10 per cent fall within the subsistence category and other 10 per cent fall within the dominant category and the remaining 10 per cent fall within weaker category. Among the Pod 48.4 per cent of the families fall within the weakest category, 38.8 per cent fall within the weaker category, 5.4 per cent fall within the subsistence level and 7.4 per cent fall within the dominant category. Among the Kolu 83.3 per cent fall within the weakest category, 16.3 per cent fall within the weaker category. Among the Dhopa 88.8 per cent fall within the weakest category, 7.4 per cent fall within the weaker category and 3.8. per cent fall within the subsistence category. Among the Keora 82.1 per cent fall within the weakest category, 14.2 per cent fall within the weaker category and 3.7 per cent fall in the dominant category. Among the Muslim

88.4 per cent fall within the weakest category and 11.6 per cent fall within the weaker category.

Labourers

Most of the labourers get the job for three months during the agricultural season. The owner cultivators also sometime serve as labourers during the agricultural season after completion of their own cultivation. If there is high demand of labour during agricultural season their daily rate rises upto Rs. 4.00 or Rs. 5.00 from Rs. 3.00 per day during ordinary season. There is no bonded labour in the village.

All the agricultural labourers are seasonal and their length of employment lasts for about three months. In other season of the year, they are compelled to adopt different types of occupations.

Share-croppers

The number of share croppers in this village is meagre and share cropping is not the primary source of livelihood of any of the share croppers. Out of six share-croppers three are workers and each of them cultivates about three to five *bigha*, one Pod cultivates five *bigha* and a Karan cultivates four *bigha* of land as share-cropper. The share-croppers incur all the expenses of cultivation, such as, labour charge, cost of ploughing, seeds etc. The paddy and straw are equally divided between the land-lord and the share-cropper. It may be noted here that share-cropping as a source of earning is gradually losing its force. The landowners are afraid of losing their right over the land if they let out their lands to share-croppers. Though share-cropping continues, this is not openly acknowledged and as such it is difficult to ascertain the number of share-croppers in the village. Leaving aside the economic condition and landholding and occupation, it was observed in the field that the people belonging to weaker sections cannot afford to eat rice throughout the year. Only after harvest did they buy cheaper variety of rice. During rainy season the cost of rice goes up and people can ill-afford to buy rice more than once or twice a month. Thus, they are compelled to eat maize flour after boiling it in water. They also partake different varieties of tubers, dried castor and tamarind seeds. Even children of the age group of 2-3 months drink a solution of arrowroot mixed with a kind of inferior quality of molasses, locally called *veligur*. Protein through food is available in the shape of cheaper varieties of fish (*simul*). During rainy season they also collect different types of fish and molluscs. The garments and clothings worn by them are very coarse and very few in number. A few cases would add insight to our observations:

1. Akbar, a Muslim boy of 15 years of age from this village refused lozenges and biscuits which were offered by the author. He said, "Please do not offer me lozenges and biscuits; instead it is better if you can pay me Rs. 5.00 by which I can atleast purchase some rice and feed myself. I have not eaten rice for last ten months". During field work the author saw him eating only very inferior quality of boiled vegetables and leaves of the cauliflowers, without any spices.
2. While enquiring about the real cause of poverty, Shri Radhanath Rahut (Karan) of this village replied "We were three brothers and we had common land and property but now we have 10 children and the lands are also divided. So division of land and property have weakened us in all respects and have forced us to lead a miserable and sorrowful life".
3. Chhiru Sardar (Keora). said, "During the last rainy season each of our family members were taking a piece of tikli (bread) only for a day. Sometimes we took the fried castor seeds, boil arums, and even tubers. As a result, I was so weak that I failed to plough the field and the overall situation of my family was so depressing that I was forced to join a group of thieves".

Social Dimension

The response on hierarchy of castes varies according to the position of caste occupied by the respondent. This is shown in table 10.

The Keora observed that the Karan of Orissa now claim a superior position and they have established ties with the Koranga. The Koranga belong to a very low caste because they are engaged on castration of bulls. The Keora also said that the Dhopa wash their clothes, so they are inferior to the Keora.

TABLE 10: Caste hierarchy

Hierarchy according to Keora	Hierarchy according to Karan	Hierarchy according to Mahisya
1. Kshatriya	1. Kshatriya	1. Kshatriya
2. Mahishya	2. Karan	2. Mahishya
3. Gandhabanik	3. Mahishya	3. Gandhabanik
4. Pod	4. Gandhabanik	4. Karan
5. Kolu	5. Pod	5. Pod
6. Keora	6. Kolu	6. Kolu
7. Karan	7. Dhopa	7. Dhopa
8. Dhopa	8. Keora	8. Keora
9. Muslim	9. Muslim	9. Muslim

The Karan said that the Kshatriya are superior to the Karan in caste status. (one respondent said that the Kshatriya are equal in social status and prestige to the Karan). The Karan are claiming their high position because in Orissa they are just below the Brahman.

The Kshatriya claim their high position because in Punjab they have been next to the Brahman.

The Mahishya gave the different pattern of the caste ranking. The Mahishya claimed that their position was next to Kshatriya. But they said, "Kshatriya are a very low caste. No body takes water from their houses. In the village the Babu are the persons who were born in the Kshatriya family due to the union between a Kshatriya father and his lower caste concubine and they claim the highest position. The villagers also support it.

It was reported by a Keora informant that two years ago Kangal (Keora), a young man of the village, offered some fruits and other things during the Durgapuja at Khorda, the adjacent village. A person from the Kshatriya family died during that time at the puja pandal. Some of the Brahman and Kshatriya then said, "it was due to the participation of a lower caste person in that festival. It was a sin. The accident took place due to the violation of the norm". From that time the Pod, the Keora and the Dhopa have kept themselves aloof from participating in the Durgapuja of the village. From the above mentioned event it is clear that the Karan and Kshatriya are superior on social position than other castes; the Gandhabanik, the Mahishya and the Kolu are in the intermediate position; and the Pod, the Dhopa, the Keora and the Muslim are in the inferior position. Some even opined that the Keora are lowest in the social hierarchy because they take part in the beating of drums and they eat different types of molluscs, these are considered to be indicators of low social position.

Religious Dimension

The Shrines of the goddess *Sitala*, *Manasa*, and *Mongal Chandi* are situated in the ward of the Karan. Here we also find the shrine of Lord *Panchananda* and the altar of the Muslim viz., Manikpir. During the village festival in the month of February-March, all the castes of Pitambara have the equal right to participate. But none of them is allowed to touch the cemented platform where the goddess *Sitala*, *Manasa* and *Mongal Chandi* have been placed. However, if some one wishes to offer something can do so by putting an earthen pot, containing fruits and sweets, called *dala*, on the steps of the platform of the goddess. After worship, the young men of the Karan families distribute ritual offerings or *dala* to the devotees. The local Muslim participate in the village festival. They offer coins after the worship is over. The service of a Muslim *Fakir* is necessary for propitiating at the Manikpir, which is also worshipped by the Hindu castes.

Members of different castes have separate priests for them. These priests come during different social and religious occasions like birth, death, marriage etc. It is said that the Karan were previously served by the Utkal Brahman. But due to non-availability of such Brahman., they are now served by the Rarhi Brahmin of West Bengal. Previously the Karan used to be served by the Malakar. But there is no function of Malakar at present. There is no *jajmani* relations between a Brahman, Dhopa, or Napit in the village.

The villagers, ranging from the dominant Karan to the weakest Keora, share the ideas of heaven (*Swarga*) and hell (*Narak*), virtue (*punya*) and sin (*pap*), *Karma, Dharma* etc. With regard to magico-religious belief, it is found that Manna Sardar, a Keora, serves as magician (*ojha*) and the villagers, irrespective of caste affiliation, respect him for his super-natural powers.

During the village festival arrangements are made for folk drama (*yatra*) where the villagers sit together despite their caste differences. For conducting that *yatra* festival, the Koran take the initiative in collecting money and other arrangements and the villagers have no hesitation in accepting their supremacy. It may be noted that the villagers are not much willing to discuss this issue as some religious values are attached to it. It is believed that Goddess *Sitala* is offended by such discussion. Besides village festivals, members of different castes observe the worship of *Manasa* or *Renna Puja* (in the mouth of *Bhadra*) *Jantal*, *Kali*, *Lakshmi*, *Paus Sankranti*, etc. either on community or individual basis. Irrespective of their caste position, the villagers attend family function or rituals like marriage, death, etc. of different castes. According to social norms, they also offer some presents on such occasions.

Political Dimension

The office of the gram panchayat consists of a Chairman and nine members. The Chairman comes from the ward of the Pod. Two representatives each were elected from the wards of Karan, Keora, and one each from the wards of Muslim, Dhopa, and Mahisya.

Function of the gram panchayat is to: (1) collect Chaukidari Tax (2) verify the exact number of the members in the family for issuing a ration card, (3) prepare list of voters (4) submit a budget for running the panchayat and (5) distribute relief grants occasionally available from the Anchal Panchayat. The village panchayat was not functioning properly due to the callous attitude of its members.

From a different view point the traditional custom of decision making is still prevalent in the village. Such cases like beating, theft, partitioning of property of a joint family, distribution of land between brothers (after death of father), and so on are settled through the participation of local elderly persons.

Function of the Developmental Agencies

The only developmental unit here is the Block Development Office. It supplies villagers with some fertilizers at cheap rates. But they are afraid that by accepting fertilizers they may be compelled to pay levy after the harvest. Sometimes a cash loan of Rs. 150.00 is available from the Block for agriculture.But this is normally granted to those having a minimum of three *bigha* of land. So members of the weaker section can not avail of this opportunity. Some of the Karan took loan for agriculture and cultivation of fish from the Diamond Harbour Cooperative Bank showing a forged account of tank and agricultural land and no body refunded this loan. Now, that particular bank has closed down business.

Conclusion

The village under study is about 200 years old. A tentative reconstruction of settlement pattern of this village can be made from the verbal statements of the villagers as well as the existing records. The Zamindar along with some Rajput Kshatriya from Punjab took possession of a vast tract of land in this area and settled in the adjacent village to Pitambara. They gradually brought different castes for various types of services. They established a social and ritual norm for running an organised community life. But after the formal abolition of the zamindari there was no central controlling authority. However, the people kept coming from various places. They enjoyed differential status in the caste hierarchy. The little land that was allotted to them could not be retained by the majority. There was no dominant peasant group in this village. So, due to all these social and economic factors a stable community life in the traditional sense could not grow. As agriculture is substantially in the hands of a few persons, and as there is an absence of substantial non-agricultural occupations, the ordinary people of the village could not cross the threshold of economic weakness. There is little individual effort in this regard.

The notion of the caste hierarchy continues to persist. But, from the functional point of view, it has considerably lost its rigidity.

Considering all these factors together, it appears that the weakness among different ethnic groups gets perpetuated primarily through the poor economic condition of the people.

5

PANCHRA : A VILLAGE IN WEST BENGAL

SATYABRATA CHAKRABORTY

Introduction

There are two problems in the present project, namely the problem of identification of the weaker sections and the problem of their development. Some administrative reports[1] identify the landless agricultural labourers and share-croppers, mainly belonging to the category of Scheduled Caste and Scheduled Tribe, as the weaker sections in the village communities throughout India. Some research reports[2] describe that various kinds of development measures could not substantially alter the conditions of life of the weaker sections. These two sets of reports pose both theoretical and applied problems which require close examination by the researchers. Inequalities in some form exist in almost all kinds of societies. It is extremely important to know the specific idiom which is acted out in the perpetuation of inequality in a particular society. For this purpose the social, economic and cultural organisation of the society concerned are to be critically analysed. This is even more necessary for successful application of knowledge for the betterment of the society. Bose[3] observed, "an anthropologist has a greater and deeper commitment, namely, that in India he has to draw a lesson from what he observes, so that he can utilize his knowledge in the attainment of the equalitarian ideal which our nation has set before itself as its goal. If he also accepts this idea, then, with his superior analytical apparatus and the use of comparisons and synthetic thinking, he can suggest many modifications in the ways in which the government or leaders of the society are trying to bring about justice where injustice prevails today. And this is where anthropology has a very significant role to play and a heavy responsibility to bear".

Scholars[4] devoted to anthropology, until recent past, have explained the phenomena of inequality in terms of an all-India Varna-Jati model which bears a rough correlation with the economically "weak" and the "strong". Recently a few scholars[5] have proposed to study inequality mainly from directly examining the nature of agrarian class structure in the context of analysing the organisation of agricultural production. The modus operandi of the present study has been specifically set to bring out the actual social, cultural, economic and political situations which constrain a sizeable section of rural Indian population in crossing the threshold of abject poverty. Initial assumption of the present work is that "the abject poverty of the people is the consequence of their being weak. . . . Decisively weak are those who have either no control or least control over local resources-economic, political, social and communicational".[6]

According to the given directives the universe of the present study was limited to peasant communities. It was suggested to study this problem intensively in a single village for the first phase. I was already working in a village at Burdwan district, West Bengal, on the "social and cultural organisation of agriculture". This village belongs to Jamalpur Block which is one of the agriculturally developed Blocks in this district. Burdwan has already undergone a massive programme for agricultural development (I.A.D.P) since 1962.[7] I stayed in the field for about nine months in three terms. This is a mixed village where the Hindu, Muslim and Tribal are living together. But I have not brought these ethnic groups as distinct entities into my immediate scope of analysis. Perhaps this would bear some relevance to the present problem. I have more or less treated them within a common peasant category at this stage.

Data were collected on the basis of broad guideline and census forms. These were largely substantiated by direct observations and conversations with various categories of people. I depended more on qualitative approach to describe the social situation.

Village

The village, Panchra, is located in south east point in the Burdwan district map and is connected by rail and bus road with district town, 30 miles away in the western side. Another market centre, Memari, is within 6/7 miles from the village in the same direction. At the eastern side, the village is connected with other market centres like Jamalpur, Sure-Kalna and finally with Tarakeswar town which stands nearly 40 miles away from the village. This area was under direct control of a kshatriya Zamindar who used to pay his rent to the Maharaja of Burdwan. Around 1932-33 two Pattanidar- one Brahman and one Tambuli of this village - took hold of this area. Subsequently they created various sub-tenants who became permanent owners after the formal abolition of the zamindary system. It is reported that all of the landowners belonged to upper and middle range castes. And the big holdings under the control of the two pattanidars were gradually divided with the split of the joint families. Some rent free lands were also distributed for performance of worship of a particular deity, *debottar*, and for certain other services (*chakran*). Rent of land varied from four anas (25 paisa) to three rupees per bigha. There was no progressive change in it after independence.

Twenty-four ethnic groups/castes/tribes, live in this village.

TABLE 1: Distribution of ethnic groups by number of families and population

Sl. No.	Caste/ Communities	Total Families	Population Male	Female
1.	Aguri	2	3	5
2.	Barui	2	3	4
3.	Baishnab	2	5	5
4.	Baidya	3	9	4
5.	Bauri	33	73	64
6.	Bagdi	44	111	116
7.	Bene	12	32	39
8.	Brahman	62	205	192
9.	Charal	5	18	16
10.	Dhopa	2	8	8
11.	Dom	2	4	6
12.	Dule	55	138	129
13.	Goala	3	11	11
14.	Hari	9	9	11
15.	Jele	8	26	22
16.	Kayastha	17	59	61
17.	Karmakar	3	8	8
18.	Moira	1	7	3
19.	Muslim	86	231	231
20.	Napit	6	16	13
21.	Suri	1	5	4
22.	Sadgope	43	129	114
23.	Santal	119	295	273
24.	Tambuli	41	126	127
		561	1531	1466

The village is divided into *Uttarpara*, *Dakshinpara*, and *Paschimpara*. The *para* or wards have no definite social boundary. Each one is specially related with the other and accommodate mixed population. The villagers apparently identify *Uttarpara* as *Chashipara* and *Paschimpara* as *Babupara*. This gives a conventional division between those who are directly engaged in cultivation and those who are not. The Muslims live in two distinctly separated wards locally known as *Sarkardanga* and *Simuldanga*. The Santal, Bauri, Dule, Bagdi, Charal, Dom, Hari, in most cases have no homestead land of their own. They usually live in huts made on land belonging to their respective Babu in some distance. The Santal generally live in huts scattered around a village tank.

I used to live with a Sadgope family at *Dakshinpara*. I found in the morning that everybody in all the families of different ethnic groups got involved in some kind of work. The labourers, cultivators, and supervisors had their routine task in the field. Housewives of upper castes and lower castes had been equally busy for their different work within and outside the residence. Even the younger boys and girls had performed different tasks in the productive activities with their parents. In the evening, men, women, and children of the labourer retired quite early. Sometime I was drawn by the recital of *madal* (drum) or flute by the Santal in the evening. I was also struck by the exchange of abusive words among the Dule or Charal during evening. This was the mode for their release of excitement - good or bad. The men of the *Babu* family would assemble in the evening in the village library for a leisurely gossip or for playing cards.

The village has a number of institutions such as two primary schools, one library, one post office, one social welfare centre, one tribal co-operative, one panchayat office. At the outskirt there is a crematorium. Besides, twelve deities are regularly worshipped in the village in separate temples. The high school, the government seed farm and the market place are within one kilometre from this village. There are a dozen public tubewells around the village which are used by various sections of the people. Recently electricity connection has reached the village. Most of the houses of the dominant section are now having electric light, fan etc.

Economic Dimension

The major source of livelihood of the people is agriculture. Two sets of people are involved in the management of land and productions. They are owner cultivator and supervisor land owners of various categories at the one hand and sharecroppers and agricultural labourers on the other. In some cases the small land owners also cultivate some amount of land on share basis and the small sharecroppers work as agricultural labourers. A table on approximate landholding is given here. Categories of holding that have been made here are somewhat arbitrary. This has been done on the basis of experience of the local situation. The first group includes entirely landless families. Next two groups include the poor and marginal owners. Subsequent two groups include small to substantial land owners. The last one includes rich owners.

TABLE 2: Pattern of landholding

Sl. No.	Ethnic Groups	Total no.of Families	Land less	Landholding in Bigha *					Total land of an ethnic group.
				0.5-1.5	2-5.5	6-10.5	11-25	Above 25	
1.	Aguri	2				2			16
2.	Barui	2	2						Nil
3.	Baishnab	2		2					2
4.	Baidya	3					3		47
5.	Bauri	33	33						Nil
6.	Bagdi	44	38	4	2				11
7.	Bene	12	8		3	1			13
8.	Brahman	62	4	1	10	15	23	9	862
9.	Charal	5	5						Nil
10.	Dhopa	2		2					1.5
11.	Dom	2	2						Nil
12.	Dule	55	53	1	1				3.5
13.	Goala	3	1	2					2
14.	Hari	9	9						Nil
15.	Jele	8	3	1	2		2		37
16.	Kayastha	17	2		2	5	4	4	392
17.	Karmakar	3			3				9.5
18.	Moira	1			1				5
19.	Muslim	86	16	10	25	8	22	5	692
20.	Napit	6	1	1	4				9.5
21.	Suri	1	1						Nil
22.	Sadgope	43	6	2	5	18	8	4	470
23.	Santal	119	115	2	2				6
24.	Tambuli	41	2		8	7	18	6	645
	Total	561	301	28	68	56	80	28	3224

* 1 bigha = 1/3 of an acre.

As already noted, the primary scope of employment for the landless people is in agricultural operations, from preparation of land to processing of harvest. This village being situated in agriculturally developed area, employment opportunity for the labourers and share-croppers has increased on account of adoption of the multiple cropping and improved method in cultivation.

On an average agricultural labourers get work for seven to eight months. It does alter depending on universal variables like bad weather and also depending on some local or personal variables like crop selection, utilization of land, physical illness and ritual engagement of the workers.

TABLE 3: Expenses and Average Production Per Bigha

Name of the crop	Average expenses of cultivation (in rupees)	Average production (in maund)	Approximate market value (in rupees)
Aman	100.00	5	200.00
Boro	200.00	15	600.00
Potato	500.00	60	1000.00
Wheat	200.00	6	300.00
Jute	250.00	7	350.00

Expenses of cultivation and rate of production often vary in individual cases. Market value of the produce is estimated in terms of the price which prevails during the harvest period. Benefit of increased price is enjoyed by the rich section only who can hold the stock for a favourable time.

Nature of engagement of the largest section of landless people in agriculture is of two kinds : as share-croppers and agricultural labourers. The share-croppers generally belong to Muslim, Santal, Dule, Bagdi, Bauri, and Charal groups. The Muslim apart, all other groups mentioned above suffer from their decisive landlessness. To own a plough and a pair of bullocks is the prime indicator for being a sharecropper, locally called as *jotedar*. The sharecropper get their lands for cultivation specially from the Hindu upper castes. The produce is equally divided between the landowner and the sharecropper. Landowners are locally referred to as *manib* or master. The sharecropper bears the cost of cultivation excepting the cost of chemical fertilizers and irrigation tax (twelve rupees per acre) which are borne by both the parties. In case of potato cultivation the cost of seed is also shared by the master and the sharecropper. The practice of manuring with cowdung and mud of pond etc. demands a different kind of interaction. In this case the manure is generally supplied by the master which remains stored in his own manure pit. Sometimes he has to purchase it from his sharecroppers. Local price of a fullcart load of indigenous manure is four rupees. Manure is carried to the field by the sharecropper for which he does not receive any payment. Usual rate of carrying a cart, loaded with manure to the field is rupees two or a little more. A sharecropper in most cases can not run the expenses required for his cultivation. He has to take loan from his master either in cash or in kind. After the threshing is over he has to repay all his dues with appropriate interest. The remaining portion of the share which a sharecropper brings home, does not in most cases meet the requirement of his household for the whole year. As a routine practice he is dragged into the system of taking loan from the master.

Sometimes, a *manib* helps his jotedar in purchasing the plough, bullock, cart, etc. It is obligatory on the part of the *jotedar* to plough in turn the land, which is directly cultivated by his *manib* at a cheaper rate. Moreover he has to supply the master agricultural labourers when it is required. Occasional free service for the master is another conventional task for the members of a sharecropper family. Besides sharecropping, the sharecropper sometimes sell their plough and work as agricultural labourers for immediate earning. To sell a plough means ploughing an agricultural plot against a fixed payment. The local practice is that a man requires about six hours or more to plough a one bigha plot on an average. It is generally done in the forenoon, which is locally called *ek dupur*. Usual charge for ploughing a one bigha plot in dry season is between rupees five and seven, whereas it rises to between rupees eight and ten in wet season. A sharecropper holds, on an average, three acres of land. It is a very common affair now-a-days that the landowners distribute their land in pieces to more than one sharecropper. They often do it verbally and on a temporary basis. Both the landowners and the sharecropper make some allegations against each other. The former allege that the *jotedar* do not cultivate their land with proper care, they are more interested to sell the plough or to work as labourer during cultivation. The jotedar, in their turn, complain that the *manib* distribute inferior quality of land to them and show little interest for proper manuring, and demand a good return. During cultivation the *manib* pay several visits to the houses of the *jotedar*. After the harvest, the scene was just reverse.

Now I will describe about the agricultural labourers who are locally called as *Kishen*. They may be divided into three categories, namely,*Nagare Kishen, Bandha Kishen,* and *Chuto Kishen*. Male and female labourers get the same pay for agricultural work. Though there is a locally standardised wage rate, yet individual cases vary according to personal need and manipulation of the situation.

1. A *Nagare Kishen* is employed for a year. He usually gets rupees two hundred and fifty to three hundred per annum plus one kilogram rice or two meals and tiffin per working day. He is given one *bigha* rent-free land in which he cultivates *aman* paddy. The *manib* supplies him the plough and bullocks for preparing the land. The *Nagare* takes the total product of that land. Besides getting occasional gift during festivals, he gets two *dhotis* and one *gamcha* (country towel) a year. The *Nagare* is supposed to do cultivation work from dawn to dusk or any other job which may be assigned by his employer.
2. A *Bandha Kishen* works under a particular employer at a fixed rate for a specified time. Unlike the *Nagare*, he is not paid if there is no work at the disposal of the employer. The wage varies from seventyfive paise to one rupee plus one kilogram rice and tiffin per working day.
3. A *Chuto Kishen* works on daily wage basis. The wage varies depending on the intensity of agricultural operations. It fluctuates between one rupee to two rupees or a little less in cash alongwith one kilogram rice and tiffin per working day. I observed that the labourers were usually given coarse variety of rice. Tiffin is generally supplied in the form of parched rice or stale rice. If an employer fails to supply tiffin, then he adjusts it with 250 gram of additional rice. A *Kishen* also gets a few number of *bidi*, one or two spoonful of mustard oil, small quantity of cheap vegetables etc. Working hours of an agricultural labourer covers nearly eight hours, from morning to late afternoon. It was observed that some of the labourers were often underpaid in terms of cash and kind. Among the Santal and the Bauri even women work as agricultural labourers.

During lean months (covering a period of about 3/4 months between August to October and between February to April)the agricultural labourers and other weaker sections of the people mostly go unemployed. They invariably go to their *manib* and take loan in cash and kind. They pay it back, as a routine practice, either by working at a cheap rate or in kind with appropriate local interest. Sometimes they keep a few utensils or ornaments in mortgage to their *manib* in exchange of loan in kind or cash. The *manib* who act as village *mahajan* (money lender) belong generally to the upper castes and include both male and female.

The debtor labourers while working in the field, during cultivation, get their wage only in kind. i.e. rice. The cash is adjusted against the previous loan. They can not consume even the full quantity of rice which they get daily against their work because they invariably sell a portion of it to a village grocer for purchasing a little quantity of kerosene oil, spices, tobacco etc. for daily use. Collected green vegetables, small fishes, and crabs form essential items of their daily food.

The women among the lower caste Hindus serve as maid servant for the upper castes. A maidservant earns two to five rupees in cash per month depending on the load of work. She is given some tiffin in the morning. She also gets a piece of cloth on the occasion of Durga Puja festival. Minor boys among them are often employed as *rakhal* (cow herd) by the cultivating families. They look after the cattle from morning till evening and get two meals a day. In some cases they earn two to three rupees per month including two meals a day. Permanent herdsmen get a shirt and a *chadar* as cotton wrapper once a year. Adult males who know and get the work of thatching, basket making, preparing *morai* (grain store house), *palui* (stacking the large pile of hay) and other such things, earn a considerable amount. Cash wages in such work are fixed at not less than two rupees, whereas the quantity of rice as wage remain the same as in the case of agricultural labourers. Adult women workers also earn a little by preparing parched rice and by boiling and drying up paddy before it is taken in to husking mill. In the first case she earns thirtyseven paise per *khola* (local measure for 3 kg. of rice), and in the next she earns three kilogram rice per *basta* (60 kg. of paddy in a sack). Members of sharecropper's family often have to do some of these work in gratis, or at a cheaper rate for their permanent *manib*.

TABLE 4: Distribution of Agricultural Labourers

Caste	Total Family	Population			Ag.Labourers*			Share-Croppers and Labo-urers**			Amo-unt of land (in Bigha)
		Adult	Minor	Sex	N	B	C				
Hari	9	5	4	M	-	1	4	-		-	x
		7	4	F	-	-	-	-		-	x
Charal	5	9	9	M	-	-	5	2	+	3	46
		9	7	F	-	-	-	-		-	x
Bauri	33	40	33	M	3	6	22	3	+	1	17
		36	28	F	-	-	19	-	+	3	x
Dule	55	73	65	M	7	9	29	14	+	11	114
		67	62	F	-	-	-	-		-	x
Bagdi	44	66	45	M	9	8	15	17	+	6	131
		58	58	F	-	-	-	-		-	x
Santal	119	154	141	M	22	31	21	59	+	29	615
		163	110	F	-	14	60	-	+	75	x
Dom	2	2	2	M	-	-	2	-		-	x
		2	4	F	-	-	-	-		-	x
	267	691	572	41	69	117	95	+	128	923	

* N + *Nagare Kishen*,
B = *Bandha Kishen*,
C = *Chuto Kishen*

** These are part-time agricultural labourers who belong to a sharecropper's family.

There are certain minor distributive mechanisms in the village which allow these sections to share the resources of the rich. For example, when the owners employ the fishermen to clear their tank a section of the people mentioned above habitually assemble around that tank. Some of them collect small fishes with *chhakni jal* (handnett), moving round the tank in knee-deep water. In some cases I observed that those who assembled during catching of fish in a tank, were given a handful of small fishes. This is known as *muthi*. These people are allowed to collect crop, specially paddy and potato if any left in the field after the harvest. This is known as *kurani*. I observed some women among them to collect paddy with a winnowing fan from the piles of straw which were left in a *khamar* (threshing ground) after the threshing was done. This is known as *panchrani*. Sometimes they sell their collected grains locally or consume it. Some of them collect cowdung, prepare dry cake with it, and sell it in the village. If anyone of them is employed by the *manib* to pluck tamarind or silk cotton from a tree, then he is entitled to an equal share of the total collection. More often than not, they have several ducks, fowls, and goats. These livestocks are a reserve source of income for them. Rearing up of pigs and cows in share is another interesting feature in this area. The system is known as poshani. A *manib* gives a female calf or a pigling to a person belonging generally to the poor families. The latter brings it up. The pig is sold normally after a year when it attains the weight of about 40 Kg.. Pork sells at the rate of three rupees a kilogram. The share is divided between the two parties. In case of cow, the *manib* receives it back after the second pregnancy, while the first calf remains in possession of the caretaker.

It has already been mentioned that improved cultivation in Burdwan has opened a greater scope for employment of agricultural labourers. As a result, labourers from distant parts of Purulia, Midnapur, Bankura, and Birbhum migrate to these areas. By this process a regular link is established between the local employers and the migrant labourers. In the village under study, altogether 59 labourers (42 Santal and 17 Bauri) came during the transplanting and harvesting operations in both *kharif* and *rabi* seasons. The employers provide them with shelter, one-way fare for their travel and in most cases granted them a little increased wage.

The pattern and construction of houses of the labouring people are very simple when compared to that of their dominant *manib*. Not a single labourer owns a building. Their huts have mudwalls with thatched roof on the top. The number of rooms is limited and functionally less specialized. The houses of the Bauri are most wretched in appearance, in contrast to the decorated and clean huts of the Santal. All of them cook in the open space in fair weather. During other times they cook in the room where they also sleep.

TABLE 5: Occupation other than Agriculture

Occupation	Engineer Doctor	Teacher	Office Workers	Technical hands	Business man	Office attendant	Traditional vacations	Maid-servant	Cowherd
1. Aguri									
2. Bauri						1			
3. Baishnab						1			
4. Baidya	2	1P	2						
5. Bauri								6	6
6. Bagdi				1		2		21	9
7. Bene			2		1	2	2		
8. Brahman	3	2C, 3H, 7P	16	2	4		14		
9. Charal								1	
10. Dhopa							2		
11. Dom								1	
12. Dule								37	10
13. Goala							3		
14. Hari							2	4	2
15. Jele							8		
16. Kayastha	1	3P, 1H	3	2	2				
17. Karmakar							3		
18. Moira							1		
19. Muslim		1P	1	1	3				
20. Napit							3		
21. Suri							1		
22. Sadgope	1		3	1	5	1			
23. Santal						2			16
24. Tambuli		2P 1H	3		12				

Some of them now-a-days use coal as fuel. The *bhadralok* informants commented, "at present the Santal also use coal; it is certain that they have been prosperous". Regarding dress, ornaments and other material belongings, they have a few items in their possession. Children among them often remain naked. Sometimes they put on garments which were used in a *Babu's* family. The adult men or women rarely have two sets of clothes *(dhoti or sari)*. They sometimes get it from their employers when these become ragged after use. The annual farm servants and maid servants get a new piece of *dhoti* or a frock each from the employers before Gajan, or Sakrad, or Durgapuja festival. Two villagers have cloth stores which remain open throughout the week. They also visit the weekly market for selling their goods. Some of the labourers and poor people purchase new cloth before Gajan and Sakrad festival. They generally purchased cloth in credit. The amount was gradually realized in cash or by employing them in the shop owners' field.

Their items of food are minimum and simple. During cultivation they get their regular meals twice or thrice a day. During lean months the number and quantity of meals decrease. They collect small fishes, various kinds of green leaves, crab, shellfish etc. for consumption. Indigeneously made liquor and fermented juice of palm tree are used very much by the landless lower caste people and the Santal.

Land is the principal source of income and security to the people of Panchra. So the pattern of landholding will itself suggest the kind of category of the families into weakest, weak, marginal or dominant sections. Of course, land alone can not always be considered for getting an idea of the economic groupings. But here in this village the range of economic diversification is limited to a few families of upper social and economic strata. Some sources of income of the landless people through non-agricultural occupations have been brought into the discussion. But those unstable and irregular income do not give them any substantial alternative means. After analysing the data the following picture emerges:

TABLE 6: Distribution of family by economic categories

Ethnic groups	Total families	Weakest	Weak	Marginal	Dominant	Remarks
1. Guri	2				2	Dominant 100%

Contd.

TABLE 6 *Contd.*

2. Barui	2	2				Weakest 100%
3. Baishnab	2	2				Weakest 100%
4. Baidya	3				3	Dominant 100%
5. Bauri	33	33				Weakest 100%
6. Bagdi	44	40	2	2		Weakest 90%
7. Bene	12	6		3	3	Weakest 50% Dominant 25%
8. Brahman	62	2		5	55	Dominant 88.7% Weakest 3.2%
9. Charal	5	4		1		Weakest 80%
10. Dhopa	2		2			Weak 100%
11. Dom	2	2				Weakest 100%
12. Dule	55	53	2			Weakest 96.3%
13. Goala	3		3			weak 100%
14. Hari	9	9				Weakest 100%
15. Jele	8	4		2	2	Weakest 50% Dominant 25%
16. Kayastha	17			2	15	Dominant 88.2% Marginal 100%
17. Karmakar	3			3		Marginal 100%
18. Moira	1			1		Marginal 100%
19. Muslim	86	4		20	62	Dominant 72% Weakest 4.6%
20. Napit	6		2	4		Marginal 66.6%
21. Suri	1				1	Weakest 100%

Contd.

TABLE 6 *Contd.*

22. Sadgope	43	2		7	34	Dominant 79% Weakest 4.6%
23. Santal	119	117		2		Weakest 98.3%
24. Tambuli	41		2	6	33	Dominant 83%
	561	281	13	58	209	

From the table it appears that a line of divide can be sharply made between the weakest and the dominant categories. These categories may more or less be correlated to lower and upper caste blocks respectively. A few families of the dominant group occupy weak position. Their total number is not very high. In the day to day interaction they enjoy higher social prestige like any other member of their respective caste. None among the weak group holds a dominant position in economic term. The weakest and the weak categories together from the "Weaker Sections" in this village. Families that belong to the marginal category include those who have some independent economic position on account of little landholding or a sizeable holding in share cultivation, some sources of income through small jobs or caste occupations. The development in agriculture has increased the working days in the field and has opened greater employment scope to the agricultural labourers. This apart, no significant development has occured to them. The wage has not increased in real term. Expenses in improved cultivation has created pressure on the sharecroppers and the poor landowners. Various land legislations, political vicissitude, profit orientation in modern cultivation have together induced the landed gentry to gradually evict the share croppers or to lessen the amount or land in share cultivation. In the absence of any alternative source of income and in the face of the growing economic crisis the weaker sections in general are being guided by the terms that are usually dictated by their dominant counterparts. When some of them were asked to comment on the result of changes in agriculture they expressed, "We were more happy when there was single crop in this area; we got our full meals. But now cultivation has improved and we can not get even two full meals".

The Weaker Sections, excepting the upper caste Brahman and

Tambuli families, basically depend on manual labour for their livelihood either in agricultural operations or in other subsidiary occupations. When there is no work they depend on personal loan, collection of food materials from the field. Cases of begging, starvation and stealing are also not unfamiliar with them; but the frequency could not be ascertained.

Social Dimension

Composition of castes in the village demonstrates elaborate hierarchical ranking system though people in general were reluctant to emphasise its importance. Lower castes took pride in establishing superiority over other lower castes. Shri Bhattacharjee, a resident of this village and an eminent Sanskrit scholar of Burdwan district, gave a picture where the Brahman were at the top. He divided the *Sudra* into pure(*sat*) and impure (*asat*). The pure include the Kayastha, Aguri, Tambuli, Napit, Sadgope, Karmakar, and the Moira. The latter include the Barui, Charal, Dule, Bagdi, Bauri, Bene, Dhopa, Dom, Hari, Jele, and the Goala.

Shri Bhattercherjee indicated that among lower castes employment of Brahman priests is one index of identifying social hierarchy. According to him the Bagdi or Dule employ priests in their ritual activities, but the Bauri do not. As per consensus among upper castes the prevalence of widow marriage among the Dule, Hari and Bauri places them below the Goala, Bagdi, and the Charal who do not practice it. The Bagdi, Bauri, Dule and Hari divide themselves into a number of subgroups and all of them in this village claim to occupy the highest position.

Besides dividing people on the basis of caste ranking one can classify them into local class categories. For example, the *kishen* and *jotedar* may be contrasted with the *manib* or *babu*. The former group is known as *chotolok* whereas the latter is known as *bhadralok*. The *chotolok* invariably mean the lower caste labouring people including the Santal. The *bhadralok* means the upper caste and middle caste land owners. The Sadgope owner cultivators are generally referred to as *chasha* (cultivator), who are neither *chotolok* nor *bhadralok*. The Muslim land owners who employ share croppers and labourers for cultivation are referred to by their employees as *manib*. A few Muslim families who have substantial economic and political power are casually referred to as *Muslim bhadralok* by their Hindu counterparts.

Besides economic relations between the *chotolok* and the *bhadralok*, there are other kind of social interactions in daily life. For example, during my stay in the field I observed on three occasions the *chotolok* carrying fire wood for cremation of dead bodies of the *bhadralok*. They were served with tea, oilcake, and country liquor on the day of cremation and were invited to attend the funeral feast. One Dule informant observed, "we perform all activities in the crematorium. Afterwards the *babu* ignite the pyre. They give us oilcake and themselves eat sweets on the day of cremation. Afterwards they care little whether we take our food in the funeral feast or not. If we go to attend the feast they serve us food at the last batch".

One day in the evening the 'morai' (meant for storing paddy) of Buno Dule suddenly caught fire. People, irrespective of being *bhadralok* and *chotolok* rushed to the spot and brought the situation under control. Without citing a large number of cases it may be said that there is close interdependence and interaction between different categories of people in the village, particularly during crisis situations.

Kinship terms are extended between members of different socio-economic categories. The *bhadralok* of the older generation address the *chotolok* by name and use derogatory term of reference even if the latter is senior by age. But the juniors of *bhadralok* families address senior members of the weaker group by terms of respect.

I observed three marriage ceremonies among the Santal, two each among the Dule,Musalman, Brahman, and the Sadgope and a funeral among the Hari. The Santal more or less follow the broad traditional customs in their marriages. Community participation is still very important but as they have migrated to Panchra from various places and have settled in the village in distinct clusters, all the Santals of the village socially do not move together. Participation is ordinarily limited to the people of the same settlement. The Dule engage a priest of lower order from a distant village to perform marriage. The rites are without much elaboration. *Jajna* (oblation) and *mantra* (incantation) which played vital role in case of the upper caste's marriage, were conspicuously absent in the marriages of the Dule. The role of Napit in a marriage was verbally reported to me by a Dule informant. But there was no Napit in actual performance. I have observed a Napit in the Brahman's marriage. He carried the ceremonial presents (tatwa) from the groom's family to the bride's family. On behalf of the groom's family he invited the village guests to marriage feast. The average expenditure of marriage among the Dule was below two hundred rupees whereas the same among the Santal was around three hundred rupees.The Dule or Santal labourers (including two share-croppers) took loan from their respective *manibs* to meet expenses of wedding. Due to want of money the Hari family could not arrange post-funeral rites and feast. The dead body was somehow cremated with the help of their kinsmen. The expense of marriage among the Muslim, Sadgope, and Brahman families were above five thousand rupees on an average. Compared to the Hindu, the expenses of marriage among the Muslim was somewhat less. Marriage among the Muslim took place between close relatives. So by mutual arrangement the expense could be controlled. In the case of the marriage of the daughter of a poor Brahman the relatives and friends of that family jointly contributed about two thousand rupees and the marriage took place auspiciously. The Dule bride and the bridegroom after marriage visited the temple of Narayana to bow before the deity. They also visited the houses of their employers to receive blessings.

The social network and family obligations are relatively less developed among the weaker sections. Baburam Hansda (Santal), Mahananda Porel (Bagdi) and Basudev Malik (Bagdi) are three exceptions in this respect. Baburam (44) was the only Santal student who read upto the high school standard. Due to family pressure he could not continue education. One Brahman of this village, who is an Engineer and stays in Calcutta, employed him as manager in their cultivation as well as in their rice mill. Thus, he is far better placed in comparison to his fellow brethren. His fluency in Bengali gave him an opportunity to mix up with rural elites of higher castes. Mahananda (35) got his training as technician in pump machines through the backing of a Vaidhya physician of his village. He is a good actor of the local Jatra party too. These two factors enabled him to extend his social horizon. He has decided to provide educational facilities to his younger brother upto the post-graduate level. Basudev(31) obtained his B.A. Part I degree. He got the unfailing economic help of his elder brother. During the United Front regime he contested from this reserved constituency as a Bangla Congress candidate and was elected M.L.A. Now he is a primary school teacher in this village and continues to be a sound social worker. Once he said that, "many *bhadralok* did not really want that I should get higher education or become an M.L.A."

Development Programme in the Village during 1972

Rural development had earlier meant the agricultural development and related aspects like co-operative movement, health improvement scheme and so on. The weaker sections had largely remained uncovered by the programmes. Only a few relief measure reached casually to some of them. The main organisation for development is the Community Development Block. During 1972 the following amount (in rupees) was allotted for Panchra village against the items indicated below :

Item	Amount	Remarks
1. Fertilizer Loan	Rs. 2400.00	People of dominant groups received it.
2. Group Loan	Rs. 750.00	None among the Weaker Section received it.
3. Cattle purchase Loan	Rs. 500.00	None among the weaker received it.
4. Shallow Tubewell	Rs. 6200.00	Recipients belong to Hindu upper caste and
5. Pump Set	Rs. 20,500.00	Muslim group. All are progressive cultivators.
6. T.R. work	Rs. 2,200.00	For this work the main force was the Santal of this village and adjacent villages. They worked for ten to twelve days on daily wage basis which included 1Kg.of wheat and Rs. 1.50 in cash.
7. Old age pension	Rs. 20.00 per month.	The weaker group (Three Persons) received it.

8. G.R.	5/6	Persons continuously get it. They come from the weaker sections. In lean months the number multiplies. They get wheat from the specified shop on production of the card issued by the Panchayat. They are allotted 2 to 4kg. of wheat per head per fortnight.

A list is prepared by the Panchayat for cloth distribution among a few family heads of the weaker group once in a year. Some *sari, dhoti*, shirt and frocks of different size were distributed. In the list of Panchra a Tambuli, a Napit, and a Jele were included, though they had some sources of income. In this way the power-holders create a section of obliged persons who remain prepared to serve them in different ways.

A *bhadralok* elite from the village once narrated to the author how they managed to make some money against the fictitious demand on behalf of two flood affected poor families of the village. This amount was spent for construction of the library building there.

After the independence Late Sukumar Roy (Vaidya by caste) alongwith his associates organized the following institutions and activities for development of the weaker sections :

(i) Panchra Tribal Co-operative (termed as *Dharma Gola* in Bengali)

Year of establishment	–	1962
Executive members	–	The local Santal
Total member	–	165
Active member	–	30

They run the paddy Co-operative and organise the distribution of bread, banana or biscuit sanctioned by the District Tribal Welfare Authority. One of the leading executive members told me that due to non-realization of the loan their paddy co-operative has been almost out of work. They only distribute food articles for children (up to 5 years) numbering about 200 when these are available. They allow 10 to 15 children from other castes of weaker group to receive those food articles.

(ii) Night School. Another school is organised at Bagdipara. In these two night schools persons above 14 years were expected to take primary education. According to the teachers Shri M. Chatterjee (62) and Shri D. Ghosh (41), "This scheme did not prove successful. They (the weaker sections) are not very serious about it,because they do not find any real utility in it".

(iii) Panchra Social Welfare Centre- established in 1958. This institute was transformed into Family & Child Welfare in 1970. Forty children of age group between three and six are selected for training. Among them 10 to 15 students are recruited from the Dule, Bagdi, Dhopa, Charal, and Hari castes. They are given tiffin regularly. This centre organises the women's camp for more than once in a year. The women from upper castes as well as from castes like Dule and Bagdi are selected for this camp which continues for 15 days at a stretch. But this effort could hardly promote social interaction in a major way.

Regarding health and medical facilities it was observed that the people of weaker sections were generally attacked with cold and fever, stomach trouble, and sometimes with critical disease like tuberculosis, cancer, leprosy etc. In general cases, they take medicine from the local charitable dispensary, from the primary health centre (which is bit far off), and from private allopaths or homeopaths according to personal convenience. They also depend on folk medicine in certain diseases. On many occasions I found them suffering without having any medicine. They do not care for minor aliments. During my stay when there was a campaign for mass Vasectomy I noted that some people from all categories accepted it. They were persuaded by the family planning promoters as well as by the local influential members of the respective community. I also noticed that the Muslim and the Santal were initially opposed to the programme. Among the upper caste Hindu also there was a apprehension regarding the ultimate physical reaction.

Members of the weaker groups could not come out with specific suggestions for improvement for their lot." What do we know about such big things?. It depends upon people like you, *Babu* please write in favour of us," some said to me. Their aspiration for life was very limited. They wanted jobs and in exchange full meals every day. They usually take a fatalistic view of life.

The *bhadralok* often described 'bad' qualities like excessive drinking, indignity of labour, lack of awareness about their own good, no sense of gratitude, unable to retain the land given to them. Conversely, they had many grievances against the *bhadralok* as they complain that they do not part with good quality of land in share cultivation, do not want to give required dose of fertilizer but want good returns, pay minimum wage, take away the relief items which are allotted to weaker sections by the government and so on.

Social Hierarchy

There was a great elaboration of social hierarchy among the people of Panchara. Among the weaker groups their identical economic positions could not obliterate their social distinctions. They take little or no education, though scope for free primary education is there. It serves no purpose to them yet. The relative positions of the weak and the dominant can be clearly seen in these interactions also. They were not much benefited out of the developmental programmes by the government. Marriage and death rituals of the weaker sections also are less elaborate and less expensive when compared with the dominant section.

Political Dimension

Only the tribal Santal have their traditional political structure. *Majhi, Jagmajhi and Goreyet* are the three officials of their political structure. Each of their 3 wards has separate set of officials.

The village Panchayat of Panchara is divided into two units. In terms of formal power structure there is no representation from the weaker sections.

During the United Front Government the so called *chotolok* were organised against the landed section of population. Their common sentiment was against the *bhadralok* in general. The Santal played the leading role in this movement. No party singularly dominate the area at present. Political leadership for the weaker group mainly comes from outside the village.

Magico-religious Dimensions

There are some festivals in this village where the people of weaker groups participate with the dominant groups viz. gajan, shiv gajan, and dharama gajan. During these festivals the Dule, Bagdi or people of middle caste groups become *sanyasi*. Sometimes they become sanyasi according to their own *'manat'* (religious vow) and sometimes peoples of upper castes who cannot undergo straneous purificatory rites (know as *dandi-khata*) engage them as their representative. The people thus engaged are paid in cash. They also get a *dhoti*, a *gamcha*, alongwith some fruits and rice for each day for more than a week. The *sanyasi* from upper castes are conventionally relaxed from undergoing hardship in *dandi-khata*. Though the Santal and the Muslim have no ritual participation in it, they join in the recreational aspect of the festival. The *gajan* is a festival of the people and the village as a whole irrespective of the group's socio-economic position. Even during Durgapuja it was observed that the ceremony was chiefly confined to the people of upper castes. Some labourers were engaged from the weaker castes for clearing the place of worship and for erecting the pandal. They were paid nothing for this service. This was the only way in their case to participate in the ceremony.

Besides common participation in some festivals mentioned above, the weaker groups organise their own festival. The Santal have their own cycle of festivals. The Dule, Bauri, and Bagdi perform 'Tusuhla-Lakshmi *puja*' during the whole month of *Poush* and assemble on the bank of the river Damodar on the 1st day of the *Magh*. A Jele is the local priest of *'Dharmaraj'* and a Dule is the local priest of *'Manasha'*. People of upper castes send their offerings to them on common occasions of ritual observance. Some people of the weaker sections are competent to give folk medicine in cases of different physical disorders including cases of snake-bite. People, irrespective of high or low caste status, use these local sources to a certain extent. The lower caste people also use folk medicine or talisman from upper caste Hindu practitioners. Thus, some of them enjoy a superior status compared to that of their community members for a limited period in the total interactional milieu.

Concluding Remarks

The preceding discussion shows the social situation of an agriculturally developed village in West Bengal. Four distinct dimensions : economic, social, political, and magico-religious have been considered for analysis. The economic aspects have been emphasised as the core of the present problem. It appears that there was a close link between the economic and social structure of the village. The concept of 'reciprocity' and '*redistribution*' may be used to explain this phenomenon. Neale[9] observed, "briefly, it can be said that relationships were reciprocative is regard to services, and redistributive in regard to agricultural produce. . . . But the reciprocative caste system as a whole was itself an element within the redistributive system of the village" (1957:227-228). The emergence of a massive techno-economic programme for rural development as well as the generation of new socio-political values since independence have not qualitatively altered the pattern of relations among the rural people which were essentially guided by a Varna-Jati frame, specially in a Hindu dominated area. Berreman[10] observed, "Even when interaction between castes is maximal and cultural differences are minimal, the ideal of mutual isolation and distinctiveness is maintained and is advertised among those who value the system. Similarly even when mobility within, or subversion of, the system is rampant, a myth of stability is stolidly maintained among those who benefit from the system" (1968 : 335).

The existing economic interactions between the landowners and the landless labourers and sharecroppers contain an element of traditional obligation though the *jajmani* system is not very much in existence in this area. It may be noted that the ideal obligatory situation has been markedly strained by the population pressure, inflation and growing market influence. Economic exploitation and social inequality mutually existed. Beteille[11] observed,"The caste system contributed to the persistence of these inequalities by providing the values and norms which were appropriate to the agrarian hierarchy" (1972 :25).

It is found that there has been no major change in the pattern of ownership of land among the weaker sections of people. The development in agriculture has only marginally benefited them. They have in general been unable to come up either by taking up education or by organised (political) movement. Cases of exceptions, which were recorded, are very few in number. These have created little impact on the vast population of the weaker sections. The objective situation around them has not helped to expand their mental and social horizon, rather this has shaped their cognitive level in a very depended manner. Continuous economic depression, political dependence and social disability, lack of social solidarity, absence of a genuine class organisation, fatalistic stand about self-emancipation, sharing of ideological thrust of the dominant sections make them less assertive and more submissive to the existing order.

In the context of what has been described so far it is imperative to think of a comprehensive programme for the development of the weaker sections. The 'package' of programme suggested by Epstein[12] seems to be relevant in the present social, economic and political situation. It consists of planning regionally integrated economic order where landowners pay progressive land taxes and landless labourers are given priority in employment outside agriculture while applied research helps to increase the productivity of small holdings and rural wage rates are tied to rewards in kind.

NOTES AND REFERENCES

1. *Report of the Study Group on the Welfare of the Weaker Section of the village community*, Ministry of C.D. etc. Govt. of India, 1963.
2. Dandekar. V.M and Rath, Nilakantha "Poverty in India" *Economic and Political Weekly*, Vol. VI, No. 1-2, 1971.
3. Bose, Nirmal Kumar "Presidential address", In *Indian Anthropology Today*, Dharani Sen (Ed.), Department of Anthropology, Calcutta University, 1974.
4. Contributions of Dumont, Leach, Srinivas may be referred to, for example.
5. For example, Beteille, A. *Studies in Agrarian Social Structure*. Oxford University Press, Delhi, 1974.
6. "Socio-economic changes among the Weaker Sections of the Indian Population since independence" (project III) *Newsletter*, Anthropological Survey of India Vol. No. 3, 1972.
7. *A short note on the Progress of the Intensive Agricultural District Programme, Burdwan*, Govt. of West Bengal, Deptt. of Agriculture and Community Development. 1972.
8. This may be compared with Peterson (1910). Peterson J.C.K. - *Bengal District Gazetteers, Burdwan*, 1910.
9. Neale. Walter C. - "Reciprocity and Redistribution in the Indian village : Sequel to some Notable Discussions", in *Trade and Market in the Early* Empires, Karl Polanyi and others (Ed.), The Free Press, 1957.
10. Berreman, G.D. - 'The Concept of Caste",*International Encyclopedia of the Social Sciences*. Vol.2, The Macmillan and the Free Press, 1968.
11. Beteille, Andre - *Inequality and Social Change*, Oxford University Press, Delhi, 1972.
12. Epstein, T. Scarlett - *South India : Yesterday, Today and Tomorrow*. The Macmillan Press Ltd. 1973.

6

MAJHIHIRA : A VILLAGE IN WEST BENGAL

GOPA BANERJEE

Introduction

This paper concerns with the present socio-economic condition of the weaker sections of Majhihira, a village in the backward district of Purulia, West Bengal. It is situated about 5.5. km. south-west of the town of Purulia.

Field investigation was carried out for about four months from December '72 to March '73. Besides applying traditional anthropological tools for collecting data, Government records of various nature were consulted and quantitative data were also collected through half-structured schedules.

The Village

Purulia is mainly inhabited by the Mahato. In the village, Majhihira, as well as in its surrounding villages, the Mahato wield political power. This region was under the Zamindary of Manbhum during the British period. The local Zamindar claims their ancestry from a Rajput clan of Rajputana. The local people consider the Zamindar to be originally a Bhumij.

During the British regime, Majhihira *mauza* was the Hikmall Estate under the *Raja* of Manbhum. But after the abolition of the zamindary system in 1952, the intermediate tenancies were abolished. The original settlers of this village were the Desoai Majhi, from whom the village derived its name. But due to some epidemic and famine during recent past most of the Majhi families left the village. Later on, the Mahato, being driven away by the Muslim from the West came and settled here. Some other castes, like Sahis and Mahali also came to live here. Locally the Mahato are regarded as good cultivators who brought a considerable amount of fallow land under cultivation. Three of their families acquired the madhyasatta zamindary right from the *Raja* of Manbhum.

There is one Basic school, one Post Office, one Veterinary Medical Hall and one Homeopathic Dispensary in this village. The main source of water is the Chakra river which is a small tributary of the river Kasai. Besides, there are eight wells, and fifteen dams, but water of most of the wells are not used for drinking purpose. These are generally used for irrigation. Most of the dams dry up during summer. One unpaved road connects the village with the Purulia-Manbazar metalled road passing about five Kms. west of the village. A bus runs from Purulia to Majhihira once a day. The villagers visit three weekly markets held within a radius of 10 kms.

TABLE 1: Distribution of population

Sl. No.	Castes	Families		Male		Female		Population	
		No.	%	No.	%	No.	%	No.	%
1.	Mahato	147	68.3	376	67.7	351	70.0	727	68.9
2.	Napit	4	1.8	11	1.9	8	1.6	19	1.8
3.	Bhumij	2	.9	4	.7	1	.2	5	.4
4.	Kumhar	4	1.8	11	1.9	6	1.2	17	1.6
5.	Garain	1	.4	6	1.0	1	.2	7	.6
6.	Kamar	3	1.3	12	2.1	9	1.8	21	1.9
7.	Desoali Majhi	14	6.5	25	4.5	25	5.0	50	4.7
8.	Kora Mudi	9	4.1	20	3.6	20	4.0	40	3.7
9.	Mahali	11	5.1	46	8.2	34	6.8	80	7.4
10.	Sahis	13	6.0	28	5.0	32	6.4	60	5.6
11.	Jolha	7	3.2	16	2.8	13	2.6	29	2.7
	Total	215		555		500		1055	

The village is divided in two neighbourhoods - *bastee* and *dih*. There are ten *parą* or *kulhi* (ward) most of which are named after the respective castes inhabiting the wards. They are Kadam Kulhi, Kacha Kulhi, Nimtolia Kulhi, Majhi Kulhi, Mahali Kulhi, Sahis Kulhi, Jolha Kulhi, Majhi Kulhi, Upor Kulhi and Namokulhi. The *kulhi* of the Mahato is centrally situated, while that of the other castes are at the periphery. The *bastee* can be divided into two wards viz. Namo *kulhi*, situated on the lower level and the Upor Kulhi where the Mahato live. The Kulhi are divided into a number of *bakhol*, a sort of spatial segments usually occupied by a single lineage.

There are ten Hindu and a Muslim castes in the village. The total population of 1055 belongs to 215 families. Among the important village functionaries who were appointed during the *raja's* rule, are the *mukhia* (Mahato), *ghatwal* (Mahali), *tabender* and *laya* (Desoali Majhi) and the *gorait* (Sahis). The old sacred places (*Gosainthan*, *Garamthan*, etc.) are still very much functioning and play an important part in the community life of the villagers.

The Mahato numerically are the most dominant (68.3%) community. Their migration to this village took place about five or six generations ago.

Economic Dimension

The village economy is mainly based on agriculture. The lateritic soil of the district is infertile and its general tendency is towards deterioration. Besides, the average rainfall is also low for rice cultivation. So, production per acre is lower than the average for West Bengal. This is mostly single cropped area. Only a few rich farmers cultivate wheat, sugarcane, potato, pulses and maize as the second crop. The small farmers usually cultivate *aus* paddy which is grown in the high land, locally termed as *baid*. But the rich farmers who have low land, or *bahal* grow *aman* paddy.

There are three types of paddy land in this region, locally known as *bahal* (low land), *kanhali* (medium), and *baid* (high land). There is a fourth type locally known as *gora* or *tann*. Paddy is not grown in this land. Mustard and pulses are generally grown there. The *bahal* and *kanhali* lands produce *aman* paddy while the *baid* land produces *aus* paddy. Average yield of *aman* paddy is about 20 mds. per acre while yield of *aus* paddy is about 12 mds. per acre.

The villagers generally practise three indigeneous methods of cultivation, viz. (1) transplantation, as done in the *bahal* and *kanhali* land, (2) *bena* or broadcasting, as done in all types of land, and (3) *thupi*, a local method of cultivation where five to six seeds are sown together six inches apart. *Boro* cultivation is not practised in Majhihira although in neighbouring villages it is practised. They say that *boro chas* required plenty of water which is scarce in this village.

The cost of production of different types of paddy varies. Table 2 presents a comparative statement for the *aus* and *aman* paddy.

TABLE 2: Main agricultural yield (per acre)

Crops	Period	No. of labour	No. of working days	Approx. yield (in Rs.)	Approx. cost after	Price (just harvest in Rs.)
Paddy	April-May	35	40	10	312.50	475.00
a) *Aus*	to August September			mds.		
b) *Aman*	June-July to November December	45	55	17.5 mds.	350.00	700.00

In agricultural organization the eleven castes of the village may be grouped into two occupational categories, owner-cultivators and labourers. Table 3 shows the number of families of different communities who are engaged mainly in agricultural operation.

TABLE 3: Distribution of castes and families in agricultural organization

Name of the ethnic-groups, castes	No. of families	Owner cultivator			Labourer	
		Cultivated by himself & hired labourers	Cultivated by himself and other family members	Munsih/ Kamin or daily labourer	Bagal o contact labourer	Monthly paid cont-contact labourer
1. Mahato	147	11 (7.4%)	42 (28.5%)	82 (55.7%)	10 (6.8%)	2 (1.3%)
2. Napit	4		1 (22.2%)		1 (22.2%)	
3. Bhumij	2			2 (100%)		
4. Desoali Majhi	14		5 (35.7%)	6 (42.8%)	2 (15%)	1 (2.5%)
5. Garain	1		1 (100%)			
6. Kumhar	4			2 (50%)		
7. Kamar	3			2 (66.6%)		
8. Mahali	11		2 (18.1%)	2 (18.1%)		
9. Mudi	9		2 (22.2%)	5 (55.5%)	2 (22.2%)	
10. Sahis	13		2 (15.3%)	8 (51.5%)	3 (23.0%)	
11. Jolha	7			1 (14.2%)		
TOTAL	215	11 (5.1%)	55 (25.3%)	112 (52.0%)	18 (8.2%)	3 (1.3%)

TABLE 4: Distribution of occupation

Sl. No.	Occupation	Bhumij		D. Majhi		Garain		Jolha		Kamar		Kumhar		Mahali		Mahato		Mudi		Napit		Sahis	
		M	F	M	F	M	F	M	F	M	F	M	F	M	F	M	F	M	F	M	F	M	F
1.	Agriculture	-	-	1	-	2	-	-	-	1	-	-	-	-	-	123	-	-	-	-	-	6	-
2.	Daily labourer	2	1	10	11	2	1	2	8	4	4	-	3	9	5	55	123	9	1	-	4	5	14
3.	Contact labourer	-	-	7	-	2	-	1	-	3	-	2	-	1	-	42	-	6	-	1	-	10	-
4.	Service	-	-	-	-	-	-	-	-	1	-	-	-	12	2	-	-	-	-	1	-		
5.	Business	-	-	-	-	-	-	2	-	-	-	-	-	-	-	7	26	-	-	-	-	-	-
6.	Traditional occupation	-	-	-	-	-	-	6	-	2	-	4	-	19	17	-	-	-	11	8	-	-	1
	TOTAL	2	1	18	11	6	1	11	8	10	4	7	3	29	22	237	151	15	12	9	4	22	15
Non labourer		2	-	7	14	-	-	5	5	2	5	4	3	17	13	139	200	5	8	2	4	6	17

N. B. M. = Male, F = Female.

The distribution of occupation by caste is given in table 4.

Besides agricultural pursuits, villagers participate in several other occupations including their traditional avocation. From their occupational point of view they may be grouped into three categories: (i) *agriculturists*, the Mahato, Bhumij, Desoali Majhi and the Garain, (ii) *artisans* Mahali, Mudi Kumar, Kamar, and the Jolha, and (iii) *servicing groups* ike Napit and Sahis. Besides, the basically agriculturists like Mahato, Desoali, Majhi, Garain, and Bhumij, the rest of the castes in the village depend primarily on their traditional callings. Exceptions are the Mudi whose traditional occupation is mat-making and the Sahis whose traditional occupation is midwifery who do not depend on their traditional occupation as these jobs are believed to be more insecured than that of the others. It may be said that as the traditional occupation of craft and menial services provide low income the people take to wage labour to supplement their income.

From table 4 it is observed that the Mahato are cultivators, service holders, and small scale traders. The Mahato, Jolha, and Desoali Majhi have petty business of grocery, sale poultry items, and milk. There are two Mahato carpenters. A few families mainly depend on their own land. Labourers mainly come from the poor Mahato, Sahis, Desoali Majhi, Bhumij and Mudi castes.

After harvest, the poor collect the residual paddy grains from the field. The pressure of lean period is met with the collection of roots and tubers. *Mahua* flowers, fruits, and the juice are consumed in various forms. Sometimes the well to do farmers give goat, fowl, pigeon, duck etc., to the poor people for rearing. The products are equally shared by them. Government relief work which generally starts in the month of April or May is another source of livelihood during lean period. For digging 100 C.F.T. of soil they get Rs. 1.00 and 1 kg. 150 Gms. of wheat. From the Forest Department a *kamin* gets Rs. 1.25 while a Munish gets Rs. 2.50 per *chua* or baskets of filled soil.

Inter-ethnic Relation

In various economic activities, the villagers are tied up with each other in various sorts of relationship, like labour-master, creditor-debtor, in *jajmani* system and so on. Through *jajmani* system a Napit earns 12 kg. of paddy per family and during any social function he gets one seer of rice. During the birth of a male child a Sahis woman gets 20 kgs. of paddy and 300 gms. of rice; while in case of a female child she gets 10 kgs of paddy and 250 gms. of rice. After completion of the pollution period, on the 9th day she gets nine kgs. of paddy. The Kamar annually gets 20 kgs paddy from each of the *jajman* family.

Usually a labourer gets regular job for four months a year from middle of September to the middle of December and middle of July to the middle of August. For the remaining months they only get occasional employment. The artisan and servicing castes earn their living from their own as well as adjacent villages. Generally the agricultural labourers prefer to work in their own village or in nearby villages.

There are 189 male and 269 female dependents in the village.

Traditionally the rich landowners are the *madhyasatta* zamindars belonging to the Mahato caste. They own the best low land like the *bahal* and *kanhali*. They got it partly from the Raja of Manbhum and partly through purchase or different mortgaging system.

From table 5 it is seen that the majority of the land is in the possession of the Mahato. The total agricultural land of the village is 1874 *bigha* and 10 *katha*, of which 1681 *bigha* are owned by the Mahato. They are followed by Desoali Majhi (61 *bigha*), the Sahis (42 *bigha* 10 *katha*) Jolha (10 *bigha* 10 *katha*), Mudi (14 *bigha*), Napit (8 *bigha* 10 *katha*), Kamar (8 *bigha*) and the Garain (3 *bigha*) respectively.

If 15 *bigha* of land is taken as the viable amount for the maintenance of five members of a family (the village average 4.7) only 1.8 per cent families satisfy the criterion and they all belong to the Mahato caste. Nearly 32 per cent own between 10 and 15 acres of land per family. Remaining 68 per cent families belong to the economically weaker section. But their degree of weakness varies.

From table 6 it is seen that all the families except 41.3 per cent of the Mahato may be labelled as the economically weak.

The rich have steadily acquired land from the poor through various types of land mortgaging, such as (i) *sud bandhaki* by which the debtor takes loan from the money lender by mortgaging land and after payment of loan with interest he gets back his land. During such period the creditor enjoys the products of the land. (ii) *khaikhalasi* where the debtor takes loan by mortgaging his land for some fixed period. After completion of that period he gets back his land.

TABLE 5: Pattern of landholding

Caste	Total family	Types of total land: Agriculture B	K	CH	Homestead B	K	CH	Non-agriculture B	K	CH	Types of land possessed	Per family land holding 1 - 2 B	K	CH	3 - 6 B	K	CH	7 - 10 B	K	CH	11 - 19 B	K	CH	20 + B	K	CH
Mahato	127	1681	-	-	19	2	-	997	14	-	Ag.	10	12	1	13	-	-	17	-	-	18	-	-	66	-	-
											Non-Ag.	5	13	2	5	14	3	57	-	-	57	-	-	19	-	2
D.majhi	11	61	-	-	-	16	-	2	5	2	Ag.	5	12	-	5	10	-	-	-	-	-	-	-	-	-	-
											Non-Ag.	-	6	3	-	5	2	-	-	-	-	-	-	-	-	-
Sahis	10	42	10	-	2	9	-	3	7	-	Ag.	3	1	-	-	9	1	-	-	-	-	-	-	-	-	-
											Non-Ag.	-	4	1	-	4	1	-	-	-	-	-	-	-	-	-
Mahali	6	28	10	-	3	1	-	9	10	5	Ag.	2	14	1	-	-	-	-	-	-	-	-	-	-	-	-
											Non-Ag.	-	18	1	-	-	-	-	-	-	-	-	-	-	-	-
Jolha	6	18	10	-	-	7	-	3	3	2	Ag.	2	12	3	-	-	-	-	-	-	-	-	-	-	-	-
											Non-Ag.	-	11	-	-	-	-	-	-	-	-	-	-	-	-	-
Mudi	3	14	-	-	1	3	-	-	-	-	Ag.	1	11	-	-	-	-	-	-	-	-	-	-	-	-	-
											Non-Ag.	-	-	-	-	-	-	-	-	-	-	-	-	-	-	-
Kumhar	4	10	-	-	1	10	-	5	1	2	Ag.	2	10	-	-	-	-	-	-	-	-	-	-	-	-	-
											Non-Ag.	1	6	2	-	-	-	-	-	-	-	-	-	-	-	-
Napit	3	8	-	-	1	12	-	2	3	-	Ag.	2	8	-	-	-	-	-	-	-	-	-	-	-	-	-
											Non-Ag.	-	14	1	-	-	-	-	-	-	-	-	-	-	-	-
Kamar	1	8	-	-	1	-	-	-	-	-	Ag.	8	-	-	-	-	-	-	-	-	-	-	-	-	-	-
											Non-Ag.	-	-	-	-	-	-	-	-	-	-	-	-	-	-	-
Garain	1	3	-	-	-	8	-	2	-	3	Ag.	3	-	-	-	-	-	-	-	-	-	-	-	-	-	-
											Non-Ag.	2	-	3	-	-	-	-	-	-	-	-	-	-	-	-
Bhumij	2	-	-	-	-	-	-	-	-	-	Ag.	-	-	-	-	-	-	-	-	-	-	-	-	-	-	-
											Non-Ag.	-	-	-	-	-	-	-	-	-	-	-	-	-	-	-

Abbreviation B = bigha, K = Katha, Ch = Chhatak, 2.5 Bigha make an acre

TABLE 5 *Contd.*

Caste	Total family	Types of land possessed	Per capita land holding B	K	CH	B	K	CH	B	K	CH	B	K	CH	B	K	CH
Mahato	127	Ag.	1	2	-	2	5	2	3	16	1	4	6	2	14	14	2
		Non.Ag.	1	1	-	1	-	-	1	4	3	3	18	2	11	3	2
D.majhi	11	Ag	1	3	-	1	10	-	-	-	-	-	-	-	-	-	-
		Non.Ag.	-	1	3	-	1	2	-	-	-	-	-	-	-	-	-
Sahis	10	Ag	-	13	-	1	13	3	-	-	-	-	-	-	-	-	-
		Non.Ag.	-	-	3	-	-	3	-	-	-	-	-	-	-	-	-
Mahali	6	Ag	-	11	-	-	-	-	-	-	-	-	-	-	-	-	-
		Non.Ag.	-	4	2	-	-	-	-	-	-	-	-	-	-	-	-
Jolha	6	Ag	-	16	1	-	-	-	-	-	-	-	-	-	-	-	-
		Non.Ag.	-	2	1	-	-	-	-	-	-	-	-	-	-	-	-
Mudi	3	Ag	-	7	-	-	-	-	-	-	-	-	-	-	-	-	-
		Non.Ag.	-	-	-	-	-	-	-	-	-	-	-	-	-	-	-
Kumhar	4	Ag.	-	8	2	-	-	-	-	-	-	-	-	-	-	-	-
		Non.Ag.	-	6	-	-	-	-	-	-	-	-	-	-	-	-	-
Napit	3	Ag	-	9	2	-	-	-	-	-	-	-	-	-	-	-	-
		Non.Ag.	-	2	3	-	-	-	-	-	-	-	-	-	-	-	-
Kamar	1	Ag	-	5	-	-	-	-	-	-	-	-	-	-	-	-	-
		Non.Ag.	-	-	-	-	-	-	-	-	-	-	-	-	-	-	-
Garain	1	Ag.	-	8	2	-	-	-	-	-	-	-	-	-	-	-	-
		Non.Ag.	-	6	1	-	-	-	-	-	-	-	-	-	-	-	-
Bhumij	2	Ag.	-	-	-	-	-	-	-	-	-	-	-	-	-	-	-
		Non.Ag.	-	-	-	-	-	-	-	-	-	-	-	-	-	-	-

(iii) *kotkoali*. In this system the debtor takes loan on condition that the capital with interest accrued thereon has to be paid within a definite date, failing which he forfeits his right over the land.

TABLE 6: Weak and dominant in terms of landholding

Sl. No.	Ethnic-groups	Weakest	Weak	Marginal	Rich
1.	Mahato	11.6%	47.1%	38.2%	3.1%
2.	Napit	75%	25%		
3.	Bhumij	100%	-		
4.	Kamar	66.6%	33.3%		
5.	Kumhar	-	100%		
6.	Garain	-	100%		
7.	Desoali Majhi	20.4%	79.6%		
8.	Mahali	45.4%	54.6%		
9.	Mudi	66.6%	33.4%		
10.	Sahis	23.1%	76.9%		
11.	Jolha	14.2%	85.8%		

Social Dimension

In this village there is a marked tendency among lineage members to live together. Every community is separated from the other by its settlement boundary. This feature is more conspicious among the Jhola, Mudi, Mahali and Sahis who live in separate *kulhi* or hamlet at the outskirts of the village.

The concept of ritual purity and pollution and the form of inter-ethnic relationship are very important in caste ranking. It also depends on the status of ritual specialists employed in their sacred ceremonies. In this village the caste hierarchy is not rigid. The concepts of *jalchal* and *jalachal*, however, persist. The high and dominant caste like the Mahato and the low and the poor castes like Mudi, Sahis, and Mahali give two different statements regarding caste ranking as shown in table 7.

Both the high and the low castes consider the Jolha as the untouchable Muslim group. The Mahato rank themselves with the Napit at the top of the caste hierarchy. They also claim their Kshatriya identity. The Napit of course, do not consider the Mahato equal to them. They place the Sahis at the lowest position in the regional hierarchy. There are, of course, differences of opinion regarding the position of the intermediate castes. The low poor castes place the Napit at the top of social hierarchy.

TABLE 7: Caste hierarchy

By the dominant caste	By the low poor castes
1. Mahato, Napit	1. Napit
2. Bhumij	2. Mahato
3. Kumhar	3. Bhumij, Kumhar
4. Garain, Kamar	4. Kamar, Garain, Desoali
5. Desoali Majhi, Mudi, Mahali	5. Mudi, Mahali, Sahis
6. Sahis	6. Jolha (Muslim)
7. Jolha (Muslim)	

In the rituals connected with life cycle rites the Brahman serve the Mahato and the Napit. Panre Brahman and Maghata Napit serve the Mahali. Bengali Napit serves the remaining castes.

The concept of occupational hierarchy is clear among the villagers. The work of midwifery of Sahis women is lower than basketry and bamboo work of the Mahali. Pottery is considered higher than smithery of iron. The Jolha (Muslim) are regarded untouchables not because of their weaving occupation but on account of their belonging to a separate faith. They however, do not regard themselves as untouchables. Agricultural operation is regarded as honourable and high and the landed aristocrats in general are respected by the mass.

The Napit do not accept cooked food from any other castes including the Mahato. The Mahato accept cooked food from the Napit. Other castes do not accept cooked food from one another except from the Mahato and the Napit.

The women of the Napit and the *Bonedi Mahato*, who belong to the *madhyastta* zamindar family, are not so much free like that of the other castes. Widow remarriage or *sanga* is not practised by them. They try to get their children married in the family of same economic status and prestige from a distant village. Marriage distance is narrow in case of the poor Mahato and low castes and they prefer to secure spouses from their fellow members, belonging to low economic position and having close proximity. A narrow kinship affiliation is found among the low castes and the poor Mahato as because they cannot afford to observe expensive rituals involving many members. The depth of kinship knowledge is limited upto three generations among them. Thus poverty is seen to corrode kinship ties.

The villagers have no clear conception of *bhadrolok-chhotolok*. It is only based on caste status and overt behaviour of the individual. Though caste distance is scrupulously maintained yet, in daily interaction, apparently the superordinate-subordinate relationship is not much evident in the village. But individual attainment of a dancer, musician, *ojha* etc., are respected irrespective of their caste affiliation. Economically well-off Mahato, the *bonedi mahato* families, and the *mukhia* get some special attention. The *bonedi mahato* families, however, do not join the low castes in gossip or marry making. But the poor Mahato are often found to gossip with them. Regarding terms of address, labourer and the landowners address each other in kinship terms, like *Dada*, *Kaka*, *Bhai* and so on.

Though the children of different castes play together or sit together in the school, yet, they always keep in mind that they are the Mahato and the others are Sahis or Jolha or Mahali as the case may be. For example, during my stay in the village a Mahato boy of seven or eight years old one day came to my room and requested for a glass of water. I gave him water and two biscuits. After drinking water he asked me "*Didi* to which caste do you belong ?" Out of fun I replied to him that I belong to Sahis caste. As soon as he heard it he threw away the biscuits and fled away. After three or four days I found him playing on the road side. A enquired, how are you, my brother?" He said, "*Didi*, you are very nice but your caste is very bad. You had spoilt my caste, too. But today my grand mother has eaten the left over of my food. So I have regained my former caste identity". The point I want to emphasize upon is that the caste feeling is very much deep rooted even in the minds of the children.

Ritual symbols of all castes follow some regional cultural pattern. It is seen that Napit are relatively more *Sanskritized* than the other castes, including the Mahato. All the castes except the Napit and the *Bonedi Mahato* prefer *sanga* or re-marriage and junior levirate. Window re-marriage and re-marriage after separation are maximally seen among the Sahis and the Mahali.

A detailed analysis of cultural traits of life crisis rituals of the various castes in the villages shows only minor differences in the employment of the specialized functionaries and certain observances. Only a broad distinction is found between the economically low and high castes. They observes all the ritual traits and engage the specialized functionaries. In most of the communal festivals both the low and high castes participate.

The low caste members are mostly illiterate. Out of the total male population only 188 are literate. Among them, 162 belong to the Mahato caste. Among the female, only 52 are literate of whom 47 belong to the Mahato caste. It is seen that - the percentages of literacy at the level of Higher education i.e. Schools Final and above is extremely low rare and it is limited only to the Mahato.

Political Dimension

Majhihira village,as has been noted earlier, was under the zamindary of Manbhum. A few Mahato families became the *madhyastta* zamindar and one family acquired the position of Mukhia under the Raja. That family continued to hold the position of Mukhia even after abolition of the zamindary system. The Mahato were controlling the village traditionally and continue to do so even today. They are also at the helm of the Gram Panchayat and Anchal Panchayat. Eleven members of the Gram Panchayat belong to the Mahato caste. In the traditional village Panchayat, '*Soloanardak*' ('The call of all'), the village *mukhia* is a Mahato of the *madhyasatta* zamindar family. Among the nine members of the Anchal Panchayat eight are Mahato.

The network of control that operated during the zamindary period was more or less as follows :

Zamindar --> Zamindary record keepers --> village level staff of the zamindar --> villagers.

At present government has taken over excess land from the Zamindar. In place of the Zamindary record keeper, block settlement office, etc., have been set up. At the village level some people belonging to the lineage of the Zamindars function as middlemen between the people and the government. It is reported that most of the benefits go to those who are not actually so poor or to those who are associated with the administrative network. Incapacity of the poor makes the middlemen very much effective. The unprivileged and the poor get very little benefit from the development activities sponsored by the Block Development Office.

Two political parties viz., Lokseyak Sangha and Congress have their followers in the village. The leadership of both the parties at the village level are in the hands of well-to-do families of the dominant Mahato caste. Some members of the lower castes work as *fanr* (middlemen) of these party leaders.

TABLE 8: Educational achievements by communities

Name of castes	Literate Male					Illiterate	Literate Female			Illiterate
	Primary	Secondary	S.F.	B.S.	B.A.		Primary	Secondary	S.F.	
1. Mahato	87	67	4		4	215	27	19	1	304
2. Napit	2	1				9		1		7
3. Bhumij	1					3				1
4. Kamar		1				10				6
5. Garain	1	1				4				1
6. Kumhar	1		1		10	1				8
7. Desoali Majhi	2	1				22	1			24
8. Mudi						20				20
9. Mahali	4	3				39	1			33
10. Sahis	2	1				25				32
11. Jolha	4	1				11	1			12
Total	104	75	5	4	367	31	20	1	448	

Discussion

I have so far given the socio-economic, political, and religious background of the village. I shall now try to identify the weaker section, describe how weakness perpetuates and why the people cannot cross the threshold of weakness.

It has been observed that both poverty and weakness are linked-up together. It seems that not only economic weakness but also socio-cultural, political and to some extent inferiority complex, etc., causes poverty. The weaker section includes those who have small landholding and all landless labourers. Village artisans and service castes fall under this category. It has been observed that those who are economically weak may not necessarily be socially weak. The Napit who enjoy the higher position in the village hierarchy are economically poor. In the true sense the dominant section of this village is informed by the three Madhyastha zamindar families who are locally respected and referred to as *Mahato ghar*, *borolok* and *mahajan*. They have high affiliations and also have control over land and power in the village. Though they do not belong to a high caste status in the Hindu caste hierarchy, they are controlling the regional hierarchical system.

Most of the lands of the poor people are on high locations and are inferior. Even those are gradually passing into the dominant section through mortgaging and various other ways.

About 35 per cent people among the weaker sections are virtually unemployed. The rate of payment of labourer is not at par with the rise of price. It also varies seasonally and according to the type of work. In both land operation and business, competition is high. As the land is controlled by the Mahato, the poor depend on them for employment and getting loans. The moneylenders exploit the situation to the maximum. Out of 40 cases of land transfer, 33 are from the lower caste to the Mahato as *sud-bandhuki khuikhulasi* and *kollowals*. One Baidya and one Brahman from another village have also taken land from other low castes. It is evident that the low castes and the poor families of the Mahato try to retain their last piece of land property but are ultimately forced by circumstances to transfer the land to the rich either through sale or through mortgage. For example, a Mahali mortgaged 5 *bigha* of land to a Baidya as *sudbandhaki* for Rs. 100 only. To get back that land he had to give a pond and Rs. 500 in cash against the principle loan and interest.

Thus, the poor Mahali lost nearly Rs. 5,500.00 in the bargain.

The system of Mahajani is very much operative in this area. Most of the Mahajan belong to high caste. They give paddy loan at the rate of 50 per cent compound interest. This compound interest gradually accumulates to such a proportion that the debtor is left with no other choice but to transfer the land to the money-lender. Poor people generally sale their land produce even when the price is low. So, in the lean period he has to buy paddy form the local shop or rich neighbour at high price or he has to take loan at the rate of 50 per cent compound interest. Beside these, during this lean period, they also mortgage their utensils or ornaments to the money-lenders with an interest of 25 per cent per month.

Various development measures were introduced for the improvement of these weaker groups. But these did not benefit them as these development programmes were mainly related with the improvement of land and agriculture over which the weak have little command.

Occasional loans that these people received did not serve any useful purpose, because due to their acute poverty, they spent the same for food.

Modern means of communication like transistor radios (altogether 5 in village) newspaper, etc. are out of bounds of the low castes and the poor. Consequently, the news of the special government measures for the weak remain unknown to them. The dominant people and even the political workers of the village do not communicate such news to the weaker section. During my stay in the village, a local newspaper carried a news item that the land which was sold since 1968 due to economic distress, will have to be returned to the seller. When attention of a leader was drawn to this and was asked to communicate it to the poor villagers, he was found careful to suppress it totally.

The local leaders can afford to maintain contact with the outside world and derive maximum benefits. For example, three wells were dug in the village by the Block office in the courtyards of the well-to-do Mahato. But the low castes were not allowed to fetch water from those wells. It is also found that all the governmental measures are mediated through these leaders. They take leadership to distribute all the relief materials such as G.R., milk, cloth, etc. to the weaker group. But in reality all the benefits go to those who do not belong to this section or are close to them.

The poor and the low castes quite often become the victim of village factionalism. The well-to-do Mahato are found to take sides of quarreling families and in the process made the weaker castes to part with their land and money. In this region *Nachni nach* is a well established traditional institution. These girl-dancers are found to be kept as concubines of the Mahato or of the other rich and high castes. Although the *Nachnis* come from the lower castes, now-a-days the Mahatos earn money through these *Nachnis*. They engage them in the market or in individual houses or during ceremonial occasion. Theoretically a Mahato girl may also become a *Nachni* or dancer. But only the low caste women are found in this profession. The institution, in a way legitimises the sexual exploitation of low caste women by the dominant castes. But when a low caste man elopes with a high caste woman, the dominant castes come down on them heavily. Say for example, a Mahali woman told me that a relative of her family some years ago eloped a Mahato girl. When the fact came to the knowledge of the Mahato they came down on that family heavily with all their power and forced them to leave the village immediately. The point is that the dominant castes not only exploit the situation, they also use their dominant position to foist their own interpretation of the value of people.

Apparently it is seen that in all secular activities of the village only some educated Mahato and the local leaders of the Mahato caste come forward. But instead of directing the efforts towards the development of the village as a whole, they try their best to improve their own lot. For example they are trying to convert the village basic school to a modern one, trying to open a health centre, improve the bus route, establish a police station in the village, etc. But these will strengthen only the interests of the dominant section leaving the poor far behind.

Besides the exploitation of the poor by the dominant, lack of knowledge, socio-cultural constraints, and indifferent attitude of the weaker section themselves to improve their own lot are the causes of their poverty.

Single - crop - cultivation limit the working days of employment of the daily wage earner. That also cause poverty to a section of the people.

The range of expectation of these poor people is very much limited. A Mudi was interviewed. He said "*Jar dhan nei tar man nei*" i.e., the poor have no prestige or status as they have no wealth. Their expectation is just to get two meals a day and a coarse cloth only.

Most of them do not want to accept the agricultural innovation. They rationalise that the high yielding variety of seeds require sufficient water supply which is very much scarce and expensive too. Use of chemical fertilizer in the field in view of low castes decreases the productive capacity of the land every year. They avoid taking any loan from the Block or voluntary agency because as soon as they get the money they have to spend it for food. The caste occupation of the artisan castes are low remunerative and as they have no capital, they cannot start a business individually. Inferiority complex also suppressed them to some extent. Though they are very much aware that they are exploited by the dominant group, they are unable to unite together to revolt against the dominant minorities. They also are aware that power is entirely vested in the hands of the dominant section and they have to depend on them in every respect. So, they accept their misery as *fait accompli*.

This poor and unprivileged group now-a-days realize the necessity of education. But their acute poverty compel them to send their children for earning money at an early age rather than sending them to school. They only send their children to the Majhihira Basic School as they get free tiffin from the school. After having their tiffin they leave the school. Educated members of the weaker section, however, feel that it is their responsibility to improve their castes' lot.

Family planning measures do not reach to the poorer section. They feel that these are useless to them. A Mudi said, "More children bring more money".

When castewise position is considered, it is found that though economically and politically weak, the Napit are high in social status, yet they may not be regarded as prestigious as that of a rich Mahato. In case of the Sahis, some of whom have land and education, do not get a high status or regarded as a *bhadrolok*. A Bhumij said that they are treated as of low social status. The Mahato do not accept cooked food from them. But in Bhumij dominating villages the Mahato accept cooked food from them and they are regarded as having higher social status than the Mahato. All the agriculturist groups and the Napit and the Sahis who also have some land claim that if they get more land their lot will be improved.

Regarding artisan group it is noticed that they prefer their caste occupation because they are skilled in it and it does not require hard labour. A Mahali and Kumhar said that during November to March they earn through basket-making and pottery respectively and do not do work in the field. The Jolha cannot compete with the fancy and cheaper varieties of mill-made cloth. They sell clothes in the months of November and December when the economic condition of the people are comparatively better after harvest. The caste occupation of the Mudi is palm mat making. The raw materials they get from other's field. So they live in an atmosphere of insecurity.

No caste wants to adopt the occupation of other caste as it is related with social status. The communities who depend on their *jajmans*, like Napit, Kamar, and other do not always get the neat amount of paddy from all their *jajmans*. Due to their poor economic condition the Kamar cannot procure the raw material. Naturally their products are very much low. As a result, many of their *jajmans* get their agricultural tools from market. In the opinion of the artisan castes, their lot may be improved if they get raw materials at cheap price and if the products are marketed immediately.

The Mahato have two broad distinct classes. As they are economically and numerically dominant they have high social rank in the regional hierarchy. Three families among them belong to *madhyasatta* zamindar family as stated before and one of them belongs to traditional *mukhia* family. Due to their traditional heritage they are controlling the village economy and political power. They are educated and have greater network outside the village and are regarded as influential and respected persons. They always see that the benefit always accrue to their own caste members. In the employment of labour they prefer to employ their own brethren. But due to factionalism a poor Mahato may be used as a tool of the exploitation game. The poor section including all low castes are remembered by the dominant castes only at the time of election and during main agricultural operation. All castes, other than the Mahato, see their position unsurmountable. They see that the power and wealth and other things that matter much in creating a network is in the hands of the Mahato.

To sum up, it may be said that since independence and after the abolition of the Zamindary system, no major change has practically taken place in the chronic poverty stricken condition of the weaker groups in this village. Precarious economy of the unprivileged section and the hierarchic nature of caste system stand as barrier to unite all the low castes together to revolt against exploitation and injustice.

7

BALIPATNA : A VILLAGE IN ORISSA

SEM TOPNO

Introduction

To study the socio-economic condition of the weaker section, a village by the name of Balipatna was selected. It is six Kilometers away from Kendrapara — a sub-division head-quarters in Cuttack District of Orissa.

Village Balipatna is within the Block Kendrapara II, known as Derabish Block. It is connected by a jeepable road from Kendrapara.

The area is within the coastal plain and there is a network of canals. A distributary of Kendrapara canal ends in the village. Its flow of water is very irregular

The settlement history of the village is not known. In the settlement of village, reclamation and distribution of land, kings. local chiefs, *thickadars*, and temples have played important roles. People in the village Balipatna have been settled by the management of temple Lachhmanji. Table 1 gives some information about the settlement of various castes in the village.

From Table 1 we find that the highest number of households have been settled by the temple management in the village.

Settlement of the village is from south of west lengthwise. Houses are found on both sides of the road. House of the Hadi and Gokha communities (both untouchables) are found just at the entrance of the village by the right hand side of the road. Close to it, at the left hand side, the lower/primary school stands. Khandait and most of the Tanti households are found away from the main road of the village. These houses are connected by a narrow way to the main road at the corner of the lower primary school. But the houses in this area too are found settled lengthwise from south to west. On the west end of the settlement, unconnected by the main road, households of the Brahman, Mali, Patra and Khandait are found. In between these two extremes, houses of a number of castes are found. No distinct sector can be identified on the basis of a particular caste in this part of the village.

TABLE 1: Acquirement of right by caste

Caste	By Purchasing (No. of house-holds)	By inheriting (No. of house-holds)	Inheriting & Purchasing (No. of house-holds)	Deotar & Jagir land of the temple
1. Brahman	-	-	-	7
2. Khandait	-	1	-	3
3. Patra	3	1	1	16
4. Guria	-	-	-	2
5. Keunth	-	-	-	1
6. Gaur	-	-	-	3
7. Bania	-	-	-	6
8. Kharura	-	-	-	8
9. Tanti	6	13	3	5
10. Sankhari	1	2	-	9
11. Barik	-	-	-	3
12. Kumbhar	-	-	-	1
13. Mali	-	-	-	1
14. Gokha	3	14	4	-
15. Hadi	-	-	-	2
	13	31	8	67

Houses have mud walls with straw roof. There is only one house belonging to Patra caste with cemented floor and tiled roof. Another house which has been recently tiled, also belongs to the Patra.

There are 120 households (1975) of 15 castes having 578 population. Distribution of families and population by caste is given in table 2.

The Tanti are numerically dominant and are followed by Patra and Gokha.

Field Experience

In Orissa I faced some difficulty in the selection of village for intensive study. Though the features of the village are similar to the village of Bengal and Bihar i.e. the main settlement consists of a number of *para* or *tola*; here no main settlement is found. Each *para* or *tola* is a main settlement.

TABLE 2: Distribution of families and population by caste

Castes	No.of families	Population	Percentage of the the total.
1. Brahman	7	37	6.40
2. Khandait	4	22	4.15
3. Patra	21	89	17.22
4. Guria	3	15	2.59
5. Keunth	1	1	.17
6. Gaur	3	12	2.11
7. Bania	6	24	4.15
8. Kharura	8	35	6.05
9. Tanti	27	143	26.74
10. Sankhari	12	69	11.80
11. Barik	3	26	4.49
12. Kumbhar	1	7	1.21
13. Mali	1	2	.34
14. Gokha	21	86	16.85
15. Hadi	2	10	1.73
	120	578	100.00

The *para* or hamlet has no administrative geographical boundary but the revenue village has. But the inhabitants of a hamlet form a close socio-religious and political entity. They have little relations in this respect with the neighbouring hamlets.

I was rather amazed to find that village people did not treat me as a stranger, as it generally happens at the first encounter. Later, when I was involved deeply with them, I came to know the reason for it. A number of villagers have visited places outside the district as well as the state. And this very contact with the outside world has shaped their behaviour in this respect.

Here I found the lower caste people, particularly the untouchables, to be indifferent about the discriminative behaviour of the upper castes. When I intensively studied their socio-economic condition, I found that they are more organised than many belonging to the upper castes. Till to-day they have active caste organisations when most of the upper caste organisations have faded out.

Economic Dimension

Land is not the primary source of income for the people. A number of agricultural castes like Khandait are ranked very low. Occupationwise there are artisan castes, service castes, and trading castes. So, the majority of the villagers are engaged in occupations other than agriculture, but a number of them have cultivable land. The land which the village people own, is located in a number of revenue villages. Land has come to the open market and there is no restriction in selling or purchasing it.

Among the 120 households, 45 households have cultivable as well as homestead land and 74 have only homestead or *gharbari* land. One family is totally landless. The size of cultivable land is small, which is within the limit of land ceiling.

TABLE 3: Size of holding in acre

Caste	Below one acre	1-1.99	2-2.99	3-3.99	4-4.99	5-5.99	6-6.99	7-7.99
Tanti	2	6	3	—	—	—	1	—
Gokha	2	2	3	—	—	—	1	—
Patra	1	4	2	—	2	—	—	—
Sankhari	3	1	1	—	—	1	—	—
Khandait	—	1	—	—	—	1	—	—
Guria	—	2	—	—	—	—	—	—
Barik	—	1	1	—	—	—	—	—
Brahman	—	1	—	—	—	—	—	—
Gaur	—	—	—	1	1	—	—	1
	8	18	10	1	3	2	2	1

From Table 3 we find that five families have land above the ceiling limit. Most of the land owners have land between one and three acres. Not all the landholding families cultivate their land. There are only four families(Khandait, Gokha, Guria, and Brahman - one from each caste) who cultivate their land and totally depend on its productions. Among them the Khandait and Gokha households have above four acres of land and the Guria and Brahman households have below three acres. One family belonging to Patra caste depends totally on his share of production from land which has been given to others for cultivation. All these households have no subsidiary occupations.

One acre of land produces about 30 to 35 mounds of paddy. But the majority of households do not get the total production from their holdings due to a number of reasons. One of the major reasons is absence of plough-cattle. Among 45 landholding families only 11 have a pair of bullocks and 15 have only one while 19 have no bullock at all. Households having small sizes of holdings and those with or without the bullock have given land on sharecropping.

Among the 74 households having homestead land, only two have taken land on sharecropping as they have bullocks. Among 45 landholding households, 10 have taken land on sharecropping and nine have given land to others on sharecropping. Among those who have taken land on sharecropping, nine belong to Gokha and Khandait castes and among those who have given land one belongs to Gokha and of the rest eight, four belong to Patra and four to Sankhari castes.

In the economic pursuit, composition of family seriously affects the economic condition of the family concerned. Out of 120 families, 10 have adopted sons (either daughter's son or son-in-laws - as they are without sons). Nine households are represented by widows only and two by males only. There are 14 households which have one male and one female only (either both are over 55 years of age or are living with minor male or female child).

Traditional occupation is the primary occupation of most of the castes. But besides their caste occupation a number of persons have adopted other occupations too. As all castes are related to land (directly or indirectly) an account of the occupational distribution of the people will reveal two things : it will give us the picture of occupational mobility and also of their sources of income. Table 4 depicts holders of homestead land only on the basis of their occupational affiliation.

TABLE 4: Occupational distribution of the landless

Sl. No.	Castes	No.of households	Economic pursuits	No.of persons
1	2	3	4	5
1.	Hadi	2	Drum beating, office peon	1,2
2.	Tanti	15	Weaving and labour, weaving:	3
			a)Household	2
			b)Powerloom(service)	3

(Contd.)

TABLE 4 *Contd.*

1	2	3	4	5
			Petty trade(seasonal product)	1
			Govt. servicc	1
			Govt. service and labour	2
			Begging	2
3.	Gokha	13	Fishing and Labour	5
			Fish trade and labour	3
			Fishing and cultivation	4
			Fishing	1
			Fish trade	1
4.	Kumbhar	1	Earthen work	2
5.	Patra	12	Labour	2
			Umbrella repairing	1
			Grocery shop	1
			Tailoring	1
			Tailoring and labour	2
			Teachership and petty business	2
			Spinning at Khadi Board	1
			Stationary vender and labour	2
			Stationary vender	1
			Jute business, stationary, grocery, cloth shop and service	3
6.	Keunth	1	Perched rice making and selling	1
7.	Kharura	8	Utensils repairing	6
			Begging	1
			Stationary selling	1
8.	Bania	6	Silver smithy and labour	2
			Tea stall	1
			Labour	3
			Sweet mistry	1
9.	Barik	1	Barber and labour	2
10.	Sankhari	6	Stationary selling	1
			Bangle trading	1
			Begging	1
			Bangle trading and cattle-plough selling in hire purchase	1
			Bangle trading and tea stall	2
			Lime stone selling	1
11.	Brahman	6	Cooking food at hotel	3
			Sewak (temple priest)	1
			Hotel cook and labour	1
			Cultivation	1
12.	Khandait	2	Labour	1
			Labour and cultivation	2
13.	Mali	1	Flower cultivation and supply to temple	2
14.	Guria	1		

From the above table we find that persons owning only

homestead lands are engaged in diversified occupations. Among them the economic condition of the three grocery shop owners (two belonging to Patra and one to Tanti) households is better than the others. Two grocery shop owners have capital input below rupees three thousands and one (Patra) has around fifty thousands. Among them two households have started business after taking loan from Mahajan. They are also the agents of stock dealers of Cuttack. Lack of capital and network of relationship (either friendly or ethnic) have prevented others to take up this sort of large scale business. There are eight households with people having permanent service while 17 persons from among them occasionally do manual labour. There are only two households who do share-cropping. These two persons are from Tanti caste. One each from Kharura and Sankhari live by begging. As many as 88 per cent of their families are poor. They earn less then Rs. 40.00 per month.

TABLE 5: Occupational distribution of the land owners

Sl. No.	Castes	No.of households	Economic pursuits	No.of persons
1	2	3	4	5
1.	Tanti	12	Weaving and cultivation	4
			Vegetable trading	1
			Cultivation, salesman	2
			Weaving,cultivation,salesman	2
			Labour	1
			Service	1
			Stationary vender	1
			Weaving	1
			Weaving and labouring	2
2.	Khandait	2	Cultivation	1
3.	Guria	2	Cultivation	1
			Sweet mistry and selling, service	2
4.	Barik	2	Cultivation and service	2
			Hair cutting and cultivation	1
5.	Sankhari	6	Bangle trade, cultivation	1
			(Living by selling land)	1
			Teacher	1
			Bangle trade	1
			Trading of seasonal product	1
6.	Gokha	8	Fishing, labour, cultivation	1
			Fishing, cultivation	5
			Cultivation, service	2
			Cultivation	1

(Contd.)

TABLE 5 *Contd.*

1	2	3	4	5
7.	Gaur	3	Cultivation, milk selling	2
			Cultivation, service	2
8.	Patra	9	Bangle trading	1
			Stationary	1
			Cultivation	1
			Cloth business, cultivation	3
			Service	1
9.	Brahman	1	Cultivation	1

It is found that out of 45 landholding households 20 still follow their traditional caste occupation. Seven persons are in service (including teachership), and eight do petty trade and business.

Thirty one per cent of the land-owning families have economic stability because of their engagement in permanent services, more capital input in trade and business and larger landholdings. Sixty-nine per cent of them are poor.

From Table 4 and 5 it can be inferred that it is very difficult to understand the people's attitude towards occupation, but a tendency is observed in some castes to stick to one's own traditional occupation. It is also observed that people follow diversified occupations even among the same caste. The majority of the households are engaged in trade and business and most of the trade is carried out by vending as well as attending local markets. Capital input in these petty trade and business is about Rs.30.00.

Effect of External Forces on Indigenous Occupations

The Tanti or the weavers, finding great difficulty in pursuing their traditional occupation in this changed situation, have formed a Weavers' Co-operative Society. It is located at village Kusiapal. Very few other castes have formed such organization. This weavers' co-operative society is aided by the State Government. All the Tanti of the village who do weaving, are its members. They have been provided with shuttle weaving apparatus and are supplied yarn regularly. They are paid for their labour according to the size, variety, and designs of cloths. Work is time consuming but they receive payment for a cloth at the rate of rupees two or five. Thus, earning from it is very meagre. Due to this reason a number of weavers of the village have discontinued membership from the society. No single family is found weaving independently with one's own capital. External forces like mill made clothes of weaver's Co-operative Society, like Kendrapara (powerloom) have liquidated the household weaving industry. The Balipatna Weavers Co-operative Society lacks the spirit of competition. Members of the society say that mill made and power loom made clothes have superior designs and fineness. So they are preferred by the people. Due to this they cannot stand in competition. Moreover, only a single trained teacher has been appointed by the government to impart training to weavers. The members complain that the teacher is not at all interested in imparting training. Again, the society has many a times placed their demand before the government for increase in the rate of payment but with no result. They also want that the Government should take full responsibility of distribution of clothes of the society and qualified designers should be appointed. Then only the society will be able to overcome these difficulties. The members finding no other alternative of income continue to pursue it. The fishing community, Gokha has also been adversely affected by the changing situation. The Block and Panchayat offices have now taken over ponds and rivers where formerly they used to fish.These ponds are now auctioned. The Gokha of the village say that as they are poor, they cannot afford to pay money for auctioning. So these ponds have now gone out of their reach. This has reduced their income considerably. The Government has asked them to form a fishing Co-operative Society but due to poverty they are unable to form one. Community fishing is still carried out in small scale in which the implements are jointly owned. Catch is partly sold out in the village and partly in neighbouring villages. Due to decrease in the fishing areas, it cannot be carried out daily. The Patra (jute traders) and Sankhari (bangle makers from lac) have been affected due to the opening of roads and spread of factory made articles. Jute cultivators now directly sell their product to the Jute Co-operative Society, 10 and 15 kilometers away from the village. Jute is purchased by jute dealers of Kendrapara and Cuttack directly from the producers. This has, on the one hand affected the Patra community adversely who were jute traders, and on the other this has benefited the cultivators as they now get the legitimate price.

This has forced many people to change occupation. A number of persons have now turned to labour work due to lack of capital to start any trade. It is reported that at this changing situation any caste can adopt any of the caste or non-caste occupation.

Occupational mobility has considerably taken place among the people of the present generation due to the changing situation. We can get a picture of occupational mobility from Table 6.

TABLE 6: Occupational Mobility

Sl.No.	Caste	Traditional Caste occupation	Present occupation other than traditional
1	2	3	4
1.	Brahman	Temple service, ceremonial function	Hotel cook, cultivation
2.	Khandait	Guard, soldier	Cultivation, labour
3.	Patra	Jute trader, making fashionable articles	Trade and business, cultivation, labour, service, tailoring.
4.	Guria	Confectionery	Cultivation, service
5.	Keunth	Parched rice making	—
6.	Gaur	Cattle herding and milk selling, *palki* bearer	Cultivation, service
7.	Bania	Trade,business	Silversmithy, sweet *mistry,* labour
8.	Kharura	Repairing (metal implements,utensils etc.)	Trade
9.	Tanti	Weaving(cloth)	Cultivation, labour service, trade
10.	Sankahari	Lac banglemaking	Trade, cultivation, service
11.	Barik	Hair cutting,ceremonial service	Labour, cultivation service
12.	Kumbhar	Potter	—
13	Mali	Flower cultivation	—
14.	Gokha	Fishing	Labour cultivation, service
15.	Hadi	Drum beating	service

The Khandait and Sankhari have left their traditional occupations completely, while the Patra have partly shifted to other occupations. The rest of the castes of the village still follow their traditional occupations along with other occupations. Table 4 and 5 give the picture of their engagement in other occupations.

Indebtedness

There are only two persons who have received loan from moneylender for investment in trade and business. Agricultural loan is given by the Block Office and Co-operative Society to such persons who hold a requisite amount of cultivable land i.e. one acre. Land below one acre is considered totally uneconomic. Thus 10 landholding families who have given land for sharecropping and eight landholders possessing land below one acre do not get loan from these sources. It is found that people do not take loan from the Mahajan or from other sources for consumption or for other non-productive pursuits. Village money lenders are the only creditors to persons engaged in trade, business and crafts; but people generally do not take loan for these occupations too.

Economic Relations Within and Outside the Village

There is no caste in the village, except the Gokha, who does not take help from others. The Gokha are very community oriented. They never take labour from the market during different economic operations such as construction of house and thatching. Roof-thatching is needed every year when the old straws are removed and replaced by new ones. Expenditure on it varies, according to the size of house, from rupees fifty to hundred.

Economy is basically market-oriented and competitive in nature. But still it has a combination of rural (agro based)-cum-urban features. This feature exists not because the village is within close proximity to Kendrapara but because there is a network of panchayat roads and markets. It is found that people have less attraction for town dwelling. For example, one Patra who is employed at Haldia, comes to the village every or alternate weekend and during cultivation he takes long leave. When asked, why he does not purchase a land at Kendrapara for construction of a house there he replied, "What is there in the town. Town people get every thing from the village and town is not very much different from village". This indicates that the people of the village have little attraction towards town life. It is observed that pucca building and tiled roofed houses are now increasingly being constructed in the village. This increase is found in irrigated areas. By-cycle, bullock carts, and sometimes scooter are seen in the village.

These very features are found in the village Balipatna. Space of economic activities and relationships have now widened. But no permanent economic relationship of the nature of *Jajmani* system between rich and poor, landowner and labourers, artisans and customers, and service rendering and receiving class is found. All the exchanges are made in ready cash payments and there is no custom of offering fringe benefit to labourers. Very few persons keep household servants and that too, in cash (though not a single family in Balipatna keeps servants). Jajmani system exists only between the Brahman and his clients. No Brahman of village Balipatna has clients in the village. Labour is available in open market.

In the field of trade and business, interaction of the people with outsiders is considerable. Hawkers visit neighbouring villages and markets almost daily on bicycle. A number of markets are held within the radius of 12 miles. Bicycle has become a very essential means of transport for persons and commodities. Under this situation, no permanent relationship of reciprocal nature can be established and weakness and dominance are not easily observable in the village. This does not mean that modern economy has fragmented intra-village relationships totally. Though traditional formal relationships (such as during details of life cycle performance inviting village people and neighbours etc.) are not found among the village people, informal interaction situations (such as gathering at tea stall and grocery shop where people of different strata and class meet and talk on different subjects) are there. Social strata is more rigidly hierarchical than we find in any traditional village.

Block and Gram Panchayat offices have now played a great role in unifying village people. During the natural calamities such as cyclone (1967), flood (1970) and fire, people help each other (not by material but by extending manual labour), though during such calamities help also comes from the government.

Role of Temple

There is a temple of Lachhmanji in the village. It has, besides religious functions, some welfare work not only for the villagers but for all the people. During summer season, drinking water is distributed to the thirsty people on market day and cattle are fed when natural fodder is not available. It also has erected Dharamsala at different places. For all these functions it has allotted lands to the people. The temple Lachhmanji of Balipatna has large amount of land (1300 acres : Balipatna and in neighbouring villages-600 acres, and Balia and neighbouring villages-700 acres). These lands have been given to people for the service of Lachhmanji and for cultivation as tenants. It is managed by a board of trustee. Distribution of temple land among people of Balipatna (within the village area) is given in Table 7.

TABLE 7: Distribution of temple land by caste

Caste	No. of families	Amount of land in acres
1. Hadi	2	.08
2. Khandait	3	2.64
3. Tanti	5	.72
4. Kumbhar	1	.36
5. Guria	2	1.90
6. Patra	16	6.12
7. Keunth	1	.16
8. Kharura	8	.69
9. Sankhari	9	2.58
10. Bania	6	.50
11. Barik	3	.66
12. Mali	1	.09
13. Brahman	7	3.57
14. Gaur	3	.84

Nearby 21 acres of land are held by 67 families of the village. Lands of 63 families are homestead. There are only four families belonging to Khandait, Guria, Patra and Sankhari castes who have been provided with cultivable land as tenants. Besides providing land to landless persons, it also helps in another way. During Dol Purnima, (in the month of March) when a series of ceremony are observed such as Dolpurnima, Thakur milan, Ramnavami, Holi etc. village people are engaged in some of the ceremonies. During Ramnavami puja, people are engaged as Hanumans and are sent out in search of Sita. In 1975, 12 persons were engaged as Hanumans at the rate of Rupees 28.00 each for a week. These Hanumans go round many villages and towns visiting door to door. They collect money varying from hundred to five hundred rupees during the period. The untouchables are never engaged as Hanuman.

Socio-ritual and Political Dimension

People of the village are hierarchically organised. The highest position is assigned to the Brahman and lowest to the Gokha and Hadi. Hierarchical order as reported by the people is given in Table 8.

TABLE 8: Caste Hierarchy

Caste	
Brahman	Upper & High
Khandait	Upper & High
Patra	Middle
Guria	Middle
Keunth	Middle
Gour	Middle
Bania	Middle
Kharura	Lower
Tanti	Lower
Sankhari	Lower
Barik	Lower
Kumbhar	Lower
Mali	Lower
Gokha	Lowest (Untouchable)
Hadi	Lowest (Untouchable)

All castes accept cooked food from the Brahman. Commensal relationship among other castes is limited to one's own caste members only. During life-cycle ceremonies and festivals, when feast is arranged, members of own castes are invited. If members from other castes are invited, a Brahman is engaged to cook food and this is arranged at some public place and not in the house of invitee.

Every caste has caste assembly or *Jatisabha*. Membership of *Jatisabha* is ascribed by birth. Caste assembly has a very wide coverage i.e. whole of Orissa. It maintains and regulates social and cultural norms. From every village a fellow casteman represents the *Jatisabha.* He is supposed to be the head of the caste members in the village and all social problems relating to caste are ordinarily reported to him. The caste council of the Gokha and Patra are better organized than that of others in the village. The *Jatisabha* of the Brahman has ceased to function. The caste councils look after the social and cultural systems of respective caste and is not concerned with the problems of the weaker sections in general.

Each caste has a series of separate socio-ritual ceremonies, festivals, and deities. It is not necessary that the Brahman of the village should conduct these ceremonies. Every household or lineage has its traditional *jajman* from whom they receive service.

The Gokha and Hadi have priests from their own community. The principal deity of the Gokha community is Ramchandi. She is worshipped individually as well as communally.

The Gokha and Hadi do not drink tea in tea stalls though almost all of them do so in their own house. The Harijans (Gokha and Hadi) cannot draw water from the wells belonging to other castes. One day a Harijan boy was about to draw water from a well belonging to a Keunth family. A person belonging to Bania caste approached him, snatched away his brass pot, rebuked the boy and asked him to stand at a distance when he would draw water for him. During summer when water is distributed to thirsty people by Lachhmanji temple authorities the Harijan are not given water in glass which members of other castes use. Water is poured down on their palm. Every household except those of the poor sections has its well and people rarely use other's well for fetching water.

In spite of all discriminations, commensal distinction, and prohibition to temple entry which has now been lifted (Gokha and Hadi neither visit Lachhmaji temple nor do they participate during Thakur Milan ceremony), people mix freely in all informal occasions. Children of all castes, sit and play together in local primary school.

The Hadi perform drum beating during ceremonies at the temple. Drums and other musical instruments are purchased from Kendrapara or Cuttack. During ceremonies, they bring out the tune from drum similar to modern band party along with clarionet. The traditional form of tune has completely been abandoned.

The Gokha have considerably improved their social condition in general but not in the eyes of the Brahman. In 1961, they started a library in a community hall constructed through cooperation of the community members. They subscribed Oriya as well as some foreign magazines such as *Soviet land, Span* etc. But due to lack of fund it could not continue. This community hall is now used as rest house for guests during marriage as well as meeting centre for the community members. No such effort has been made by other castes of the village.

The Gokha and Hadi observed almost all the festivals which are observed in the area. They, however, do not play colour during Holi. The upper castes Hindu avoid them during such occasion.

Literacy is nil among the Keunth, Kumbhar and Mali. Table 9 gives the distribution of literacy by caste.

TABLE 9: Distribution of literacy by caste

Caste	Population	Literacy standard					
		I-III	IV-V	VI-VII	VIII-X	Matric	College
Brahman	37	—	2	1	1	—	—
Khandait	22	1	1	3	1	—	—
Patra	89	10	7	9	6	3	—
Guria	15	1	1	1	—	—	—
Keunth	1	—	—	—	—	—	—
Gour	12	—	—	—	—	—	—
Bania	24	—	1	2	—	—	—
Kharura	35	1	1	1	—	—	—
Tanti	143	10	7	16	3	2	Pre-University-1
Sankhari	69	1	3	2	2	—	B.A.-1
Barik	26	—	—	1	—	—	—
Kumbhar	7	—	—	—	—	—	—
Mali	2	—	—	—	—	—	—
Gokha	86	4	8	5	1	2	B.A.fail-1
Hadi	10	—	—	1	—	—	—
	578	28	31	42	14	7	3

The average percentage of literacy among the villagers is 11 per cent whereas the proportion of the Harijan is 1.90 per cent. The highest proportion of literacy is found among the Tanti and they are followed by the Patra, Gokha, and Sankhari in order. Three villagers have got college education. One Sankhari has graduated, a Gokha is a B.A. plucked and a Tanti has got pre-University education. The Sankhari family holds four acres of land but has given it to others for sharecropping. The Gokha family does fishing and has taken land under sharecropping, and the Tanti family has one acre of land under sharecropping and a member of this family is having a permanent service. From the table we find that low castes are also getting education along with other castes.

The Gokha and Hadi are staunch supporters of the Congress(R), though the area is under the influence of Lok Dal (Utkal Congress). They contest Panchayat election. One person from the Gokha community remained a ward member for about 25 years. He is literate up to fifth standard and his economic background is not sound. No member of the Harijan is found in Panchayat Samity at the Anchal level or in the District Board. No cases (*faujdari* and *dewani*) are either reported to the Police Station or the Court. Political parties are found to be very active during Panchayat elections.

Developmental programmes have on the surface made some impact on the people but have not impressed upon them very much. People say that these developmental programmes have made no good to the poor people. Persons who are well-off, are the real beneficiaries. The common people, not finding these programmes is conformity to their requirement and immediate need, look upon it as *taila munda re taila dhara houchhanti*. The village has been electrified but only those persons are getting benefit who can afford to pay. The Health Centre which was constructed in the year 1965, is still lying unoccupied. A branch of the Mahila Samity for the adult education of women has been opened but it has done little so far. People get grain and manure regularly. Even high yielding variety of paddy is distributed to the people. But as there is no irrigation facility, people cannot reap its benefit. Though the number of cattle population is not much, still at every Panchayat there is a hospital for animal husbandry and veterinary where artificial insemination is extensively carried out. People have been somewhat benefitted from these programmes.

No discrimination on the basis of caste is made by the Panchayat and Block Office when aid and facilities are given to the people. All information regarding these programmes and facilities are made open in the Panchayat. That is why all communities are well aware of such programmes.

Conclusion

From this analysis it is clear that poverty affects all the communities equally. No family or group of families or caste in the village is found holding an overall dominant position. Persons and households which are economically well-off pay no attention at all to power politics and village affairs. They do not excrt any influence upon the village people. The Tanti, though hold numerical dominance in the village, due to other handicaps are not in a position to convert it into power or authority. Due to lack of control over the means of production, people have become poor which has led to weakness. The poor are out of the shadow of dominant persons or groups, in the village, but they have been highly influenced by external forces, like price rise, natural calamities, spread of factory-made articles, and immigration of outsiders into the region. Though the Harijan are still fighting against the social constraints and stigma which have prevented their integration with national life, they are, improving their socio-economic condition steadily.

8

SIKRI : A VILLAGE IN SOUTH BIHAR

SEM TOPNO and PIJUSH CHOUDHURY

Introduction

Sikri is situated in Chotanagpur plateau of South Bihar within the jurisdiction of Thana and Anchal Barkagaon of Hazaribagh District. It is about five Kilometers away from the town Barkagaon.

The region is hilly, forest clad, and undulating. Total area of the village is 5780.52 acres of which about 3889.08 acres (67.36%) is covered by hills and forest. A tributary of the river Damodar flows down through the village from North-West to South-East.

Agriculture is the main occupation of the villagers. The majority of them are poor and rely on various subsidiary occupation.

All the people of the village are "Utharu" i.e. immigrants. Mahra, Dusadh, Dhobi, Bhuinya, and Kurmi (not all of the present generation) are the descendants of the earliest settlers of the village. The first four communities, it is said, owned most areas of land prior to the settlement of upper castes in the village. The upper castes are relatively late comers.

In Sikri low castes occupy one end of the settlement, while the upper castes occupy the other. This division is based not as mush on caste distinction as on ownership of land.

The village has 305 household and 1897 people (as in 1972-73). Two hundred ninety four households belong to the Hindu and 11 belong to the Muslim.

There are 16 distinct Hindu castes. Muslims of the village belong to Momin group of the Ansari clan. Number of households and population of each caste/community is given in Table 1.

TABLE 1: Distribution of caste/community

Caste/Community	No. of household	Male	Female	Total
1. Pandey/Brahman	2	10	10	20
2. Gossain	7	14	14	28
3. Rajput	16	67	54	121
4. Lala	2	13	16	29
5. Bania	13	54	53	107
6. Barhi	19	52	63	115
7. Kurmi	160	528	498	1026
8. Kumhar	4	13	7	20
9. Sundi SC	7	27	30	57
10. Kandu	13	16	11	27
11. Teli	1	-	1	1
12. Nauwa	5	17	18	35
13. Bhuinya SC	3	13	11	24
14. Dusadh SC	11	24	20	44
15. Dhobi SC	7	23	22	45
16. Mahra	24	65	67	129
17. Momin	11	37	32	69

In this village the Kurmi form the majority (160 household). They are followed by Mahra (24 households) Barhi (19 households), and Rajput (16 households) in order.

Methodological Approach and Experience

When we carried out field work in the village, the most talked about subject among the villagers was land reform (ceiling and distribution of surplus land) by the Government of Bihar. Because of this, when we arrived at the village we encountered a mixed reception. It made us careful about the selection of location of camp and as we felt that there existed a socio-economic line of divide among the people. Though we were offered rooms for stay by a number of householders, we preferred to occupy a vacant house in the area of the low castes. Thus, we avoided the situation of neglecting either of the groups and soon the camp became club house for all.

We purposely avoided taking information on land alongwith household census. This helped us in establishing a very good rapport with all sections of village people.

As rich and poor both realised the utility of our work (sensing that Government is going to help them in their favour) we feared the possibility of over statement of fact by one group while suppression of it by the other. We solved this intricacy through cross interview.

The people do not keep record of income and expenditure. We had to wholly depend on their information on these items as we found no way out to test its reliability.

We collected qualitative information and opinion on particular topic through interview of selected informants.

Economic Dimension

As there is no irrigation facility in the village, agricultural operation is wholly dependent on monsoon.Its operation is carried out by traditional plough technology. Cattle wealth is the second to land in importance. More than 25 per cent of cultivating families have no plough or bullock. They get their land cultivated either by sharecroppers or by hiring plough and cattle. About five per cent of the households have only one bullock. It is generally found that families who have no plough or only one bullock either give land for sharecropping or cultivate it by taking loan from Mahajan.

Of the total cultivable land 35.94 per cent is fallow and 16.56 per cent is at present under cultivation. Agricultural holding per capita is 0.54 acre in which paddy land comes to 0.25 acre. This amount of land cannot fulfil yearly requirement of a person.

Distribution of 1495.41 acres of cultivable land among the castes and community is given in Table 2.

TABLE 2: Distribution of land by caste/community

Caste/ Community	No. of landholding households	Total amount of land in acres	Average holding per family in acre
1. Pandey/Brahman	2	18.94	9.47
2. Gossain	7	41.27	5.89
3. Rajput	16	355.43	22.21
4. Lala	2	101.36	50.68
5. Bania	10	66.08	6.06
6. Barhi	18	95.01	5.27
7. Kurmi	159	530.69	3.33
8. Kumhar	4	21.44	5.36
9. Sundi	7	50.50	7.22
10. Kandu	13	47.33	3.64
11. Nauwa	5	18.88	3.77
12. Bhuinya	3	16.56	5.51
13. Dusadh	11	73.29	6.66
14. Dhobi	7	23.09	3.29
15. Mahra	16	9.84	0.61
16. Momin	11	26.70	2.42

From the table we find that land is held unequally by different castes. Thus we find the Lala and Rajput holding the highest and second highest average (50.68 and 22.21 acres) respectively. The Mahra, who are placed at the lowest of the ladder of social hierarchy hold the lowest amount of land. They have the highest number of landless families. The other landless families belong to Kurmi, Barhi, and Teli, having one family each, and the Bania having three landless families. Kurmi, Barhi and Mahra are dependent on casual labour. The later also do drum beating during socio-religious ceremonies. The Teli family is supported by its sons who are engaged in manual labour in West Bengal. Two Bania families do petty trade of local products and the other one is supported by a member who is employed in a shop in West Bengal.

In the village, it is found that highest number of families, mostly belonging to low castes, are dependent on small size of landholdings. Small landholding is one of the indices of poverty, particularly in Chotanagpur, where people are wholly dependent on primitive method of cultivation. So, an assessment of poverty of the people can be made by the classification of village people on the basis of size of landholdings. Table 3 may explain the situation.

TABLE 3: Size of landholding

Caste/ Community	Below 1 acre no of families	1-5.99 acre No. of F.	6-10. 99 ac. No. of F.	11-15. 99 ac. No. of F.	16-20 99 ac. No. of F.	21 ac. above No. of families
1. Pandey/Brahman	-	-	2	-	-	-
2. Gossain	-	3	4	-	-	-
3. Rajput	-	9	4	-	-	3
4. Lala	-	-	-	-	-	2
5. Bania	2	7	-	2	1	-
6. Barhi	-	14	1	2	1	-
7. Kurmi	29	102	24	4	-	-
8. Kumhar	-	4	-	-	-	-
9. Sundi	-	5	1	-	1	-
10. Kandu	-	11	2	-	-	-
11. Nauwa	-	4	1	-	-	-
12. Bhuinya	-	2	1	-	-	-
13. Dusadh	1	8	1	1	1	-
14. Dhobi	-	5	2	-	-	-
15. Mahra	12	4	-	-	-	-
16. Momin	5	5	1	-	-	-
Total	49	183	44	9	4	5

Production of crops per acre, on the basis of the estimate of local cultivators, is 30 and 24 maunds in low and upland respectively.

It is found that the production of crops in 10 acres of land is sufficient to support a family consisting of six members (average size of family of the village) in normal situation (sufficient rain fall, less contingent expenditure etc.). But no family holding land below 10 acres is immuned to abnormal situation. Thus, 276 households having land between below one to ten acres are susceptible to difficulty due to abnormal situation. These households generally depend on subsidiary occupations and require outside help to support themselves for the whole year. Labour supply mainly comes from these categories of landholders and a good number of them are found in various jobs and services, temporary and permanent, within and outside the village. Besides labour work, they depend on sharecropping, traditional occupations and loan. The maximum number of cases of land alienation is found among these categories of landholders.

Rajput and Lala big landholders give loan in cash and kind to small landholders and also provide land for share-cropping. They are the major source of credit for the villagers as well as for the neighbouring villages. This is one of the reasons for the concentration of land in their possession. Two highly rich families among them are engaged in trade and business also.

TABLE 4: Distribution of share-croppers

Caste/Community	No. of persons gave land for share-cropping	No. of persons acquiring land for share-cropping
1. Pandey/Brahman	-	2
2. Gossain	1	3
3. Rajput	4	4
4. Lala	2	-
5. Bania	2	6
6. Barhi	3	3
7. Kurmi	11	70
8. Sundi	2	4
9. Kandu	1	6
10. Nauwa	-	2
11. Kumhar	-	2
12. Dusadh	3	4
13. Dhobi	-	3
14. Mahra	-	11
15. Momin	-	5
Total	29	125

For small or uneconomic landholders (below 10 acres), the first source of supplementary income in the village is by sharecropping. Landless persons, who have plough, also practise sharecropping. A share-cropper gets 50 per cent of the production but as the best quality of land is not given for sharecropping and the amount of land which he gets is very small, he gets very small income. Castewise classification of persons who gave and those who acquired land for sharecropping in the year 1971-72 is given in the Table 4.

From the table, we find that only 29 landholders had given some portions of their land for sharecropping to 125 persons of the village. Among the landless only two Mahra had secured land for share-cropping as they have plough. The number of sharecropper is increasing as the size of land from individual's possession is decreasing due to complex land transactions by sale, mortgage, *rehan*, exchange, and division. The Rajput and Lala provide the major amount of land for sharecropping mostly to low castes i.e. Mahra, Kurmi, Kandu, Dhobi, Dusadh, and Momin.

Other source from which some income is derived is traditional occupation. Importance of traditional occupation has considerably declined, particularly on part of the artisan castes due to influx of urban or factory made articles. Another reason cited is the change in traditional socio-cultural environment and the taste of people. Old occupation today does not provide the respective castes required livelihood. The number of families who still follow their traditional caste occupation is given in Table 5.

Castes, namely Rajput (military service) Sundi (distiller of liquor), Kandu (perched rice making), Teli (oil pressing), Momin (weaving) and Bhuinya (tending of pig) have given up their traditional caste occupation and have adopted agriculture. Kurmi and Dusadh are considered agriculturist traditionally.

Traditional occupations of the artisan and service castes do not provide them work for the whole year.

Adoption of new occupation is guided either by the attitude and values of the caste themselves or availability of capital. Choice of the untouchables in the selection of occupation in the village, particularly in trade and business is still decided and regulated by the upper castes. They cannot engage themselves in trade and business due to the social stigma on the one hand and lack of capital on the other. But the upper castes are free in the selection of their own trade and occupation. The three Rajput families who are economically the most dominant in the village and control socio-religious and political matters are found in trade and business of local products. One Rajput family has a fair price shop and the other has a husking cum grinding machine (diesel operated).

TABLE 5: Distribution of traditional occupation

	Caste/ Community	Traditional caste occupation	Total no. of family	No. of family performing traditional caste occupation
1.	Barhi	Carpentry, masonry, black smithy	19	9
2.	Nauwa	Ritual function, hair-cutting and shaving	5	4
3.	Pandey/ Brahman	Ceremonial service	2	2
4.	Mahra	Leather work, lifting dead cattle, midwifery drum beating	24	21
5.	Kumhar	Pottery	4	4
6.	Dhobi	Ceremonial functions	7	2
7.	Bania	Trade and business	13	8
8.	Gossain	Jajmani, consulting horoscope, astrology etc.	7	2

Persons who have small landholdings follow traditional caste occupation which still has its importance in present situation such as, carpentry, hair clipping, pottery, and trading. Ceremonial or ritual functions of Pandey, Nauwa, Dhobi, and Gossain provide very little income to them.

The jobs within the village which do not require any training and in which the village people are found engaged, at least for a short period, are :

a. Agricultural operation : Ploughing, sowing, transplanting, weeding, harvesting, storing etc.
b. Construction and repairing work : house, road, well, small irrigation schemes etc.
c. Others : Kup, Rope-making, wood collection, household servant, gorkhia, attendant to traders etc.

TABLE 6: Employment situation

Caste/ Community	Landless			Below 1 acre			1 to 5			6 to 10			11 to 15			16 to 20			21 & above			Total		
	Sc.	C.	P.	Sc.	C.	P.	Sc.	C.	P.	Sc.	C.	P.	Sc.	C.	P.	Sc.	C.	P.	Sc.	C.	P.	Sc.	C.	P.
Kurmi	-			25	31	4	45	41	14		4	7			4							70	76	29
Mahra	2	15		9	4	3			1													11	19	4
Barhi							3	10	3													3	10	3
Rajput							4				2											4	2	-
Kandu							6	2	1													6	2	1
Momin				4			1	6	4		1											5	6	5
Bania			2				5				1		1									6	1	2
Dusadh							4	6	2		2	2			1							4	8	5
Gossain							1		1	2												3	-	1
Sundi							4		2													4	-	2
Dhobi							2	6		1												3	6	-
Nauwa							2	2														2	2	-
Kumhar							2	1														2	1	-
Bhuinya								9														-	9	-
Pandey/ Brahman										2												2	-	-
Lala																						-	-	-
	W	(1)								(2)											(3)	125	142	52

INDEX Sc = Share Cropper
C = Casual
P = Permanent

In agricultural operations mostly the Mahra, Dusadh, Kurmi, Sundi, and Momin are employed. Agricultural operation and construction work of the landholders who give land for sharecropping are done by sharecroppers. They get a meal but no payment from landholders. Construction works (wells, road, small irrigation scheme) taken up by Block and Panchayat are generally done by outside labourers. Eleven persons belonging to Kurmi and Bania castes are found in Kup. In rope-making some families from Mahra and Kurmi castes are found. It is only the household servants and Gorkhia (shepherd) who are found engaged for the whole year. In such jobs the Mahra, Kurmi, Dusadh, and Bhuinya are generally engaged. Four Rajput and one Lala family employed household servants from Kurmi, Bhuinya, and Rajput castes. Only two persons, one each from Dusadh and Nauwa, are found as attendants of village traders on daily payment basis. Household servants receive payment daily. The Gorkhia receive payment annually at the rate of ten and twenty seers of paddy per head of bullock and buffalo respectively.

Apart from engagement in caste occupations and jobs available within the village, a good number of people belonging to landholding groups of below one acre are engaged in other skilled and unskilled jobs, such as teaching, and service (government and colliery). These persons have a better standard of living in comparison to their fellow villagers. Some of them are now purchasing land or reacquiring their own land which had been sold out earlier. They are slowly coming out of the poverty condition. Table 6 presents an over-all picture of employment situation of villagers as in 1972.

The people with landholdings below 10 acres sell out after harvest considerable proportion of grain at low prices to meet many of their requirements, e.g., clothes, agricultural implements, bullocks, and payment of loan to *mahajan*. Loan of the government and *mahajan* are generally paid after the harvest. Cases of sale of land and cattle are very frequent among the small landholders and sometimes ornaments and utensils are also put under mortgage. A good number of them (90.82%) are still found under debt. As indebtedness is inherited, a person with fixed income finds it hard to get out of it. People are sometimes forced to borrow money to tide over natural calamities such as drought. Some persons have not yet been able to pay off their loan taken during the drought of 1966-67. Normally loan is taken for meeting household expenses, cultivation, payment to rent, house construction, life cycle, ritual expenditure, trade and business, court cases, education, treatment, travel, and 'bribery'. This indicates that the people take loan for immediate need. It is also found that the same family has taken various types of loan from different sources.

During lean period (beginning from February) landless and landholders below five acres, very often live on *ghataleto* (soup prepared from makai and bajwar). Mahua flower is also eaten as food by these people. Few persons of these categories, particularly from Mahra community, prefer drinking liquor than eating *ghataleto* for they can remain without the knowledge of hunger for the whole day. Poor people do not take refreshment in the morning but they eat staple food, and molasses during summer. Economically better off families of Rajput, Bania, and Kurmi eat either stale rice or *chapati* in the morning. Two Rajput families eat *chapati* with *ghee* regularly. Table 7 gives the number of families under deficit income and saving after calculation of net annual income and expenditure.

TABLE 7: Balance sheet of deficit and saving

Size of land	No. of families	Deficit in agriculture	Deficit in net income	Saving in net income
Below 1, acre	49	49	39	10
1 to 5.99 acres	180	138	120	60
6 to 10.99 acres	44	28	9	35
11 to 15.99 acres	9	1	Nil	9
16 to 20.99 acres	4	1	1	3
21 of above acres	5	Nil	Nil	5
Total	291	217	169	122

From the table we find that 217 out of 291 families suffer from deficit in agriculture. As the people have subsidiary occupations, the number in net deficit comes down to 169. There are 122 families with saving in net income. But the saving of families holding land below 10 acres is not enough. The Rajput and Lala have large landholdings and sufficient saving. From the table, it is clear that 60 per cent of the villagers are constantly living under poverty, it is only the 40 per cent who can save, of which about five per cent may be called well off. The poor belong to different castes and communities but the highest number of such people comes from the low castes.

No distinction in the pattern and design of houses are found in the village. The house designs of two Rajput families (who are highly rich) are distinguishable from other houses in the village, as they are brick walled structures. No marked difference in the style and quality of dress between upper and lower castes is visible. It is between the educated and illiterate only that such difference is clearly visible.

Shoes are worn by all castes and none is found without it. *Charpai* is used by all for sleeping as well as sitting purposes. Some Rajput, Lala, and Kurmi families possess wooden cot. A number of families possess bicycle, radio, and watch etc. People who live under subsistence economy do not long for these articles at all.

The two Rajput families who have pucca building, do trade and business of local products. One Bania family having not much land (fall in the land holding size of 11 to 15.99 acres) is also engaged in trade and business. They sell local products, maintain a grocery, liquor shop, and a fair price shop. The forefathers of these Rajput and Bania families were landlords and Jagirdars and the Lala families were in the service of the king of the area. These families try to maintain the dignity of their forefathers but village people do not pay much respect to them. They possess fire arms and one of the Rajput family occasionally employs wrestlers to scare the village people. The head of these two Rajput families belong to the same lineage and have identifiable nicknames as "Malik Saheb" and "Chhot Jan". They are the major creditors of the village and the area. Due to this *mahajani* profession, they possess land in a number of villages. They also employ servants from Kurmi, Mahra, Dusadh, and Bhuinya castes. All these factors have made them decisively dominant.

The economic relationship of the landholders and share-croppers, creditors and debtors affect the decision making processes. In the village the major decision makers are the landholders and creditors who also belong to the upper castes. Sharecroppers are sometimes engaged as labourers without wages by the landholders and in such situation the later cannot withdraw his service. In loan transaction if the debtor is unable to pay it back, the whole amount is divided into two halfs and date of payment is fixed. But if there is no good relationship between the two parties, the debtor is not given this facility.

The Block and Irrigation Department have been made responsible for economic upliftment and eradication of poverty of the villagers. But the people are yet to reap benefit. The seed that the poor borrow from the grain gola and Co-operative Society are usually consumed. It is found that people generally do not like to take loan from these sources due to a number of reasons such as intricate procedure and demand of bribery. This is why the Kurmi of the village have formed their own co-operative Society. Its membership is limited only to lineage members and tola members. This is an effort of the people against the *mahajani* system to save their fellows from indebtedness and exploitation. The rich persons belonging to Rajput and Bania castes have easy approach to development and welfare agencies of the Government. They are the real beneficiaries. Caste status and better economic position help them in gaining such advantage. The poor people do not know what the government is doing for them. Land have been provided to landless Mahra community through Bhoodan movement, but these lands are actually controlled by rich upper castes (Rajput and Lala) of the village. The Mahra approached the B.D.O. but with no result.

Socio-cultural and Political Dimension

In rural situation, weakness among a social group is easily observable by examining such group's control over local resources of income, status, and power. These resources are possessed unequally by the village people. In the study of weaker section, it is important to trace out the mechanisms by which this inequality is maintained and by whom and what are its consequences in inter-personal and social relationship of the people. In economic sphere, we identified the poor people and analyzed their relationship with others in intra and extra village situation. Now we shall analyse their status and power in socio-ritual and political sphere.

As has been said earlier, village Sikri is a multicaste village where castes of all Varna categories are found. There is also a Muslim family belonging to Momin group of Ansari clan.

TABLE 8: Caste and Varna hierarchy

	Varna Order	Caste Order
1.	Brahman	Pandey, Gossain
2.	Kshatriya	Rajput, Lala (Kayastha)
3.	Vaisya	Bania
4.	Sudra	Barhi, Kurmi, Kumhar, Sundi, Kandu, Nauwa, Teli, Bhuinya
5.	Untouchable Caste	Dusadh, Dhobi, Mahra.

Categorization of castes in the above order is based on interview with the members of each caste. Pandey, Gossain, Rajput, Lala and Bania are said to belong to higher or upper castes. Among the Sudra controversy regarding order of relative position is found. In their categorization the Bhuinya are given the lowest ritual ranking and are treated like untouchables. Among the untouchable castes, Dusadh is agriculturist by profession and Dhobi and Mahra are washerman and Chamar. The Dusadh receive better treatment from upper castes, almost equal to the Sudra castes. But the Sudra, along with the untouchables in general, receive a number of socio-religious indignities.

Inter-relationship between the rich and poor is not guided purely by the factor of difference of wealth. Behavioural attitude of the rich belonging to upper castes towards the poor and lower castes is generally based on socio-ritual considerations.

Caste distinction based social inequality gets reflected in behaviour and activities of the people. Inequality in terms of socio-ritual statuses is maintained through the concept of purity and pollution. Social status is determined by birth to a particular caste and is maintained by prohibition imposed through the rules of intra-caste commensality, caste endogamy and binding of traditional occupation.

Cooked food of the upper castes is taken by lower and untouchable castes but no cooked food of the later is accepted by the former.

Discrimination is observed the upper castes against the lower castes in certain activities. After immersion of Durga during Ramnavami Puja *shantijal* (water of peace) is distributed to all except the Mahra, Dhobi, and Bhuinya. Untouchability is still observed by the upper castes. With regard to drinking water facility, the Dhobi and Mahra get it from their own well. Other castes do not take water from these wells. Momin (Muslim) are also treated like untouchables by the Hindu. They have no well of their own, so either they get water from the Panchayat well or from the well belonging to the Nauwa caste. When a Hindu draws water they are made to stand at a distance. The Bhuinya have got no well of their own. So they get drinking water from the river. Though the well belonging to the Kurmi caste is close to their houses, they are not allowed to take water from it.

Inter-caste social stratfication is clearly observed during

socio-religious feast and sharing of *chillum* during smoking of *ganja*. During marriage ceremony at the house of upper castes, services of the Mahra, Dhobi, and Nauwa are essential. At the time of feast, they are made to sit at a distance from the rest of the people.

Tobacco is shared by Kurmi, Nauwa, (both Sudra) and Dusadh among themselves (untouchable) but they do not share it with Bhuinya (Sudra) and Mahra (untouchable). Upper castes (Pandey, Gossain, Rajput, Lala and Bania) never receive tobacco from the hands of Dusadh, Nauwa, Mahra, Bhuinya, and Dhobi; Mahra, Bhuinya, and Dhobi never share the cot or mat occupied by other castes.

No instance of exchange of greeting and coloured water during Holi festival between upper and lower castes is observed. Some people touch the feet of Gossain but never greet the Pandey and Rajput. Kinship terms are not used beyond one's lineage members.

Attempts of social mobility among the low castes particularly the Kurmi and Dusadh are reported. Individual caste identity is maintained by the *jatisabha* which every caste of the village has. Wearing of sacred thread is an indicator of belonging to upper caste. But the lower caste think and say that it belongs not to the upper caste only, it is an indicator of being Hindu and of purity. A man can wear sacred thread if he keeps its sanctity. Sanctity of the thread is preserved by abstaining from eating non-vegetarian food and avoiding drinking of intoxicants and by keeping oneself away from social vices. When asked whether the upper castes have lost their social positions as they are found indulging in many social vices the reply was that "they are loosing caste characteristics but not the social position. It is determined by birth, so how can they loose. It is not related to wearing of sacred thread". An imitation caste characteristics or wearing of sacred thread does not provide or help a person or a community in gaining higher social position. Mahra, Dhobi, Bhuinya etc. neither known the myths related to Hindu Gods and deities nor do they believe in rebirth.

Thus, the upper castes hold the prestigious social position enabling or placing them in comfortable bargaining position (on economic ground) when dealing with the villagers, while low social position has prevented the lower castes from acquiring such position. Thus, low social position has made the poor weak. Under this situation, ideology and world view of the two social groups are contradictory to each other.

Amidst caste distinction and social disabilities, there is a common participation in limited sphere. When village deities are worshipped, all obey the advice of Naya, the village priest. Similarly when divination is performed at the courtyard of Kali temple, whatever the diviner says is obeyed by the people. The village priest belongs to the Kurmi caste and the village diviner is a Bhuinya. Both these posts are hereditory and these specialists are each attached to a piece of land for this service. Besides, there are spirit doctors belonging to Mahra, Dusadh, Nauwa, and Kurmi castes, whose services are sought by all castes, irrespective of distinction in social-ritual status. But this has not helped these castes in gaining prestige. Moreover, community ceremonies are regulated and guided by Rajput, Lala, and Bania. So, ultimate control of socio-religious affair is in the hands of the upper castes.

A high percentage of illiteracy is found among the villagers. But the position of those in the upper castes is better than those in the lower castes. Literacy distribution has been given in Table 9.

Among the upper castes Rajput, Lala, and Bania have comparatively high literacy. Low castes, particularly the Mahra, Dhobi, Nauwa, Kumhar, and Teli are totally illiterate. The reason of this low level of literacy is not that the people do not understand the value of education. For this state of affairs teachers, people, and the dominant upper castes are equally to be blamed.

Low caste people think that the dominant castes do not want to see them as literate or educated. There is a middle primary school in the village but it has no building. All the efforts of the people as well as of the Education Board for construction of a school building have failed due to intrigue. Very few children of the low castes attend the village school; firstly, because of the economic stringency of their parents and secondly, very often children of the low caste receive illtreatment from the children of the upper castes. Members of upper castes, also send their children to school at Barkagaon. The low castes are thus kept away from education, knowledge, and communication media. Illiteracy, thus, adds to their weakness.

New political system, after the independence has not brought any marked relief to the lower caste. Poor people belonging to low castes find it difficult to accommodate in new situation but the upper castes, particularly the dominant group are in an advantageous position.

TABLE 9: Standard of literacy

Caste/ Community		Population	I - III	IV - V	VI - VII	VIII - X	XI Matri-culate	College Education	Total	Perce-ntage
1.	Pandey/ Brahman	20	1	-	-	-	-	-	1	5.00
2.	Gossain	28	2	2	1	1	-	-	6	21.42
3.	Rajput	121	8	5	10	6	6	-	35	28.00
4.	Lala	29	-	-	1	1	6	3 B.A.	11	37.93
5.	Bania	107	6	2	2	2	3	-	15	14.01
6.	Barhi	115	3	3	2	-	3	-	8	6.95
7.	Kurmi	1026	15	15	14	5	-	1 B.A,B.Ed:	52	4.87
8.	Kumhar	20	-	-	-	-	2	-	-	100.00
9.	Sundi	57	1	1	-	1	-	-	3	5.26
10.	Kandu	27	1	3	-	-	-	-	4	14.81
11.	Teli	1	-	-	-	-	-	-	-	100.00
12.	Nauwa	35	-	-	-	-	-	-	-	100.00
13.	Bhuinya	24	-	1	-	-	-	-	1	4.33
14.	Dusadh	44	3	1	2	3	-	-	9	20.45
15.	Dhobi	45	-	-	-	-	-	-	-	100.00
16.	Mahra	129	-	-	-	-	-	-	-	100.00
17.	Momin	69	1	-	1	-	-	-	2	2.89
	TOTAL	1897	41	33	33	19	17	4	147	

Dominant section (rich upper caste) now control the village politics. Though problems are settled through traditional method by village elders, the people get no free and fare judgement. The statutory Gram Panchayat has been formed by the government comprising of five villages. Village people, however, have no confidence over the elected panchayat leaders. Since the inception of statutory panchayat, only two cases have been reported to it and these two are still pending, while more than twenty cases were reported to Police Station from the village during this period.

The upper castes and the Kurmi fight election of office bearers of the statutory Gram Panchayat. The lower castes have not yet contested the election. This is why during the last Panchayat election there were six candidates from the village for the post of *mukhia*, two from Rajput, two from Kurmi, one from Gossain and one from Bania caste. Though during these elections the low caste people are much sought after but this has not resulted in any gain.

Village people support two political parties — Jana Sangh and Congress (R). They are aware of the objectives of these two parties. As the area was under the influence of *raja* of Ramgarh and his party (Janata Party), the landed aristocrats (Zamindars and Jagirdars) supported this party. The objective of the Janata Party was to restore the Zamindary system to dominant groups. The Bania, Rajput, and Lala supported the party. Later this party was amalgamated to Jana Kranti Dal and at present Jana Sangha has taken its place.

The Congress received support from the lower caste people. This has divided the people into two camps and has greatly affected the socio-economic development of the people. Every attempt of the government to uplift the poor and low caste people is opposed by the dominant groups. In 1969, electric line of the D.V.C. was being drawn through the settlement of the village. The dominant group of the village did not allow the workers to do that. For the socio-cultural development, the government assisted the people by various ways. For eradication of illiteracy, adult education was started. Later, dance drama and party of Bhajan and Kirtan were organised by the people. All the poor, irrespective of caste distinction, were members of the organisation. These activities and get together of village people were taken by the dominant groups as ensuing danger to their status and authority. So, they tried to liquidate the organisation. These activities were being organised at the house of a Dusadh who was active supporter of the Congress. Once, after the performance of a dance-drama, someone belonging to the dominant group set fire to the godown of the Dusadh. Every one knew the culprit and the members of the organisation were determined to take revenge but the head of the household did not allow them, lest he would become the key figure and target of anger of the dominant group. This organisation automatically came to an end.

The poor and low castes avoid open conflict with the dominant castes because these people have no control over resources of income. If anyone ever dared to speak for these people, he is left alone.

All these examples illustrate how the aspirations of the poor and low caste are curbed by the dominant group thereby keeping the former under constant pressure.

Conclusion

From the foregoing analysis it becomes easier to identify the weaker section. In the village "dominance" is not identifiable in terms of caste groupings because no caste has absolute control over resources of income as well as on socio-ritual and political affairs. These are rather controlled by few persons from Rajput, Lala, and Bania castes. A few households belonging to these castes are also poor. So, they somewhat support the poor people belonging to other castes in village affairs. Pandey and Gossain, though belonging to upper caste, have more qualities of weakness than dominance and align themselves with the low caste people in village affairs. Kurmi, who are in majority numerically do not claim dominance, firstly, because they fall in the lower level of caste hierarchy and secondly, they fall in several economic levels, thirdly, their level of literacy is low and fourthly, unity among them is not of the corporate nature. All these drawbacks have stood in the way of the Kurmi from attaining dominance in the village. Mahra, who are the second largest caste, belong to the lowest social stratum. Percentage of landless families is also the highest among them. They lack all the attributes which are required for attaining dominance. So, no single caste claims absolute dominance in the village. The low castes in general, lack the unity due to various reasons as mentioned earlier and so they cannot claim dominance in the village. They form the weaker section.

In the analysis it is found that socio-economic condition of the weaker section of Sikri is still pathetic. It is further observed that they are facing two types of problems : (a) poverty and (b) socio-cultural disabilities and barriers due to low social-ritual status and prevalent ideologies, norms, and world view of the upper castes which are against them.

As Hindu socio-economic structure is based on interdependence regulated by the *Jajmani* system (though not reciprocal and egalitarian in nature), there is a possibility to bargain at each dealing. In other words, man to man dependency in religio-economic field with clear social distinction of individuals has given birth to interest group. Though agricultural pursuits and modern profession have lessened this dependency of man on man to some extent in Sikri village, the decreasing quantity and quality of land, lack of irrigation system, indebtedness, and lack of job opportunities have worsened the situation. It is thought that poverty of the low castes would be solved and ameliorated through the proper operation of the *jajmani* system, but the low castes never derived any economic benefit from it and their aspirations are lowered down by upper castes who have command over the resources.

So, socio-economic conditions of the weaker sections can be tackled in two ways : by providing diversified economic opportunities and by reviewing socio-religious ideologies and norms of the upper castes in favour of the low castes. Dependence on land and forest provides little solution. Ameliorative measures taken by the government are not very effective. At this changing situation, the low caste or weaker sections lack adaptability and command over power and resources, while the socially privileged class who posses the necessary knowledge and have the ability are in far better position.

[illegible] social mobility [illegible] is based on [illegible] experience [illegible] the [illegible] system [illegible] though [illegible] and [illegible] possibility to [illegible] at each [illegible] would [illegible] to [illegible] who [illegible] of individuals [illegible] given birth [illegible]. [illegible] Five Year [illegible] pursued [illegible] have [illegible] the dependency of [illegible] and to some extent in [illegible] village [illegible] quality and [illegible] of land, lack of irrigation [illegible] and lack of job opportunities have worsened the situation. It was thought that poverty of the low castes would be [illegible] through the proper operation of the [illegible] system but the low castes never derived any economic benefit from it and their [illegible] are lowered down by upper castes who have [illegible].

9

HAMIDPUR : A VILLAGE IN NORTH BIHAR

ANSHU PROKASH NANDAN and SUNIL RANJAN MAITRA

This paper is based on the data collected from Hamidpur, a village in Muzaffarpur District of North Bihar. Field work was carried out for a period of five months from January to May, 1973.

Field Experience

On the first day of visit to the village, the authors were warmly received by the villagers who were curious to know the reason for visit. We explained that the reason was to study the village, particularly the conditions of the weaker sections. There was a mixed reaction. This interaction helped to know the nature and behaviour of some individuals and groups.

A Bhumihar (landowning caste) wanted to know the details of the study. A Matriculate teacher, Kayasth by caste, was of the opinion that this piece of research was bogus and wastage of government money. He asserted, the members at the bottom of the society cannot be uplifted. The Kurmi and Dhanuk felt proud as only their village in North Bihar, was selected for the purpose of study. In Harijantola (a ward of the village where the Harijan reside) a Mehtar (scavenger) expressed scepticism about any improvement in the condition of the backward class.

Except the Bhumihar and the Kayasth, the inhabitants of the village are depressed and frustrated due to long neglect, poverty and illiteracy

Our long stay in the village was not liked by the Bhumihar and the staff of the Block Development Office. They often asked about our programme for departing the village. They feared that our long stay in the village might expose some facts which would be detrimental to their interest.

Method

The unit of study was the village but detailed information was collected from 51 selected households.

It was difficult to get exact information on annual income and expenditure of the villagers. The rate of daily wage varies in the village and town and expenditure also varies depending upon the needs etc. Only an approximation about income and expenditure could be made and possible care was taken to overcome omissions and errors. Data on landholding was verified from all possible sources. Members from each caste were asked to arrange the castes of the village according to hierarchical position.

The Village

Hamidpur is situated within Bochaha Block under Sadar Police Station and is connected with Muzaffarpur town by Muzaffarpur - Darbhanga road that passes through Bochaha proper.

Formerly this village was owned by a Bhumihar Zamindar. The earliest inhabitants of the village were the Yadav and only one family of the Koiri caste. The present settlers are immigrant from the neighbouring villages — Peer Mohammedpur, Roshanpur, Akbarpur, etc. Due to the continuous damage caused by flood of the river Gandak the people were bound to move out.

The Brahman and the Bhumihar immigrants were already having some quantity of land at Hamidpur. For the other settlers, the Government of Bihar purchased a portion of the village land from a Bhumihar and distributed among them in 1958. Besides land, they also received cash from the Government for erecting huts of their own.

Social Layout

The old settlement of the Yadav and the Koiri is known as Purana-tola and the settlements of the immigrants is known as Naikatola. The settlements are segmented into different *tola* and named after castes of the inhabitants. The Yadav are the original settlers of the village and occupy relatively a larger area. Their settlement is known as Goar-tola. The Bhumihar and the Brahman are living on the eastern side of the village along the main road of the village boundary. In the southern part there are the Kurmi and Dhanuk settlements known as Kurmitola and Dhanukputty. The Dusadh, Chamar, and Mehtar live in a small area in the south-west corner and their settlement is called the Harijantola. Members of the remaining castes are less in number and settled in the south-east corner of the village.

The settlement of the untouchables is considered unclean by others.

The Bhumihar, Brahman, a few Yadav, and a Kurmi have brick-built houses with tiled roofs. Others have huts. Most of the houses are without any window. The Bhumihar, Brahman, Koiri and some of the Yadav have a courtyard, a covered verandah, and a separate kitchen in their houses. Others have single-roomed houses.

The Brahman, Bhumihar, and most of the Yadav have tube-wells of their own. There were three old wells which cannot be used by the Harijan. The public tube-wells at Naikatola are used by those who do not have tube-wells.

There is a primary school in Naikatola established in 1970.

Caste Composition

The village has a population of 939 living in 195 households. There are 18 castes amongst whom the Brahman are at the top of the hierarchy and the untouchable Mehtar are at the bottom.

The eighteen castes are classified into three broad categories viz., upper castes, intermediate castes, and untouchables.

The upper caste group consists of the Brahman, Bhumihar, Rajput, and Kayasth. This group consists of 54 individuals living in 14 households. They constitute only 5.75 per cent of the total population.

The total population of the intermediate group is 514. They live in 100 households. They constitute 54.73 per cent of the total population. In this group there are the Yadav, Koiri, Kanu, Nunia, Teli, Hajam, Kurmi, Dhanuk, Turah, and the Mallah.

The untouchables are the Pasi or toddy tapper, Dusadh or pig-rearer, Chamar or cobbler and Mehtar or sweeper. This group consists of 371 individuals living in 81 households. They form 39.52 per cent of the total population.

Numerically, the Yadav, the original settlers, are at the top and the second position is held by the Dusadh, an immigrant caste.

TABLE 1: Distribution of population by caste and caste hierarchy

Sl. No.	Castes	No.of house hold	Aver-age house-hold size	Population Male	Population Female	Total	Percen-tage	Remarks
1.	Brahman	2	5.0	4	6	10	1.07	
2.	Bhumihar	10	3.7	20	17	37	3.94	UPPER
3.	Rajput	1	1.0	1	-	1	0.11	CASTES
4.	Kayasth	1	6.0	3	3	6	0.63	
5.	Yadav	38	5.7	112	106	218	23.21	
6.	Koiri	6	4.8	16	13	29	3.09	
7.	Kanu	11	4.8	28	25	53	5.64	
8.	Nunia	7	4.3	18	12	30	3.20	INTER-
9.	Teli	4	3.5	7	7	14	1.49	MEDI-ATE
10.	Hajam	1	4.0	3	1	4	0.43	CASTES
11.	Kurmi	13	5.2	37	30	67	7.14	
12.	Dhanuk	9	6.0	27	27	54	5.75	
13.	Turah	2	3.0	4	2	6	0.63	
14.	Mallah	9	4.3	17	22	39	4.15	
15.	Pasi	1	7.0	5	2	7	0.75	UNTOU-
16.	Dusadh	43	4.4	93	98	191	20.34	CHABLES
17.	Chamar	34	4.7	86	77	163	17.36	
18.	Mehtar	3	3.3	5	5	10	1.07	
Total		195	4.4	486	453	939	100	

Land

The Bhumihar, who were the Zamindar in the past have lost much of their land. The Yadav and the Koiri, who belong to intermediate group, acquired land in course of time and are now contestants for economic power.

The total agricultural land in the village is 279.08 acres and the average land holding per household is 1.43 acres

The Brahman are at the top in respect of land holding per household (10 acres) and the next successive position are held by the Bhumihar (8.16 acres), Rajput (4.09 acres), Koiri (3.56 acres) and Yadav (2.85 acres). The only Kayasth family of the village possesses 1.31 acres of land. The other castes belonging to the intermediate group hold less than onc acre of agricultural land. The Nunia, Dhanuk and Kurmi are almost landless and the Turah and Hajam arc absolutely landless.

TABLE 2: Distribution of land

Sl. No.	Caste	No.of house-hold	Popul-ation	Average size of house-hold	Land hold-ing in acre	Land holding per house-hold in acre	Percen-age of landless household
1.	Brahman	2	10	5.0	20.00	10.00	Nil
2.	Bhumihar	10	37	3.7	81.61	8.16	Nil
3.	Rajput	1	1	1.0	4.09	4.09	Nil
4.	Koiri	6	29	4.8	21.36	3.56	Nil
5.	Yadav	38	218	5.7	108.25	2.85	7.9
6.	Kayasth	1	6	6.0	1.31	1.31	Nil
7.	Mallah	9	39	4.3	8.12	0.90	44.4
8.	Kanu	11	53	4.8	7.75	0.68	18.2
9.	Teli	4	14	3.5	2.54	0.63	Nil
10.	Nunia	7	30	4.3	2.34	0.33	28.6
11.	Dhanuk	9	54	6.0	3.00	0.33	33.3
12.	Kurmi	13	67	5.2	2.29	0.17	61.5
13.	Turah	2	6	3.0	Nil	Nil	100
14.	Hajam	1	4	4.0	Nil	Nil	100
15.	Dusadh	43	191	4.4	14.56	0.34	62.7
16.	Chamar	34	163	4.7	1.86	0.05	61.7
17.	Pasi	1	7	7.0	Nil	Nil	100
18.	Mehtar	3	10	3.3	Nil	Nil	100
	Total	195	939	4.4	279.08	1.43	40.5

Among the untouchables the Dusadh possess 0.34 acre and Chamar .05 acre of land per household. The Pasi and the Mehtar are landless.

The percentage of landless households is very low among the Yadav (7.9%) and high among the Dusadh (62.7%), Chamar (61.7%) and Kurmi (61.5%). Landless households among some intermediate castes are below 50 per cent, e.g. the Mallah (44.4%), Kanu (18.2%), Nunia (28.6%), and Dhanuk (33.3%). All the Turah, Hajam, Pasi, and Mehtar are landless. In contrast there is no landless family among the Brahman, Bhumihar, Rajput, Koiri, Kayasth, and Teli.

Types of Land (Agricultural)

Agricultural land is classified into three types based on the position of the land. They are 1) *veeth*, 2) *dhanaur* or *manihar* and 3) *dhab*.

1) *Veeth*

This type of land is located at the high altitude location, it is fertile, and never flooded.

2) *Dhanaur* or *Manihar*

This type of land is located at the comparatively low land area and is suitable for rice cultivation.

3) *Dhab*

This land is very low, sandy, and unproductive, situated on the bank of the river Gandak and gets flooded every year. If standing crops is not harvested before flood, it becomes a total loss. Since this type of land is sandy, it requires much water for cultivation. It is considered as the most inferior type of land by the villagers.

The Yadav have the maximum quantity of *veeth* or high land (83 acres). In terms of average holding per household the Brahman (3.18 acres) are at the top to be followed by the Yadav (2.18 acres), Koiri (1.89 acres), Rajput (being one member of the only household holding 1.59 acres) and Bhumihar (1.55 acres) in order. Remaining castes hold negligible amount of *veeth* land ranging from .29 acre to .02 acre.

The maximum *dhanaur* or paddy producing land per household is possessed by the Bhumihar (2.30 acres) who are closely followed by the Brahman (2.27 acres). The Koiri and the Yadav possess .75 and .34 acre respectively whereas, the Kanu and Dusadh have only .07 and .02 acre per family respectively.

Dhab or the sandy low land is mostly in possession of the Bhumihar, Brahman, Rajput and Kayasth. Rest of the castes hold less than one acre of this type of land.

Thus, most of the good quality land is possessed by the upper castes like Brahman, Bhumihar, Rajput etc. whereas poor infertile lands are owned by the lower castes, that too in very negligible quantity.

TABLE 3: Distribution of landholding by type

Sl. No.	Caste	No. of house-hold	Types or Land					
			Veeth		*Dhanaur* or *Manihar*		*Dhab*	
			Total holding in acre	Aver-age	Total holding in acre	Aver-age	Total holding	Average
1.	Brahman	2	6.37	3.18	4.54	2.27	9.09	4.54
2.	Bhumihar	10	15.56	1.55	23.00	2.30	43.05	4.30
3.	Rajput	1	1.59	1.59	-	-	2.50	2.50
4.	Kayasth	1	0.18	0.18	-	-	1.13	1.13
5.	Koiri	6	11.36	1.89	4.55	0.75	5.45	0.90
6.	Yadav	38	83.00	2.18	13.25	0.34	12.00	0.31
7.	Kanu	11	1.98	0.18	0.79	0.07	4.98	0.45
8.	Nunia	7	-	-	-	-	2.34	0.33
9.	Teli	4	1.18	0.29	-	-	1.36	0.34
10.	Hajam	1	-	-	-	-	-	-
11.	Kurmi	13	0.54	0.04	-	-	1.75	0.13
12.	Dhanuk	9	-	-	-	-	3.00	0.33
13.	Turah	2	-	-	-	-	-	-
14.	Mallah	9	1.14	0.12	-	-	6.98	-
15.	Pasi	1	-	-	-	-	-	-
16.	Dusadh	43	0.77	0.01	0.79	0.02	13.00	0.03
17.	Chamar	34	0.68	0.02	-	-	1.18	0.03
18.	Mehtar	3	-	-	-	-	-	-
	Total	195	124.35		46.92		107.81	

In most of the *veeth* and *dhanaur* type of land both Kharif and Rabi crops are grown. In *veeth* wheat and maize are grown better. In *dhanaur* rice is grown if there is sufficient water. The average yield of these two types of land, if properly cultivated is twenty maunds per acre. In *dhab*, onion, wheat, sweet potato, *khesari*, etc. are cultivated. Sometimes maize, millet etc. are also cultivated but the yield is generally very poor.

The condition of the Brahman, Bhumihar, Rajput, Yadav, and Koiri, who are holding a good quantity of *veeth* and *dhanaur* land, are much better than the rest of the castes. The Bhumihar, in addition to *veeth* and *dhanaur*, hold the maximum quantity of *dhab* land (43.05 acres) and they are utilizing them wholly with diesel pump sets and bore wells of their own.

A family consisting of five members can meet the minimum need for survival from three acres of agricultural land, either *veeth* or *dhanaur* type without any other source of income. The average yield is 20 maunds of crops (wheat, maize, millet, etc) per acre, the market price of which was Rs. 500 (in 1973). Households which do not have three acres of land may thus be considered weak.

TABLE 4: Distribution of households by size of landholdings

Sl. No.	Caste group	No. of house-hold	Land-less	Up to 1 acre	Above 1 but less than 3	3 - 5 acres	5 - 7 acres	7 - 9 acres	Above 9 acres
1.	Bhumihar	10	-	-	-	3	-	1	6
2.	Brahman	2	-	-	-	-	-	-	2
3.	Yadav	38	3	7	16	3	7	1	1
4.	Koiri	6	-	-	5	-	-	1	-
5.	Rajput	1	-	-	-	1	-	-	-
6.	Mallah	9	4	2	3	-	-	-	-
7.	Kanu	11	2	7	2	-	-	-	-
8.	Kayasth	1	-	-	1	-	-	-	-
9.	Dusadh SC	43	27	13	3	-	-	-	-
10	Teli	4	2	1	1	-	-	-	-
11.	Dhanuk	9	3	5	1	-	-	-	-
12.	Nunia SC	7	2	4	1	-	-	-	-
13.	Kurmi	13	8	5	-	-	-	-	-
14.	Chamar SC	34	21	13	-	-	-	-	-
15.	Hajam	1	1	-	-	-	-	-	-
16.	Turah	2	2	-	-	-	-	-	-
17.	Pasi	1	1	-	-	-	-	-	-
18.	Mehtar SC	3	3	-	-	-	-	-	-
	Total	195	79	57	33	7	7	3	9
Percentage			40.51	29.23	16.92	3.59	3.59	1.54	4.62

Table 4 reveals that out of 195 households, only 116 are in possession of agricultural land and the remaining 79 are landless. Fiftyseven families have land below one acre, 33.83 per cent of which is *dhab* land. Therefore, these 79 landless and 57 marginal peasants constitute the weaker section, which together constitute 69.74 per cent of the total population. The households holding land above one acre but less than three acres are weak and constitute 16.92 per cent of the total population. From three to five acres owning landholders may be regarded as neither weak nor dominant and landholders possessing above five acres are dominant. The dominant section constitute only 9.75 per cent of the total population.

It is observed from the above that the Bhumihar and the Brahman are dominant castes in respect of land holding. Nine households from the Yadav and one from Koiri are also dominant.

The Bhumihar is the landowning caste but during our investigation they had lost much of their land. In spite of the fact that they are minority in number they still control a sizeable amount of land, which enables them to remain dominant socially and economically. The Yadav and the Koiri belong to the intermediate group who acquired land in course of time and are now contestants for economic power.

The main source of finance for agricultural production is the nationalized bank that provides loan to agriculturists against land through the Block Office. The amount of loan depends on the quantum of land in possession of the borrower. There is one Co-operative Credit Society, sponsored by the Block Development Office. Any agriculturist may be a member of this Society and avail of loan amounting to ten times of his share capital in the society. Only the Bhumihar go to the bank for loan. The Yadav and Koiri do not visit any of these agencies, lest they cannot refund the amount with interest in time. They prefer money lenders for loan.

The landowners of the village get labour forces for performing various agricultural operations from the village itself. Most of the agricultural labourers are from the Dusadh and Chamar castes. Members from other castes also have taken up work of agricultural labourers as the primary occupation.

The land owners viz. the Bhumihar and Yadav, and the labourers – the Dusadh and Chamar have a close economic relationship. Normally an agricultural labourer has employment opportunity for four to five months in two agricultural seasons of a year.

Exploitation of the labourers by the landowners is a regular feature. One labourer has to work in the landowner's field from dawn to dusk and the wages received is incredibly low, i.e., Rs. 1.25 to Rs. 1.50 plus tiffin like boiled sweet potato (1/2 seer) & salt or crushed *khesari* and salt. The government approved rate is Rs. 2.50 per day (i.e. during 1973). Furthermore, they are watched in the field and any slackness in work may cause severe threat. Sometimes, the labourers are provided with loans by the landowner, which can never be repaid. As a consequence, the capital and interest together mounts up resulting in their bonded status.

TABLE 5: Distribution of labourers

Sl. No.	Name of the caste	No.of ag.lbr.	Percentage	Labour seasonal	Labour Permanent
1.	Dusadh	41	39.81	1	3
2.	Chamar	36	34.96	5	12
3.	Nunia	6	5.83	-	-
4.	Kurmi	5	4.85	-	-
5.	Kanu	5	4.85	-	-
6.	Yadav	4	3.88	-	1
7.	Mallah	3	2.91	-	-
8.	Turah	2	1.94	1	1
9.	Dhanuk	1	0.97	-	-
	Total	103	100.00	7	17

A Yadav landowner admitted that he used to provide loans to his labourers so that they remained fixed. Thus, the trouble of searching labourer every year would be eliminated. That landowner has got a permanent labourer in the Purana Chamartola who for all practical purposes has became a bonded labourer.

The local term used for sharecropping is *batai*. Those who are not in a position to cultivate their total land, arrange for sharecropping. Generally, the land which is unproductive due to lack of proper irrigation, or if a piece of land is too far off is given for sharecropping. The entire cost of agriculture is borne by the sharecropper and the yield is divided between the landowner and sharecropper on fifty-fifty basis.

The landowner may take away the land from the share-cropper according to his convenience. Sometimes, the share-croppers are forced to return the land even with standing crops on payment of a paltry amount.

A Chamar labourer reported that in 1970 he had got about two acres of land from a Bhumihar for sharecropping. The crop was very good and that is why the landlord paid him the cost of cultivation and took away the land with standing crop.

It is obvious that only the dominant section is enjoying the new agricultural innovations, such as bore wells, diesel pump-sets for irrigation, and fertilizer at reasonable rate from the Block Office.

They can invest a good amount from the loan taken from the agencies against their land. While the small landholders irrigate their land with manually operated shallow tubewells and purchase fertilizers like 'Grow more Urea', etc. from the black market.

In the village the Bhumihar family, (at present splitted into nine) are owning seven deep bore wells and three diesel pump-sets, two of which have been financed by Bank. One Yadav, also owns a deep bore well and a diesel pump-set acquired through Block Office.

It is observed that most of the castes have changed their traditional occupation. Among the Yadav about 47 per cent took agriculture as the primary occupation for the last three generations. Besides, they also follow their traditional occupation of milk-selling.

Most of the Chamar left their traditional occupation of leather-dressing and shoe-making for the last three generations. The primary reason was the growth of population and acute competition in the traditional occupation. The profession of shoe-making and repairing degrades one in the society for which they have adopted new occupations. Nunia, Mallah and Dhanuk employed themselves in wood-splitting in Nepal for most of the days in a year.

The occupations of the different castes may be classified under six categories. Owner cultivator, sharecropper, business (grocery, vegetable-selling, tailoring, and surveying), profession (milk and curd selling, *muri*-selling toddy tapper, sweeping, leather dressing, palanquin carrier and teacher) agricultural labourer and daily labourer including service.

In the table 6, details of different occupations practised by the villagers are given with percentage in brackets.

There are 297 working hands in the village of which 30.97 per cent are owner cultivators, 34.67 per cent agricultural labourers and only 2.02 per cent are sharecroppers. Thus, these three categories constitute 67.66 per cent of the total working force who are engaged in agriculture.

Only seven persons (2.35%) are engaged in business. Two of three Yadav are running two grocery shops and the other deals in rice within the village importing from Nepal. One each from the Teli, Kurmi, and Mallah sells vegetables, parched rice (*muri*) and milk respectively in the town and one Dusadh is surveyor (*amin*).

TABLE 6: Distribution of occupations

Sl. No.	Caste	No. of male worker	Owner cultivator	Share-cropper	Business-man	Profession-al	Age labourer	Daily lab.& service
1.	Brahman	3	2 (66.66)	-	-	-	-	1 (33.33)
2.	Bhumihar	10	9 (90.00)	-	-	-	-	1 (10.00)
3.	Rajput	1	1 (100.00)	-	-	-	-	-
4.	Kayasth	1	-	-	-	1 (100.00)	-	-
5.	Koiri	10	9 (90.00)	-	-	-	-	1 (10.00)
6.	Yadav	63	46 (73.01)	-	3 (4.95)	2 (3.17)	4 (6.34)	8 (12.68)
7.	Kanu	16	3 (18.75)	-	-	4 (25.00)	5 (31.25)	4 (25.00)
8.	Nunia	11	2 (18.18)	-	-	-	6 (54.54)	3 (27.27)
9.	Teli	4	3 (75.00)	-	1 (25.00)	-	-	-
10.	Hajam	1	-	-	-	1 (100.00)	-	-
11.	Kurmi	23	2 (8.70)	-	1 (4.35)	6 (26.10)	5 (21.73)	9 (39.13)
12.	Dhanuk	15	2 (13.32)	-	-	3 (19.98)	1 (6.66)	9 (59.94)
13.	Turah	2	-	-	-	-	2 (100.00)	-
14.	Mallah	13	4 (30.77)	1 (7.69)	1 (7.69)	-	3 (23.08)	4 (30.77)
15.	Pasi	3	-	-	-	1 (33.33)	1 (33.33)	1 (33.33)
16.	Dusadh	66	5 (7.57)	-	1 (1.51)	-	41 (62.12)	19 (28.78)
17.	Chamar	51	4 (7.84)	5 (9.80)	-	1 (1.96)	35 (68.62)	6 (11.76)
18.	Mehtar	4	-	-	-	3 (75.00)	-	1 (25.00)
	Total	297	92	6	7	22	103	67
	Percentage		30.97	2.02	2.35	7.40	34.67	22.55

In daily labour and service category it is observed that there are 19 from the Yadav, Dusadh, and Chamar, who are mason, hume pipe maker, and mossaic polisher in Muzaffarpur. Nine Dhanuks, four Mallahs, three Nunias, and a Kurmi are engaged in wood splitting in Nepal, and two Chamars, one Dusadh and one Kurmi are rickshaw pullers. A few Kurmi and Dhanuk are household servant, cook, hotel boy, peon and bus-cleaner. One Mehtar youth is employed in the municipality water works. One Brahman is in the Railway water supply service, one Bhumihar is serving in a cloth store at Muzaffarpur and a Dusadh is in the Military service.

Professionals altogether form 7.4 per cent showing that the traditional occupations are in a process of slow decline.

Jajmani System

There is only one person of Hajam caste in the village who renders ritual service (hair cutting and others) through *jajmani* system to the villagers. Agriculturists take service of black-smith, carpenter, and washerman who live in the adjacent villages, through *jajmani* system. These servicing castes are paid in kind twice a year.

No. of Working Days

The agricultural labourers get about four month's employment during various agricultural operations in a year. The details are given below:

March	-	30 days
April to May	-	20 days
June to July	-	30 days
Sep. to October	-	30 days
Nov. to Decembe	-	30 days
Total		140 days

TABLE 7: Distribution of earners and dependents

Sl. No.	Caste	Total population	Earners	Dependent	Earner dependent ratio
1.	Brahman	10	3	7	2.33
2.	Bhumihar	37	10	27	2.70
3.	Rajput	1	1	-	-
4.	Kayasth	6	1	5	5.00
5.	Koiri	29	10	19	1.90
6.	Yadav	218	65	153	2.35
7.	Kanu	53	26	27	1.03
8.	Nunia	30	17	13	0.76
9.	Teli	14	7	7	1.00
10.	Hajam	4	1	3	3.00
11.	Kurmi	67	31	36	1.16
12.	Dhanuk	54	21	33	1.57
13.	Turah	6	4	2	0.50
14.	Mallah	39	27	12	0.44
15.	Pasi	7	3	4	1.33
16.	Dusadh	191	101	90	0.89
17.	Chamar	163	78	85	1.08
18.	Mehtar	10	5	5	1.00
	Total	939	411	528	1.28

The upper castes have a higher dependency ratio (1.90 - 5.0) than that of the lower castes. Still they remain dominant because they have easy access to the economic resources. The intermediate group (excepting the Yadav and Koiri) and the untouchables have low dependency rate (0.76 - 1.57), as they have little control over the economic resources.

Income and Expenditure

Castewise per capita income from the selected fifty one household of different castes is given in Table 8.

TABLE 8: Distribution of per capita income

Caste	Per capita income in Rs.
Bhumihar	1943.40
Brahman	857.90
Yadav	690.00
Koiri	684.85
Kurmi	668.72
Kayasth	604.66
Kanu	516.58
Dusadh	449.93
Dhanuk	407.70
Hajam	403.25
Pasi	387.35
Mehtar	355.33
Chamar	276.84
Mallah	204.60

From Table 8 it is observed that the highest per capita income is found among the Bhumihar followed by the Brahman. The per capita income of the Brahman family is comparatively less because the only adult head of the family is very old and as a result most of the lands is given on sharecropping. The next positions are hold by Yadav, Koiri, and Kurmi in order, their range of per capita income being Rs. 600 - 700. In cases of Kanu and Kayasth it is only Rupees five to six hundred. Among the Dusadh, Dhanuk, Hajam, Pasi, Mehtar, and Chamar it is only Rs. 200-450.

Castewise percentage of the total expenditure towards the major items like food, clothing, housing, rituals, education, and cultivation is given in Table 9.

It is observed from the table that the upper castes spend comparatively less on food and clothing than the intermediate and the untouchable castes but spend more on housing, education, and cultivation which helps them to remain dominant. In respect of rituals the percentage of expenditure is at a very low variance level in average. The maximum expenditure of the poor untouchables is on food. The Brahman and Kayasth invest nothing on cultivation as they

TABLE 9: Distribution of expenditure

Sl. No.	Sample castes	Food		Clothing		Housing		Rituals		Education		Cultivation	
		% of total expenditure	Average	% of total expenditure	Average	% of total expenditure	Average	% of total expenditure	Average	% of total expenditure	Average	% of total expenditure	Average
	UPPER GROUP												
1.	Brahman	77.01		5.93		7.26		3.30		1.20		-	
2.	Bhumihar	58.35	68.86	8.08	7.01	1.82	4.16	5.46	4.71	0.40	0.94	15.57	5.44
3.	Kayasth	71.23		7.02		3.41		5.39		1.22		0.76	
	INTERMEDIATE GROUP												
4.	Yadav	69.81		8.00		2.20		4.23		0.43		8.70	
5.	Koiri	66.62		10.03		3.16		4.65		0.79		7.92	
6.	Kurmi	73.93		9.67		3.77		3.86		0.33		2.11	
7.	Dhanuk	68.69	72.39	8.32	8.89	4.31	2.59	6.29	4.72	0.42	0.29	1.79	3.25
8.	Kanu	68.24		6.97		3.46		4.30		0.04		2.26	
9.	Mallah	77.80		9.90		-		5.65	-	-		-	
10.	Hajam	81.69		8.60		1.28		4.09	-	-		-	
	UNTOUCHABLES												
11.	Pasi	82.20		5.90		-		4.23		-		-	
12.	Dusadh	70.67		7.91		0.88		4.27		0.11		2.07	
13.	Chamar	76.69	76.99	7.81	7.70	2.08	1.01	5.19	4.15	0.37	0.12	2.74	1.20
14.	Mehtar	78.40		9.59		1.10		2.70		-		-	

give out their land on sharecropping. Except the Yadav and Koiri in the intermediate group and the untouchables, the percentage of investment on agriculture is very low.

There are 18 castes in the village. The social hierarchy along with traditional calling are given in Table 10.

TABLE 10: Distribution of traditional calling

Sl. No.	Name of castes	Traditional calling	Remarks
1.	Brahman	Priesthood	UPPER GROUP
2.	Bhumihar	Agriculturist	
3.	Rajput	Warrior	
4.	Kayasth	Writer	
5.	Yadav	Milk-man	INTER-MEDIATE GROUP
6.	Koiri	Agriculturist	
7.	Kanu	Sweet-maker	
8.	Nunia	Salt-dealer	
9.	Teli	Oil pressurer	
10.	Hajam	Hair cutting and shaving	
11.	Kurmi	Household servant	
12.	Dhanuk	Household servant	
13.	Turah	Palanquin carrier	
14.	Mallah	Fisher-man	
15.	Pasi	Toddy tapper	UNTOUCHABLES
16.	Dusadh	Pig rearer	
17.	Chamar	Leather dresser	
18.	Mehtar	Sweeper	

It is seen told that the castes are broadly grouped into three clusters : upper, intermediate, and untouchable categories. The Brahman is at the top followed by the Bhumihar, Rajput, and Kayasth in order. There is no disagreement about their relative position.

The villagers, however, are of different opinion about the relative position of castes belonging to the intermediate cluster. The Yadav and Koiri are given the first and second positions respectively, and all the remaining castes claim the third highest positions. According to village consensus the hierarchy may be arranged as below : Yadav,

Koiri, Kanu, Nunia, Teli, Hajam, Kurmi, Dhanuk, Turah, and Mallah.

The hierarchical order of the untouchable castes is rigid and based on their traditional occupations and also exchange of food and water between castes. Their order is as below : Pasi, Dusadh, Chamar, and Mehtar. Thus, the social hierarchy in this village is based more or less on the purity of traditional occupation.

Verbal Behaviour

The weakest section (e.g., the untouchables) and some other weaker castes from the intermediate group such as the Kurmi, Dhanuk, etc. serve as labourers in the fields of the dominant sections. During socio-economic interaction the weaker and weakest of the village population address the dominant person as *malik* (means Lord) while they are contemptuously addressed as *heh,hoh* etc., by the latter.

Education and Communication

The children of the dominant and the weak castes get school education in the village primary school and in the middle school located in an adjacent village.

The over-all percentage of literacy in the village is 21.97 per cent. It is very high among the upper castes (50% - 80%). Among the intermediate castes it is between 11.1 to 31 per cent and it is 7.3 to 15.1 per cent among the untouchables. Four castes viz., Rajput, Nunia, Teli, and Turah are hundred per cent illiterate. Though the Scheduled Caste students, which includes the untouchables are provided with stipend from the government, yet they are very much indifferent. Abject poverty is the primary reason which compels them to enter into earning at an early age. Despite such hindrances, a few who got educated are yet to get any white collar job. An Intermediate passed Dusadh youth was compelled to work as wage labourer to save his family from starvation. Another undergraduate Dusadh is also seeking for a white collar job.

Literacy among the various castes of the village with percentage is shown in Table 11.

TABLE 11: Distribution of literacy

Sl. no.	Caste	No. of household	Population	Percentage of literacy	Remarks
1.	Brahman	2	10	80.0	
2.	Bhumihar	10	37	72.9	UPPER
3.	Kayasth	1	6	50.0	
4.	Rajput	1	1	Nil	
5.	Koiri	6	29	31.0	
6.	Hajam	1	4	25.0	
7.	Kanu	11	53	22.6	
8.	Kurmi	13	67	22.3	INTER MEDIATE
9.	Yadav	38	218	18.8	
10.	Mallah	9	39	15.3	
11.	Dhanuk	9	54	11.1	
12.	Nunia	7	30	Nil	
13.	Teli	4	14	Nil	
14.	Turah	2	6	Nil	
15.	Dusadh	43	191	15.1	
16.	Pasi	1	7	14.2	UNTOU-HABLE
17.	Mehtar	3	10	10.0	
18.	Chamar	34	163	7.3	
	Total	195	939	21.97	

The weaker sections have got different opinions regarding education. Some are of the opinion that it is of no use to get their children educated. Instead, if they can earn something, it may help them to survive. The others are of the opinion that their children are getting educated to keep the statement of their income and expenditure straight and at the same time they may earn money by taking up jobs in offices.

Frequently, the villagers make use of postal facilities. The local daily Hindi newspaper published from Muzaffarpur town is read by the literate villagers when they go to Bochaha and important news are communicated to the villagers by them. There are three transistor-sets in the village which enable the villagers to be acquainted with the current news of the state and the nation.

Community Role in the Village

In order to build a school in the village members of all the castes contributed ungrudgingly. The Brahman donated the plot of land, the Yadav and the Koiri supplied the material required for the construction of the school (in 1970), and the Chamar and Dusadh donated labour free of charge. Not only that, the villagers fed the teachers (two) in turn in different houses when no aid was available from the government.

Social Organisation of the Dominant and Weak Castes

Except the Bhumihar all the castes have both joint and nuclear families. Among the Bhumihar, nuclear family is the predominant type. About 60 per cent households in the village are nuclear. Among the untouchables 41.02 per cent are nuclear families. The Yadav and the Koiri are still maintain joint families. They are in the process of building up assets to uplift their position in economic sphere by joint endeavour. But among the Bhumihar, who are decisively dominant, the process of splitting of joint family structure into nuclear type is mainly due to land fragmentation and worsening of the economic condition.

The weaker sections are not capable of tracing their lineage beyond the second ascending generation. They do not have any clan organisation and marriage also takes place within the village. All the lineage and kin members are equally poor. Thereby the range and net-work of kinship is very narrow among them. On the other hand the dominant section have got elaborate clan organisation and village exogamy is strictly observed by them. They can trace their lineage to a sufficient depth and their kin net-work is wide. Thus, the dominant and the weaker sections have nonidentical net-works of kinship.

Wide social net-work of the dominant section helps them in various ways in maintaining their dominance. Its absence adversely affect the untouchables and other weaker castes.

Social Mobility

Every member of the the low caste aspires to raise his position in the social hierarchy. He employs various means and one of them is to change the surname. The surname of the Kurmi is Mahato, but nowadays some of them have become Mandal. In this matter one Kurmi family is one step ahead and uses the surname Rai which is ordinarily used by the Yadav. Previously, the Kurmi were serving in the *darbar* (the house of the Bhumihar Zamindar) as household servant and were not allowed to enter into the kitchen and water was not accepted from them. Now they are allowed to cook meals for the family of ex-Zamindar.

One Teli has taken up agricultural work though he still adheres to his traditional occupation of oil pressing. This, however, did not change his social position.

The Yadav are still practising the traditional calling (milk-selling) along with the agricultural occupation. Recently some of the Yadav have started wearing sacred thread. Trends of change in ritual hierarchical positions are seen among all castes of intermediate and untouchable caste clusters. In some cases, however, these could not crystalise owing to traditionalism.

The village Hamidpur is under the Mirzapur Panchayat which comprises sixteen villages. The village Panchayat has two wings — the Developmental wing and the Judiciary wing. These two wings are headed by the *mukhia* and *sarpanch* respectively. The overall incharge of the Panchayat is the *mukhia*. These two wings consist of eight members each, of which four are elected by vote of the villagers and remaining four are nominated by the *mukhia* and the sarpanch in their respective wings. Among the nominated members two must be from the backward or scheduled castes and one must be a female candidate. The election of the Panchayat takes place after every three years.

A Yadav replaced a Bhumihar in 1972 from the statutory Panchayat and became Mukhia. Inspite of the numerical strength of the weaker section, the facilities and amenities sponsored by the Block Development Office are mostly enjoyed by the dominant section. There are representatives of the weaker section communities in the Panchayat but they are non-vocal. The two dominant castes, the Bhumihar and Yadav, are controlling the political power and utilizing facilities provided by Block Deveelopment Office and Panchayat institutions, depriving the weaker sections

The village politics is centred round the village Panchayat. All villagers are conscious about it and take active interest in its formation and activities. The youth club of the untouchables has established political linkage beyond the village, with the Socialist

Party, but is inactive in the village scene and serves no cause of the weaker section.

Power in true sense is controlled by a Bhumihar, the richest man in the Block. The entire office of the B.D.O. and the *mukhia* are controlled by him and his family members. The richest Bhumihar, B.D.O., and Mukhia have formed a clique for mutual benefits. The net result is that it acts as a barrier to the usual flow of development aid to the poor and needy. It is reported that a few dominant members were exempted from levy whereas small landowners were forced to pay levy. The entire structure and its operational principles act as a barrier instead of as a bridge, keeping the weaker section in perpetual poverty.

All castes participate in village festivals but the extent of participation by different castes is regulated by the norms of the caste groups which are determined by their relative positions in caste hierarchy and the concept of purity of the worship. Offerings are distributed by the castes of the intermediate group. The untouchables remain outside the main stream. They play music from a distance. Even during *Holi*, which is caste free and is supposed to integrate all, the untouchables cannot smear coloured powder on the face of the members of the upper caste.

Dominant and Weak

The upper castes of Hamidpur, particularly the Brahman and Bhumihar emerge as the dominant castes of the village in respect of land ownership, high literacy, high social status, and political control, although they are a minority numerically. The intermediate castes are generally weak but the Yadav and Koiri among them have uplifted themselves and are competitors for economic and political power. This was possible for them more because of their acquisition of land and educational attainment and less on account of *Sanskritization* of their ritual behaviour.

The rest of the castes in the intermediate group and the untouchables are weak on all counts. Particularly the Dusadh and the Chamar, inspite of their numerical strength, remain where they were.

Thus, in the village, the upper castes dominate over the lower castes by virtue of power derived from control of resources, ritual status, and social ascendancy, and political supremacy. About 70 per cent of the population, who are landless or nearly landless and depend mostly upon wage labour constitute the weaker section.

World View of the Weaker Section

The philosophy of the weaker section population is *khao, peeo aur jeeo* (eat, drink and be merry). This acts as hindrance to cross the line of poverty. It has been observed that when there is money with them, the poor want to exhaust it as early as possible. Often they go extravagant. They do not think for their future. Their ideology is *aaj ki baat aaj socha, kaal ki baat kaal sochega* (present affair is to be thought today and the future will be taken care of tomorrow). They spend for their neighbours, too. The Nunia, Dhanuk, and a few Kurmi visit Nepal for wood-splitting. On return they bring a lot of money which is spent lavishly by performing *puja* and feeding co-villagers. They accept everything as *fait accompli*. The older generations think that living in *kaliyug* cannot otherwise be better.

Development Programmes

The Block Development Office is the main development agency in the village. Several plans and programmes such as small scale industry, school for leather technology, deep bore well irrigation, etc. were undertaken for the betterment of the weaker sections but failed due to lack of finance. The landowners and members of the agricultural co-operative society have the privilege to enjoy the benefit of some pump-sets, fertilizers, and loans for agricultural purpose. The landless weaker section have received nothing except some ordinary tubewells installed by the Block Office within their settlement. The only personal benefit received by the weaker section from the Block Office is sugar at a controlled rate. But none of them has the purchasing capacity. The Scheduled Caste students of the village primary school were provided with stipend for the first time in 1973 ever since the inception of the school (in 1970). There is fund but the weaker section cannot enjoy it due to manipulation of agencies and of the dominant landlords.

Causes of Poverty

The weaker sections have nuclear families as frequent quarrels due to poverty break up joint family institution. The weak wear dirty and torn clothes, short *dhoti*, and no shoes or slippers. They are fully dependent upon the dominant landlord (*malik*). Low social position, nuclearisation of domestic organisation, and narrow range of kinship network, besides the socio-political pressure, have made them more dependent.

Internal weakness caused by poverty and conflict and factionalism within the caste are the great handicaps for the weak to organise themselves against the dominant. Extravagant expenditure, dependence on loan and low aspiration level stand on their way to progress.

The opportunity for employment being limited, the landless weaker sections depend upon wage labour. One can get work for about 150 days in a year and earn about Rs. 200 annually, beside something in kind. He accepts a lower wage, than prescribed rate because their is no other opportunity in the village. The employer sees that the labourer always remains in debt. Want of work in the village makes a large contingent of labourers sometimes to move to town.

Having no choice the weaker section continues to live in the village even under grinding pressure, humiliation, and exploitation.

Conclusion

The upper castes are dominant in respect of land holding, literacy, and political control, although they are weak in numerical strength.

The intermediate castes are generally weak excepting the Yadav and Koiri, who are now competing with the upper castes for social and economic power. Moreover, the Yadav have also the numerical strength.

The Dusadh and Chamar, being and untouchable weak on all counts such as landholding, education and low ritual status remain where they were before independence, inspite of their numerical strength.

Both the Yadav and the Koiri have Sanskritized themselves and elevated their socio-ritual status. But the other castes and particularly the untouchables have not been able to overcome the social-ritual and political pressure. Their weak economic resources, poor education, support of thin and narrow kinship network, low social status — all combine together to perpetuate their miserable social state.

10

BAMORI : A VILLAGE IN MADHYA PRADESH

P.C. HEMBRAM

Introduction

This study aims at depicting the condition of a village in Madhya Pradesh with particular reference to changes that have taken place among its weaker sections since independence. The principal objectives of the study are to identify the weaker sections, to make their social disabilities and stigma explicit, and to spell out the constraints on account of which economic development among them do not seem possible. Though our observations are based on the intensive study of a single village viz. Bamori from Sagar District, castes or ethnic groups form the main unit of detailed analysis.

Bamori with a population strength of 871 and 18 castes were selected for intensive investigation.

Settlement History of the Village

The village is approximately one hundred and fifty years old. Members of the Dangi-Chattri caste came first to settle here from Garhpaira, a place situated about ten miles away from the present village. People say that prior to permanent settlement of the village, the Banjara, a nomadic group used to halt at the site temporarily on way to important trade centres of the region. They had dug an well and made several stone platforms for facilitating their halt there. The reminiscents of these are still found in the outskirt of the village. In local dialect the stone platform is called the *chabutar*. The old well which is still the main source of drinking water supply for villages is known as Motital-Banjara well. Adjacent to the well towards the north-west at a distance of about one hundred yards the reminiscent of an old *Mokvara* is still seen. According to villagers, this was made in honour of a Muslim General who died in an encounter here, further details about whom could not be traced.

The settlement record of castes in the village is as follows :

1. Dangi Chattri(Thakur) settled five generations back.
2. Brahman (Sonakonia) settled four generations back.
3. Lohar (Iron Smith) settled four generations back.
4. Brahman (Baseria) settled three generations back.
5. Chamar (Ladiya) settled three generations back.
6. Sonr (Tribal group) settled three generations back.
7. Chaddar (1st group) settled three generations back.
8. Chaddar (2nd group) settled two generations back.

Some other castes like Kachi (vegetable grower), Yadav (milkman), Naua (barber), Dhobi (washerman), Nona-Chamar (monkey chamar),Kuchbondi (rope maker) and Dhanok (drummer) settled in the village nearly 30 years back and a few others came to live here during the last ten years.

The Sonakonia Brahman, have moved out to another village around 12 miles away. The village is divided into two hamlets : Bamori, the main settlement and Tori or Bhatua, the new settlement. Tori is situated at the southern part of main settlement at a distance of about a kilometer. From Sagar, the district headquarters, the distance of the main settlement is about 10 kilometers.

In the main settlement there is a primary school that imparts education upto fifth standard. Adjacent to the school there are two temples devoted to Sankarjee and Hanumanjee standing side by side. On a nearby hillock the shrine of Bhoibaba is located nearly one mile away from the main settlement of the village.

In the new settlement there is also a temple of Hanumanjee. Besides, the shrine of Goroyababa is located on the top of Bhatua, about half a mile away in southward direction from the new settlement.

Altogether 18 different castes live in Bamori. Thirteen of them live exclusively in the main settlement, three live exclusively in the Tori, and other two groups, namely Ladiya and Dhanok, live in both the settlements. Castes found in the main settlement and the new settlement with their traditional profession are listed below:

Main settlement :

1.	Brahman	(priesthood)
2.	Chaddar	(agricultural labourer)
3.	Chattri	(warrior)
4.	Dhanok	(drummer)
5.	Dhobi	(washerman)
6.	Gond	(tribal)
7.	Kachi	(vegetable grower)
8.	Kabirpanth	(follower of Kabir)
9.	Kori	(weaver)
10.	Kumhar	(potter)
11.	Ladiya	(chamar or leather worker)
12.	Lohar	(iron smith)
13.	Naua	(barber)
14.	Sonr	(tribal)
15.	Yadav	(milkman)

New settlement:

1.	Dhanok	(drummer)
2.	Kuchbondi	(rope maker)
3.	Ladiya	(chamar)
4.	Nona-Chamar	(monkey chamar)
5.	Teli	(oil presser)

Out of the village population of 871 (472 males and 399 females), the Ladiya, numbering 359 souls (190 males and 169 females) form the single largest group. They form 41.20 per cent of total population of the village. The Sonr with 82 persons (44 males and 38 females) occupy the second position in this respect.

The Lohar numbering 77 (46 males and 31 females) closely follow the Sonr. The Kabirpanth being represented by a single soul occupies the lowest position. Details of population composition is given in Table 1.

Communication

As regards the transport and communication, residents of the new settlement have better facilities than the people of the main settlement as the former live close to Sagar-Bhopal highway.

During the rainy season people of the main settlement suffer a considerable disadvantage. At that time use of bullock cart and bicycle are not possible due to accumulation of mud on the road. Horse is their only means of transport during rains. Transistor radio as a mass media agent is quite popular among the villagers and newspapers are yet to gain popularity among them.

TABLE 1: Population composition

Sl. No.	Community	Total male	per cent	Total female	per cent female	Total male & female
1.	BRAHMAN	17	54.84	14	45.16	31
2.	CHADDAR	24	52.17	22	47.83	46
3.	CHATTRI (Thakur)	19	52.78	17	47.22	36
4.	DHANOK	10	58.82	7	41.18	17
5.	DHOBI	1	20.00	4	50.00	5
6.	GOND	8	72.73	3	27.27	11
7.	KABIRPANTH	1	100.00	-	-	1
8.	KACHI	26	50.00	26	50.00	52
9.	KORI	25	50.00	25	50.00	50
10.	KUCHBONDI	2	66.67	1	33.33	3
11.	KUMHAR	3	60.00	2	40.00	5
12.	LADIYA	190	52.92	169	47.08	359
13.	LOHAR	46	59.74	31	40.26	77
14.	NAUA	6	75.00	2	25.00	8
15.	NONA CHAMAR	13	50.00	13	50.00	26
16.	SAHU (Teli)	6	66.67	3	33.33	9
17.	SONR	44	53.66	38	46.34	82
18.	YADAV	31	58.49	22	41.51	53
	TOTAL	472	54.19	399	45.81	871

A railway track connecting Sagar with Bhopal runs between the new settlement and old settlement. The nearest railway station is, however, 10 Kms away at Sagar. Tori, the new settlement being adjacent to the highway is in a better position in this respect as the people there can use bicycles, horses, tangas, and carts for their transport throughout the year.

The village comes under the control of a village level worker (VLW), an official agent of change who resides at Sagar. Neither the VLW nor his programmes are much liked by the villagers.

Distribution of Land

Land is one of the main economic resources of the villagers. To the landless the art of bidi-making is very important and to members of certain castes this is the main source of income. Casual labour in the agriculture fields, on road building, and other construction is also important but as subsidiary sources of income. Besides, some people are engaged in stone cutting and brick manufacturing.

The total area of the *mouja* is 757.995 Hectors, out of which 296.403 Hectors are uncultivable. A government seed farm occupies 160.20 acres of cultivable land in the village. The area of main settlement is 3.326 Hectors.

Out of the total 130 households, only 36 (belonging to different caste groups) possess cultivable land. Thirteen of them possess between one and five acres, four possess between six and 10 acres, 17 possess between 11 to 20 acres and the remaining two possess between 21 and 41 acres of land. The total cultivable land owned by the villagers within the mouja is 389.86 acres. Besides, some non-resident farmers own a substantial amount of cultivable land in the village.

The Brahman possess the highest amount of land, that is 122.35 acres. Per capita landholding among them is 3.947 acres. Next come the Yadav and Chattri who hold 84.63 acres and 55.07 acres of land respectively. Per capita land holding of chattri is 1.597 acres and that of the Yadav is 1.530 acres. The total land holding of the Lohar is 57.35 acres which is higher than that of the Chattri but in terms of per-capita land holding the former's share is even less than half of the latter.

Table 2 gives the distribution of land and per capita land by caste. There are nine castes or ethnic groups in the village who do not possess any land. Table 2 does not incorporate them.

Category of Farmers

The farmers of Bamori can be categorised according to the size of landholding into small, medium, and big farmers. Those holding one to ten acres come under small farmer, having 11 to 30 acres are medium and those who own between 31 to 50 acres are big farmers.

There is only one big farmer in the village who is a Brahman. Five medium farmers and one small farmer belong to the same community. The Yadav consist of four medium farmers and Chattri have three medium and two small farmers. The Lohar include three medium and three small farmers. The Ladiya consist of three medium and small farmers. The Chaddar, Kori, and Dhobi have one small farmer each and the Kachi have five small farmers.

Proportion of landowning families and the distribution of various categories of farmers can be seen from Table 3.

TABLE 2: Distribution of land/per capita by caste

Sl. No.	Community	Total Population	Total land in Acres	Per capita land in Acres
1.	BRAHMAN	31	122.35	3.947
2.	CHADDAR	46	2.59	0.056
3.	CHATTRI	36	55.07	1.530
4.	DHOBI	5	3.50	0.700
5.	KACHI	52	5.00	0.098
6.	KORI	50	8.46	0.169
7.	LADIYA	359	50.89	0.142
8.	LOHAR	77	57.35	0.745
9.	YADAV	53	84.63	1.597
	TOTAL	709	389.84	0.4475

TABLE 3: Distribution of big, medium, and small farmers

Sl. No.	Community	Tot.No.of household holding	Tot.No.of family land	Small farmer	Medium farmer	Big farmer
1.	BRAHMAN	9	8	2	5	1
2.	CHADDAR	8	1	1	-	-
3.	CHATTRI	6	5	2	3	-
4.	DHOBI	1	1	1	-	-
5.	KACHI	9	5	5	-	-
6.	KORI	9	1	1	-	-
7.	LADiYA	66	5	2	3	-
8.	LOHAR	12	6	3	3	-
9.	YADAV	10	4	-	4	-
	Total	130	36	17	18	1

Transfer of Land

At Bamori transfer of land occurcd from castes having higher ritual status to the lower. Some Ladiya, who bought cultivable land recently had purchased them from non-resident high caste landowners. A non-resident big land owning Ladiya from Bhatna sold 20 acres of land to his community members in 1954, where a new settlement has developed.

Type of Occupation

Thirty-six households are directly involved in agriculture as owner-cultivators. Members of a few households work for the absentee landlords and other few as casual agricultural labourers. Some agriculturists manufacture *bidi* as the subsidiary source of income. To many landless families, as already stated, this is the primary source of income and they practise it throughout the year.

Prior to the introduction of *bidi* industry the landless depended for employment upon agriculture-labour only. As the agricultural activities were conditioned by the amount of rainfall received the employment situation was uncertain. So, the people used to migrate seasonally in search of employment. *Bidi* making provides a sacred and certain employment opportunity. As a result the people do not migrate any more.

Distribution of Labour and Worker by Community

The village population is classified into twelve occupational groups. They are (1) farmer, (2) *saldar* (annual farm servants), (3) *Bidi* manufacturer, (4) casual labourer, (5) cattle keeper, (6) service holder, (7) small traders, (8) business-men, (9) contractor, (10) professional of traditional occupation, (11) dairy keepers and (12) craftsmen. Out of total population of 871, only 469 are engaged in various occupations. Among the total employees, 303 are bidi-makers, 87 are casual labour, 41 are farmers, five are *saldars*, four are cattle keepers, two are small traders, eight are service holders, four are businessmen, two are contractors, three are followers of traditional profession, one is a dairy keeper, and nine are craftsmen. The highest proportion of farmers belong to the Brahman caste, that is 55 per cent. They are closely followed by the Yadav having 52 per cent and then by the Chattri having 30 per cent farmers. Thirteen per cent and ten per cent farmers are from Lohar and Ladiya castes respectively. The highest percentage of *bidi* manufacturers belong to the Ladiya community, that is 81 per cent. They are followed by the Kori and Lohar having 66 and 61 per cent respectively. Cent per cent of the Nona-Chamar employees are casual labourers. They are followed by the Sonr having 41 per cent casual labourers. The Saldar are found among the Gond, Sonr, Kumhar, and Kachi communities.

Distribution of Employer and Employee by Community

Out of the total 18 castes only three act as employers. They are the Brahman, Yadav, and Chattri. They engage the Sonr, Gond, Kumhar, and Kachi on annual terms. Table 4 gives details of employers and employees. All the employees belong to the landless category. They are engaged for agricultural work, household duties, and herding cattle. The Ladiya are not engaged by the Brahman, Chattri, and Yadav for doing household work as they are considered untouchables. They can be engaged for attending agricultural jobs.

TABLE 4: Employer — employee relationship

Employer	Employee					
	Kachi	Kabir-panth	Kumhar	Sonr	Gond	Total
BRAHMAN	1	1	1	-	-	3
CHATTRI	-	-	-	-	1	1
YADAV	-	-	-	1	-	1
Total	1	1	1	1	1	5

Census of Livestocks

Cows, buffaloes, horses, goats, and fowls are the domesticated animals of the villagers and birds are also found at Bamori. Ritually higher castes do not keep goats or fowls.

The total number of domesticated animals in the village is 367 among whom there are 106 cows, 92 oxes, 65 calves, 29 buffaloes, 29 goats, 20 fowls, 23 chickens and three horses.

The largest herd of cows, oxen, and calves are possessed by the Ladiya (149). Next comes the Brahmin (61) closely followed by the Yadav (56). The Chattri with 26 heads of cattle occupy the fourth position in this respect. The possession of other groups is rather negligible. Out of the total 29 buffaloes in the village, the Yadav, the Brahman, and the Chattri have 17, 11 and one respectively.

The goats are possessed by the Sonr, Dhanok, and Ladiya and the poultry birds are possessed by the Ladiya (27) and Dhanok (3).

The Kuchbondi and Dhanok possess 3 and 5 animals respectively. Two animals each are domesticated by the Nona-Chamar, Naua, and Dhobi. Three groups namely, the Sahu, Kumhar and Kabirpanth do not possess any animal.

Income and Expenditure

Information regarding income and expenditure was collected from 52 sample families belonging to various castes. Items for expenditure on food, clothing, medicines, and house repair have been called basic items of expenditure and the expenditure related to education, religion, and conveyance are called other items of expenditure. It was found that seven communities did not spend money on education and twelve families did not incur expenditure on agricultural operations.

The income and expenditure of Brahman is higher than that of other groups. Then comes the position of the Chattri, Lohar, and Yadav in order.

TABLE 5A: Annual income and expenditure

Community	Per capita income in *Rs.*(approx)	Per capita expenditure in *Rs.* (approx)
1. BRAHMAN	1052.00	827.00
2. CHATTRI	464.00	430.00
3. LOHAR	415.00	342.00
4. YADAV	381.00	362.00

The Brahman spend 36 per cent of income on education; the Chattri spend eight per cent, the Lohar spend three per cent and the Yadav spend five per cent. These groups have a small amount of annual saving since their income is higher than the expenditure. The Sonr, Chaddar, Nona-Chamar, and Ladiya show a deficit, that is lower income than the expenditure. Per capita income and expenditure of these groups are given in Table 5B.

TABLE 5B: Annual income and expenditure

Community	Per capita income in Rs. (approx.)	Per capita expenditure in Rs. (approx.)
1. CHADDAR	171.00	174.00
2. SONR	185.00	204.00
3. NONA-CHAMAR	280.00	296.00
4. LADIYA	304.00	316.00

It is seen from the Table 5B that per capita income of Nona-Chamar and Ladiya is considerably higher than that of the Sonr and Chaddar. This indicates the higher consumption expenditure of the former groups. So far as the expenditure on education is concerned the Ladiya spend eight per cent of income in education and the Chaddar spend six per cent. No money is spent for education by the Nona-Chamar and Sonr.

Average family income of village per year is Rs. 211.00 (approx.) and expenditure is Rs. 1981.00 (approx.). Again average per capita expenditure of the village is (approximately) Rs. 321.00 against per capita income (approximately) Rs. 341.00.

The Sonr, Chaddar, and Dhanok are ritually as well as economically handicapped. Though the position of the Ladiya and Nona-Chamar from economic point of view is somewhat better, inspite of that they are handicapped as their expenditure is bigger than their income. They are also the untouchables.

The economic condition of the Kori, Kumhar, Dhobi, and Nona-Chamar is not very favourable but their economic status is somewhat higher than that of the Sonr, Chaddar, Dhanok, Ladiya, and the Nona-Chamar. Ritually they also belong to unclean groups.

Indebtedness

The poor villagers who can not earn sufficient money for their livelihood come under clutches of Mahajan and other lenders. Once a poor man gets into the hand of a Mahajan, he never comes out of it.

In Bamori,most of the families are poor (as their expenditure is higher than their income). So, they borrow money from Mahajan and other money lenders.

Introduction of *bidi* industry has brought some relief to the poor villagers who found an alternative employment avenue over the year round. This enabled them to get some money in advance from the *bidi* dealers which can be adjusted later on. No interest is charged for such advances. The money thus obtained is also not often sufficient. As a result people are compelled to borrow money from other sources in order to meet expenses on immediate necessities and liabilities.

Land owning groups can get loan from government agencies for digging irrigation wells, buying pumping sets etc. The landless people sometimes mortgage utensils or household plot for obtaining loan.

Type of Loan with their Interest

In Bamori if any one borrows money he enters into a contract with the moneylender to work at his residence or field till he repays the whole amount. The borrower works at the house of moneylender in return of interest. As a result, he is never in position to return the actual amount of loan and so spends his life tied up with his moneylender.

The moneylender takes two per cent interest per month. Interests on growing interests is also of the same rate.

Loans taken in kind is also converted into cash for repayment. In most of the cases, the creditor pays the interest but fails to repay the original amount of loan. Thus they become bonded labourers, such borrower from Bamori belong to Sonr, Kumhar, and Gond communities.

The terms and conditions in case of advance payments made by the *bidi* merchant are similar in the sense that if the borrower fails to repay through *bidi*-manufacturing, two per cent interest per month is charged for. But such cases have not been reported from the village.

Bulk of cash loans are given against surety i.e. mortgage of land, house, and ornaments. There are a few governmental agencies to provide loans. Such loans are given only against surety of land. So, the landless groups cannot take advantage of such sources. Distribution of loan is given in Table 6.

TABLE 6: Distribution of borrowers by caste and reason for borrowing

Purpose of loan	Caste	Percentage of loan
1. Necessities	Brahman,Dhanok,Kuchbondi, Ladiya,Lohar,Nona-Chamar, and Sonr.	19.85
2. Agriculture	Ladiya,Lohar,Chattri and Yadav.	63.82
3. Liabilities	Ladiya,Lohar and Sonr	9.55
4. Industry	Ladiya	6.82
TOTAL		100.04

Among the borrowers 36.22 per cent got loans from Mahajan or other local money lender and 63.82 per cent obtained loan from governmental sources like co-operative credit society. The borrowers belong to the Brahman, Dhanok, Kuchbondi, Ladiya, Lohar, Nona-Chamar, Sonr, Chattri and Yadav communities.

Innovation

The most important change brought about in the agricultural sectors is through introduction of some pumping sets. There are five such sets in the village, two owned by the Chattri, other two by the Yadav, and the remaining one by a Ladiya.

The Village Level Worker assigned to work at Bamori never meets poor farmers. However, interested farmers collect informations through other agencies like seed-farm. Farmers are familiar with the use of chemical fertilizers namely Grow-more, Uria, and Potash. As their rates are sometimes beyond their ability to buy (Rs. 135 per Quintal) their use is limited. In 1972 only three farmers used chemical fertilizers. They belonged to the Brahman, Yadav, and Ladiya communities. The Brahman farmer use two varieties of chemical fertilizers, uria 1/2 Quintal and potash 1/4 Quintal. The Yadav farmer used 1/4 Quintal grow more and the Ladiya farmer used one quintal grow more. Four farmers possess iron plough, two of them are Brahman, one each is from the Ladiya and Chattri group. Besides, there is a threshing machine owned by a Brahman farmer and a [1]wheat grinding machine owned by a Ladiya farmer.

From examination of the economic variables a clear cut division of the caste or ethnic groups of the village becomes apartment. Whether it is the question of control over resources or their economic performance, the division between "haves" and "haves nots" is conspicuous and their line of divide is more or less in congruence with hierarchical division of the society based on ritual purity and pollution.

The ritual ranking of 18 caste groups of Bamori has been given in Table 7. The superior most three castes have their exclusive positions. The remaining others share positions occupied by some other groups. As a result, 18 caste groups could be arranged into eight strata.

TABLE 7: Different communities and their local ritual hierarchy

Sl. No.	Ethnic group	Local ritual hierarchy	Total population
1	BRAHMAN	1	31
2	CHATTRI (Thakur)	2	36
3	YADAV	3	53
4	LOHAR	4	77
5	KACHHI	4	52
6	GOND(Tribal)	4	11
7	SAHU(Teli)	5	9
8	NAUA	5	8
9	KORI	6	50
10	CHADDAR	6	46
11	KUMHAR	6	5
12	SONR(Tribal)	6	82
13	KUCHBONDI	7	3
14	DHOBI	7	5
15	KABIRPANTH	7	1
16	NONA-CHAMAR	8	26
17	LADIYA	8	359
18	DHANOK	8	17
		TOTAL	871

Demarcation of Settlement on the Basis of Ethnicity

Most of the Brahman families live in the heart of the main settlement of Bamori. Other caste groups are scattered around them. The Ladiya and the Dhanok live in the outskirts of the village. The Sonr live on the slope of the adjacent hillock, Molalipahar. On the same slope there also live a Dhobi, a Gond, and two Chaddar families. Houses of other clean castes are intermittently spreadout between ritually unclean groups. Thus, the village is not strictly compartmentalized on the basis of the concept of ritual purity and pollution. Houses in the new settlement are scattered without any discrimination. There is a well in the new settlement and all draw water from the same well.

In the main settlement untouchables have a separate well for drawing water. They are not allowed to use wells wherefrom members of the higher castes draw water.

Tribals are grouped under the Hindu fold and the Gond occupies a fairly high position in the local ritual hierarchy. The Sonr, another tribe, is considered unclean but superior to untouchables.

Family Composition

Village families on the basis of constituent members have been grouped as extended, nuclear, nascent, and broken. An extended family is one where more than one consanguinally related nuclear unit live and eat together. The total number of extended families in the village is 47 (29.01 p.c.). A nuclear family consists of husband and wife and their unmarried children. The total number of nuclear families in the village is 70, which makes 43.21 per cent of the total families. Families consisting of husband and wife without issues have been called nascent. There are 16 nascent families which forms 9.88 per cent of the total families of the village. Absence of one of the spouses of a nuclear family makes it broken. There are 29 broken families in the village which forms 17.90 per cent of total families of the village.

The average size of family in the village is 5.4.

A large number of extended families is found among the Chattri, that is 50.00 per cent. They are followed by the Lohar and Yadav having 33.00 per cent and 30.00 per cent respectively. The highest number of nuclear family is found among the Chaddar having - 62.00 per cent. They are followed by the Lohar and Yadav both having 50.00 per cent. Among the Sonr and Ladiya the nuclear family consists of 47.00 and 40.00 per cent respectively.

An examination of family composition shows that the nuclear type of family is the most prevalent type though the proportion falls below

45 per cent.

Access to Facilities

Every family possesses a house of its own. The houses of Bamori can be grouped as big and small. A few big houses have brick walls and others have stone walls plastered with lime paste called *atari*. The roof is made with tiles. Some brick houses have reinforced concrete roof. In the main settlement three *ataries* are found belonging one each to a Brahman, a Kachhi, and a Yadav. In Tori also there are three *aṭaries* and all belong to the Ladiya. The plan of *atari* is simple. The wall is made of stones abundantly available in the locality after cutting into sizes. The walls are plastered with sticky - soil-paste. The floors of houses are bedded with the plates of cut stones and is covered with soil-paste. An *atari* is a two storied house. Big houses are divided into compartments as per necessity. Some houses have boundary walls and open court-yards. The room at the entrance is the living cum guestroom. The kitchen is separated by a wall from the main house. Cowsheds are separately constructed by the well-off families. Walls of 90 per cent of the houses are constructed of stones. The design and pattern of housing are similar across castes. Only the houses of the Sonr have some speciality and can be identified and separated from the others. The size of their house is small (12 feet in length, 8 feet in breadth, and 6 feet high). They are divided into compartments, one bedroom, and a kitchen. After cooking and partake of meals the kitchen is also used as a bedroom. An extended roof of the house is used as the cattleshed.

There is no laterine facility in any of the houses in the village. But there are bathrooms in five Brahman, two Chattri, and four Yadav houses.

Electricity is not available in the main settlement but seven families of the new settlement enjoy this facility.

Concept of Clean and Unclean with Relation to Pure and Impure

The terms clean and unclean connote ritual purity and impurity respectively. The Brahman, Chattri, Yadav, Lohar, Kachi, and Gond are considered clean. The unclean stands for the impure as well as the untouchables. The former consist of the Sonr, Chaddar, Kori, Nona, Kuchbondi, Kumhar, Kobirpanth, and Dhobi and the latter consists of the Ladiya, Dhanok, and Nona-chamar.

A distance is maintained by different caste groups in relation to one another on occasions of village meetings and gatherings during observances of rituals. Greater the distance greater is the degree of purity and impurity. The Brahman are considered the purest.

The clean and unclean castes have limited interactions. Interdining is possible only between Brahman and Chattri including the *pucca* food. The Brahman refuse to eat *pucca* food in the houses of other communities unless the food is prepared and served by another Brahman.

The position of the untouchables is particularly derogatory. Even in local recreational functions their presence is not welcome. Other unclean castes are not forbidden to attend the same. The untouchables organise separate functions at Tori or the settlement where they can move freely being away from the clean castes.

The unclean and untouchable castes maintain religious as well as in economic interactions not as masters and servants but as fellow workers. *Bidi* manufacturing has brought many castes closer through economic interaction. During the religious ceremonies some clean castes visit the houses of unclean groups. But as the untouchables are looked down upon, they themselves avoid attending any religious ceremony held at the house of clean groups.

It has been observed that the people belonging to different caste groups do not address each other in same manner. High caste groups, specially the Brahman and the Chattri address the lower caste members by names. But the lower caste people address a Brahman as *maharaj* and a Chattri as *Saheb*.

Literacy and Education

Literacy level in the village is rather low. Out of 871 persons in the village only 181 (including schooling children) are literates. Ninety of them have read up to the primary standard, 30 upto the middle standard, 15 upto the secondary standard, six upto the graduation and three upto the post graduate standard. The average proportion of literacy in the village is 18.14 per cent in case of male and 2.64 per cent in case of female.

The highest proportion of literates is found among the Brahman, 48.39 per cent among male and 12 per cent among female. The lowest proportion of literacy is seen among the Nona-chamar among whom 3.83 per cent male and no female are literate.

There are two post-graduates in the village, belonging one each to Chattri and Lohar caste. Besides, there is a post-graduate student among the Brahman.

TABLE 8: Distribution of literacy by caste and community

Sl. No.	Ethnic group	Total popula-tion	No.of male literate	Percent	No.of female literate	Percent	Total litera-tes	Percent
1	BRAHMAN	31	13	48.39	4	12.90	19	61.3
2	CHADDAR	46	10	21.74	1	2.17	11	23.9
3	CHATTRI (Thakur)	36	9	45.00	4	11.11	13	36.1
4	DHANOK	17	1	5.88	Nil	Nil	1	5.8
5	DHOBI	5	Nil	Nil	Nil	Nil	Nil	Nil
6	GOND	11	1	9.09	Nil	Nil	1	9.1
8	KACHI	52	18	34.62	2	3.85	20	38.4
9	KORI	50	10	20.00	2	4.00	12	24.0
10	KUCHBONDI	3	Nil	Nil	Nil	Nil	Nil	Nil
11	KUMHAR	5	1	20.00	Nil	Nil	1	20.0
12	LADIYA	369	45	12.53	4	1.11	49	13.6
13	LOHAR	77	20	25.97	4	5.19	24	31.1
14	NAUA	8	4	50.00	-	-	4	50.00
15	NONA-CHAMAR	26	1	3.85	-	-	1	3.85
16	SAHU (Teli)	9	5	55.56	1	11.11	6	66.6
17	SONR	82	7	8.54	1	1.22	8	9.6
18	YADAV	53	11	20.57	-	-	11	20.57
	Total	871	158	18.14	23	2.64	181	20.78

Social Mobility

In closed stratification system of Indian castes, climbing social ladder is almost an impossible job. This, however, does not rule out the existence of mobility movements in India which frequently occur. The Ladiya movement of the Chamar of Bamori and its neighbourhood makes such a case.

In the village context the Chamar had performed the traditional role of lifting dead animals, a very low profession that made the people ritually unclean. As a result, members of other castes of the village looked down upon them. Even 30 years after the independence this was the situation.

They however, form a band of good workers. As dead animal lifting was not a full time job they used to engage themselves as agriculture labourers. They also developed expertise in stone work, particularly in shaping stones to sizes, construction of houses and well etc. When bidi manufacturing was introduced in the area they were very quick to master the art. People had appreciation for their hard work and naturally as workers they were in good demand. This gave them economic solvency but the social stigma remained firm.

They could not protest even if they were insulted as they could hardly depend on public protection in case of any confrontation as Government Officials, mostly belonging to upper castes, had scarce regard for their honour. Economically solvent Chamar families could not tolerate this situation any more. They internally organised themselves to give up their name Chamar and replace it by Ladiya which in local vocabulary means a skilled craftsman. They joined together and purchased a plot of 20 acres land one mile away from the main settlement of the village and migrated there. At first seven families moved out of the main settlement and settled in the new one. In the year 1957, they organised a caste *panchayat* (meeting) which the Chamar from other villages also participated. There they unanimously passed two important resolutions: 1) to call themselves the Ladiya henceforth; 2) not to remove dead animals from houses of other caste groups. Thus they came to call themselves the Ladiya. This incident resulted in petty quarrel and physical violence in many villages. But ultimately they could repel the force that wanted them to lift dead animals and get their Ladiya name accepted.

Now, the Chamar call themselves the Ladiya and even the other ethnic groups call them so. This, however, could not alter the inter-caste ritual positions of the village, though the economic independence of the people allowed them to protect their self respect. Now a days, they are in a position to engage services of the Brahman priests in their ritual ceremonies which was a dream to them during 1950s. The Ladiya now show interest in getting their children educated. This will resolve many of their problems. The Ladiya are now equally interested in the local politics. Though they can not take full advantage of their population strength in the village politics, they participate in the panchayat elections and there is a reserve seat in the Gram Panchayat for them.

Welfare Schemes

The village Bamori is under Sagar Community Development Block that extends rural reconstruction facilities to the people. Every year the Government seed farm organises an exhibition where use of hybrid seeds, appropriate dosage fertilizers, and modern farm equipments are demonstrated. All big and small farmers visit the exhibition of seed farm though the material benefit generally does not flow to the poor.

A co-operative credit society is very much active in the village. Middle class farmers usually obtain loan for agricultural purposes from the said society. But the poor are not benefitted by it.

There is no dispensary, mobile unit or a hospital in the village. Nevertheless people are alert about necessary medical treatment and rush to Sagar General Hospital. Malaria Eradication unit visits the village from time to time and sprays D.D.T. in every house.

Different Caste Panchayats and their Efficiency

The traditional caste panchayat is present and functional among the Sonr and the Ladiya. The Panchayats have authority over their respective castes and settle disputes arising out of breach of social norms. Divorce, betrothal etc., also need caste panchayat's sanction. Heads of caste panchayats inherit the position through the principle of male primogeniture, though it may not necessarily confine to one family. For resolving other disputes the assistance of Panchayat is essential. The head of the caste panchayat is assisted by a few respected members of the caste in his work. In the Ladiya community there are five members in caste panchayat including the caste head and in the Sonr panchayat four members are there including the caste head. There was no major incident brought before the caste panchayat during the last several years.

Statutory Gram Panchayat

Statutory Gram Panchayat is present in the village. The village comes under Bathoriahatt Gram Sabha, a village situated five miles away from Bamori.

The Gram Sabha consists of 18 members belonging to 13 different villages, five members including two members of executive committee are from Bamori village.

TABLE 9: Distribution of membership of the Gram Sabha by caste/community

Sl. No.	Caste/community	No. of members
1	BRAHMAN	3
2	CHATTRI	4
3	Lady Representative (1 Brahman & 1 Kayastha)	2
4	YADAV	3
5	LADIYA	3 (Reserved seats)
6	LOHAR	1
7	KORI	2
	TOTAL	18

The Sarpanch belongs to the Chattri community and the Up-Sarpancha is a Brahman. Besides them, five executive committee members are there who came from different ethnic groups like two Brahman, two Chattri and one Yadav. Though there are reserve seats for tribals, no tribal member is found elected to the Gram Panchayat. On account of their indifference towards politics and lack of education they do not show interest in election. As a result, a reserved seat is treated as open. The Ladiya caste has elected its members from reserve seats. But they do not have much voice in the Gram Sabha. Two lady representatives are from Brahman and Kayastha community.

All meetings of the Gram Sabha, either of executive or of general body are presided over by the *sarpanch* and in his absence by the *up-sarpanch.* Every village has a *patel*, traditionally a revenue collector and headman. In the village Bamori the position of *patel* is hereditary who belongs to the Brahman caste. The *patel* is also a member of the executive committee of statutory Gram Panchayat. Previously the *patel* used to collect taxes of land of the village. But now it is done by *patwari*.

The *patel* is concerned with peace and security of the village. Besides, he holds a duplicate record of the village land. Usually a Patel gets elected to the Statutory Gram Panchayat but it is not compulsory.

So far as the Panchayat representation is concerned, the higher castes, namely the Brahman, Chattri and Yadav are very much conscious. Scheduled Caste members, though represent the Panchayat, have little role to play in its decision making. Tribals are far more backward in this respect. They seem to have a general apathy towards politics.

Party politics has entered the village scene. But many do not have sufficient awareness about the existence of various political parties. Knowledge of the upper castes is definitely more complete in this respect.

Conclusion

The 18 caste or ethnic groups of the village, on the basis of their control over resources, power structure, communication network, hierarchical position, literacy distribution, economic performance etc. independently or together may broadly be divided into three segments called high, middle, and low. Segmentations are generally congruent with one another. As already shown, the Brahman, Chattri and Yadav have more or less absolute control over resources and production mechanism. In the village power structure also whether traditional or statutory, these groups enjoy the lion's share of power. In literacy they occupy the top positions. In the regional communication network it is these groups from the village who operate maximally. Their ritually prescribed superior position is undisputed. In the overall economic performance these groups are on the positive side in the sense that their income expenditure ratio is always more than one. The Kori, Sonr, Nona-Chamar, Dhobi, Dhanuk, Kuchbondi, Kabirpanth, Chaddar and the large majority of the Ladiya occupy low positions in this respect. They have practically no control over resources or production mechanism. In the village power structure though one or two representatives from these groups are there, this neither gives them any authority or any political maneuverability, though as a single group the Ladiya has the highest population strength and votes for election purposes. Except the Ladiya among them no other group is interested to operate politically and even the Ladiya move with some restraint in order to avoid confrontation that might enhance their misery particularly because they are still treated as untouchables. Members of these castes have little or no participation in the communication network of the area. As a result, they are little aware of development of the region.

They are mostly illiterates, occupying a very low position in the ritual hierarchy and their overall economic performance is poor. They spend more than what they earn and are mostly indebted. This is the circle around which they revolve.

Thus, as it emerges at Bamori, with the exception of a few caste and ethnic groups like Gond, Lohar, Kumhar etc., who occupy the undifferentiated zone between rich and poor, sometimes included with the former and sometimes latter, the village, more specifically the ethnic and caste groups of the village, on the basis of the factors already discussed, are sharply divided into two distinct classes : the "haves" and the "have nots".

Limited economic changes are, however, observable among the untouchable Chamar families who by virtue of their achievement in economic sphere through adoption of a non-traditional profession could emancipate themselves economically. But this did not elevate their social position, in the local caste hierarchy, though they did abandoned "their" old caste name and adopted a new name – "Ladiya". Ultimately, in order to avoid the social pressure created by their search for a new identity they had to emigrate and settle down in a new locality.

NOTE

1. Wheat grinding machine of the Ladiya is given in an annual contract to a non-resident Sahu (Teli), who pays Rs.90 per month to the owner of the machine for operation of the same.

11

BARBADI : A VILLAGE IN EASTERN MAHARASHTRA

DIPALI G. DANDA and D.K. SAMANTA

Introduction

The village Barbadi in Wardha District of the Vidarbha region of Maharashtra was purposively selected for the present study. It is multiethnic with a population of 1312, a large proportion of whom belong to the weaker sections. The special reason for its selection as a study village is its proximity to Sewagram, an important centre associated with Mahatma Gandhi's name. His dedication to the service of Harijan and untouchables is proverbial. Barbadi being within a mile and a half from Sewagram had many experiences of Gandhian programmes. It was intended through this study to examine how such programme could make a difference in terms of weakness and strength when compared with other situations in the country.

The duration of field work, on the basis of which this reporting has been done is from March 1973 to July 1973.

Inspite of its close proximity to Wardha and Sewagram the village remains mostly disconnected with these centres during rainy months because of its poor communication system. Foot tracks surrounding cultivable fields connect Barbadi with neighbouring villages which get flooded in case of heavy rains. In fair weather, the primary means of transport are bullock carts and bicycles. During rains, having no approach roads, physical mobility is limited.

Wardha is its nearest market centre, district, and tahsil headquarters; so villagers visit it for various reasons. Medical facilities available here are mostly used by villagers. They also send their children for high school and college education here. Thus,

Wardha plays a significant role in the villagers' life.

There are three Maruti temples, one Vitthal Rukma temple, one Buddha temple, two shrines of Nal Saheb and one shrine of Mata (seat of the goddess of small pox) in the village. Public buildings in the village include a primary school and the Panchayat house. There is an open space in front of the latter where the people arrange flag hoisting during Independence Day and Republic Day celebrations. The cremation ground is in the southern outskirt where the Chambhar, the Mang, and the Bouddha dispose of their dead bodies at one end and the higher castes at the other. There is no public graveyard for the Musalaman who use their respective agricultural fields to bury their dead.

Social Layout of the Village

Barbadi, for Panchayat election purpose is divided in to four wards named after Nehru, Gandhi, Subhash, and Hanuman to which the villagers do not give much cognizance. They conventionally divided the village into a number of hamlets (*pura*) naming them after various castes as per their concentration in respective cases such as Malipura, Telipura, Rajputpura, Gondpura, Kalarpura, Musalmanpura, Bouddhapura, Chambharpura, and Mangpura. There are a few castes like Mahali, Warthi, Vadhai, Khati-Wadhai, and Bhui, represented by one or two households only which are scattered around. There is no *pura* after their caste names. Malipura is the biggest in area, the Mali are also the most numerous in the village.

Barbadi is a compact and congested village. areas inhabited by its castes are closely situated and even the so-called untouchables are not very far off. There settlement is farthest from that of the Rajput, the highest caste of the village and nearest to that of the Gond and Bhui. Previously the settlement of the Bouddha used to be referred to as Dherpura by the members of high castes though the people living their called it Maharpura. Since their conversion to Buddhism there is a common name for this settlement, that is Bouddhapura.

Areas inhabited by the untouchables were considered unclean and formerly no member of high caste used to visit their places. Now a days people are less discriminative and whenever necessary they visit those places. Though women still largely hold their traditional concept of purity and pollution.

The village is inhabited by numerous lanes and bylanes. Every house thus opens to a lane howsoever narrow or wide it may be. With the exception of school and panchayat buildings which are made of bricks, all houses in the village are mud-built and roofed with country tiles. The general ground plan is rectangular having a big all purpose room with attached kitchen-cum-store and a covered verandah. In a poor man's house, the kitchen-cum-store is absent and the verandah serves such purpose. The house of every rich villager has a courtyard bounded by mud or brick walls, at one corner of which the cowshed is located. Irrespective of whether they belong to rich or poor, houses are clean. All big houses of the village are owned by the Rajput, Gujar, and Teli. A few well-to-do Mali families also have big houses with large compound walls.

Malipura and Bouddhapura give a general appearance of poverty. Here huts are low, small, congested and without any courtyard. There are no kitchens and a corner of the single-room house is multipurpose in use and house the cattle during rains. Fittings of these houses are also inferior when compared to that of the Rajput, Teli, and other well-off sections. Houses of the rich have private wells. There are none at Malipura and Bouddhapura. Special reference has been made about the Mali and Bouddha as they form the major bulk of the population. Bhui, Warthi, Mahali, Mang, Chambhar, Gond, and Goari also share poverty to the same extent, if not more and in their case also it gets reflected through their housing and settlement pattern.

Well is the only source of drinking water in the village. In Bouddhapura there are three public wells and Gondpura, Chambharpura and Mangpura have one well each. The Bouddha, Mang, and Chambhar are not allowed to draw water from the wells belonging to higher castes and Musalman. The Kalar, Teli, and Maratha can fetch water from the well of the Musalman but the reverse is not in practice. In each of the Kalarpura and Musalmanpura there is a well. Similar is the case at Rajputpura. But most of the Rajput families have their own private wells. Well-to-do families, irrespective of their caste affiliation, have wells.

Electricity has been introduced to the village in 1962 for irrigation purposes and subsequently for the domestic consumption. Street lights have also been provided. Altogether 23 houses (9 Teli, 5 Rajput including Gujar, 4 Mali, 3 Kalar, 2 Bouddha) have energy connections. Public places like panchayat house, school building, and Vitthal Rukma temple have lighting arrangements.

Public sanitation is poor in the village. Many individual houses have soakpits to absorb water from kitchen and bathroom. But the extra water flows down to the village lanes. As a result at many places water gets clogged and makes the area dirty. There is no public latrine or urinal there and only three houses have private latrines. People, particularly women and children, use village roads for attending the nature's call. Men and young boys go to some nearby places, a little away from the village for such purposes. The Rajput and Gujar women maintain some privacy in this respect. Other women of the village, in general, are uninhibited in this respect.

Nobody cares to clean or sweep the village roads, though people are particular in cleaning their respective courtyards. As a result, the village approach presents a filthy and squamish appearance. The situation could be worse if the village cattle and dogs had not served as nature's scavengers. During rains the situation worsens.

Caste Composition and Social Hierarchy

The Mali are the oldest inhabitants of the village. They have been followed by the Teli, Rajput, and other communities in sequence. The Mali, Teli, and the Mahar (presently Bouddha)[1] are the major communities of Vidarbha. The Kalar estimate to have come to Barbadi about hundred years ago. The Rajput claim to have come nearly three hundred years ago. Still they have some loose link with Rajasthan and a Bhat or genealogy maker visits once a year or so. The Rajput, specially the Gujar section have nearly assimilated themselves to the regional culture. The untouchables are also the early settlers and a slow but continuous process of their immigration and emigration is in process. People who came and settled in the village during the last fifteen years are all agricultural labourers. The population distribution by caste/community is shown in Table 1.

Barbadi is a Hindu majority village and all castes/communities inhabiting here are ranked as per the regional Hindu hierarchical system. This also includes the Musalman and the Adivasi who traditionally do not conform to the Hindu system of hierarchy. The villagers apparently do not make any distinction among themselves on account of religion. To them the village is a single entity, and each caste or religious group has a definite hierarchical position. The Musalman enjoy a fairly high social status and live in the midst of the village among other Hindu groups. They are allowed to visit any Hindu house and invite the Hindus on special occasions.

The two Adivasi groups of the village viz., Gond and Goari have completely lost their tribal identity and have become part of the local

Hindu peasantry. Until recently, they were least conscious that they had a non-Hindu origin. They still operate in the socio-cultural network of the Hindu but have become conscious about their special privileges provided by the constitution of Independent India. As a Gond observes, "After Independence we have been declared *adivasi* by the *sarkar* and we are given certain facilities". This new consciousness does not, however, lead to any revivalistic movement and to the fellow villagers they are very much Hindu having all privileges and handicaps of a caste society. The Gond and Goari are both of tribal origin, though, the former, because of their better economic standing enjoy a superior hierarchical position in comparison to the latter. Ordinarily a status is assigned in view of the nature of occupation of a community. As the tribals did not have any traditionally prescribed occupation, economy played the important role in determining their status (vide Table 1).

TABLE 1: Population composition

Sl. No.	Names of communities	Number of household	Percentage	Total male	Total female	Total
1.	Bhui (fisherman)	4	1.54	10	13	23
2.	Bouddha (agricultural-labourer)	52	20.07	138	117	225
3.	Chambhar (leather-worker)	4	1.54	16	12	28
4.	Goari (agricultural-labourer)	3	1.16	12	6	18
5.	Gond (cultivator)	6	2.32	18	13	31
6.	Kalar (distiller)	10	3.86	25	27	52
7.	Khati-wadhai (black-smith)	2	0.77	4	9	13
8.	Kosthi (weaver)	1	0.39	3	3	6
9.	Mahali (barbar)	1	0.39	2	1	3
10.	Mali (cultivator)	84	32.43	213	194	407
11.	Mang (drummer and basket maker)	3	1.16	6	8	14
12.	Maratha (cultivator)	2	0.77	2	8	10
13.	Musalman (cultivator)	9	3.47	20	21	41
14.	Rajput (cultivator)	8	3.09	22	25	47
15.	Gujar (cultivator)	13	5.02	41	36	77
16.	Shimpi (tailor)	3	1.16	8	6	14
17.	Teli (oilpresser)	48	18.53	125	115	240
18.	Wadhai (carpenter)	5	1.93	13	17	30
19	Warthi (washerman)	1	0.39	2	1	3
	Total	259	680	632	1312	

Though there were minor differences among respondents regarding hierarchical position of various castes or communities of the village, they are in exact agreement in clustering of castes/communities into four identifiable segments. The Brahman have the highest position in caste hierarchy[2].

Next comes the Rajput represented by 21 families. Their two sections, Chhatri and Gujar, though interdine, do not intermarry[3]. So, for our analysis they have been treated as two different groups. Gujar practise cultivation. The Maratha, represented by two households, occupy the next lower position.

Then come the Mali and Teli in order. Though the economic condition of the Teli is better than that of the Mali, the Mali are considered superior to the Teli. Traditionally the Teli are oil pressers and the Mali are agriculturists. Both the groups now practise agriculture as their means of subsistence. In earlier days they did not interdine. For the last fifteen years they practise interdining. But even now a Brahman drinks water supplied by a Mali but not by a Teli.

The position of the Kalar in the village society is dubious. Their traditional occupation was distilling and wine selling hence they were considered very low. But now they are mainly engaged in agriculture. According to their traditional caste occupation the members of higher castes like the Brahman and Chhatri or Rajput assign to them a low position far below that of the Mali and Teli. But as they are very well-off, to the poor villagers like Bouddha, Gond, Musalman, and even to the impoverished section of the Mali, the Kalar occupy a higher position than that of the Mali or Teli. This implies a new line of thinking in respect of caste ranking. to the impoverished lot, ritual purity or pollution has little meaning. Their regard for their food supplier is the highest, no matter what the food supplier's ritual position might be. As a poor Mali puts it, "The Kalar have money so they are superior". Thus, the de facto caste stratification is not very sharp in the village, Clustering of castes is, however, conspicuous. Various castes/communities of Barbadi may be grouped into four clusters as in Table 2.

All castes/communities have been put in a vertical order though the inter-caste/community distance is not always uniform. Reasons for and nature of differences vary. Generally it is the ritual status of a community that plays an important role, sometimes it is the economic consideration that matters (which is true for the Kalar) or both matter simultaneously. Those who are economically dominant also occupy the very high social (overall ranking) position in the village. The impoverished lot, in contrast, are ranked socially very low.

TABLE 2: Clustering of castes/communities in terms of dominance and weakness

Cluster of the communities	Ritual status	Economic status	Overall ranking
Rajput,Gujar,Maratha	Very high	high	decisively dominant
Mali,Teli,Kalar	high	high	dominant
Shimpi,Wadhai,Kosthi, Khati-wadhai,Bhui,Gond, Goari,Musalman,Mahali, Warthi	medium	medium to low	weak
Chambhar,Bouddha,Mang	low (un-touchable)	medium to low	decisively weak

Of the two carpenter families of the village, one is vegetarian and its male members wear sacred thread. They think themselves superior to non-vegetarians and identify themselves as Geneo-Wadhai. These two section do not intermarry.

Though the Mahali and Warthi are not treated as untouchables, they are not considered very clean. In the weaker cluster they occupy the top most position. All castes in this cluster have their respective wells, whereas in former days mutual exchange of facilities was not permissible. Now a days the Chambhar allow the Bouddha and Mang to draw water from their well when it is needed by them but they themselves do not use the well of the Mang or Bouddha. Still they consider themselves superior to these two groups. The Mang are the drummers and basketmakers and their women work as midwives.

The Bouddha traditionally were engaged for lifting dead animals. In addition, they were agricultural labourers. Before conversion to Buddhism they were Mahars. At present they are mostly agricultural labourers and since their conversion in 1956, they have advanced in many respects. Though in Table 2 they have been categorised as decisively weak, in economic terms their position would be between the Gond and Musalman.

Literacy and Network of Communication

In the village the decisively dominant groups, i.e., the Rajput and the Gujar come under the highest literacy bracket with 74.5 per cent and 52 per cent of literacy. The minimum literacy is observed among the Khati-Wadhai (7%) and Bhui (13%) both belonging to the weaker section. The overall litcracy of the village is 42.38 per cent. With the exception of Kosthi (100%) and Mang (50%), none among the weaker sections have crossed the average literacy percentage of the village. This high proportion may not be the true representativo of these two communities as a whole as their population in this village is very small. The Bouddha show 41.6 per cent literates among them, which is closest to the village average. Table 3 gives details of literacy distribution and educational attainment.

TABLE 3: Dominance and weakness in terms of educational attainment

Community and population	Illiterate (in percentage)	Literate (up to primary in percentage)	Moderately educated (beyond primary but up to higher secondary in percentage)	Highly educated (beyond higher secondary in percentage
1. Bhui 23	86.95	13.05	—	—
2. Bouddha 255	38.43	23.92	14.91	2.74
3. Chambhar 28	64.28	25.00	10.71	—
4. Goari 18	61.11	27.78	11.12	—
5. Gond 31	67.74	16.13	16.14	—
6. Kalar 52	32.69	36.54	28.85	1.92
7. Khati-Wadhai 13	92.31	7.69	—	—
8. Kosthi 6	—	83.34	—	
9. Mahali 3	66.67	33.33	—	—
10. Mali 407	62.90	23.10	13.52	0.49
11. Mang 14	50.00	28.57	21.43	—
12. Maratha 10	60.00	40.00	—	—
13. Musalman 41	63.41	24.40	12.20	—
14. Rajput 47	25.53	34.04	38.30	2.13
15. Gujar 77	48.05	29.87	19.49	2.60
16. Shimpi 14	42.86	35.72	21.44	—
17. Teli 240	55.42	27.08	16.66	0.83
18. Wadhai 30	70.00	26.67	3.33	—
19. Warthi 3	66.67	33.33	—	—

All highly educated people are rich. Exceptions are the Bouddha who being otherwise low have a large number of graduates and post-graduates in the village. In general literacy, the Bouddha occupy a lower position than that of the Rajput. Even the proportion of moderately educated people among the Rajput is more than the Bouddha. It indicates that literacy distribution and literacy attainment broadly follow the same hierarchy. This set pattern received a jolt with the sudden thrust presented by the Bouddha in the educational field and this is definitely a post-independence development. The Bouddha availed themselves of all opportunities provided by the governmental programmes. The Bouddha are trying hard to do away with the wage earning and have started securing good positions among the educated communities, while for the bulk of the village population the situation remains as before.

To all groups, dominant or weak, the primary object of education is to get a white collar job. Education for making a better farmer or home maker is beyond their comprehension. The dominant sections go for it perhaps in order to keep themselves in power. No women among the weaker sections is educated.

The educated people from the weaker sections do not have much communication with their fellow brethren. They remain busy in their own world. If they are consulted by others, they patiently hear them and offer opinion and suggestion. Rarely do they volunteer or display any initiative. The illiterates among the weaker sections though maintain a distance from them, feel proud of their educated fellow castemen.

No newspaper comes to the village and neither the dominant or the weak read any newspaper. Only few educated unemployed Bouddha youth read newspaper when they visit Wardha town. Their interest is in classified advertisements of job opportunities and sports information. There are a number of radio sets in the village, belonging to different individuals. In Bouddhapara there are three of them. Nobody in the locality shows any interest in listening to the news. They tune to the Vividh Bharati programmes. Cinema going is very popular among the young boys of the village and they spend a good amount of money and time on account of cinema.

Social Organization of the Weaker Sections

Most of the castes/communities are endogamous and divided into various *kur* represented by specific surnames like Lade, Shende, Sonaye, Zambre etc. *Kur* regulates marriage within an endogamous group. The Gond divide themselves by the cluster of deities they worship.

Linege as a corporate group is not much functional among the weaker sections as it is among the dominant groups. For them neighbourhood members mostly participate in marriage and accompany the bridegroom. Their marriage distances, of-course, are relatively less. The dominant sections have greater marriage distances and for these lineage affiliation is much more important than neighbourhood affiliation.

Among the poor people irrespective of community affiliation a family consists of husband, wife, and their unmarried children. It works like a cell having limited network of relationship that does not extend beyond the primary relations. The well-off section has the maximum frequency of extended family. The reason behind seems to be economic. Cultivation needs more hands and its cost is minimum when the holding is big enough for a pair of bullock. Further, women labour is needed for various agricultural operations. If there is an old mother in the family to attend young children, other women can go out to work.

With the exception of the Rajput, maternal cross cousin marriage is allowed among all communities. The Musalman have fraternal and maternal types of cross-cousin marriage.

Widow marriage is permitted among all groups other tan the Rajput, though such cases are rare in the village. Cases of desertion both by man and woman and remarriage are more among the poor Mali and Bouddha. It appears more to be related to poverty than their respective social organisations. Monogamy is the usual pattern irrespective of caste or community affiliation. Kinship terminology is almost similar among all groups but their manifestations differ between the dominant and the weak.

Social Mobility

In this part of Vidarbha, the Mahar are numerically dominant[4]. They used to be considered very unclean and treated as untouchables by the upper caste Hindus. They had no right of entrance to the village temple or drawing water from the village wells. They were so much discriminated by members of other Hindu castes that they could hardly feel that they also belonged to Hinduism. As a Bouddha retorts, "Before conversion to neo-Buddhism we were Mahar only. We were never treated as fellow Hindu by the high castes".

The Mahar reacted to the indignity and social injustice *en masse*. Eventually, neo-Buddhist movement initiated by Dr. Ambedkar and subsequent formation of the Republican Party of India gave the Mahar a new identity. Under the leadership of Dr. Ambedkar they organised themselves as a formidable force of national importance and *en masse* embraced neo-Buddhism in 1956 at Nagpur. It is estimated that nearly two and half lakhs Mahar[5] converted themselves to neo-Buddhism in one day. One of the objectives of the movement was to throw away the age-old pressure of being low born. They wanted to eradicate social injustice and promote economic betterment.

The Mahars of Barbadi also insisted on social justice. As a Bouddha recalls, "We are aware that one can improve one's economic condition by dint of hard labour and perseverance or by the help of governmental programmes. But stigma of being low born is difficult to eradicate. It is the social context that is important in this respect". They are very much inspired by Ambedkar, though very few are familiar with the preachings of Bouddha or Ambedkar. They, however, known that the year 1956 was a turning point, though none among the villagers was ceremonially ever converted to neo-Buddhism. As they say, *"Baba saheb pukar diye our ham sab Bouddha ban gaye"* (Baba saheb proclaimed and we became Bouddha). Since 1956, they have given up the practice of lifting dead animals and eating beef or carrion. In the village, they gave up participating in the *bhajan* at Nal Saheb's place. They also replaced idols of Vitthal and Rukma by that of Lord Buddha. Change has been effected in the marriage incantations also. Another important attempt made by the Bouddha was for eradication of mass illiteracy. They are aware that control over land, which is a source of power in an agrarian society cannot be immediately achieved but they can have control over communicational resources through education, and mobilise themselves as an important pressure group which in a democratic set up is always advantageous. They know that there are reserved vacancies in Government departments for them and they try hard for achieving them. Some of them now hold good positions and as a result, though in the village they are not treated at par with higher caste groups, in their respective offices they are not discriminated.

As a result of this achievement, there has been a significant change in the identity of the people even at the village context. People who used to be called *dher* for their traditional occupation are Bouddha even to the members of upper castes. Some of course, think that what is the harm if we call them so". But the fact is that though the demand for the new identity is intense the members of higher castes purify their house if a Mahar entered there. Now that situation has also changed and an educated Bouddha can enter into the courtyard of a high caste freely. In Panchayat meetings the Bouddha members used to be served tea in earthen cups and thereby discriminated from others. They protested against this and are now served tea in cups along with other members. Still there is a difference as the Bouddha members have to wash the cups they use. The educated and leaders among the Bouddha sit on the same *dari* (cotton carpet) or very close to the upper caste members when there is any important meeting concerning the village affair held at any house of the higher castes. The latter show courtesy to them and even serve tea in plastic cups though mentally they still seem to have reservations.

Formerly on occasions of wedding or other feasts in the house, members of higher castes used to invite the Mahar as well, though they were entertained with discriminated treatment. Now, as they demand equal treatment, this practice has been stopped. As a member of the dominant section remarks, "Every man has his own sense of humour and pride and is eager to preserve the same. They demand that we should honour their pride at our cost. That is not possible. So, we stopped inviting them to any feast". The dominant section does not put much importance to the new religion of the Bouddha. To them, it is just a change of name. They observe, "Those who are educated and have contract with the outside world have to some extent changed. The bulk are still as backward as they used to be. Even they eat beef privately".

Conversion of the Mahar to neo-Buddhism did not give them the social status they aspired for. The educated Bouddha youth though are aware of this phenomenon but they do not accept it as truth. Their religious transformation is also more symbolic than concrete. By renouncing Hinduism they are becoming more orthodox, more *sanskritized*. Only outwardly did they replace the Hindu idols by the image of Buddha. Otherwise, they are trying to shape their way of living in the model of upper caste Hindus.This is the real crux of the problem of their attaining higher social status. The new religion and the new identity fail to emancipate the people because of their upper caste Hindu reference model which make them the victim of Hindu system of hierarchy. It is a sort of vicious circle and the people in their attempt to come out of the system, have fallen back into its fold again.

The village society is rather rigid and not only the dominant groups expressed indifference in extending recognition to the Bouddha, even many belonging to the weaker groups are unwilling to accept their elevated status inspite of their significant progress in many aspects of life. The Chambhar still consider the Bouddha inferior though to the higher caste Hindus both are untouchables.

The Bouddha being numerically dominant care little whether the Chambhar admit their elevated social position. Their efforts, particularly that of the youth, are indomitable. The older generation still cling to the age old values and have regard for the set norms of the village society. The younger generation, in this respect has totally alienated itself. A great many of them are thinking of moving out of village so as to free themselves from the pressure of tradition and that would enable them to establish themselves as an emancipated group.

Dynamics of Social Relationship

Dominance can be defined in terms of numerical strength, economic and political power, and social and ritual status. In Barbadi, no group is dominant on all counts. In numerical strength the Mali are the dominant in the village. Thus, they had the potential for absolute political dominance though they could not attain it. The Teli and Kalar, inspite of much low representation, have a greater say in the village politics. Economically the Rajput, Teli and Kalar dominate the scene and in socio-ritual status the Rajput occupy the topmost position in the village. Thus we find multiple important pressure groups operating in the village and who would dominate in village affairs largely depends on the context and maneuverability of these groups.

The Rajput and Gujar maintain a distance from other villagers except during religious functions. They never join any feast entertainment organised by the Mali, Kalar, or Teli. In the village contextual weakness or strength is identified in terms of ethnicity or caste affiliation and not in terms of family or any other unit. According to control over landholdings the bulk of the Mali belong to the weaker group. But the villagers in general are more concern about ritual position of the community than their economic achievement. On the other hand, inspite of their high numerical strength, high literacy, and moderate control over landholdings, the Bouddha suffer most on account of the stigma attached to being low born. However, the Chambhar, Bouddha, and Mang appear to be the weakest and they are referred to as Harijan by the dominant castes. Due to the influence of Sewagram and Gandhiji on the social life of the villagers the untouchables are referred to as Harijan. This, however, is not liked by the young Bouddha any more. As one of them reported, Gandhiji did damage to us by calling us Harijan. Are we alone the children of Hari? Who are others then? Why should we be discriminated from others"?

There are other groups in between the dominant and the weakest like Vadhai, Khati-Wadhai, Shippi, Kosthi, Mahali, Warthi, and the two *adivasi* groups, Gond and Goari, and the Musalman. They are not untouchables and have very little resources under their control.

Social interaction among members of various groups may be observed through their participation on important occasions like marriage, funeral etc. During our stay in the village a number of marriages took place and we analysed the pattern of interaction across the community through nature of invitation extended to different members sand their responses in the form of participation. Such cases in brief are presented in the Table 4.

An examination of facts reveals that people with high economic and social status do not invite those belonging to low social status. People with somewhat better economic condition sometimes invite, as it is in the first case, poor people. One man invited three friends from Bouddha community but had to treat them separately. After eating they had to lift their own used plates. They did not mind this on personal consideration. Their younger boys do not accept such invitation as they consider it derogatory or insulting to lift used plates after eating. Another Mali invited the Gond, Goari and Musalman. Inspite of his socialistic bent of mind, he failed to invite the Bouddha for fear of adverse public opinion. As he is a rich man, he is more susceptible to public criticism which was not there in the former case. There are many in the village who personally wish to entertain

TABLE 4: Composition of host and invitees

Name and caste of the marriage party	Economic condition	Invitation extended to (other than caste member)	Actual attendance by	Remarks
Madhukar Lende (Mali)	Medium	Teli Gond Musalman, Bouddha	all attended	The Gond and Musalman were entertained in the same row. The Bouddha were treated separately and had to lift their used leaf-plates after meals. They paid no gift.
Namdeo Gaotre (Mali)	High	Mali,Teli Kalar, Rajput Maratha	all attended	Only the high castes were invited and gifts were accepted from them.
Changdeo (Bouddha)	Poor	friends from Mali Gond,only important persons from Kalar, Teli,Rajput	Gond attended the marriage feast.	He is a graduate so he distributed invitation letters to all important persons of the village. Nobody but a Gond attended, even his intimate friends from other communities did not turn up.
Premdas Jangam (Bouddha)	Medium friend	One teli attended	Not	
Ajab Shende (Mali)	High	Kalar, Teli, Rajput, Khati, Musalman, Gond, and Goari	all attended	Khati, Musalman Gond, and Goari did not present any gift.
Govind Sonaye (Gujar)	High	Teli,Mali Rajput	all attended	All the invitees presented some gift.
Kamal Dhamane (Gujar)	Medium	Teli,Mali, Rajput, Kalar,Gond.	all attended	All the invitees presented some some gift.
Dhamaji Nagose (Goari)	Poor	Musalman, Teli,Mali, Kalar.	Musalman, Kalar attended	A gift was given by the Kalar.

friends irrespective of their caste or community affiliation but dare not doing that publicly. Once we observed that a Teli could not invite his Bouddha friend on a particular occasion. He entertained him in his house the next day with sweetmeats and himself washed his used plates. He did not offer him cooked food as in that case the plates used by him could be more defilling. We never found any member of higher caste, even of younger generation, visiting friends in Bouddhapura. However, when such a friend visits them they extend all cordiality and offer betel leaves. If ever invited by the high caste people, the people with low social status cannot give any gift to the bride as the same is not acceptable by the higher caste people. The people of low ritual and economic status never invite the Rajput and Gujar. Among the dominant section, the Kalar because of their ritually low position are more approachable in this respect.

The members of the weaker and the weakest sections refer to those of dominant section as *malak* or *sarkar* but there is no opposite generic term. *Malak* and *sarkar* indicate respect. Members of weaker sections are referred to by their individual names.

The weaker and dominant do not have much social interaction, though there is enough economic interaction between them. Socially they have their respective domains. There is however a common place where they meet without any inhibition and caste consciousness, that is the shop of illicit liquor. There is such a shop in the Bouddhapura and liquor is distilled by a Bouddha. The Mali, Teli and Kalar visit the place and drink together, even from the same glass with the Bouddha. One Mali even takes his food along with drinks in the house of Rama Bouddha, the distiller. At that time they forget their socio-ritual statuses though during community feasts they carefully maintain it. There are some other distilleries run by Rajput, Gujar, and Kalr where the affluent Rajput, Gujar and Teli meet to have the drinks. Many Mali also indulge in illicit distilling. It may be incidental that the distilleries maintained by the Rajput are visited only by the Rajput, Gujar, and Teli who belong to the higher income bracket and enjoy very high social position. A liberal Kalar and a Maratha argue that if the people of high caste can drink liquor distilled and served by the Bouddha and even when they can share the drink from the same glass what is wrong if they take water from them too. Once these two gentlemen drank water from the well of Chambhar at night. At this, the members of upper castes got annoyed but they could not do anything to the deviants as they were very wealthy. But even the deviants, by violating the set norm could not bring about any perceptible change in the existing system of the society.

The exploitation of the weaker by the dominant is primarily organizational in character. In comparison exploitation of the weaker by their fellowmen is direct. A rich Bouddha extends loan to the poor fellowmen at a very high rate of interest. As these people do not have any other sources to borrow, he exploits the situation to his maximum advantage. There is a Gond who works as *mate* in the road construction work. It is his duty to engage daily wage labourers, maintain the muster roll, and disburse weekly payments. He shows many names in the register who actually work elsewhere and not in road construction. On the day of payment they gather to receive salary. Out of Rs. 2.25 per day per labourer the Gond *Mate* takes Rs. 2.00 for himself against each 'bogus' labourer. By supporting his corrupt practice they insure themselves of his reciprocal help during lean days. The Gond *mate*, however, does not consider it unfair as according to him,there is a long chain of corruption in the construction work which involves almost everyone engaged in the job. In this chain, he considers himself a very small fry who is incapable of bringing about any change in the practice.

Inspite of co-existence of abject poverty and relative affluence side by side in the village situation, people in general have accepted their life ways for granted. The impoverished do not accuse any body for their deprivation, not do they try to seek the reason thereof. Poverty has pushed them to such a sub-human level that most of them lost the courage of expressing their problematic existence. Exceptions are the Bouddha, but they too are not as vocal for economic parity as for social equality. There is no apparent tension in the village though one can feel their suppressed discontentment when one speaks to them. The dominant sections are so secured in their position that they put little importance to the discontentment of the poor.

A few noticeable changes have, however, occurred during the post-Independence period in the village situation. Perhaps the most important one is the awareness of the poor of equal rights for living. Due to awakening of the Bouddha community the dominant sections felt pressurised to accept the former as full member of the society which was denied to them for centuries. Communication net work played an important role in this respect. Besides, introduction of

Panchayati Raj based on adult franchise provided a forum even to the weak to express themselves which was not possible in earlier days. The dominant sections are not very happy about the developments though they have accepted the change.

Ethics and World View of the Weaker Section

In comparison to the dominant sections, the world view of the weaker section is narrow and is confined only to their immediate boundary. They are less aware of the country and its greater tradition. The weaker section do not show any typical ethical norm which can be considered to be the product of their weak conditions. They share the same ethical norms prevalent in the society at large. They show the same kind of notion towards sympathy, cooperation, fellow feeling etc. Due to their poverty they cannot be always sufficiently generous to offer *supari* to their visitors. Those who are comparatively well off among them, offer *supari* or even tea to the guest. Whether dominant or weak, the people are very much busy with their own work. There is not much scope for community gathering. Not much co-operation is observed in the village in any sphere of life. At the time of wedding of a Bouddha, we observed that no body from his community gave him electricity connection for playing the electrically operated amplifier set. He had to hire battery operated amplifier at a higher rate. Similar treatments are very common in the village.

Alcoholism cannot be said to be related to the condition of weakness. The people in the village, irrespective of their caste or creed or economic condition, are very much addicted to liquor. The dominant sections indulge in it as they can afford to spend and to the poor it is the only source of enjoyment. Gambling by card is very much prevalent among the poor Mali. Rich people also gamble during festivities. The habit of gambling and drinking liquor is relatively less among the Bouddha. But they too, do not spend their leisure hours for any constructive purposes. Most of the evenings we used to observe school going children gossiping near the Bouddha temple. For doing something constructive, they think it is the government's responsibility. Whether educated or not, their themes of gossiping centre around Hindi films and sex.

There are two different explanations for the weakness, one offered by the weaker sections belonging to high or non-untouchable group and the other by the untouchable groups specially by the

Bouddha. To the former weakness is mainly economic. They do not suffer from any feeling of inequality on account of their birth, whereas the Bouddha feel that they suffer mainly for their being low born. The weaker sections of the intermediate caste think that there would be high and low in the society and the birth in a particular caste or community depends on one's own fate. So, on their part there is no effort to overcome this. On the contrary, the Bouddha think that by birth all men are equal. It is the dominant Hindu who make them untouchables and ascribe a low social status. Unlike the other groups, they think that they can improve their condition and their attempts are quite visible in many respects. To improve their condition they put 50 per cent individual endeavour. According to them, religious movement speed up the change. Though very much individualistic, because of common religion they can organise group activities like the celebration of Buddha Jayanti or cleaning of any area in their neighbourhood. It is very difficult to organise the youth of the other weaker sections. Often the latter differ on many issues and pick up quarrels among themselves which is not so among the Bouddha.

Economic Organisation

Economy of the village is land-based and majority of the people are dependent on land directly or indirectly. Out of 259 households, 68 households (26.6%) are wholely dependent on cultivation and 119 households (46.5%) are dependent on labour only. The rest are engaged in service, trade or traditional occupation along with cultivation or labour as their secondary source of income. Those who have sufficient access to land, 50 per cent of them do not put their own labour in production mechanism. People having minimum or no land have labour as the primary economic resource.

The economy of the labour households are also dependent mainly on agriculture, i.e. 68 per cent of the households sell their labour to 26 farm households. In fact, this proportion will be even less as 26 per cent comprises all farmers, big or small, and in the village, the ratio of small farmers with limited capacity to employ is high. The people of the village are engaged in (i) labour — agricultural and non-agricultural on daily wage basis (ii) agricultural labour and allied jobs on annual contract, (iii) small trade and craft (iv) service.

Organisation of Labour

In the village, the Mali and Bouddha are the main suppliers /of labourers. The Rajput, Gujar, Teli, Kalar and a few rich Mali are engaged in cultivation of their family farm. Among them, only the poor Teli households go for labour. Except the two male heads among the Gujar, none is engaged in labour on daily wage basis. Their women work in their own field but never as hired labourers. A significant proportion of women belonging to the Mali and Bouddha work as agricultural and non-agricultural labourers.

Next to daily paid labourers, the jobs of *saldar* (annual farm servant) and *gurakhi* (annual cattle keeper) are important. A *saldar* is employed on contract for one year on the first day of Chaitra. The remuneration for the whole term varies from Rs. 400 to 600 in cash and 600 to 720 kgs. of Jowar, depending on the capability of the farm servant sand ability of the employer. Ordinarily, the labourers do not like the job of *saldar* as there is practically no leisure and no freedom of work for a *saldar*. He is expected to work for the master for 20 hours a day, rest at night either at the master's place or in his field. No leave is due to him during the whole service period. Salary for the period of absence on account of any exigency is deducted. Payment is made on monthly basis.

The cattlekeeper or dairy servants on annual contract are paid less than the *saldar*. Only big farmers having more than 20 acres of land employ them. The Mali provide the maximum number of saldars to the big farmers in the village and they are followed by Bouddha in this respect. It is observed that often *saldars* change their masters. Breach of contract and going to serve the other master is a common occurrence and in such cases the employer suffers. In earlier days such servants used to serve a master for several years. Now they prefer to change masters almost every year. Usually the same set of employers engage the same set of servants with some interval readjustment. In most of the time right of choice lies with the servants.

Among the non-agricultural labour, work in road construction and loading-unloading of goods in market or railway station are important. Specially the youngmen of the Bouddha community prefer this kind of labour to agricultural labour which they consider very time consuming. The young Mali boys also prefer such jobs while the elderly members of the community prefer to work in agricultural fields.

Differences are observed between the two sets of labourers (agricultural and non-agricultural). Both receive weekly payments but those engaged in road construction spend the whole amount of their earning on liquor and mutton on the day of payment. They never think for their future. The only aspiration they have is to set a source of regular daily wage earning. The agricultural labourers always try to invest their money as capital expenses like buying a pair of bullocks, cultivating others' land on share-cropping basis etc. though in most cases the return they get is incompatible to what they invest. Agriculture provides opportunities to labourers for full employment for six months a year. During the remaining six months they are underemployed or unemployed.

In Barbadi though the labourers are dependent on farmers, specially the big farmers, they do not suffer from any feeling of subordination or deprivation. The labourers are mostly poor, sometimes they remain on the verge of starvation for two to three days a week. As a result, they get accustomed to such living. Even when starving, as it was observed in case of some Goari and Mali families, they do not go to any cultivator for employment. When asked a Goari replied, "How can I go if somebody does not call me for work"? Many a times we observed that the Rajput women came to poor Mali houses to call the women for agricultural work on daily wage. For engaging them as labourers a cultivator has to go to the labourers personally.

The working hour for a day labourer is from 10 0' clock in the morning to 5 O' clock in the evening with a break between 1.00 p.m. and 2.00 p.m. The wage rate for a man is between Rs. 2.50 and Rs. 3.00 per day and for the woman it varies from Rs. 1.25 to Rs. 1.75. The relationship between the labourer and master is commercial and contractual. Presence of the master in the field is a must, otherwise the labourers would do as minimum work as they can.

Control Over Resources

Jowar and cotton are main agricultural crops in this area. The soil of this area is suitable particularly for cotton cultivation. The best cotton soil Kali I is not in abundance in the village. Here most of the lands are Kali II and Morand I that are locally called *bhari* and *sadharan* respectively. All superior quality lands are in the hands of big farmers belonging to high castes.

Villagers of Barbadi possess 1724.99 acres of cultivable land the distribution of which is shown in Table 5.

TABLE 5: Dimension of weakness or dominance in terms of control over resources

Sl. No.	Caste/ community	Total house-hold	Landless house-hold No.		Land owning house-hold No.		Total land acre		Total land per capita (in acre)
1.	Bhui	4	4	100.00	—	—	—	—	—
2.	Bouddha	52	31	59.62	21	40.38	196.62	11.4	0.771
3.	Chambhar	4	3	75.00	1	25.00	8.30	0.5	0.296
4.	Goari	3	3	100.00	—	—	—	—	—
5.	Gond	6	2	33.33	4	66.67	31.85	1.8	1.027
6.	Kalar	10	3	30.00	7	70.00	193.87	11.2	3.728
7.	Kosthi	1	1	100.00	—	—	—	—	—
8.	Khatiwadhai	2	2	100.00	—	—	—	—	—
9.	Mahali	1	1	100.00	—	—	—	—	—
10.	Mali	84	51	60.71	33	39.29	339.96	19.7	0.835
11.	Mang	3	2	66.67	1	33.33	5.41	0.3	0.386
12.	Maratha	2	1	50.00	1	50.00	29.89	1.7	2.909
13.	Musalman	9	3	33.33	6	66.67	51.61	3.0	1.299
14.	Rajput	8	1	12.50	7	87.50	191.11	11.1	4.066
15.	Gujar	13	2	15.38	11	84.62	156.98	9.1	2.039
16.	Shimpi	3	2	66.67	1	33.33	26.34	1.5	1.881
17.	Teli	48	19	39.58	29	60.42	486.72	28.2	2.028
18.	Wadhai	5	4	80.00	1	20.00	2.13	0.1	0.071
19.	Warthi	1	0	0.00	1	100.00	5.00	0.3	1.667
Total		259	135	52.12	124	47.88	1724.99	99.9	1.315

The Bhui, Goari, Kosthi, Mahali and Wadhai do not have any land. Out of a total of 259 households, 135 are landless. Among the 124 landholding households, the Teli possess the maximum amount of land. The other important land holding communities are the Rajput, Gujar, Kalar, and Mali. Among the untouchables the Bouddha own substantial amount of land though of inferior quality. Per capita landholding is highest among the Rajput i.e., about five acres. Among the Kalar and Teli it is three and two acres respectively. Per capita landholding among the Mali and Bouddha is about an acre each. Thus, the Rajput, Gujar, Kalar, and Teli control the major landholdings of the village.

TABLE 6: Intra & inter community pattern of distribution of landholding

Sl. No.	Caste/ community	Size of the landholding										Total number of household owning land
		Upto 10 acre		10 - 20		20 - 30		30 - 40		Above 40 acre		
		No.	%	No.	%	No.	%	No.	%	No.	%	
1.	Bouddha	14	23.33 66.67	6	15.38 28.57	1	9.09 4.76	—	—	—	—	21
2.	Chambhar	1	1.67 100.00	—	—	—	—	—	—	—	—	1
3.	Gond	2	3.33 50.50	2	5.13 50.00	—	—	—	—	—	—	4
4.	Kalar	1	1.67 14.29	4	10.26 57.14	—	—	—	—	2	66.67 28.57	7
5.	Mali	21	35.00 63.64	8	20.51 24.24	1	9.09 3.03	3	27.27 9.09			33
6.	Mang	1	1.67 100.00	—	—	—	—	—	—	—	—	1
7.	Maratha	—	—	—	—	1	9.09 100.00	—	—	—	—	1
8.	Musalman	5	8.33 83.33	1	2.56 16.67	—	—	—	—	—	—	6
9.	Rajput	3	5.00 42.66	1	2.56 14.29	—	—	2	18.18 28.57	1	33.33 14.29	7
10.	Gujar	3	5.00 27.27	6	15.38 54.55	1	9.09 9.09	1	9.09 9.09	11		
11.	Shimpi	—	—	—	—	1	9.09 100.00	—	—	—	—	1
12.	Teli	7	11.67 24.14	11	28.21 37.93	6	54.55 20.69	5	45.45 17.24	29		
13.	Wadhai	1	1.67 100.00	—	—	—	—	—	—	—	—	1
14.	Warthi	1	1.67 100.00	—	—	—	—	—	—	—	—	1
	Total	60	48.39	39	31.45	11	8.87	11	8.87	3	2.42	124

6. Upper percentages compare between communities and lower percentages compare within communities.

Intra and inter community pattern of distribution of landholdings indicates the relative weakness and dominance of individual communities. Out of the 124 land owning households, 60 households (48.39%) have landholding up to ten acres. A family can barely subsist on ten acres of land. So, no cultivator takes the trouble of cultivating land by himself if he happens to possess five acres or below. Those who have land up to ten acres may be called small or marginal farmers. The major bulk of this category comes from the Mali and Bouddha. Farmers belonging to the dominant section have greater concentration in the categories of medium, big, and very big landholdings. So they devote full time and energy in agricultural work. Further, most of the land of the small cultivators are inferior in quality because of which these families cannot solely depend on cultivation..

In respect of land holding the Mali need special mention as they present a different picture from others. The Rajput, Gujar, Teli and Kalar have less small farmers and more medium and big farmers. Conversely, the Bouddha have more small farmers and less medium and big farmers. Among the Mali, 63.64 per cent are small farmers and nine per cent big farmers. Thus, among the dominant, wealth is distributed in a uniform fashion and among the Bouddha and other weaker groups poverty is spread out in a uniform manner. The Mali present uniform distribution of wealth as well as poverty.

Organisation of Production

In Barbadi different systems of cultivation are prevalent. They are locally called *kastekari*, *bhare* and *theka* or *makta*. When one cultivates his family farm by self labour and supervision that is known as *kastekari*.

A small farmer having no bullocks usually gives land to other small farmers having bullocks for ploughing on cash payment. Similar contracts are negotiated with others for weeding sand harvesting. Overall supervision is the only job left with him. This system of cultivation is known as *bhare*, which means cultivation through hired labourers. In such cases the farmers are primarily engaged in some other works like tailoring, or running a grocery shop etc.

Cultivation through *theka* or *makta* is also practised by the small farmers. This is a lease of land for one year against cash payment and the lessee is known as *maktadar*. Owners of small landholdings prefer to give land to tenants or sharecroppers having small landholding, also a pair of bullocks. Most of the time such farmers take contract of ploughing land of non-cultivating small farmers or sell self labour and bullock labour to big cultivators on daily wage basis. Now a days, due to the new Tenancy Act the term *makta* has been replaced by *bhare chittee*. It is shown in the document as a sort of contract between the owner of the land and a tenant or *maktadar* as if the farmer is paying some amount of money to the latter for cultivation of a piece of land. But in fact, the money is given by a *maktadar* to the owner of the land as rent.

Sharing of crops is known as *batoi* and the share cropper is called *batoidar*. The cost of production is wholly borne by share croppers and the yield is equally divided. In all cases whether he is a *maktadar* or *batoidar* he refers the owner of the land as *malak*.

Kastekar, *maktadar* or *batoidar* are not exclusive categories because a small cultivator is also a *kastekar*, and at the same time he cultivates others' land on share or *makta*. We can make exclusive category of the farmers on the basis of certain criterion like degree of involvement in the work of cultivation and dependency on it, quality of land and the yield pattern etc. *Kastekari* means agricultural job but *kastekar* are those who are full time farmers or owner-cultivators. In local usage, a *kastekar* has to have sufficient cultivable land for one pair of bullocks. Marginal farmers are characterised by small land holdings of inferior quality and low yield. The owner-cultivators have capabilities and resources which they can gainfully utilise in the mechanism of production. All of them are equipped with better bred bullocks, irrigation wells, electric pump sets and can manipulate sources of credit agencies essential for meeting financial needs. Marginal farmers depict an opposite picture. Their production technology is ill-equipped, ill-financed, and the people are least resourceful to tap external assistance.

On the basis of their nature and extent of involvement in the organisation of production the village population may be divided into several categories as (i) owner-cultivators (ii) non-cultivating small farmers, (iii) marginal farmers, and (iv) landless agricultural labour. Distribution of households in terms of agrarian hierarchy is given in Table 7.

As it could be seen from the Table, most of the *kastekars* belong to upper castes. Out of a total of 114 farmers, 92 have their respective pair of bullocks and 50 have their respective irrigation wells. Thirty-six of them are beset with electric pumps. Among the remaining 14, water is drawn by cattle power through indigeneous device called *moat*. As there is no canal irrigation facilities in the area, a farmer has to make his own arrangement of water supply.

Government loans distributed through different welfare agencies were utilised in most of the cases for digging wells or buying a pump set. Some of these wells do not have sufficient water to irrigate even 10 acres of land during summer months. The distribution of wells by caste is given in Table 8.

TABLE 7: Weakness and dominance in terms of agrarian hierarchy

Caste/ community	Owner	Non-cultivator	Marginal/ small farmer	Labour farmer	Others	Total
Bhui	—	—	—	4	—	4
Bouddha	2	10	9	25	6	52
Chambhar	—	—	1	—	3	4
Goari	—	—		3	—	3
Gond	—	3		3		6
Kalar	10	—	—	—	—	10
Kosthi	—	—	—	—	1	1
Khati Wadhai	—	—	—	—	2	2
Mahali	—	—	—	—	1	1
Mali	11	9	6	52	6	84
Mang	—	—	1	—	2	3
Maratha	—	—	—	—	1	2
Musalman	1	2	—	6	—	9
Rajput	5	3	—	—	—	8
Gujar	10	—	—	2	1	13
Shimpi	—	—	1	1	1	3
Teli	18	7	2	18	3	48
Wadhai	—	—	1	—	4	5
Warthi	—	1	—	—	—	1
Total	58	35	21	114	31	259

TABLE 8: Distribution of wells by caste/community

Caste/ community	No. of farmers	Well with pump	Well with moat	Only well	Total
Mali	26	11	3	4	18
Teli	27	9	2	—	11
Rajput & Gujar	18	9	2	—	11
Kalar	10	3	1	—	4
Maratha	1	1	—	—	1
Bouddha	21	3	—	1	4
Musalman	3	—	1		1
		36	9	5	50

As the Table indicates, most of the wells with pumps belong to farmers belonging to higher castes. The village credit cooperative society (established in 1946) is operative in distributing loans for meeting expenses of farming at the rate of nine per cent interest per year and ten per cent interest for credit balance. Eighty-eight farmers of the village are members of the society. Besides, there are many governmental sources like Panchayat Samiti, Land Revenue Department, Bhubikash Bank etc. from where farmers obtain loans for digging wells, installation of pump sets, purchase of bullocks etc. As lands are to be mortgaged for obtaining such loans, only big farmers can easily avail themselves of these facilities. Poor cultivators still borrow money at a very high rate of interest from *mahajan* of the village or outside for meeting their agricultural expenses. The local Patwari ordinarily acts as a contact man between villagers and governmental credit agencies for negotiating distribution of loans. Many rich farmers have direct contact with the officials and in addition the Patwari also acts in their interest. Marginal farmers, who need assistance most ordinarily fail to receive Patwari's assistance.

Economic distinctiveness among villagers is conspicuous though this does not get reflected in their social behaviour. Mutual economic cooperation (hiring of bullock etc.) are restricted within the respective categories i.e. big farmers hire the bullocks from the big farmers only and small farmers give their land on share or *makta* to the small farmers or hire bullocks from them. However, the big farmers are respected and invited to all village functions not so much as the representative of a class, but due to their personal qualities, wisdom, and resourcefulness. All, however, irrespective of rich or poor work. Here, women from all castes or communities put their manual labour in production process, no matter whether they are rich or poor. The big landowners do not hesitate to employ their near relatives when necessities arise. This is a favour to relatives who do not have adequate financial support. In this rural set up, inspite of the existence of economic categories, no perceptible distance between groups could be observed.

Access of the Weaker Sections to Agricultural Innovations

As Barbadi is a big village and also close to the Panchayat Samiti office, it received adequate attention of extension agents and had enough exposure to various agricultural innovations. Even then the farmers of the village have shown little initiative in adoption of agricultural innovations other than in employing electric pump sets. At the time of study, only ten big farmers had iron ploughs and six had sprayers. None from the weaker sections had any. Twelve farmers of them belonged to the higher income bracket. Peoples' reaction to programmes are unwelcome. Once in 1969, Government pushed high yielding jowar with a loan of Rs. 200 for meeting cultivation expenses. The programme was pushed to many farmers including several small cultivators who had neither good soil nor the requisite irrigation facilities. So for them it was a case of complete failure.

Dominant sections exploit the governmental sources even in unfair ways. They do not refund loan in time. But as they have plenty of land in different titles they can manage to obtain loans every year. The weaker sections are handicapped in this respect and wait till the previous loan is repaid. Chemical fertilisers as such are not popular among the cultivators. Even the successful cultivators believe that chemical fertilisers spoil the inner strength of the soil. None in the village uses recommended dosages of fertiliser. No farmer from the weaker sections applies chemical fertiliser to their agricultural fields. They use cowdung as manure.

State Cotton Trading Corporation is very disadvantageous for marginal growers as it does not pay loan instantly. The recently introduced Tenancy Act did not help them either. Previously tenant cultivators could grow something at their own cost. Now the system has been replaced by *bhare* and under this system the tenant cultivators have been transformed to agricultural labourers.

Such experiences frustrate farmers belonging to weaker section and make them apathetic to governmental programmes. Often they say "Experiences of the last 25 years convince us that all governmental programmes are only for the rich. They have nothing to do with the poor".

Occupational Mobility

For a caste or community as a whole no occupational mobility has taken place in the village except the abandonment of lifting of dead cattle by the Mahar. There is, however, an extra-ordinary urge among the agricultural labourers for possession of agricultural lands. Since Independence some landless people could buy land and thereby some labourers have been transformed to small cultivators. Details of land transfer in the village is given in Table 9.

TABLE 9: Transference of land since Independence

Sl. no.	Caste/ community	Number of buyer			Amount of land bought			Number of sellers	Amount of land sold
		Without land	With land	Total	Without land	With land	Total		
1.	Bouddha	7	8	15	37.24	47.48	24.72	1	7.35
2.	Chambhar	—	1	1	—	8.30	8.30	—	—
3.	Gond	1	—	1	7.00	—	7.00	—	—
4.	Kalar	1	—	1	3.78	—	3.78	—	—
5.	Mail	3	8	11	10.74	33.14	43.88	1	9.55
6.	Mang	1	—	1	5.00	—	5.00	—	—
7.	Maratha	—	—	—	—	—	—	1	9.00
8.	Musalman	1	—	1	7.00	—	7.00	—	—
9.	Rajput	—	5	5	—	95.60	95.60	3	59.60
10.	Shimpi	—	1	1	—	19.00	19.00	—	—
11.	Teli	3	15	18	26.25	114.54	140.79	3	23.65
12.	Wadhai	1	—	1	2.13	—	2.13	—	—
	Total	18	38	50	99.14	318.06	417.20	9	109.15

From among the weaker sections only the Bouddha could buy some land. Three landless families of Mali also bought land. Most of the buyers already had sufficient land in their possession. This suggests that changes which have occurred in this respect are marginal.

The number of sellers of land is obviously very few among the weaker sections. Major land transactions have taken place among the Rajputs. In earlier days, they bought land beyond their requirement at a cheaper rate. Now, observing the landhunger among the landless they avail themselves of the opportunity of selling inferior quality and distantly located lands to them. Thus, even when the landless weaker sections buy land, the major benefits of transaction go to the well-off.

Consumption Pattern and Material Life Style

Jowar is the staple food of the people. It is cheaper than wheat and rice sand the majority of the villagers and nearly cent per cent of the weaker sections live on it. Well-to-do families of the village consume wheat and rice.

Villagers start the day with morning tea. As milk is very scarce and expensive, the poor have tea without milk. With the exception of infants, villagers do not drink milk. The rich prefer to have curd and buttermilk

The well-off families of higher caste usually do not have breakfast. An adults' eating breakfast is looked down upon. Most of them, however, have launch by 11 O'clock before going to the field for work. Labourers eat some left over food of the previous night before going for work. As both the sexes from the weaker sections go for labour, they individually carry their respective food packets. Small children who stay back home have their food by themselves whenever they like. Children of well-off families are made to observe fixed time schedule in this respect.

The main items of meals for the majority is *chun bhakar chatni bhakar* i.e., curry prepared out of powdered gram *(besan)* and *roti* of *jowar*. Curry is sometimes substituted by seasonal vegetables. Variation of food items can be correlated with the socio-economic condition of the community concerned some details of which are given in Table 10.

TABLE 10: Variation of food items according to economic category

Economic class	Food items
Very poor	*Chana, bhakar, chatni,* tea without milk.
Poor	*Chuna, bhakar,* tea without milk.
Medium	*dal, bhaji, bhakar,* or roti, tea with milk and jaggery.
Rich	*dal, bhaji, bhakar,* mango juice, (seasonal), tea with milk and jaggery.
Very rich	*dal, bhaji, bhakar* or *roti,* rice, buttermilk, milk,mango juice(seasonal),tea with milk and jaggery.

The impoverished lot mostly survive on *bhakar* and *chatni* (pasted chilli). When they do not get any employment for days together, they live on boiled gram *(chana)*.

The Rajput and Gujar are vegetarian by habit. Though there is no restriction for the Teli and Mali against eating non-vegetarian food usually their well-off sections observe vegetarianism. The poor are non-vegetarian and like to eat mutton which they can seldom afford.

The food situation remains almost uniform throughout the year in case of higher economic class. For the labourers, sowing and harvesting seasons are the best as they can afford to buy sufficient food from their earning. During the remaining period, the labourer families live on the threshold of starvation.

The major portion of the expenditure of the poor is on cereals. Even then most of the labourer families do not get sufficient cereals to eat. In local standard, an individual needs one kg. *atta* a day which they can rarely have. Sometimes the lady of the house borrows a minimum quantity of cereals required for the family from neighbours, which is also not easily available.

The next major item of expenditure of the poor people is on spices, specially chilli which serves as a substitute for pulse and vegetables. They spend minimum on milk and milk products. When they cannot have two meals regularly, the question of nutritive diet is superfluous. Per capita expenditure on food is much higher among the rich and very rich in comparison to the landless people.

Per capita annual income is found to be highest (Rs.1035) among the Kalar and minimum is among the Bhui (Rs.218), the average of the village being Rs. 451.91. Ten communities namely Shimpi, Goari, Kosthi, Bhui, Chambhar, Gond, Khati-Wadhai, Gujar, Wadai and Mali have income below the average. The Rajput, Teli, and Kalar have fairly high annual income ranging between Rs. 600 and Rs. 1000. It is generally observed that people with high social status have higher income. The majority of the community earn up to Rs. 500. Seven communities have per capita income beyond Rs. 500. Among them the Rajput, Teli, Kalar and Maratha are dominant in every respect. Though in low social status, the Bouddha have made much progress in economic sphere. Their per capita income is Rs. 574. On the contrary, the annual per capita income of the Mali is Rs. 413 only.

Except very rich families, no one has surplus in the village. The landless people spend little on consumer articles. Their income is so meagre that they can save nothing. Expenditure on investment is maximum among the economically dominant groups like Kalar, Teli, and Rajput. Those who have more investment also have more loans. The labourers borrow for meeting consumption expenses whereas the dominant sections borrow for investment purposes. Thus, they are not indebted in the sense as the weaker sections are.

Almost all loans for cultivation purposes are obtained from governmental sources. Persons who provide loan for meeting consumption and other necessities are the money lenders. Two persons, one from the Teli and the other from the Bouddha, extend loan for such purposes. As they are not licensed brokers, they maintain the document in such a way as if they are not lending money but are giving money to friends without charging any interest. Usually for heavy amounts such documents are maintained. For petty loans like Rs. 10 or so no document is maintained. Transaction takes place on the basis of mutual trust in this case and the rate of interest is exorbitantly high. Once a poor Mali borrowed Rs. 40 from the village money lender for a week at the rate of interest Rs. 10 for the week, failing which one rupee extra for each remaining days. The need was so urgent that the poor man could not imagine the rate of interest he had to pay. The interest amounted to Rs. 950 p.a. Usually they try to repay the sum within the stipulated period and never consider it exploitation. These money lenders charge from the poor a higher rate of interest and when a wealthy man takes loan they uniformly charge 25 per cent p.a.. People also borrow money from *saukar* of Wardha. Money lending business is conducted across the boundary of caste or community.

Village Panchayat

The traditional Panchayat system which was once in operation to deal with all important matters relating to major aspects of village life has now become defunct for all practical purposes. In earlier days it used to govern village politics to a considerable extent and this was responsible for the village as a whole. It did not have any formal organisation. Elderly persons of the village acted as its members and decided cases. After Independence, the statutory panchayat under the Panchayati Raj system has been introduced to the area. It has a three tier structure. The Zilla Parishad occupies the top at the district level and the Gram Panchayat is at the bottom at the village level. The Gram Panchayat consists of nine members including a coopted lady member. A secretary is there for conducting the panchayat duties like recording activities of the Panchayat and collecting house tax. The village level worker is the ex-officio Secretary of the Gram Panchayat and he is paid for his service by the State Government. Other than the Secretary, all members are elected and honorary. The office of the Sarpanch is also elected. Eight members are elected from 4 wards of the village. There is one *sipahi* attached to the Gram Panchayat belonging to the Mali caste to clean the panchayat building. He is a paid servant.

At present the Gram Panchayat is responsible only for the development work in the village like repairing roads, digging and redigging wells and soakpits, making lighting arrangement of the village lanes, distribution of land to the landless etc. Sixteen persons got land from Gram Panchayat for constructing their houses. All of them, however, were not landless. The well-off high caste people also managed to get land due to their contact with the higher authorities.

If we analyse the representation of different communities in the Panchayat it would throw some light on dominance or weakness of different communities in the sphere of power structure of the village.

TABLE 11: Representation by different communities in Gram Panchayat

Year of Panchayat election	Rajput	Maratha	Mali	Teli	Kalar	Bouddha	Total
1949	3	1	1	2	1	1	9
1959	—	1	3	2	2	1	9
1962	1	—	5	1	1	1	9
1966	1	—	3	3	—	2	9
1970	2	—	3	2	—	2	9

Among the dominant groups, the Rajput, Mali and Teli together are almost uniformly represented to the Gram Panchayat since the introduction of statutory panchayat. From the weaker groups only the Bouddha is regularly represented. Initially the Rajput, as a single group had more control over the Gram Panchayat. Gradually the Mali, Teli and Bouddha came into prominence and their proportion of representation improved. The same set of people with few changes represent the Gram Panchayat consecutively. This suggests formation of coterie of well-off section for holding control over the authority structure of the village. Leadership quality is secondary to this consideration. Only one or two members of the village panchayat has some leadership qualities. Perhaps due to this reason that the Gram Panchayat could not have the desired impact.

Among the weaker sections, except the Bouddha no group has any leader. The economic condition of the Bouddha leaders is fairly good. They are very much careful to exert their Bouddha identity and resentful about the rest of the villagers specially the dominant section. There are a few unemployed youth among them having some leadership qualities who attend the panchayat meeting regularly and are quite vocal. There is only one among them who may be considered a village leader. Leaders command respect from their fellow castemen. But across the community with the exception of the one, they suffer from inferiority complex. They like to remain confined within their own cell as an isolated self-styled leader without any accommodation for others whether weaker or stronger than them.

People display enthusiasm and interest in the village panchayat during the time of election. Otherwise they are indifferent about panchayat activities. There is a community radio-set in the panchayat hall. No important villager ever goes to listen to the news or any other programme, not even those of the common rural people. Only young boys gather there to listen to film songs broadcast from the Vibidh Bharati. Most of the people do not bear a high opinion about the activities of the Panchayat. Villagers are under the impression that the Panchayat members misappropriate public money in the plea of undertaking public work. Though they are unhappy with the functioning of the Panchayat, they have not shown initiative in attending meetings of the panchayat, or gram sabha nor make their grievances public. On an average, one gram sabha meeting is held a year and as record shows it was never attended by more than 7 villagers. The budget meeting is also attended by a few. Even all elected members of the panchayat did not attend the meeting. It may be mentioned here that the Bouddha show a great interest in attending the meetings regularly when compared with other communities. The dominant group, as a whole is apathetic to attend meetings. The economically weaker sections represented by the poor Mali, various artisan castes, Gond and the Musalman do not feel it necessary to attend panchayat meetings as they think that the panchayat has nothing to do for the poor.

The panchayat does not entertain any case of dispute regarding property rights or the like. Disputes of civil nature are mostly decided by the elders of the neighbourhood. Whenever there is any case regarding physical assault or theft it is reported to the police through the Police Patel.

There are some minor groupings in the village but no clear out factions. The Panchayat election does not follow any faction or party line. At the district level various political parties viz., Congress, CPI, and Republican parties are active during general election. But none of the parties have any base in the village. The party candidates or their representatives visit the village only during the election campaign. All parties pledge fulfilment of aspirations of the villagers but no concrete programme follow the election. In general, villagers understand little of election or government and 'Independence' means only replacement of '*sarkar*' to them.

During the last general election except some Bouddha all voters of the village supported the Congress (R). Those Bouddha voted for the Republican party which is considered by them as their own party. The knowledgeable members of the dominant section were familiar with the name of the National Congress and Mahatma Gandhi and said to have voted for Indiraji. The other section of the dominant group with a leaning towards socialism also voted for the Congress (R). Many of them commented, 'Independence is good, our leaders paid for it. But now-a-days administration is too corrupt. The corruption is so all-prevading that nobody can escape it. Any person who comes into power nourishes it. It has now become a part of our system. So electing X, Y, or Z does not make any difference'. Those who are poor, irrespective of their caste affiliation also voted for Congress (R), because election as such has no meaning to them. Many of them told that as they were requested to vote for Indiraji, they did accordingly. It means little to them whosoever comes into power.

Due to various plans and programmes of the government, now-a-days the villagers come in contact with different government officials and their experience in this respect is not happy. All villagers, irrespective of economic status are almost unanimous about the corrupt behaviour of the officials and specially talked about bribery. This, according to them, has spread at all levels ranging from *chaprasi* to *saheb*. People who can bribe have their purpose served. The poor suffer as they cannot afford to get things done by bribing. During pre-Independence period the interaction between the officials and the people was very limited, so they think that in those days there was more justice and fair administration and therefore the British Raj was perhaps better for them.

Development Programmes for the Weaker Section of the Village

Now-a-days government is solely responsible for all developmental works in respect of the weaker sections of the area. It works through

Panchayat Samiti. The Gram Panchayat has done some work by repairing the wells of the village including the wells belonging to the untouchables or weaker section. But the people specially the Bouddha are not happy about the Panchayat. They complain that the panchayat employs labourer for well digging from the Mali and Teli community. For similar work they have to go outside the village. Whatever may be the community affiliation, some of the villagers get certain labour employment opportunity through panchayat activities.

The people are not very happy with the welfare programmes of the government. It can be illustrated by the case of one Chambhar. He told "Now government is giving *sarki* (cotton seed). Today only I got it after visiting Wardha for three consecutive days for which I have to lose my daily income from leather work. On the first day *babulog* (clerks) told us to wait. We waited for hours together. After a long waiting we were asked to come the next day. The next day was a closed holiday and again we returned disappointed. All the programmes of the government are for the rich people and not for the poor as they are capable of bribing officials for getting things done".

There are other non-government organisations around the village. Most important of these are Sevagram Ashram of Mahatma Gandhi and Paunar Ashram of Vinoba Bhave. Once the *bhoodan* programme was also taken up in this area and a few landless were given land. Around 1952, Sewagram Ashram took up a programme for village sanitary problem and constructed a few public latrines. But these had not any lasting impact on the villagers. The Sewagram Medical college of Kasturba Health Society introduced a programme of health insurance. Few rich villagers have become its members but no one was from the weaker group. Annual premium of this insurance is Rs. 25 which a daily labourer cannot pay at a time. More so, they cannot conceive of the idea of health insurance when there is no ailment. They pay for treatment when it is serious and essential. In general, people have less confidence on government hospitals. Specially, the poor people cannot visit hospitals as they have to borrow or hire a bullock cart for attending it and lose the wage of the day. To commemorate the Silver Jubilee of the Independence of India, Maharashtra Government had taken up a programme of developing model villages through intensive development programme. Villagers selected for such purpose are called Jayanti village. One of the important programmes of such villages is the distribution of loans for construction of houses to the backward people. A major bulk of the Bouddha population of the village are taking initiative in this programme.

Ritual Interaction Across the Community

Scope of ritual interaction across community is very limited. The services of a Brahman is hardly needed. Since the last twenty years, people are getting accustomed to solemnise their marriage and funeral etc. without engaging a Brahman. At present only the Rajput employ *pardeshi* (not local) Brahman at their marriage and funeral. Services of a barber is essential for mortuary rites. But he does not serve the untouchables. One of the Bouddha does the job for them when such occasion arises. The midwife belonging to Mang community serves all the communities.

The regional worship of festivals are common to all the Hindu villagers, rich and poor. Now-a-days the younger generation of the Bouddha do not observe the traditional worship of the Hindu.

Most of the worships have two sets of nomenclatures – one is sanskritic and the other is local. The Rajput and Gujar are acquainted with all the sanskritic nomenclatures and use them while referring to rituals. The weaker sections are not aware of those sanskritic names. Those in between, know all sanskritic as well as local names, but use only the local names. The dominant sections have better knowledge about the important pilgrim centres and the network of the Hindu religion. The middle segment does not have so wide knowledge either about pilgrim centres or the scriptures.

The important festivals in the village are the Ramjanam Utsav, Hanuman Jayanti, Pola, and Holi in which the villagers participate. Ramjanam Utsav is celebrated for seven days by community feast. *Bhajan* is continued for seven days in relay. Anybody may join it. It is observed that the rich people do not participate in the *bhajan* though they visit the temple during the occasion. The poor Mali, Teli, and other artisan groups are main participants to this.

In the celebration of Hanuman Jayanti the Mali take an important role. One of them officiates as the priest. The procession carrying images of gods does not enter into the area inhabited by the untouchables. Prasad (contained food) is distributed to everyone and untouchables' touch is avoided while giving them *prasad*.

During the Holi and Pola, arrangements of lighting the Holi fire and constructing gate for Pola is done by the kotowal, belonging to the Bouddha community. The food articles offered to the Holi fire is collected by him. Neither the Bouddha observe Holi or play with colour water, nor do other people go to them for playing colours. Communal prayer is observed to Lord Buddha on that day. Their old members do not take much interest in it but the younger generation is very much enthusiastic about this. Onc festival still cuts across the community barrier. On the day of Holi young men and boys of the village irrespective of caste affiliation drink country liquor and almost everyone gets drunk. The Bouddha have given up observing Holi but not the tradition of drinking liquor during this occasion.

Observance of Nal Saheb on the day of Muharram is important to the villagers. Nal Saheb was a Muslim faquir who became renowned in this area for his deep meditation. Since long the Gond have been acting as the main devotees of Nal Saheb and the Kalar as the chief patron. The rich people from the Rajput, Gujar, Teli, and Mali caste do not participate in it. The chief devotee is believed to have been possessed by some supernatural spirit during the observance and through such power he establishes communication link between the supernatural agencies and the common people. Those who gather there, high or low born, do not hesitate to touch the feet of the chief devotee. This suggests that when possessed his caste or community identity becomes immaterial and he gains status because of spiritual support.

The concept of heaven and hell, *pap* (sin) and *punya* (virtue) are very important to the people irrespective of their caste and economic status. It is observed that most of the people except the Bouddha, depend more on fate than on their deeds. Among the dominant sections, particularly the educated people, *karma* (deed) is a determining factor. Some of them believe that birth in a particular community is a matter of chance and the caste system is man's creation. It has nothing to do with the religion. It can be said that among the dominant sections those who advocate and attempt to initiate change in the society are not governed by fatalism. The older generation of the Bouddha consider that a birth in a low caste is a chance factor and it also depends on one's fate. But the younger generation think that nobody can be low by virtue of his or her birth. It is only the situation and environmental factor that make a man high or low.

Conclusion

Considering the degree of dominance and weakness the population of Barbadi can be divided into four categories.

1. People with high social status, economic status, ritual status, and better academic attainment viz., the Rajput, Gujar, Teli and a small fraction of Mali. With fair social, ritual and economic status the Kalar has also found its place in this category.
2. People with high social and ritual status with poor economic condition and education viz. bulk of the Mali, Artisan castes. Musalman, Gond and Goari with their fair socio-ritual status also belong to this category.
3. People with low social and ritual status but with fair economic condition and educational attainment viz. the Bouddha.
4. People with low social, ritual and economic status and illiteracy viz. the Chambhar, Mang.

The first category stands for all high (with the exception of Kalar) and thus in the context of the village, this category is decisively the dominant. The last category being all low, represents the decisively weak of the village. The other two categories i.e., the second and the third represent different degrees of weakness or strength. In the village society the decisively dominant are those who have these four qualities which provide them with the authority in the power structure of the village. Of these factors, the most important combination is the high social ritual status coupled with better economic condition. High social status as such cannot make a community dominant. The bulk of the Mali who belong to the second category are, on the whole, rather weak inspite of their high numerical strength and fairly high social status. The community of the third category has many qualities of dominance though it is considered low because of its low socio-ritual status. The fourth group is the weak on all counts.

It becomes clear from the description that a single factor as such does not determine weakness or strength. A set combination of factors can neither determine this in all situations as their possible impact may very from context to context. What is crucial in this respect is the cumulative impact of multiple factors in appropriate contexts.

As we examine the four factors like social status, economic status, ritual status and literary status, when it is all plus for a community, its dominance is certain. But when it is minus one, whether the community will be considered as dominant or weak will depend on the situational context. At Barbadi the Bouddha have some control over economic resources. They are also fairly strong in numerical strength and literary performance. Even then they are considered weak. Nearly similar is the condition of the Mali who inspite of their high numerical strength and fairly high social status are weak. On the contrary, the Kalar are poor in numerical strength, their traditional ritual status is also very low. Even then with fair literary attainment sand high control over economic resources, they have a fairly dominant position in the village situation. This gives the general impression of high importance of economic and literacy factors, though the case of the Buddha does not lend support to this. A question that crops up here is whether any one factor may have a relatively more decisive role in this respect than the others. Economy is definitely a very important factor, though in certain situations it is no match to the ritual status. Otherwise, being the second richest group in the village, the Kalar would have been ranked higher and even the Bouddha could have been assigned on overall superior position. Having the background of their association with traditionally unclean professions, they are yet to project a better image to the villagers.

With the introduction of adult franchise and democratic decentralisation, the numerically dominant groups are likely to have an edge over other communities, particularly with respect to power and associated factors. But the single largest group at Barbadi, the Mali oscilate in the shadow zone between dominance and weakness. The other numerically important groups like the Buddha and Teli are in no way superior in this respect. Thus even ranking of factors responsible for determining weakness and strength, in order of importance, appears dubious.

It may, however, be pointed out here that though the Mali and Teli of Barbadi largely failed to utilise their numerical strength to their advantage, the Bouddha scored a fairly high performance in this respect. As already indicated, during the pre-Independence days even with all support from Gandhiji and his followers and having the experience of several reform movements initiated by Sewagram, the

Bouddha (the then Mahar) of Barbadi could not cross the threshold of impoverishment. Among all communities of Barbadi perhaps the Bouddha have progressed maximum during the post-Independence period and in this endeavour their numerical strength was of great advantage. At the village level they are not the majority, though in the regional context they form one of the strong groups which puts them politically in an advantageous position. Governmental programmes for spread of literacy and special provisions for the backward communities for supporting education were successfully utilised by the Bouddha to their advantage. As a result, they have been able to create the background for a major breakthrough.

Their dependence on land-based economy is the impediment in this respect. With a precarious land-man ratio, there is very limited opportunity for much economic improvement. Along with their other improvements if they can detach themselves from the land-based economy and diversify their economic activities, they are likely to advance at a faster pace. However, the poor artisan groups and the poorest of the poor, the Chambhar and Mang are yet to show any sign of betterment.

NOTES

1. Buddhism embraced by Dr. B.R. Ambedkar and his followers is referred to as neo-Buddhism or Nava-Buddha.
2. The only surviving member of the only Brahman family that once lived in the village now stays elsewhere and scarcely comes here. So, this Brahman has not been considered as a resident of the village.
3. The Chhatri have been referred to as Rajput throughout the report.
4. The Mahar are enumerated as Bouddha in 1961 Census. Their population in Wardha district is 95,635.
5. "The Religious quest of Ambedkar", by B.A.M. Paradkar in *Ambedkar and Neo-Buddhist Movement*. T.S. Wilkinson and N.N. Thomas, (eds) Madràs, 1972.

12

TASGAON : A VILLAGE IN WESTERN MAHARASHTRA

D.K. SAMANTA

Introduction

Inequality is a universal phenomenon commonly found in most of the human societies. It results in the formation of stratification within them. With the back-drop of caste system, India is found to have an elaborate stratified structure. The strata, within this framework are found to be legitimised by the concept of ritual purity and pollution. Inequality is observed in different degrees in all the major aspects of life social, economic, political, and communicational. From this point of view the Indian population may broadly be divided into dominant and weak sections depending on the nature of their access to and control over the local resources. With the independence of India, various constitutional and organizational measures have been taken up to help the downtrodden and thereby to reduce the gap of such inequality. The present objective is two fold – first, to identify those groups which are decisively weak, and second, to define the social situations responsible for such weakness and to find out the constraints that stand in their way of crossing the threshold of weakness and the disabilities they suffer from.

Our study village, Tasgaon, comes under the Hatkanangle taluka of Kolhapur District in the south-western part of Maharashtra. The taluka lying in the Krishna-*panchaganga* basin belongs to a rain shadow area, though the western part of the district receives heavy Sahyadry offshoots.

The village is at a distance of about 21 kms. from Kolhapur and is about 15 kms. away from the taluka headquarters. The nearest urban centre at Vadgaon-Peth is at a distance of four kms. and has been recognised as a municipal town since 1887.

Tasgaon was selected for intensive study on purposive basis as per criteria fixed for the purpose. Accordingly, the village is fairly representative of the area and has some unique features of its own. This part of the state has received special attention for extensive cultivation of sugarcane. Availability of better irrigation facilities, technology, and improvement in agriculture, coupled with extensive cultivation of sugarcane have set in a series of changes. Construction of roads for transportation of sugarcane from interior parts to the factories has brought villages of the area closer to the urban influence. But Tasgaon has not received many of these facilities so far. The nearest river flows about eight kms. away from the village. Cultivation here is still largely dependent on monsoon rains. Until 1973 the village had only foottracks connecting it to the neighbouring villages. These roads helped the village in maintaining its traditional rural characters.

There are regular bus services to Vadgaon-Peth from Kolhapur and other neighbouring towns. The Poona-Bangalore highway is only four kms. away from the village and connected by a link road. From Vadgaon-Peth one had to walk down the distance to reach the village. In 1973, two unpaved roads have been constructed under the programme of drought relief work to connect the village to its surrounding villages including Vadgaon-Peth. The nearest railway station is at Rukdi, about eight kms. away from the village. In 1972, a telephone has been installed at the village Panchayat Office. The village comes under the branch Post Office of Tope. The Postal peon is supposed to visit the village once a week, but he seldom does so. Villagers mostly avail themselves of the services of the Post and Telegraph Office at Vadgaon-Peth.

In transportation of goods, bullock carts play the main role. Trucks and tractors are also used for transporting heavy loads. Light loads are carried on head or bicycles.

There are in all eighteen radio sets in the village of which the Navi,the Muslim, and the Mahar have one each and the remaining belong to the Maratha. The Public Library at Vadgaon-Peth subscribes all the important dailies in Marathi and also some Hindi and English dailies. The villagers casually read them.

There is a permanent as well as a weekly market at Vadgaon-Peth The cattle market at Vadgaon-Peth is the biggest in the district. It attracts traders from nearby districts. A government medical dispensary, a maternity home, a high school, the state transport bus terminus, several banks, a police station and a cinema hall are located at Vadgaon-Peth. The villagers visit this place to sell their surplus agricultural produce and also for shopping. It also serves as the meeting place for friends and relatives coming from neighbouring villages. So, it plays an important role in the life of the villagers. Even for recreational purposes they often visit this place.

The Village population is composed of nine castes viz. Maratha, Navi, Sutar, Gurao,Lohar,Ramoshi, Chambhar, Mahar, Mang, and the Musalman. All of these castes and communities can be divided into two main clusters in terms of their position in the ritual hierarchy.

One cluster includes, Maratha,Sutar, Navi, Gurao, and Lohar, all belonging to the high castes. The other cluster comprises untouchables viz., Ramoshi, Chambhar, Mahar, and Mang. The Muslim of the village, though do not strictly confirm to the Hindu system of caste hierarchy, enjoy a better status than the untouchables and as such are ranked high. Members of high and the low castes have separate wells for drinking water.The well for the high caste groups is well constructed and has sufficient supply of water for most part of the year. The well meant for the untouchables is very shallow and devoid of cemented wall and pulley. It dries up by the middle of April. A light post is provided near the well belonging to the high castes and as a result people can fetch water from there even after dusk. The untouchables are to fetch water before dusk as there is not such lighting arrangement.

There are two cremation grounds, one for the high castes and the other for the untouchables. The high caste people always cremate their corpse. The Muslims have no separate burial ground. They bury their dead in their private land. The untouchables practise both cremation and burial depending on the means to meet expenses. The Christian Mahars bury the dead in the common cremation ground.

The Maratha claim that the village was founded by three uterine brothers who were Maratha of Chauhan lineage and were of Kshatriya origin. This is not denied by the other high caste people. The Mahar and the Chambhar also claim themselves to be the early settlers of the village. The members of the remaining caste groups migrated to the village in recent past.

The village settlement is divided into three wards for the purpose of the Gram Panchayat election, each having nearly equal number of households. But the villagers do not take much note of it and divide the village settlement into three hamlets each named after the numerically dominant caste living there. Maharwada is in the east, Chambharwada is in the north-east, and Marathwada of *gaon* is at the centre of the village settlement. The Mang and the Ramoshi reside outside the main concentration towards its northern fringe, and away from each other. The area of settlement under Maharwada and the Chambharwada are considered to be defiling by the high caste people for any sacred procession to pass through. Women of high castes avoid these areas for fear of pollution. The grocer's shop, the grinding mill, and the bicycle repairing shop are all located in the *gaon*.

The village settlement is intercepted by lanes and bylanes in such a way that every house opens to a lane or bylane. The lanes are spacious and have road gutters on both sides for easy drainage of rain water and used water in case of *gaon*. But in other two hamlets the lanes are relatively narrow and are provided with road gutters in some parts only. There are 18 street lights being energized since 1968. Out of these, three are in Maharwada, one in the Chambharwada, and near the well of the high castes, and the rest are in the *gaon*.

The general cleanliness of the village is noticeable. The approach roads and the village lanes are well maintained. The village scavenger keeps these roads and drains clean. The *gaon* is more clean as compared to the other hamlets. In the *gaon*, each of the households sweeps the part of the lane that comes in front of the respective houses and sprinkles water daily. The villagers use the agricultural land for defecation. There are areas for the untouchables separate from that of the high castes. Women usually go to defecate either early in the morning or after the dust.

Generally, houses do not have any courtyard. In Gaon, there are some open space around a house. In other two hamlets the houses are huddled together.

The ground-plan of a house is rectangular. Houses are devoid of any window and consist of single all purpose rooms with floors separated into two or three sections at different levels. The walls are made of stone slabs plastered with mud. The roof is double sloped and made of country tiles. Houses located in the *gaon* are, in general, well constructed. Some of them consist of more than one room and are provided with wooden door panels. House in the other two hamlets are poorly built with the exception of a few. Every house belonging to a high caste is with a covered bathroom where female members have their bath. Some have cemented floors. The Mahar and Chambhar women go to the nearby irrigation well to have their bath. In Marathwada separate cattle sheds are common but in Maharwada and Chambharwada cattle are kept inside houses. Two public urinals one near the school and the other behind the Panchayat building have been recently constructed. Twentyseven houses are provided with electricity, out of which one belongs to a Mahar and another to a Gurao, the rest being owned by the Maratha.

The sacred spots of the village include a Mahadeo temple, a Maruti temple, a dilapidated Mosque, a sacred spot of Pir, and a temple of Margubai (goddess of cholera and small pox). The Margubai temple is located in Maharwada and the other shrines are located in the Gaon. A temple of Biroba is about one km. outside the village and a temple of Sidhola is situated on the top of a hillock within the revenue village.

Public establishments in the village include the Gram Panchayat house, the Co-operative Credit Society, the Milk Co-operative Society, and the school. Buildings for a dispensary and a residential quarter for the village Gram-sevak are under construction. The Panchayat house has two rooms, one being used for the office and the other contains the wrestling ground. The wrestling room is reserved for the high caste people and the Muslims. The Harijan Ksheti Society has constructed a *talimghar* (room for wrestling) for the use of the untouchables.

The village school coaches upto the seventh standard and run by the Zilla Parishad. Education is free there. For higher school education one has to go to Vadgaon-Peth. For graduation and post-graduate studies, students go to colleges at Varnanagar and Kolhapur city.

There are ruins of a structure at Maharwada which they call Takia. It was the meeting place for the Mahar caste Panchayat in former days. Their traditional caste Panchayat now ceased functioning for the last thirty five years approximately.

Population Composition and Ritual Hierarchy

Table 1 details communitywise distribution of the village population. As already stated,there are nine caste groups besides the Muslims.

The Maratha are numerically the most dominant group forming 59.82 per cent of the total population. Next in position come the Mahar forming 25.72 per cent of the total population. Chambhar occupy the third position in this respect (4.52%).

TABLE 1: Population composition

Sl. no.	Community	Households		Population			
		Number	Percentage	Male	Female	Total	Percentage
1.	Chambhar	10	5.38	30	23	53	4.52
2.	Gurao	4	2.15	7	11	18	1.53
3.	Lohar	2	1.08	5	9	14	1.19
4.	Mahar	49	26.24	170	131	301	25.72
5.	Mang	1	0.54	4	5	9	0.76
6.	Maratha	108	58.06	369	331	700	59.82
7.	Muslim	3	1.61	14	6	20	1.70
8.	Navi	5	2.69	14	13	27	2.30
9.	Ramoshi	1	0.54	2	1	3	0.25
10.	Sutar	3	1.61	12	13	25	2.13
	Total	186		627	543	1170	

The nine caste groups may be arranged in the following order from higher to lower social position in accordance with the village caste hierarchy.

1. Maratha
2. Sutar (High caste cluster)
3. Gurao
4. Lohar
5. Navi

---

6. Chambhar
7. Ramoshi (Untouchable cluster)
8. Mahar
9. Mang

The members of the high caste groups in the first cluster are free to fetch water from the common well meant for them, have the right to enter the village temples, and interdine. The caste groups of the second cluster have a separate well common for the group. Their entry to the village temple is considered sacrilegious with the exception of their entry to Margubai temple. They do not practise interdining amongst themselves.

The Muslims are included in the first cluster as they enjoy similar privileges and status. Their position within the caste hierarchy is not precise. They, however, are generally considered below the Maratha.

The local term for the artisan and service castes is *balutdar*. Except the Maratha who are traditionally agriculturists, all other castes are balutdars. They render service to the Maratha and other high caste people including the Muslim on annual payment of grain for all sorts of repair works and take cash payment for making anything new. The high caste *balutdars* like Lohar and Sutar receive cash payment from the untouchables. The Navi and the Gurao do not render any service to the untouchables. High caste *balutdars* among themselves exchange services on reciprocal basis.

The Maratha occupy the topmost position in the ritual hierarchy. The *patils*, i.e., the heads of the village were from them in the past and the present police *patil* (agent of the police at the village levels) also belongs to this caste. They command the highest respect in the village. Sutars (the carpenters) hold the next immediate position in the ritual hierarchy. Guraos (suppliers of leaf plate for any communal feasts) serve as the priest at the Maruti temple and are entrusted with the duty of cleaning the temple daily. For their services they have been given by the Maratha two acres of land. They also get special food items prepared by the members of the high castes on any festive occasion. They belong to Lingayat sect and are vegetarian. Traditional occupation of the Lohars is smithery of iron and the Navis are barbers.

The Chambhars are the shoe makers who occupy the highest position among untouchables. Kolhapur sandals are famous because of their variety and durability. Earnings of some of the Chambhars is reasonably good on this account. The Ramoshi were originally farm guards. The payment for their service was dependent on the yield and so their earnings were not fixed. This might have put them under hardship, ultimately leading them to criminal activities. The head of the Ramoshi household and his son are now in jail on the charge of a murder. Their position in the ritual hierarchy is just below the Chambhar. The housewife is now living as mistress to a Maratha.

The Mahars are the main supplier of farm labourers in the village. Their traditional services that they gave up about twenty years back included: (1) lifting of dead cattle, skinning and selling the hide in the market, the sale money being given to the owner of the cattle, receiving instead one and a half seer of jawari per cattle; (2) carrying the message of any death in the village to the near relatives of the deceased, fetching the dried cowdung cake and pyre wood to the cremation ground; (3) sweeping the village lanes; (4) lifting of the leaf plates after use in any feast (5) fixing ropes at the village entries on some particular occasions and (6) lighting of Holi and *Hola* fire during the Holi festival. They were thrown out of their services following a conflict with the Maratha on the issue of their demand for an increase in their remuneration. Twelve Mahar households are Christian converts. Conversion to Christianity could not alter their position in the ritual hierarchy. The traditional calling of the Mang is rope making. They are also the drummers. The jobs which were once traditionally done by the Mahars, have now been assigned to the Mang by the Maratha of the village. The housewife of the present household is an employee at the Gram panchayat.

The Maratha of the village have presently five exogamous divisions or *kurs*, namely, chauhan, jadav, Sindhe, Kokate, and Gadbe. Among the Chauhans, those who are *patil*, occupy the highest position among the Maratha. Monogamy is the rule. Polygynous marriages have also been reported, usually when the first wife does not conceive within two to three years after marriage. Maternal cross-cousin marriage is the preferred type of union. There is no case of paternal cross-cousin marriage, though it is not prohibited. Cases of uncle-neice (Si Da) marriage is found. junior sororate is the preferred type for secondary marriage, specially when the deceased wife leave young children. Widow remarriage and divorce are strictly prohibited.

Except the Maratha, divorce and widow remarriage are practised by all other high castes, though they also have the *kur* system. As the high caste people look down upon the practice of divorce and widow remarriage the people of other castes who practise so are considered low. The system of bride-price is common among the Gurao and the untouchables but at present, dowry is gradually replacing the bride-price among the untouchables. The Maratha and the remaining high caste people have only the dowry system.

Table 2 details the family composition in the village community. We find in the table that there are one hundred and eighty six families in all. The families have been classified into four types,namely nascent consisting of a couple in child bearing age without any issue; nuclear, having a couple with unmarried children; extended, a nuclear family with other additional members; and broken, in which spouses are dead or it may occur due to separation divorce or desertion.

TABLE 2: Family composition

Sl. no.	Community no. of	Average size	Type of family(with percentage)			
			Nascent	Nuclear	Extended	Broken
1.	Chambhar	5.3	-	7	2	1
	10	70.00	20.00	10.00		
2.	Gurao	4.5	-	1	2	1
	4	25.00	50.00	25.00		
3.	Lohar	7.0	-	2	-	-
	2	100.00				
4.	Mahar	6.1	1	23	21	4
	49	2.04	46.94	42.86	8.16	
5.	Mang	9.0	-	-	1	-
	1	100.00				
6.	Maratha	6.5	1	52	55	-
	108	0.93	48.15	50.93		
7.	Muslim	6.7	-	-	2	1
	3	66.67	33.33			
8.	Navi	5.4	-	3	2	-
	5	60.00	40.00			
9.	Ramoshi	3.0	-	1	-	-
	1	100.00				
10.	Sutar	8.3	-	-	2	1
	3	66.67	33.33			
Total	136	6.3	2	89	87	8
			1.08	47.85	46.77	4.30

As it appears from the Table, the frequency of both nuclear and extended family types is close (89 and 87). The percentage of extended family is the highest among the Maratha; the Mahar come next and the Chambhar have the lowest percentage. The percentage of nuclear family is highest among the Chambhar, the Maratha come next, followed by the Mahar. In case of the high castes, there is a preponderance of extended family. The Mahar have a sizeable proportion of broken (8.16%) families, of which the Chambhar have one and the Maratha have none. The other high castes have two broken families in all. The average family size among the three numerically dominant caste groups, Maratha, Mahar, and Chambhar is 6.3, 6.1 and 5.3 respectively.

Social Implication of Family Types

Among the dominant section, the frequency of extended family is high. The Maratha are primarily agriculturists. In agriculture, more hands are needed for various types of agricultural operations. The care that a member of a household takes cannot be expected from a hired labourer. So there is a tendency among the brothers to live jointly in common family even after the birth of their children. Another factor plays a significant role in this respect. The fragmentation of a family farm following separation always brings lower yield. But extended families are resistant to this. Brothers in general are engaged in cultivating their ancestral land jointly even after getting separated from one another. Those who have considerable amount of land, mostly belong to extended family. The weaker sections are the agricultural labourers. They also go to industrial complexes in search of jobs. They have little amount of land which they usually get as gifts under some governmental scheme. They seldom take any serious note of such facilities extended to them. So, among the weaker sections we find that there is preponderance of nuclear family.

Those who work in the industrial complexes around Bombay visit their families once in three or four months. So, the family cohesion in such cases is lost to a certain extent. Among the dominant sections, there is more land and they are in a habit of investing their savings towards the improvement of agriculture. Among the weaker sections, social obligations are limited to the minimum and that too are in relation to the immediate family members. The condition in case of the dominant sections is somewhat different as their social obligations extend even beyond the family circles.

Social Mobility

Mobility movement as such has not taken place at the village level. However, an attempt had been made about twenty years back by the Mahars demanding a raise of their rate of payment. The Maratha suppressed this movement and as already stated, threw them out of their traditional services. The Maratha brought a Mang family from a neighbouring village and assigned it with those job which were traditionally pursued by the Mahars. A tense situation prevailed for about a year in the village on this account and some members of the Mahar caste were beaten up during this period.

Shahu Chhatrapati, the Maratha king of Kolhapur state, initiated the movement directed against the domination of the Brahmans in the early present century. He advocated not to appoint Brahmans for priestly services. He tried to unite all non-Brahman castes and abolish untouchability. In this venture he also employed some members from the untouchables in his court. A Mahar from this village got appointment there. This he did to unite the non-Brahman forces to stand against the Brahmin domination. A parallel movement largely Anti-Brahminic in character was also initiated by Mahatma Jotirao Phulley, approximately in the middle of the last century. Phulley himself hailed from a non-Brahman caste. Due to these movements some perceptible changes have occured in respect of the rigidity of caste rules, particularly regarding untouchability. The general tendency among all the castes here is to imitate the Maratha life style as the model.

Social Relations

It has already been stated that castes/communities in the village form two main clusters, the untouchables and the high castes including the Muslim. The Members of these two clusters interact rather discordantly among themselves in respect of all important matters concerning the life cycle activities, like marriage, birth, and death. Members of high castes rarely invite an untouchable on such occasions. If any untouchable is ever invited, he is very much discriminated. Among untouchables invitations are restricted to untouchables only. Selection of invitees among high castes depends on the nature of personal ties that exist between the families concerned, irrespective of their caste affiliation.

When an untouchable meets a Maratha, it is obligatory on his part to offer salutation to the Maratha, who may or may not respond to it. The high caste people call the untouchables by their names and use their caste names instead of the surnames. It does not matter even if the untouchable happens to be older in age.

The villagers when meet at some common public place like

market, segregate themselves according to cluster identity. On occasions untouchables may offer tea to members of high castes but such treatment is never reciprocated by the latter.

In any intercaste dispute, when a Maratha is at fault his fellowmen do not raise any voice against him.

When an untouchable visits the house of a high caste member, he sits on the floor maintaining a distance. When a Maratha goes to the house of an untouchable, he sits on a cot.

There is no discrimination between high and low castes in the village school. There are teachers, clerks, bank officers, and local leaders who sometimes hail from untouchable castes. In such cases, rigid caste rules automatically get relaxed and even the people of high caste do not hesitate in entertaining them when any opportunity comes. Reservation of seats in the village Panchayat has brought them to the forefront of the village politics, though primarily as supporting agents to the dominant group. They sit on the same *dari* (cotton carpet) with members of the high caste in Panchayat meetings or during visit of any government officials or political leaders. Long acquaintance develops intimacy at individual level.A domestic servant or a permanent farm labourer enjoys some relaxation of caste rules in the day-to-day dealings from the master.

Education

Table 3 depicts the literacy composition of the village by community. We find from the table that the average proportion of literacy in the village is 41.5 per cent. About 57 per cent males and 24 per cent females are literate. As it appears from the table, the Maratha have the highest rate of literacy at all levels of educational standard. Among the Maratha, there are graduates, engineers, and a post graduate student. The Mahar and Maratha who otherwise occupy opposite poles, have come very close in respect of proportion of literacy. There are a few graduates among the Mahar and Chambhar. The proportion of female literates is 8.31 per cent among the Mahar and 13 per cent among the Maratha. The Maratha have eight male and one female graduates, the Mahar have one male and two female graduates, and the Chambhar have one male graduate. It needs a mention here that the Chambhar have one male graduate. It needs a mention here that the Christian Mahar have shown the maximum proportion of literates and educated among them as compared to other castes. Educational facilities provided by the Christian missionaries have made this possible. Educated Mahar girls are mostly taking to nursing as profession when their Hindu counterparts are still in the darkness of illiteracy. The change due to conversion is marginal in their over-all life style. The Hindu and the Christian Mahar are not segregated from each other. They interact among themselves in economic as well as social matters.

TABLE 3: Literacy composition

Sl. no.	Community	Illiterate	Literate	Educational performance (upto)							
				Primary		Middle		Secondary		Graduation tion & above	
				M	F	M	F	M	F	M	F
1.	Chambhar	29 54.72	24 45.28	10	5	2	—	5	1	1	—
2.	Gurao	10 55.56	8 44.44	3	2	3	—	—	—	—	—
3.	Lohar	12 85.72	2 14.28	2	—	—	—	—	—	—	—
4.	Mahar	214 71.9	87 28.00	38	12	11	6	12	5	1	2
5.	Mang	9 100.00	—	—	—	—	—	—	—	—	—
6.	Maratha	367 52.53	333 47.44	130	59	59	27	44	4	9	1
7.	Muslim	12 60.00	8 40.00	3	—	5	—	—	—	—	—
8.	Navi	15 55.56	12 44.44	7	5	—	—	—	—	—	—
9.	Ramoshi	2 66.67	1 33.33	1	—	—	—	—	—	—	—
10.	Sutar	14 56.00	11 44.00	4	2	3	—	2	—	—	—
Total		684 58.46	468 41.54	198 40.74	85 17.49	83 17.08	33 6.79	63 12.96	10 2.06	11 2.27	3 0.62

Role of the Educated Among Weaker Sections

Role of the educated among the Maratha, the Mahar, and the

Chambhar reveals some important features. In the case of the Maratha, agriculture is considered an important occupation. The educated Maratha, even when employed in white-collar jobs occasionally visit the village and do plan for better farming and invest their saving for the development of their farm land. Improvement of irrigation facilities and introduction of sugarcane as cash crop, as well as availability of loans from various sources have made farming a profitable enterprise. Besides, they have the age old tradition as landowning agriculturists. So their attachment to land is conspicuous. Sentiment to keep the extended family intact also brings them back to their kin and they help each other at times of needs. In the case of the Chambhar, as traditional shoe makers they were mostly landless. The educated Chambhar look for jobs in urban areas and do not feel like coming back to the village. Many of them have gone to Bombay where they work in some shoe factories. The educated youth among the Mahar do not keep touch with their kinsmen. They were mostly landless farm labourers and are, at present, holders of meagre amount of land. This does not induce much attachment to agricultural occupation. They often conceal their caste identity in social gatherings.

Economy

The village economy is mainly based on agriculture. The Maratha are traditionally agriculturists and the Mahar are the main suppliers of farm labourers. The remaining castes extend services to the Maratha farmers, for which they receive annual payment of grains. The educated villagers aspire for white-collar jobs. A few of them are teachers in the local middle high schools, and very few have gone to Bombay to work in factories.

Soil Types

The village land is undulating and intersected by two hillocks. The cultivable land may be categorized on the basis of thickness of surface layer, the amount of stone content, and the soil composition which have direct bearing on the proportion of yield. There are three types of land namely (i) *bhari*, *kali*, or *uttam*; it is alluvial soil, medium to deep black, and most fertile; (ii) *tamdi* or *madhyam* it contains brown soil, it is also rich and fertile where sugarcane can be grown successfully; (iii) *buddi* or *kanisth*, it is the inferior quality soil with rocky bed and very thin surface layer, the capacity of its yield is very low.

The principal crops grown here are jawari, wheat, Bengal gram, ground-nut, a variety of pulses, and small quantity of rice. Sugarcane is the main cash crop grown in plots which have irrigation facilities. Chilli and vegetables are also grown.

Farmers mainly depend on monsoon rains for cultivation. There are only 45 irrigation wells in the village. Out of these, the Maratha have 39 (86.67%), the Mahars have 5 (11.12%), and the Navi have one (2.22%). Only nine or ten wells retain water during summer months and the same are used for irrigating small plots of sugarcane and vegetable fields. All such wells belong to the Maratha and one to a Mahar. Besides, there are twelve wells owned by the Maratha which are fitted with diesel pump sets.

All farmers are owner cultivators and take active part in agricultural operations. Share cropping is no more present in the village since the implementation of Land Requisition Acts. Former share croppers have now become owners of the land in most of cases.

Control Over Resources

Nine castes/communities own land, though the amount of possession of land castewise varies considerably. The Table 4 details the distribution of cultivable land in the village and the source from which it is obtained.

As it appears from the table, the Maratha own more than 73 per cent of the village land, most of which they have acquired through (89.97) inheritance. The Mahar hold the immediate next position, who have 18% of the village land in their possession, more than 61 per cent of which they have got as gift, either directly from the government or due to the Tenancy Act. The next in position are the Chambhar who own about 3.5 per cent of the village land, 57 per cent of which they have received from the government as gift. The Navi own 2.34 per cent of the village land and stand next to the Chambhar. They have inherited more than 98 per cent of their land. The Ramoshi have 0.87 per cent of the village land which they have been gifted by the State Government.

TABLE 4: Possession of land

Sl. no.	Group		Inherited	Through Tenancy Act	Gift	Purchase	Total % of village land
1.	Chambhar	acre	15.67	-	20.55	-	36.22
		%	43.26		56.75		3.43
2.	Gurao	acre	7.40	-	-	1.00	8.40
		%	88.10			11.90	0.79
3.	Lohar	acre	0.88	-	-	-	0.88
		%	100.00				0.88
4.	Mahar	acre	72.20	59.85	57.30	-	189.35
		%	38.13	31.61	30.26		18.00
5.	Maratha	acre	672.97	50.08	36.01	5.92	764.98
		%	87.97	6.55	4.71	0.77	73.16
6.	Muslim	acre	2.17	-	2.05	-	4.22
		%	51.42		48.58		0.40
7.	Navi	acre	24.02	-	-	0.04	24.12
		%	98.36			1.64	2.34
8.	Ramoshi	acre	-	-	9.25	-	9.25
		%			100.00		0.87
9.	Sutar	acre	9.38	-	-	-	9.38
		%	100.00				0.89
	Total	acre	804.69	109.93	125.16	7.32	1047.10
		%	76.85	10.50	11.95	0.70	100.00

Sale and purchase of land is negligible. Nearly five per cent of the land owned by the Maratha was received through the scheme 'Land to the ex-military personnel'. In case of Mahar and Chambhar, the gift of land has come under the scheme 'Land to the landless Harijans'. Thirty-one per cent of the land owned by the Mahar have been acquired through the Tenancy Act, all of which were under possession of the Maratha farmers.

There are in all nineteen landless households. Twenty per cent of the Mahar, 10 per cent of the Chambhar, and 5.5 per cent of the Maratha households are landless. The Mang household has no land either.

As has been stated earlier, there are three qualities of land in the village. Table 5 details per capita holding of land by type.

TABLE 5: Per capita land by types

Sl. no.	Community	Population	Per Capita land (in acre) Uttam	Madhyam	Kanistha	Grazing	Total	Field
1.	Chamber	53	—	0.513	0.170	—	0.683	
2.	Curao	18	—	0.235	0.232	—	0.467	
3.	Lohar	14	—	0.064	—	—	0.064	
4.	Mahar	301	0.130	0.293	0.207	—	0.630	
5.	Mang	9	—	—	—	—	—	
6.	Maratha	700	0.304	0.520	0.269	0.008	1.101	
7.	Muslim	20	—	0.211	—	—	0.211	
8.	Navi	27	0.123	0.251	0.542	—	0.916	
9.	Ramoshi	3	—	3.083	—	—	0.083	
10.	Sutar	25	0.080	0.128	0.167	—	0.375	
	Total	1170	0.220	0.434	0.241	0.005	0.900	

As it appears from the table, the Ramoshi have the highest per capita land holdings. That is one of the gift lands distributed by the government. It, however, does not indicate better economic condition of the Romoshi as their population size is small in the village and the land under their possession is rocky and very much unproductive. Otherwise the Maratha surpass all other communities in per capita land holdings. Next to them are the Navi who inherited the land. Each of the Maratha, Navi, and Sutar own some amount of *uttam* quality of land, and the Maratha stand above all in respect of per capita holdings in this regard. In respect of *madhyam* quality, leaving apart the Ramoshi, the Maratha have the highest per capita land. The Chambhar hold the next position and the Mahar follow next.

The farmers of different communities may be classified into different groups on the basis of the size of land holdings. The range of such holdings from one group to the next is 10 acres. There is one Maratha in each case having 30 to 40 acres and more than 40 acres of land. In the 20 to 30 acre range there are four Maratha and one Mehar. In the 10 to 20 acre range there are 12 Maratha while the Mahar and the Navi are there one each. In the first group the highest number of farmers are Maratha (84). The Mahar come next (37), followed by Chambhar (9) and the Navi respectively.

Of the total 165 households having land the Maratha form about 62 per cent, the Mahar 23 per cent, followed by the Chamber 5.5 per cent and the Navi 3 per cent.

The various occupations pursued by different communities of the village may be grouped under four broad categories, viz., agriculture (owner-cultivator and agricultural labour), professional (domestic servant, cattle keeper, craftsman, leather worker and petty trader) and non-agricultural labour and service (contract labourer other than those in agriculture service etc.). Table 6 details the distribution of occupation by caste/community.

TABLE 6: Occupation composition

Sl. No.	Community	No. of workers	Agriculture (owner cultivator)	Agricultural labourer	Profe-ssionals	Non-agricul-tural and service
1.	Chambhar	18	5(1.25)	—	2(0.5)	11(2.75)
2.	Gurao	8	6(1.50)	1(0.25)	—	1(0.25)
3.	Lohar	4	—	—	—	4(1.00)
4.	Mahar	139	38(9.50)	71(17.75)	10(2.5)	20(5.00)
5.	Mang	6	—	2(0.50)	1(0.25)	3(0.75)
6.	Maratha	203	179(45.75)	3(0.75)	14(3.50)	7(1.75)
7.	Muslim	6	4(1.00)	1(0.25)	1(0.25)	—
8.	Navi	7	5(1.25)	—	—	2(0.05)
9.	Ramoshi	1	—	—	—	1(0.25)
10.	Sutar	7	—	1(0.25)	—	6(1.50)
	Total	399	237(59.25)	79(19.75)	28(7.00)	55(13.75)

As it appears from the table 6,79 per cent of the working force are absorbed in cultivation and seven per cent in agricultural service. Only 13.75 per cent of the total earners are in occupations independent of agriculture. So, the main bulk of the working force are involved in agricultural economy. Most of the owner cultivators are the Maratha followed by Mahar. The highest number of professionals are the Marathas, the immediate next position is that of the Mahar. Maximum number of agricultural labourers are comprised by the Mahar. All the female labourers in agriculture are from the Mahar. In the non-agricultural labour and service the Mahar top the list. They are followed by the Maratha and the Sutar in this respect.

There are two main types of agricultural labourers : labourers on annual contract basis and daily wage labourers on weekly payment basis, locally known as *gadi*. In all, there are only five labourers on annual contract, of whom three are Mahar and two belong to the

Mang caste. A few Mahar cattle keepers are there in the village on annual contract. The employer is always known to be a Maratha. Some of the daily wage labourers in agriculture are in continuous service with their masters for a number of years. Some of the big farmers employ one or two labourers of supervisory cadre. The rate of payment even of them is the same as that of the other daily labourers. Usually such labourers are employed from higher castes. The normal labour rate is Rs. 2.50 per day for a male labourer and Rs. 2 for a female labourer. The rate varies with the agricultural season.

TABLE 7: Earner-dependent ratio

Sl. no.	Community	Total population	Earner	Dependent	Number of dependents per earner
1.	Chambhar	53	18	35	1.94
2.	Gurao	18	8	20	1.25
3.	Lohar	14	4	10	2.50
4.	Mahar	301	139	162	1.16
5.	Mang	9	6	3	0.50
6.	Maratha	700	203	497	2.44
7.	Muslim	20	6	14	2.30
8.	Navi	27	7	20	2.85
9.	Ramoshi	3	3	—	—
10.	Sutar	25	7	18	2.57
	Total	1170	401	769	1.90

As it appears from the table, the dependency rate is highest among the Maratha, followed by the Navi and the Sutar, respectively. The Lohar and the Muslim come next. Among the untouchables the dependency rate is very low. The dependency ratio for the village is 1:1.9 of the three numerically dominant groups viz. the Maratha, Mahar, and Chambhar. The Mahar have lowest ratio and the Maratha have the highest ratio.

Income and Expenditure

As the Maratha and the Mahar are the two numerically dominant groups, there differential expenditure have been compared. It has been found that both the groups spend nearly the same proportion of their income on food. The Maratha spend more in items like medicine, education, and house construction in comparison to the Mahar. The Maratha spend more for the capital investment also. The Mahar have actually nothing to invest. For this reason the Maratha are found to be more indebted than the Mahar, which indicates their higher capability of borrowing and that too from governmental sources. The sample households may be classified into three groups on the basis of their income range. The Maratha families are mostly on the higher income groups, while the Mahar families belong mainly to the lower income group. The per capita income for the Maratha is nearly double that of the Mahar.

Indebtedness

The Maratha were found to have borrowed the largest sum of money, most of which was for agricultural purposes, petty trade, and construction of houses. The Mahar took less loan and most of which they spent for prime necessities. So, in the case of the Maratha, the greater portion of expenditure is for capital investment, whereas in case of the Mahar it is mainly outright consumption. More than 92 per cent of the loans taken by the Maratha is from government sources and so they have to pay very low rate of interest. About 30 per cent of the loan taken by the Mahar is from private source and that the rate of interest is exorbitant. The rate of interest they pay is sometimes 120 per cent per year as against to 11 per cent per year for any government loan.

Distribution of Livestock

The main live-stock in the village includes cows, bullocks, and buffaloes. Cows and buffaloes are domesticated for milk. Bullocks as well as the he-buffaloes are used as draft animal. Bullocks form the major portion of the total draft animal. The he-buffaloes are only a few in number. Table 8 shows the distribution of principal live-stock by community in the village. As it appears from the table, the Maratha own about 73 per cent of the total live-stock of the village. They are followed by the Mahar who own nearly 19 per cent of livestock.

Agricultural Innovations

The high yielding varieties of seeds were first introduced in the village in the year 1966 and the Maratha were the first to adopt them. There are only a few from the Mahar and the Chambhar who took up improved seeds for cultivation. The Maratha farmer many a time procure improved seeds from the Mahar or the Chambhar farmers to meet their own need as the latter (Mahar and Chambhar) sometimes sell out the same to big farmers.

TABLE 8: Distribution of livestock by community

Sl. no.	Community	Cow	Bullock	Buffalo	Male Buffalo	Total
1.	Chambhar	1(1.45)	—	2(10.00)	5(1.42)	5(1.42)
2.	Gurao	1(1.45)	—	3(1.68)	—	4(1.12)
3.	Lohar	—	—	—	—	—
4.	Mahar	20(28.99)	17(19.10)	27(15.08)	6(30.00)	70(19.61)
5.	Mang	—	—	—	—	—
6.	Maratha	45(65.22)	72(80.90)	32(72.74)	12(60.00)	261(73.11)
7.	Muslim	—	—	3(1.68)	—	3(0.80)
8.	Navi	—	—	8(4.47)	—	8(2.32)
9.	Ramoshi	—	—	1(0.56)	—	1(0.21)
10.	Sutar	2(2.90)	—	3(1.68)	-	5(1.41)
	Total	69(100.00)	89(100.00)	179(100.00)	20(100.00)	357(100.00)

Out of 119 farmers, who took hybrid jawar in the year 1974, 99 farmers were Maratha, 15 were Mahar and five Chambhar. The high yielding paddy was cultivated by 111 farmers, of which 94 were Maratha, 12 were Mahar and five were Chambhar. The farmers who cultivated hybrid wheat were 52 in all. The highest number of them were also Maratha. The other hybrid corn and sunflower was also found to be cultivated by the Maratha only.

Mainly the Maratha farmers use chemical fertilizers and pesticides as they can afford the same. The rationing system is there for the distribution of these articles. To meet the deficit of their actual requirement, the Maratha farmers procure these articles through the Mahar farmers. The spray machines and other various agricultural equipments are available from the government sources. Lack of contact and awareness are the main reasons for the Mahar and the Chambhar farmers for not availing of these privileges. They cannot afford to gratify the corrupt government officials for acquiring them when such demands are made at times due to their bad economic condition.

The nationalised banks and various other governmental as well as private organisations extend loan to the farmers. But the weaker groups could not avail themselves of those privileges. The Land Development Bank is mainly responsible for providing loans for well digging, land development, etc. The highest number of debtors in the list of this bank that comes from village are Maratha with only four Mahar. The three Chit Fund Societies in the village also extend loan in small scale. A composite list of members of these Chit Fund Societies reveals that the majority of the members are from the Maratha group.

Two big irrigation projects have been undertaken for the village, one by the Zilla Parishad and the other by the Irrigation Department of the State Government. The Zila Parishad has constructed an agricultural tank. The land that comes under the command of this tank is owned mainly by the Maratha and by a few high caste farmers. The other project has been taken up to lift water from the nearby and to drain it to the village lands through pipe lines. Both the projects are on the verge of completion. These would not help the Mahar and the Chambhar farmers in any way as their lands are on high ridges. Their land is of *kanisth* variety having very thin surface layer.

To improve the condition of the chambhar, a Co-operative Society was established with government aid. But due to unscrupulous policy of some of its members, it liquidated.

To develop the economic condition of the Mahar and the Chambhar, another Co-operative Society has been formed which got a gift of about one hundred acres of land, alongwith financial assistance for development of the same. The plot is at an altitude of about 700 ft. Irrigation is a problem there, though the quality of the land is good. The members divided it into small plots and are cultivating the same independently.

The *sarpanch* and the Deputy *sarpanch* of the existing committee belong to the Maratha caste. Both the factions largely have faith in the ruling Congress Party. These factions exist only at the village level. If one faction supports a political party, the other usually supports the opponent without consideration of any merit.

The sarpanch is the President of the Local Block Congress (Ruling) Committee and also a member of the local Panchayat

Samiti. The police *patil*, a Maratha, is also well known in the area though in a limited scale. There are others from the Maratha caste who form the second line of local leadership. The Mahar and the Chambhar have no such involvement.

Even, in other organisations like Milk Society, co-operative Credit Society, chit Fund, the participation of the Mahar and the Chamber, both as committee member as well as ordinary member, is negligible. From a composite list of committee members from time to time, it is noted that one Mahar got elected as a member of the committee, once in the case of the Milk Society. Other members were the Maratha. The Mahar member of the Milk Society has been replaced by a Navi in the present committee. There has been no substitution for the Maratha.

The President and Vice-President of the local Panchayat Samiti during different periods were mostly the Maratha. Only once the President was a Mang and the Vice-President has been a Jain. The present Chairman and the Vice-Chairman of the Zilla Parishad are Maratha and the previous incumbents also belonged to the same group.

The local constituency has been declared as a Scheduled Constituency for the present term and consequently the present member of the Legislative Assembly is from a Scheduled Caste. This is not a Permanent Scheduled Constituency. The sitting member of the Parliament for the area is a Maratha.

It may be mentioned here that of the eleven members of the Legislative Assembly in the district, seven are Maratha, two are Jain, one Brahman, and the other is from the Dhor caste.

Religious Groups and Sects

It is stated earlier that the villagers of Tasgaon belong to three religious groups, namely, the Hindu, the Muslim, and the Christian. The Sutar and Gurao are of Lingayat sect. They are strictly vegetarian.

The Hindu festivals which are observed in a year are as follows : (i) Padba (ii) Shimga (iii) Ramnavami (iv) Hanuman Jayanti (v) Akiti (vi) Bendur (vii) Panchim (viii) Nabaratri (ix) Gokul Astami (x) Diwali and (xi) Sankrant.

Padba is observed on the first day of the year of the local Maratha calendar, which corresponds to the *saka* era. On this day the farmers of all the castes erect a *gudi* and observe the ritual for a good harvest. In *shimga,* the fire is lighted to *holi* and *hola* by the Mang widow. This festival corresponds to the Holi festival. Other Hindu castes take their term by putting some fire wood to be guided by the Mang. Significantly, playing of colour is restricted usually to individual caste groups, with some relaxation within the respective clusters. This restriction, is, however, strictly observed in respect of the members belonging to the high and untouchable clusters. Other festivals mostly observed by the high castes, leave minimum scope for the lower groups to participate or to play any role in it. Even during the Diwali festival, the interactions between them is minimum, and besides *gudi* and *shimga* it is the only festival in which the members of the untouchable groups participate, though not in a much significant manner. On all other occasions when the high caste observe their festivals, the untouchables simply prepare and eat special food as a mark of festivity without observance of any ritual. Untouchables are not permitted to enter the temples and any religious procession is not taken through their inhabited area. The high caste people keep the untouchables away from the ritual observances of their own. On some ritual occasions the untouchables receive some food articles from the high caste houses which the former take as *prasad*.

Mention may be made here of the worship of *Bhauka*, the village God, which takes place in the month of *Jaisth* (May-June) every year. *Bhauka* is considered to be the God of rains and is worshipped by the *balutdars* (both clean and unclean). The Mang and the Mahar who are also the *balutdars* by virtue of their occupation, are not allowed to participate in it though the Ramoshi and the Chambhar, both untouchables, are allowed to participate in it.

It is the duty of the Mang to keep the temple of *Margubai* clean and look after it. If there is an epidemic of cholera offerings are made to the deity by the Mahar. In case a Maratha needs and wants to offer any *puja*, he does so only through the Mahar priest. The *prasad*, provided through the offerings of the Maratha is shared by the Mahar only and Maratha do not take any.

There are some sects of the lower denominations. There are as many as forty individuals who are the follower of *Suint Tukaram*. Most of them are Maratha, with a few from the high castes, and none from the untouchables. The devotees arrange to meet periodically and sing *bhajan* in praise of their religious teacher. A Dhanger (low caste) of another village, who happens to be the secretary of the Panchayat, sometime participates in it. It appears that the rigidity of caste prohibitions prescribed for untouchables in general can be relaxed for outsiders. In a feast arranged by a Maratha on the eve of *Tukaram Saptah*, the school teachers of the village some of whom are Mahar were entertained and even their leaf-plates were lifted by a Maratha. On this occasion a drama was staged and songs were sung which the untouchables alongwith other villagers witnessed.

Some Mahar beg once a week taking the image of their deity along. Each of the households belonging to the high castes gives some quantity of jawari to the devotee.

Some of the untouchables who have *Khandoba* as their lineage god, observe a day in a year as the *jatra* day. The devotee belonging to different untouchable castes gather at a place and worship the god.

The Muslim of the village observe only two major festivals, Muharram and Bakrid, in which no Hindu participates. They prepare and eat special food (puranpoli) on these occasions. During the month of Ramjan, they observe fast only for five to ten days. During these festivals and on some other occasions they go to a neighbouring village (2 kms. away) for mass prayers, where there is a sizeable Muslim population in that village and which has a well maintained mosque. During the early part of this century, some of the Mahar got converted to Christianity at Vadgaon-Peth. At present baptism rarely takes place. Some of the important ceremonies they observe include *Natal* (Christmas) and *Nabinbarsa* (new year's day). On these occasions the head of the household with children go to the chapel at Vadgaon-Peth to attend the mass prayer. They are Roman Catholics. They also prepare special food items which are in no way different from that which is prepared by members of other faiths during their respective festive occasions. Besides their own festivals, they also prepare special food during any important Hindu festival as per demand of their children.

Conversion and its Implication

A section of the Mahar in the village got converted to Christianity in the early part of the present century. With the establishment of the British rule in India, the activities of the Christian missionaries became obvious in various parts of the country. They started their mission in India as a part of their global strategy, with the support of the then British rulers. With their selfless service in the educational and medical fields which were particularly extended to the backward communities, the missionaries were soon able to attract members of the down-trodden classes to get converted into Christianity. The Mahar of the area were in no way exception to this.

As per the nature of the caste-based society in India, it is elaborately stratified on the basis of ritual concept of purity and pollution. The castes in the lower rung are the most sufferers. Being branded as untouchables, they are subjected to all sorts of humiliation by the high caste people. They always suffer from the stigma of low-born status. Their Hindu identity is even put in question at times by the members of the high caste groups. Their economic condition is also, in general, pitiable as they mostly suffer from chronic impoverishment. The Mahar of the area represent a true example of such groups. The Mahar of the village were mostly landless (till 1955) and depended mainly on agricultural labour. Their ritual status is also very low in the caste hierarchy. So, when the activities of the missionaries were operative, the Mahar were also attracted by it and some got converted between first and second decade of the present century.

This conversion can in no way, be considered in the light of any mobility movement. A mobility movement, in the Indian context is characterised by the indigeneous incentive surcharged within a group itself with an ulterior motive to move upward in the caste hierarchy. But here the question of such conversion does not offer any such motive. Further, Christianity does not accept any stratification on the basis of caste. There was no indigenous incentive in the process of conversion, rather it was an extraneous influence. Though the Mahar occupy the position numerically next to the Maratha, only a few families got converted. There was also no uniform response to such conversion. It has been found that the Hindu Mahar do not prefer to get themselves converted now. Though there are marriages between the Hindu and the Christian Mahar, some of the Hindu Mahar are reluctant to give their daughters in marriage to the Christian boys. As there is no caste distinction in the church, members of the castes which are lower in status than the Mahar enjoy the same status with those of the Mahar.

Of the other untouchable castes in the village, the Chambhar occupy the highest position. They were not so much discriminated as in caste of the Mahar. The Chambhar were shoe makers when the

Mahar were lifters of dead animals. They were also used to consume the flesh of carrion which gave them a very low position. Though some Chambhar got converted in other parts of the state they were in general particularly in this part of the State not attracted by the services offered by the missionaries. The shoe making industry here has an age old reputation in the country and as such, the economic condition of the Chambhar was not that miserable as that of the Mahar. The other two untouchable castes viz., the Mang and the Ramoshi have one family each and they are recent migrants to the village.

The conversion could not bring to the Mahar a higher social status. As has been stated earlier, the converts have availed of the educational facilities extended by the Christian missionaries and show a high rate of literacy. Some of the educated Maratha do recognize such achievement but never did they grant any concession to them. The ritual position of these converts and non-converts is largely the same and their interaction with the high castes are restrained. To the other castes as well as to their Hindu counterpart they are Mahar first and then Christian. The converts themselves have the similar impression. While taking household census when asked about their caste, the Christian Mahars' reply was that they are Mahar by caste and Christian by religion.

Conclusion

In the preceding discussions we have examined the position of different castes with reference to their relative control over the local resources, social, economic, political, and communicational. In most parts different positions of a caste do not exactly correspond. The numerical dominance has also been accounted for, as in a democratic set up it has a pronounced importance. On the whole, however, none of these facets is less important than the other.

Taking all these criteria in view, the two positions: decisively dominant and decisively weak, are fairly recognisable.

If we analyse the condition of the untouchables in general, we observe that until Independence they were mostly landless and without any control over the power structure. Provision of reservation of seats in the village panchayat has compelled the dominant groups to part with some privileges and share control of the village power structure with them. Various other developmental schemes specially laid for the untouchables could not precipitate. They could not make use of these privileges to any extent due to lack of awareness as well as as resourcefulness.

Since Independence, various developmental programmes have been taken up, the fruits of which are being enjoyed by the dominant group as well as the weak. But because of the edge over the weak, the dominant group is in an advantageous position in comparison. The special interest in educational programmes on part of the weaker castes is a welcome development in this respect which is likely to provide awareness as well as communicational network in order to derive benefits out of governmental programme. Extension of additional employment facilities will be of help in this respect. Proper implementation of different schemes and review and adjustment of the developmental programmes from time to time may help in weeding out the handicaps.

13

VINZAR : A VILLAGE IN WESTERN MAHARASHTRA

N.N. KUNDU

Introduction

The field work for this study was undertaken in Vinzar during the period from July, 1973 to December 1973. The village is situated in Havel Tahsil of Poona District, Maharashtra. The village was selected as it satisfied all the criteria laid down in the guideline for the present study. To state briefly the study proposes to describe the socio-economic condition of the weak in the rural areas and to show whether any significant changes have taken place among them since independence.

Data were collected from Vinzar on the basis of the guideline and through different schedules, interview, participant observation and case history. Village census has been collected from the head of each family of the main village and its hamlets. Some households have left for Poona and Bombay cities and these families have not been included for this study. Data on income and expenditure was collected from selected 58 households irrespective of caste. Information about indebtedness was also collected from the people of different castes who were in debt to the money-lenders.

Description of Location

Vinzar is an interior village surrounded on its northern and southern sides by hills having height more than 4,000 feet. The hills in the north and the south are respectively two miles and four miles away from the main village. The hills in this area are the extension of Sahayadri ranges and the area comprises of ups and downs here and there in the northern side of the village and the cultivable land of the village starts from the foot of the northern hills.

Vinzar is a dispersed village having four hamlets i.e., (a) Tamkar wadi in the north-west direction and approximately four furlongs away from the main village, (b) Bhuruk wadi in the north-east direction, near the hill and one mile away from the main village, (c) Dhangar wasti in the north direction, situated at the top of the hills, houses constructed in dispersed way and more than two miles away from the main village and (d) Harijan wasti is situated in the east and one furlong away from the main village.

Vinzar is named after Vinjhai debi situated in the south-West direction near the main village. This is an old deity of the village and one goat is sacrificed before the goddess during worship. Tamkar wadi is named after the surname - *Tamkar* of a Maratha who came from the main village to settle in this area, but the Tamkar family is no more here. Bhuruk wadi is named after the surname - Bhuruk of the Maratha who are still living in this hamlet. Danger wasti is named after the Dhangar who are still living in that area and Harijan wasti is named after the Harijan who still live there.

In the main village the people of eighteen communities excluding the Belder, Chambhar, and Mahar are living. The Maratha and Belder live in Tamkar wadi, only the Maratha in Bhuruk wadi. only the Dhangar in Dhangar wasti and the Harijan wasti is inhabited by the Mang, Chambhar and Mahar.

Language

Language of the people is Marathi which is the regional language of Maharashtra state. Some educated persons also understand Hindi and English. A few Brahman families are immigrants to this village and they speak Konkani dialect.

Communication, Transportation and Public Places

Vinzar with 1864 people is one of the largest villages in this area. Poona - Bangalore national highway bifurcates near Nasrapur where from a metalled and motorable road goes upto Velhe - Mahar taluka headquarters. The Nasrapur - Velhe-Mahal road passes through Vinzar. Every two hours State Transport buses ply between Poona city and Velhe-Mahal Taluka headquarters.

TABLE 1: Population composition

Sl. No.	Group	Total no. of family		Total Male	Total Female	Total Male and Female
1.	Beldar	1	No.	3	4	7
			%	42.86	57.14	(0.38)
2.	Brahman	13	No.	33	31	64
			%	51.56	48.44	(3.43)
3.	Dhangar(Sc)	24	No.	55	52	107
			%	51.4	48.6	(5.74)
4.	Dhobi(Sc)	4	No.	18	20	38
			%	47.37	52.63	(2.04)
5.	Gurao	7	No.	17	28	45
			%	37.78	62.22	(2.41)
6.	Jain	1	No.	1	—	1
			%	100		(0.05)
7.	Kasar	1	No.	11	8	(1.02)
			%	57.89	42.11	3
8.	Koli-Mahadeo	1	No.	2	1	(0.16)
			%	66.67	33.33	2
9.	Lingayat	1	No.	1	1	(0.11)
			%	50	50	233
10.	Mahar(Sc)	33	No.	113	120	(12.50)
			%	48.5	51.5	9
11.	Mali(Sc)	3	No.	6	3	(0.48)
			%	66.67	33.33	42
12.	Mang(Sc)	7	No.	23	19	(2.25)
			%	54.76	45.24	1095
13.	Maratha	185	No.	498	597	(58.74)
			%	45.48	59.52	30
14.	Mochi	5	No.	15	15	(1.61)
			%	50	50	17
15.	Muslim	4	No.	7	10	(0.91)
			%	41.18	58.82	33
16.	Nhavi	4	No.	13	20	(1.77)
			%	39.4	60.6	1
17.	Panchal	1	No.	1	—	(0.05)
			%	100	18	
18.	Ramoshi	2	No.	11	7	(0.97)
			%	61.11	38.89	27
19.	Sonar(Sc)	7	No.	16	11	(1.45)
			%	59.26	40.74	39
20.	Sutar(Sc)	6	No.	23	16	(2.09)
			%	58.97	41.05	34
21.	Teli	5	No.	18	16	(1.82)
			%	52.94	47.06	
	TOTAL	315	No.	885	979	1864
			%	47.48	52.52	(100.00)

In the village there are two primary schools i.e., one in the main village and another one in Tamkar wadi, one high school in the main village, a dispensary, hotel, bus stand, flour mill, village panchayat office, talim (gymkhana), Vairabnath temple, Maruti temple and Vishnu temple. A primary school teacher is running a sub-post office in the village and a Maratha has been appointed as a postman in this sub-post office. On the right side of the metalled road, there is a milk collection centre for the Dairy Society. Altars of Masoba and Maskoba deities and two household temples are found in the locality of the Mang. Cremation grounds of different higher castes are situated in the north-east and north-west sides of the main village. Three cremation grounds for the three Scheduled Castes and burial place for the Muslim are situated near the eastern side of the Harijan wasti. The Dhangar bury the dead body in the hills.

Population Distribution

The population of Vinzar is composed of members of several castes, which include the Maratha, the Brahman and a number of other castes such as the Beldlar, Dhangar, Gurao, Jain, Kasar, Koli-Mahadeo, Lingayat, Mali Muslim, Nhavi, Panchal, Parit (Dhobi), Ramoshi, Sonar, Sutar, Teli, Mang, Chambhar and Mahar. In the village 16.35 per cent people are Scheduled Castes i.e., Mang, Chambhar, and Mahar having 160 persons together and 0.16 per cent people are a Scheduled Tribe i.e., Koli-Mahadeo having three persons and the other caste groups having 1701 persons and constituting 83.48 per cent of the total population. There are altogether 315 families, out of which the Maratha are having 185 families with a population of 1095, 33 Mahar families having 233 persons, 24 Dhangar families having 107 persons, 13 Brahman families having 64 persons, and the Guaro, Mang, and Sonar families having 45,42 and 27 persons respectively. There are six Surat families having 39 persons, five each of Chambhar (Mochi) and Teli families having 30 and 34 persons, four each of Parit (Dhobi), Muslim and Nhavi having 38, 17 and 33 persons respectively, three Mali families having nine persons, two Ramoshi families having 18 persons and one each of Belder, Jain, Kasar, Koli-Mahadeo and Lingayat Panchal are having seven, one, nineteen, 32, and one person respectively. Table 1 shows the population composition of Vinzar. Out of the total population 47.48 per cent are male and 52.52 per cent are female, the sex ratio being 1106 females per thousand males.

One of each Beldlar, Jain, Koli-Mahadeo, Lingayat, Mang, Muslim, Panchal, Sonar, Teli. two Mali and eight Maratha families are immigrants to the village. The Jain, Koli-Mahadeo, Lingayat, Panchal, Sonar, one Mali and eight Maratha are school teachers in this village. The Maratha are numerically dominant in comparison to other communities in the village. Second and third positions are held by the Mahar and Dhangar respectively. The remaining communities are having less population.

Economic Dimension

Vinzar is a revenue village having an area of 2251 acres and 17 3/4 gunthe of cultivable land, out of which the villagers of Vinzar are holding 1800.56 acres of cultivable land and the rest is occupied by the outsiders. There are 150 acres and 34 1/4 gunthe of land under river, canal, and fallow land, 13 acres 26 gunthe for gaonthan (Village courtyard), 11 acres 16 gunthe for marg (road), 10 1/4 gunthe for cremation and burial ground, four acres 12 1/4 gunthe under Kharak (rocky area) and 1119 acres are forest area.

The soil of the village is locally classified into four types.

1. Kali — Black soil — best quality for growing *Bhat* (rice), *Gehu*, *Harbara*, *Masur* and Hybrid *Jawari*.
2. Telangi — Brown soil — inferior to black soil and growing *Salu* (local variety of *Jowar*), *Bhat* (rice), *Harbara*, *Masur*, Hybrid *Jawari*.
3. Tambdi — Red soil — inferior to brown soil and growing the same crops as in *telangi* soil.
4. Safed — Whitish soil — inferior to red soil and growing only *gawat* (grass) and it is generally grazing ground for domestic animals.

There are 21 communities in the village but people of only 14 communities i.e., the Brahman, Dhangar, Gurao, Kasar, Mahar, Mali, Mang, Maratha, Nhavi, Parit, Ramoshi, Sonar, Sutar and Teli are having cultivable land. Table 2 gives the distribution of various types of land held by various communities. Kali Jamin is the best quality of land and its total quantity in the village is 110,59 acres.

TABLE 2: Land — Type held by various communities

Sl. No.	Community		Landless family	Landless members	Land owning family	Land owning members	*Kali* Acres	*Telangi* Acres	*Tambdi* Acres	*Safed* Acres	Total	Per capita
1.	Brahman	No.	3	6	10	58	0.45	44.01	175.74	142.73	362.93	5.67
		%					(0.41)	(8.78)	(18.66)	(57.74)	(20.16)	
2.	Dhangar	No.	15	58	9	49	—	0.72	53.05	—	53.77	0.5
		%						(0.14)	(5.63)		(2.99)	
3.	Gurao	No.	—	—	7	45	2.53	6.29	32.09	—	40.9	0.91
		%					(2.29)	(1.25)	(3.41)		(2.27)	
4.	Kasar	No.	—	—	1	19	—	0.54	—	—	0.54	0.028
		%						(0.11)			(0.03)	
5.	Mahar	No.	4	112	29	221	1.14	27.76	31.6	—	60.5	0.26
		%					(1.03)	(5.54)	(3.36)		(3.36)	
6.	Mali	No.	2	8	1	1	—	0.06	—	—	0.06	0.007
		%						(0.01)			(0.003)	
7.	Mang	No.	4	127	3	15	—	0.65	—	—	0.65	0.015
		%						(0.13)			(0.04)	
8.	Maratha	No.	20	60	165	1035	98.87	384.65	596.99	91.54	1172.05	1.07
		%					(89.40)	(76.75)	(63.40)	(37.03)	(65.09)	

(*Contd.*)

(Contd.)

Sl. No.	Community		Landless family	Landless members	Land owning family	Land owning members	*Kali* Acres	*Telangi* Acres	*Tambdi* Acres	*Safed* Acres	Total	Per capita
9.	Nhavi	No.	—	—	4	33	1.12	7.15	—	—	8.27	0.25
		%					(1.01)	(1.43)			(0.46)	
10.	Parit	No.	—	—	4	38	5.04	16.41	30.85	6.89	59.2	1.56
		%					(4.56)	(3.27)	(3.28)	(2.79)	(3.29)	
11.	Ramoshi	No.	—	—	2	18	—	0.24	—	—	0.24	0.013
		%						(0.05)			(0.01)	
12.	Sonar	No.	5	20	2	7	0.51	3.63	3.01	—	7.16	0.27
		%					(0.46)	(0.72)	(0.32)		(0.40)	
13.	Sutar	No.	—	—	6	39	0.93	1.19	—	0.63	2.74	0.07
		%					(0.84)	(0.24)		(0.25)	(0.15)	
14.	Teli	No.	1	1	4	33	—	7.9	18.23	5.42	31.55	0.[illegible]3
		%										
	TOTAL	No.	54	392	247	1611	110.59	501.2	941.56	247.21	1800.55	0.97
							(6.14)	(27.84)	(52.29)	(13.73)	(100.00)	

89, 40 per cent of Kali land is held by the Maratha, 4.56 per cent by the Parit (Dhobi), but the Brahman, Gurao, Mahar, Nhavi, Sonar, and Sutar are having insignificant quantity of Kali land. All the 14 communities are having 501.20 acres of *telangi* land, out of which the Maratha are holding 76.75 per cent, 8.78 per cent land are held by the Brahman and other communities are holding insignificant amount of Telangi land. Eight communities i.e., the Brahman, Dhangar, Gurao, Mahar, Maratha, Parit, Sonar, and Teli are holding 941.56 acres of *tambdi* land in the village. The Maratha are holding 63.40 per cent of *tambdi* land, 18.66 per cent are owned by the Brahman and the rest are held by other six communities. Only five communities are holding 247.21 acres of safed land, out of which the Brahman are holding 57.74 per cent, the Maratha are holding 37,03 per cent and the other three communities are holding the rest amount of *safed* land. It is seen that the Maratha are holding the maximum amount of four types of land, the second position landholding wise is held by the Brahman. The other twelve communities each is having less than four per cent of land. The Beldar, Jain, Koli-Mahadeo, Lingayat, Chambhar, Muslim, and Panchal families are landless.

There are 315 families of different communities but only 247 families (78.41%) are holding cultivable land and 68 families are (21.59%) landless in the village. Out of 247 families *kali* land is held by 120 families, Telang land by 179 families, Tambdi land by 163 families and Safed land by twentytwo families. Only ten Brahman families, out of 13 are having cultivable land. Distribution of four types of land among the Brahman is not equal.

Kali land is held by only two Brahman families, *telangi* land by eight families, *tambdi* land by nine families and *safed* land by six families. Out of 185 Maratha families, only 165 families are having cultivable land. *Kali* land is held by 95 families, Telangi land by 11 families. Only nine families, out of 24 Dhangar families are having *telangi* and *tambdi* types of land. Possession of land by the other eleven communities is very much less.

In the village the amount of land per head is 0.97 acres. Out of the fourteen communities the Brahman are having per capita the maximum quantity of land i.e., 5.67 acres. The Parit hold the second position with 1.56 acres, the third position is of the Maratha holding 1.07 acres per head and the other eleven caste groups are having less than one acre of per capita land.

Thirty three families belonging to Brahman, Maratha, Mahar,

Gurao, and Parit caste groups are having 85 acres 32 1/4 gunthe of cultivable land in a neighbouring village called Malwali.

In the village the Beldar, Jain, Koli-Mahadeo, Lingayat, Chambhar, Muslim, and Panchal families are landless and among them the Jain, Koli-Mahadeo, Lingayat, and Panchal families and one Muslim are immigrants. Except these immigrants, one Brahman family, two Mali families, a few Maratha families, one Sonar, one Dhangar and one Teli are also immigrants. The head of the Jain, Koli-Mahadeo, Lingayat, Panchal, Brahman, one Mali and Maratha immigrant families are school teachers, another Mali is a village doctor, one Muslim is a forest rounder, one Maratha is a veterinary doctor and one Dhangar is an attendant in the veterinary hospital in the village. These employees are not considered as poor villagers because, they are having landed property at their native places.

Formerly, the Beldar family was moving from one village to another wherever they used to get traditional jobs. In this village this family has settled for the last six years. And they get job from the villagers every month. But by this income they cannot maintain their family properly.

The Muslim and the Chambhar are living in this village for generations together but they are not having cultivable land. The Muslim are traditionally butchers and get *balut* (annual payment) from the villagers for their job. They are also the agricultural labourers in this village. Through these two sources of income they cannot maintain their family properly and are passing days under hardships. These three Muslim families come under poorer section in the village. The Chambhar also are not having cultivable land in the village. They are still practicing their traditional occupation i.e., making new shoes or repairing the old ones. For performing traditional jobs in the village they get *balut* per year from the villagers. They also work as farm servants to the landowning cultivators in the village and perform their traditional jobs outside the village. Whatever they earn through traditional occupation and agricultural labour, is not sufficient for them to maintain their families. They are very poor in the village.

Agriculture is the principal basis of economy of land-owning villagers and agricultural operations are performed by them on various types of soil during Kharif and Rabi seasons. In Kharif season, the villagers grow the main crops like paddy, nachni, hybrid jawari, and argar (varieties of pulses), and other crops such as *singdana* (groundnut), *karba* (Til), *urid* and *chauri*. In Rabi season, they grow main crops such as *masur, pawta* and *batana*.

Agricultural Innovation

Except in rainy season, the river in the southern side of the main village and two canals i.e., one in the eastern side of the main village and the other one in the eastern side of the Harijan wasti remain dry. The water of this river and canal cannot be used for irrigation purposes. There is heavy rainfall during rainy season which supports to grow paddy in this area. Out of 15 wells, two have been constructed by the help of B.D.Office and the rest of the wells are constructed by twelve villagers belonging to the Brahman and Maratha communities. During scarcity period in the year 1972, one well was constructed by B.D.Office for the Harijans in their cultivable field for irrigation purpose. The other caste groups are not having wells for irrigating their cultivable fields.

Village carpenters also perform the job of smithery of iron and they supply and repair the agricultural implements to the villagers. They get *balut* per year after the harvest season for performing the job of smithery. As regards modern technology, B.D.Office has supplied two spray pumps to the Gram Panchayat Office of Vinzar village. In Vinzar there is a co-operative society named "Vinzar Vividha Karyakari Seva Sahakari Samstha Ltd" and it is having one spray pump and one improved hoe locally called *Kolpa*. Only the members of the co-operative society can use two articles. But all the cultivators can use two spray pumps of Gram Panchayat Office.

B.D. Office and cooperative society supply to the villagers during Kharif and Rabi seasons chemical fertilizers such as Diamophosphate, Sufala, Nitro-phosphate, Ammonium Sulphate, organic manure and Urea.

B.D. Office and co-operative society also supply pesticide, insecticide and herbicide to the villagers. But the quantity is so less that it does not fulfill the demand of all cultivators. The big cultivators purchase these articles from the market at their own costs but the petty land owners cannot purchase these articles due to want of cash money. Here we find that the petty land owners are economically depressed and cannot grow more yield in their field.

Employer-Employee Relationship

The villagers of Vinzar have employer-employee relationship of four kinds i.e., permanent, annual, seasonal and occasional. The members of all Brahman and Maratha families having land more than 15 acres do not go for agricultural labour anywhere. Occasional labourers are available in the village from the remaining communities and also from the landless and petty landowning Maratha families. They are paid at a daily wage of Rs. 2.00 per head in case of men and Rs. 1.50 in case of women. Whenever the petty land owners possessing upto five acres of land do not have agricultural work in their field go for daily labour to another cultivator of the village. Exchange of labour is also performed among near relatives. The landowners having five to 15 acres of land also employ farm servants during Kharif and Rabi season. In the village three Brahman families have employed three seasonal employees, four annual employees and nine permanent employees for agricultural activities. Fourteen Maratha families have employed four seasonal employees, six annual employees and four permanent employees. Only one Parit family holds sufficient amount of land and has employed one permanent employee belonging to the Mahar community. These seasonal, annual and permanent employees are given clothes, food and remuneration ranging from Rs. 10.00 to Rs. 125.00 per month. During harvesting time, most of the cultivators employ daily labourers. Generally the employees belong to the Maratha, Dhangar, Muslim, Sonar, Rashomi, Mahar, Mang, and Katkori communities. Only one Katkori, eight Maratha, three Mahar and one Dhangar have come here from neighbouring villages as agricultural labourers and the other labourers belong to this village. Table 3 has given the distribution of employees to the land owners.

In dairy farm the rich Brahman family has employed 14 permanent servants whose pay varies from Rs. 130.00 to Rs. 180.00. Nine temporary servants and their wage ranging from Rs. 90.00 to Rs. 100.00, 59 part-time servants and their wage ranging from Rs. 42.00 to Rs. 100.00 and four daily labourers at the rate of Rs. 3.50 per head per day are also employed. In transport business eight permanent workers are employed with the wage ranging from Rs. 110.00 to Rs. 220.00 and three temporary employees with the wage ranging from Rs. 75.00 to Rs. 90.00. The employees of the dairy farm and transport business belong to Brahman, Maratha, Ramoshi,

Teli, Harijan (Mahar), Chambhar, Kumbhar, and Muslim communities. Landless villagers and petty landowners always try to get labour work in the village itself. But five Mahar are employed in industries at Poona city and four Mahar are employed in cloth mills and private firms in Bombay city. It is thus seen that the petty landowners and landless villagers are agricultural labourers in the village.

TABLE 3: Farm servants

Employer (Caste)	No. of employers family	Seasonal employees	Annual employee	Permanent employee
Brahman	3	3	4	9
Maratha	14	4	6	4
Parit (Dhobi)	1	—	—	1
Total	18	7	10	14

Other Servants

Dairy farm

Employer (Brahman)	Perma nent servant	Pay Scale	Tempo rary servant	Pay Scale	Part-time servant	Wages	Daily labour	Wage
Seeram Hari & Phadke & his brothers	14	Ranging From Rs. 130 to Rs. 180 p.m.	9	Ranging from Rs. 90 to Rs. 100 p.m.	59	Ranging from Rs. 42 to Rs. 100 p.m.	4	Rs. 3.50 per head
Transport Business								
-do-	8	Ranging from Rs. 100 to Rs. 220	3	Ranging from Rs. 75 to Rs. 90				
Total	22		12		59	4		

Sharecropping in the Village

Four types of sharecropping are practised by the villagers and these four types are locally termed as a) *ardhalini*, b) *tijhaini*, c) *chowthaini*, d) *khandani*.

TABLE 4: Sharecropping

Landowner (caste)	No.	Sharecropper (caste)	No.	Contract in local term
Brahman	5	Maratha	1	
		Mang	3	
		Ramoshi	1	
		Sutar	2	
		Chambhar	1	
Maratha	3	Maratha	1	
		Dhangar	1	Ardhalini
		Maratha	1	
Mahar	1	Sutar	1	
Sutar	1	Sutar	1	
Brahman	1	Maratha, Parit, Sutar	11	
				Tijhaini
Maratha	1	Dhangar	1	
Brahman	3	Chambhar	3	
		Mahar	8	Chowthaini
		Mahar	9	
Brahman	1	Maratha	4	Khandani
Maratha	6	Dhangar	3	
		Dhangar	3	
		Dhangar	1	
		Dhangar	1	
		Dhangar	1	
		Brahman	1	
Teli	1	Dhangar	1	
Mahar	2	Mahar	1	
		Mahar	1	

Ardhalini means 1/2 share of the yield is taken by the sharecropper and the other 1/2 by the landowner. *Tijhaini* means 2/3 share is taken by the landowner. Chowthaini means 3/4 share of yield is taken by the sharecropper and 1/4 share is taken by the landowner. Khandani means a kind of mortgaging the land. After taking money, the landowner gives away the land for cultivating for a fixed period. The landowner without taking money gets certain fixed amount of yield but not as a share from the mortgage. Table 4 gives the data on land-owner-tenant relationship.

Under the *ardhalini*, five Brahman have given their plots of land to one Maratha, three Mang, one Ramoshi, two Sutar together and one Chambhar for cultivating them. Three Maratha have given each plot of land to one Maratha, one Dhangar and one Maratha. One Mahar has given his land to one Sutar and one Sutar has given his land to another Sutar in the same terms. In terms of *tijhaini* one Brahman has given his land to eleven persons of Maratha, Parit, and Sutar together and one Maratha has given his land to one Dhangar. In terms of chowthaini three Brahman have given their three plots of land separately to a group of three Chambhar together, eight Mahar together and nine Mahar together. Under Khandani one Brahman has given his land to four Maratha together, six Maratha similarly have given their land to three Dhangar together, three Dhangar separately and one Brahman and one Teli gave land to one Dhangar, and two Mahar to other two Mahar separately. All terms and nature of contract are fixed verbally and the landowners do not agree to hand over their land to the sharecroppers in writing, lest, the sharecroppers may occupy the land under the Land Tenancy Act. In the table 4 it is seen that the landless villagers and petty landowners go for sharecropping due to their economically distressed condition. It is proved that the landless villagers and petty landowners irrespective of castes are very poor in the village.

Occupational Mobility

Agriculture is the principal basis of economy of the villagers who are having only cultivable land. The landless people earn their livelihood through agricultural labour or through their traditional occupation. The last two ascending generations were cultivators and did not go outside the village for accepting new occupation. The villagers of the present generation do cultivation in their field but many villagers have accepted new occupation is Poona and Bombay cities. The dominant landowners of the Brahman and Maratha communities are getting sufficient yield from their fields to maintain their families. They are educating their children properly and after getting higher education the male persons are getting jobs in Poona and Bombay cities. Many educated persons have settled in cities and do not come to their village for performing agricultural activities. Some employed Maratha come back to the village on leave or during Kharif and Rabi seasons for agricultural operations. From the families of petty landowners and landless villagers, one Parit is working in the defence factory and another one is in a private firm, one Sutar in a private firm, and one Muslim as a watchman in the Reserve Forest. A few Mahar are working in cloth mills, electricity board, government office, and as school teachers. One Chambhar is working in the army as a soldier, two Gurao are in a newspaper press, (Tarun Bharat), one Dhangar boy is in cloth mills, and 52 Maratha are working in cloth mills in Bombay city. Many have returned to the village after their retirement from the mill and their sons have got employment in the same mill. Economic factor influences the villagers to choose new occupations outside the village.

Livestock

The landowners of Vinzar keep bullocks as draft animals for ploughing their fields. In agricultural seasons they sometimes give bullocks on hire to the co-villagers who do not have their own. The Maratha are having 143 bullocks, which is the maximum number. The Brahman are having only 16 bullocks and the Dhangar, Garao, Mahar, Parit, Ramoshi, Sonar, and Teli communities are having less than 10 bullocks each. Table 5 gives the census of live-stock among different castes.

Gauri Dhangar — a shepherd group have a good number of cows and she-buffaloes and milking is their traditional occupation. The other villagers rear cows and she-buffaloes for running their milk business. The Maratha are rearing maximum number of domestic animals and the next positions are occupied by the Dhangar and Brahman in order of precedence. The other communities are rear a limited number of domestic animals. One Brahman and six Maratha dairymen are supplying milk from the village directly to Poona city. At first the Brahman dairyman started supplying milk to Poona and then the Maratha took up the job. The Brahman dairyman supplies on an average 300 litres of milk in summer season and 125 litres of

TABLE 5: Livestock census

Community	No. of cows	No. of calf she	No. of calf he	Bull	She buffalo	He buffalo	Calf buffalo She	Calf buffalo he	Hen	Cock	Goat	Sheep	Total
Beldar	—	—	—	—	—	—	—	—	—	—	—	—	—
Brahman	11	8	5	16	23	1	3	—	—	—	—	—	67
Chambhar	—	—	—	—	4	—	—	—	7	—	—	—	1
Dhangar	89	58	22	9	38	—	13	4	34	1	—	—	268
Gurao	5	1	1	6	5	—	1	—	16	—	—	—	35
Jain	—	—	—	—	—	—	—	—	—	—	—	—	—
Koli-Mahadeo	—	—	—	—	—	—	—	—	—	—	—	—	—
Kasar	—	1	—	—	1	—	1	—	—	—	—	—	3
Lingayat	—	—	—	—	—	—	—	—	—	—	—	—	—
Mahar	4	3	3	11	33	—	11	—	76	4	—	2	147
Mali	—	—	—	—	—	—	—	—	—	—	—	—	—
Mang	—	—	—	—	3	—	2	—	6	—	—	—	11
Maratha	96	44	53	143	182	—	75	8	353	88	—	4	980
Muslim	—	—	—	—	3	1	—	—	9	—	1	—	14
Nhavi	2	—	2	—	2	—	—	—	16	—	—	—	22
Panchal	—	—	—	—	—	—	—	—	—	—	—	—	—
Parit	2	4	—	7	7	—	2	—	10	4	—	2	38
Ramoshi	2	—	1	2	1	—	1	—	—	2	—	—	9
Sonar	1	—	2	1	—	—	—	—	5	—	—	—	9
Sutar	—	—	—	—	2	—	—	—	11	2	—	—	15
Teli	1	—	3	1	2	—	2	—	18	2	—	—	29
TOTAL	213	119	92	196	306	2	111	12	561	37	1	8	1658

milk in winter season. The other six Maratha dairymen supply five to 60 litres of milk in summer seasons and five to 25 litres of milk in winter season. In Poona city there is a private organization named District Milk Federation, Poona which is having its branches in many villages of different tahsils of Poona District. A Vinzar Sahakari Dairy Society has been established in 1964 and its managing committee consists of one Chairman (Sabhapati) belonging to Brahman group and five members (*panches*) belong to Maratha group. Its accountant belongs to the Teli. A Maratha has been employed in this dairy society for collecting milk between 7.30 a.m. and 11 a.m. and his remuneration is Rs. 50.00 p.m. 110 villagers have been members in this dairy society with the interest of getting higher rate for one litre of milk than the rate given by the village dairymen. But most of the villagers are cultivators and do not always have cash money with them. Whenever cash money they need the dairy society cannot give them loan but the village dairymen could pay them loan at the time of their need. That is why the milk suppliers are more inclined towards the village dairymen than the dairy society. This is the new course of income and the landless families and the petty landowners also earn through selling of milk.

Sources of Income

Fourteen out of 21 castes in the village are holding total 1800.56 acres of cultivable land. Out of seven landless communities, five are immigrants in this village and the rest two i.e., Muslim and Chambhar are not having cultivable land.

Table 6 shows approximate income (gross) per acre of land per year by types of land.

TABLE 6: Approximate income (Gross) per acre of land per year by type

Type of Land	Name of crops	Yield per acre (in quintals)	Rate per quintal (in Rs.)	Income Rs. P.
Kali Jamin	Paddy (transplanted)	8	105	840.00
	straw	5 (bundle)	10 each	50.00
	Gehu	4	85	340.00
			Total:	1,230.00

Contd.

TABLE 6 *Contd.*

Telangi Jamin	Paddy (transplanted)	8	80	640.00
	Straw	4 (bundle)	10	40.00
	Shalu	4	100	400.00
	Stalk & Chaff	—	—	—
			Total:	1,080.00
Tambdi Jamin	Paddy (transplanted)	8	75	600.00
	Straw	4(bundle)	10	40.00
	Harbara	1	100	100.00
	Chaff	—	—	—
			Total:	740.00

From table 6 it is seen that the villagers derive maximum income from *kali jamin*. Next comes Telangi and *tambdi jamin* in order of precedence. Table 7 gives some idea of approximate expenditure (in Rs.) per acre of land per year by types of land.

The table of expenditure shows that amount of investment necessary for cultivation of *kali* land is higher than that of other types. Then comes investment on *telangi* and *tambdi* in order. However, when we compare the income derived from each type of land we find that the villagers get maximum return from *kali* land. Then comes *telangi* and *tambdi* in order or precedence. The annual net income of *kali* land is as high as Rs. 490.00 per acre. Next comes *telangi* and *tambdi* with Rs. 441.00 and Rs. 147.00 income respectively. Petty landowners having upto five acres of land cannot maintain their family properly for the whole year. Hence, they, alongwith landless people are considered poor in the village.

Sources of Finance

B.D. office, Panchayat samity, Tahsil office, different banks and Vinzar Co-operative Society are the sources of finance for agricultural production, running business and purchasing cattle. In the year 1975 and 1968 B.D. office offered loan of Rs. 500.00 each to

TABLE 7: Approximate expenditure (in Rs.) per acre of land per yearly type

Items of expenditure	Types of land			
	Kali	Telangi	Tambdi	Safed
1. Rent of Land	3	2	1	0.50
2. Cost of labour for preparation of seed bed (including ploughing, manuring, broadcasting, charges for irrigation) and uprooting of seedlings	60	50	40	00
3. Charge for ploughing (first, second, third & so on) including cost of human and bullock labour)	100	75	75	00
4. Labour charge for manuring	100	75	75	00
5. Labour charge for transplantation	90	75	75	00
6. Labour charge for weeding	40	40	30	00
7. Labour charges for treatment of plants, if any		—	—	—
8. Labour charge for harvesting including transportation cost	60	60	50	00
9. Labour charge for thrashing including cost of preparation of thrashing ground	30	30	30	00
10. Labour charge for storing including treatment of grains	5	5	5	00
11. Labour charge for irrigation, if any	12	12	12	00
12. Labour charge for contour bunding	5	5	5	00
Cost of material				
Seed	100	75	60	00
Manure & Fertilizers	100	100	100	00
Plant protection chemicals	20	20	20	00
Average cost of tools and implements	15	15	15	00
Total expenditure (in Rs.)	740	639	593	50

two Maratha and one Nhavi for milk business. In the years 1968 and 1970 two maratha received loan of Rs. 1000.00 each for constructing well (*bihir*). In the years 1958 and 1959 three Maratha, one Teli and one Nhavi received loan ranging from Rs. 200.00 to Rs. 500.00 for construction of bunds in their agricultural fields. In the year 1970-71, the Panchayat Samiti of Poona District gave loan ranging from Rs. 95.00 to Rs. 99.00 to six Maratha, one Parit, and one Gurao for agricultural operations. The Maharashtra Bank, Bhumi Vikash Bank, and Poona District Central Co-operative Bank Ltd., gave loan to the villagers of Vinzar co-operative society and among them 130 were landowners. To be a member it is required for the person to pay Rs. 5.00 to the society. This co-operative society has offered loan till now to 95 members belonging to Brahman, Maratha, Parit, Teli, Nhavi, Gurao, Sutar, and Mahar communities. Loan for Rs. 29000.00 i.e., Rs. 15000.00 for fertilizer (khat) and Rs. 14000.00 for cash payment has been distributed among these 95 members with the 9 per cent interest annum and 12 per cent interest per annum if not repaid in the first year.

Six Maratha, two Brahman and one Gurao moneylenders of this village give loan to the villagers. The rich Brahman does not receive any interest from the borrowers but the other moneylenders take interest ranging from six per cent to 10 per cent p.m. from the borrowers. Three Maratha and two Marwari of the neighbouring villages also gave loan to the villagers of Vinzar with three per cent to six per cent interest.

Table 8 indicates distribution of families according to annual income. The amount of income has been categorised into five slabs i.e., upto 1000, 1001 to 2000,2001 to 3000, 3001 to 4000, 4001 to 6000. Nearly seven per cent of the families come under the slab of upto Rs. 1000, 56.9 per cent families under the slab of Rs. 1001 to 2000, 25.9 per cent families under the slab of Rs. 2001 to 3000, 6.9 per cent families under the slab of Rs. 3001 to 4000 and 3.4 families under the slab of Rs. 4001 to 6000.

Rs. 2000.00 of income can be considered as poverty line and the average size of the family is 5.9 in the village. So, Rs. 33898 p.m. is the income of per capita per annum by which the person cannot meet up the demand of essential needs in his family. Table 9 indicates path among 58 selected families 89.6 per cent are within the poverty line, out of which 32.96 per cent are the poorest and 56.9 cent are poor. Only 10.34 per cent families are rich in the village.

In the village the economically well-off families irrespective of caste possess costly and good number of utensils and ornaments. The Brahman and the landholding Maratha are better in their economic condition and their male members are working in Poona and Bombay cities. The service holders bring new utensils from the city when they visit their home. A few families of Parit, Sonar, Sutar, Gurao, and Nhavi are having a good number of utensils but not so

TABLE 8: Distribution of families according to annual income

Sl. No.	Community	Upto No.	1000%	1001- No.	2000 %	2001- No.	3000 %	3001- No.	4000 %	4001- No.	6000 %	Total
1.	Brahman	—	—	—	—	—	—	—	—	1	1.7	1
2.	Chambhar	—	—	—	—	2	3.4	—	—	—	—	2
3.	Dhangar	—	—	7	12.1	2	3.4	—	—	—	—	9
4.	Gurao	—	—	2	3.4	1	1.7	—	—	—	—	3
5.	Kasar	—	—	—	—	—	—	—	—	1	1.7	1
6.	Mahar	—	—	3	5.2	3	5.2	—	—	—	—	6
7.	Mang	1	1.7	3	5.2	—	—	—	—	—	—	4
8.	Maratha	1	1.7	15	25.9	4	6.9	3	5.2	—	—	23
9.	Muslim	1	1.7	—	—	—	—	—	—	—	—	1
10.	Nhavi	—	—	1	1.7	—	—	—	—	—	—	1
11.	Parit	—	—	—	—	1	1.7	—	—	—	—	1
12.	Ramoshi	—	—	—	—	1	1.7	—	—	—	—	1
13.	Sonar	—	—	1	1.7	—	—	—	—	—	—	1
14.	Sutar	1	1.7	1	1.7	1	1.7	—	—	—	—	3
15.	Teli	—	—	—	—	1	1.7	—	—	—	—	1
	Total	4	6.9	33	56.9	16	27.6	3	5.2	2	3.4	58(100%)

TABLE 9: Level of economic conditions – communitywise

Sl. No.	Community	poorest	poor	rich
1.	Brahman	—	—	1(100%)
2.	Chambhar	1(50%)	1(50%)	—
3.	Dhangar	7(77.78%)	2(22.22%)	—
4.	Gurao	1(33.3%)	2(66.67%)	—
5.	Kasar	—	—	1(100%)
6.	Mahar	6(100%)	—	—
7.	Mang	3(75%)	1(25%)	—
8.	Maratha	—	20(86.96%)	3(13.04%)
9.	Muslim	1(100%)	—	—
10.	Nhavi	—	1(100%)	—
11.	Parit	—	1(100%)	—
12.	Ramoshi	—	1(100%)	—
13.	Sonar	—	1(100%)	—
14.	Sutar	—	2(66.67%)	1(33.33%)
15.	Teli	—	1(100%)	—
	TOTAL	19(32.76%)	33(56.90%)	6(10.34%)

much costly ornaments. The Dhangar, Ramoshi, Mahar, Mang, Chambhar, Beldar are poor in terms of their material possession and they can be considered as very poor.

Differential Expenditure

Table 10 shows per capita expenditure on essential commodities. The information about expenditure has been taken from selected 58 families of the village.

The Muslim, Parit and Ramoshi incur less expenditure on food in comparison to other communities. In case of housing, fuel and incidental expenditure the higher caste groups incur more expenditure than the lower caste groups. All children of the Dhangar, Muslim, Parit, Ramoshi, and Teli are not going to the school. Dhangar, Kasar, Mahar, Maratha, Muslim, Nhavi, Ramoshi, and Sutar incur more expenditure for medicine, Now-a-days the lower cast people also have started wearing terrycot pant and shirt. Kasar, Parit, and Ramoshi incur less money for clothing in comparison to the other communities. The highest expenditure on clothing is made by the Maratha and Brahman people than the other groups.

TABLE 10: Per capita expenditure on essential commodities

Sl. No. 1	Community 2	No. of families 3	No. of members 4	Food 5	Housing & fuel 6	Incidental 7	Educational 8	Medicine 9	Clothing 10
1.	Brahman	1	9	20.21	2.77	1.50	22.22	5.55	44.44
2.	Chambhar	2	16	36.69	2.57	1.52	7.50	9.38	31.25
3.	Dhangar	9	45	31.41	0.61	0.64	—	14.29	30.00
4.	Gurao	3	21	33.75	1.47	1.15	4.76	8.33	42.86
5.	Kasar	1	19	31.44	1.05	1.68	—	10.52	26.32
6.	Mahar	6	59	36.51	0.46	1.02	8.81	11.86	37.29
7.	Mang	4	33	36.15	1.05	1.06	4.55	7.73	36.36
8.	Maratha	23	167	41.52	1.82	0.99	11.47	20.96	50.90
9.	Muslim	1	7	17.61	4.24	0.18	—	28.57	28.57
10.	Nhavi	1	7	38.23	2.63	0.57	14.28	21.43	35.71
11.	Parit	1	11	16.37	0.07	0.50	—	9.09	18.18
12.	Ramoshi	1	14	10.40	0.67	0.27	—	25.71	28.57
13.	Sonar	1	7	44.95	0.91	1.43	28.57	3.57	42.86
14.	Sutar	3	21	34.54	1.62	0.88	4.76	10.71	30.95
15.	Teli	1	13	39.13	0.52	0.85	—	7.69	38.46
	Total	58	449	35.71	1.37	0.97	7.58	15.22	40.19

Note: First 3 items (5-7) are monthly expenditure and the last three (8-10) are yearly expenditure.

Indebtedness

The people of the Vinzar village have debtor creditor relationships with local moneylenders. At the time of their special needs they come to the moneylenders and borrow money from them. This transaction is based on mutual trust and no surety is needed for establishing such relationship. In this village two Brahman, six Maratha and one Gurao lend money to the villagers. Only the rich Brahman do not receive interest from the debtors. But one each among Brahman, Maratha, and Gurao receive interest ranging from six per cent to ten per cent per month from the debtors. Three Maratha and two Marwari of neighbouring villages also lend money to the people to Vinzar with the interest ranging from three to six per cent per month. Data have been collected on indebtedness from the villagers irrespective of castes who had borrowed money from the moneylenders. In table 11 it is seen that eight castes viz. the Dhangar, Gurao, Mahar, Mang, Maratha, Mochi, Nhavi, and Sutar borrowed money from the moneylenders at the time of their needs. Needs have been classified into five categories i.e., (a) necessities, (b) liabilities, (c) house construction, (d) agriculture and (e) industry. The villagers also receive loan from B.D. Office, Panchayat Office, Tahsil office, different banks and Vinzar Cooperative society. It is found that affluent landowners get loan from B.D. Office, Panchayat Office, tahsil office and different Banks but the landowners who are members of Vinzar Cooperative society, get loan from it for agricultural operations and livelihood. The petty landowners and the landless people take loan from the moneylenders for the above mentioned five reasons. The Mahar have taken loan of Rs. 15681.00 for all five reasons. The second position comes of the Dhangars who borrowed a total amount of Rs. 7980.00 for similar reasons of necessities, agriculture and industry. Next comes the Nhavi, Mang, Maratha, Mochi, Sutar and Gurao in order or precedence.

In Table 11 it is found that the seven communities except the Mang have taken loan for meeting necessities and only four communities except the Gurao, Mang, Chambhar and Sutar have borrowed money for agriculture. Loan for industry was taken by the Dhangar, Mahar, Mang, and Chambhar people only and loan for house construction taken by the Mahar and Nhavi.

TABLE 11: Distribution of indebtedness by reason

Sl. No.	Group	Total No. of house holds	Total No. of debtor	% age of debtor 100	Necessities					Liabilities					House construction					Agriculture					Industry					Total
					— 500	101 1000	501 2000	1001 5000	2001 100	— 500	101 1000	501 2000	1001 5000	2001 100	— 500	101 1000	501 2000	1001 5000	2001 100	— 500	101 1000	501 2000	1001 5000	2001 100	— 500	101 1000	501 2000	1001 5000	2001	
1.	Chambhar	5	2	4.26	100																				300	300				700
																									42.86	42.86				100.00
2.	Dhangar	24	9	19.15	830	850	1600																2000			700		2000		7980
					10.40	10.40	20.05																25.06			8.77		25.06		99.99
3.	Gurao	7	1	2.13		300																								300
						100.00																								100.00
4.	Mahar	33	28	59.57	2872	5703				100	200	500			150	1000	1500			156	1000	1000				50	1350			15681
					18.31	36.37				0.64	1.28	3.19			0.96	6.38	9.56			0.99	6.38	6.38				0.96	8.60			100.00
5.	Mang	7	2	4.25						500																	1000			1500
										33.33																	66.67			100.00
6.	Maratha	185	3	6.38	100															300		1000								1400
					7.14															21.43		71.45								100.00
7.	Nhavi	4	1	2.13	650										500					200			2000							3350
					19.40										14.93					5.27			59.70							100.00
8.	Sutar	6	1	2.13	250	400																								650
					38.45	61.54																								100.00
	Total				4152	7903	1600			600	200	500			650	1000	1500			656	3000	5000			300	1150	2350	2000		31561
					13.16	25.04	5.07			1.90	0.64	1.58			2.06	3.17	4.75			2.08	9.51	15.84			0.95	0.95	7.44	6.35		100.02

Two Dhangar, one Mang and three Mahar borrowed a large amount of money for doing business of cattle and buffalo in the village and the amount of loan has been categorised in the column of industry. After analysing the data of indebtedness it is found that the Dhangar, Gurao, Mahar, Chambhar, Maratha, Nhavi and Sutar had borrowed money for their daily livelihood. It is found that either they are landless or petty landowners and having limited sources of income they cannot maintain their families properly. At last they go to the moneylenders for borrowing money. The people of these eight castes including the Mang also borrowed money for these reasons i.e., liabilities, house construction, agriculture and industry. It can be generalized that the borrowers of these eight castes are either landless or petty landowners and have limited sources of income.

Different Communities and their Social Hierarchy

In Vinzar there are twenty one ethnic groups which are given below alphabetically:

1 Beldar
2 Brahman
3 Chambhar
4 Dhangar
5 Gurao (Sagar)
6 Jain
7 Kasar
8 Koli Mahadeo
9 Lingayat
10 Mahar
11 Mali
12 Mang
13 Maratha
14 Muslim
15 Nhavi
16 Panchal
17 Parit
18 Ramoshi
19 Sonar
20 Sutar
21 Teli

On the basis of commensality, untouchability and purity 21 ethnic groups have been divided into two categories; lower castes and the higher castes. The lower castes consist of the Mang, Chambhar and Mahar. The higher castes consist of the Brahman, Maratha, Sonar, Sutar, Mali, Kasar, Dhangar, Teli, Beldar, Parit, Gurao, Nhavi and Ramoshi and the Muslim. The three caste groups i.e., the Jain, Lingayat, and Panchal and one tribe i.e. Koli-Mahadeo are recent immigrants to this village. They are school teachers here and are respected by the villagers. The Brahman are considered the highest in rank among all ethnic groups and they do not accept food and drinking water from other ethnic groups.

But the people of other ethnic groups take food from the house of the Brahman. The Marathas hold the second position hierarchically and they accept food only from the Brahman but not from other groups. They can accept drinking water from the hands of Sonar, Sutar, Kasar, Dhangar, Teli and Beldar but not the food. They do not accept food and drinking water from the houses of the rest of the ethnic groups. Sonar, Sutar, Kasar, Dhangar, Teli and Beldar place themselves in changing order of precedence. They do not accept food from each other's house and also from the houses of scheduled caste groups but accept both food and drinking water from the house of the Brahman and Maratha. Only they accept drink from each other's house and also from the hands of Parit, Gurao, Nhavi, Ramoshi and Muslim but not from Mang, Chambhar & Mahar people. Parit, Gurao, Nhavi, Ramoshi and Muslim are having equal rank to each other but they do not accept food and drink from each other's house and also from the houses of Mang, Chambhar and Mahar. Mang, Chambhar and Mahar place their ranks themselves in that order. They do not accept food and drink from each other's house and also from the houses of Parit, Gurao, Nhavi, Ramoshi and Muslim; but they always accept food and drink from the houses of the other higher caste groups. Mang, Chambhar and Mahar are considered as unclean castes.

In communal feast, the Brahmans maintain restriction and sit separately from other caste groups at the time of taking their meal. But no restrictions to sit in the same line (*pankti*) for taking food is maintained by other ethnic groups except Mang, Chambhar and Mahar who must sit a little far away from the other groups. The Mang, Chambhar and Mahar also sit a little away from each other.

Political Dimension

There is no traditional or informal village panchayat in Vinzar village and also no formal caste panchayat is found in any community of the village. But the meeting of informal caste panchayat is held when the case is of a particular caste group. Membership of the informal caste panchayat is given to elders of the particular caste group of the village and the elders of the same caste are also called from the neighbouring villages for the meeting. There is only Koli-Mahadeo,

Lingayat & Panchyal panchayat. Except Kasar and one each of Beldar, Jain, Kasar, all groups are immigrants in this village and do not have informal caste panchayat. The remaining ethnic groups are having informal caste panchayat in the village. In Poona City the Mang and Chambhar have their own organisation for the welfare of their community. The name of the organisation of the Mang people in known as "Matang Samaj" and meeting is held once in a month for their welfare activities. The samaj has some office-bearers elected by them. The Chambhars have their large organisation on all Indian basis and it is named as "Akhil Bharatiya Charmakar Parishad". Jagjivan Ram, the then Central Cabinet Minister was the president of this Parishad. In state also they have one organisation known as "Maharashtra Charmakar Parishad" which is founded in Poona City. They have also talukwise caste Panchayat, the members of which meet together once in a month for the welfare of their people.

Statutory Gram Panchayat

In Vinzar village statutory Gram Panchayat has been set up in the year 1956. The First *sarpanch* of this Panchayat belonged to Maratha group and served for two terms i.e., from 1956-61 and 1962-66. The second *sarpanch* also belonged to Maratha and his tenure was for only one term from 1967-72. Again in the month of December, 1972 there was a panchayat election conducted in the B.D. Office. In this election all the previous members including *sarpanch* were defeated. Nine members i.e., 6 males and 2 females belonging to Maratha group and one belonging to Mahar were elected. There is only one reserved seat represented either by the scheduled caste or the tribe. Formerly, one Mang was representing the Mang, Chambhar and Mahar for the last three terms. The Gram Sevak belongs to Maratha group and is employed by the B.D.Office. He comes from Bhor taluka and is also secretary of Gram Panchayat.

In case of drinking water, all the higher caste groups including Brahman, except Mang, Chambhar, and Mahar may draw water from each other's well (*bihir*). Mang, Chambhar, and Mahar cannot touch the bucket of higher castes to draw water from the well of the higher castes. The water of such well is considered polluted if these three caste people have drawn water from that well. The concerned person is threatened by the well-owner with severe consequences if he draws water again in future. The whole water is fetched out from that well and when water springs again fill that well, the people of higher caste groups start using that water. Formerly Mang, Chambhar, and Mahar used to draw drinking water from the nearby canal adjacent to their wasti. After the introduction of the Panchayat Raj, Block Development Office constructed two brick built wells in the locality of the Harijan and now-a-days they are drawing drinking water from that well.

The Brahman, Sonar, Sutar, and Kasar have one cremation ground (*mashan*) and the other higher castes (expect Dhangar, Muslim, and Scheduled Castes) have another cremation ground. The Dhangar are living in the hilly area and bury the dead at Hati-dant-a hillock. The Muslim have a separate burial ground near their habitation. Nearby their bustee, Mang, Chambhar, and Mahar have their own separate cremation grounds adjacent to each other.

All people irrespective of castes visit Vinzar main village, Tamkar wadi, Bhuruk wadi, and Dhangar wasti but not the Harijan wasti. In olden days, the Mang, Chambhar, and Mahar people were not allowed to walk through the main streets of the main village and other three hamlets. After introduction of the untouchability Act, social distance between higher caste and untouchables has been lessened. Now-a-days, a few higher caste people visit the Harijan wasti. The children belonging to scheduled castes enter the temple compound to attend their classes, although there is demarcation of sitting areas between the children of the scheduled castes and that of higher castes.

Family Composition

In Vinzar village there are 12 ethnic groups and 315 families, out of which the Maratha are having the highest number of families i.e., 185. The Mahar hold the second position consisting of 33 families and the third position comes of the Dhangar having 24 families. The fourth position is of the Brahman having 13 families, fifth position comes to the Gurao, Mang and Sonar, each having 7 families; sixth position goes to the Sutar having 6 families, seventh position is for the Chambhar and Teli each consisting of 5 families, eight position goes to the Dhobi, Muslim, and Nhavi each having 4 families, ninth position is of the Mali consisting of 3 families, tenth position goes to the Ramoshi having 2 families and eleventh position is held by the Beldar, Jain, Kasar, Koli-Mahadeo, Lingayat, and Panchal each consisting of one family.

The average size of the family in Vinzar is 5.9 which resembles the average size of Maratha family. The average size of the Brahman is 4.9.

Families in the village have been categorised into 5 types : 1) Nascent, b) Nuclear, c) Extended, d) Broken and e) Polygamous as shown in Table 12.

There are 11 (3.49%) nascent families in Vinzar. The Brahman, Dhangar, Lingayat, and Mahar each is having one nascent family and only the Maratha are having 7 nascent families. There are 109 (34.60%) nuclear families, 145 (46.03%) extended families, 45 (14.29%) broken families and 5 (1.59%) polygamous families. Only 5 Maratha are having such families in the village. The Brahman, Maratha, Dhangar, Mang, Chambhar, and Mahar are having more extended families in number than other types of families. Many villagers prefer extended family whereby they can maintain their social obligations properly.

Literacy and Education

There are two primary schools in Vinzar. One is situated in the main village established in 1948 and another in Tamkarwadi established in 1972. Generally the children of the main village, Harijan wasti and a few from Bhuruk wadi go to the primary school of the main village. All children from Bhuruk wadi can not come to the primary school due to distance (one mile from the main village). The Dhangar are having their settled tract at the top of the hills and their wasti is far away from the main village. It is very difficult for the Dhangar children to come to the school through the jungles and also from a long distance. Anyhow, very few children from Dhangar wasti come to the school sometimes. The children of petty land owners and landless families do not study further after completion of their primary education due to involvement in their household work and lack of incentive.

A high school is also situated in Vinzar and established in the year 1961. The name of this school is "New English School" which belongs to the organization of Shri Swami Vivekananda Shikshan Sanstha. There are teachers including Headmaster and the total number of students in the school is 114. Students from neighbouring villages also come to this school i.e., from Malawali, Dapodi, Khondoli, Sakhar, Lavi, Maravani, Khamsodi, Margashni, and Kharur and they belong to the caste groups Brahman, Maratha, Mang, Chambhar, Mahar and Koli-Mahadeo,

TABLE 12: Composition of family

Sl. No.	Community	Total No. of family	Total population	Average size of family	Type of Family									
					Nascent		Nuclear		Extended		Broken		Polygenous	
					No.	%	No.	%	No.	%	No	%	No.	%
1.	Beldar	1	7	7.0	—	—	1	(100.00)	—	—	—	—	—	—
2.	Brahman	13	64	4.9	1	(7.69)	2	(15.38)	8	(61.54)	2	(15.38)	—	—
3.	Dhangar	24	107	4.5	1	(4.17)	8	(33.33)	10	(41.67)	5	(20.83)	—	—
4.	Dhobi	4	38	9.5	—	—	—	—	4	(100.00)	—	—	—	—
5.	Gurao	7	45	6.4	—	—	2	(28.57)	3	(42.86)	2	(28.57)	—	—
6.	Jain	1	1	1.0	—	—	—	—	—	—	1	(100.00)	—	—
7.	Kasar	1	19	19.0	—	—	—	—	1	(100.00)	—	—	—	—
8.	Koli-Mahadeo	1	3	3.0	—	—	—	—	—	—	1	(100.00)	—	—
9.	Lingayat	1	2	2.0	1	(100.00)	—	—	—	—	—	—	—	—
10.	Mahar	33	233	7.1	1	(3.03)	9	(27.27)	18	(54.55)	5	(15.15)	—	—
11.	Mali	3	9	3.0	—	—	2	(66.67)	1	(33.33)	—	—	—	—
12.	Mang	7	42	6.0	—	—	1	(14.29)	4	(57.14)	2	(28.57)	—	—
13.	Maratha	185	1095	5.9	7	(3.78)	70	(37.84)	83	(44.86)	20	(10.81)	5	(2.70)
14.	Mochi(Chambh)	5	30	6.0	—	—	2	(40.00)	3	(60.00)	—	—	—	—
15.	Musalman	4	17	4.2	—	—	2	(50.50)	2	(50.00)	—	—	—	—
16.	Nhavi	4	33	8.3	—	—	2	(50.50)	2	(50.00)	—	—	—	—
17.	Panchal	1	1	1.0	—	—	—	—	—	—	1	(100.00)	—	—
18.	Ramoshi	2	18	9.0	—	—	1	(50.50)	1	(50.00)	—	—	—	—
19.	Sonar	7	27	3.9	—	—	2	(28.57)	1	(14.29)	4	(57.14)	—	—
20.	Sutar	6	39	6.5	—	—	5	(83.33)	1	(16.67)	—	—	—	—
21.	Teli	5	34	6.8	—	—	—	—	3	(60.00)	2	(40.00)	—	—
	TOTAL	315	1864	5.9	11	(3.49)	109	(34.60)	145	(46.03)	45	(14.29)	5	(1.59)

TABLE 13: Literacy composition

Sl. No.	Community	Literates		Literates		Total literates	Percent-age
		Male	Female	Male	Female		
1.	Beldar	2	2	1 + 0	0 + 2	3	42.85
2.	Brahman	5	4	20 + 8	16 + 11	55	85.93
3.	Mochi(Chambhar)	9	15	3 + 3	0 + 0	6	20.00
4.	Dhangar	51	52	3 + 1	0 + 0	4	3.73
5.	Gurao	8	23	5 + 5	0 + 4	14	31.11
6.	Jain	—	—	1 + 0	0 + 0	1	100.00
7.	Kasar	2	4	4 + 3	2 + 4	13	68.42
8.	Koli-Mahadeo	—	1	1 + 1	0 + 0	2	66.67
9.	Lingayat	—	—	1 + 0	1 + 0	2	100.00
10.	Mahar	76	113	25 + 21	3 + 5	54	23.18
11.	Mali	3	1	2 + 1	1 + 1	5	55.56
12.	Mang	12	15	4 + 4	6 + 1	15	35.71
13.	Maratha	213	484	134 + 150	33 + 81	398	36.34
14.	Muslim	5	9	1 + 1	1 + 0	3	17.64
15.	Nhavi	7	19	1 + 4	0 + 2	7	21.22
16.	Panchal	—	—	1 + 0	0 + 0	1	100.00
17.	Parit(Dhobi)	11	15	2 + 5	1 + 4	12	31.57
18.	Ramoshi	8	6	2 + 0	2 + 0	4	22.22
19.	Sonar	7	6	5 + 4	1 + 4	14	51.85
20.	Sutar	10	11	7 + 6	2 + 3	18	46.15
21.	Teli	9	11	8 + 1	5 + 0	14	41.18
	TOTAL	438	791	231 + 218	196	645	100.00

The total population of Vinzar is 1864, out of which 365 (34.07%) persons are literates and 1229 (65.93%) persons are illiterates according to the Table 13. Among 645 literates, there are 449 males and 196 females and the proportion of literacy has increased by 12.30 per cent during the last decade. The highest percentage (85.93%) of literacy in the village is found among the Brahman and next comes the position of the Kasar having 68.42 per cent. The other higher caste people are having better percentage of literacy than the Scheduled Castes. Table 13 of literacy and education shows literates and illiterates among different communities.

Number of literate is more among the Mahar than that of the Mang and Chambhar people. Insignificant percentage of literacy is found among Chambhar, Mang, Dhangar, Muslim, Nhavi, and Ramoshi.

Social Mobility

Among the 21 communities in the village, only the Mahar have been converted into Buddhism about 25 years ago and have become followers of Dr. Babasaheb Ambedkar. The higher caste people specially the Brahman advised the Mahar not to convert. But the Mahar did not obey the advice of higher caste people and accepted Buddhism. Formerly, the Mahar were ranked the lowest in social hierarchy among Mang, Chambhar and Mahar. The Mang and Chambhar were ranked in 1st and 2nd position respectively. After conversion the Mahar have left their traditional occupation and are better of economically. They now consider themselves superior to the Mang and Chambhar. But the Mang and Chambhar do not protest against the demand of the Mahar for making their rank higher and the other higher caste people also do not pay heed to the demand of the Mahar. The Mahar do not equalise their rank to any higher caste. They are having some amount of cultivable land and do agricultural labour for the higher caste people. They are passing their daily life in a better way than that of the Mang and Chambhar. No such mobility is observed among other communities in the village.

Liquor Consumption

Most of the villagers irrespective of castes except the Brahman are habituated to drinking liquor. In the village there are seven illicit liquor makers belonging to the Maratha group. Formerly one poor Muslim was preparing liquor illicitly at his home but he was caught by the police when he was preparing it. A case was going on in the court against him. Other seven liquor-makers are preparing liquor illicitly in their hideouts. They supply liquor to their own villagers and also to the people of the neighbouring villages. There are two authorised agents for selling factory made liquor in the village, the secretary of the co-operative society is one agent and the village medical doctor is another agent. Some village women of different communities also drink liquor in little quantity whenever they get chance to have it. No major members of alcoholic or drug addicts are found in this village. Some Dhangar and scheduled caste drink liquor daily, although their earning is less. The members of these families suffer more owing to this type of expenditure incurred by their earners.

Development Scheme

Development agencies like Primary Health Centre, Block Development Office sponsored by the Government and one voluntary agency i.e. A.F.F. are initiated for welfare of the villagers. There is one private medical practitioner in this village and he is an immigrant here. He also visits neighbouring villages. Except this village doctor, the villagers also get medical facilities from the primary Health Centre which comes under the jurisdiction of Block Development Office of Velhe Mahal taluka. Actually this village comes under the jurisdiction of Haveli taluka; but it is situated very far away from Poona City and very near the border of Velhe-Mahal taluka. The taluka headquarters of Velhe-Mahal is 6 miles away from the village. For medical facilities, three villages i.e., Vinzar, Oangni, and Antrauli of Harveli taluka have been included within the jurisdiction of primary Health Centre of Velhe-Mahal taluka where two medical doctors-one for family planning and the other for public health, auxiliary nurse, midwife, one vaccinator and one cholera inoculator are appointed. Auxiliary nurse, midwife, vaccinator and cholera inoculator visit Vinzar every month. There was no epidemic in this village during the last decade. Only one aged Brahman male is suffering from leprosy and another Mahar female, 40 years of age, is suffering from T.B. Three months before the present investigator's arrival in this village, one middle aged Maratha male had died of dog-bite. That person did not take anti-rabies injection which was available in Primary Health Centre of Velhe-Mahal taluka and Sasoon Hospital in Poona. After one month he went mad and then died. Generally, the villagers are in favour of going to Sasoon Hospital, Poona instead of going to the Primary Health Centre, Velhe-Mahal where they do not get proper medical facilities. During emergency the village medical doctor is called for and if the village doctor proves failure to cure the patient, the villagers prefer to take the patient to Sasoon Hospital, Poona.

Voluntary Agency

A.F.F. stands for Association of Friends in France, the office of which is situated in Poona. This Organisation extends help to the Harijan of Poona District. Dr. Muruk, a private medical doctor and a social worker is residing at Khanpur, 14 miles away from Poona. He is in touch with their A.F.F. and visits Vinzar off and on. Under his influence, A.F.F. has taken a decision to help the Harijan (Mahar) of Vinzar in digging out one well (*bihir*) in their agricultural field for irrigation purpose. But during the scarcity period in the year 1972, the B.D.Office helped the Harijan, giving them work for digging one irrigation well in their agricultural field. So, one irrigation well has been constructed during scarcity period in the fields of the Mahar. Now A.F.F. decided to supply them one pump set with oil engine for the new irrigation well. Gradually A.F.F offered them two ploughs with share, four bullocks and one bullock-cart for their cultivation.

Block Development Office

After the introduction of the Panchayat Raj in Maharashtra, only one Block Development Office has been set up in each taluka of Poona District. The function of B.D.Office is to do welfare activities for the people of Haveli taluka. During summer season B.D. Office supplies improved variety of paddy seed (Ratnagiri 24 and I.R. 8) and hybrid Jawari to the Gram Panchayat of Vinzar village. Any landowning villager can purchase these improved variety of paddy seed and hybrid *jawari* for sowing in his field. During my stay in the village, I have seen that no scheduled caste person purchased paddy seed from the Gram Panchayat Office due to want of money in their hand. The rich and large landowning Brahman family help the scheduled caste in cash or kind at the time of their needs. The rich Brahman supplied hybrid *jawari* seeds to three Harijan for sowing in their field. Later on, these Harijan would repay the cost of hybrid *jawari* seed to the rich Brahman at their convenient time. During winter season, high yielding variety of wheat was supplied by the B.D. Office to this Gram Panchayat. The cultivators irrespective of caste, including the Mahar, took wheat seeds for sowing purpose. There are 35 wells (*bihir*) in Vinzar. Twenty wells (*bihir*) are constructed for supply of drinking water and 15 wells for irrigation. The B.D. Office constructed only six *bihirs* for drinking water in the village. Out of these six, one for the Mang, one for the Mahar, one in Bhurukwadi — a hamlet, one in Tamkarwadi — a hamlet, and two for the main village — Vinzar. Out of 15 irrigation wells, the B.D. Office constructed three wells only and the rest were constructed by the villagers by their own efforts. In 1972, one irrigation well was constructed by the B.D. Office for the Harijan. Except this, the B.D.

Office gave loan to the higher caste people for running dairy farm and constructing well and bunding in the agricultural field. The scheduled caste people did not get any loan from the B.D. Office. No employee from the social welfare section of the B.D. Office ever visited Vinzar village for the welfare of the scheduled caste.

The Panchayat Samiti, Haveli taluka gave a small amount of loan ranging from Rs. 95.32 to Rs. 9918 to the eight higher caste persons but the Scheduled Caste people did not get loan from this Panchayat Samiti. Vinzar Vividh Karya Savasad Society Ltd., is having 184 members irrespective of caste and they are shareholders in this co-operative society. Purchasing of share in this society requires only Rs. 5.00 (Five rupees only) and a person may purchase as many shares as he can. Ninetyone persons irrespective of caste including the Mahar took loan with little interest from this co-operative society for agricultural operations and livelihood.

It is seen that from the development programmes that have been sponsored by the State Government for the welfare of the village people, the higher caste people are the maximum beneficiaries of these programmes.

There is no traditional village panchayat in Vinzar and also no formal caste based panchayat of the village. But the meeting of informal caste *panchayat* is held when the situation demands. Membership of the informal caste *panchayat* is held by the elders of the particular caste of the village and the elders of the same caste are also called from the neighbouring villages for the meeting. There is only one such panchayat operating among the Beldar, Jain, Kasar, Koli-Mahadeo, Lingayat, and Panchal. Except Kasar, all these groups are immigrants in this village and do not have informal caste panchayat. The remaining ethnic groups are having informal caste panchayat in the village. In Poona City the Mang and Chambhar have their own organisation for the welfare of their community.

In Vinzar, statutory gram panchayat has been set up in the year 1956. The first *sarpanch* of this Panchayat belonged to Maratha group. The second *sarpanch* also belonged to the Maratha and his tenure was for only one term. Again in the month of December, 1972, there was Panchayat election and nine members i.e., six males and two females belonging to the Maratha group and one belonging to the Mahar were newly elected. In this village Maratha are numerically dominant. Eight Maratha and one Mahar from the scheduled caste people were elected. The Brahman of Vinzar are dominant in all respects but they do not participate in the Gram Panchayat election although they are alert about it. The other caste people do not contest the Gram Panchayat election due to their less numerical strength and poor economic condition. In the last three terms no Sipahi was appointed in the Gram Panchayat Office. But the present working committee of Gram Panchayat has appointed a Sipahi and Rs. 20.00 had been fixed as his salary. In the Gram Panchayat Office at least one meeting should be held every month. But the Sarpanch and Upa-Sarpanch do not organise a meeting every month. The villagers get help from Block Development Office through Gram Panchayat for agricultural innovations i.e., supplying of improved seeds and chemical fertilizer; and monetary help for purchasing bullocks, construction of lift irrigation well, bunding and house construction, and also for running business and dairy farm.

During general election, the agents of Congress (O), Ruling Congress, Jan Sangh, Praja Socialist party, Nagrik Sangathana and Shivasena came to this village for political canvassing. Some Maratha persons are working in Bombay city and participating in the political activities of CPM. When they come to the village, they apprise villagers about CPM programmes. There are some channels of political communication in this village through agents of different political parties, daily newspaper (*Tarun Bharat*) and radio. Factions are formed in the village at the time of Gram Panchayat election and during land disputes.

Rashtriya Swayam Sewak Sangha

R.S.S. has been established in the village since 1955. At first two persons of the rich Brahman family became members of R.S.S. when they were studying in the school at Poona City. After completion of their study in the school, they established the R.S.S. in their village after returning to the village. Seoram Hari Phadke, a member of the rich Brahman family has been made Sangha Chalak of the R.S.S. for Velhe-Mahal Taluka and Jnaneswar Dhondo Phadke, a member of another Brahman family has been Karyabahak of that organisation. In the village the followers of R.S.S. meet every evening in the compound of Vairabnath or Maruti temple and perform prayer, exercise, and hold discussions on activities of R.S.S. after hoisting the R.S.S. flag of *bhagwa* colour. Only school going children, irrespective of caste and some elder villagers belonging to the Brahman and

Maratha attend this gathering. Children of scheduled castes are allowed to join this organization but they do not come to attend it.

Emergence of Elites

There are a few elites among the scheduled castes in the village. Only a Mahar boy graduated from Poona University and is now employed in a Government office in Bombay. The *ojha* (diviner) — a Mahar, cures the snake-bite-patients and is allowed to enter into the temple. All villagers irrespective of caste pay him attention. One aged Mahar, called Mukaddam is considered the headman and respected by the Mahar. The higher caste people contact him at first to get agricultural labourer from amongst them. One Chambhar has been employed in transport business of the rich Brahman family and another Chambhar man is a cobbler and running a good business of mending shoes in the village. Though these elites are economically, to some extent, better, they are not interested for the welfare of their own community. There are no elite among the Mang, Changar, and Muslim. Among the poor people, children are sent to school and their parents have aspiration that after the completion of school education their sons would earn money through employment somewhere. The elites from scheduled castes are not so much valued by the dominant sections. Because, they are lower in social status and cannot take leading part in political and religious functions. Their brethren always depend upon the higher caste people for earning their livelihood.

Magico-religious Belief

In Maharashtra, the calendar year starts from the month of *chaitra.* The first day of *chaitra* is observed as *Varsa- Pratipada* or Gudi Parba by the people of all communities. On the new year day, *jotish* (astrologer) is called by the people of some higher caste for reading Panchank (future of the new year) and the listeners offer money and *sidha* (eatable articles) to the *jotish.* On that day females of the Brahman families put *halud kumkum* on the forehead of each other and wet gram and sweets are distributed among the participants.

It is found that some religious festivals are observed by the whole village community, some by the higher caste groups, some by the lower caste groups, and some by only a certain caste group. Gudi

Parba, Chaitra Suddha Navami, Chaitra Suddha Purnima, Akshaya Tritia, Vairabnath, Mukai devi, Mali-cha-Masobadeo, Wagjai debi, Mengjai debi, Vinjai debi, Bendur, everyday fast in religious month of Srawana, Nagpanchami Puja, Kojagara Purnima, Bachhu Barash, Krishna Caturdashi, Diwali, Tulsi-Cha-Lagna, Makar Sankranti, Ganapati Puja, Pitri Paksha, Vijaya Dashami, Holi Purnima and *Urus* are observed and deities are worshipped by all communities except the Buddhist Mahar who only participate in the community festivals. In the month of *ashad,* all non vegetarian people except the Brahman observe *gattar amabasya* or *ashad krishna paksha amavashya*. On that day he-goats and sheep are killed in the village and the villagers enjoy mutton. The Brahman are vegetarians and do not observe this festival. During the community religious festivals the scheduled caste cannot enter the temple. After the worship if there is a common feast the scheduled caste people are not allowed to sit with the higher caste people at the time of taking meal. They sit far away from the higher caste people and also follow the restrictions. Jibantika Puja, Narsubaji puja, Mahalakshmi puja, Haritalika barta, Rshi Panchami, Ananta Chaturdashi, Vasant Panchami are observed by the Brahman only and Bata Briksha puja is performed by the female of higher caste groups. Marial debi, Ankhari, and Kakni (F), Masuba and Mallar deities are also worshipped by the Mang only. Bappujiba deo, and Marial debi are the god and goddess of Chambhar and the Dhangar worship Mukai, Janni, Kumbharajai, Mengjai, Magjai, Masoba, Kotharjai, Kuldeo deities. The Mang, Chambhar, and Dhangar sacrifice he-goats or sheep before the deities at the time of worship. After conversion to Buddhism the Mahar have left worshipping Hindu deities. They, however, participate in the community religious festivals.

The Mahar diviner needs to pray before Maruti and Vairabnath deities for curing the patient. So he is allowed to enter into the temple and incantations. He does not receive any money for curing patients. There is not a single case where a patient could not be cured by him. He also cures patients of headache, stomach-ache, thron-struck, and other minor diseases by receiving incantations. He is a very important person and all villagers have affection for him. Snake-bite patients from nearby villages also come to him.

Choka-Mela, belonging to Mahar community, was a great saint. Among the Chambhar, Rohidas was a great saint. Ajamera belonging to Mang community was also a great saint. He was buried at

Pandharpur which is an important pilgrim centre in Maharashtra.

The scheduled caste follow restrictions imposed by the higher caste people. They are always supressed and neglected by the higher castes. Generation after generation religion acts as a barrier and makes them weaker in the village.

Concluding Remarks

In the preceding discussion I dealt with the economic, social, political, and religious aspects of the people of Vinzar. A major source of production in the village is land. After analysing the field-data it is found that 22 per cent of the families are landless in the village. Out of these landless families, one each is from Jain, Bingayat, Mang, Koli-Mahadeo, Muslim, Teli, and Sonar community, two Mali families, eight Maratha families and three Brahman families are recent immigrants to this village. Some are school teachers, some are government employees and one is a medical doctor. The rest of the landless families include one Beldar, five Chambhar, 15 Dhangar, four Mahar, three Mang, 14 Maratha, three Muslim and four Sonar families. The landowning Dhangar, Gurao, Mahar, Nhavi. Parit, Ramoshi, Sonar, and Sutar families except a few are petty landowners in the village and are economically depressed due to the meagre incomes as they get from their land. Only a few families of these groups have somewhat a better economic condition. Thus the landless people and the petty landowners are weaker sections in the village. Among the Maratha, about 89 per cent families are landowners and 11 per cent are landless. The landowning Maratha are having 65.9 per cent of the total land, out of which 38.33 per cent families are having upto 5 acres of land and whatever yield they get from their field is not sufficient for their family consumption. These Maratha petty landowners are also considered weaker sections in the village, although they are socillay not so. In the village all the Brahman families are dominant in respect to economic, social, political, and religious matters.

Landlessness, less quantity of land, employer-employee relationship, indebtedness and limited sources of income are the factors responsible for economic weakness of certain people. The Beldar, Chambhar, Mang and Muslim are totally landless people. Employer-employee relationship is a factor responsible for weakness of the agricultural labourers in the village. The seasonal and permanent agricultural labourers do not get enough remuneration for their labour. Some agricultural labourers belong to the scheduled caste and some are from other caste groups of the village and neighbouring villages. These seasonal and permanent labourers get food daily in their master's house and limited clothes for the whole year but whatever remuneration each agricultural labourer gets, it is a meagre amount for him to maintain the members of his house. So, these labourers always suffer from economic hardship.

The people of Vinzar have debtor creditor relationship with money-lenders. At the time of their special needs they go to the moneylenders of their village or neighbouring villages and borrow money from them with high rate of interest. This transaction is based on mutual trust and no surety is needed for establishing such relationship. Sometimes the borrowers get money from the moneylenders after pledging their articles like brass, bronze or steel utensils and silver or gold ornaments. Table of indebtedness indicates that the Mahar and Dhangar borrowed more money than the other groups did. The borrowers always remain in debt to the moneylenders and are able to repay only the interest every month but they cannot repay the capital at a time. Limited sources of income compel the people to borrow money from the moneylenders. Whatever the debtors earn, it is spent for maintaining their families and they cannot repay the capital at a time to the money lenders.

Factors like social layout of habitation on the basis of clean and unclean zones, social status, immigration, less education, and scant attention given to the scheduled castes in ameliorating their conditions by governmental welfare agencies are responsible for weakness among a large section of the low caste villagers.

The scheduled caste people do not have any political role in Gram Panchayat. There is only one reserved post for them. They can never think of winning a Panchayat election by competing with the higher castes. The service caste people, viz., Beldar, Dhobi, Gurao, Nhavi, Ramoshi, and Sutar do not compete in Gram Panchayat election and cannot provide leadership in the village affairs. They are also numerically and economically weak. Politically, the Brahman and Maratha are dominant sections in the village.

In magico-religious affairs, the higher caste people maintain restriction and social distance against the scheduled caste during the community festival. Therefore, the scheduled castes are weaker sections on religious count. Certain changes have taken place in case of religious customs. The scheduled caste people are not allowed to enter the compound of the temple except on the days of community religious festivals. Only the Mahar diviner can enter the rooms of the deities of Vairabnath and Maruti temples at the time of curing the snake-bite-patient, but the other scheduled caste people are not allowed to enter any deity room. But the children of the scheduled castes can attend the Primary school which are held in the compounds of the temples.

Way of Emancipation

Weakness is measured by landlessness, low income, indebtedness, unskilled men in the labour force, low education, substandard housing, and disability of social distance imposed by higher caste people. The weaker people do not have enough resources to meet up their essential needs daily. To uplift their condition, compulsory education is required among all the villagers whereby the weaker people can understand their problems and resist the oppression made by the dominant sections. Distribution of land to the landless people is a prerequisite for providing proper means of their livelihood and reducing their poverty. Adoption of agricultural innovations would help the petty cultivators to get more yield from their land. Exploitation of the weaker people by the unauthorised moneylenders must be stopped. Standard of housing should be improved with the help of the government. The higher caste people should never maintain social distance or untouchability with the scheduled caste people. The economically well-off families of the village should pay wages to their agricultural labourers as per the government prescribed rate and should not cheat and exploit them. Helpful attitude should be shown towards the weaker people in all respects for improving their condition.

REFERENCES

1. *Peasant Life in India*. 1967. Anthropological Survey of India.
2. Beteille, A. : *Inequality and Social Change*. 1972.
3. *District Census Handbook*, Poona, Census of India, Maharashtra, 1961.
4. Dube, S.C. : *India's Changing Villages*, 1961.
5. Epstein, T.S. : *Inequality and Social Change*. 1972.

14

PEHAR : A VILLAGE IN EASTERN UTTAR PRADESH

SADHAN SENGUPTA

Introduction

Data presented in this paper were collected the investigator when he was working on the project entitled : "Untouchable and untouchability in rural and urban situations - the Helas of eastern U.P. and Calcutta stum". During my work the higher caste people regarded me as 'Hela' i.e. sweeper (more specifically as 'Bangal Hela' as I happen to be a Bengali). The rural Hela were sympathetic to me. I shared a mud hut (12' X 10') alongwith a Hela family consisting of seven individuals during winter of 1973. I used to take the same food which they consumed.

Field Situation

The village Pehar is located in the Utraula Tahsil of Gonda District in Uttar Pradesh. The data used here were collected by the author during 2nd February to 24th July, 1973.

Pehar is a large village inhabited by 233 families (139 Hindu and 94 Muslim) containing a total of 1221 individuals. The Hindu are divided into 18 *jatis* namely : Brahman, Jat, Murao, Kayasth, Ahir, Bania, Sonar, Lohar, Barai, Kurmi, Nau, Bhuj, Teli, Kahar, dhobi, Kori, chamar, and Hela. Similarly, the Muslim have 11 *Quom*[1] groups, as : Pathan, Sheikh, Barhai, Halowai, Darji, Nau, Ansari, Manihar, Dhuniya, Fakir, and Mirasi.

Economic Condition

Total area of village Pehar is 552 acres. Out of it, the Gan Samaj land containing water sources and drainage system includes 27 acres, site for habitation 47 acres, fallow land 16 acres and the rest 462 acres are used for agricultural purposes.

Agricultural lands are of two broad categories viz - a) *Upruhar* or high land, and b) *Dabar* or low land. Due to lack of irrigation most of the agricultural lands of this village depend on rain.

According to *Owajibul - aar*; (i.e., old settlement record) this village was owned by the Jat and Pathan Zamindars in terms of equal share. These landowners brought several artisan and service castes, who were referred to as *asami*. Service castes were given *inami* (tax-free service tenure land) land for their services. The other castes either used to give *lagan* (tax) and practised cultivation as tenant or worked in the fields of the Zamindar as agricultural labourers.

In previous years, all the lands of this village were exclusively owned by the Zamindar. After abolition of the Zamindari system some of the members of the other castes also owned some land. Present picture of land holding is given in table 1.

Previously we have stated that the village possesses 462 acres of agricultural land. If we just count the amount of land given in the table, the total would be 651 acres. The excess amount of 189 acres are in the neighbouring villages and owned by the ex-Zamindars. On comparing the family landholdings, we find that the Jat, Pathan, Kurmi, and Kayasth have the largest holding which when taken collectively does not change the respective groups' superior land holding power. On the other hand this kind of similarity between the group holding and the familywise land holding is not seen among the rest of the communities. Except Jat, Bhuj, Chamar, Kalowar, Sheikh, Lohar, and Brahman all the communities have some landless families.

Analysing the data, the author found the following three factors responsible for landlessness among the residents of the Pehar village.

i) Due to poverty:

People of this category were very poor, so they could not acquire land from the Zamindars on lease. Some of the poor communities are Pathan, Mirasi, Bhuniya, Murao, Kori, Barai, Ansari, and Fakir.

TABLE 1: Distribution of land by community

Sl. No	Community	No. of family	Land held		Approx. family average		Percentage of landless families
			Bigha	Bissa	Bigha	Bissa	
1	Pathan	55	1340	19	24	00	23.63
2	Jat	4	735	10	183	17	Nil
3	Kurmi	21	328	19	15	12	4.06
4	Kayesth	8	103	00	12	18	12.5
5	Kori(Sc)	12	95	10	8	00	8.33
6	Kalowar	10	90	00	9	00	Nil
7	Murao	17	80	04	5	00	5.88
8	Teli	9	69	10	7	14	11.11
9	Bhuj	5	56	05	10	17	Nil
10	Darji	6	58	00	9	13	33.33
11	Ansari	9	41	11	4	12	55.55
12	Barai(Sc)	11	41	10	3	16	36.36
13	Nau *	6	33	15	5	12	16.66
14	Bhuniya (Sc)	6	29	05	4	18	33.33
15	Lohar	5	28	05	5	13	Nil
16	Barhai (Sc)	5	27	00	5	08	20.00
17	Hela (Sc)	9	25	03	2	16	11.11
18	Chamar (Sc)	2	20	10	10	05	Nil
19	Sonar	6	20	00	3	07	33.33
20	Dhobi (Se)	8	18	10	2	06	12.5
21	Sheikh	2	16	00	8	00	Nil
22	Ahir (Sc)	2	12	00	6	00	50.00
23	Halowai	3	11	08	3	16	33.33
24	Brahman	3	8	09	2	16	Nil
25	Manihar	2	5	00	2	10	50.00
26	Fakir	4	3	02	0	15	75.00
27	Mirasi	1	0	00	0	00	100.00
28	Kahar	2	0	00	0	00	100.00

* Single Muslim Nau family included.
1 Bigha = 1/5 acre
1 Bissa = 1/20 bigha

ii) Willingness to continue with traditional occupation :

Previously all people were not interested in agriculture, as the income of their traditional occupations could subsist them well. Although there was a service tenure system in the past, it was found that this was not very popular with the service castes. The reason attributed for this was that it was found difficult to cope with two occupations simultaneously, namely - traditional craft and agriculture. It was noticed that in this particular district in the Himalayan foot hills of *Tarai*, agriculture is round the year industry. So most of the people are landless now. e.g. Some among Kayasth, Halowai, Kahar, Dhobi, Manihar, Sonar, Nau and Ahir. Willingness to stick to traditional occupation is one of the main reasons for the low family income average among different artisan and service castes (vide-Table-1, on land holding).

iii) Due to family reason :

This situation emerges during the splitting up of the joint families, specially when father is alive as the head of the family and is the sole proprietor of the family land. Examples are some Hela, Kurmi, Darji and Barai individuals.

Occupation

On the basis of occupation, the villagers can be classified into 3 distinct groups, namely-

a. Those who prectise cultivation.
b. Those who are in traditional/caste occupations and
c. Those who practise other occupations.

a. *Cultivation*

Table 2 shows the different categories of the villagers who derive their livelihood directly from cultivation.

TABLE 2: Different categories who derive their livelihood from agriculture

Category	Total	Male	Female
1. Supervisor Landowner	40	36	4
2. Owner cultivator-cum-share cropper	325	197	128
3. Agricultural Labour	163	85	78
Total :	528	318	210

Most of the supervisor landowners also happen to be higher caste people. They have much land and hire the services of agricultural labourers. A few persons having small amount of land are also in this category. They are primarily engaged in other occupations.

Except Sheikh, Kayasth, Mirasi and Kahar, owner cultivators are found in all the communities. Some of these people also do share cropping on *adha batta* (1/2 share) basis.

TABLE 3: Number of sharecroppers (communitiwise) among the owner cultivators

	Community	No.of Individuals
1.	Kurmi	10
2.	Murao	9
3.	Bhuj	6
4.	Pathan	5
5.	Kori (untouchable)	4
6.	Nau,Jat,Dhuniya, Lohar,Barai	10 (2 in each group)
7.	Kalowar,Ahir,Ansari,Barhai,Halowai	5 (1 in each group)
	Total :	49 Individuals.

Among the untouchables we only find the Kori as share croppers because they are very laborious and hardy.[2] There are three reasons for not preferring the other untouchable communities like Dhobi, Chamar and Hela for sharecropping because :

i. They are all marginal farmers having very low economic condition (Vide table 1).
ii. They are having a very low social status.
iii. The local higher castes also think that these communities are lacking sufficient proficiency in cultivation as compared to other agricultural castes. The non-cultivating landowners prefer small farmers. (owning 6-10 bighas of land) to cultivate their land on share cropping basis.

Agricultural labourers are of three different categories, namely - *Majdoor*, *Bhataha* and *Tankhaiyah*. Both male and female can work as *majdoor* (daily labourer). But female are tabooed from ploughing land. They are paid either in cash or in kind.

TABLE 4: Wages of daily labourers

Nature of work	Medium of payment	Down by (sex)
Tilling and Levelling	Rs.2/- per bigha in cash	Male
Broadcasting, Trans-plantation, weeding, threshing,storing,etc.	75 paisa to Rs.1.00 in cash or 3 seers(kachcha) Wheat or 5 seers(kachcha) Paddy in kind	Male/Female
Harvesting	1 bundle (*pura*) out of every 20 bundles in case of paddy and wheat. In case of *arahar* they receive only dried stalk. In case of sugarcane they get only leaves. In the case of other crops they are paid in cash.	Male/Female

Those who work as contract labourer and receive grain as allowances for their services are known as bhataha. Males are selected for this type of work. With different agricultural activities they have to take care of bullocks and agricultural implements. They get meal from the employers along with 1/6 of the total produce annually. Besides they also get tips (*bakhsis*) during any social ceremony from their employers. Each *bhataha* is entitled to get one set of clothes annually namely one *dhoti* and *kamij*. There is no *bhataha* in the village now.

Thankhhaiyah labourers are like *bhataha*. Instead of payment in kind they receive monthly salary. It ranges Rs.50.00 to Rs.60.00 per month. They neither get the usual set of clothes, nor any share of the harvest nor food. There are three *tankhaiyah* (1 Kurmi and 2 Pathan) in this village.

b. *Traditional/Caste Occupation*

In Pehar nearly 50 per cent of the different caste groups follow their traditional occupation. They are paid mostly in kind and during some socio-religious ceremonies in cash also.

To describe the various mode of interactions of these groups mention of *jajmani* system can be made. Incidentally, though the economic interactions are there, yet that particular term (i.e.

jajmani) is absent at Pehar. The early Zamindars had brought these service rendering castes according to their necessity. Later the families of these people increased in number. So they divided the total families of this village mutually among themselves. Each of these divisions are termed as *halka*. They usually refer to lower caste members of the *halka* as *asami* and the big landlords of the higher caste are addressed as *malik*.

Now let us describe about the caste groups and their caste occupations alongwith their wages.

a. *Darji* : They are tailors. They get 1 mound (kachcha) [3] grain, half yearly, from each house of their *halka*. During marriage they make *jora-jama* (special orange coloured tunic of the bride-groom) and get Rs.10.00 extra in cash as *bakhsis* (tips) along with the usual cost of the material. In some cases their clients supply them raw material for making jora-jama. Now they are facing certain difficulties, because now-a-days the villagers prefer to buy cheaper ready made garments from the weekly market (*hat*). The younger boys who go to the secondary schools at Utraula town also prefer to buy garments of up-to-date fashion[4] from town.

b. *Teli* : They prepare oil and get the oil cakes as their remuneration. They are not paid in cash.

c. *Sonar* : They are Goldsmiths. In the case of gold ornaments they charge @ 12 paisa per rupee on the total value of the raw material. In case of silver it is 6 paisa per rupee. Repairing charge depends on the nature of work (usually ranging from 10 paisa to Rs. 2.00, sometimes even more).

d. *Lohar* : They make different articles of iron used for agricultural and domestic purposes. Raw materials are supplied by their clients (*asami*). Besides they fix the share of ploughs and during harvesting season sharpen the sickles of their clients once in a weak. They get 1 mound (kachcha) grain half yearly as their remuneration (*jaura*) from each house.

e. *Bruhman* : During the worshipping of the Lord Satyanarayana and other deities they get 25 paisa as the charge of their priestly service and the amount which the other villagers give in the name of god as *parnami*. In marriages they get Rs.5.00 to Rs.10.00 for their priestly services. Moreover they get one new cloth and *sidha* (food stuff) consisting of 5 seers (kachcha) rice, 3 seers (kachcha) wheat flour, some salt, *ghee* (butter oil), mustard oil, green vegetable and spices. They do not serve the untouchable castes of the village.

f. *Barhai* : They make different wooden articles for agricultural and domestic purposes. Raw materials are supplied by their clients. Their remuneration are same as the Lohars.

g. *Nau* : They get 4 passeri grains half yearly for shaving from each adult male. They accompany *barat* (marriage party of the bride-groom) for carrying several articles of marriage in case of clean castes only and receive tips. At the end of pollution period they pare the nails and get Re. 1.00. During *muran* or *mundan* (first hair shaving ceremony of the male child) they get Re. 1.00. Six days after child birth Nau women smear the body of the child with mustard paste (*bukka*) and oil (*tel*). They get *sidha*, consisting of 250 grams rice/wheat flour, 125 grams pulses, some salt and oil daily. During marriage Nau women decorate the bride and receive tips. Services of the Nau women are rendered to the clean castes only. The Muslim Naus have to cook and serve food during marriage ceremony among the Muslims only.

h. *Dhobi* : They are washermen. Per married woman they get 4 passeri grain twice in a year. They do not get anything for washing the clothes of the unmarried girls or whose *gaona* (second marriage ceremony after attaining puberty) is pending. During *gaona* they get Rs. 5.00 in cash, new cloth and 10 seers (kachcha) grain as tips. At the end of the pollution period the Dhobi women sprinkle water for the purpose of purification in clean caste houses and get Re. 1.00.

i. *Kahar* : They work as domestic servants in Jat and Kayasth houses. Previously they were paid in kind. Now all of them get monthly salary which ranges from Rs. 4.00 to Rs. 6.00 per house. They also get two meals from their employer's house.

j. *Manihar* : They sell glass bangles and other cosmetics used by the women and young girls. All of their transactions are done strictly in terms of cash.

k. *Bhuj* : They are grain parcher. They get 1/5 of the amount of grain parched as remuneration.

l. *Hela* : They are sweepers. Per married family they get 4 passeri grain half yearly. The Hela women act as midwives. For cutting the umbinical cord they get Rs.2.00 in cash and receive hand full of rice or other grains (*anjuri*) which are presented to the newly born by the kinsmen. Upto six days after child birth they receive *sidha* (same as

Nau) for smearing body of the child with mustered paste and oil. The Hela males also play musical instruments during various social ceremonies. For that they are paid in cash along with food.

So far, we have been discussing about various caste occupations and their wages. They are mostly paid in kind and during some socio-religious ceremonies in cash also. Even today they are receiving the same amount which they used to get during Zamindari period. These amounts are certainly too small to meet their requirements. As such they have to look to other avenues of employment for supplementing their income. Being tradition bound their education with reference to modern standard is vastly inadequate (vide appendix table-1 on literacy). This keeps them confine to their village. Here in the village the only avenue thus open to them is that of agricultural labourer. Moreover the mode of payment in reality varies from caste to caste. For example, the services of the Lohar (black-smith) and Barhai (carpenter) are highly needed in agriculture, so they are regularly paid in correct weight by wheat or paddy.

On the other hand the Dhobi (washerman) and Hela (sweeper) are paid by kodo (a type of cereal) and barley.

Generally no individual of one caste follows the occupation of the other castes. Occupations of Nau, Dhobi and Hela are considered to be low, so nobody logically opts for them. Similarly the occupations of Brahman, Lohar, Bahai, etc., require much specialised skill which can not be acquired without proper equipment and training.

Tradition undoubtedly die hard and as we have seen above these traditional occupations are self generating and reinforcing. We may cite here the case of an Ansari who has taken up oil-pressing by the orthodox method of using the rotatory wooden oil-press driven by a single bullock. In this case we observe that economic insecurity compelled this Ansari to adopt a new profession. If we look at this case from a different angle it will be worth nothing that the Ansari, being a Muslim his faith did not stop him from adopting a new occupation.

C. *Other Occupations*:

There are various business and services, traditional and modern, in which the villagers are involved. These are described below:

Business

Grocer's shop	....	4	individuals
Sweet meat shop	....	2	"
Tea stall	....	3	"
Meat selling	....	2	"
Flour Mill	....	3	"
TOTAL	....	14	individuals

*Service**

Service in wine shop	....	3	individual/s
Medical compounder	....	1	"
P.W.D. Labourer and Peon	....	9	"
Teacher (Pri. & Sec)	....	8	"
Sweeper	....	7	"
In water supply works	....	1	"
In Baker's shop	....	2	"
Pound Keeper	....	2	"
Post Master	....	1	"
Settlement Clerk	....	1	"
Police	....	3	"
Dealers of utensils	....	3	"
Mason	....	1	"
Lawyer	....	1	"
Government Clerk	....	4	"
TOTAL:		47	individuals

Transport

Ekka driver (horse cart)	....	1	individual/s
Truck driver	....	1	"
Rikshaw Puller	....	2	"
TOTAL	....	4	individual

* Among the service holders 33 individuals live outside the village.
Truck driver and Rikshaw pullers live outside the village.

Begging

There are three beggars (Ansari, Patha, and Hela) in this village. They are too old to do any physical work and do not have any close relative to support them. Out of the three beggars two are Muslims. The Muslim institution of charity (*jakat*) and its management should have looked after them but charity institution seems to have undergone a drastic change and lost its original purpose.

Dancing

There are two men of the Kori people who are attached with *nautanki* (open air theatre) as dancers. It is temporary occupation which starts from later part of October and continues upto March.

General economic condition of the rural poor

The share croppers and agricultural labourers do not have favourable attitude towards the higher caste people. In the opinion of the share-croppers, the landowners generally give them inferior quality of land. Inspite of their hard toil they cannot get much profit. On the other hand the landowners get half of the amount produced without investing labour or money. The labourers also have the same complain against the landlords. In their opinion, the landowners make them to work much, yet pay them poorly. In case of payment in kind they give less in weight . The labourers have not agitated for an increase in wages particularly because they fear, this will render them unemployed, and the landowners will hire labourers from the adjoining village.

According to the agricultural labourers, their condition has gradually worsened since independence. Their wages are hopelessly inadequate. It can hardly meet the bare requirements. The question of having any saving is beyond imagination particularly with the spiralling price rise. Yet the agricultural labourers (specially the untouchable groups) now feel happy as they do not have to render *begar* (forced labour) to their landlords now-a-days. The following words of Sri Darsan Hela of Pehar village may help us to understand how horrible the *begar* system was.

> "*Jara eya garmi, chahe pani girhe chahe bajjar parhe, jab gohoraot tab he jayeke parat raha. Tanni derme ekho juti bhuiyam nahi girat raha*."

("Weather it is extremely hot or cold, or it is raining or thundering, whenever they shouted - we had to be present. On delaying a little we were severely beaten by shoes").

In agriculture, the rural people get earning opportunity for less than six months. Though a few subsidiary occupations are there, but they have to depend on borrowing. The existing methods of borrowing are known as *derha* and *soai*. In the first case the interest is 50% and in the second case it is 25%. This may be in cash or in kind. Such credit facilities are available from the Bania and big landowners. If anybody fails to clear up his dues, he has to work in the moneylenders field until the whole amount is cleared up. If utensils or ornaments are mortgaged they have to pay 120% interest per annum.

Like the agricultural labourers, marginal farmers also face the same difficulties. Usually during harvesting season the price of the agricultural produce remain low. But due to the pressure of the creditor they have to sell their produce to the local whole seller at a low price right from the threshing ground (*khalihan*). Two/three months after harvesting, prices again go up, so the marginal farmers again have to go to the *Mahajan* or moneylender for taking loan.

Local B.D.O. Office and Co-operative society have several schemes to give loans for the benefit of the poorer people at lower rate of interest but it is a lengthy process for getting loan, moreover they have to spend a lot of money at various steps to get their loans sanctioned. So they go to the local *Mahajans* knowing that he charges considerably higher rate of interest. According to them, *Mahajan* is the saviour of the poor who comes to their rescue in the time of distress without lengthy formalities. He, thus, according to them, has legitimate claim to charge higher interest. The use of kinship terms in a reciprocal manner by both debtors and creditors and the social idiom under which transactions take place not only have given a familial touch to this institution of rural financing but also a relaxed and informal meaning.

With the implementation of land consolidation Act in Uttar Pradesh, the rural poor have lost some of their land and job opportunities. It was reported that :

i) The poor people were given inferior quality of lands which were officially recorded as having higher valuation. On the other hand, the ex-zamindars (as they provided shelter and food at cheaper rate to the settlement clerks and officers and space for their office) got superior land on lesser valuation.

ii) On account of land consolidation, the land which the big landlords had given to the poor farmers on share cropping because they were situated far away from their area of residence, they are now self cultivating.

iii) Land consolidation has helped the big landlords to cultivate their land by using lesser number of agricultural labourers in comparison to the previous times when they had to employ more labourers in their scattered plots. So it limited the scope of earning of the agricultural labourers.

From these points it will be clear that the poor have become poorer while the rich have become richer. This surely was not the intention of the legislation which gave birth to 'Land Consolidation Act'. The objective is undoubtedly creditable yet the implementation by the corrupt officialdom results in nullifying the objective. When a big landlord consolidates his far flung and isolated bits of little holdings his production efficiency certainly increases. This increase is a welcome feature which results in higher production. From the point of view of employment, the one time share-croppers of these small and distant holdings are thus rendered destitute. It is this fact that has to be considered seriously and at the higher levels of policy making whether the present trend should continue or be modified. It will perhaps not be out of place in the context of the weaker sections to mention that the events before and after the implementation of the land consolidation act have helped in widening the economic gap between the ex-zamindars and the share-croppers.

During Zamindari period, the poor people virtually had to lead an uncertain life like serfs. With the abolition of Zamindari system the poor people got opportunity to own some agricultural and homestead land officially. But the amount of land given to them were so scanty that this virtually gave rise to a number of marginal farmers.

TABLE 5: Distribution of agricultural land by family

		Small	Medium		Big	
Total Family	Landless	Up to 5 Bigha	6-10 Bigha	11-20 Bigha	21-50 Bigha	Above 50 Bigha
233	46	76	43	35	19	14

According to the villagers atleast 5 Bighas of agricultural land will more or less suffice in normal conditions to meet the expenses of a family consisting of 5 members. Then without any finer calculation it can be said that at Pehar village approximately 54.4% (122 out of 233) families are below the subsistence level.

In fact in all the communities we find economically rich and poor families. But when we speak in terms of communities (weather rich or poor) then invariably we have to make some sort of generalization on the basis of certain fixed criteria. So on the basis of average per family landholding (as it happens to be the most important determinant of economic status) the following groups, namely Murao, Ansari, Dhuniya, Barai, Halowai, Sonar, Hela, Brahman, Manihar, Dhobi, Fakir, Mirasi and Kahar can be stated as 'economically poor' though some of them have very high social position (vide Table-1).

Nature of Social Interaction

We find that at present the higher and lower caste houses are located side by side, though at Pehar the houses of the Hela sweepers are situated at the western boundary of the village. This area is termed as *Helaun-dih* and is not usually visited by the other Hindu and Muslim communities of the village.

The Hindus of this village are divided into 18 *jati* groups. Their respective social positions in the village society are primarily determined by - i) purity and pollution of their traditional occupation, ii) food habit, and iii) acceptance of food from the other caste groups. The Hindus of the Pehar village are sharply divided into two groups on the basis of food habit. Vegetarian groups have more social prestige than those of the non-vegetarian groups. Social-ritual ranking pattern of Pehar is given in the Table 6.

Among all these *jatis* the vegetarian groups have the higher position and the Brahmans have the highest position among them. They may take water from the Ahirs but not from the Muraos (who are also vegetarian). But the vegetarian people never accept water or any kind of food from the non-vegetarian people.

Among the non-vegetarian castes, the Jats are at the top of the list followed by the Kayasthas. Though the Jats originally are agriculturists (like the Kurmis) now they claim themselves as Thakur (Kshatriya). As they were Zamindars and are very powerful even today so nobody dares to challenge their social position. Let us quote the words of Sri Shiw Karan Kurmi told to Sri Ram Ratan Kalowar to explain this situation :

> *"Ar-re bhai, woh loge Zamindar hoi, malik hoi, ham sabko eha basaya hai. To Kaise ham unka barabar hoi jab ?"*

(Listen, they are Zamindars, they are masters, they gave us land to settle here. Then how we could be equal to them ?)

TABLE 6: Showing caste ranking among the Hindu

VEGETARIAN			NON-VEGETARIAN		
Caste		Traditional Caste occupation	Caste		Traditional Caste occupation
1. Brahman	Clean high caste	1. Priesthood			
2. Ahir		2. Milkman			
3. Murao		3. Vegetable grower.			
			1. Jat	Clean high caste	1. Agriculturist
			2. Kayasth		2. Village Clerk
			3. Bania	Clean caste	3. Businessman
			4. Sonar		4. Gold Smith
			5. Lohar		5. Black Smith
			6. Kurmi		6. Agriculturist
			7. Nau	Clean low caste	7. Barber
			8. Barai		8. Betel leaf seller
			9. Bhuj		9. Grain parcher
			10. Kahar		10. Domestic Servant
			11. Teli		11. Oil pressure
			12. Dhobi	Untouchable caste	12. Washerman
			13. Kori		13. Weaver
			14. Chamar		14. Leather worker
			15. Hela		15. Sweeper

The Jats can take *kachcha/pucca*[6] *Khana* from the Kayasth houses and vice-verse. Bania, Sonar, Lohar and Kurmi are all clean castes, having more or less equal social status. Similarly Nau, Barai, Bhuj, Kahar and Teli are having more or less same social status and are referred to as clean low castes. Clean high caste people will not take water from these groups except from the hands of a Kahar, Kahars can also cook food without salt for the high caste people other than the vegetarian groups. Each constituent unit of the social hierarchy, that is *jati*, functions as an autonomous unit for regulating its internal affairs.

Dhobi, Kori, Chamar and Hela are considered as untouchable *jatis.* Socially their positions are very low and on the basis of polluting nature of their occupation, i.e. sweeping, the Hela occupy the lowest rung of the social ladder. There is a great controversy among the untouchables regarding their social status. Since independence due to some political reasons they are exhibiting themselves as better Hindus than before to the higher clean castes. They have abandoned eating carrion, beef, etc. They have also abandoned accepting cooked food from the Muslims publicly. Dhobi, Kori, Chamar and Hela have far excelled the upper castes in the practice of discrimination when it comes to untouchability amongst themselves.

System of social ranking among the Muslim in comparison to that of the Hindus seems to be little fluid, because Islamic tradition never allowed social inequality. Yet some traits akin to the *jati* system can be noticed among them. Similar to the Hindu *jati* groups the Muslim refer to their different endogamous groups as *quom*, Muslim *quoms* are broadly divided into two categories as i) *asraf* and ii) *atrab* (i.e. Sophisticated and rustic, while laterally meaning - gentle or well-bred and rude or ill-bred).

TABLE 7: Social Ranking among the Muslim

Quom	Social Status	Traditional Occupation
1. Pathan	Asraf	1. Not specific.
2. Sheikh	..	2. .. ..
3. Barhai	Atrab	3. Carpenter.
4. Halowai	..	4. Sweet meat seller.
5. Manihar	..	5. Bangle seller.
6. Darji	..	6. Tailor.
7. Nau	..	7. Barber.
8. Dhuniya	..	8. Cotton Carder.
9. Ansari	..	9. Weaver.
10. Fakir	..	10. Mendicant/Beggar.
11. Mirasi	..	11. Musician.

Pathan and Sheikh people belong to the *asraf* category. Though there is a controversy regarding their social position, the Pathans are considered to be the highest. They were the owner of this village. The Pathans feel proud of their *haddi* (lit. bone, meaning purity of descent). The *haddi* of the other *quom* are supposed to be inferior.

All the Muslim *quom* theoretically can pray and dine together. But the local Pathans never accept water and food from the hands of the Mirasi and the Muslim Dhobi because of their occupation. To keep their *haddi* pure local Muslims do not allow inter-*quom* marriages. Violation of this rule of endogamy would lead to ostracization, locally referred to as *hukha bandh/hukha pani bandh*. Relating this instance with other published cases (Russel & Hiralal - 1916 : 4, 215-33; Alexandar - 1972 ; 160-61; Fiske - 1972 : 140-41) we may infer that the Brahminic concept of purity-pollution is so deeply intrenched within the core of Indian Civilization that it has influenced almost all the religious groups in the country.

The Muslim, following the Hindu practice of discrimination, regard the Dhobi, Kori, Chamar and Hela groups as untouchable. In turn, collectively the Hindu castes regard the Muslims as impure (rather than as inferior) as the later take beef.

Though the economic conditions of the poor clean caste and the poor untouchables are identical yet on the basis of jati ranking they get differential treatment. A clean lower caste individual can go inside the houses of higher castes, he can have his meal there. The utensils thus used can be made fit for using again by washing it. On the contrary, no process of purification is considered to be sufficient to purify the utensils used by the untouchables in similar situation. In some life cycle rituals (e.g. child-birth) the clean low castes are allowed to cross the threshold of the higher castes as share-cropper unlike the untouchable farmers.

The untouchable *jatis* have to suffer a host of other social discriminations. These are:

1. An untouchable individual is not allowed to sit along with higher caste individual, not at the same level. As a token of respect, he must stand up from his seat in the presence of a high caste individual. The educated youth of the untouchable communities continue to observe the same practice. However, it was noticed that the untouchable youths are now developing a different attitude towards social discrimination.

2. In the social ceremonies of the higher castes they usually go there. The untouchables are not served food within the house of any higher caste. They are given food outside the house, which in most cases happens to be the leftover from the food of the clean caste.
3. Currently there is no restriction for the untouchables in fetching water from the village well. They are, however, not allowed to draw water at the same time alongwith the higher caste Hindus and Muslims. The private wells of the higher *jatis* are totally forbidden to the untouchables even today. The effective control is excerised by having the wells located within the compound of the higher caste house.
4. The untouchables are not allowed to set foot in the courtyard of the higher castes when boiled paddy for the preparation of consumable rice is being dried.
5. In sweet meat shops they are served in leaf plates and in the tea-stalls they are given earthen cups instead of glass tumbler. In some shops special cups are kept for the untouchables.
6. Ritual services of the Brahman are never available to the untouchables. Previously, they were not allowed to enter any temple. Government now by legislation have removed this restriction. The author, however, found that the untouchables dare not go within 'Dookh Haran Nath' and 'Jwala-mai' temples. When vows are to be fulfilled and notice offering are to be made by the untouchable, it was observed that they used the services of Ahir or Murao as intermediaries, to arrange worship for them. During 'Barawati-mai' worship in the month of Asadh (June-July) their offerings are kept below the platform of the village shrine.
7. In village panchayat meetings the untouchables keep themselves at a respectful distance from the higher castes and sit on the ground as mere spectators.

Physical contacts and touch of the untouchable groups are not considered as polluted now-a-days as it was in the past. In public places like school, college, hospital or in the public vehicles they go along with other castes freely.

In the activities of day to day living the untouchables have more interaction with the lower clean castes than with the higher castes. The lower clean castes follow the principles of discrimination much more rigidly and always remind the untouchables about their low origin through their words and deeds. These words and deeds give rise to *jati* distance phenomena directly proportional to the degree of discrimination. This word and deed complex is apparently the boundary maintaining mechanism and contributes directly against possible union of the socially low (both clean and unclean) against the socially high landlords.

The ambivalent attitude of the lower caste people towards the higher castes can easily be found out by the depth interview and group discussion. The lower castes address the higher caste by several kinship terms, like-*Nana* (Mo Fa), *Mama* (Mo Br), *Chacha* (Fa Br), *Fufa* (Fa Si Hu), etc., and vice-versa. Greetings and salutations are very freely exchanged. It was, however, observed that the exchange of salutation always commenced from the lower castes. Though both the high and low castes use the same local dialect yet some differences in the mode of address are found.

On comparing the economic condition with the respective social position of the different *Jati* and *quom* groups it can be said that, there is apparently a close correlation between the economically weak status and the socially inferior position of *jatis* or *quoms* at Pehar.

Political Life of the Rural Poor

In political sphere we will discuss certain aspects of change in the local power structure and the impact of democratic decentralisation policy on the rural society.

Previously this village did not have any panchayat.In case of any dispute the joint verdict of the local Zamindars were the last words. Nobody dared to disobey them as that could endanger their existence. Social disputes were settled by the respective *Jati* groups among themselves.

Statutory village panchayat of this village was established in 1949 after the enactment of 'Panchayati Raj Act'. At that time some youth of the poorer section (namely, Abdul Majid Khan, Chhangeur Murao and Raja Ram Kurmi) became interested in political matters and tried to organise the poor people of the village, so that dominating higher castes may not get elected to the 'Panchayat Executive Committee'. The Zamindars reacted by exerting pressure on the poor people and took away all the lease lands. The poor tenants and the labourers got frightened and they withdrew their support to this new movement against the Zamindars. Thus, a Pathan of Zamindar's family became the uncontested village *Pradhan* (Headman). Not only the village headmanship, the higher caste people also captured all the important offices of this village, as described below:

1. Village pradhan ... Pathan
2. Local representative in the *Anchal Panchayat* ... Pathan
3. Local representative in the Land-development Bank ... Jat
4. Regional representative in Block Development Office ... Sheikh
5. President, Local Co-operative Society ... Pathan
6. Secretary, Local Co-operative Society ... Pathan
7. Treasurer, Local Co-operative Society ... Sheikh
8. Seed store -in-Charge, Local Co-operative Society ... Jat
9. Post Master ... Pathan
10. Village Patwari(Settlement Clerk) ... Kayasth
11. Head Master, Local Primary School ... Pathan

Thus the monopoly over all the important offices by the higher castes or the socially higher people resulted in the poor people to depend entirely on the mercy of the former.

In case of allocation and distribution of government relief funds the opinion of the village *Pradhan*, being the elected representative, is final. This criteria for distribution may be made effective for indirect purchase of votes during some future election. Similar things are happening in case of giving loan at lower rate of interest from the local co-operative society. If the village *patwari* comes to investigate any case of dispute of land, then he charges some money from both the parties. The village post master charges @ Rs.1.00 per hundred rupees as his commission in the cases of money-orders. The headmaster of the local primary school sells the *dalia* (soyabeen flour) and soyabeen-oil to the sweetmeat shop instead of distributing them among the students.

There are several instances which will show how the poor villagers are deprived of materials intended for them by the socially and politically powerful high caste people. They, have thus, not benefited from the 'Democratic Decentralisation' policy of the government aimed at gradual amelioration of the masses who live in poverty.

Another thing which requires a special mention, is the role of the rich individuals emerging from within the weaker sections. All of them are medium landowners having 10-20 Bighas of land. They do their cultivation themselves and have made cultivation a profitable concern. To get high yielding variety seed, chemical fertilizer, etc., and other facilities, they generally try to remain in association of the local power elites consciously betraying causes of the other poor people. Besides sycophancy (locally referred to as *Chamchabazi*) some seasonal business also enable them to earn cash money. So their economic condition is gradually improving. On pointing to a pucca bulding of a lower caste member, a member of the ex-Zamindar family stated the following:

> "*Jahan par dekhio bade makan-lekin edhar udhar tuta hai, pani girat hai, to samjh liho u khandani bade admiko kothi hai. U loge avi garib hoin jat hai, merammat nahi kar paot hai. Ar-re bhai, ab to sab koi paise kamana suru kiya. Chamar bhi bahut kamaot hai. Ab pucca building ka kya ijjat rah giya*? "

(Whenever you see a big house which is dilapidated and leaking you can take it for granted that it belongs to a traditional rich man of high caste. They have now become poor and they are unable to get their houses repaired. Now everybody has started to make money, even the Chamars earn a lot. Now what is the respect for a pucca building ?).

It is seen that the rural poor in most cases have low social status and virtually lacking any political power to combat various types of economic exploitation in the rural situation.

It is the low social status alongwith some carefully designed and imposed social restrictions which never allowed the rural poor to acquire wealth and power. This also helped the higher caste people to exploit the lower castes and continue this process.

It may be argued that the *Varna* and *Jati* present an unique system of social stratification. Here Mencher's observation is very relevant (1974:15,4 : 469-93). Quoting from Harris, she pointed out that, the caste system in India had functioned in two different manners, as :

i) an institution that controlled the content of ideology *to legitimise social inequality on the basis of religion and,*

ii) an institution that physically suppressed the subversive, rebellious and revolutionary actions of alienated individuals and groups.

REFERENCES

1. Alexandar, K.C. "The Neo-Christians of Kerala", in *The Untouchables in Contemporary India.* Edited by J. Michael Mahar, P. 160-61. Tucson, Arizona. The University of Arizona Press, 1972.
2. Fiske, A. "Scheduled Caste Buddhist Organizations", in *The Untouchables in Contemporary India.* Edited by — J. Michael Mahar, p-140-41. Tucson, Arizona The University of Arizona Press. 1972.
3. Mencher, J.P. "The Caste system upside down, or the The not-so-mysterious East". *Current Anthropology.* 15:4, 469-93, 1974.
4. Russell, R.V. & Hira Lal *The Tribes and Castes of the Central Provinces of India.* p. 215-33. Volume — IV. London, Macmillan & Co. Ltd. 1916.

NOTES

1. The term *Quom* literally means "nation", But the Muslim of Pehar village use this term to denote different endogamous groups.
2. There is a local proverb about the Kori people. It says, *"Kurmike dhan aur Korike jangar kavi nahi oraot hai."* (Kurmi's wealth and Kori's strength are never lost.)
3. *Local measures for weight.*
   1 seer (Kachcha) = 6 chittacks (370 gms. approx.)
   5 seers (Kachcha) = 1 passeri (1 kg. 800 gms. approx.)
   8 passeri = 1 mound (kachcha) (9 kg. Approx).
4. Locally referred to as "hero-cut" dresses.
5. Dr. P.K. Misra pointed out that in Uttar Pradesh — "Kodo" is considered to be an inferior variety of cereal. In common purlance it is said that those who consume *Kodo,* become dull.
6. Kachcha Khana = boiled food. Pucca Khana = fried food.
7. Italics added :
8. Only 25.2% of the villagers are literate. Literacy in case of males is higher than that of females. Literacy is nil among the Chamar, Dhobi, Kahar and Mirasi. Percentage of literacy among the Brahman, Jat, Kayasth and Manihar is more than 40.0%. The Fakir, Pathan, Sheikh, and Sonar have literacy percentage between 30.0 to 39.0%. The Ahir, Ansari, Darji, Halowai, Kalowar, Lohar, and Nau have the literacy percentage between 20.0 to 29.0%. Percentage of literacy among the rest of the community ranges from 3.0% to 15.0%.

Appendix I

Level of literacy among the villagers of Pehar

Community	Illiterate	Literate	without schooling	Primary		Secondary		Higher		Total	Percentage	
	M	F	M	F	M	F	M	F	M	F		
Ahir	3	5	—	—	1	—	1	—	—	—	10	20.0
Ansari	12	16	2	2	3	—	3	—	—	—	34	26.0
Barai	23	19	1	—	3	—	1	—	—	—	47	11.0
Barhai	8	14	1	—	1	—	—	—	—	—	24	8.0
Bhuj	10	14	—	—	1	—	2	—	—	—	27	11.0
Brahman	2	4	—	—	3	—	1	—	—	—	10	40.0
Chamar	5	8	—	—	—	—	—	—	—	—	13	Nil
Darji	13	20	2	1	2	1	5	—	—	—	44	25.0
Dhobi	18	17	—	—	—	—	—	—	—	—	35	Nil
Dhaniya	17	14	—	—	—	—	1	—	—	—	32	3.0
Fakir	7	10	7	2	—	—	1	—	—	—	27	37.0
Halowai	4	10	1	1	—	—	3	—	—	—	19	26.0
Hela	20	16	—	—	1	—	2	—	—	—	39	8.0
Jat	2	12	—	1	1	1	8	—	—	—	28	50.0
Kahar	6	3	—	—	—	—	—	—	—	—	9	Nil
Kalowar	15	27	1	—	3	—	7	—	—	—	53	21.0
Kayasth	7	3	—	3	3	7	16	10	4	—	53	81.0
Kori	18	26	—	—	2	—	5	1	—	—	52	15.0
Kurmi	50	61	4	—	6	—	8	—	—	—	129	14.0
Lohar	11	18	—	—	3	—	6	—	—	—	38	24.0
Manihar	3	5	2	3	2	—	3	—	1	—	19	58.0
Mirasi	4	2	—	—	—	—	—	—	—	—	6	Nil
Murao	27	41	—	—	5	—	6	—	—	—	79	14.0
Nau	13	13	1	—	3	—	3	—	—	—	33	21.0
Pathan	71	114	2	24	21	11	33	1	9	—	286	35.0
Sheikh	4	7	—	—	3	—	3	—	—	—	17	35.0
Sonar	8	6	—	—	4	3	1	1	—	—	23	35.0
Teli	14	13	—	—	3	—	1	—	—	—	31	13.0
Total	395	518	24	37	74	23	120	15	14	1	121	25.0
Grand Total	913		61		97		135		15		121	25.0

Appendix II

Landholding Pattern at Pehar (communitywise)

Community	No.of family	Landless	Upto 5 Bigha	6-10 Bigha	11-20 Bigha	21-50 Bigha	Above 50 Bigha	Total and held	
								Bigha	Bigha
Ahir	2	1	—	—	1	—	—	12	00
Ansari	9	5	3	—	—	1	—	45	11
Barai	11	4	4	3	—	—	—	41	10
Barhai	5	1	3	—	1	—	—	27	00
Bhuj	5	—	—	2	3	—	—	58	05
Brahman	3	—	3	—	—	—	—	8	09
Chamar	2	—	—	1	1	—	—	20	10
Darji	6	2	—	2	1	1	—	58	00
Dhobi	8	1	7	—	—	—	—	18	10
Dhuniya	6	2	1	3	—	—	—	29	05
Fakir	4	3	1	—	—	—	—	3	02
Halowai	3	1	1	1	—	—	—	11	08
Hela	9	1	6	2	—	—	—	25	03
Jat	4	—	—	—	1	1	2	735	10
Kahar	2	2	—	—	—	—	—	—	—
Kalowar	10	—	4	4	1	1	—	90	00
Kayasth	8	1	2	2	—	3	—	103	00
Kori	12	1	5	2	4	—	—	95	10
Kurmi	21	1	—	6	9	5	—	328	19
Lohar	5	—	2	3	—	—	—	28	05
Manihar	2	1	1	—	—	—	—	5	00
Mirasi	1	1	—	—	—	—	—	—	—
Murao	17	1	10	5	1	—	—	80	04
Nau	6	1	3	—	2	—	—	33	15
Pathan	55	13	14	3	6	7	12	1340	19
Sheikh	2	—	1	—	1	—	—	16	00
Sonar	6	2	3	—	1	—	—	20	00
Teli	9	1	2	4	2	—	—	69	10
Total	233	46	76	43	35	19	14	3298	165

1 Bigha = 1/5 Acre 1 Bissa = 1/20 Bigha.

15

MIRPUR : A VILLAGE IN EASTERN UTTAR PRADESH

HASAN ALI

Mirpur, located about 25 kms. away from Allahabad city, is a multiethnic Harijan dominated village under the Chail Block and Manauri Police Station.

The first general reaction of the villagers against us was that we had come from Delhi from the family planning department for conducting operation concerning birth control. It happened so mainly for the reason because the family planning drive during those days was going on in full swing in the whole area. However, we were able to convince them about the nature of our work and this helped to remove fear from their mind. Also, they came to realise that we had no connection with the family planning department, when our inquiries moved further.

But when we started enquiring about land, another problem cropped up. The villagers, especially the landowners, suspected that our inquiries would raise the rates of their land tax as well as the amount of levy. Again we had to convince them that we did not belong to the tax or levy department. The village Pradhan and a young Moslem doctor, who belonged to a village about 10 kms. away from Mirpur and the educated youth helped us greatly in removing the villager's apprehension.

We showed some of the monographs published by the Survey to the villagers, particularly to the educated youth and explained that our research work would result in the publication of a book. This seemed to work well upon them and they became very cooperative.

Concerning data on the household income and expenditure, we had to face certain difficulties. The villagers though unable to give an exact account of their household income and expenditure, showed a common tendency to conceal their income. We rechecked our data on these points over and over again and thus got an approximate picture.

Information have been collected in accordance with the guide line prepared in advance for our research. The methods employed are interviews and observations. The period of field work was about four months during January to May '73.

Ethnic Composition and Settlement Pattern

The population of Mirpur is divided into 14 castes, nine Hindu castes, five castes among the Harijan and eight endogamous groups among the Moslem consisting of 856 individuals. Out of a total of 154 households, 69 households are those of the Harijan viz. Kori, Dhobi, Pasi, Khatik or Sonkar, and the Chamar.The upper and intermediate castes together constitute 39 households. They are the Brahman, Yadav, Bania, Chourashia or Barai, Bhunjwa, Lohar, Teli, and the Kumbhar. Among the 46 Moslem households there are Sayyad, Pathan, Ansari, Chick, Jogi, Faquir, Nai, and the Kayasth.

For the convenience of comparison and understanding, the village population may be trifercated into the caste Hindu,Harijan, and the Moslem.

The most striking feature of the settlement pattern is that unlike the usual pattern, the Harijan here do not have separate cluster of their own. However, in a village adjacent to Mirpur, the Hela (sweeper) lived in a separate cluster, at a distance from the main village.

In Mirpur the houses of the Dhobi are at the main entrance of the village, connected with those of the houses of the Brahman and the Chourashia. The houses of the Kori and Khatik are also within the village. The Pasi and the Chamar though have their houses on the other end of the village, are well connected. The Moslem are also within the village. The overall settlement pattern may be said to be of nucleated type.

Economic Dimension

The primary economic pursuit in the village is agriculture and a majority of the villagers are directly or indirectly dependent on it. Land is important symbol of prestige and power.

The total amount of land possessed by the villagers is 180 acres, distributed among 85(54.9%) households. The remaining 69 households (45.1%) are landless. Out of a total number of 39 households among the clean castes, 31 households possess land in varying amounts while only eight households are landless. The total amount of land possessed by these 31 households is 72 acres, having on an average 2.32 acres per household.

Castewise distribution of land among the Harijan households shows that out of a total of 69 households, 33 possess land while other 36 are landless. The total amount of land possessed by the 33 households is 70.5 acres, coming to an average of 2.13 acre per household.

Among the Moslem, 21 households out of a total of 46 households possess land and the remaining 25 households are landless. The total amount of land among them is 37.5 acres (average 1.78 acre per household). The detail of the land distribution described above has been presented in Table 2.

Table 3 shows the number of landowners according to the size of land they possess. It shows that 71 households possess land between one and three acres, land between three and five acres is possessed by nine households and land above five acres is possessed by only five households. They are caste wise as follows; Yadav (5.50 acres), Chourashia (6.50 acres), Kori (5.50 acres) and Khatik (6.00 acres).

Thus on the basis of the size of landholding one household in the village is decisively dominant. On the basis of the average out-put per acre it is found that an average of five acres of land is required for maintaining a family of five members, which is the average family size of the village. Thus taking five acres as the economic holding in the village only five households possess land between 5.50 to 6.50 acres (only a slightly above the economic holding) and the rest have land below five acres. Thus all the land owners in this village may be regarded as belonging to marginal and small categories of farmers.

The major crops of this area are wheat and paddy. Chana, matar and arhar are also cultivated among the Rabi crops. Agriculture depends almost entirely on monsoon. Tube wells are very few and far between. Only one household belonging to the Kori caste owns one deep tube well.

Apart from agriculture the villagers are engaged in a number of occupations, traditional or otherwise. There are a number of itinerary traders of cloth, footwear, and stationary articles who

TABLE 1: Ethnic composition and traditional/present occupation

Sl. No.	Ethnic Group	No. of house hold	Population	Traditional Occupation	Present Occupation
1.	Brahman	6	31	Priesthood	Priesthood, Agriculture, Service.
2.	Bania	4	27	Business	Business & Agriculture.
3.	Yadav (Gowala)	4	18	Milk selling	Agriculture, Service Labour.
4.	Barai (Chowrashia)	5	27	Betel selling	Agriculture, Labour.
5.	Kurmi	1	2	Agriculture	Agriculture, Labour.
6.	Bhunjwa	2	9	Grain frying	Grain frying, Agriculture & Labour
7.	Lohar	3	12	Black smithy	Black smithy, Carpentry & Labour.
8.	Teli	5	23	Oil pressing	Business, Agriculture, Labour.
9.	Kumbhar	9	54	Pottery	Pottery, Agriculture, Service, Labour.
10.	Kori	38	171	Weaving	Agriculture, Labour
11.	Khatik (Sonkar)	5	23	Vegetable selling	Vegetable selling & Agriculture, Labour
12.	Dhobi	9	42	Cloth washing	Cloth washing, Agriculture & Service, Labour.
13.	Pasi	11	56	Pig rearing	Pig rearing, Agriculture, Service, Labour.
14.	Chamar	6	56	Leather work	Shoe making & Agriculture, Labour.
15.	Sayyad	1	6	Not wedded to any specific service.	Service and Agriculture.
16.	Pathan	1	4	-do-	Agriculture, Labour
17.	Kayastha	4	30	Patwari	Service & Agriculture.
18.	Ansari	15	121	Weaving	Agriculture, Labour
19.	Chick	9	62	Meat selling (Mutton)	Meat selling, Agriculture, Labour.
20.	Faqir	8	52	Mendicancy	Agriculture, service Labour, Tailoring.
21.	Nai	2	18	Hair cutting	Hair cutting, Labour
22.	Jogi	6	37	Begging	Begging and Labour utensils repairing, tailoring.
	Total	154	856		

TABLE 2: Distribution of land

Ethnic group/ Cluster	Total no. of house hold	Number of landless household	Number of landowning household	Total amount of land in acre.	Average land per household in acre.	Remarks
Harijan						
Dhobi	9	6	3	6	2.00	
Khatik	5	3	2	7.50	3.75	
Chamar	6	4	2	3	1.5	
Pasi	11	3	8	18	2.25	
Kori	38	20	18	37	2.05	
Total	69	36	33	70.50	2.13	
Caste Hindu						
Bhonjwa	2	1	1	1	1.00	
Brahman	6	Nil	6	17	2.83	
Barai	5	1	4	19	4.75	
Teli	5	2	3	2	0.66	
Lohar	3	3	Nil	Nil	Nil	
Bania	4	Nil	4	12	3.00	
Kumbhar	9	1	8	8	1.00	
Kurmi	1	Nil	1	2	2.00	
Yadav	4	Nil	4	11	2.75	
Total	39	8	31	72	2.32	
Moslem						
Jogi	6	6	Nil	Nil	Nil	
Nai	2	2	Nil	Nil	Nil	
Ansari	15	5	10	20	2.00	
Faquir	8	2	6	6	1.00	
Sayyad	1	-	1	2	2.00	
Pathan	1	1	Nil	Nil	Nil	
Chik	9	5	4	8.50	2.12	
Kayastha	4	4	Nil	Nil	Nil	
Total	46	25	21	37.50	1.78	

TABLE 3: Distribution of landowners by size of holding

Ethnic groups	Total no. of household possessing land	Range + 1-3 acres	Range 3-5 acres	+5
Harijan				
Khatik	2	1	—	1
Chamar	2	2	—	—
Dhobi	3	3	—	—
Pasi	8	8	—	—
Kori	18	15	2	1
Total	33	29	2	2
Caste Hindu				
Bhonjwa	1	1	—	—
Brahman	6	4	2	—
Barai	4	1	1	2
Teli	3	3	—	—
Bania	4	3	—	1
Kumbhar	8	8	—	—
Kurmi	1	1	—	—
Goala	4	3	1	—
Total	31	24	4	3
Moslem				
Ansari	10	9	1	—
Faqir	6	5	1	—
Sayyad	1	1	—	—
Chik	4	3	1	—
Total	21	18	3	—

peddle around the surrounding villages. A number of persons belonging to various ethnic groups among the Hindu and Moslem are engaged in service in various public and private sectors. One Bania household deals with cycle accessories, having a shop at Manauri about five kms. from Mirpur. A good number of Moslem are engaged in tailoring business. Moslem household is running the only flour mill in the village. The details of occupations, ethnic, groupwise, has been presented in Table 4.

TABLE 4: Occupational classification

1	2	3	4	5	6	7	8	9	10	11	12	13	14	15	16	17	19	20	21	22	23	24	25	26	27	28	29	30
1. Bhonjwa	—	—	—	—	—	—	—	—	4	—	1	—	—	—	—	—	—	—	—	—	—	—	—	—	—	3	—	—
2. Dhobi	1	—	—	—	—	5	—	3	—	—	—	—	—	13	—	—	—	—	—	—	—	—	—	—	—	10	—	—
3. Brahman	5	1	—	—	—	—	—	—	—	—	—	—	—	—	5	—	—	—	—	—	—	—	—	—	—	5	—	—
4. Barai	2	—	—	—	—	4	—	3	—	—	—	—	—	—	—	—	—	—	—	—	—	—	—	—	—	5	—	—
5. Teli	1	—	4	—	—	2	—	—	—	—	—	—	—	—	—	—	—	—	—	—	—	—	—	—	—	4	—	—
6. Kori	4	—	4	—	—	30	—	15	—	3	7	—	—	—	—	—	—	—	—	—	—	—	—	—	—	39	—	—
7. Goala	1	—	—	—	—	—	—	3	—	—	—	—	—	—	—	—	—	—	—	—	—	—	—	—	—	1	—	—
8. Lohar	—	—	—	—	—	—	—	—	—	4	—	—	—	—	—	—	—	—	—	—	—	—	—	—	5	1	—	—
9. Khatik	—	—	—	—	—	—	—	4	—	—	—	—	—	—	—	—	—	—	—	—	—	8	—	—	—	3	—	—
10. Bania	—	—	8	—	—	—	—	—	—	—	—	—	—	—	—	—	—	—	—	—	—	—	—	—	—	5	—	—
11. Kumhar	2	—	—	—	—	3	—	2	—	—	—	—	—	—	—	10	—	—	—	—	1	—	—	—	—	8	—	—
12. Pasi	3	—	—	—	—	8	—	6	—	—	—	—	—	—	—	—	—	—	—	—	—	—	—	—	—	8	—	—
13. Kurmi	—	—	—	—	—	—	—	2	—	—	—	—	—	—	—	—	—	—	—	—	—	—	—	—	—	—	—	—
14. Chamar	1	—	—	—	—	9	1	3	—	—	—	—	—	—	—	—	—	—	—	—	—	—	—	—	—	3	2	—
15. Jogi	1	—	2	2	—	0	2	—	—	—	—	4	1	—	—	—	—	—	—	—	—	—	—	—	—	2	—	—
16. Kayasth	—	2	—	—	—	—	—	—	—	—	—	—	—	—	—	—	—	1	—	1	—	—	—	—	—	18	—	—
17. Nai	—	—	—	—	—	—	—	—	—	—	—	—	—	—	—	—	—	—	—	—	—	—	—	—	—	3	—	—

(Contd.)

TABLE 4: *(Contd.)*

1	2	3	4	5	6	7	8	9	10	11	12	13	14	15	16	17	19	20	21	22	23	24	25	26	27	28	29	30
18. Ansari	3	—	1	5	1	8	1	6	—	—	—	—	—	—	—	—	1	—	8	—	—	—	—	—	—	25	—	1
19. Saiyad	2	—	—	—	—	—	—	—	—	—	—	—	—	—	—	—	—	—	—	—	—	—	—	—	—	—	—	—
20. Sheikh	—	—	—	—	—	2	—	—	—	—	—	—	—	—	—	—	—	—	—	—	—	—	—	—	—	—	—	—
21. Fakir	—	—	1	1	—	3	—	3	—	—	4	—	—	—	—	—	—	—	1	—	—	—	3	—	—	5	—	—
22. Chikua	—	—	4	2	8	0	1	4	—	1	—	—	—	—	—	—	—	—	—	—	—	—	—	—	—	6	—	—
TOTAL	26	3	24	10	9	74	5	51	4	8	12	4	1	13	5	10	1	1	9	1	1	8	4	5	5	154	2	:

1. ETHNIC GROUP
2. SERVICE
3. SCHOOL TEACHER
4. BUSINESS
5. TAILORING
6. MEAT SELLING
7. AGRICULTURAL LABOUR
8. CYCLE REPAIRER
9. AGRICULTURE
10. GRAIN FRYER
11. CARPENTER
12. RAJGIR (MASON)
13. UMBRELLA AND UTENSIL REPAIRER
14. BEGGING
15. CLOTH WASHING
16. PRIESTHOOD
17. POTTERY
18. SHOE REPAIRING
19. SHOE MAKING
20. DR. (HOMEOPATH)
21. ITINERARY TRADING
22. PAINTER
23. MILK SELLING
24. FRUIT & VEGETABLE SELLER
25. MOTOR MECHANISM
26. HAIR CUTTING
27. IRON WORKS
28. STUDENT
29. DAI (MID WIFE)
30. TANGEWALA

Analysis, however, reveals that income from sources other than agriculture is generally more among the landowning households themselves.

Traditional Occupation and Jajmani Network

Though the relationship between the caste and traditional occupation is in a process of dissolution all over peasant India, nevertheless there are a number of artisan and service castes viz. Lohar, Chamar, Kumbhar, Dhobi, Nai and Brahman who are still continuing their traditional occupations in varying degrees.

There are three Lohar and two Nai households in the village. They are landless. The Lohar have combined smithy of iron with carpentry while the Nai have centered mainly around their traditional occupation of hair cutting. Apart from their daily cash earnings they are also paid in kind during the harvest season from their *Kisan* or landowners in return of their services based on the traditional jajmani relationship. They have clients from the neighbouring villages also.

Among the Dhobi, out of nine households six are landless. Excepting one person who is serving in the Indian Army, all are engaged (including women) in their traditional occupation of cloth washing. Six persons among them jointly run a laundry at Bombay and visit the village by turn.

The Kumbhar are traditionally pot makers and are still continuing it. Eight Kumbhar households out of nine possess land on an average of one acre each. Thus, they depend largely on their traditional occupation as well as labour. Among the Chamar, out of a total of six households four are landless while only two households have land 1.5 acres each. Two persons are engaged in their traditional occupation of leather work and two elderly women act as midwives for the villagers irrespective of their caste and communities.

Among the six Brahman households all possess land on an average of 2.83 acres each. In return of their traditional ritual services four households receive payments in terms of crop from their clients. During marriage ceremonies they receive payment in cash and clothes.

The two households of the Bhunjwa caste also pursue their traditional occupation of grain frying. Among the Bania all the four households are engaged in business on small scales. The other castes have abandoned their traditional occupation and are depending primarily on other sources for their livelihood.

Among the Moslem in the village those who are carrying their traditional occupation partially or fully are the Nai, Chick, and Jogi. All others have abandoned it. The Nai and the Chick are still to a larger extent bound by their traditional occupation of hair cutting and selling of meat (mutton). The Jogi (traditionally beggars) have abandoned the profession excepting one elderly person and have taken to utensil and umbrella repairing works. The Faqir (traditionally religious mendicants) have taken various pursuits including agriculture.

The above illustrations show that a number of ethnic groups depend upon their traditional occupations along with new occupations related to land, labour, service, business etc. The number of persons engaged in various occupations is shown in Table 4. It should be noted, however, that all the ethnic groups excepting the Brahman, Bania and the Sayyad supplement or depend greatly on wage labour, and also that the artisan and service castes are somewhat in a better economic position compared to those landless who have no other alternative than depending upon labour.

Organization of Agricultural Labour

The landless and marginal landowning households most of whom are the Harijan with no other dependable source of income sustain themselves greatly on wage labour. The normal rate of payment for a male labourer is Rs. 2.50, whereas Re. 1.00 only for the female labourers. Payment during harvest season is generally made in terms of grains. For wheat harvesting one labourer (male or female) gets two Kg. of wheat and Re. 1.00 per day. During paddy harvest, one labourer (male as well as female) generally collects about six to eight Kg. of paddy during the whole day. The harvest of *arhar* is done mainly by the male labourers as it requires more of physical labour. A male labourer gets six Kg. of *arhar* as his remuneration whereas a female labourer, if employed, gets only three Kg. for a day. Sowing operation is mainly done by the females, for which they get one Kg. of the grain sown and 0.25 paise for a day. Weeding, locally known as *neerai*, is also carried out by the female labourers for which they get Re. 1.00 only for a day.

Apart from the agricultural labourers who work on the daily wage basis, a few labourers have been employed by the landowners as farm servants locally known as *'halwaha'* on annual basis. There are three *halwaha* in the village, one Moslem and two Kori being employed by the Barai, Bania, and Brahman respectively. The first two receive Rs. 800.00 per annum including food while the third receives Rs. 900.00 per annum including food.

Along with these two categories of agricultural labourers mentioned above another category is formed by those of the skilled labourers who mostly work outside the agricultural field viz, Mason,Carpenter, Blacksmith (Lohar) etc. The remuneration of these skilled labourers ranges from Rs.6.50 to Rs.8.00 per day.

During various agricultural operations a labourer gets work for four months and 10 days (Table 5). During the rest of the period, the labourers generally go to the subdivisional town about five kms. away as well as to Allahabad. But they do not get regular work there. Some, however, get occasional work in and around the village, such as repairing and construction of house, digging of well etc.

Share-cropping and Landowner-Tenant Relationship

The total number of share-croppers in the village was ten and the total land under share-cropping amounted to 24 acres. Share-cropping was done mainly by the marginal farmers taking land from the farmers having larger holding. As none in this village could be mentioned as big farmer, generally landowners cultivated their land themselves with the help of their respective family members and through employment of labourers.

The local rules of share-cropping is that the cost of seed and manure is shared equally by both the parties while only 1/3rd of the total cost of irrigation, if there is any, is shared by the landowner. The entire cost of harvesting, threshing, and winnowing is borne by the share-cropper. The output is divided equally. Along with this general rule, some deviations were also observed. In one case share cropper received only 1/3rd of the total produce. In that case the total cost was shared equally by both the parties.

Sources of Agricultural Finance

The most popular source of agricultural finance among the local peasants was the Cooperative Credit Society. The other sources being Block Development Office and the nationalised banks Along with loan in cash farmers receive seeds and fertilizers at subsidised rates from the Cooperative Credit Society. The number of members of the society is very low. Out of a total number of 85 landowning households only 33 are members. The majority of the members belong to upper caste Hindu and Moslem communities and only five members are from among the Harijan (Table 6). The poor marginal farmers who do not hold share often have to obtain seeds, fertilizers etc. from the shareholders for which the former have to return double the quantity.

TABLE 5: Length of employment for agriculture labourer

Operation	Period	No. of days getting Employment
Ploughings: Sowing	15th June-August	45 days
Neerai (Weeding)	September	15 days
Kharif Crop Harvesting	From last week of November to December	30 days
Rabi crops sowing (Wheat, chana, matar)	After the paddy harvest During November to December	10 days
Rabi crop harvesting	From last week of March to April	30 days
		130 days

TABLE 6: Distribution of members of the cooperative society

Sl. No.	Ethnic Group	Total Number of land owing house hold	No. of members
1.	Brahman	6	3
2.	Bania	4	2
3.	Yadav	4	2
4.	Bhunjwa	1	2
5.	Barai (Chorashia)	4	5
6.	Kumbhar	8	4
7.	Moslem	21	10
8.	Pasi	8	1
9.	Kori	18	4
10.	Dhobi	3	Nil
11.	Khatik	2	Nil
12.	Chamar	2	Nil
13.	Teli	3	Nil
14.	Kurmi	1	Nil
	Total	85	33

Income and Indebtedness

Table 7 shows the distribution of per capita annual income among the ethnic groups and castes in the village. Out of a total of 154 households, 41 households representing all ethnic groups in the village were selected for detailed investigation on the economic aspect. The Bania have the highest per capita income followed by the Chowrashia or Barai, Sayyad, and the Brahman. The lowest per capita income is recorded by the Jogi (Moslem). The Chamar have the next lowest per capita income in the village.

According to Minhas, the per capita income of Rs. 20 at 1960-61 prices was considered to be the minimum level of living in India. Since 1960-61, there has been a phenomenal increase in the prices and it needs Rs.40 per month i.e., Rs. 480 per year as the minimum level of living. Thus we find that a great majority at Mirpur are living below the poverty line.

Data on indebtedness was collected from a sample of 41 households. Thirty-two of them turned out to be under debt (Table 8).

TABLE 7: Per capita annual income

Sl.No.	Ethnic Group	Income in Rs.
1.	Dhobi	400 = 00
2.	Khatik	492 = 00
3.	Chamar	312 = 00
4.	Pasi	325 = 00
5.	Kori	450 = 00
6.	Bhunjwa	388 = 00
7.	Brahman	676 = 00
8.	Barai	750 = 00
9.	Teli	435 = 00
10.	Lohar	375 = 00
11.	Kurmi	485 = 00
12.	Bania	890 = 00
13.	Kumhar	365 = 00
14.	Yadav	496 = 00
15.	Jogi	262 = 00
16.	Nai	400 = 00
17.	Ansari	480 = 00
18.	Faqir	362 = 00
19.	Sayyad	703 = 00
20.	Pathan	345 = 00
21.	Chiks	350 = 00
22.	Kayastha	353 = 00

TABLE 8: Indebtedness

Sl. No.	Ethnic Group	Total no.of household	Sample size	Total amount of debt. (in Rs.)	Average amount of debt (in Rs.) per household
1.	Dhobi	9	2	600=00	300=00
2.	Khatik	5	1	100=00	100=00
3.	Chamar	6	2	650=00	325=00
4.	Padi	11	3	300=00	100=00
5.	Kori	38	9	450=00	50=00
6.	Bhunjwa	2	1	Nil	Nil
7.	Brahman	6	1	50=00	50=00
8.	Barai	5	1	Nil	Nil
9.	Teli	6	1	100=00	100=00
10.	Lohar	3	1	20=00	20=00
11.	Kurmi	1	1	Nil	Nil
12.	Banai	4	1	Nil	Nil
13.	Kumhar	9	2	400=00	200=00
14.	Yadav	4	1	Nil	Nil
15.	Jogi	6	2	600=00	300=00
16.	Nai	2	1	Nil	Nil
17.	Ansari	15	4	200=00	50=00
18.	Faqir	8	2	100=00	50=00
19.	Sayyad	1	1	3000=00	3000=00
20.	Pathan	1	1	Nil	Nil
21.	Chiks	9	2	250=00	125=00
22.	Kayastha	4	1	Nil	Nil
	Total	154	41		

The poorer households obtain loan for their daily consumption as well as for discharging certain magico-religious obligations from the local money lenders. The prevalent rate of interest is six per cent per month. Very often the labourers obtaining loan from the village *mahajans* have to work for them during agricultural seasons at cheaper rates. The money lenders in the village are those whose income are comparatively high. They are the Bania (2), Chowrashia (1), Moslem (2), and Khatik (1). The highest burden of debt was shown by the only Sayyad household in the village. He had taken the loan for treatment of his wife. A higher incidence of debt was shown by the Moslem and the Harijan. The moneylenders demand a security against their loans and so the poor villagers mortgage their ornaments and sometimes the households utensils. This is locally known as *rehan*. Sometimes in order to get some heavy amount as loan land is also kept as *rehan* with the *mahajan*. As his interest in such case the *mahajan* gets the harvest till he gets his money back.

Only one case of this kind, the Sayyad household, was found in the village to have kept two acres of his land with the Khatik money lender of the village in 1970 for Rs.3000.00.

Consumption Pattern and Material Style of Life

The poorer households, as their consumption pattern suggests, spend a larger proportion of their income on the consumption of food. Due to their low income, most of them were found unable to spend on education of children, medicine, construction of house, etc. Those having comparatively higher level of income have a balanced budget. They spend towards educating their children, on house construction, purchase of dresses, and household belongings.

The inequalities of income get reflected in the material conditions of the economically dominant and the weak in terms of their dress, house type, household belongings etc. Though there is no *pakka* house in the village (the construction of one *pakka* house had been started by one Bania during the time of investigation), the houses of the economically better families are comparatively much larger.

Social Dimension

Though there is much controversy regarding the relative ranking of castes in the caste hierarchy, it is not difficult however, to locate three blocks of castes among them. They are upper, intermediate and lower blocks. Tentatively, the hierarchical order of various castes is as follows:

Brahman : Bania :	- Upper
Yadav : Barai : Kurmi : Bhunjwa : Lohar : Teli : Kumbhar :	- Intermediate
Kori : Khatik : Dhobi : Pasi : Chamar :	- Lower

Exchange of ritual services is considered an important the parameter in the general context for judging the ritual status of castes.

Although long residence and close association have brought the Hindu and the Moslem closer to each other, still they maintain their separate socio-religious boundaries and separate identities.

The Moslem are considered by the Hindu as a separate group of people, having a separate religious faith. The commensal interaction across the two broad sections of the population is almost nil. The Hindu do not in general receive water or food from the Moslem as they are ritually considered a separate community. The Moslem do not receive water or food from the Harijan.

Though the local Hindu are aware of the presence of various endogamous groups among the local Moslem, they do not have any clear cut notion about the hierarchy among the Moslem. The equivalence of all groups in the religious field, lack of commensal distance, the absence of the vegetarian and non-vegetarian categories of food on caste basis, as well as the absence of priestly caste, restricted the Hindu to conceive a notion of hierarchy among them.

The Sayyad are often compared with the Brahman and accorded the highest position. The big zamindars in that area among the Moslem were mostly the Sayyads. Pathan, Kayastha, Ansari, Chick, Faqir and Nai tentatively followed the Sayyads in the hierarchy, while the Jogi are placed at the bottom.

The Moslem divide themselves into three broad categories of high, middle and low statuses guided mainly by descent, nature of traditional occupation, and existing economic and educational standing of the ethnic groups. The secular factors play a more decisive role in evaluating the hierarchy among the Moslem.

Among the Hindu the Brahman are considered by general consensus to occupy the top position in the ritual hierarchy followed by the Bania. The castes within the intermediate ranking order are, Banis, Yadav, Bania, Kurmi, Bhunjwa, Lohar, Teli and Kumbhar.

The third block constists of the Harijan castes viz., Khatik, Dhobi, Kori, Pasi, and Chamar. The Chamar are considered the lowest in the hierarchy. Next to them are the Pasi followed by the Dhobi and the Khatik and Kori at the top.

Complete equivalence in commensality prevails only among members of the same caste and even among the Harijan castes commensal restriction was observed to be well maintained which suggests existence of untouchability among the untouchables themselves.

During the ceremonies among the caste Hindu and the Moslem, the Harijan are generally not invited, nor do the Harijan invite the former. However, during a *sradh* ceremony sponsored by a Yadav a few selected Harijan (Dhobi, Kori, and Khatik) were invited, who were served separately.

In day to day life also a strict distance is maintained by the high caste Hindus as regards the sitting arrangements with the members belonging to the Harijan castes. A Harijan, as per prevailing social norm, can not sit together with any member of a caste of high or intermediate status on the same cot or bench. This distance, however, is said to have been reduced during the recent years. The Harijan also now sit together with other castes, especially with members of intermediate status during the village panchayat meeting. The vice-president of the statutory village panchayat, a *Khatik* (Harijan) was seen sitting during the panchayat meeting together with other officials belonging to middle caste status. He was also quite vocal and played often a decisive role though the upper hand in decision making was vested with the *pradhan* (Barai), who was generally influenced by the Brahman and the Sayyad. During the meeting, a few Dhobi, and Kori were also observed sitting at a little distance from the upper castes. One member of the Panchayat belonging to the Chamar caste was observed sitting silently at one corner.

The Harijan, especially the Dhobi, Kori, and the Khatik were frequent visitors to the invesstigator's camp and used to sit together with the members of the caste Hindu and the Moslem on the same cot or bench. The exception was the Brahman. Very often, the Khatik Vice-President of the village panchayat sat together even with a young Brahman on the same cot in the camp. The Brahman worked for the Railways at Aligarh and had a wider outlook. The same Khatik, however, never used to sit with the elderly Brahman. Another Brahman, a school teacher, also did not hesitate sitting together with the members of the Dhobi, Khatik, and the Kori castes. However, one old Brahman remarked that "the village pradhan had destroyed the habits of the Harijan, otherwise they never dared to come closer to us". Moreover the Brahman or other higher castes who used to sit together with the low castes in our camp did not like to sit together with the same persons at their own houses.

The youngsters belonging to various castes were found to be well aware about their high or low caste statuses and seemed particular about accepting or refusing food or water from each other. The children of upper and intermediate caste clusters were found playing together with the Harijan children (Dhobi, Kori, Khatik). The children of the Pasi and Chamar castes, by virtue of living at the other end of the village, did not mix freely with the children of upper castes and played separately.

One important point to be noted is that there had been no separate wells for separate castes in the village and the Dhobi, Kori and the Khatik were observed to use the same wells. But a Harijan cannot draw water from the well at the time while any member of the high caste was drawing water. They have to wait till all others have taken water, with the preference to the higher castes. This is a matter of daily observance. The Chamar and the Pasi claim that they could use the same well, but the settlement pattern did not allow them to do so.

The mode of address often reflects the relative superiority or inferiority of castes. It was observed that the Brahman were always addressed by the members of lower as well as the intermediate castes as *Panditjee* or *Maharaj*.

The educated individuals among the Harijans get a better treatment from their own caste members and from all the villagers in general, as was observed in case of a member of the Dhobi caste, who read upto matric standard and was serving in the Indian Army. During our stay in the village he came on leave for one month. He was treated differentially and with respect. The youth among the Dhobi by virtue of living in Bombay have adopted some urban traits viz. wearing of clean cloths, shoes, and watch etc. and thus get some differential treatment. But their overall socio-ritual position remains still at the bottom.

Upward Mobility among the Untouchables

There was an effort on the part of the untouchables to raise their status in the social scale by adopting the style of life of the higher castes, especially of the Brahman.

The Chamar, who are considered the lowest both socially and ritually, in order to gain honour and higher status of their caste, have abandoned to a large extent their traditional occupations of leather work, tennary, midwifery, and also their dietary habits such as eating of pork, beef and carrion, that accounted for their lowest status. A ban has been put on these by their *jati panchayat*. As a result, no one now eats pork, carrion and beef. However, two old women among them still continue to do midwifery, while other two make shoes.

One Chamar family has become *bhagat* and thus family members do not use meat and liquor. The members of the Chamar caste as well as other Harijan have started wearing the sacred thread as the symbol of the twice born castes since 1968. The 'sacred thread' or *janeu* (as known in the local language) is not given to the Harijan by the village Brahman and hence they purchase it from the market. Though no violent objections were put over it, the Harijan were often ridiculed by the upper caste Hindu on this count.

Though the Harijan claim and some members of the high castes admit as well that the former could enter the temple made by the high castes within their settlements, it was not observed in actual practice. Moreover, Mirpur had no common temple. Various temples have been constructed by individuals of specific castes. The Harijan have a separate small place of worship.

Some changes are reported to have occurred in the interaction pattern of the high castes vis-a-vis the lower ones during recent years. During marriage, a Brahman is consulted by the Harijan also, regarding the date and *lagan* or marriage. But the Brahman do not perform the marriage rituals of the Harijan excepting that of the Kori and the Dhobi, which they have started doing since 1970. Among the Dhobi this has started since 1972.

There are four Hela families in adjacent village. Being landless, they mostly work in the city. As it has been stated earlier, their settlement in the village is a bit detached from that of the main village. They have their separate well. During marriage, mundan, bhandara (feast sponsored after pilgrimage to Badrinath or Puri etc.) they are called by Mirpur high caste members for sweeping and cleaning purposes. They collect the left-overs and take home the same for their consumption. They also substantiate their income through basket making and drumming.

It seems that though some minor change has occurred in regard to inter-caste relations between the Harijan vis-a-vis the higher caste Hindu, the basic structure of the society based on caste organisation has remained unchanged. The old traditional relations of exclusion continue to persist and the untouchables remain the untouchables. However, during Holi festival the Harijan were also observed to be singing songs together with members of the upper castes. Smearing of colour and greetings were also inter-changed between the upper caste Hindu and the Harijan. Previously the untouchables were not allowed to do so, especially, the Kori, Dhobi, and the Khatik. The

Pasi and the Chamar are not allowed entry even into the courtyard of high caste Hindus.

The Chamar at some places have gone out of the Hindu fold and become Buddhists. But so far, the Buddhism has not been a successful answer to their social problems, and in the eyes of others they continue to be the same degraded and depressed people.

Among the Kori, efforts are being made towards upward social mobility. As a result they now claim to be the *Rajput*. But they have been denied their acceptance as such in general by the upper caste Hindu in the village or area.

Boundary Maintenance

Boundary may be understood in two ways, viz. between the upper castes vis-a-vis the lower ones and between the rich and the poor.

Boundary maintenance however, was more visible along the caste line than along the class line. Each caste maintains a social boundary vis-a-vis the other one through the practice of endogamy, traditional occupation, commensality habits etc. Alongwith these almost each caste has its own *jati-panchayat* with extra village affiliation, which deals with the cases of marriage, divorce etc., among the members of their own *jati* or caste as well as organising reform measures and social mobility (esp. among the Harijan) among its own caste members. The extra-village affiliations of the *jati-panchayat* includes only members of its own caste.

The socio-religious boundaries at caste level is internally accompanied by numerous interest groups which make them ethnocentric and parochial. This does not allow the poor and the weak to unite together and make any concerted effort for improving their lot.

Political Dimension

The political scene at the village level has always been dominated by the economically dominant section of the village, belonging to the upper and intermediate caste status.

The Shukla family and later the Sharma family (both Brahman) dominated the village political scene as village heads during the pre-independence period. However, during the 1969 election, a member of the Barai or Chourashia caste got elected as the village Pradhan, who is now considered as the most powerful and dynamic person in the village.

After independence, the first Pradhan elected was a Harijan (Khatik) who was succeeded by another Harijan pradhan (Kori). The existing Pradhan i.e., the head of the statutory panchayat is holding the office for over last thirteen years (being re-elected during 1971 election). The posts of village panchayat is occupied by members of following castes.

Chowrashia or Barai — One (Pradhan)
Sonkar or Khatik — one (Up-pradhan)
Pasi — one !
Ansari — one !
Bania — one !
Members
Kori — Two !
Chikwa — one !
Kumbhar — Two !

Though there have been three members from the Harijan castes and the Vice-president is also a Harijan, the decisive role regarding all matters is played by the Pradhan, though, of course, Uppradhan was also quite influential. It should be noted however, that the Uppradhan though belonged to the economically dominant section, was never regarded by the upper and intermediate castes as socially dominant.

Moving out of the village and taking a little wider perspective we find that out of a total number of 85 Pradhan in the entire Chail Block, the number of Harijan Pradhan among them was only 10 which obviously shows that in the political field the Harijan could not do better in the regional context due to low ascribed status and poverty. Ten Harijan Pradhans caste wise were Kori (2), Sonkar or Khatik (2), Chamar (3), Dhobi (1), and Gadra (2). The number of Pradhans in the region among the upper caste Hindu is 53 and among the Moslem 22.

The other important official at the Block level above the Pradhan is the *Pramukh*. During the first election held during 1961, one Bania was elected as the *Pramukh* and during the last election (1973), a Yadav (principal of a school) had been elected to the position. Thus, in this office also the Harijan could not make any place of their own.

Education

Education may well be considered as one of the important determining factors of weakness or dominance. Education directly affects one's standard of living through opening service opportunities. Educated individuals, irrespective of caste, are held in respect by the villagers which affects their personal status.

When we analyse the level of literacy among various ethnic groups, we find that the highest percentage of literacy of the village is among the Sayyad (83.33%) followed by the Kayastha (76.66%), Pathan (75.00%), and Ansari (71.90%). The percentage of literacy among the Brahman is 58.06.

Among the Harijan the percentage of literacy is like this, Chamar (50.00), Dhobi (47.61), Khatik (27.48), and Pasi (23.21) (Table 9). The lowest percentage of literacy in the village is among the Yadav (16.66%) followed upward by Kumbhar (20.37%), Jogi (21.62%) and Pasi (23.21%). Considering the male and the female literacy separately we find that the highest percentage of male literacy is among the Sayyad (100%) (being three males only) and among the Kurmi (100%) (being one male only). The highest percentage of female literacy is among the Pathan (100%) (being two females only). The lowest percentage of male literate is among Yadav (16.66%) and the lowest percentage of female literate is among the Chamar (nil).

The only graduate in the village completed his degree course in 1972 and is doing his B.T. course. He comes from the Bania caste. There are altogether five intermediate pass in the village of which two are Moslem (Sayyad, Ansari), two Brahman and one Pasi (Harijan). There are two matriculates, one Moslem (Ansari) and one Dhobi. Similarly, there were three who read upto 10th standard, (one Kori, one Kayastha, and one Ansari).

Thus it is seen that even in the field of education the people belonging to lower social strata in the village on an average possess a poor position. The poor families could not afford to send their children to schools due to poverty. There is a good number of drop outs among them. As soon as the children attain some age, they are encouraged by their parents to work as labourers and contribute to the family income.

World View

The poverty has made the poor apathetic and fatalistic towards life.

A person born in a poor family is naturally deprived of all the privileges enjoyed by the privileged class of the society.

TABLE 9: Distribution of Literacy by Ethnic Groups

Sl.No.	Ethnic Group	Percentage of Literacy
1.	Bhunjwa	66.66
2.	Brahman	58.06
3.	Barai	26.64
4.	Teli	42.42
5.	Lohar	66.66
6.	Bonia	72.96
7.	Kumbhar	20.37
8.	Kurmi	50.00
9.	Yadav	16.66
10.	Jogi	21.62
11.	Nai	31.25
12.	Ansari	71.70
13.	Faqir	55.76
14.	Sayyad	83.33
15.	Pathan	75.00
16.	Chik	59.81
17.	Kayastha	76.66
18.	Dhobi	47.61
19.	Khatik	27.48
20.	Chamar	50.00
21.	Pasi	23.21
22.	Kori	27.68

The semi starved and semi-clad poor look forward to have two square meals a day, a pair of cloth and roof above their head. They seem to have only a limited aspiration, and want a little more than what they have, and do not aspire for an alround development and a higher standard of living. The poor seem to have a poor opinion about good-life.

The youth now having contact with the outside world, and knowledge of the present day situation do not maintain poverty as ordained by God but consider it the result of the perpetual exploitation of the poor by the rich and the dominant Zamindar. The Zamindar in general did not allow the Harijan especially the Dhobi, Chamar, and the Khatik to cultivate land as tenants but employed them largely as agricultural labourers. As a result, they do not have adequate land even to-day.

A section among the Harijan, especially the youth did not

consider the Varna structure of caste as God-ordained or sacred, but creation of the *samaj* (society) through which the upper castes have obtained the ritual supremacy. They maintain that the government sponsored development programmes and spread of education in massive scale might bring about a change in their life.

The poor, landless or marginal farmers among the Harijan, Moslem and intermediate caste Hindu in general maintain that absence of land and inadequate holdings, lack of regular employment, and proper educational facilities are the primary causes of poverty. They maintain that there should be redistribution of land.

The opinion of the villagers was that the system of agriculture should be revolutionised in the sense that better facilities for cash loans, seed, manure, irrigation etc. should be made available. Educational facilities and communicational network be improved.

The upper caste Hindu in general observed that the government should help all those who are poor irrespective of caste and community affiliation, instead of helping only the Harijan in matter of education and other aids.

Dominant *Versus* Weak

On the basis of the description in the preceeding pages, if we seek to identify the dominant section considering the major dimensions of our study viz.- economic, social, political, educational, and numerical strength, we find that no single caste or ethnic group at Mirpur could be regarded as the decisively dominant one. Numerically the Harijan taken together (44.83%) dominate over other, but socially as well as economically to a larger proportion they fall within the category of the weaker section. Economically, the most dominant are the Bania but numerically they are quite negligible (four households only), while the political power on the village level was wielded by the Chowrashia caste.

In terms of per capita annual income as well as possession of land,on an average we may consider the Bania, Barai, Brahman, Khatik, and the Sayyad as the dominant, while the rest may be put under the category of economically weak. Considering the non-Harijan caste Hindu, Moslem, and the Harijan as three sections of population in the village we find that the percentage of landlessness is more (54.03%) among the Moslem, followed by the Harijan (52.17%), while among the caste Hindu the percentage of landlessness is 20.51 per cent. No great difference could be observed in terms of average land holding per family among the land owners i.e. 1.68 acres per household among the Moslem, 2.13 acres per household among the Harijan and 2.32 acres per household among the caste Hindu. The difference in terms of average land holding between the Harijan and the caste Hindu is only marginal, while the Moslem have a comparatively lower average. But in terms of per capita income the Moslem stand in a slightly better position when compared with the Harijan in general. The caste Hindu show better position in this respect when compared with the Moslem and the Harijan.

Though a number of households belonging to these broad three categories of Harijan, other caste Hindu, and the Moslem suffer from acute poverty, the Harijan castes on the whole may be put under the category of the decisively weaker section. They are facing a two fold problem simultaneously. One is that of poverty and the other is that of their social backwardness.

Rampant drinking on the part of the Harijan is considered by others as well as by themselves as one of the major causes for their miserable plight. A complex network of religious beliefs and practices and a highly emotional attachment towards its observances also seem to be one of the important constraints for the poor villagers towards improving their lot. A fairly large amount is channeled out in the name of religious rituals. The superstitious villagers also spend a large amount on the *ojha*, *sadhu*, etc. for treatment of diseases.

The poor households among the Harijan castes as well as among others due to their low income seem unable to have any saving. Their hard struggle for existence does not offer any chance for future planning. Poverty itself has put them in such a deprived situation that they find themselves unable to get out of its rut. Along with lack of resources and opportunities, they sometimes seem also lacking an urge for moving up. Misery and scarcity, in which the Harijan live, seem to have become a part of their tradition.

REFERENCES

Fonseca, A.J. *Ed., Challenge of Poverty in India*. Vikas,Delhi, 1971.

Beteille, Andre, *Studies in Agrarian Social Structure*, Oxford University Press, London, 1974.

Beteille, Andre, *Inequality and Social Change*, Oxford University, Press, Delhi, 1972.

Minhas, B.S., "Rural Development for Weaker Sections : Experience and Lessons" in *Rural Development for Weaker Sections,* Bombay,1974.

Myrdal, Gunnar, *The Challenge of World Poverty*, Penguin International edition, 1969.

16

KILHORA : A VILLAGE IN WESTERN UTTAR PRADESH

SUKUMAR BANERJEE and S.P. LALA

Introduction

Apart from the fact that the term 'Weaker Section' has been used in the Article 46 of the Constitution of India to cover various groups among India population, for promoting their economic interests as also protecting them from various social injustice and exploitation, the expression does not clearly delineate the categories that are to be brought within its purview. While various groups of Indian people like the Scheduled Tribes, Scheduled Castes and Other Backward Classes have been brought within this 'inclusive category', there is a sizeable section of Indian population living in rural and urban areas who may not belong to the Scheduled Tribes and Scheduled Castes but yet may possess the attributes of weakness that may deserve attention.

The question has assumed considerable significance after the findings of Prof. Dandekar and Rath (1971) who have shown that 40 per cent of the Indian population now live below the poverty line. It is, therefore, all the more essential to known the circumstances under which these weaker people are compelled to lead a life that reflects growing inequality, want, and social deprivation as a result of their involvement in a social order prevalent throughout the country.

As the traditional caste system is basically hierarchical in nature, it is widely believed that these people have been allotted a low position for belonging to groups considered ritually impure. Being not in a position to have significant hand in means of production, they could not acquire the corresponding facilities as availed of by the dominant groups and are exploited by the latter with the sole purpose of enjoying the fruits of their labour by making them an integral part of their productive base.

Finding themselves in such a situation where every body has to encounter tremendous obstacles in improving his status, those who occupy a position either just below those of Brahmans or occupy a higher position in the middle order of the traditional hierarchy, have gained some success in improving their position by acquiring necessary economic power together with the control of various socio-political institutions. We can cite here the case presented by Bailey (1958) who has found an untouchable caste having followed ritually impure occupation of distiller, has not only improved its material conditions but has been able to raise its social position equal to the level of dominant caste (warrior) by internalising some of the patterns of their ritual life so also due to secularisation of the existing social order brought about by the extension of the economic frontier.

Working on the identical line among the rural population in the Birbhum district of West Bengal, Sinha and Bhattacharya (1969) emphasize bhadralok-chhotolok dichotomy in the existing social system of caste hierarchy. Characterised by its simplicity and flexibility, the two-fold division of the present social stratification has taken place on the basis of 'style of life' and the 'extent of control over socio-political institutions'. Having turned themselves more as an interested group in possession of means of production with corresponding 'style of life' both the bhadralok and chhotolok divisions have come to pursue different qualities of cultural life, which are not only contrary to each other but the former group is said to cultivate superior habits than the latter. Inspite of their disadvantageous position for being low castes and occupying the lower rung of the new social hierarchy, the chhotolok group has found the new existing arrangement as an adaptation of the traditional caste hierarchy to facilitate their day-to-day interactions.

Categorising them in this way, we may now pin-point the various constraints that prevent them either to cross the line of dominance or findout how much they have been culturally improvised as to feel helpless in gaining any advantage to their favour. Examining their culture of poverty which definitely corrodes their initiative to cross the line of divide, that exists between them, we may consider that these people owing to the sharing of common traits bearing with poverty, may constitute a 'sub-culture' that stands on their way to identify themselves with total cultural system. While this may be one of the reasons for their being weak, variations in this respect may indicate some groups to label them as weaker or may be classified as weakest in village setting. It is the purpose of this report to analyse the socio-economic context in certain groups that tends to persist in a state of weakness and also the trends of improvement of the condition of the chronic weak, if any, since independence on the basis of intensive field study of a village in western U.P.

Layout of the Village

Situated on the midway between the industrial town of Modinagar and the commercial town of Hapur, we came to this place, Kilhora, by local state transport service, after covering a distance of twenty-five miles from Ghaziabad, where we had to mark a temporary halt to meet the Sub-Divisional Officer for necessary official formalities in this connection. We also came to know that the village Kilhora is located within the jurisdiction of the Pilakhwa Police Station and the work of development is being looked after by B.D.O. from his head quarters at Bhojpur located on 4th mile of Modinagar-Hapur road.

The village Kilhora is located on the northern side of the main road at the ninth mile stone from Modinagar. Walking through the agricultural fields, we reached the first settlement- Bambapar, occupied exclusively by a section of the Jat. We came to know that it came into being after the formation of the original sector located at the other side of the canal. Connected with a small bridge, the road extends further northward passing through the heart of the main sector referred to as 'Mandirwala' as the houses are clustered all round the temple of the village. Thereafter the road extends further linking two of its neighbouring villages Torih and Kheri Raghunathpur in which the latter is situated at a distance of onc mile.

While the main sector is the residential area for all the castes of this village, the dwelling house of the untouchable castes comprised of the Chamar (leather workers) and Chuhra (sweepers) are found to be located on the northern fringe. Their houses being confined within the village, the settlements of the untouchable groups and other caste-groups are found adjacent to one another. The settlement of the former is referred to as the quarters 'meant for the Chura and Chamar', the common name applied to the untouchables by the villagers.

We visited a few neighbouring villages situated on both sides of the Modinagar-Hapur road for the purpose of comparison.

The pattern of settlement of the two villages (Kheri and Bhadola) situated on the northern side of the main road lying at a distance of one mile north and west of Kilhora respectively, is found to be similar as prevalent in the village Kilhora. These are multi-caste units where the dominant groups, the Jat and Gujar are in possession of better sites, leaving the northernmost fringe of the village to the lot of the untouchable castes who are subjected to the same sort of inconvenience as meted out by their brethren in Kilhora. In Hahali and Isapur lying on the southern side of the main road, we noticed a variation in the arrangement of houses. The untouchables have occupied the southern most fringe of the village and the pattern is just the reverse of what has been observed in the villages situated on the northern side of the main road.

It is thus clear that while establishing these villages, due care was taken by the dominant castes to acquire better sites. Such an arrangement does indicate a priviledged position of the dominant caste and the contention was confirmed when we visited Isaquenagar, a neighbouring village of Nahali. On enquiry of the reason for setting up the untouchable quarters on the southern side of the main road, they explained that the variation was the result of the location of the village near to the Kasba-Faridnagar instead of main road (Modinagar Hapur). Hence the selection of the site by the dominant caste in this village has been made accordingly on the western side leaving the eastern half to the lot of the untouchable. The dominant castes in this region have therefore been able to retain all the advantages as available in the existing ecological conditions leaving out the unfavourable sites to the castes like the Chamar and the Chuhra.

Social Hierarchy of the Castes in the Village Kilhora

The village Kilhora has twelve Hindu caste-groups (*jat* or *jati*) and four ethnic-groups or *kaum* among the Muslim. The local people have categorised them into three orders, the Higher, the middle, and the lower- on the basis of traditional caste-hierarchy. The following table gives the distribution of 209 households with a population of 1478.

TABLE 1 : Distribution of population by caste, household and population

	Number of Houses	Population per cent	
Highest groups			
Jat	87	633	
Gujar	31	256	
Brahman	3	23	64.6%
Tyagi	1	14	
Vaish	3	28	
Middle order			
(a) (Hindu Caste Groups)			
Saini (Mali)	15	95	
Gadaria	8	54	
Kumhar	2	10	12.1%
Dhimar	1	14	
Aheria	1	6	
(b) *Muslim ethnic groups*			
Faquir	2	23	
Julaha	11	59	
Barhai	4	25	11.3%
Lohar	4	34	
Dhuna	2	27	
Lowest order			
Chamar	19	111	12.0%
Chuhra	15	66	

Highest Group

All the important spokesmen of different caste-groups individually and collectively have assigned the Jat the top-most position in the exiting hierarchy. Beside their numerical preponderance (45%), they were the peasant-proprietors controlling rights over the land. Thus, with an appreciable income from land, they are now diverting their surplus manpower to take up different occupations like business, mechanic, teaching, industrial workers, transport workers and military service. Having additional income from other sources, they have been able to adopt a better style of life as observed partly from their material possessions. Apart from belonging to a marital race, they have not failed to acquire refinement and sophistication in the estimation of the villagers.

The Gujar though stand on same footing with the Jats on the basis of these important criteria have been assigned the second position on the consideration of their being less 'sophisticated' and for securing land from the zamindars through the system of 'mourusidari' which is less prestigious than the role of a zamindar, as played by the Jat.

The Brahman, Tyagi and Vaish who constitute four per cent of the total population cannot stand on equal footing with the Jat and Gujar, in relation to their numerical strength and economic power. Having lost their prestige for not having enough land, some of them are compelled to release their land-holding to share-croppers for want of power. Inspite of their numerical weakness than those castes in the middle order, their incorporation in this level is due to their belonging to higher varna-order of the Hindu society.

Intermediate group :

(a) *Hindu Section*:

The list of groups in the middle order includes the ritually clean castes of the Hindu as well as Muslim section. Starting with the account of the Sainis in the Hindu section the reason on the part of forefathers to shift their residence from the original village, was to free themselves from the clutches of the landholders, for these people used to inflict immense troubles on them for their inability to clear off their arrears of land revenue. As a result of their numerical strength being not small for they stand next to Gujars, they have been placed at an advantageous position for possessing a reputation of good cultivators. The original settler was able to procure a piece of land from zamindars on 'mourusidari' basis for which his descendants are still land-owners. Having got the right to sell their lands even in view of their being *Bhumidars* for depositing an amount ten-times of the prevailing rent to the Government after abolition of zamindary in 1952, all of their brethren could not avail of this facility. Many of them have secured land as share-croppers but they would have received more prestige if they happened to be actual owners of land. Even then, mere possession of it in any capacity with the facility of augmenting the income has been found in keeping with the prevailing notion of assigning a better status to such families. They have been placed not only at the top of the intermediate group but considered as occupying a place on the border line between land-owners and landless, in which Gadarias (shepherds), Kumhars (potter), Dhimers (vegetable sellers), Aherias (basket makers) are included.

Excepting the potter, members of the other three caste groups are still carrying on their traditional occupation. The fore-fathers of the present potter family was brought from the neighbouring area to serve the villagers on the basis of service relationship. Inspite of following their traditional occupation for the last few generations, they never received a steady flow of annual grains (*faslana*) from their patrons. Being aware of substantial profits that one gets from the business of driving carts in this region, the present heads of the families of the potter started their career in this way replacing it later by tonga.

(b) *Muslim Section*

All the four ethnic groups occupy parallel position in relation to the Hindu. Being members of Islamic religion they live mostly in socio-religious world of their own with least inter-actions in the socio-religious ceremonies of the Hindus. Living along with the Hindu communities for generations together, they could not free themselves from the notion of caste-hierarchy. The hierarchy may not be so conspicuous among them as among the Hindu castes but it has slowly crept in. As a result of economic independence, Faquir gained status in the Muslim society consisting of artisans such as Julaha, Barhai, Lohar and Dhuna.

Lowest Section

The untouchable Chamar and Chura, stand just on the other side of the scale, possessing all the negative attributes. Besides their low numerical strength (12%) and being landless, they occupy the lowest position in the ritual status as their occupation is very low.

The local Chamar are original inhabitants of the village. Having obtained necessary permission from the zamindar to cultivate a portion of village land on rent, no less than seventy or eighty Chamar families settled down here at some point of time by clearing the forest. Though the Chamar at that time were not getting adequate return from their primary occupation relating to the work on hides, most of them took up the occupation of farming. Having failed to pay their rent, the zamindar not only confiscated their lands but compelled them to leave their villages. They settled in villages that were free from such suppression. The condition did not improve when the Jat stepped into the scene as the zamindar. The Jat allowed them to remain in the village rent free but introduced the system of obtaining free forced labour (*begar*) from them As these agricultural labourers were less in number, without any property or land, they dared not to oppose them. As a result of their poverty, they had no other alternative but to seek loans from the cultivators (*kisan*) or from their patrons to meet their social obligations. Being illiterate and ignorant they never understood the intricacies of the accounts which showed them as perpetual debtor who were required to compensate it by paying labour. Being turned into bonded serfs (Kamere) many of the Chamar families made a fresh exodus to neighbouring villages. Thus, only nineteen families (7%) are left in this village. After abolition of zamindary they have formally got themselves freed. This to some extent has reduced their miseries but the *kisan*, or *kastkar* (Jat and Gujar) are still dominant in every walk of life not only in this village but in all the villages wherever they are found.

Chuhra

The history of this caste-group is somewhat different. Occupying the lowest position in the existing caste-hierarchy they have not been subjected to same treatment as meted out to the Chamar (who have sanskritised themselves and changed their caste name as Jatav). Distributing the patron-families among themselves, they are conducting the work in terms of service-relationship (*tahel*) by receiving payment of grains (*faslana*) after every harvest or local crops (*Rabi* and *Kharif*).

Though they continue to carry on with their traditional occupation which gives economic viability for the existence of service relationship, they are despised for the prevalence of few stereotypes. This brings about an image of their locality being dirty without any sense of hygienic conditions. They prefer to maintain their daily subsistence of one bread from each patron-house in exchange for their services. They eat left over from the leaf plates used by members of other castes. They also collect materials thrown away during disposal of the dead by others. They are considered degraded to such an extent that they are not allowed to enter the house of clean-castes or sit on the same level. Adoption of a new name Balmiki has not come to their advantage, particularly in improving their status.

Identification of Weaker Groups

In the light of above discussion, it is clear that the Jat and Gujar are dominant castes. The Brahman, Tyagi, and Vaish (traders) maintain their subsistence in a modest way and are somewhat subservient. While these castes need not pay any special reverence to the dominant castes, the other castes have to obey them and pay due respect. The other castes like the Saini and Chuhra, were in one way or the other dependent on them.

As all the criteria for assigning a status have operated to their disadvantage, the untouchables have been allocated the low position. While the extent of such relationship have lessened after independence particularly after the abolition of Zamindary, the same is still continuing in a somewhat subdued fashion in the rural sector of this region.

We can distinguish two sets of people in this village. These are dominant castes, who are not only in possession of economic resources, but also in control of socio-political institutions, whereas the other section is composed of landless groups and among whom a small section is suffering from various social disabilities that act as great barriers to cross the line of divide. The existence of such a dichotomy in the rural society of western U.P. is clearly reflected from the local use of two words namely 'reya' and 'kisan' while the latter term is reserved for the dominant, the 'reyas' are those groups who apart from numerically smallness and landlessness, are also considered backward. On the basis of this definition, castes like Saini and Chuhra are considered 'reya' and are considered weaker section in the village.

Material Culture

The existence of social stratification in the village and an estimate of the affluent condition of the dominant section can be ascertained from the size of the homestead land (average 1370 sq. ft) as also from various house types. Each house has a big compound where they have an out-house (*gher*) meant for guests. The compound is also utilised by them as shed for their livestock.

While 86 per cent of the total domiciles among the dominant section have pucca houses, they have acquired other prerequisites essential for maintaining a particular style of life. They have modernised their living not only by installing hand-pumps for their drinking water or shallow tube-well for irrigating their fields but they have also procured all types of furniture, mill-made clothes, transistors, cycles, and other modern agricultural equipments like tractors, pump-sets from nearby towns and markets with the availability of improved facilities in communication and transport.

The material condition of the artisans is slightly better than those of the untouchable groups but they have not attained the level of that of the Jat and Gujar. The other caste-groups make use of hand-pumps or wells for their drinking water. About 88 per cent of the total domiciles among the untouchable live in *kaccha* houses. The average size of such holding is one fifth of the total area occupied by one of the dominant sections. Though a few domiciles of weaker sections are fenced by mudwalls of low height the majority of them, have of course no such arrangements. The people have no hand pumps in their houses. They depend on the wells meant for respective caste groups.

Economic Dimension

The total area of the village as mentioned in the records of the Patwari is 760 acres approximately. Walking through the inhabited area of the village (30 acres), we can also form an idea about the respective wards being inhabited by the people who can be placed in various economic categories like rich, poor and very poor. Turning to the Jat and Gujar, whose respective localities do give an indication of their better economic positions, let us examine the pattern of their control of various resources through which they have been able to maintain dominance in varying proportions to their economic advantage.

TABLE 2: Primary occupation (men) (excluding non-workers)

Caste Groups	Traditional Occupation		Cultivation		Agricultural Labour	Service	Teacher	Business	Household industry	Trans. Driver	Total
			own Cult.	Share Cropper							
Highest											
1. JAT	Agriculture		135	—	—	45	3	—	—	—	183
2. GUJAR	Agriculture		59	—	1	10	2	5	—	—	77
3. BRAHMIN	Priest		5?	—	1	3	—	—	—	—	9
4. TYAGI	Agriculture		4	—	—	3	—	—	—	—	7
5. VAISH	Trader		4	—	—	1	—	2	—	—	7
Inter Mediate Groups											
6. SAINI	Gardening		6	7	3	7	—	2	—	—	25
7. GADARIA	Shepherd	8	—	—	1	5	—	—	—	—	14
8. KUMHAR	Potter	—	—	—	—	—	—	—	—	2	2
9. DHIMAR	Veg.seller	2	—	—	—	2	—	—	—	—	4
10 AHERIA	Basketmaker	2	—	—	—	—	—	—	—	—	2
11. FAQUIR	Mendicant	—	3	—	1	3	—	—	—	—	7
12. JULAHA	Weaver	9	5	—	1	—	—	—	—	1	16
13. BARHAI-LOHAR	Carpenter-cum-blacksmith	6	5	—	—	1	—	3	—	—	15
14. DHUNA	Cottoncader	1	—	2	—	2	—	—	—	1	6
Lowest											
15. CHAMAR	Leather-worker	2	1	2	16	6	—	—	1	—	28
16. CHUHRA	Sweepers	8	—	—	7	5	—	—	—	—	20
		38	227	11	31	93	5	12	2	3	422

TABLE 3: Distribution of land by caste

Castes	Landholding families	Landless families	Total
Jat	81	6	87
Gujar	26	5	31
Brahman	3	0	3
Tyagi	1	0	1
Vaish	2	1	3
Saini	6	9	15
Gadaria	0	8	8
Kumhar	0	2	2
Dhimar	0	1	1
Aheria	0	1	1
Faquir	2	0	2
Julaha	4	7	11
Barhai	0	4	4
Lohar	4	0	4
Dhuna	0	2	2
Chamar	1	18	19
Chuhra	0	15	15
Total	130	79	209
Percentage	62	38	100

Sixty-three per cent of the families in the village are land-owners. The Jat and Gujar constitute 82.3 per cent of the land-owners. This gives an indication of polarisation of economic resources. Table 4 shows the size of the land-holdings among the different groups of landowners.

TABLE 4: Distribution of landholdings by size

Size of land holdings (in acre)	Jats	Gujars	Tyagi	Vaish	Brahmin	Saini	Faquir	Lohar
Less than an acre	4	3	—	—	1	2	—	2
1 + to 5	39	18	—	1	2	4	2	2
5 + to 10	22	3	1	1	—	—	—	—
10 + to 15	11	2	—	—	—	—	—	—
15 + to 20	5	Nil	—	—	—	—	—	—
Total	81	26	1	2	3	6	2	4

On account of control of economic resources to a greater extent than what has been observed among the other caste-groups in the village and coupled with their favourable position in the socio-political institutions in the village, and Anchal Panchayat, (C.D.Block-level) the Jat and Gujar have been able to secure many facilities like canal irrigation, agricultural loans from the C.D.Block, improved variety of seeds, and fertilizers. A few among them have constructed tube-wells which require less expenditure for availing of water at low depth in this region. Not only did the land pay them a good dividend in the form of food and cash crops (sugarcane) but the increased income from land has also helped them to utilize other economic resources. Their affluent condition has enabled them to get hold of various orchards in this region which have again proved to be good source of income. Depending on their annual return from their lands, a few members of the respective dominant castes have been able to free themselves from the cultivation work for taking up the services in the military as also in the factories in the nearby Modinagar town. Income from such external sources have further improved their conditions and helped them to maintain a more decent style of life.

The detailed study of the economic life of the various castes has clearly shown a higher per capita annual income for a person belonging to dominant group. It is quit obvious that the figures in this respect for other castes are lower as they are not in receipt of various economic resources. The Saini case is an exception. Although nine out of a total of fifteen families have been shown as landless, six families among them have procured land on share-cropping basis. While these families have got the opportunity to augment their income through these means, two other landless families have availed of an alternative course by getting jobs in the industrial town of Modinagar and also by engaging themselves in business of selling milk, leaving one family to depend entirely on agricultural wage labour in the village. Having diversified their occupations in a manner of the dominant groups, the Saini have improved their economic position more than other caste-groups belonging to middle order as evident from their per-capita annual income of Rs. 747.00. For this reason, the villagers have conceded more prestige to them and the people hesitate to declare them in public as a group belonging to 'reya', for they have extorted their social relationship with the dominant groups with the result that they are no longer considered as belonging to weaker group.

While some difference relating to per-capita annual income is perceptible between various castes in the middle order and the lowest section (untouchables) as per our figure this is Rs. 585.00 and Rs. 516.00 respectively. Yet those are not of such an order as to place them above the level of poverty based on 1971-73 prices. Having no access to any tangible economic resources, there is no other alternative than to build up their meagre capital from the labour only. The following section will show that the weaker section are exploited in this field. As they have no other way out, to have a decent living they had to suffer all these inconveniences for they depend on the dominant castes who happened to be land-owners.

Social Organisation of Labour

Consolidating their economic position in this way, the landowners were in a comfortable position till legislation of the Bhumidhari Act in 1952. While they were concerned about earning more income from external sources by giving lands on share-cropping or on rent, they received a jolt when the Government declared the right of ownership to be conferred on tenant in possession of land for a continuous period of five years. As this legislation has given scope to misappropriate the official records, cases have arisen where tenants in possession of lands for two years only have preferred to claim it in their favour after bribing the revenue officials.

To save themselves from these troubles, small cultivators have decided to cultivate their own lands, compelling the big land owners to undertake their own supervision of various operations with the help of labourers on daily-wage basis. While the bulk of such labourers come from neighbouring villages like Nahali, Bhadola, and Kheri, a glance at Table 2 indicates that the only people that can be recruited from this village are the Chamar as this is the only caste left for them after giving up their traditional occupation. But the other caste-groups who still cling to their own traditional occupation, sometimes find their income being too meagre which required to be supplemented by means of such labour.

While the land owners are really prosperous because of the prevalence of two crops (Rabi and Kharif) they also realise a third crop (*jaid*) by reaping maize, pulses, and fodder in August, September, and October, released from sugarcane cultivation to be sown again after six months. Usually the labourers are engaged by big landowners either for conducting the work of hoeing the fields or for weeding, for which each of them is required to devote 10 to 12 hours of work in a day with half-an-hour recess. As the weaker sections from other villages are in no way dependent on these landowners, they agree to work only when they receive advance payment in this respect. Having developed a reputation for being laborious and efficient labourers, they are preferred to undertake these casual work and are paid @ Rs.5.00 without any meal whereas the local labourers are given a sum of Rs. 2.00 as daily wage together with a meal consisting of one *chapati* to be taken with a little *dal* (pulses) and *gur* (mollases). No doubt, the local workers resent very much a lower rate for them they have no other alternative but to accept it as not only do they stay in the same village but they are also dependent on the employers in various other ways. All those difficulties are ignored with the expectation that they are the only workers to be engaged during harvest receiving their wage in grains (maize or wheat) on the basis of their labour. It is also noticed that they try to maximise their gain as much as possible on this occasion but the prevalent rate do not allow a person to earn a quantum of grains worth more than Rs. 4.00 at the existing prices. Over and above these duties, the demand for labour is maximum when small cultivators are also in need of them for looking after the saplings of paddy or maize during kharif season. In order to protect them from the depredations of jackals and birds, they are engaged to keep a watch on these fields for day and night.

The employer instead of paying on daily wage basis, enters into a contract with the labourer, in which the latter gets a share of the yield on the basis of 3:1. In order to get this benefit, the employers entangle them in such a way as to prevent them from leaving their job till the completion of harvest. As the labourer needs rest after continuously attending to his duties for a few days and nights, he had to depute other members of his family to replace him. The nature of his duties demand round the clock attendance to the work because the seedlings are to be protected at night.

But even then, the labourers who are usually of low caste without having any control of economic resources are denied their due share at the appropriate time. Many of the Chamar have given evidences of exploitation by their respective patrons in this respect. Any protest in this respect is returned by assaulting them. Being numerically weak, neither they dare to raise any objection nor can they do anything under the circumstances owing to their dependence on them for the livelihood of their family. They have no other alternative than to depend on them in times of need, particularly for seeking loan to meet the cost of their medical treatment and social obligations.

A careful perusal of the schedules relating to indebtedness indicates about the prevalence of heavy debt among the families belonging to weaker sections, particularly, the Chamar. Each family has taken a loan of Rs. 500.00 on an average which has to be returned every month with two to three per cent interest thereon, failing which the principle would be adjusted on the expiry of a fixed period of service to be rendered by the debtor either in the house of creditor or in the fields of the employer.

Thus, in course of time they are turned into bonded-labourer. There is no way out for them except by running away from the village. In order to save themselves from tyranny many of the Chamar have run away to distant villages to be entangled there by a new patron in the same process when their positions in the original villages are taken up by another immigrants arriving there under similar conditions. While the intensity of such tortures has come down, there are persons who can vouch about the tyrannies they have undergone in different villages before coming over to this place and they can also narrate the incidents which compelled some of the Chamar to emigrate from this village to save their life and honour.

Social Dimension

The behaviour between the dominant castes and the weaker ones with reference to mode of addressing, entry in the house of others, use of wells etc., is based on superordination-subordination relationship. While the members belonging to weaker group address the dominant persons with due respect mentioning them rich and eminent person, possessing all power, the behaviour of the latter is just the contrary who use all sorts of derogatory terms that are repeated and stressed more when they meet one belonging to lower caste.

In order to give an impression about the suspension of untouchability, an old Chuhra was requested to hoist the national flag in the temple compound on the occasion of our independence day celebration. But such an outburst of enthusiasm has never been witnessed thereafter. Not only the weaker sections (untouchables) are kept at a 'safe' distance from the temple, they are not allowed to enter the houses of other castes either. Though the rigidity is maintained against the Chuhra (sweeper) on account of their work being polluting in nature, some relaxation is observed in regard to their behaviour with the Chamar. The same sort of attitude is shown in the use of wells. Introduction of modern hand-pumps has brought some change in the usual practice even then there were three sets of wells meant for exclusive use of clean castes, Chamar, and Chuhra.

A total exclusiveness is observed in the use of the cremation grounds. For a 'reya' to use a common plot of land is unthinkable nor the location of the grounds adjacent to each other can be approved of. Having been given the extreme end of the caste hierarchy, the same sort of arrangement has been made in regard to the location of their cremation ground. All castes other than the untouchables have occupied a common ground on the southern fringe of the village whereas the allotment to the untouchables has been made on the northern end of the village.

While these practices are followed for the purpose of boundary maintenance between the dominant and weaker sections, there are few more social usages that bring about further segmentation between castes included in the highest category. As an example we can cite the use of hubble-bubble (*hooka*) or the use of *kachha* and *pucca* meals. While the interaction pattern between the Jat and Gujar reflects a clear solidarity to preserve their privileged position, the same sort of behaviour is not executed with others. It varies in degree in terms of ranking in the caste hierarchy. Of late, members of the Gujar and Saini castes exchange *hooka* (hubble-bubble) contrary to the general practice in which even a Brahman is not allowed to have this privilege. Keeping in view the support that the Gujar receive from the Saini in their day-to-day life as also in socio-political affairs of the village, these two groups have now come to form a closer association. Such concession is an indirect acceptance of the Saini with a higher status in the village social hierarchy, as a result of improvements in their style of life after possessing economic resources. Having gained some success in the educational sphere in a manner of the dominant groups, the present trend shows the smooth incorporation of the Saini into dominant section after occupying a place on the border line between landowners and landless. All these are devices or mechanisms to maintain the distance between different segments so as to act as a buffer against each other, consolidating the position of the dominant section. It can be said further that the weaker section as a whole may not endanger the position of the dominant groups by the process of the coalescence. Thus, social inequality maintains the separate identities of these castes, and such a condition is favourable to the dominant section which acts as an interest group.

In conducting the studies on the families, lineages, and clan-organisations, we noticed some variations in between the dominant and weaker sections of the village. The former have a preponderance of joint families on account of the dependence of the members on the common farm. In the absence of such a facility and for maintaining their subsistence by wage labour, the respective families among the weaker sections have to function as a small consumption unit in the form of nuclear family.

Having grown up in different situations, the children imbibe the characteristic norms of the groups to which they belong. In the case of marriage, the rules of village and regional exogamy are followed by all the castes but these two sections conduct their own affairs in a slightly different manner. While the dominant section particularly the recent immigrants among the Jat are referred to by the names of their original villages like the Bhatonia and Atoria etc., they actually belong to two different clans occupying separate portions in their own locality of Bambapar. But we do not find this feature among the weaker section. Neither they are aware of their original villages nor there exists any sub-locality in their sector. The reason is that clan is not a very significant trait to be taken care even in conducting their marriage relations except to avoid the villages considered subservient to them for being 'wife-giver'. All these indicate that the notion of clan is very strong and active among the dominant section whereas it is conspicuous by its prominence among the weaker sections particularly among the Chamar. Accordingly the dominant section has been able to extend the kinship network at a considerable distance far beyond the village, whereas the weaker section has lost all contact with their distant kins, and conduct their marriage relationship within a limited circle which hardly extends beyond the area covered by the neighbouring villages that form their *biradary* (extended lineage).

Finding the area of operation being within the zone of the dominant section, the latter finds itself in an advantageous position.

Whenever any member of the weaker section used to run away to take shelter in the resident of a kin, it was not very difficult on the part of dominant section to trace him out on account of the network which has created a strong unity and solidarity among them. It is for this reason, that the dominant section was able to keep the weaker section, particularly the agricultural labourers under its control by making them an integral part of their productive organisation without any possibility of any freedom from it for a considerable period even after the abolition of Zamindary system in 1952.

It would not be out of place to mention here about the pattern of interaction between different castes during marriage ceremonies. The members of first five groups constituting the highest order in the society participate in the marriage function of each other on an equal basis but the pattern of behaviour with the other groups is based on superordinate-subordinate relationship. While members of many of the castes in the village are not invited at all, they call for the barber (Nai), Saini, Dhimar, and Churha, and allot some essential work to them. The barber are required to take up the work of inviting guests belonging to higher castes and also to carry on other errands relating to marriage functions. The Dhimar bring water for helping the cook in preparation of meals for the guests. The Churha play musical instruments in lieu of meals or cash for their services. But an improvement in the inter-caste relationship has been witnessed through extending invitations to the Saini. Having been placed in between landowners and landless, the Saini, on account of their capacity to augment their income for being share croppers, and diversifying the occupation pattern in a manner of dominant groups, have persuaded the dominant section to make some adjustment with the Saini. Following the local custom of inviting through barbers, and to convey a sense of their belonging in the groups of landowners, the Saini are again involved in some part of work relating to marriage. The action on the part of the dominant section seems to be of compromising type, so far as their behaviour towards the Saini is concerned.

Magico-religious Dimension

Observing the same set of ceremonies, the actual functions of these two groups of people (i.e. cleaner castes and untouchables) are conducted at their respective altars situated at different places in the village. Comparatively, the celebrations among the dominant section are more elaborate not only for their affluent condition but due to participation of the Brahman priest. In their performance of rituals, they bring together those features into relief that indicate the set-pattern of the Hindu life. It is for this reason that we witness more *sanskritic* elements in the functions of the higher castes. Such features are at a low key among the weaker sections.

Having lost the diacritical marks of a dominant group, the low castes included in the category of weaker section have at the first instance 'sanskritised' their respective caste names from Saini to 'Bhagirathi Saini', from Gadaria, to 'Pal-Khatriya', from Kumhar to 'Prajapat', Chamar to 'Jatav' and Churha to 'Balmiki'. As it has not made any impact in their day-to-day interactions, a few Chamar, particularly from the adjoining village of Sarawa, converted themselves to Buddhism to wipe out their social stigma of belonging to an untouchable caste. Finding no economic base as also the required prestige of esteem, they preferred to return to their old faith (Hinduism) rationalising their present lot of unsatisfactory condition through various myths prevalent among the respective communities.

Political Dimension

Except the Chamar in the village, no other group has reported the existence of traditional caste-panchayat at any point of time. While such bodies had gone defunct in not very distant past, secular duties of the village used to be carried out by the traditional officials like mukhia, lambardar, chowkidar and few important personalities of the dominant castes who were members of such an organisation for proper maintenance of peace and order in the village.

But the modern panchayat system has brought about a separation of powers at the village level. Each village maintains its entity by controlling the executive and development work through the institution of *gram-sabha*. It consists of nine members from the village, headed by a Pradhan, whereas ten or twelve neighbouring villages have been grouped to form the judicial organisation - *nyaya panchayat* making one of the villages of the region as its headquarters. Each constituent unit delegates two members from the *gaon sabha* to form the body of *naya panchayat* headed by the Sarpanch. He distributed the work by constituting a number of benches from among its members and proper records of his proceedings are maintained by the panchayat secretary, and employee of the state government.

Necessary reservation has been made to appoint the scheduled castes as members of these bodies, but the Churha seem to remain outside such membership as no Churha was taken in these bodies since its incestion in 1952. The privilege is, therefore, availed of by members of the Chamar caste.

In earlier days, members in the traditional village panchayat used to be selected on the basis of village consensus. Now the process has changed. They prefer to contest now through election. Inspite of the fact that the Jat are numerically preponderant in the village, the post of Pradhan has gone to the Gujar. It is due to the manoeuverings of the latter that their candidate came out successful. While two factions among the Jat always come to some understanding, the combined strength of this alignment is neutralised at the first instance when the Gujar joined hands with the third faction among the Jat. Being sure of the strong support that would be available from the weaker section, the Gujar instructed the respective voters in the weaker group to cast votes in favour of their candidate. Being aware of their small numerical strength, the weaker section follow all these strategies in expectation of certain advantage that may be available when aligned with one of the constituent units of the dominant section. Not only these people are sometimes referred to by the Gujar as younger brother (chotebhai) but the Saini, Julaha, Lohar and Chamar have found their respective places inside the Gram Sabha. They form a block with the two representatives of the Gujar to prevent the Jat to assert their dominance through these socio-political control institutions. Past exploitation and undue dominance on part of the Jat are some of the reasons that act as a great impediment in enlisting their support.

Even then the representatives of the weaker sections belonging to other castes and the Chamar act mostly as observers in the meetings and they do not usually open their mouth in presence of members belonging to the dominant section. It is for this reason that they cannot plead the case of their fellowmen nor can they draw any sympathy from others relating to their difficult position. The dominant sections, the Jat and Gujar are in majority in this body. This is also the picture in the next higher bodies like *nyaya panchayat* and *panchayat samity*.

Apart from their lack of economic resources, their educational level is lower than that of the dominant section. No doubt, illiteracy is present in large measure in both these groups but it is rampant among the weaker sections (80%). On a comparative level, primary education among these two groups has not shown any significant difference. In secondary education there is a considerable fall among the weaker sections (8%) as the corresponding figure for the higher caste groups is 23.6 per cent. There may be many reasons for this state of affair but it is also a fact that the students of weaker section faced many a hardships and the dominant section prevented the weaker section to avail of higher education. As such the number of matriculates among the weaker section is now only three when the number among the higher caste groups is forty-three. There are seven graduates among the dominant castes and two persons have secured post-graduate degree also, when nobody from the weaker sections could avail of such opportunity. It is for this reason that proper leadership could not grow among the weaker section to improve their present lot. They do not expect to get any sort of amelioration or betterment from any where. Having been frustrated in this way for generations together, they now depend on the present ruling party (Indian National Congress) and according to their opinion, they will deliver the goods some day as they did by abolishing the Zamindary in 1952. It is difficult to say how long they would remain in this manner but they have a conviction that things would not remain as they exist now.

Summing Up

It is clear from the above description that while the dominant section of the village has a very strong economic base, the condition is just the opposite among the weaker sections. Consistent with their strong socio-economic base, the organised life of the dominant section has provided them with a matching strength that is generated from its cultural context. This super-ordinate position demands the presence of sub-ordinate levels in the society. Finding the cultural life being not of the same order as compared with the dominant group, the life of the weaker section has assumed the nature of a sub-culture which cannot maintain its relationship in an integrated fashion with the total cultural milieu. The dominant section has used the system to its advantage and all sorts of disparities are maintained not to allow the weaker section to attain a comparable level because such an attempt on its part would debar the dominant castes from enjoying the status and position they occupy.

REFERENCES

Bailey, F.G. *Caste and Economic Frontier*. Oxford University Press. Bombay, 1958.

Dandekar, V.M. "Poverty in India : Dimensions and Trends", *Economic and Political Weekly*. January 2,1971.pp.25-48,1971.

Sinha, S. and Bhattacharya, R. "Bhadralok and Chhotolok in Rural Area of West Bengal", *Sociological Bulletin*. Vol.18. No.1, pp.50-66, 1969.

17

BHAMAIYA : A VILLAGE IN SOUTH GUJARAT

WILLIAM EKKA

There is an assumption that the rural Indian society is broadly divided into dominant and weak sections. Theoretically, the dominant section is composed of the people who have control over local economic, social, political, and communicational resources. Conversely, the people forming the weak section have the least or practically no control over these resources. Keeping the dichotomous proposition in view the present paper attempts at bringing about the factors of dominance and weakness among the people of different castes of a village in Surat district, Gujarat.

The Village and its People

The village under study is Bhamaiya. It is located in Bardoli Taluka. By road it is about 11 Km. away from Bardoli, the taluka headquarters, in the north-eastern direction.

The 776 people of the village composed of four Bhausar, five Brahman, 36 Dhedha, 470 Dubla, one Hajam, 246 Kanbi, 13 Soni and a Suthar. Of these ethnic groups the Dhedha are a Scheduled Caste, the Harijan and the Dubla are a Scheduled Tribe. In the past, the Dhedha lifted dead cattle and skinned them. The Dubla are called Halpati, meaning one who ploughs. This name has been given to them by Mahatma Gandhi and Sardar Vallavbhai Patel.

Economy

The village economy has primarily an agricultural base with a small number of landowners and a large number of landless agricultural labourers. This is indicative of a vast economic disparity between them. This is all the more so as the latter do not have any alternative employment and agriculture has become more capital-intensive and less labour intensive in this area.

Landholding

Out of 702.11 acres of arable land of the village, the villagers hold 597.52 acres collectively. In the following table number of landowning and landless households of different castes and the amount of land held by individual castes are given.

TABLE 1: Distribution of Land

Sl. No.	Castes		Total No. of house-holds	No. of land owing households	No. of landless households	Total amount of land held in acre
1.	Bhausar	No.	1	—	1	—
		%			(100.00)	
2.	Brahman	No.	1	1	—	2.28
		%		(100.00)		(0.4)
3.	Dhedha	No.	5	4	1	14.03
		%		(80.00)	(20.00)	(2.3)
4.	Dubla	No.	95	22	73	44.98
		%		(23.2)	(76.8)	(7.5)
5.	Hajam	No.	1	1	—	3.13
		%		(100.00)		(0.5)
6.	Kanbi	No.	39	36	3	533.10
		%		(92.3)	(7.7)	(89.2)
7.	Soni	No.	1	—	1	—
		%			(100.00)	
8.	Suthar	No.	1	—	1	—
		%			(100.00)	
	Total	No.	144	64	80	597.52
		%		(45.1)	(54.9)	

The Kanbi owning 89.2 per cent of the village land have more or less absolute control over economic resources of the village. Members of other castes have very small amount of land in their possession. It may be mentioned here that the land held by the Brahman belongs to the temple of the village.

Per capita landholding for the whole village is 0.88 acres. For landowning castes like the Brahman, Dhedha, Dubla, Hajam, and Kanbi it is 0.46, 0.39, 0.10, 3.13 and 2.17 respectively. The Hajam have the highest per capita land and smallest population in the village. Though the Kanbi have the second highest population, their per capita land is large. The Dubla have the smallest per capita land. They are very large in number and hold a small amount of land. The difference in per capita land between the Brahman and the Dhedha is only 0.7 acres. But the former being represented by a single household with only five members are economically far better off than the latter.

The Bhausar, Soni, and Suthar are the landless castes. The Suthar had some land which he had sold out along with his house to a Kanbi of the village on the understanding that he would live in his house as long as he is alive. Landlessness is significantly high among the Dubla. Nearly 77 per cent of their total households are landless. In contrast, 92.3 per cent of the Kanbi households have land. One of the three landless Kanbi households is in reality not a landless. The head of the household, with wife and children, lives away from his parents and has a share over his parents landholding.

Forms of Production

In general the landowners cultivate their land themselves. Only three instances of share-cropping, known as *adhbhag,* was found in the village. In all these instances the landowners are Kanbi.

In share-cropping costs of fertiliser, water, and seed are borne equally by the landowner and the cultivator. The cost of labour, however, is entirely borne by the cultivator. The produce is equally divided between them.

Because of small landholding the Dhedha and Dubla refrain from giving their land for share-cropping. It is not profitable to them either, as in share-cropping they have to share the expenditure of fertilizer, seed, and water with the cultivator. Being poor they cannot do so. In the past, they used to mortgage and lease out their land to the Kanbi. Now they seldom do so. They themselves cultivate their land as the irrigation facility, besides eliminating the chances of crop-failure, enables them to produce double crops. The rising price of foodgrains also has urged them to cultivate their land by themselves.

Landowner and Labourer

In the past, *halipratha* (the local name for a system of bonded labour under which an indebted labourer was bound to serve the landowner from whom he borrowed money until the repayment of debt) existed between landowners and landless agricultural Dubla labourers. The landowner-moneylender and the indebted labourer were known as *dhaniama* and *hali* respectively. A *dhaniama* could sell or transfer his *hali* balance of his debt (Shah, 1958). Under such circumstances the landowners were in complete control of the economic situation and the indebted labourers or *hali* having no means of paying back the loan were forced to render unconditional services to the landowners. In the absence of alternative means of subsistence, they were completely at the mercy of the landowners in respects of their working-hours and rate of wages. Such a situation excludes the possibility of the wages of bonded labourers to be above the minimum subsistence level, so that they could get rid of debt bondage.

According to Shah, *hali* system was abolished by law on 17th June, 1948. But in practice it lingered because the Dubla had no other means of subsistence. Jan Breman (1974) holds that the "commercialization of agriculture" and "depatronisation of relationship between the parties concerned" are responsible for the disappearance of *hali* system. These had, in fact, disintegrated the system. It was brought to an end by the Minimum Wages Act. It changed the nature of relationship between the landowner and the labourer. Under the present Act the labourer is free to work for anyone, and get Rs.3.00 for eight hours' of work a day. But the Act has not been desirably beneficial to the labourers. In this regard a special correspondent of *Economic and Political Weekly* has aptly observed that change in the pattern of crop has hit the labourers, and in the absence of alternative employment they are vulnerable to exploitation in spite of the fixation of rate of wages and hours of work by the government. This is true of the condition of agricultural labourers of Bhamaiya. Now the farmers grow such cash crops as sugarcane and banana which require less labour. It leaves many labourers out of employment who, having no alternative employment, are forced to sit idle many days a month. Observing the Act in all details also is a matter of doubt as describing a similar situation in Uttar Pradesh, S.M.Hale says that the landowners, having monopoly over employment opportunities, control the wages paid. To some extent it applies to the landowner of Bhamaiya. The labourers insist on the implementation of the Act. But the landowners unscrupulously employ short time migrant Choudhury and Gamit labourers in summer from neighbouring areas having no irrigation facilities at a cheaper rate and for long working hours.

Sometimes the labourers are deprived of the opportunity of earning some money, on account of being poor. From around February to June, a large number of labourers come to sugarcane producing area of Surat district from Khandesh area of Maharashtra with their bullock-carts. They harvest sugarcanes and transport it to sugar factories. For harvesting one ton of sugarcane and transporting it to sugar factory they are paid Rs.11.50. The local labourers are not employed for this work, because they do not have bullock-carts. They can not afford to have them also with their meagre income.

Now the labourers are free to work for anyone. Hence, the landowners have stopped giving loans to them, because they are not sure of getting their money back, and they cannot get the labourers to work for them for the repayment of loan. Therefore, money is contributed by each Dubla household of the village for the fulfilment of certain necessities. For instance, for marriage ceremony and for the performance of death rites of every member of the tribe, each Dubla household contributes one rupee, and fifty paise respectively.

Mainly the Dublas supply the agricultural labourers in the village. 206 or 79.54 per cent of 259 Dubla earners are primarily agricultural labourers. The only other caste supplying agricultural labourers is Dhedha. It has 16 earners, 7 of them being agricultural labourers. Thus there are 213 agricultural labourers who form 60.68 per cent of the total number of earners in the village. There are only 60 persons in the village who are primarily agriculturists. The number of agricultural labourers per agriculturist works out to be 3.55. The number of agricultural labourer per agriculturist will go up if seven Dublas and as many Dhedha agriculturists, who rarely employ labourers, are excluded, and the secondary agricultural labourers are taken into account. The village, thus, tends to have a surplus supply of agricultural labourers It is more so when even among the Kanbis all the farmers do not have equal labour employing capacity. The situation of supply of labour is more or less the same in the village around Bhamaiya. Hence, the labourers do not go outside the village to seek employment. The surplus labour supply, absence of alternative employment and low rate of wages partially account for the poverty of the agricultural labourers.

Occupational Pattern

The Bhausar are a trading caste and have a shop in the village. The head of the Brahman household is the *pujari* (priest) in the village Rama temple. He uses the field attached to the temple and supplements his income by collecting milk from the Kanbi households who are members of a milk cooperative society which sends milk to Surat. Besides seven agriculturalists and as many agricultural labourers among the Dhedha there is a diamond cutter and a service holder. The latter is a peon in a local college. Among the Dubla the number of agricultural labourers is followed by 19 diamond cutters. They have 17 contract labourers, 14 of whom are cattle graziers and three are crop-watchers of the Kanbi. Only seven Dubla are primarily agriculturists. Five Dubla have been employed as *chakar* (annual labourers) by the Kanbi. Of the remaining five Dubla earners, one is a government servant (Kotwar), one tractor driver, one daily labourer in the irrigation department, one carpenter, and one domestic servant in a temple of a nearby village. Though the Hajam is barber by occupation but the lone Hajam woman in the village is an agriculturist. Out of the 67 Kanbi earners, 45 are agriculturists and 13 are diamond cutters. Four Kanbi are in service. One of them is a professor of History heading the department of a local college. Of the remaining three, one is a school teacher, one is a mechanic in a sugar factory, and the last one works under a building and construction contractor. Two Kanbi are contract labourers, one serving as agricultural supervisor and the other as a cook of an old Kanbi couple. There is a Kanbi contractor who takes up the job of road construction. He owns a truck and supplies road metal also to other contractors. There is one Kanbi car-driver and a domestic servant. Both are under the employment of a rich Kanbi of the village.

Traditionally the Soni are the goldsmiths. But three of the five Soni earners are diamond cutters. The remaining two follow their traditional occupation in a small way. The traditional occupation of Suthar is carpentry. The lone Suthar of the village has given up his occupation because of his old age.

It may be mentioned here that except the two contract labourers, one car-driver and one domestic servant, among the Kanbi earners all the other have agriculture as their household occupation. In most cases their employment in other occupations is meant to increase the income rather than to support the subsistence of their households. Some Kanbi have lucrative secondary occupations also. Thus a Kanbi, who is also the Police Patel of the village, runs a diamond cutting factory in the village. There are ten Kanbi households who are members of a cooperative milk society and sell milk through it. The ceremony of the Kanbi is further buttressed by the money earned in foreign countries also. At present there are 17 Kanbi from Bhamaiya working in foreign countries.

Agricultural Innovations

Agricultural innovations are limited mainly to the Kanbi. Four Kanbi farmers have tractors, three hand operated blowers for blowing chaff, four pumps for spraying insecticide, and seven electric water pumps. They use large quantity of chemical fertilizer, especially for sugarcane cultivation. In 1973, ten Kanbi farmers had used chemical fertilizer worth Rs.24,800.00. The amount spent on it by the Dhedha, Dubla, Brahman, and Hajam during the same year is Rs.850.00, Rs.125.00, Rs.2000.00, and Rs.100.00 respectively. Farmers of all castes avail themselves of the irrigation facilities provided by Kaprapar dam. But where the canal water does not reach, the Kanbi irrigate the land with electrical water pumps. With the help of electricity and chemical fertilizer they cultivate even those land which would otherwise have remained fallow.

Source of Finance for Agricultural Production

There are several cooperative societies which advance loans to the farmers in cash as well as in kind (chemical fertilizer) and sell their agricultural produce. All the Kanbi farmers are members of different cooperative societies at a time. The Hajam woman has her membership in two cooperative societies. The Brahman is not a member of any cooperative society as he is not the actual owner of the land he cultivates. But he manages to get loans from these societies on the shares of the Kanbi of the village. Among the Dhedha and Dubla the number of members of cooperative societies is three and two respectively.

These cooperative societies are run by the Kanbi and small landholders of other castes are discouraged to become members. Even otherwise, the Dubla farmers do not appear to be interested in becoming members because they grow foodgrains only for domestic consumption which does not require large quantity of chemical fertilizer. They can do even without it. And as they themselves work on their fields, they do not need money to pay hired labourers. They have doubt also in their ability to pay back the loan. If they fail, they would lose their land because loan from the cooperative societies are essentially backed by borrower's land. If at all they need, they borrow money from private sources, often from the Kanbi for agricultural purpose. There are nine Dubla and one Dhedha who have borrowed money for this purpose from private money lenders. Loans from such sources are returned in kind after the harvest. According to terms, the price of the commodity is fixed at 25 per cent less than the prevailing market rate. No other interest is charged for the loan.

Earners and Dependents

In the low and high income groups, the dependency load tends to decrease and increase respectively. It has been found to be applicable to the three castes of Bhamaiya : the Dhedha, Dubla, and Kanbi.

TABLE 2: Earner-dependent ratio

Sl. No.	Castes	Population	No.of earners	No. of dependents	Ratio
1.	Bhausar	4	1	3	1 : 3.00
2.	Brahman	5	1	4	1 : 4.00
3.	Dhedha	36	16	20	1 : 1.25
4.	Dubla	470	259	211	1 : 0.81
5.	Hajam	1	1	—	1 : 0.00
6.	Kanbi	246	67	179	1 : 2.67
7.	Soni	13	5	8	1 : 1.60
8.	Suthar	1	1	—	1 : 0.00
	Total	776	351	425	1 : 1.21

All the castes taken together, the village has 351 earners and 425 dependents, the ratio being 11.21. Of the three groups mentioned above, the earners among the Dubla exceed the number of dependents. They have 259 earners and 211 dependents. More earners may earn more money. But when the income per earner is very low in a caste, most of its members have to work. This is the case with the Dubla. The Dhedha have more dependents per earner than the Dubla. This is so because seven of the 16 Dhedha earners are agriculturists and have low income. Economically they are slightly better off than the Dubla. Among the Kanbi there are 2.67 dependents per earner. They have very high income from agriculture and are able to maintain the dependents without much difficulty.

Income-expenditure

An assessment of income of different castes reveals that the Kanbis are the richest people in the village. Having almost absolute control over land the major portion of their income comes from agriculture. Irrigation facility and consequent production of sugarcane have considerably increased their agricultural income. The Dubla are the poorest people in the village. The major portion of their income comes from agricultural labour. Their income from other sources is meagre. With regard to income the Dhedha are slightly better than the Dubla. They also earn their major portion of income from agriculture. The Bhausar, Brahman, Hajam, and Soni have a moderate income with which they can live comfortably and save something from it for rainy days.

The assessment of the expenditure on different necessities made by different castes shows that the Dubla and Dhedha spend greater portion of their income on food and clothes. But in spite of this they eat food of poor quality and wear coarse clothes. They spend very small amount on religious observances, education, medicine, conveyance, and house repair. As the Dhedha earn the major portion of their income from agriculture they spend a significant amount on it. Though the Kanbi spent a very small amount of their income on food and clothes, they eat nutritious food and wear fine clothes. They spend a handsome amount of money on education, medicine, religion, conveyance, and house repair. The major portion of their income is spent on agriculture. All this indicates their affluence. On the basis of their income, expenditure, and savings the Kanbi occupy the highest position. They are followed by the Soni, Bhausar, Brahman, Hajam, Dhedha, and Dubla in order. The Dubla have a deficit budget. The Dhedha can potentially save something. But they declare that they could hardly save anything from their income. The

Suthar has been left out of the treatment as his income and expenditure are uncertain.

Indebtedness

Indebtedness has been observed among all landowning castes. But the Brahman, Hajam, and Kanbi borrow money from cooperative societies only for investment in agriculture. Hence they may not be treated as being indebted. If the loan for agricultural purposes is not treated as debt then only two Dhedha are indebted. One of them has bought food articles on credit which has accumulated into a large amount over three years. The other purchased clothes on credit.

In the past the Dubla usually borrowed money from the Kanbi. But now the Kanbi have stopped giving loan to them. That may be one of the reasons for low indebtedness among the Dubla. If the loan for agricultural purposes, even from the private sources, is excluded, then there are only nine indebted Dubla. Eight of them purchased clothes on credit. The remaining one, a diamond cutter, has borrowed a large amount of money from his employer and spent it on buying a cycle, a wrist watch, a transistor radio and a cot.

Livestock

In Bhamaiya only Kanbi, Dhedha, and Dubla have livestock and out of 461 heads of cattle they have in possession 209, 236 and 16 cattle respectively. While the Kanbi and Dhedha have only buffaloes, cows, and oxen in addition to this the Dubla have goat also. This accounts to largest number of cattle among them. They have 128 goats in total. If the goats are excluded, they would have only 106 heads of cattle. The Kanbi have a large number of buffaloes. They are 121 in all and are reared mainly for milk. The Dubla look after 34 buffaloes, 20 of whom belong to the Kanbi. The Dubla rear them for small unspecified amount of money or food grains. When they have calve, they are taken away by their owners. In the same way two cows of the Kanbi are being reared by the Dubla.

Social Dimension

At present caste system is not rigid in its operation in the village as was in the past but caste distinction and self-identity are still maintained. In certain aspects of social life economic disparity between different castes finds expression in their social intercourse.

Settlement Pattern

The settlement pattern of the village being broadly based on caste distinction serves to perpetuate social difference between high and low castes. The area occupied by the Kanbi is situated on a slightly higher level and is directly connected with a tar road running between Bardoli and Kadod by a broad and about half Km long approach road. The Bhausar, Brahman, Hajam, Soni and Suthar also live in this area. It is spacious and has wide village lanes where the houses have been constructed in rows.

The settlements of the Dubla are known as Dubalwada. There are three of them in the village. The main or original Dubalwada is situated on a lowlying area in the western side of the Kanbi area. During rainy season it turns into a sort of marshy land and the lanes become so muddy that people place large stones on them for stepping on. The situation worsened after the construction of a canal near the northern side of the village. Because of rains and canal water, the mud-floor of the Dubla huts get wet. This forced some of the Dubla to move to two different settlements situated on slightly higher level of land in the north of the village.

The settlement of the Dhedha, known as Dhedwada, is in the extreme west of the village beyond the main Dubalwada. Dhedwada and Dubalwada are connected by a narrow path. Dhedwada has large single house with many rooms that accommodate all the five Dhedha households.

All the three Dubla settlements and the Dhedwada have one well each. Every Kanbi household has its own well in the kitchen garden. Besides, there are three wells in the village for common use. Then the well of the main Dubalwada goes dry in summer and the Dubla go to fetch water from one of the three wells situated in the Kanbi area. The well of the Dhedha also dries up in summer. Then they fetch water from the well of the school of the village and not from the well of Kanbi area though it is close to their place. It seems that they still are inhibited by their past untouchability status.

A typical characteristic of this area of Surat district is that in every village where the Kanbi live there is a separate settlement of the Dubla. The reason lies in the fact that the Dubla earn their livelihood primarily by working as agricultural labourers on the fields of the Kanbi.

Social Relationship

Following Srinivas (1955), the Kanbi may not be called the dominant caste in every sense of the term. But economically they are decisively dominant. Socially, they may be called relatively dominant. Numerically and ritually they are next only to Dubla and Brahman respectively. The Kanbi also wield considerable political power in the Gram Panchayat of the village.

In the local "caste hierarchy", the Brahman occupy the highest position. They are followed by Kanbi, Soni, Bhausar, Suthar, Hajam, Dubla and Dhedha in order. The lowest position of the Dhedha in the village is associated with their past untouchable status. Though untouchability is not legally in practice, their social and ritual position has remained unchanged. The social position of the Dubla is just above that of the Dhedha. Though they are numerically dominant they do not get any benefit from it because of their poverty and low social position.

The social interaction between the Dhedha and Dubla on the one hand and the other castes of the village on the other is limited. No Dhedha or Dubla comes to the Kanbi settlement without any work. The Kanbi arc also seldom seen in the Dhedha or Dubla areas. When invited, the Dubla may attend the marriage ceremony of the Kanbi. But thc Kanbi would not reciprocate. They do not take part in the birth or death ceremonies of each other. People of different castes assemble together only once a year on the occasion of Holi festival to burn the heap of wood (*Holka*). But they do not celebrate together the festival of colour the following day.

This sort of exclusiveness is observed with regard to commensality also. Except the Dhedha and Dubla, all the remaining castes accept food and water from each other. All castes, including the Dubla, observe commensal pollution with the Dhedha. In the past, the Kanbi treated the Dhedha as untouchables, so much so that a physical touch would require a Kanbi to have a bath. They did not allow the Dhedha to step into their varandah. Now they allow them to sit on their varandah. This change may be ascribed to the efforts of Mahatma Gandhi and to the growing literacy among the people. The Dhedha have contributed to the removal of their status of untouchability by giving up defiling traditional occupations like lifting of dead cattle and skinning them.

The Kanbi accept water from the Dubla and the Dubla also

accepted water from the Kanbi in the past but those days they did not accept food from them. Now they are willing to do so if the food served to them is cooked clean. All the Kanbi, however, do not hold this egalitarian view. The old Kanbi would not accept food from the Dubla because they are non-vegetarian and they drink liquor.

Both the Dhedha and Dubla are more or less the equal in their day to day life. In other words, they have the same style of life. But the Dubla observe commensal pollution with the Dhedha because they were untouchables. That is the reason why they object the Dhedha to draw water even from the well of Kanbi area from where they themselves fetch water during summer. They themselves are socially low and as a result appear to be overconscious in maintenance of their hierarchical superiority in relation to the Dhedha.

After the abolition of the *hali* system, the relationship between the Kanbi and Dubla has undergone a significant change. Prior to it the Dubla were treated virtually as 'slaves' and were scolded and even beaten by their Kanbi-masters. They were a group of submissive people having no courage to object to the inhuman treatment met out to them by the Kanbi. Things have now changed and the Dubla have a competitive attitude towards the Kanbi which found expression in two recent violent incidents. Perhaps only on such occasions their numerical dominance proves to be a great help to them. On both occasions the Kanbi had to withdraw. The Dhedha being numerically, socially, and economically low as well as backward are still humble and submissive to the Kanbi.

Family Composition

Table 3 describes the family composition among different castes of the village.

A great majority of the Kanbi families are extended. It can be related to their better economic condition. They have a large amount of land in their possession which produce enough to feed a large number of members. Family-property particularly land, binds them together. It is just the opposite among the Dubla who have large number of nuclear families reflecting their poor economy. They do not have enough land and earnings to maintain large families. The majority of the Dhedha families are also nuclear.

TABLE 3: Family composition

Sl. No.	Caste	No. of family		Types of family				Total
				Nascent	Nuclear	Extended	Broken	
1.	Bhausar	1	No.		1			1
			%		(100.00)			(0.69)
2.	Brahman	1	No.		1			1
			%		(100.00)			(0.69)
3.	Dhedha	5	No.		3	2		5
			%		(60.00)	(40.00)		(3.47)
4.	Dubla	95	No.	8	52	31	4	95
			%	(8.42)	(54.74)	(32.63)	(4.21)	(65.97)
5.	Hajam	1	No.				1	1
			%				(100.00)	(0.69)
6.	Kanbi	39	No.	3	8	27	1	39
			%	(7.69)	(20.51)	(69.23)	(2.56)	(27.08)
7.	Soni	1	No.			1		1
			%			(100.00)		(0.69)
8.	Suthar	1	No.				1	1
			%				(100.00)	(0.69)
	Total	144	No.	11	65	61	7	144
			%	(7.46)	(45.14)	(42.36)	(4.86)	(100.00)

Ethics and Worldview of the Dhedha and Dubla

Both the Dhedha and Dubla have a hateful attitude towards crimes. But in their day-to-day life they do not live up to their ethical concepts. They, especially the Dubla, are accused of dishonesty, laziness, stealing, drinking, sex-immorality, lying, gambling and many other vices by the Kanbi. Some such vices are of course, found among them.

Both the Dhedha and Dubla have almost identical conditions of life. But they seem to be neither sympathetic nor apathetic to each other. They find no ground of cooperation. This and their indifference to each other are mainly due to their different social positions in the caste hierarchy. Not being better than the Dhedha in any way, the Dubla jealously try to guard their social ritual position and maintain it. Besides, there is a lack of initiative among them for betterment of their lot. This has resulted from the combination of complete lack of their control over the local economic resources and their low social status. They seem to have no ambition, and look resigncd. They do not known how to get out of the rut of poverty and social inferiority. In essence, all this has drivcn them to take a fatalistic view of life.

The Dubla hold the Kanbi responsible for their present plight. They call themselves *Adivasis* by which they mean original settlers. They regard the Kanbi and all other non-tribals as outsiders who,particularly the Kanbi, have usurped their land.

The Dhedha and Dubla do not think that by hard work they can improve their condition. Only a few of them have negligible amount of land. Most of them are agricultural labourers and whether they work hard or not get the fixed amount of wages. They have no capital to invest. They have nothing to work hard in order to improve their economic condition.

Education and Communication

Disparity in economy may explain high and low literacy among at least three groups : the Kanbi, Dhedha, and Dubla of Bhamaiya. Table 4 shows the distribution of literacy in the village.

TABLE 4: Literacy Composition

Sl. No.	Caste	Total Population		Literate	Illiterate
1.	Bhausar	4	No.	4	—
			%	(100.00)	
2.	Brahman	5	No.	3	2
			%	(60.00)	(40.00)
3.	Dhedha	36	No.	22	14
			%	(61.11)	(38.89)
4.	Dubla	470	No	59	411
			%	(12.55)	(87.45)
5.	Hajam	1	No	—	1
			%		(100.00)
6.	Kanbi	246	No.	197	49
			%	(80.08)	(19.92)
7.	Soni	13	No.	9	4
			%	(69.23)	(30.77)
8.	Suthar	1	No.	—	1
			%		(100.00)
	Total	776	No.	294	482
			%	(37.89)	(62.11)

According to the table the Dubla have a small number of literates. They explain it in terms of their inability to send children to school which has resulted from economic impoverishment. As the parents go to earn wages, older siblings look after the younger ones. By the time the younger children grow up the older generally cross the school age. Besides, as they live in rural areas, they do not see any job opportunities for educated persons. Further, as they cannot afford to give high education to their children they feel that they might as well not go to school at all. Those who go to school are occupied with bare necessities of life, and thus, arc not in a position to continuc studies. They have to leave the school at an early stage to earn their livelihood. School registers also support this fact showing that the number of Dubla students goes on decreasing as they go from lower to higher classes.

Among the Dhedha literacy is quite high. They are economically somewhat better off than the Dubla and hence can spare their children to go to school.

Among the Kanbi the percentage of literacy is very high, and some of them are highly educated. Having sound economic condition they spend large amount of money for education.

The literate persons among the Dubla and Dhedha are so little educated that they hardly play any role in maintaining ties with members of their community and the village community. Almost all the Dubla diamond cutters are literate. They are respected by their tribesmen not for their education but for the salary they earn through their job. As they are poor, intellectual achievement has no meaning to them.

The village has a post office, and members of all castes make use of postal facilities. Every Kanbi household has either a transistor or a radio set. They listen to songs, and local as well as notional news. The Dhedha and Dubla have one transistor each which is used for the purpose of entertainment only. Nine Kanbi households subscribed different Gujarati news papers. The Soni and Bhausar household also subscribe one news paper each.

Development Programmes

The State government has a number of provisions for the educational and economic development of the backward people. It gives legal and medical aid also to them. But the response of these people to the welfare and development measures is very poor. The Dhedha and Dubla are not at all aware of them except the housing scheme under which 20 Dubla of the village have been beneficiaries in 1973.

In the sphere of educational development of the Dubla, the efforts of the Halpati Seva Singh, a voluntary agency, are commendable. It came into existence in 1961 at Bardoli and runs various Ashram School, Balwadi(nursery school); and hostels all over Surat District. The nearest Ashram school from Bhamaiya is about 2 1/2 km. in Vaghecha village. Education, boarding, and lodging are free in the school. Besides, every student is given two sets of dress, one small carpet, one chadar (bed sheet) and one rough blanket.

Though the school is so close no Dubla student from the village is studying there. It implies their lack of interest in education. The students studying mostly belong to the Gamit,Choudhuri, Vasavi, and Dhodia tribes from far off villages.

Political Dimension

In Bhamaiya the Dubla and Dhedha are politically weak. Their political weakness may be related to their economic backwardness and social inferiority. Their numerical dominance has not helped the Dubla to get anywhere even in the present democratic political set-up.

The village never had any collective village panchayat for all its castes in its true sense. Perhaps the necessity for having such a panchayat did not arise because of great social economic differences between the three main groups : the Kanbi, Dubla, and Dhedha. Being at the lower end of the social hierarchy the Dubla and Dhedha have minimum social interaction with the Kanbi. The economic inequality between them is as great as that of the social. Socially and economically they had or have nothing in common in making the collective village panchayat effective.

Caste Panchayat

The Dubla have a caste panchayat which deals with their social issues such as divorce, dissolution of marriage, social customs, and petty disputes of the tribesmen. With the passage of time and exposure the organization has become loose. Now they do not have formally selected functionaries. An old man presides over the meetings of the panchayat. He has acquired the leadership among the Dubla of the village by virtue of his personal qualities.

The Dhedha do not have any caste panchayat in the village. When any social issue is to be dealt with they request some elderly and influential members of their own caste of neighbouring villages to assemble at a convenient place and settle it.

Regional Caste Panchayat

The Dubla and Dhedha do not have such an organization now to manage their social affairs through it. Of these two groups only the Dubla had a sort of regional tribal panchayat encompassing 12 to 15 neighbouring villages. It is defunct now. It was never concerned in any way with their economic or social uplift.

It is evident that the Dubla and Dhedha do not have recognised leaders among them. The lack of leadership may to some extent be explained in terms of their illiteracy and poverty.

Gram Panchayat

The village has a statutory Gram panchayat with its office located in Kanbi area. It has nine members of which four are Kanbi, other four are Dubla and one Dhedha. The seats of the Dubla and Dhedha are reserved. The Dubla are, however, not represented in the *gram panchayat* proportionately. They are almost double in numerical strength to the Kanbi but they have as many members as the Kanbi have. The leadership of the Gram panchayat is in the hands of the Kanbi. Its *sarpanch* and *upsarpanch* were and are from the Kanbi community. Because of their poverty, illiteracy and ignorance they can not utilise their democratic rights in their favour.

The functions of the gram panchayat are the development of the village and general welfare of the villagers. The development and welfare activities accomplished by the gram panchayat are electrification of the village roads, construction of an approach road connecting the village with a tar road, construction of wells and teachers' quarters. The gram panchayat has an electric water pump to draw water from a well for the cattle. It pays electric charges for the street light and maintains a small library for the villagers. But all these development and welfare activities have been beneficial to the Kanbi rather than the Dhedha and Dubla. The gram panchayat intends to have a telephone line in the village. If ever it materializes, it will serve the purposes of the Kanbi only.

Political Parties and Affiliation to them

In general the Kanbi are supporters of the Congress (organisation). This is due to the fact that the enactments of some of the rules by the Congress (R) government such as Minimum Wages Act, Land Ceiling Act, and imposition of levy on paddy has run counter to their interest. The association of a prominent leader of Gujarat to Congress(O) is also responsible for their support to this party.

The Dhedha and Dubla do not have political awareness as that of the Kanbi. They are never heard discussing about politics and political condition of the country. They are too busy to make their two ends meet. They, however, support the Congress(R) not because they understand its policies but because they believe that the government has done something for the amelioration of the backward people. They look upon the Halpati Seva Sangh as an organisation for their welfare. It may be mentioned here that its secretary was an M.L.A. during the ministry of Chimanbhai Patel. This also accounts for their support to the Congress (R).

The Brahman, Bhausar, Hajam, Soni and Suthar align themselves with the Kanbi in supporting the Congress (O) as they are otherwise very close.

Religious Dimension

The Kanbi and the other castes of the village except the Dubla and Dhedha worship Hindu gods and goddesses and celebrate Hindu festivals. The Dubla and Dhedha say that they follow Hindu religion. But their religious beliefs and practices do not support it.

Deities of the Dubla and Their Worship

The Dubla have two main male deities : Bharam Dev and Balia Kaka and many female deities. Some of the female deities are Manima, Veraima, Bhawanima, Akasima, Shitlama, Ingraima, Phulbaima, Khutaima, Petfodima etc. When a large number of persons suffer from any disease, Bharam dev is worshipped with the sacrifice of goats and chickens. Balia Kaka and Shitlama are associated with pox and are worshipped by other castes also. The female deities are all associated with different diseases. If anyone suffers from any disease he makes a vow to one of them to offer certain things after the recovery and if one of them is found responsible for causing illness by the *bhagat* (magico-medicine man) she is appeased with the sacrifice of goat or chicken and liquor as advised by the *bhagat*.

Belief in Evil Spirits

The Dubla believe in another set of spirits who are called *bhutmama*. A few of them are Himariya, Khajaria, Satbhutmama, and Ankulmama. These spirits are both benevolent and malevolent. If anyone displeases them they would keep him wandering in lonely and deserted place or keep him under water or sitting on tree. The victim may die if not treated by the *bhagat*.

The Dubla believe in *churail* (ghost of a pregnant women) and *dakin* (witch). Both of them are capable of causing harm and disease to the human beings. The victim can get rid of their evil effect through the intervention of the *bhagat*.

Some Dubla worship their deceased ancestors also a day before the full moon day of Chaitra (March-April) sacrificing a chicken and offering a coconut and liquor for the welfare of members of their lineages.

Festivals Celebrated by the Dublas

The main festival of the Dubla is Divasa which they elaborately celebrate on the day of *amavashya* of Asadh (June-July) month. At night marriage ceremony of a pair of male and female dolls is performed by the unmarried girls. In the morning they are kept in a new earthen pot to float away in a river. The day is spent in festivity.

Because of their contact with the Hindu (Kanbi) they celebrate some Hindu festivals such as Diwali, Holi, Dashara, Navratri, Makar Sankranti etc. But the social and ritual significance attached to these festivals are lacking in their celebration by the Dubla. In these festivals they are not hired to work as labourers and in the past when they were *halis* they were not asked to go to work. Hence, they treat these days as days of festivals. According to Shah the Dubla celebrate Hindu festivals because of their contact with the Kanbi. But he further says, the Dubla do not believe in Hindu gods even for obtaining relief from their ailments and although they go to the fairs held at religious centres of the Hindus, they do so to spend time in merry-making and sight-seeing and making purchases if they have money and not to visit temple (1958 :145).

Religious Beliefs and Practices of Dhedha

The Dhedha celebrate some such Hindu festivals as Holi, Diwali, Dashara,Navratri, Shitla Sati, Badev Ramanavami, Mahasivaratri etc. But like the Dubla, they regard them as mere festivals and do not perform any ritual associated with them. They rather worship their household deity, *kuldavi*, on these festive occasions with flowers, lighting oil lamps and burning incense. Though the Kanbi do not have any objection to their going to the village temple they never go there to worship. They have great faith in *Haribaba*,a deity worshipped for cure from snake bite. His seat is in the Dhedha locality of a township, Madhi, and his *pujari* is a Dhedha. They acknowledge the existence of deities of the Dubla. But they do not worship them except at the instance of the *bhagat* to get rid of diseases. Like the Dubla they believe in evil spirits,*churil*, and *dakin*.

Concluding Remarks

The Dubla and the Dhedha are economically weak in the village. Their economic weakness results from their small landholding or landlessness. Most of the Dubla are agricultural labourers. Taken together, there is a surplus supply of agricultural labourers in the village. These agricultural labourers do not have alternative employment. On top of it with the mechanization of agriculture they cannot save anything for the days when they do not get jobs. All this account for their poverty which is reflected on their small and poorly constructed dilapidated huts and few material possession, expenditure of major portion of their income on their poor quality food and coarse clothes, on their inability to spend much on religion, medicine, education, conveyance etc. and on the large number of earners among them.

The Dubla and Dhedha are inferior in the local caste hierarchy. The Dhedha are Harijans. They were untouchables in the past due to their defiling works of lifting dead cattle and skinning them and their non-vegetarian diet. Though the untouchability among them has considerably weakened to which they had contributed by giving up their traditional defiling works, they are still at the lowest position of the caste hierarchy. The lower social position of the Dubla also is associated with their non-vegetarian diet and their addiction to liquor. All other castes of the village observe commensal pollution with these two socially low castes on ritual grounds. However, now some young Kanbi express their willingness to accept food from the Dubla. But they refrain from doing so for hygienic reasons.

The settlement pattern of the village serves to segregate the Dhedha and Dubla from the other castes in the village. As they have separate settlements they have little social interaction. No Dubla or Dhedha is seen in the Kanbi area of the village without any work. The Kanbi also are seldom seen in the Dubla and Dhedha settlements. Except for burning the heap of wood on the occasion of Holi festival there is no other occasion when the villagers get together. The Kanbi, Dubla and Dhedha do not attend to or participate in the social function or ceremonies of each other. When invited the Dubla may attend the marriage ceremonies of the Kanbi. But the Kanbi do not reciprocate.

The Dubla and Dhedha have a large number of nuclear family. This social fact has an economic explanation. As they are poor having no economic interest to bind them together, they have family of smaller size. Their poverty-stricken condition is such that every potential earner is forced to work. Hence the large size family does not suit them. It often leaves the aged members of those castes without having any saving with no social security. Low literacy among them, especially among the Dubla also is an outcome of their poverty. Because of their poverty they fail to avail themselves of the educational facilities extended to them by the government and the Halpati Seva Sangh. The government has various schemes for the uplift of the backward people. But none of the Dubla and Dhedha of the village has been benefited from them except the housing scheme under which twenty huts have been constructed for the Dubla. They are not aware of the other government measures of welfare meant for them.

Politically the Dhedha and Dubla are weak. Their political weakness is associated with their poverty, illiteracy, and lack of leadership. Because of these reasons even the numerically dominant Dubla cannot wrest the posts of *sarpanch* and *upsarpanch* of the gram panchayat from the Kanbi and do not have any say in making decisions in the gram panchayat in spite of having the same number of representative in it as that of the Kanbi. The development and welfare activities of the *gram panchayat* also has not benefited these castes as it has done to the Kanbi. For instance, the *gram panchayat* has electrified the village. While except one Kanbi house all the other have been electrified, only one Dubla and not a single Dhedha house has been electrified. Because of their poverty they can hardly afford to electrify their houses. The water tank for the cattles of the village which is filled up with water drawn by the electrical water pump of the panchayat is situated at such a place that the cattles of the Kanbi only have an easy access to it. The gram panchayat has a small library. But the Dhedha and Dubla being illiterate do not make any use of it. Same is the case with the approach road constructed by the gram panchayat. It is mainly used by the Kanbi. The Dubla and Dhedha lack initiative and leadership to organise themselves to improve their condition. Had there been any recognized leader among the Dubla, their numerical strength would have been helpful for them. Sporadically the Dubla have organized themselves to fight with the Kanbi on certain issues. But only the retaliatory sort of instinct had spurred on them to organize themselves politically. They could be organized for constructive purposes if they had capable and competent leaders for their own economic and social uplift.

From the religious point of view the Dhedha are neither Hindu nor tribals. They form a part of the Hindu social system but being untouchables they could not share its religious beliefs and practices. That is why they make a sort of pretense of celebrating Hindu festivals but the rituals associated with them are not known to them. Temples were closed to them and they did not have much social interaction with the Hindu castes. Hence, they had no means of knowing Hinduism. Even now they care little to know about it though they are not restricted to go to the temples and to listen to religious discourses.

The Dubla have a tribal background, of religious beliefs and practices. They worship their deities for getting physical well-being or cure from diseases. As they have to group along it is important for them that they do not suffer from diseases so that they may work and earn wages for their daily subsistence. Thus their religious beliefs and practices are concerned with their life crises, their physical wellbeing rather than with spiritual attainment. That is the reason why they are ignorant of Hindu gods and goddesses and various other things associated with the Hinduism, in spite of their long association with the Kanbi. Their ignorance about Hinduism is further accounted for by the social distance lying between them and other Hindu castes of the village.

A great deal has been said about and some efforts have been made for the removal of poverty of and social inequality from among the masses of rural India. But still poverty persists and social inequality exists. An overall economic improvement of the country may help the rural economy take a turn for better. Social inequality is associated with caste system, and one may wishfully think that it will go out of existence if the caste system is done away with or disappears of its own accord.

Coming specifically to the socio-economic condition of the weaker section, the Dubla and Dhedha of Bhamaiya are in great need of economic rehabilitation. In their present circumstances they can not help themselves economically. They need extraneous economic assistance in the forms of alternative employment or means of subsistence, vocational guidance, and monetary assistance. What is immediately needed is the increased rate of wages for the agricultural labourers, for the alleviation of their economic sufferings. Besides, it has to be ensured that all the official measures for their welfare arc sincerely implemented and the monetary assistance meant for them truly reaches them. Due attention should be paid to their education also. A slightly better economic condition and education among them may reduce the social distance between them and the higher castes. It has been observed that the Chowdhari and Dhodhia, both Scheduled Tribes, are treated well by the Kanbi because their economic condition is somewhat better and the proportion of literacy is quite high among them.

REFERENCES

Srinivas, M.N "The social system of a Mysore village",in *Village India* Mc Kim Marriotted *Ed*. 1955

Shah, P.G. *The Dublas of Gujarat* Delhi, 1958.

Hale, S.M. "Development & Underdevelopment at Village Level", *The Eastern Anthropologist*. Vol.28, No.1,1974

Breman, J. "Mobilisation of Landless Labourers : Halpatis of South Gujarat", *Economic and Political Weekly*. Vol. 9, No. 12, 1974.

Special Correspondent "Gujarat : Landed and Landless in Surat District", *Economic and Political Weekly*. Vol.9, No. 25, 1974.

18

NANGAL SOOSAWATAN : A VILLAGE IN RAJASTHAN

BAGESHWAR SINGH

The main objective of this study is to delineate the factors responsible for weakness and to identify the weaker sections. The field work was carried out between February and May, and between August and September, 1973.

Selection of the Village

The village Nangal Soosawatan was selected for intensive study on the basis of the following four criteria : (1) away from the urban-industrial complex, (2) sizeable population of the weaker sections, (3) an approximate over-all population of 1,000 persons and (4) multi-ethnic composition. The village, Nangal Soosawatan, is away from urban centres,and had low impact of industrialization. The village population is dominated by the Mina, a Scheduled Tribe. The village had 1337 people belonging to nine castes.

Nangal Soosawatan is situated at a distance of about 13 kilometers from Jaipur, the capital of Rajasthan. The village is surrounded by hills of varying heights between 350 meters and 372 meters which in the north-east and south from a part of the Aravalli range. This village along with the neighbouring villages, namely, Natata, Saidad, Chimanpura, Khoh, and Shiswas, are inhabited principally by the Mina. The village has river kukas in the north and east and is linked with Jaipur-Delhi highway by an unpaved track through the river bed which remains dry for the major part of the year.

Population Composition

There are nine castes/communities living in the village. Their numerical strength is given in the table 1. The Brahman occupy the highest ritual status and are represented by three households in the village, one of which looks after one of the village temples and the other two live on income from agriculture. The Mahajan are traders-owner-cultivators. The Mina are numerically the most dominant group in the village. They are primarily owner-cultivators having most of the village lands under their possession. They form the largest Scheduled Tribe of Rajasthan and are mostly concentrated in its eastern reign of which the Jaipur district forms a part. The Mali are also cultivators who grow and sell vegetables. The Jaga or Brahm Bhatt are traditionally genealogists. At present they are mostly engaged in various government service. Only a few old male members still carry on their traditional occupation. The Khati are carpenters who still serve farmers through *jajmani* relationship. The Jogi represented by a single household are religious mendicants. The Rana or Dhoi, the traditional drum beaters, are represented by two households. They are landless contingent labourers and to a limited extent practise cattle herding. The Balai occupy the lowest position in the ritual hierarchy of the village. Previously they used to deal in skin and hide, make shoes for the villagers, and lift the dead cattle. At present they are landless labourers.

TABLE 1: Population composition[1] (Feb-March'73)

Sl. No.	Community (in alphabetical order)	Number of household	Number of persons	Percentage of total population
1.	Balai	14	85	6.4
2.	Brahman	3	26	1.9
3.	Jaga	12	69	5.2
4.	Jogi	1	7	0.5
5.	Khati	12	85	6.4
6.	Mahajan	1	8	0.6
7.	Mali	17	102	7.6
8.	Mina	147	944	70.6
9.	Rana	2	11	0.8
	Total Nine	209	1337	100.0

The Mina constitute 70.6 per cent of the total village population. They are followed according to the order of numerical strength, by the Mali (7.6%), Balai (6.4%), Khati (6.4%), Jaga (5.2%), and Brahman (1.9%). The remaining three communities viz., the Rana, Mahajan, and Jogi constitute less than one per cent of the village population. The Rana are represented by two households, and the Mahajan and Jogi are represented by one household each.

Communication

Because of its close proximity to the state capital, tahsil headquarters, and an important urban centre, the over-all communication system of the village is relatively good. But visit to the neighbouring settlements makes a difficult trekking, particularly during bad weather. Villagers usually walk down distance when they are to visit nearby villages. Besides, they also travel on camel's back, or by bullock-cart. There is a branch post-office in the village. There are some transistor radio sets in the village, and nobody subscribes any newspaper.

Institutions

The village has a school, panchayat samiti, cooperative society, post-office, and grocer's shop.

The primary school is upto the fifth standard. It is run by the state government through the panchayat samiti. The school has a two-roomed building. It is located at one end of the village. Both boys and girls, altogether 73 students, attend the school. The school has two teachers. It has ample open space for game activities.

The Gram Panchayat, which includes six other neighbouring villages has its headquarters here.

The village has a cooperative credit-cum-multipurpose society which owns a two-roomed building and has hired another two-roomed building. They are used as seed godown and office. The Society had 113 members on 13th April 1973. There were 137 wells in the village out of which 31 had electrically operated irrigation pumps.

The village has a branch post office housed in an one-roomed building. Its activities are managed by a single person. It has only one delivery service per day. It comes under the sub-post and telegraph office of Amer.

The village has a fare price ration shop managed by the Mahajan family. It also serves as a provision (grocery) shop. The Rajasthan State Electricity Board, Forest Department, and Rajasthan Public Works Department operate within the vicinity and have influence on the village by way of providing electricity to the irrigation pumps, allocating grazing lands for the village cattle, and providing employment opportunity to the villagers as road labourers.

The grocer family of the village manages another business establishment at Amer which the villagers are constantly in touch with. Through that the villagers gain knowledge of grain trade, government policies regarding redistribution of food grains, and of other essential commodities. Villagers are also exposed through the shop to many commodities manufactured and processed in different parts of the country.

Economic Dimension

Nangal Soosawatan is one of the twelve villages given to the Mina by the then ruling Rajput king of Jaipur under the *jagir* system. The land was owned and cultivated by the Mina. Other communities living in these villages depended upon them, to whom they provided their specialized services like priesthood, carpentry, smithery of iron and agricultural labour. The Mina in their turn used to serve the royal palaces as guards. In a few cases, the land owing Mina gave their land to other Mina, or on occasions to members of other communities for cultivation. This did not provide cultivators with the occupants entitlement to the land as the title, by virtue of being *jagir*, remained with the Mina landlords. No major change has taken place in respect of distribution of land in the village since then.

Table 2 gives the distribution of village-land per capita by community.

The Mina possess nearly 90 per cent of the village land. The other five landowning communities together have 10 per cent of the land. The per capita land possession is highest among the Mahajan (1.922 acres) while the Mina own less than half of this amount.

People cultivate their own land, employing the agricultural labourers only occasionally, particularly during harvesting time. Table 3 gives occupational break-up of the village population, indicating radio of dependence of males and females upon various economic pursuits.

TABLE 2: Distribution of land

Sl. No.	Land owning communities	Population	Land owned (acres)	Percentage land	Per capita
1.	Balai	85	19.966	2.62	0.235
2.	Brahman	26	7.937	1.04	0.305
3.	Khati	85	8.497	1.15	0.708
4.	Mahajan	8	15.375	2.02	1.922
5.	Mali	102	29.988	3.94	0.294
6.	Mina	944	679.075	89.24	0.719

TABLE 3: Occupational pattern

Sl. No.	Community	Population	Earner	Cultivation			Agricultural labour	Other labour	Crafts (male only)	Other
				Total	M	F				
1.	Balai	85	44	3	1	2	—	31	5	5
2.	Brahman	26	11	8	2	6	—	—	1	2
3.	Jaga	69	25	—	—	—	7	2	—	16
4.	Jogi	7	1	—	—	—	—	—	—	1
5.	Khati	85	32	11	1	10	1	—	20	—
6.	Mahajan	8	3	1	1	—	—	—	—	2
7.	Mali	102	38	25	11	14	—	10	1	2
8.	Mina	944	553	444	178	266	3	48	4	54
9.	Rana	11	5	—	—	—	—	2	—	3
	Total	1337	712	492	194	298	11	93	31	85
	Percentages				27.07	41.93	1.54	13.18	4.5	11.98

The table makes two things clear. One, the majority of the workers are primarily engaged in agricultural production (about 70%). Two, involvement of women in agricultural work is much higher than that of men (41.33% female to 27.07% male). Women workers belong to all communities of the village. Men usually go elsewhere to seek jobs for supplementing family income from land. Womenfolk naturally share the major burden of agricultural work. There is no industry in the village, neither is there any other avenue for employment except house construction and agricultural labour. As a result, villagers' primary dependence in general is on agriculture. Some are engaged in non-agricultural jobs outside the village.

There are no absentee landlords, tenant-cultivators, share-croppers or permanent farm-servants in the village. Landowners' participation in the production system is direct. Under some exceptional circumstances share-croppers or permanent farm-servants are required to be engaged. For example, a widow with minor children usually has to get her fields cultivated through such arrangements. On account of small landholdings with poor yield, an owner-cultivator occasionally seeks employment to supplement his income from agriculture. The landless labourers who depend mainly upon the owner-cultivators for seasonal employment as agricultural labourers also seek employment elsewhere during the lean season when their services at agricultural farms are not required.

Category of Farmers

Those who own land may be grouped into different categories on the basis of their size of land-holdings per family, namely, big farmers, who own more than 10 acres of land, medium farmers, who own between 5 to 10 acres of land and the small farmers who own less then 5 acres of land. Table 4 shows the distribution of different categories of farmers by community.

Nearly 11 per cent of the Mina families belong to the farmers category. Other 13 per cent of them fall in the medium category of farmers and the remaining 76 per cent belong to the small farmer's category. All the 3 Mahajan and one of the Mali families are in the medium category. The remaining families of the village are either landless or small farmers. The analysis shows that the farmers of the village are unevenly divided into these three categories. More numerous are the small farmers followed by medium farmers, the big farmers being the least.

TABLE 4: Category of farmers

Sl. No.	Community	Number of landowners	Category (with percentage)		
			Big farmers	Medium farmers	Small farmers
1.	Balai	12	—	—	12(100.0)
2.	Brahmin	2	—	—	2(100.0)
3.	Khati	9	—	—	9(100.0)
4.	Mahajan	3	—	3(100.0)	—
5.	Mali	19	—	1(5.3)	18(94.7)
6.	Mina	187	21(11.2)	24(12.8)	142(75.9)

The landless people are in extremely poor condition and depend upon opportunities of employment for their survival. The Balai are one such people in the village. They go for contingent labour. A few among them know the art of masonry and work in the site of house construction. The daily wages vary from Rs. 8.00 for a mason are, for their helpers the rate is Rs. 1.50 to Rs. 3.50 per day depending upon the age and sex of the person employed.

Other Occupation

Non-agricultural occupations that the various communities of the village practise are genealogy making (the Jaga), government service (the Mina and the Jaga), small trade (the Mahajan and the Mina), carpentry (the Khati) and masonry including the job of helper (the Mina and the Balai). These apart, people also work as contingent labourers from time to time. One Brahman family exclusively depends upon priesthood and one Rana family depends on cattle herding. The people's employment outside the village has not led to any mass migration either seasonal or otherwise. The village economy remains largely dependent upon the agriculture, inspite of some outside employment.

Earner-dependent Ratio

Earner-dependent ratio among different communities which are clustered according to their ritual status is given in table 5.

TABLE 5: Earner-dependent ratio

Dependent earner		Clusters of ritual status	
Brahman	Mahajan	Mina	High
1.36	1.67	0.75	
Jaga	Khati	Mali	Medium
1.68	2.27	1.68	
Balai	Jogi	Rana	Low
1.12	2.50	2.67	

As it can be seen from the table, the Mina with high ritual status have the minimum number of dependents when compared with other communities, and in this respect they are closest to the Balai of the lowest ritual status. This suggests that the ritual status may not have any direct relation with the earner-dependent ratio. The Mina are the only community to have more earners than the dependents. The Balai are, though close to the Mina in this regard, have more dependents than earners. The agricultural people show a tendency of even distribution of male-female earner ratio, differing from those engaged in non-agricultural pursuits. Among the Jaga there are 17 male earners against 8 female earners, showing maximum dependence of the females on their male counter-part. Among the Mina there are 277 male earners to 276 females earners, showing minimum dependence of the females on the males. The Jaga genealogy makers or engaged in some government service. Both these occupations provide minimum employment opportunity to the females. The Mina being largely agriculturists, their females have enough scope to participate in the economic pursuits.

As it has been said earlier, there is no industry in the village. Cattle herding is done by only one Rana family and animal breeding is almost negligible. Cow and buffalo are domesticated primarily for the milk supply meant for household consumption. Nevertheless, the male calves of the cow and buffalo when grow old may be used as draft animals besides the bullocks which are extensively used tilling the land. Community wise per capita income is given in table 6.

TABLE 6: Per capita income (annual)

Sl. No.	Community	Income Rs.
1.	Balai	398.40
2.	Brahman	699.80
3.	Jaga	282.61
4.	Jogi	249.28
5.	Khati	373.04
6.	Mahajan	1275.00
7.	Mali	324.82
8.	Mina	453.28
9.	Nai	500.00
10.	Rana	116.67

The Mahajan have the highest annual per capita income and the Rana occupy the lowest position in this respect. The average income pattern generally corresponds with the ritual position of a community, one exception in this respect being the Mahajan who have the highest average income with relatively low ritual position.

Expenditure pattern in relation to major items like food, clothing and housing by community is given in table 7.

We find that the Brahman spend minimum (proportionately) on food as compared to other communities in the village. They spend almost one fourth of their total expenditure on food when compared to the Nai who spend more than four-fifths in this respect, the Balai spend a little less than three-fourth of their total expenditure. Other communities show little variation in this regard as their proportion of expenditure on food does not vary much compared to the average of such expenditure of all communities which is 53.26 per cent of the total expenditure.

TABLE 7: Expenditure on major items (annual, per family)

Sl. No.	Community	Expenditure item (Percentage of total expenditure)		
		Food	Clothing	Housing
1.	Balai	73.70	10.31	0.72
2.	Brahman	24.21	11.53	0.69
3.	Jaga	54.42	6.82	0.38
4.	Jogi	41.72	17.19	20.67[2]
5.	Khati	57.74	8.93	0.97
6.	Mahajan	52.04	5.03	1.21
7.	Mali	62.84	10.30	0.60
8.	Mina	50.51	9.57	2.67
9.	Nai	84.18	11.18	1.01
10.	Rana	50.91	4.86	2.45
All communities		53.26	9.26	2.20

As regards the expenditure on other two items, namely clothing and housing, the communities show low variance among themselves, housing being of lower variance than clothing. The Jogi make an exception in this regard. Food is the most important item of expenditure among all communities. Exceptions are the Brahman who spend maximum on production and investment items (vide table 8). Economically poorer communities spend comparatively greater portion of their total expenditure on food.

Poor communities like the Jaga, the Rana and the Nai have no capital expenditure, Balai too have little to invest. The capital expenditure is found to have increased proportionately with the social position of the communities. The Brahman invest maximum followed by the Mahajan, who in turn are followed by the Jogi and the Mina.

TABLE 8: Expenditure on investment (annual, per family)

Sl. No.	Community	Expenditure items (percentage of total expenditure)	
		Cultivation, industry, business	Education
1.	Balai	3.67	0.17
2.	Brahman	48.03	7.68
3.	Jaga	Nil	2.36
4.	Jogi	17.19	0.98
5.	Khati	8.60	1.01
6.	Mahajan	30.19	3.02
7.	Mali	12.81	2.98
8.	Mina	16.28	0.68
9.	Nai	Nil	Nil
10.	Rana	Nil	Nil

Indebtedness

Out of 50 households selected for detailed study of their economic condition, 41 households turned out to be under debt. The amount of debt varies considerably from Rs. 100 to Rs. 6,000. The following table gives the information about the amount of total debt and average debt by community.

The Brahman took loan for the purpose of investment in some industry, while the Mahajan were under debt for meeting expenses on agriculture. The Mina spent 25 per cent of their loan for the purpose of some industry and 11.64 per cent for agricultural purposes. The Mali took loan and spent 25 per cent on house construction, 16.67 per cent agriculture and rest 58.34 per cent on other necessities. The Jaga spent 30 per cent of their loan on house construction, while the Mina spent 8.64 per cent of their loan for that purpose. The major items of expenditure of all the communities comprise the important incidental liabilities like marriages, funeral feasts or other such things. The Rana and the Nai took loan only to fulfil the demand of such obligations while the majority of the Balai (75%), the Jaga (60%) and the Jogi (55.56%) spent the major portion of their loans on such liabilities. The Khati (30.56%) and the Mina (19.22%) on the other hand, spent quite a good amount of their loan or liabilities. The basic necessities of life also compel the people to take loans, the Khati (69.45%) and the Mali (58.34%) spent a significant amount out of their loan on these necessities. The Jogi and the Mina also spent on necessities 44.44 per cent and 35.12 per cent of their loan respectively. The Jaga with regular income from service spent only 10 per cent of their borrowed money on necessities while the landless labour group, the Balai, spent 25 per cent on this score while rest was spent on account of liabilities.

TABLE 9: Indebtedness

Sl. No.	Community	Total number of households	Sample size	Debtors	Percentage	Total amount of debt in rupees	Average per family
1.	Balai	14	3	2	66.67	400	200
2.	Brahman	3	1	1	100.00	6500	6500
3.	Jaga	12	3	3	100.00	5000	1667(App.
4.	Jogi	1	1	1	100.00	100	100
5.	Khati	14	3	3	100.00	3600	1200
6.	Mahajan	1	1	1	100.00	3000	3000
7.	Mali	17	6	4	66.67	6000	1500
8.	Mina	147	30	26	86.67	92600	3561(App.
9.	Nai	1	1	1	100.00	4000	4000
10.	Rana	2	1	1	100.00	2000	2000

It is evident from the above description that the economically better off communities take loans to invest on agriculture and industry while the poor communities mostly take loans as to fulfil the liabilities and for the basic necessities like food. The amount of loan taken though gives some general ideas about the economic condition of individual communities, but it makes it more clear in indicating the specific reasons for which the loans are taken. The itemwise distribution of the loan hints at the general economic condition of the communities and at the same time it also shows how the same is linked up with the communities' economic condition, independent of the factors involving indebtedness.

Economic Classes and Class Formation

On the basis of size of landed property, differential income and expenditure pattern, along with the reasons for incurring the debt, the communities may roughly be placed in different categories or classes. But in categorising the people on the basis of all these three criteria, the communities may show an amount of variance within and among themselves and exceptionally show a tendency to be in a different set of groupings if done on the basis of a single criterion. By taking all three criteria together, three groupings emerge. The high economic class is formed by the Brahman, Mahajan and Mina, the middle economic class is formed by the Jaga, Khati and Mali, and the low economic class is formed by the rest of three communities viz., the Jogi, Nai, Rana and Balai. The fact, however, remains that these economic classes tend to closely correspond to the socio-ritual classes as well, namely high, middle and low castes. But, while the ritual ranking is rigid on placing an individual community in some specific position, the economic classes (or groupings) do not operate in a rigid manner.

Our data, further, confirm that these economic groupings do command authority in terms of caste affiliations in the context of other villages in the neighbourhood as well. The Mahajans carry on with the business, trading and money lending, the Brahman carry on with their priestly services to other castes, besides which they have also taken up agriculture and low-paid government employment. The Jaga pay attention to educations and try to get into service, the Khati do the carpentry and agriculture and the Mali remain agriculturists. The economically poor communities, the Rana, Jogi and Balai continue to lead the life with poverty in these villages. The Mina have not shown any tendency of class formation as some families among them belong to weaker section. Inter-dining, inter-marriage and free interaction among economically differentiated sections of the Mina is indication of their greater social cohesion. The marriages were reported to have taken place without any consideration of the economic condition of the contracting families. The kin relations are maintained without any consideration of the economic condition of the individuals concerned. Inter-dining is prevalent irrespective of the clan affiliation and the economic condition. During festivals, the Mina do not make any distinction among themselves.

Social Dimension

The nine communities living in the village are all endogamous and belong to the Hindu faith. Their respective ritual positions and traditional occupation are given in table 10.

TABLE 10: Communities in the village

Sl.No.	Community (in order of ritual ranking)	Traditional occupation
1.	Brahman	Priesthood
2.	Mahajan	Village record keeping and trade
3.	Mina	Agriculture
4.	Jaga	Genealogy making
5.	Mali	Agriculture
6.	Khati	Carpentry
7.	Jogi	Religio-medicinemanship
8.	Rana	Drum beating
9.	Balai	Lifting dead cattle and shoe making.

At present some castes have taken up different jobs other than their traditional occupation. The Brahman do agriculture and go for government service; the Mahajan have taken up agriculture; the Mina and the Mali go for seasonal employment besides doing agriculture; the Khati have taken to farming; the Jaga go for government service, and other communities also go for employment as labourers. The Balai have totally given up their traditional occupation and are at present landless agricultural and contingent labourers. Among the villagers only the Balai have severed all connections with their traditional occupation. The Mina, though a scheduled tribe on formal ground, have been articulated within the regional Hindu caste hierarchy.

Ritual Hierarchy

The observance of differences among the communities are not always equally firm or rigid. The first three communities viz., Brahman, Mahajan, and Mina are in each case distinctly separate from one another and they differentiate themselves from others in the tribal order of stratification or caste hierarchy of the village, while the next three communities, namely the Jaga, Mali and Khati do not have very rigid lines of differentiation among themselves. The dividing lines between the Balai and other unclean communities are again very rigid.

On this basis, we may categorise the communities under three clusters, namely,

(1) The high castes including the Brahman, Mahajan and Mina.
(2) Other clean castes including the Jaga, Mali and Khati, and,
(3) Unclean castes including the Jogi, Rana and Balai.

The Balai are the only people in the village who are considered untouchables and are not allowed to enter into the house of other communities, nor permitted to touch their utensils. They are not permitted to draw water from the wells meant for other communities.

Physical Layout

The physical layout of the village does not necessarily segregate the people according to their ascribed ritual ranking. Nevertheless, the communitywise houses are clustered together more as a matter of convenience rather than any compulsion.

Differences are, however, observed in social interaction among the communities. In the village gathering, the different communities are to occupy seats as per their ritual position. Entry to a temple is restricted only to the high and clean caste people. Unclean castes are not allowed to enter the temple. During any village festival inter-caste differences appear more prominent wherein the High castes and clean castes get a priority over the unclean castes in all respects.

The unclean castes are looked down upon by the higher castes and their differences are so apparent that even the children segregate themselves on the basis of their ritual statuses in games and other activities, and refer to the children of unclean communities by their community names rather than by their individual names.

Family Composition

Table 11 shows the composition and size of families by community in the village.

TABLE 11: Family composition

Sl. No.	Community	Number of house-hold	Population	Average family size	Family composition 3			
					Nascent	Nuclear	Extended	Broken
1.	Balai	14	85	6.1	—	21.43^{3}	74.43^{10}	7.14^{1}
2.	Brahman	3	26	8.7	—	33.33^{1}	66.67^{2}	—
3.	Jaga	12	69	5.8	—	41.67^{5}	50.00^{6}	8.33^{1}
4.	Jogi	1	7	7.0	—	—	100.00^{1}	—
5.	Khati	12	85	7.1	—	33.33^{4}	56.34^{7}	8.33^{1}
6.	Mahajan	1	8	8.0	—	—	100.00^{1}	—
7.	Mali	17	102	6.0	5.88^{1}	41.18^{7}	52.94^{9}	—
8.	Mina	147	944	6.4	6.80^{10}	16.73^{54}	48.38^{72}	7.48^{11}
9.	Rana	2	11	5.5	—	50.00^{1}	—50.00^{1}	
Total		209	1337	6.4	5.26^{11}	38.89^{75}	$51.67^{1\text{-}8}$	7.18^{15}

As it appears from the table the variation among the communities is low as regards the average family size which is 6.4 for the village, ranging from 5.5 among the Rana to 8.7 among the Brahman. In family composition, however, they differ from one another considerably. Family types of the village have been classified into four categories. Nascent, consisting of a couple in child bearing age but without any issue. Nuclear, having a couple with their unmarried children. Extended, a nuclear family with other, additional, members. Broken, in which either or both spouses are dead. A broken family may occur due to separation, divorce or desertion also. Nuclear and extended families together show a preponderance over the remaining two family types. The Mali have 41.18 per cent nuclear families and 52.94 per cent extended families and 5.88 per cent nascent families and the respective percentage of the Mina are 36.73, 48.38 and 6.80. In addition they have 7.48 per cent broken families.

Access to the Facilities

No differences on caste lines are observed in the village in respect of availability of general facilities like accommodation, latrine, bath-room etc. Nevertheless, a marked difference can be observed in terms of average living space occupied by different communities. Intra-caste differences in this respect are also observed on account of economic capabilities of the individuals, and the Mina show the maximum variation in this respect. Analysing by caste, the Brahman are found to have enough living space in their possession and the Mahajan have one of the best houses in the village. Some Mina also live in very big house. In comparison, Rana houses are very small with single rooms.

The size and accommodation differ from house to house rather than from community to community. It is generally observed that the economically weak and ritually low people in the village have less living space.

Concepts of Clean and Unclean

The Mina are considered ritually clean. They are numerically and economically dominant. They were traditional landowning aristocrats of the region, called Jagirdars. The agriculturalists like the Mali, the genealogy makers like the Jaga and the artisan castes like the Khati are in the middle tier with whom high castes interact freely and maintain minimum distance. They are treated as clean castes and water from their hands is accepted by the high castes. The last three communities the Jogi, Rana, and Balai are considered unclean and the high and clean castes maintain a distance from them and do not accept water from their hands. The Balai, because of their traditional profession of lifting of the dead animals and dealing in skin and hide, are given the lowest position in the caste hierarchy of the village and are considered polluted. The members of the high and clean caste groups, even the Jogi and the Rana of the unclean group, maintain a distance from the Balai.

The Brahman, on the other hand are always given a respectable position irrespective of their economic status. On the basis of cleanliness and ritual ranking the communities may be placed into the following order.

Brahman	Highest
Mahajan, Mina	High
Jaga, Mali, Khati	Middle
Jogi, Rana	Low
Balai	Lowest

In the day-to-day interactions of villagers, their respective caste affiliation appears to be very important. Individuals are ordinarily referred to by their caste names. An outsider while on visit to the village is also identified by his caste affiliation. Children while quarreling, accuse and abuse a child of lower ritual rank by referring to his caste name. In village gathering, people cluster themselves according to their caste identity. During village festivities social interactions among its members are also regulated by caste affiliation. On the occasion of Holi the high caste people are privileged to get a priority to offer their prayers at the holy fire-place before the people of lower castes get their turn. Thus, in their day-to-day behaviour the caste affiliation plays a very significant role and those who belong to the higher castes continue to enjoy the time honoured privileged position.

Literacy and Education

In respect of educational performance the village may be called a backward one, though there is a primary school within the village and there are two other primary schools and a middle school in the vicinity, and a high school not very far off. The following table shows the distribution of literates by sex and community.

The literacy percentage by community differs from 11.76 to 62.50, the Mahajan being on the top and the Balai being at the bottom. The Brahman have 53.85 per cent literates. The average literacy percentage of the village is 18.02 and four castes are much above the average in literacy performance, one (the Rana) is very close to the village average and other four are considerably below the village average.

TABLE 12: Literacy in the village

Sl. No.	Community	Total Population	Literates			Percentage
			Male	Female	Total	
1.	Balai	85	10	–	10	11.76
2.	Brahmin	26	12	2	14	53.85
3.	Jaga	69	30	3	33	47.82
4.	Jogi	7	1	–	1	14.28
5.	Khati	85	29	1	30	35.30
6.	Mahajan	8	3	2	5	62.60
7.	Mali	102	18	–	10	17.65
8.	Mina	944	127	1	128	13.57
9.	Rana	11	2	–	2	18.18
Total		1337	232	9	241	18.02
Percentage			17.35	0.67		

The four castes having better educational records than the village average belong to the high or middle caste clusters. The only community having high ritual, social and economic position to display poor literacy performance is the Mina. The Jaga show a high literacy percentage (47.82) and many of them are in government service and otherwise better off though being landless.

If we analyse the figures further we find that there are 106 persons who have completed the education and there are 127 in schools. The school going children (i.e., education continued) also show a disparity among the communities : while 3.53 per cent children are in school from the Balai community 23.09 and 25 per cent children from the Brahman and the Mahajan community respectively are in the school. The Mina are educationally poor because their school going children form 8.58 per cent among children attending school. Education upto the level of graduation could be attained only by one Mina and one Jaga. The female literacy is extremely poor (less than 1%) among most of the communities, except the Brahman, Jaga and Mahajan castes.

Social Mobility

The Jaga wish to identify themselves as Brahm Bhatt and claim the status of the Brahman or placement just below it. They are genealogy makers which they claim to be the profession of a priestly class. The villagers do not admit their high position, on the contrary ridicule their claim because of their non-vegetarian habit, which the Brahman and the Mahajan do not have. The Mina and Mali, who patronise the Jaga take objection to their claim of higher socio-ritual position.

The Balai were traditionally engaged in lifting the dead animals in the village and used to make shoes for which they were looked down upon by other communities. They have now given up the occupation completely in order to elevate their position, but they still remain in the same position in ritual hierarchy where they were in the past. They have no resources, either economic, being largely landless, or communicational as they are mostly illiterates and consequently they are no better than what they had been in the past. Rather, they have been further pushed backward economically. They once provided essential service to the village folk and were dependent upon other communities. The mutual inter-dependence and economic ties with the agriculturists which existed in the past have broken.

Political Dimension

Informal Village Panchayat

The Mina, having 70 per cent of total village population and the background of being *jagirdars*, have the absolute control over the power structure. The village was divided in four divisions and there were four Patels (the Mina) who looked after the interest of the individuals in their respective divisions. Even now the Mina decide about any major issue for the village as a whole, whether it concerns the village as such or it is an inter-village matter.

Different Caste Panchayat

Various castes of the village have their respective panchayat at the inter-village and the intra-village level. These panchayats deal with the cases in respect of specific social norms pertaining to the breach of any social rule. These panchayats hold meetings at the time of marriage and funeral feasts when there is a gathering of caste members; hence there are no defined places for the meetings nor there is any periodicity. The cases of elopement and adultery are settled by these Panchayats at the place of the concerned parties (generally the aggrieved party) and person-to-person intimation is sent to the different villages where the caste people inhabit.

The Mina caste panchayats effectively work at the regional level, inter-village level and at village level because of their numerical preponderance. With the introduction of statutory panchayats, political activities have increased at the village level.

Statutory Gram Panchayat

The statutory Gram Panchayat is named after this village, though it includes six more nearby villages in its jurisdiction. All the offices in the Panchayat committee are held by the Mina excepting one (co-opted member) which is held by an individual of the Balai community. The statutory gram panchayat helps implement government programmes.

Conflict and Cooperation

The multiple factors that lend the Mina a dominant and comfortable position in the power structure, have some impact on other communities who seek assistance and cooperation from the Mina in respect of various political matters.

Magico-Religious Dimension

As all castes of the village belong to the Hindu faith, they all apparently share the festivals and religious functions together. The Mina, though a Scheduled Tribe, have been assimilated and integrated into the Hindu fold without leaving any trace of their tribal identity, particularly in case of religion. The weaker sections which are economically poor and ritually low do not participate in the religious functions and the ritual calendar of the clean and high castes. As a result, they remain simply on-lookers in many festivals of the clean castes. The latter have many household observances as well in which also the unclean castes have no roles to play. They however, receive some food-stuff on such special occasions from the high and clean castes. The villagefolk in general are religious minded and God fearing and that gets reflected in their day-to-day interactions. They believe that their destiny is determined by their Karma or actions and they also believe in rebirth. This is in line with their idea that the weaker sections or the low castes are impure and polluted because of their misdeed in the previous birth. The services of the Brahman priests are in general not available to the weaker sections.

Development Schemes

The schools and the health and other development schemes are now in operation but fruits of these schemes reach to the economically better off more than the poor mass largely because of economic constraints. Even the possible access to these schemes is of no help to the weaker sections as they can not make sufficient use of them on account of economic backwardness. The older children are engaged to look after the younger ones, rather than spared for school. And children before attaining maturity, start looking for some kind of job. At no juncture do they have enough money to pay for medicine and other facilities. The development schemes in agricultural sector necessarily provide the better facilities to those who have control over resources (i.e., land) and since the weaker sections have negligible control over resources they are least or not benefited by any such scheme. The 'grow more food' programmes help those who have land. The weaker sections do not have land and thus the agro-based programmes are of no help to them. These programmes, on the other hand, widen the gap between the rich and the poor.

Sociology of poverty

As it appears from the discussion, the landless and illiterate, and ritually low castes have no means to improve their social, economic and ritual positions. The Balai no more lift the dead animals and nor do they anymore deal in skin and hide in order to remove the stigma of the unclean profession, but that has hardly resulted in bringing about any significant change in providing them a higher ritual position in the village or regional context. Their position is the lowest in this regard and are looked down upon as before. Moreover their traditional economic ties with the cultivators are broken and that has pushed them into economic insecurity and more hardships. They could not attain even literacy mainly due to their economic constraints; the development schemes and land legislation could not bring benefit to them in anyway. They are largely dependent on their manual working capacity and earn their livelihood as daily wage-labourers. There is no security of job and consequently have no regular income. That situation forces them on occasions to borrow money for their necessities. Since government agencies do not grant any loan to such people, they borrow from private agencies and these moneylenders charge a high rate of interest. This makes them further poor and they are hardly in a position to either overcome the debt or to earn better livelihood anywhere. The poverty perpetuates on account of several interlinked factors and unless there are changes introduced in respect of employment facilities and education, the poverty would persist.

Conclusion : Dominant and Weak

We observed that the communities could be arranged in multiple hierarchical orders of which the most important is the ritual hierarchy. The highest position in the ritual hierarchy is occupied by the Brahman, who command ritual superiority over all other communities in the village. The second in order are the Mahajan and the Mina, who acknowledge the ritual superiority of the Brahman and claim themselves superior to others. The immediate next order is represented by the Jaga, Mali and Khati who accept their ritually inferior position in comparison to the Brahman, Mahajan and Mina in the village. The fourth position is occupied by the Jogi and Rana, who claim ritual superiority only over the Balai, the untouchables.

Numerically the village population may be divided into three clusters, the high, the middle, and the low. The Mina with 70.65 per cent of the population strength of the village occupy the high position. The middle position is occupied by the Balai, Brahman, Jaga, Khati and Mali together and the low position is occupied jointly by the Jogi, Mahajan and Rana. The numerical superiority which in a democratic set up with adult franchise is the source of political power is so decisive that even the combined strength of all other castes and communities is no match before the Mina.

In the over-all economic assessment the Brahman show their superiority. But due to their very low population strength in the village (1.96 percent), their affluence does not reflect upon the over-all economic condition of the village as such. Similar is the case of the Mahajan who have a smaller population strength. The Mina, rank third in terms of over-all economic prosperity. It may, however, be pointed out here that in economic terms there could be nearly as many patterns of stratification in the village as there are the castes. In this respect various castes and communities of the village display more differences than similarity. The Rana are, however, the poorest caste in the village and they are closely followed by the Balai and Jogi in this respect.

When we take the educational attainment into account, the Mahajan rank the highest position in the village and they are closely followed by the Brahman, Jaga and Khati. All remaining castes score very poorly and the attainment of the Balai, Jogi and Mina is the poorest in this respect.

Considering all the factors together, the Balai are by far the worst placed as they do at the level of destitution and the Jogi and Rana closely follow them in this respect.

It becomes clear from the above description that no single factor is responsible for determining weakness or strength. From the discussion this also becomes clear that following the various factors no one can be considered superior or inferior to the other as the intensity of respective factors is likely to vary from context to context.

When we review the extent of change that weaker sections of

Rajasthan have undergone since Independence, Nangal Soosawatan presents rather a dismal picture. No developmental programme has reached the poor and the destitutes. The village got electrified during the post Independence era, several irrigation pump sets have also been installed in the village following the energy connections but the impoverished lot have remained uncovered and untouched. The problem of poverty due to the nature of the development programme as such. Because of the predominance of agriculture in rural India's economic scene, any developmental programme for rural India weigh heavily towards agricultural development. Though most of our rural population live on agricultural economy, the great majority of them are simply agricultural labourers having no right over the land in which they invest their labour. Under the circumstances if the developmental programmes are made land-based, the great majority of the people remain uncovered by the programme.

NOTES

1. A couple belonging to Nai community came to live in the village sometime between the two phases of field investigations, that were carried out in early and late 1973. They are described elsewhere. Their ritual position is between the Jogi and the Rana.
2. The Jogi household constructed a new house and hence the average expenditure is so high for them. The information was collected on random sampling basis from selected households and actual expenditure during the year of investigation (i.e. 1973) was noted.
3. Calculated percentages are given below the number of figures.

19

GOVINDGARH : A VILLAGE IN PUNJAB

SUKUMAR BANERJEE and D.B.MONDAL

Introduction

Materials on which the present paper is based were collected by the authors during their fieldwork in 1975 (from February to April) in Govindgarh, a village situated fourteen kilometers east of Ludhiana, Punjab. The present study highlights the impact on the villagers of the opportunities available due to their proximity to the industrial city of Ludhiana and the impact of 'green revolution' particularly on the weaker sections.

Govindgarh is a Sikh village where the weaker and the dominant sections have equal numerical strength. The village has two main wards or sectors; the northern occupied by the Jat-Sikh having pucca houses with modern outfits and the southern occupied by the Chamar living in ordinary houses. North-South orientation is the usual settlement pattern of the non-Chamar and Chamar in this region. As the Chamar at one time were engaged in their tradition strong occupation of dressing raw-hides, such a plan helps prevent spread of strong smell into the locality of others.

The sector of Jat-Sikh is called as *pind* or the village-proper. The locality of the Chamar is *berah*. The *berah* is considered ritually unclean, where due to weakness of the inhabitants the homesteads are small and nearly devoid of any arable land or adequate material possession.

The six caste groups professing Sikh-religion, and other two groups belonging to Islam form three district hierarchical divisions as shown in Table 1.

TABLE 1: Hierarchical ranking of caste

Name of the Caste		Hierarchical order	No. of Families	Population	Percentage
Jat-sikhs (Landowners)		I	66	401	40.58
Tarkhan	Sikh	(artisans)	5	50	5.06
Nai	Sikh	(artisans)	3	13	1.31
Mehra	Sikh	(artisans)	5	32	3.23
Gujar	Muslim	II	1	9	0.91
Mirasi	Muslim	II	1	1	0.10
Chamar		III	68	446	47.01
Chamar (Landless agricultural labourers)		III	6	36	2.60
Total			158	988	

Principles of Caste-ranking

Numerical strength linked with ownership of land or *sarmoidar* primarily determine the status of a caste. Income, style of life, ritual rank, tradition, and prestige play secondary role in this respect.

Landowners and farmers

Jat-Sikh migrated to the area from the east about one hundred and fifty years ago. Members of Aujla clan had initially settled in the adjoining village Niche Mangal. Later, they along with member of Khakh clan shifted to the present site. In early days there were frequent raids by the Muslims from the south. The Jat then were given protection by the local governor Govind Jash, after whom they named the village.

Though the Chamar are numerically dominant in the village, by virtue of their control over economic resources and fairly high numerical strength the Jat-Sikh occupy the most dominant position.

Landless Artisans

The original Jat-settlers, in order to meet requirements of some specialized jobs, had invited a few families of artisans to settle there. As ritually clean, the first settlers among them were allowed to construct houses in the common *mushtrakas* and located in the Jat-sector.

The carpenter-cum-blacksmith (belonging to Ramgariya caste) are known as Tarkhan. The barbers or Nai and the water-carriers or Mehra occupy low position in the traditional hierarchy. When they agreed to render their service, receiving fixed quantum of grains or *sepi* from landowners after harvest, this further lowered their position.

The Tarkhan repair agricultural and house-hold equipments, receiving full payment in cash. Before the introduction of Sikh religion, Nai used to serve the patrons by turn. Now they are required for pairing nails only. Need for traditional services of Mehra has decreased with the installation of hand-pumps in households. The Nai and Mehra have some socio-ritual roles to perform in their patrons' place.

The artisans are *Lagi* to their patrons. This indicates the semi-obligatory relationship that exists between them. The Nai and Mehra receive from the patrons 15 kilograms of foodgrains after every harvest. The Tarkhans' payment depends on the total output of landowner. The Tarkhans also enjoy a better status than the Nai or Mehra. Among themselves, the artisan castes exchange reciprocal services. The Tarkhans sometimes attend to jobs of Chamar free of charges. The Nai and Mehra do not serve them.

Landless Muslim

There are two Muslim families in the village, a Gujar and a Mirasi. The Gujar used to tend cattle of the Jat-Sikh, and as remuneration received a handful of flour from every cattle owner. Now the Gujar have taken up buffalo trade and cultivation by reclaiming land or on the basis of rent or *jabti*.

The Mirasi are bards. They were consulted by Jat-Sikhs for matrimonial information. With the improvement of communication system in the area there is less demand for such specialised services. As a result, the Mirasi have taken to other cundry jobs. One adult Mirasi works as a peon in the Punjab Agricultural University.

Landless Untouchables

The lowest order is constituted by the untouchable Chamars (leather workers) and Chuhras (sweepers). Numerically the Chamars form the single largest group (47%). But being landless and having a low ritual position their numerical strength could not place them high in the caste hierarchy.

The Chamars belong to two clans, Sandhu and Sandiley. Having provided one agricultural labour to each of the Jat house on a semi-permanent basis, the Chamar have developed a sort of patron client relationship with the Jat-Sikh. Traditionally they are responsible for lifting dead animals. At present in addition to agricultural work they also attend sundry jobs. The Chamar are referred to as *Lagi* by the Jat-Sikh and the latter are lender to the former. Some Chamar were engaged in dressing raw hides and supplying them to leather merchants in the nearby city. Later on under patronization of Muslim traders of Ludhiana, they took up shoe making. With the partition of India, as the Muslim traders left for Pakistan, there was a decline in the business of shoe-making.

As a non-cultivating caste, the Chamar were debarred from getting any land according to land Acquisition Act 1901. As a result of an amendment brought about in this Act in 1947, the Chamar are now free to buy land. The Chamar are responsible for cleaning cattle sheds of their Jat-Sikh patrons. In exchange they receive a *roti* per family per day. They also supplement their income by working as agricultural labourers.

Identification of weaker groups

The Jat-Sikh form the dominant group in the village. The Artisans are landless and dependent on the Jat-Sikh. But some changes have occured in this respect due to green revolution and expansion of small industries in the nearby town of Ludhiana. In general, however, the lender are dominant and the *Lagi* are weak.

Literacy

The Chamars are somewhat behind the Jat-Sikh in terms of literacy though the difference is not very sharp. As untouchables, their performance appears very satisfactory.

TABLE 2: Levels of literacy of Jat-Sikhs and Chamars

Levels of Literacy	Jat-Sikh (in Percentage)	Chamar (in percentage)
Illiterates	42.0	50.0
Primary level	17.7	26.0
Secondary level	26.6	20.0
Matriculates	9.8	3.0
Pre-University	2.0	0.5
graduates	1.7	0.2
Post-Graduates	0.2	Nil

Economic Dimension

Arable lands of the village are divided into three categories namely, *malkiat* (owned by individuals), *samlat patti* (common clan land), and *samlat dey* (village land under control of the Gram Panchayat). The first two types are exclusively owned by the Jat-Sikh. They own 310 acres of *malkiat* land of the village. However, 74 per cent of the Jat-Sikh belong to small or middle farmer category and the remaining 26 per cent posses 7.5 acres to 16 acres of land.

The Chamar have little land. Due to lack of infrastructure to support modern farming, the Jat-Sikh discourage them to take up land on *batai* or share-cropping basis. This leaves little opportunity for the weaker sections but to work as agricultural labourers.

History of Agricultural Development

Prior to independence, there were huge sand-dunes around the villages that proved a great impediment to agriculture. Due to poor soil condition and lack of irrigation facilities, the landowners used to get little return from this land. The sand-dunes were later cleared by the contractors to meet their needs of construction in Ludhiana. With the removal of sand dunes developments in the field of agriculture began. For a sharp assessment of the developments, the post-independent era may be divided into three phases :

1) *Pre-C.D.P. Period* (1947-1953)

Incentives were provided through Agriculture Department, Govt. of Punjab, by granting loans for digging wells, for buying fertiliser, reclaiming wastelands and for purchasing tractors.

2) *C.D.P. Period* (1954-1962)

In 1954, Govindgarh came under the jurisdiction of Ludhiana Development Block. Fresh loans were distributed for purchase of various implements like tractors, sowing drills, sprayers, insecticides, fertilisers, and harvesters. Three important steps taken by concerned authorities were responsible for bringing about green revolution at a later date. They are : (i) electrification of the village in 1958, (ii) consolidation of landholding on the basis of the Govt. order issued in 1948 (vide East Punjab Holdings Consolidation and Fragmentation Act. 1948), (iii) extension of irrigation facilities by construction sub-canal from the main Sirhind canal.

3) *I.A.D.P. Period* (1962 to this date)

The Agricultural University, Ludhiana gave a great filip in the agricultural production by distributing, through its trained extension agents, seeds of high yielding varieties (Kalyan 227,334) to the farmers from the year 1964-65. As a result of better agricultural production, corresponding development took place in other ancillary industries and seventeen public corporations were formed in the state (Punjab Agricultural University Hand Book). These agencies helped in mechanisation of agriculture and provided necessary inputs. In Govindgarh, the village cooperative bank, helps farmers by issuing the required quantity of fertilizers on credit by requisitioning the total requirement from the sub-agencies of the MARKED organisations. The farmers make after sale of their products.

Average production in the area is fifteen quintals of wheat per acre in ordinary soil and more than twenty quintals in fertile lands (from one crop). Yield has increased through multiple cropping with the adoption of rotation of crops.

Social organisation of labour

A Jat-Sikh farmer works in his field with the Chamar, engaged in terms of *sanjhi* and *beet*. Under both systems the workers are farm-servants. The former would work throughout the year receiving a share, either one-fifth or one-sixth of the production. A *beet* gets a fixed salary monthly or yearly, and food.

As agricultural plots are distributed in wide area the owners are not in a position to devote full attention to each of them. Under the circumstances, they engage *sanjhi* who pays full attention to cultivation which also increases his share over production.

With the introduction of agricultural innovations in the area, the production cost has gone up. As a result the *sanjhi* do not find it much profitable to cultivate land under the existing terms. So, the *sanjhi* system has more or less been replaced by *beet* system. The latest trend among the agricultural labourers is to work as *dehari* on daily wage basis @ Rs.8.50 per day. The landowners, however, prefer employment of *beet*, and many of them engage *bhaiya* (labourers from Uttar Pradesh) as 'beet' @ Rs.100.00 or Rs.120.00 per month plus food and accommodation. Nearly 80 per cent of farmers of the village are in possession of six acres of land or above and 62 per cent among them have engaged a *beet*. Labourers from Uttar Pradesh constitute 80 per cent of the total farm servants of the village.

Daily wage labourers look forward to the harvesting time when they earn maximum. Before the introduction of high yielding varieties a labourer after 12 hours work was allowed to carry a bundle of wheat stock *bhari* weighing about 30 kgs. as his wage. As there used to be disagreement about the exact weight of the bundle the system was replaced in 1965 by *penga*. This was not found very satisfactory either. In 1970, the *penga* system of payment to daily wage labourers had been replaced by *'banga'*, according to which a labourer got @ 70 Kgs. threshed wheat per acre.

The daily rate of labour during this period was between Rs. 14.00 and Rs. 15.00 per day. Quantity of wheat earned by a labourer during harvesting season is sufficient to feed his family for seven to eight months a year. The remaining period is managed by earning as agricultural labourers or following some other occupation. Not a single Jat-Sikh is an agricultural labourer (vide Table 3), whereas 43.8 per cent Chamar live on this profession. As employment opportunities are available in nearby industrial centres, a good number of these people have engaged themselves in service (25.5%), as industrial labourer (20.4%), and in business (10.2%). Detailed probing in this respect shows that barring a few, who are drivers or mechanic, 88 per cent of the Harijan in the service category are class III and class IV employees in various government and public undertakings. They also work as labourer in industrial establishments like cycle and spinning factories. Some have taken to trade and one has a tea-stall near one of the factory establishments.

TABLE 3: Distribution of occupation of male work

Caste groups	Trade Occupation	Cultivation	Ag. Labour	Industrial Labour.	Business	Service	Selling milk	Poultry	Total
Jat-Sikh	—	53	—	6	2	31	—	3	95
Tarkhan	2	—	—	6	1	1	1	—	11
Mehra	—	—	3	5	—	—	—	—	8
Nai	—	—	2	3	—	—	—	—	5
Gujar	—	1	—	—	—	—	—	—	1
Chamar	—	—	43	20	10	25	—	—	98
Churha	2	—	7	—	—	—	—	—	9
Mirasi	—	—	—	—	—	1	—	—	1
Total	4	54	55	40	13	58	1	3	228

A good number of economists and other researchers have conducted studies in Punjab during 1969-73, relating to problems of labour and wages (Bardhan 1970), mechanisation (Billing, 1969-70, Mandal 1970), differential income and distribution in rural areas (Bardhan and Srivastava 1971), class conflicts and tensions (Lade Jinskey 1970), and landless rural labour (Aggarwal 1973). No doubt a wide difference continues to persist between per capita income of a Jat-Sikh and a Chamar, the respective figures being Rs. 1572.00 and Rs. 600.00 per month (based on 25 per cent sample), the Chamar in Govindgarh are still economically much better off than their counterpart elsewhere. A detailed analysis of the data shows that the Chamar included in the sample can, according to their income, be divided into three categories as below :

Categories	Total number of families	Total no.of members	Total income of all families annual	Percapita income
A	3	15	Rs.5280.00	Rs.352.00
B	6	39	Rs.17329.00	Rs.444.00
C	7	52	Rs.41067.00	Rs.789.00

It may be mentioned here that families both in category A and B earn their living as agricultural labourer. As category B has more people then category A, the former could earn a larger amount of wheat during harvest. Their average income got inflated due to the inclusion of two members in regular service. The difference of per capita annual income between category A and B is, however, not that wide as between category B and C. The condition of families in category C has improved as, in addition to their earning sufficient wheat during harvest, most of them are also engaged in service, business, and working as industrial labourers. Their educational attainments have helped them in such matters. Their per capita annual income is still lower than that of the state average, which, in 1970-71, was Rs. 881.00. But their income was then much higher than the state average of West Bengal, that is Rs. 539.00 and the all India average of Rs. 633.00. Thus, some benefits of agrarian changes and farmers' prosperity in Punjab did trickle down to the poor.

Social Dimension

Even to a casual visitor of Govindgarh the distinction between settlements of the dominant section and the weak is conspicuous. Now-a-days all have access to hand-pumps for fetching water. Previously they had separate source and the Jat-Sikh also allowed Muslims to fetch water from their wells, a facility, which was only casually available to the Chamar. The Jat-Sikh and Chamar had separate cremation grounds. Out of the three Gurdwaras in the village, two are used by the Jat-Sikh and artisans, and third by the Chamar.

In spite of egalitarian doctrine of the Sikhism the Jat-Sikh never accepted food from the Chamar or Churha nor did they attend socio-religious functions of the latter.

Owing to their inferior position in the caste hierarchy and having no control over means of production, the Chamar are completely dependent on the dominant group.

Magico-religious Dimension

Sometime between 1910 and 1915, the Jat-Sikhs of Govindgarh embraced Sikhism. Until then they were Hindus. The new faith organised the people who took interest in religious and secular instructions. They utilized the network of Gurdwara organisation to their benefit. Gradually they adopted secular principles and picked up traits of westernisation.

After independence the Chamar began to adopt the Sikh-model in a bid to elevate their social status. They did not disown their past and adopted Ramdasi (sevak of their Guru Rabidas or Ramdas) as their caste name. They turned Sikh by adopting the diacritical marks undergoing a simple process of conversion. Apart from celebrating some of the Hindu-festivals in their own fashion, they also started performing various ceremonies relating to the Sikh-Guru. This, however, did not elevate social status of the Chamar in relation to the Jat-Sikhs and other castes.

Political Dimension

Except the Chamar no other caste has any traditional panchayat. This Chamar panchayat has gone defunct and the people get their disputes settled through traditional village panchayat which was under the control of the Jat-Sikh and three *Lambardars* (revenue collectors) from three streets (*pattis*) constituted it.

With the introduction of Panchayat Raj system the Chamar have realised the value of their numerical strength. But as they are economically tied-up with the Jat-Sikh, they prefer to elect a Jat-Sikh as the Sarpanch. They in return, receive the protection from exploitation by the dominant group.

Recently, having drawn inspiration and support from the Congress, the Chamar have started asserting their rights for their own benefit. They have also demanded a higher social status, at par with the Sikh, based on greater egalitarianism.

REFERENCES

Aggarwal, P.C. Impact of Green Revolution on Landless Labour, *Economic and Political Weekly*. Vol. VI, Nov. 20, 1971, 2363-2365, 1971.

Bardhan, P. Green Revolution and Agricultural Labour, *Economic and Political Weekly*. Vol.5,No.29-31, Special Number and Vol.5, No.46, 1970.

Govt. of West Bengal *Draft Fifth Five Year Plan : West Bengal*. Dept. of Development & Planning, Aug.,1973.

Ladejinsky, W. *Agrarian Reform in Asia, the Green Revolution and the Reform Effects*. 28th Int.Cong.of Orientalists. Canberra, 1971.

Singh, P. *Punjab Agricultural Handbook*. Punjab.

Grewal, K.S. Agricultural University, Ludhiana, 1975.

20

BASANTPUR : A VILLAGE IN HARYANA

HASAN ALI and ASIM MAITRA

Basantpur is located about 11 kms. away from Rohtak city on the Gohana road under the Rohtak Block and Rohtak P.S.

In the beginning of our research work despite our clarifications, the villagers became suspicious and confused about the purpose of our work. We had to face scores of questions concerning the actual purpose of our enquiry through a prolonged stay for about three months. We told them that we came for studying their way of life in its total perspective viz. social, economic, political, educational, magico-religious etc. so that it may be published in a book form and people in other parts of India or outside may know them. We showed them few books we had with us. This helped greatly to reduce their suspicion. Still then the landowners, especially the big ones became concerned and thoughtful that our enquiries would increase tax on their land, agricultural tax as well as quantity of levy. However, we could convince them through the help of the educated villagers, especially the youth. Instead of living in someone's house we decided to stay in the village panchayat house locally known as *press* or *choupal*. It was freely accessible to all and hence it facilitated our work.

While enquiring about land in most of the cases it was found that the landowners understated the amount. On the basis of our earlier field exposure we were prepared for this problem. Hence with the help of the village *patwari* the data on land were thoroughly rechecked and corrected. Regarding tenure of share cropping, lease, and mortgage etc. having no official records we depended on the villagers only. The rural households do not keep account of their family budget, hence exact account of household income and expenditure was not obtainable. Thus we got only an approximate picture about them. The economic scarcity was well reflected through the villagers' style of life and material possession.

Data were collected on the basis of a guideline prepared in advance. The main tools were observation and interviews. Some schedules were also administered. The duration of field work was about three months during February to May '75.

The total population of Basantpur is 998. There are 124 households, 72 of which are of the upper caste Hindu and 52 of the Harijan castes. There are ten castes. Among the caste Hindu are the Brahman, Jat, Bania, Sonar, Nai, Lohar, and Chipi (tailor). Among the Harijan castes are Dhanak, Chamar, and Chura (Table 1).

The upper and the intermediate castes maintain some physical distance from the Harijan. The Dhanak and the Chamar, though living in one cluster, their settlements are divided. The Chura or sweeper have their settlement almost in isolation to the main cluster, socially thus the gap is wide.

The houses are linear and open to the lanes. Each of the Harijan castes (Dhanak, Chamar, and Chura) has separate wells while the upper and the intermediate castes use common wells.

The basic economy of the village is based on agriculture and a majority of villagers directly or indirectly depend upon it. The Jat and the Brahman here are traditionally agriculturists. The Sonar and the Bania are traditionally business communities and while the latter is continuing business the former has entered into service. The Nai, Lohar, and the Chipi are continuing their traditional occupations, supplemented by wage labour. The Harijan castes supply the bulk of the agriculture labour force. A few educated persons are engaged in service in various government departments. A few persons are serving in Indian Army (Table 9).

Control over resources

In the rural sectors where agriculture remains the basic source of economy, the ownership and control over land means economic power. At Basantpur the entire cultivable land (774 acres) is in the hands of the Jat and the Brahman. Among these two the larger concentration is among the Jat (712 acres), distributed among 52 households (13.7 acres per household) while only 62 acres are owned by the six households among the Brahman which comes to an average of 10.3 acres per household. The remaining villagers are landless (Table 2). The Jat and the Brahman (farmers, big or small

TABLE 1: Population composition castewise

Sl. No.	Caste	Traditional Occupation	Total no. of house holds	Total population	Percentage of the total	Male population	Female popula-tion	Separate settle ment	Social dis-crimination disability	Regueren-tation in Panchayat	Reform movement
1.	Brahman	Priesthood	6	45	4.50	27	18	Y	N	Y	N
2.	Jat	Agriculture	52	542	54.10	305	237	Y	N	Y	N
3.	Bania	Business	1	5	0.50	2	3	Y	N	NA	N
4.	Sonar	Gold smithy	2	11	1.10	7	4	Y	N	NA	N
5.	Lohar	Iron smithy	7	40	4.00	21	19	Y	N	NA	N
6.	Chipi	Tailoring	1	4	0.40	2	2	Y	N	NA	N
7.	Nai	Hair cutting	3	28	2.92	10	18	Y	N	NA	N
8.	Dhanak	Sheep rearing Weaving	33	203	20.35	115	88	Y	Y	Y	N
9.	Chamar	Leather work	14	89	9.02	48	41	Y	Y	N	N
10.	Chura	Sweeping	5	31	3.11	14	17	Y	Y	N	N
	TOTAL	—	124	998	100.00	551	447				

locally known as zamindar) are not only controlling the local means of production but the distribution mechanism is also under their control. Thus 58 households out of 124 are controlling the local economic resources while 66 households (53.33%) are landless.

According to the local classification as well as on the basis of the average family size (10 members) among the landowners and the average out-put per acre, the landowners in the village may broadly be classified into 5 categories viz., marginal, small, medium, big, and very big (Table 3). The minimum size of holding is two acres and maximum is 60 acres.

The major crops grown here are wheat and sugarcane, the later being the main cash crop. The subsidiary ones are jowar and bazra. Barsim and gowar are the two main fodder crops. Bullock carts, Jhota (cart pulled by buffalo) as well as tractor are the main means or transporting the surplus produce to market.

According to available means of irrigation, the land is classified locally into three categories viz., *nehri* (canal irrigated), *chachi* (tube well irrigated) and *baram* (depending on monsoon). The main source of irrigation is canal. The soil is classified into three types viz., *dakar, domath*, and *raie. Dakar* is considered the most fertile for all crops, followed by *domath. Raie* is considered unsuitable for any crop. The greater amount of land in the village belonged to the first two qualities, and roughly about 15 per cent of the total land belonged to *raie* variety.

Organisation of Agricultural Labour

Though labour is provided by the landless households of all castes excepting the Bania and the Sonar, the bulk of labour comes from the three Harijan castes. The Harijan almost entirely depend upon labour and constitute the majority of the landless labour class. They decisively constitute the weaker sections of the local society.

The agricultural labour may be classified into three major categories. Some agricultural labourers were found to have been engaged by the big landowners especially the Jats to work in their farms. The farm servants are locally known as *basandir*. There were altogether 8 persons working as *basandir*. They were castewise as follows; Chamar (4), Dhanak (3) and Chura (1).They all belonged to Basantpur excepting the Chura, who came from an outside village. They were paid remuneration ranging from Rs.800 to 1200 per

TABLE 2 : Distribution of land

Sl. No.	Caste	Total no. of house hold	Household possessing land	Total land in acre	Average land per household
1.	JAT	52	52	712	13.7
2.	BRAHMAN	6	6	62	10.3
3.	SONAR	2			
4.	BANIA	1			
5.	NAI	3			
6.	LOHAR	7 Land less.			
7.	CHIPI	1			
8.	DHANAK	33			
9.	CHAMAR	14			
10.	CHURA	5			
		124	58	774	

TABLE 3: Landholding of Zamindar of Jat and Brahman

RANGE	JAT	BRAHMAN	TOTAL
Upto 5 acres	8	3	11
5 to 10 acres	24	1	25
10 to 15 acres	4	1	5
15 to 20 acres	6	1	7
Above 20 acres	10	-	10
TOTAL	52	6	58

TABLE 4: Wage

Sl. No.	Nature of work	Remuneration paid	Remark
1.	Wheat harvest	One puli or bundle (2 to 3 kgs. of grain) out of 20 bundles	
2.	*Jowar* and *bazra*	Re. 1 and one bundle approx. containing 2 kg. *bazra/jowar* grain per day	
3	Sugarcane	*agola* (upper end of the Sugarcane)	done by the female
4.	Sugarcane binding into bunches	Rs.2 and 2 meals per day	
5.	Ploughing	Rs.5 per day	done by male

annum including three meals and a measure of milk. In the second type labourers are engaged on a contract basis mainly during the wheat harvesting for the entire season. Three labourers, one Chamar and two Dhanak were found engaged on this basis on a remuneration of 56 mds. of wheat. The third type of agricultural labourers are those who work on daily wage basis. The remuneration for the daily labourers differ according to the nature of agricultural operations (vide Table 4).

The normal rate of payment for a male labour is Rs. 5 per day and for the female Rs. 4 per day. The skilled labourers like the mason and carpenter get Rs. 10 per day. The Lohar of the village works as carpenter on *jajmani* basis. There is no mason in this village.

The number of days during which all the labourers get full employment comes to nearly 25 (about 15 days during wheat harvest and 10 days during *jowar* and *bazra* harvest). Agricultural labourer collect nearly three months' food grain during the wheat harvest. Approximately 20 kgs of jowar and bazra are collected by each household.

Some of the labourers from this village specially the youth among them go to other districts like Karnal, Kurukshetra etc. to work as agricultural labourers during the paddy harvest. This continues for about a month. As remuneration one labourer gets three kgs of paddy out of every 37.5 kgs generally harvested. One labourer normally gets 7.5 to 9 kgs of paddy a day.

Occupational mobility and the landless

Among the landless people the economic condition of the Harijan is considerably bad compared to the other landless castes. The traditional socio-economic background seems to be one of the most important factors resulting in the existing economic difference between the two.

The only Bania household belonging to a typical business community runs a grocery shop in the village. The two Sonar households, who are traditionally ornament makers, have also a business background. There has been, however, a shift of occupation among them and they have entered into service. The Nai and the Lohar (2 households) have *jajmani* relationship with the Zamindar and they receive a fixed quantity of crop twice a year. One Chipi or tailor household was found engaged in tailoring.

Thus, the demand for the traditional services of Nai, Chipi, and Lohar have not been reduced with the advancing years.

The Lohar also have enough pressure of work as still now mechanization in the agricultural sector has not been widely popular among all the categories of farmers. Moreover, they have combined carpentry with iron works.

Among the Harijan the Dhanak and the Chamar with their traditional occupations could not compete with the changing situation and simultaneously could not catch up with some other paying occupations. As a result, they turn as labourers in large numbers. The Dhanak traditionally followed the occupation of sheep rearing and weaving. Sheep rearing has been abandoned completely due to deforestation and consequent lack of grazing space. Weaving also declined sharply due to increasing popularity of mill made cloth. Out of the total population of 203 among the Dhanaks only 14 elderly persons followed weaving. Among the new generation no one showed any interest in it. Moreover weaving was done in full swing only during the winter season.

Similar was the case with the Chamar of this village. Only one person was found engaged in shoe-making. Among the Chura the women still continue their traditional sweeping and cleaning occupation. Men among them worked mainly as labourers. Their traditional occupation of sweeping and cleaning has never been a paying one in the local rural set up.

One subsidiary source of income especially followed by the Harijan is to keep buffaloes (being kept with them by the dairymen, mainly the refugees living at Rohtak city), for which the Harijan charges a fixed amount per month ranging from Rs. 50 to 100. The system is locally known as *charai*. Households keeping buffaloes on this basis were castewise as follows : two Lohar households (3 buffaloes) one Nai, 9 Dhanak households (13 buffaloes), 4 Chamar household (6 buffaloes).

Income and indebtedness

Out of the total 124 households, information on income and expenditure were collected from a sample of 33 households. The Jat have the highest percapita income followed by that of the Bania, Brahman and the Sonar (Table 5). The Harijan in this respect are on the other extreme recording a very low percapita income. The Lohar, Chipi, and Nai show a slightly higher per capita income than that of the Harijan, but still much below than that of the Jat, Bania, Brahman, and the Sonar. The income seems to correspond closely with the ritual status of a caste. It is observed that the low caste status and poverty go together.

A large number of landless labourers do not get regular employment in agricultural field and outside it also there is not much demand for them.They lived under a condition of underemployment. Whatever they earn as manual labourer does not suffice their bare necessities of life. Their low income and tough struggle for existence does not offer any scope for future saving or future planning. They virtually live consuming the earning the same day. They were largely under debt of the local *mahajans*. The data on indebtedness was also collected from a sample household of 33.

The proper households due to low income fall into the clutches of the local *mahajan* or money lenders. The Harijan have the highest burden of debt and all the 13 sample households among them turned out to be under debts (Table 6). The local rates of interest is 20 per cent per annum. The loans taken by the big and medium categories of landowners from the Banks have not been taken into consideration here, as that is rather an index of prosperity. Along with the Harijan the Chipi and Lohar also bear heavy burdens of debt upon them. The rest viz. Jat, Brahman, Bania and Sonar have no debt.

TABLE 5: Per capita annual income

Caste	Income in Rs.
JAT	1163.00
BANIA	1065.00
BRAHMAN	1050.00
SONAR	545.00
LOHAR	267.00
DARJI (CHIPI)	256.00
NAI	283.00
DHANAK	240.00
CHAMAR	224.00
CHURA	193.00

TABLE 6: Indebtedness

Sl. No.	Caste	Total no.of household	Sample size	Total amount of debt in Rs.	Average amount of debt per household in Rs.
*1.	DHANAK	33	8	15,200	1,900
2.	CHAMAR	14	3	8,800	2,933
3.	CHURA	5	1	1,500	1,600
4.	CHIPI	1	1	3,000	3,000
5.	LOHAR	7	2	3,200	1,600
6.	NAI	3	1	400	400

Consumption pattern and material style of life

The consumption pattern shows that the poorer households spend a higher proportion of their income on food. Because of their low income most of them are unable to spend money on education, medicine, construction of house etc. For these as well as for meeting expenses of the socio-religious ceremonies often they borrow money at a high rate of interest.

The Jat as well as other castes belonging to higher income category could distribute their income in a somewhat balanced way. They take care of the schooling of their children, spend on house construction, dress, and for other household articles.

The inequality of income gets well reflected in the material condition of the economically dominant and weak in terms of dress, food, housetype, household belongings etc. There is a world of difference in these regards, especially between the landowners and the landless Harijan.

The landless Harijan mostly live in one-roomed mud built small houses with only a very few exceptions who have brick-built small houses. By contrast, the dominant landowning Jat and Brahman with the exception of only three have fairly large, mostly double storied brick-built spacious houses. They have separate *baithak* as well. The Bania and Sonar have also well constructed houses, whereas the Nai, and Chipi as well as the two households among the Lohar have kachha-pakka or mixed type of small houses.

The staple food in the village among low caste people is wheat, jowar, which is used mainly as fodder by the well-to-do households, being cheaper than wheat. The poor households could not afford to use milk or milk products which are largely used among the dominant landowning Jat and Brahman as well as among the Bania and the Sonar. *Bazra* which was used as fodder for their cattle by the well-to-do households, being cheaper than wheat is also commonly used by the poor landless households.

Green revolution

The greater beneficiaries of "green revolution" have been the big farmers in terms of the use of high yielding seeds, fertilizers and improved technologies like tractor, tube-well, thrasher etc. Though high yielding varieties of seeds and fertilizers were found to be equally popular among the medium as well as small farmers, the use of tractor, tube-well, and thrasher etc., remained exclusively confined to the big farmers. The six tractors in the village are owned by the big farmers. Further, most recent varieties of seeds like Sonalika which requires comparatively more water were cultivated by the big farmers only with the help of tube-wells. The big farmers owning tractors, apart from their own land, have been able to bring more areas under cultivation through the system of lease. Mechanization also reduced the need for the small farmers to give land on share-cropping basis. The small farmers engaged in share-cropping do not receive their proper share of 2/3rd in most of the cases, but receive mostly 1/3rd only. The small as well as medium categories of farmers used mostly the old technologies of agriculture. However, the overall impact of the green revolution on the landowners of all categories has been considerably good. It increased the production several folds.

With the start of sugar mill at Rohtak city, sugarcane cultivation became increasingly popular during the last 15 years. A tendency to bring more areas under sugarcane cultivation was also observed among all categories of farmers. The increase in the wheat production, and intensive cultivation of sugarcane as the main cash crop have conspicuously improved considerably the general economic condition of the landowners. As a result, the large *pucca* houses have started replacing the *kaccha* houses since 1960.

The green revolution has though increased the production several folds through double cropping, improved inputs, and mechanization, it did not help improve the condition of the landless in the same way. When double-cropping increased the demand for labour the mechanisation reduced such demand. Though the normal rate of wage increased from Rs.3 during 1973 to Rs. 5 in 1975, in the real term it did not make any significant difference as the number of days a labour gets work in the agricultural field has decreased. Whatever they earn through agricultural works is not enough to pull them through out the year. They have to seek employment in non-agricultural sectors. In the non-agricultural sector also there is not much demand for labour and hence they remain under a condition of underemployment.

One important reason for less demand of labour in agricultural sphere which holds true particularly for this part of the country was the Jat landowner's zeal to carry out all agricultural operations themselves with the help of their respective family members. This further reduced the scope for labourer's employment. The incidence of joint/extended family among the Jat is also considerably high (22 out of 52 households). The Brahman landowners also, unlike those in many other parts of the country carry out all agricultural operations by themselves, keeping less scope for labour employment.

Social Dimension

Social inequality occupies an important place in our value system. The Indian society traditionally "provides the most powerful and ideological justification for social inequality through its institution of 'caste'". (Beteille : 1974:64). Caste system has divided people into various unequal ritual statuses. Each caste occupies a distinct ritual status in the caste hierarchy.

Tentatively, the various castes in this village according to their ritual positions may be arranged as follows :

Brahman	Highest
Jat Bania Sonar	High
Nai Lohar Chipi	Intermediate
Dhanak Chamar Chura	Low

Though in respect of wealth and power as well as numerical strength the Jat predominate over all the others, the highest position of the Brahman and the lowest position of the Chura is agreed upon by all.

Complete equivalence in commensality prevails only among the members of one's own caste. No castes receive water or food from the Harijan. Hukka and bidi are very common smoke in this area among all sections of people. The castes belonging to high and intermediate statuses share *hukka* and *bidi* among themselves. The Brahman do not share these with any other caste. *Bidi* was observed to be accepted by all castes from the Harijan.

As it has been stated earlier, all the three castes among the Harijan have separate wells for themselves. They were not allowed to draw water from the wells common for all. They do not accept water or food from each other nor do they share *hukka* or *bidi* among themselves. Members of high and intermediate castes rarely invite the Harijan during any important socio-ritual ceremonies.

The Harijan in general do not enter the houses of the other castes, especially the upper ones. The farm servants, however, enter the houses of their masters. The Harijan, however, have free access to the *baithak* of the upper castes.

The Harijan, with the exception of the Chura, are allowed to sit together with the members of all castes, except the Brahman. They generally occupy the foot end of the cot. The children also seem to be all well aware about the ritual distance between Harijan and Harijan castes and maintain it. The children of the upper castes do not play with the Harijan children. The Harijan children play in their own wards.

The Harijan of the village were not observed to enter the village temple, though they claim to do so. The Brahman do not perform marriage rituals of the Harijan.

During the panchayat meetings the Harijan sit at a distance from the rest. As *hukka* smoking is very common in all this area, they carry it to the meeting also. Thus the Dhanak, Chamar, and the Chura, as they do not share *hukka* among themselves, form exclusive clusters of their own around *hukka*.

One M.L.A. belonging to the Chamar caste started some sort of a movement a few years back, demanding land for the landless Harijan and removal of untouchability in actual practice. But the movement did not fetch any viable result and ultimately failed, because the

Dhanak and the Chamar in general refused to come to equal terms with the Chura in their day to day interaction.

There has not been any organised movement for an upward social mobility or for a higher social status among the Harijan of this village or area. There have been attempts, however, on part of the Dhanak and the Chamar to *sanskritize* their way of life through adoption of vegetarian diet.

All castes maintain boundaries amongst each other in terms of endogamy, commensality, *jati-panchayat* etc. The boundaries along the caste line is so overriding that it does not allow the poor and the landless to unite together as "*the* poor" and make concerted efforts toward improving their lot. A poor Jat will not unite with a poor Chamar but he would find it more cordial and comfortable to identify and unite himself with the rich Jat.

Political Dimension

Like differentiation in the control over the local resources resulting in inequality of property and income, inequality pervades also in terms of control over the local political power and authority. Though democratic institutions have been set up within the village itself, all castes do not have equal access to power in the real sense. The weaker sections due to poverty and social disabilities do not have any independent voice of their own. Their representatives in the village panchayat are just pawns in the hands of the economically dominant upper castes upon whom they are economically dependent also to a large extent.

The Jat being the most dominant economically as well as numerically have always had control over the power structure at the village, Block, or Anchal level.

The *sarpanch* or the head of the statutory Panchayat of this village is a Jat. He is holding the office since 1968. He happens also to be one of the richest persons in the village. The Harijan member in the panchayat is a Dhanak. He has practically no voice in any matter. The position of other castes is also no better in this respect. In whole of the 40 villages within the Rohtak Block there is no *sarpanch* from among the Harijan castes. At the Block level one Chairman and one Vice-Chairman are elected every five years. These offices also have been dominated by the dominant landowning castes. The existing Chairman is a Jat, while the Vice-Chairman is a Brahman.

The village panchayat has 27 acres of cultivable land in its name, which is sanctioned every alternate year. 1/3rd of the total of 27 acres has been earmarked for the Harijan. But so far none among the Harijan could have their share of land due to lack of money and means to cultivate the same. So their share of land also goes to the landowners, especially the Jat.

There is no elite or leader of any considerable stature among the Harijan at the village level. One belonging to the Chamar caste is said to be an emerging leader among the Harijan. He attempted to contest the panchayat election during the last election as a Harijan member but was failed by the dominant Jat.

Education

Table 7 presents the castewise percentage of literacy in the village. The highest percentage (80.00%) is found among the only Bania family in the village, followed by the Jat (45.57%), Sonar (45.45%) and Lohar (42.50%). The Brahman have 35.55% literates (closer to the average percentage of literacy in the village which is 39.17%). The lowest percentage of literacy is recorded among the Chura (6.45%). Considering the level of education, from matriculation and above, we find the Jat scoring better than any other in the village.

TABLE 7: Literacy in the village

Sl. No.	Caste	Total no. of population	Literate	Percentage	Illiterate	Percentage
1.	BRAHMAN	45	16	35.55	29	64.45
2.	JAT	542	247	45.57	295	54.57
3.	BANIA	5	4	80.00	1	20.00
4.	SONAR	11	5	45.45	6	54.55
5.	LOHAR	40	17	42.50	23	57.50
6.	CHIPI	4	1	25.00	3	75.00
7.	NAI	28	9	32.14	19	67.86
8.	DHANAK	203	63	31.03	140	68.97
9.	CHAMAR	89	27	30.38	62	69.67
10.	CHURA	31	2	6.45	29	93.55
	TOTAL	998	391	38.98	607	61.02

TABLE 8: Education level in the village

Sl. No.	Caste	Total No. Popula- tion	(I-IV) Pass	(V-VIII) Pass	(IX-X) Pass	Matric	I.A.	B.A.	Above
1.	Brahman	16	4	5	2	3	2	—	—
2.	Jat	247	78	66	54	35	7	5	2
3.	Bania	4	2	2	—	—	—	—	—
4.	Sonar	5	2	2	—	1	—	—	—
5.	Lohar	17	9	6	2	—	—	—	—
6.	Darji (Chipi)	1	1	—	—	—	—	—	—
7.	Nai	9	5	4	—	—	—	—	—
8.	Dhanak	63	30	27	4	2	—	—	—
9.	Chamar	27	14	9	3	1	—	—	—
10.	Chura	2	1	1	—	—	—	—	—
	TOTAL	391	146	122	65	42	9	5	2

We find relatively a lower percentage of literacy among the poorer households, most of whom incidentally belong to the lower castes. They express their economic inability to educate their children. The economic inability coupled with a general apathetic attitude towards education have kept them at a low level of literacy. There is a good number of drop outs among their children due to parents' inability to provide books, dress etc. for their children. The children of school-going age are also engaged by their parents to look after the cattle and/or younger siblings.

Summing Up

On the basis of the description in the preceding pages we find that the Jat of Basantpur village emerge as the decisively dominant community in terms of wealth, power, prestige, and numerical strength. They control the larger proportion of land and thereby the local economic resources are greatly under their control. In terms of per capita annual income they are at the top. The percentage of literacy and level of education are comparatively high among them. The local power structure is also controlled by them. Economically the Brahman, Bania, and the Sonar may also be regarded as dominant. Ritually the Brahman are at the top, but it is well undermined by the overall dominance of the Jat.

TABLE 9: Occupational classification

Occupation	Brahman	Jat	Bania	Sonar	Lohar	Dorji	Nai	Dhanak	Chamar	Chura	Remarks
Agriculture	28	280	—	—	—	—	—	—	—	—	
Service	2	13	—	2	3	—	—	9	2	1	
Teacher	—	8	—	—	—	—	—	—	—	—	
Shop-Keeper	—	1	1	—	—	—	1	—	1	—	
Cattle-business	—	2	—	—	—	—	—	1	—	—	
Lecturer	—	1	—	—	—	—	—	—	—	—	
Lawyer	—	1	—	—	—	—	—	—	—	—	
Scooter Driver	—	1	—	—	—	—	—	—	—	—	
Tailor	—	—	—	—	—	1	—	2	—	—	
Labour	—	—	—	—	13	3	12	85	35	5	
Hair cutting	—	—	—	—	—	—	2	—	—	—	
Shoe-repairing	—	—	—	—	—	—	—	—	1	—	
Thikadari	—	—	—	—	—	—	—	—	1	—	
Sweeping	—	—	—	—	—	—	—	—	—	5	
Tonga-Driving	—	—	—	—	—	—	—	—	—	3	
Pig Rearing	—	—	—	—	—	—	—	—	—	1	
Mid Wife	—	—	—	—	—	—	—	—	—	1	
Weaving	—	—	—	—	—	—	—	14	—	—	
Rickshaw-puller	—	—	—	—	—	—	—	1	—	—	
Blacksmith	—	—	—	—	2	—	—	—	—	—	
Total	30	307	1	2	18	4	15	112	40	16	Total=545

The Harijan being weak on all counts stand at the opposite pole. They are at the bottom both economically as well as socially. They form the bulk of the weaker section. The other castes such as Nai, Lohar, and the Chipi though fall within the category of the weaker section economically, socially or ritually their position is above the Harijan. Educationally also, the Harijan score poorly, though in respect of education the position of Nai, Lohar, and Chipi also is not much better.

The Harijan, thus, have to face a dual problem at the same time, economic as well as social.

The green revolution did not improve the lot of the poor landless labourers. Among them there is a total lack of business enterprise. Cases show that quit a few persons among the Dhanak and Chamar being the Harijan, had been engaged in the cattle purchase and sale business but presently only one Dhanak household was found continuing it. The others had to abandon the same due to heavy financial loss. They could not reorient this job due to lack of capital. The poor Harijan also generally do not get any financial help from their kin during crisis because, as stated, their kin were also equally poor. The Harijan of this village also have the highest burden of debt.

Though some obvious changes in the interactional and behavioural pattern between the high castes *vis-a-vis* the low castes have occurred during recent years, the basic structure of the society based on caste stratification remains unchanged. It is interesting to note that though the low castes are bitter about the existence of high and low castes and the social discrimination made against them by the upper castes, they also maintain caste distance among themselves fairly rigidly.

The concentration of land among a few persons and its absence among so many others has created a wide economic gulf between the rich and the poor. While analysing the causes of poverty on the psychological level the weaker section seems to be swayed by a fatalistic attitude, living in a state of poverty and social weakness for centuries. They seem to possess a very 'limited aspiration'. Of course, sometimes, the youth maintain that if they receive cultivable land, their condition might be improved. Education is also viewed by some as another important factor that might change their fortune.

The dominant section in general hold the view that weaker soction's condition especially those of the Harijan cannot be improved. Even if the Harijan are given land, they would not be able to keep it with them because they lack proper means for cultivation. They cannot have large land holdings of their own as they do not have the purchasing capacity. Drinking rampant was also stated to be one of the important causes which contributed to their misery.

The poor Harijan not only lack resources and opportunities for going up they also lack a sincere drive for removing poverty. Poverty, thus, seems to be a self-perpetuating phenomenon.

REFERENCES

Beteille, Andre *Studies in Agrarian Social Structure*. Oxford University Press, London, 1974.

Fonseca, A.J.(ed) *Challenge of poverty in India*. Vikas Publication, Delhi, 1972.

Myrdal,Gunar *Challenge in the World Poverty*.

Nair, Kusum *Blossoms in the Dust*, London. 1961.

Singh, Tarlok *Poverty and Social Change in India*, Bombay, 1969.

Lay, Muni *Haryana : on High Road to Prosperity*, Vikas, 1974.

Minhas, B.S. *"Rural Development for Weaker Sections : Experience and Lessons"* in *Rural* Development for *Weaker Sections*, Bombay, 1974.

21

HEMA-REVELLY : A VILLAGE IN ANDHRA PRADESH

T.N.PANDIT

Andhra Pradesh, with an area of 2,75,209 Sq. Kms. and a population of 4,3502708 (Census 1971), is the fifth largest state in India. Contiguity to the sea has given the state nearly 1000 km. long coastline in the east. Andhra Pradesh was the first state in India to be created on linguistic basis. Originally it consisted of eleven districts of the coastal and Rayalaseema regions. In 1956, the state was enlarged to include nine Telugu speaking districts of erstwhile princely state of Hyderabad. These nine districts together constitute what is known as the Telangana region. Based on geographical, political, historical and cultural Telangana has a distinct personality as compared to the other two major regions of the state.

The field research on which this paper is based was conducted from March to August 1973 in a village, here named Hema-Revelly, in Mahbubnagar district in Telangana. Mahbubnagar District is situated south of the city and District of Hyderabad and is further bounded by Raichur and Gulbarga districts of Karnataka in the west and by the districts of Karnataka in the west and by the districts of Nalgonda, Guntur and Kurnool in the north east and south respectively.

With an area of 18258 Sq. Kms. and a population of over 19 lakhs (1971 figures), Mahbubnagar is one of the larger districts of Andhra Pradesh. (Dist. Stat. Officer : 1971). Though large rivers like Krishna, Dindi (a tributary of Krishna), and Tungabhadra flow through this district not much benefit is derived from these here although there were plans to make use of these waters to irrigate additional 60,000 acres of land.

Like the rest of Telangana it is relatively hot and dry area with a normal rainfall of 721.6 mm. The soil is mostly of red loamy (regard) with a sprinkling of the black cotton type (*chalka*). Nearly 50 per cent of the land is under cultivation.

The district is divided into 12 taluk that cover 1456 inhabited villages and 14 towns. Further there are 16 Development Blocks, 16 Panchayat Sammity and 754 Gram Panchayat.

Village Hema-Revelly belongs to Shadnagar taluk and is placed under Shadnagar Block and Panchayat Sammity.

Shadnagar taluk has an area of 1263 kms. and in 1961 had a population of about 1,44,000 which must have risen to nearly 1,75,000 by 1971 (growth rate for the district for the decennial 1961-71 has been + 21.31%). Shadnagar town, the taluk headquarters, is situated on the national highway and is about 57 kms. away from Hyderabad city. Hema-Revelly is about 65 km. from Hyderabad, about 28 kms. from Shadnagar, and 10 kms. off the national highway to which it is connected by a *kutcha* road that branches out from the latter at Balnagar village. Mahbubnagar town, the district headquarters, is about 53 kms. away from Hema-Revelly.

The regional centre of Anthropological Survey of India at Mysore had been entrusted with the responsibility of conducting field-studies in the four south Indian States. I chose Andhra Pradesh gladly though I did not have the advantage of knowing the regional language, Telugu.

The choice of Telangana was made on the basis of some historical reasons and operational advantage. Telangana had been the scene of a violent communist movement from 1948 to 1951. Certain degree of bilinguilism prevalent there also drew me to this area. Sections of population here speak both Telugu and Deccani (Urdu), especially the upper caste educated groups and the Muslim. With my knowledge of Urdu this was of some advantage to me.

On the face of it any district of Telangana seemed as good as any other to study the theme of "weakness and dominance" in the backdrop of rural poverty in the region. However, Mahbubnagar was finally chosen because of the relatively high incidence of landless labourers i.e. 17.5 per cent (Census 1961 figures) and the very helpful attitude of the district officials towards my work. The relative population of landless labourers was treated as a good indicator of the relative population of the weaker sections. Besides, different parts of the district had suffered drought conditions in varying degree for the third year in succession. This we thought might have given a greater edge to the "weak-dominant" syndrome and naturally would contribute to greater clarity in our observations.

Shadnagar taluk was highly recommended by the district officials as this had received some early and special attention with regard to development activity and the establishment of Panchayati Raj and as such was generally regarded as a progressive taluk. Since we were also interested in studying the impact of developmental activity on the "weak - dominant" situation, it was essential that the area of our study should in an appreciable measure be exposed to it. Hence the suggestion was accepted.

II

Selection of the village needed care as it had to meet with several criteria such as :

1. It had to be a multi caste village with high and low castes being properly represented.
2. Its population had to be around 1000 or so.
3. It had to be fairly representative of the area.
4. It had to be away from a city or a major town to have retained its rural character in all important respects.
5. It must have witnessed some developmental activities.
6. It had to provide reasonably good activities for field work.

Making Shadnagar a base, we visited seven villages to gather first hand impressions and information. After comparison of information we chose Hema-Revelly which met all our requirements in good measure and the villagers too generally welcomed our presence amongst them with varying degrees of comprehension regarding the purpose of our study and investigations.

Hema-Revelly has 22 *jatis* (caste) ranging between high and low. The population turned out to be 1422 (714 males and 708 females). The most dominant caste (*kulam*) is the Reddy and there are three Harijan castes. In economic terms the villagers can be divided into the rich, well off, moderately well off, poor, and very poor. The village has electricity, a milk centre, a veterinary dispensary, a family planning center-cum-dispensary, a senior basic school, and a privately owned rice and flour mill etc. The village had been the home of the old *deshmukh* (*Jagirdar*) of the area and by all accounts it is an old settlement, though its exact antiquity could not be traced. The village is connected with the main road (national highway) at Balanagar by a 10 km. motorable but unpaved road. The normal mode of transport and transportation on this road is by bullock carts which sometimes go beyond Balanagar with grains etc. Milkvan comes to the village to collect milk and sometimes private trucks and hired buses ply on it.

III

The field-work was done for about six months from early March to end of August (in 1973). Except for two or three short breaks for visits to Shadnagar, Hyderabad, and Mysore the stay in the village was continuous. We stayed in a room at the edge of the village. During our stay we visited every household in the village several times, had long chats with many of the villagers in their homes, in the shops, in the Panchayat ghar, in our room and out in the fields. The meetings were both with groups and individuals of the same *kulam* or of various *kulam*. Often we found it profitable to talk to people of different *kulam* separately. That way the people tended to be more frank and forthright in their views about others. Sometimes we joined the *bhajan meeting* where members of the clean castes gathered for prayers and for singing *bhajan*. Travelling by bullock carts or on foot we spent time with the cultivators and the labourers in the fields. We also participated in folk singing and dancing sessions held in various parts of the village where members of some clean castes joined with the Harijan to dance and sing. We also attended marriage ceremonies of various castes including the Harijan. We made it a point to visit the *Harijan-wada* almost daily to keep in touch with them. We also chatted and played games with the school children sometimes. It was in this manner and through this kind of participant-observation with members of all *kulam*, children of all ages that we gained the confidence of the villagers and an insight into their life, social, and religious practices and their aspirations.

This work was supplemented by formal individual and group interviews, direct observation and case-studies, information being noted on a diary or sometimes on a taperecorder (lesser reliance was placed on the latter because the informants sometimes lost their spontaneity on seeing the small mike and recorder). However, most of the quantitative data regarding household census, demography, land ownership, literacy, assets, income, expenditure, and indebtedness were collected with the help of mainly two kinds of schedules. Additional nine schedules were canvassed in about 50 households. Quite often, supplementary information, was also noted down in the schedules.

Visits were also paid to nearby villages and hamlets to get a feel of their relationships with the main village. Information was also collected at Shadnagar, Mahbubnagar, and Hyderabad.

The information regarding age and assets, income and expenditure may not be accurate because of the well-known difficulties encountered by most field-workers studying Indian villages.

IV*

1

Hema-Revelly, a village having 1420 people is situated in Mehboobnagar district of the Andhra Pradesh. It has 23 different castes. The settlement is compact and shows division on caste lines.

On the basis of ritual status the whole population in Hema-Revelly can be conceived of as farming three segments, the lowest being the Harijan. The contrast between the living areas of the upper and lowest segment is clear. Literacy is high among the people of higher segment which has enabled them to achieve some degree of occupational mobility. But literacy and occupational mobility for the people in lower segment has been nominal. Reddi from the upper caste alone control 65 per cent of land of the village whereas the Harijan who form about 30 per cent of total population of the village have only six per cent of land with them. Since the area is drought prone having a well is a definite asset. But digging a good well costs around 12,000 to 15,000 rupees and a mechanised well costs more than that. In Hema Revelly 88 per cent of the mechanised wells were owned by the people of the upper segment. The same pattern continues in the distribution of live stock. Incidentally the village belongs to the 'progressive' taluk of the district. Most of the development programmes have benefitted the people of upper segment and more particularly one single household belonging to

---

1. * *Editor's Note*:

Due to various reasons the author was not in a position to complete reporting and submit a finished paper. Section IV of the present report has been adapted from Dr. P. K. Misra's general discussion on the "Weaker Sections in South Indian Villages". To a patient reader this and the unanalysed tables will supplement valuable information.

upper segment, who is the ex-Deshmukh of the village. Nearly 1/6 of the fertilizers, insecticides etc., allotted to the village are utilised by this household.

TABLE 1: Distribution of occupations, households, population, and land

Clusters	Sl. no.	Name of Kulam/ Jati	Traditional occupation	No. of house-holds	Popula-tion	Land owned (in acres)
A (Three)	1.	Komati	Traders	1	9	Nil
	2.	Lingayat	Traders & Farmers	7	39	66
	3.	Reddy	Farmers	49	284	1760
B (Seven)	4.	Aiyavaru	Low Category Temple Priest	1	2	4
	5.	Ausula	Goldsmiths	3	17	Nil
	6.	Kammari	Blacksmiths	2	8	2
	7.	Vodla	Carpenters	7	30	12.5
	8.	Kattika	Butchers	3	24	55
	9.	Gauda	Toddy-tappers	14	71	143
	10.	Turaka/ Muslims	Petty traders/ Public servants	14	78	33
C (Six)	11.	Bogam	Temple servants & Debadasis	2	8	45
	12.	Muthirashi	Hunters and fishers and village servants	28	134	39.5
	13.	Kuruva	Sheep & goatherds and blanket makers	11	45	4.5
	14.	Golla	Shepherds & milk vendors	21	109	192
	15.	Kummari	Potters	6	38	22
	16.	Bhata-Raju	Bards	2	8	9
D (Three)	17.	Mangali	Barbers	1	10	5
	18.	Chakali	Washermen	6	35	13
	19.	Vodderu	Stone-breakers	5	41	26
E (Three)	20.	Mala	Agricultural labourers, grave-diggers & removers of dead dogs	18	71	40
	21.	Madiga	Agricultural labourers, remove dead cattle & make shoes	75	339	104.5
	22.	Baindla	Village musicians & ritual specialists for Melas & Madigas	4	22	4.5
Total	22			280	1422	2580.5

TABLE 2: Distribution of literacy by cluster and sex (population below 5 years excluded)

Cluster	Male			Female			Overall literacy
	No.	No. of literates	%	No.	No. of literates	%	%
A	146	106	73	147	85	58	65
B	99	62	63	106	29	27	44
C	153	26	17	133	4	3	10
D	33	3	9	39	0	0	4
E	193	8	4	186	0	0	2
Total	624	205	33	611	118	19	26

	Total population (5 years & above)	=	1235
	Total No. literates	=	323
	Literacy rate for the village	=	26.11%
	Males	=	32.85%
	Females	=	19.31%
	Literacy rate in Andhra Pradesh	=	24.57%
	Males	=	53.18%
	Females	=	15.25%
	Other South Indian States Literacy rate in Karnataka	=	31.52%
	Tamilnadu	=	39.46%
	Kerala	=	60.42%
India	Overall literacy	=	29.46%
	Males	=	39.45%
	Females	=	18.72%

Source: For information on South Indian States and India : Census of India 1971).

TABLE 3: Levels of educational achievement by cluster and sex

Cluster	Male					Female				
	B.A. & above	High school	Middle school	Primary school	Total	B.A. & above	High school	Middle school	Primary school	Total
A	6	25	7	68	106	1	9	14	61	85
B	0	6	9	47	62	0	0	1	28	29
C	0	0	1	25	26	0	1	0	3	4
D	0	0	1	2	3	0	0	0	0	0
E	0	0	3	5	8	0	0	0	0	0
Total	6	31	21	147	205	1	10	15	92	118

TABLE 4: Distribution of school going children

Cluster	Population	%	1973-74 Admission time		1972-73 Admission time		1972-73 Examination time		1972-73 % of dro-ponts
			No. of children	%	No. of children	%	No. of children	% of total	
A	332	23.3	80	51.6	76	50.3	49	66.2	36
B	230	16.2	53	34.2	46	30.4	21	28.4	54
C	342	24.0	10	6.4	17	11.3	3	4.0	82
D	86	6.0	3	1.9	4	2.6	0	0.0	100
E	432	30.4	9	5.8	8	5.3	1	1.3	88
Total	1422	100	155	100	151	100	74	100	51

TABLE 5: Distribution of school girls

Cluster	Population of Women	%	1973-74 session Admission time No. of girls	%	1972-73 session Admission time No. of girls	%	1972-73 session Examination time No. of girls	%	1972-73 % of dropouts
A	169	23.9	44	73.3	37	63.8	24	92.3	35.1
B	117	16.5	13	21.6	13	22.4	2	7.7	84.6
C	166	23.4	2	3.3	5	8.6	0	0.0	100
D	46	6.5	1	1.6	2	3.4	0	0.0	100
E	210	29.6	0	0.0	1	1.7	0	0.0	100
Total	708	49.8	60	38.7	58	38.4	26	35.1	55.2

TABLE 6: Ownership of agricultural land by socio-ritual status

Cluster	Households		Population		Total land owned	% of land owned	Land owned per head	Socio-ritual status
	No.	Average membership	No.	%				
A	57	5.9	332	23.3	1826 acres	70.0	5.5 acres	High
B	44	5.2	230	16.2	250 acres	9.7	1.0 acres	Medium
C	70	4.9	340	24.0	319 acres	12.3	0.9 acres	Low medium
D	12	7.1	86	6.0	44 acres	1.8	0.5 acres	Low
E	97	4.4	432	30.4	149 acres	5.7	0.3 acres	Very low
Total	280	5.0	1420	100	2588 acres	100	1.8 acres	

TABLE 7: Ownership of wet agricultural land

Cluster	Population %	Total land owned	Percentage
A	23.3	220 acres	63.2
B	16.2	41 acres	11.8
C	24.0	50 acres	14.0
D	6.0	13 acres	3.7
E	30.4	24 acres	6.9
Total	100	348 acres	100

(a) Total agricultural land = 2580.5 acres
(b) Area of natural wet agricultural land = 348 acres (13.4%)
(c) Area of well irrigation land = 302 acres (11.7%)
(d) Area of dry agricultural land = 1938 acres (74.9%)

TABLE 8: Distribution of landholdings by households and cluster

Nature land holding Cluster	Large		Medium		Small		Very small		Landless or near landless		Total Households	
	15 acres & above		10 to under 15 acres		5 to under 10 acres		2 to under 5 acres		0 to under 2 acres			
	No. of household	%	No.of household	%	No.of household	%	No.of household	%	No. of households	%	No.of house-hold	%
A	35	76.0	7	53.0	8	26.6	2	4.2	5	3.5	57	20.3
B	7	15.2	0	0.0	2	6.6	7	14.9	30	20.5	44	15.7
C	4	8.7	4	30.7	7	23.3	23	49.0	32	22.2	70	25.0
D	0	0.0	1	7.7	3	10.0	1	2.1	5	3.5	12	4.3
E	0	0.0	1	7.7	10	33.3	14	29.8	72	50.0	97	34.6
Total	46	14.6	13	4.6	30	10.7	47	16.8	144	51.4	280	100

TABLE 9: Ownership of irrigation wells

Cluster	Mechanised wells using electricity		Using kerosene oil		Ordinary wells		Total		Agricultural area irrigated	
	No. covered	Area covered	No. covered	Area	No.	Area	No.	%	Acres	%
A	29	178 acres	7	40 acres	1	4 acres	37	64.8	222 acres	73.5
B	2	12 acres	0	0	0	0	2	3.8	12 acres	4.0
C	1	6 acres	0	0	7	34 acres	8	15.0	40 acres	13.0
D	0	0	0	0	3	11 acres	3	5.7	11 acres	3.6
E	1	0	0	0	2	12 acres	3	5.7	17 acres	5.6
Total	35	196 acres	7	40 acres	13	61 acres	53	100	302 acres	100

TABLE 10: Distribution of livestock

Cluster	Cows and buffaloes		Goat & sheep	Fowls
	No.	%		
A	457	56.9	169	218
B	57	7.0	55	111
C	148	18.3	305	16
D	44	5.4	33	17
E	100	12.4	38	30
Total	806	100	600	392

TABLE 11: Income, assets and indebtedness (1972-73)

Cluster	Average annual income (approximate)		Average value of Assets per house hold (approximate in rupees)	Average indebtedness per household (in rupees)
	Per household (in rupees)	Per capita (in rupees)		
A	4464	757	7,057	1,667
B	1756	336	1,865	275
C	1184	244	768	210
D	1022	141	1,445	737
E	825	185	448	141

A. Average Annual Income per household = Rs. 1810
B. Average annual per capita income = Rs. 356

22

VITHALGERA : A VILLAGE IN NORTH KARNATAKA

S.G. MORAB

Introduction

The problem of poverty is not peculiar to India alone. In advanced industrial countries like the United States and Britain there are a considerable number of people living below subsistenced standards (Townsend, 1970; ix). Infact, the seriousness of poverty made the U.S. Government to declare a formal "War of poverty" with its Economic Opportunities Act of 1964 (Harp and Hofley, 1971; 15). Not long ago, in India, a call "Garibi Hatao" (removal of poverty) was given by the Prime Minister, Smt. Indira Gandhi.

Anthropologists and sociologists were more concerned with rural social stratification during 1960s. Since 1970 onwards, however, there has been a spurt in the studies on poverty. In this regard, Dandekar and Rath's work on *Poverty in India* may be considered as a pioneering study. Poverty is socio-economic phenomena and hence the entire problem of poverty and consequently of weakness of people have to be viewed from a broader framework of economic, socio-cultural and political dimensions. The Anthropological Survey of India had proposed intensive village studies in many parts of India with a view to bring into relief the nature and extent of weakness in rural India and also how it is perpetuated.

A village in Karnataka was intensively studied with this broad objective. Fieldwork for the study was conducted during 1973 in the village for a period of more than six months (15-2-73 to 24-8-73) and subsequently a short revisit to the area for 3 weeks (18-12-74 to 5-1-75) was made. During the initial phase, the fieldworker had to face several difficulties as the area then was affected by severe drought. Attempts of the field worker to stay nearer the settlements of labour castes was met with hostile responses by some individuals of higher castes and belonging to well-to-do families. Certain timely actions, like starting of the soil conservation work and opening up of a fodder centre by the government for which the field worker had met the concerned authorities, were taken. It had helped to establish good rapport with the poorer sections to collect the data.

The data was collected by observation, intensive interview and case studies. A few charts to give quantitative data were also used.

The Area

The Bidar District in North Karnataka was in the erstwhile Nizam's territory of Hyderabad State which was annexed with the Indian Union in 1948. The land is mainly dry and rainfed. The crops grown are chiefly groundnut, pulses and millet (*jowar*). Prior to the abolition of Zamindary, most of the village lands were in the control of Deshmukh of Chitguppa, a sub-taluk place situated about twelve miles, but the tenants had acquired full rights and become permanent owners after the Zamindary abolition. The numerically dominant people in the district are a mixed one. They belong to Lingayat, Kurubagond, Kabbaliga, Harijan, and Maratha. Muslims are also in significant number.

The Village

Vithalgera (pseudonym) village is situated about 22 kms from Humnabad, a taluk town in Bidar District which could be approached by a *kachcha* road connected to the Sholapur-Hyderbad national highway.

Population

The village has a population of 1067 distributed in 137 independent households and in 16 communities as shown in Table 1.

Table 1 indicates that numerically the Kurubagond and Kabbaliga are dominant with 24.6 and 16.9 per cent respectively. Due to their preponderance, the village is referred to as the 'Kuruba-Kabbaligara Uru' in common parlance. The four scheduled castes are Christian Madaru, Dhor, Hindu Madaru, and Holeya, who constitute 23.8 per

TABLE 1: Distribution of the population by community and traditional occupation

Sl No.	Community (Alphabetical order)	Traditional occupation	No.of households	Percentage	Population	Percentage
1.	Banajiga (Lingayat)	Trade and agriculture	4	2.1	30	2.8
2.	Brahmin	Non priestly; Landlord (supervision of land)	3	1.6	14	1.3
3.	Christian Madaru	Agricultural labour & village functionary	9	4.8	64	6.0
4.	Dhor (Sc)	Agricultural labour & leather worker	1	0.5	5	0.5
5.	Hindu Madaru	Agricultural labour & village functionary	16	8.6	69	6.5
6.	Holeya	-do-	18	9.6	116	10.8
7.	Jangam (Lingayat)	Priestly & agriculture	8	4.3	41	3.8
8.	Illiga	Toddy tapping & selling	1	o.5	7	0.7
9.	Kabbaliga	Agriculture	35	18.7	180	16.9
10.	Kudu Vokkal-iga (Lingayat)	Landlord (Supervision of land)	3	1.6	14	1.8
11.	Kumbar	Pottery	6	3.2	36	3.4
12.	Kurubagond	Agriculture, sheep rearing & blanket weaving	42	22.5	263	24.6
13.	Muslim	Agriculture & agricultural labour	22	11.8	110	10.3
14.	Panchal	Carpentry	6	3.2	39	3.7
15.	Varik	Barber	3	1.6	19	1.8
16.	Waddar	Stone cutter	10	5.4	60	5.6
	Total	187	100.0	1067	100.0	

cent of the population. I am referring these people in a generic term as Harijan. The Waddar, once a nomadic group, have settled down in the village, although on many occasions they go to other places in search of seasonal work. They comprise five to six per cent. The servicing castes are the carpenter, potter, and Lingayat barber who form 8.7 per cent. In some other villages, the Lingayat are found in large number. But in Vithalgera, they are 7.9 per cent distributed in three castes, viz. Jangam, Kudu Vokkaliga, and Banajiga. There is only one Brahmin family but this family has divided itself into three nuclear households about a decade ago, obviously to effect separation of property. There is the case of an Illiga household, which migrated to the village two years ago from Chitguppa for doing the work of toddyselling.

The social layout indicates that there are clear cut boundaries for certain communities. For instance, the Holeya and Madaru (both Hindu and Christian) have their own separate streets called as *holageri* (for Holeya) and *madargeri* (for Madaru). Similarly the Waddar have their own street (*waddargeri*). These communities are supposed to be living outside the village (*uru horaginavaru*) and all others belong to the village proper (*uru olaginavaru*). Though in terms of physical proximity the distance is very little between those who live outside and those who are in the village, there is considerable social distance.

The service castes like the potter, carpenter, and barber live in a separate street (*aagarara beedi*) which is close to the centre of the village. In the central portions, high castes like the Brahman, Lingayat, reside who are surrounded by the Kurubagond and Kabbaliga on either side respectively. The Muslim live close to the Kurubagond [1] and Kabbaliga.

There are separate wells for drinking water for the Holeya, Madiga, and Waddar for their exclusive use. Even during drought when the wells of the Holeya had dried up, the wells of the other community i.e. Madaru was not made use of, as it was against custom. The government had provided a borewell then, which eased the situation. The Waddar were previously not allowed to draw water from the wells of the Kurubagond. During drought I observed that they were permitted to draw water for the first time. Though the Kurubagond could not give any satisfactory answer for this sudden change, I gathered that although the Waddar were regarded as unclean, they were not untouchable like the Harijan. When the Waddar settled near the Kurubagond street, there was no opposition. Many of the higher castes have their own family wells and where there is no well water is drawn from wells belonging to any community. For instance, water from the well of a Muslim was freely drawn by the Jangam, Kurubagond, and barber.

Economic Dimension

Agriculture provides the basic subsistence to villagers. Most of the occupations, therefore, revolve round farming. There are also service castes who are bound to their patrons. Besides agriculture, the other main economic pursuits are blanket weaving, stone-cutting, masonry, etc.

Occupation

The data from the household survey on primary occupations is given in Table 2. The table shows the highest percentage is of the non-workers (32%), followed by agricultural labour (23%), household work by women (12%), and agriculture (10%). Out of the remaining 23, six per cent are school going, other six per cent tend cattle, and the remaining 11 per cent do miscellaneous jobs. One important point that is revealed from the table is that nearly 56 per cent of the people in the village are those who lack sufficient capacity to earn, being engaged in household, school going activities, and consisting of olds, infants, and invalids. In other words, they are dependents. The earner-dependent ratio is 44:56.

Communitywise analysis shows that mostly the Brahman and some families of Jangam, Kabbaliga, and Kudu Vokkaliga are engaged in the supervision of land which means agriculture is done by hired labour. The Kurubagond and Kabbaliga have a high percentage as agriculturists i.e., self cultivators. The first two categories of occupations are considered as superior. Agricultural labour is considered inferior to agriculture. Doing agriculture by oneself has connotation of being in possession of land and bullocks, which provide social status. Occupations like village service rendered by the Harijan, the Dhor, and barber are regarded as low.

It may be seen from Table 2 that nearly 23 per cent are agricultural labourers. Among them the highest is that of the Harijan with about 47 per cent that is, nearly half of the entire agricultural labour force. The Kabbaliga have 23 per cent agricultural labourers while Kurubagond and Muslim have nearly 13 per cent each. Among

TABLE 2: Occupational distribution of the population by communitywise

Occupations / Communities	Banajiga (Lingayat)	Brahman	Christian Madaru	Dhor	Hindu Madaru	Holeya	Jangam (Lingayat)	Iliga	Kabbaliga	Kuduvokka (Lingayat)	Kumbar	Kurubagond	Muslim	Panchal	Varik	Waddar	Total population and percentage
1	2	3	4	5	6	7	8	9	10	11	12	13	14	15	16	17	18
1. Supervision of land (No manual work)	—	3 (42.8)	—	—	—	—	1 (14.3)	—	2 (28.6)	1 (14.3)	—	—	—	—	—	—	7 (0.66)
2. Agriculture	6 (5.6)	—	—	—	1 (0.9)	—	11 (10.3)	—	27 (25.3)	3 (2.8)	—	40 (37.4)	16 (14.9)	1 (0.9)	2 (1.9)	—	107 (10.04)
3. Agricultural Labour	1 (0.4)	—	33 (13.6)	1 (0.4)	34 (14.0)	47 (19.3)	1 (0.4)	—	56 (23.0)	—	—	31 (12.9)	33 (13.6)	—	4 (1.6)	2 (0.2)	243 (22.78)
4. Farm Servant	—	—	1 (5.6)	1 (5.6)	3 (16.7)	3 (16.7)	—	—	—	—	1 (5.6)	5 (27.6)	4 (22.2)	—	—	—	18 (1.67)
5. Tending Animal	—	—	5 (8.8)	—	6 (10.5)	8 (14.0)	—	—	3 (5.3)	—	3 (5.3)	19 (33.3)	8 (14.0)	—	—	5 (8.8)	57 (5.34)
6. Household Work	8 (6.1)	3 (2.3)	3 (2.3)	—	1 (0.8)	2 (1.5)	10 (7.6)	2 (1.5)	20 (15.3)	3 (2.3)	—	47 (35.9)	6 (4.6)	9 (6.9)	2 (1.5)	15 (11.4)	131 (12.28)
7. Non-Worker (old, children etc.)	10 (2.9)	5 (1.5)	15 (4.4)	3 (0.9)	18 (5.3)	43 (12.6)	15 (4.4)	4 (1.2)	59 (17.2)	3 (0.9)	13 (3.8)	79 (23.1)	40 (11.7)	7 (2.0)	6 (1.7)	22 (6.4)	342 (32.06)
8. Going to School/College	3 (4.5)	2 (2.9)	5 (7.3)	—	6 (8.8)	5 (7.3)	2 (2.9)	—	9 (13.3)	4 (5.9)	—	17 (25.0)	2 (2.9)	9 (13.3)	4 (5.9)	—	68 (6.37)
9. Weaving and Sheep rearing	—	—	—	—	—	—	—	—	—	—	—	18 (100.00)	—	—	—	—	18 (1.67)
10. Service, Govt., Private	1 (33.3)	1 (33.3)	—	—	—	—	—	—	1 (33.3)	—	—	—	—	—	—	—	3 (0.28)
11. Servicing (Carpentry, Pottery and Barber	—	—	—	—	—	—	—	—	—	—	19 (61.3)	—	—	11 (35.3)	1 (3.2)	—	31 (2.9)
12. Flour Mill	—	—	—	—	—	—	—	—	—	—	—	2 (100.0)	—	—	—	—	2 (0.19)
13. Masonry	—	—	—	—	—	7 (100.0)	—	—	—	—	—	—	—	—	—	—	7 (0.66)
14. Stone cutting	—	—	—	—	—	—	—	—	—	—	—	—	—	—	—	16 (100.0)	16 (1.50)
15. Trading etc. (Not included in 1-14)	1 (5.9)	—	2 (11.8)	—	—	1 (5.9)	1 (5.9)	1 (5.9)	3 (17.6)	—	—	5 (29.3)	1 (5.9)	2 (11.8)	—	—	17 (1.59)
Total	30	14	64	5	69	116	41	7	180	14	36	263	110	39	19	60	1067 (100.0)

the farm servants 39 per cent belong to the Harijan. The Kurubagond and Muslim have about 28 and 22 per cent respectively. Mostly young boys are engaged for tending cattle on a very meagre remuneration. It may be noted that nearly 33 per cent each of the Harijan and Kurubagond youngsters tend cattle and the proportion for the Muslim is 14 per cent. Most of the service castes like the carpenter, potter, barber, and also the Kurubagond and Waddar have retained their traditional occupation.

The traditional patron-client relationship between the various service castes have been breaking down. The carpenter, especially, were not enthusiastic to maintain ties with smaller land holders. Some of the bigger land-holders want to pay their artisan client in cash in lieu of kind as the price of grains has increased enormously. The quality is also reduced. Therefore the artisans prefer job-work instead of the yearly contract work. The worst affected is the barber. Many of the patrons would go to towns for hair cut. A few well to-do-individuals of high castes still seek services of the barber, but this does not give him enough work. Members of his family may have to go in for wage labour. Traditionally, all the service castes were given *inam* (service) lands for which they did not have to pay taxes. Even now they enjoy that land. Because of fragmentation at different generations, there are smaller land holdings and hence this situation has put them into difficulties. It was observed that some of the service castes were going in for labour work, which they never did previously.

Landholding and its Extent

In Bidar district, three fold classification of land ownership is made for the purpose of granting development loans by the Small Farmers Development Agency (SFDA), CO-operative Banks and Cooperative societies etc., i.e. 1.Marginal Farmers are those who own less than 2 1/2 acres; 2.Small Farmers having land between 2 1/2 acres and 10 acres; and 3. Those owning more than 10 acres are Big Farmers. In view of the dry nature of the land, the limits indicated above are too small. My enquiries have shown that at least five acres may be considered as somewhat economically viable unit. During the normal year, the production and expenditure on land measuring five acres would be as given below :

A. *Kharif crops:*

(i) Groundnuts.	
Usually for 5 acres,	
2 quintals. Approximate value	Rs. 1,200
(ii) Pulses like green gram and black gram.	
3 quintals.	Rs. 300

B. *Rabi crops:*

(i) Millet (Jowar). 8 Quintals.	
Approximate value	Rs. 1,200
(ii) Toor pulse. 2 Quintals.	
Approximate value	Rs. 300
	Rs.3,000

Expenditure:

(i) Manure costs and transporting. approx.	Rs. 200
(ii) Labour for ploughing,	
wedding and other jobs. "	Rs. 100
(iii) Harvesting-All the crops. "	Rs. 250
(iv) Fodder and bullocks. "	Rs. 150
	Rs. 700

Production	Rs. 3,000
Expenditure	Rs. 700
	Rs. 2,300

Thus, normally, a farmer is supposed to get a net amount of Rs.2,300. There could, however, be variations depending upon the intensity of agricultural operations, use of manure, less menacc of pests and good rains.

Basing on the above calculations, we may regard an amount of five acres as a viable unit which would usually meet the minimum basic needs of a household with five members on an average. Those who have less than this amount, may, therefore, be regarded as *Marginal Farmers*. Those who own more than 5 acres and less than 10 acres may be considered as *Small Farmers*. Further two categories of

TABLE 3: Classification and distribution of landholdings into different categories by community

Occupations *Communities*	Banajiga (Lingayat)	Brahman	Christian Madaru	Dhor	Hindu Madaru	Holeya	Jangam (Lingayat)	Iliga	Kabbaliga	Kudu-Vokkaliga (Lingayat)	Kumbar	Kurubagond	Muslim	Panchal	Varik	Waddar	Total with percentage	
1	2	3	4	5	6	7	8	9	10	11	12	13	14	15	16	17	18	
1 2	1 2	1 2	1 2	1 2	1 2	1 2	1 2	1 2	1 2	1 2	1 2	1 2	1 2	1 2	1 2	1 2	1 %	2 %
1. Upto 5 acres (Landless & Marginal Farmers)																		
a. Landless	1 7	— —	5 38	— —	6 20	5 28	— —	1 7	6 24	— —	1 4	4 17	— —	— —	— —	9 49	41 21.9	210 19.7
b. Upto 1 acre	— —	— —	— —	— —	— —	3 17	— —	— —	8 26	— —	— —	3 10	— —	— —	1 4	— —	15 8.0	57 5.3
c. Above 1 acre & upto 5 acres	— —	— —	4 26	— —	8 36	10 71	— —	— —	9 55	— —	4 23	14 81	7 34	3 23	— —	— —	59 31.5	349 32.7
d. Above 3 acres & upto 5 acres	— —	— —	— —	— —	2 13	— —	1 2	— —	1 2	— —	1 9	11 67	4 18	— —	2 15	— —	22 11.6	126 11.8
2. 5 to 10 acres	1 7	— —	— —	— —	— —	— —	5 26	— —	3 19	— —	— —	4 39	8 42	2 11	— —	1 11	24 13.0	155 14.5
3. Above 10 & upto 20 acres	1 7	1 3	— —	1 5	— —	— —	2 13	— —	7 47	2 4	— —	6 49	— —	1 5	— —	— —	21 11.0	133 12.5
4. Above 20 acres	1 9	2 11	— —	— —	— —	— —	— —	— —	1 7	1 10	— —	— —	— —	— —	— —	— —	5 3.0	37 3.5
Total	4 30	3 14	9 64	1 5	16 69	18 116	8 41	1 7	35 18[illegible]	3 14	6 36	42 263	22 110	6 39	3 19	10 60	187 100.0	1067 100.0
Average acreage per household (in acres & guntas)	8.3 —	53.0 —	1.00 —	12.0 —	1.2 —	1.09 —	6.0 —	— —	5.21 —	30.27 —	2.07 —	5.0 —	5.13 —	9.07 —	3.0 —	0.32 —	— —	— —

Note: Columns 1 and 2 refer to the number of households and the population covered in them respectively.

TABLE 3a: Distributions of landholdings among household of different classes

Classes/ categories	Landholding (acres)	No. of households	Percentage of households
I	Landless and Marginal Farmers		
	(i) Landless	14	21.9
	(ii) upto 1 acre	15	8.0
	(iii) 1-3 acres	59	31.5
	(iv) 3-5 acres	22	11.6
	Total	137	73.0
II	Small Farmers (5-10 acres)	24	13.0
III	Big Farmers (10-20 acres)	21	11.0
IV	Very Big Farmers (Above 20 acres)	5	3.0
	Total	187	100.0

bigger farmers could be identified, that is, those having between 10 and 20 acres are *Big Farmers*, and the *Very Big Farmers* could be those having more than 20 acres. With this four fold classification the data on land holding is presented in Table 3 according to the various communities. The detailed land holdings given in Table 3 is retabulated into the above classes in Table 4.

Table 3a shows that nearly 73 per cent of the households are below the minimum land holdings, out of whom 22 per cent are landless. Nearly 39.5 per cent of the households hold land between one acre and three acres. On the other hand, five households are very big farmers. In, fact these five households (2 Brahman, 1 Kabbaliga, 1 Kudu Vokkaliga, and 1 Banajiga) own about 251 acres (i.e. 21 per cent) of the total cultivable land of the village. Table 3 shows that the Brahman and the Kudu Vokkaliga hold on an average 53 and 21 acres, (mostly fertile land (*kali regad*) per household respectively. It is interesting to note that the Brahman joint family had nearly 150 acres of land a decade ago and now due to partition the land is shared among the individual households. The Panchal (carpenter) and Banajiga have eight acres each while the Kurubagond, Jangam, and Muslim have about five to six acres. The Harijan (except the Dhor) and Waddar have very meagre land holding, i.e. the average household land holding is 1.10 and 0.32 respectively. In the case of the Waddar, they are almost landless except in one case. A Waddar happened to buy about seven acres with the help of the headman. The Harijan (Dhor) had traditionally acquired 11 acres of land but it is *lal kharab* (loose sandy soil with less fertility) land.

TABLE 4: Distribution of population in different income categories by community

Income catego- ries / *Commu- nity*	Banajiga (Linga- yat)		Brahman		Chris- tian Madaru		Dhor		Hindu Madaru		Holeya		Jangam (Ling- ayat)		Iliga		Kabba- liga		Kudu- Vokka- liga (Ling- ayat)		Kumbar		Kuru- bagond		Muslim		Pan- chal		Varik		Waddar		Total	
1	2		3		4		5		6		7		8		9		10		11		12		13		14		15		16		17		18	
	1	2	1	2	1	2	1	2	1	2	1	2	1	2	1	2	1	2	1	2	1	2	1	2	1	2	1	2	1	2	1	2	1	2
Upto Rs.100	1	7	—	—	2	21	—	—	2	10	2	16	—	—	—	—	4	26	—	—	1	5	1	3	—	—	1	9	—	—	1	10	15	107
101-200	—	—	—	—	5	34	1	5	10	44	14	81	—	—	1	7	14	63	—	—	5	31	16	111	10	62	2	15	2	11	7	30	87	494
201-300	1	9	—	—	2	9	—	—	3	14	2	19	—	—	—	—	3	6	—	—	—	—	9	53	5	27	1	6	1	8	2	20	30	171
301-400	1	7	—	—	—	—	—	—	1	1	—	—	3	15	—	—	2	12	—	—	—	—	5	31	4	17	1	4	—	—	—	—	17	87
401-500	1	7	—	—	—	—	—	—	—	—	—	—	2	11	—	—	—	—	—	—	—	—	2	3	1	3	—	—	—	—	—	—	6	24
501-600	—	—	—	—	—	—	—	—	—	—	—	—	—	—	—	—	—	—	—	—	—	—	4	30	—	—	—	—	—	—	—	—	4	30
601-700	—	—	—	—	—	—	—	—	—	—	—	—	1	8	—	—	—	—	—	—	—	—	—	—	1	1	—	—	—	—	—	—	2	9
701-800	—	—	—	—	—	—	—	—	—	—	—	—	1	2	—	—	2	14	—	—	—	—	2	13	—	—	—	—	—	—	—	—	5	29
801-900	—	—	—	—	—	—	—	—	—	—	—	—	—	—	—	—	1	9	—	—	—	—	—	—	—	—	—	—	—	—	—	—	1	9
901-1000	—	—	—	—	—	—	—	—	—	—	—	—	—	—	—	—	3	21	1	2	—	—	—	—	—	—	—	—	—	—	—	—	4	23
Above Rs.1000	—	—	3	14	—	—	—	—	—	—	—	—	1	5	—	—	6	29	2	12	—	—	3	19	—	—	—	5	—	—	—	—	16	84
	4	30	3	14	9	64	1	5	16	69	18	116	8	41	1	7	35	180	3	14	6	36	42	263	22	110	6	39	3	19	10	60	187	1067

Note: Column number 1 and 2 indicate the number of households and the population covered in the households respectively.

TABLE 4a: Distribution of households into different classes population showing percentage

Classes	Income categories in (rupees)	Sections (poor/rich)	No. of households covered	Population	Percentage of the population
I	Upto 400	Very poor	149	859	30.50
II	401 - 600	Poor	10	54	5.00
III	601 - 1000	Rich	12	70	6.50
IV	Above 1000	Very Rich	16	84	8.00
	Total		187	1067	100.00

Income

Prior to my study i.e. during the year 1972-73, the area was affected by drought which had continued with its severity. But the government tackled the issue of drought relief with much seriousness and had provided the people in the village and other places employment like road building, metal breaking and soil conservation work etc. Thus, the data on income of all earning members from each household accruing out of the economic activities were collected for the year 1972-73 (February- March). However, I may point out here that this may not exactly represent a picture of the normal year. In terms of income, perhaps, this drought year was able to provide employment to landless people to some extent which in a normal year, the people might not have much scope for rural employment.

Data on household income was collected and per capita income was calculated. As the averages were taken, no weightage to children and non-workers was given. the data is given in different income groups according to the various communities in Table 5.

It was considered useful to construct family monthly budget of a few people of the poorer section. When information on budgets were asked, it was not possible for them to exactly give such information. However, attempts to collect information on some families were made. The case of Shri Tukkapa of the Harijan (Holeya), a nearly landless household is cited here to know the pattern. The informant said that, for a family of two adult members and three young children usually his needs are as given below. He, however, cautioned that this budget may undergo changes depending upon increase of members, arrival of some guests, or any other extraneous circumstances.

TABLE 5: Family budget of a Harijan household

		Approx. Cost in May 1973.
1. Food — Millet (*jola* & Maize)	About 50 kgs of *jowar* & 5 kgs of Maize (for gruel and uppittu)	Rs. 96.00
2. Rice	About 5 kgs sometimes broken rice also used	Rs. 10.00
3. Pulses — *nenki, toor*, greengram etc.		Rs. 10.00
4. Jaggary, tea leaves etc.		Rs. 6.00
5. Oil (cooking groundnut).		Rs. 5.00
6. Kerosene Oil		Rs. 2.00
7. Vegetable (onion etc).		Rs. 2.00
8. Chillies, salt, spices, meat etc.		Rs. 15.00
9. Miscellaneous like *bidi* betel leaves, travelling etc.		Rs. 10.00
		Rs.156.00

(Usually articles are brought bit by bit)
Rs. 156 X 12 months = i.e. Rs. 1872.

Family budget of a Harijan household (Continued)
Other expenditures for the year

1. Clothes (on credit) (1 pair of dhoti, 2 shirts, 2 sarees, blouse pieces & dress of children).	Rs.150
2. Rituals (for festivals).	Rs. 50
3. Medical care.	Rs. 50
	Rs.250
Total expenditure for the household i.e., Rs. 1872 + Rs. 250 =	Rs. 2,122.

From the above family budget it may be seen that the per capita monthly expenditure workout to be more than Rs.400.00 i.e., nearly Rs. 424 (2122/5). Normally, people were expected to spend what they usually earned. Otherwise they incurred debt. We have already given the data on the incomes in table 4. It is surprised that an income of Rs. 2000.00 per annum for a household consisting of five members is not sufficient to meet the bare requirement as shown by the case illustrated above and hence, we may consider those whose income is Rs.2000.00 per annum or below as very poor. Poverty line may be considered at Rs 400.00 or less percapita annual income. Almost the same amount works out in the 2 case of other estimates. The Karnataka per capita income survey puts a daily income of Rs. 1.10 in rural areas as poverty line and this means the calculation per year would be Rs. 401.50. Dandekar and Rath (1971) fix the poverty line at Rs. 15.00 according to 1960-61 prices. If it is calculated for 1972-73, it may work out a little more than Rs. 30.00 per month, and for an year, it would work out more than Rs. 360.00 and nearly Rs. 400.00.

Table 5 shows that the percentage of people who are very poor, that is, who are living below poverty line is about 80 per cent. The estimates of Indian population living below the poverty line in rural areas differ.

TABLE 6: Percentage of rural population below the line of poverty

Year	Ojha (Rural)	Bardhan (Rural)	Minhas (Rural)	Dandekar and Rath (Rural)
1960-61	51.8	38.0	46.0	40.0
1967-68	70.0	53.0	37.1	40.0
Criteria of poverty line	Monthly per capita consumption Rs. 15-18 (1960-61 prices)	Monthly per capita consumption of Rs. 15 p.m. at 1960-61 prices	Monthly per capita consumptions of Rs.17 at 1060-61 prices	Rs. 15 per monthly per consumption (at 1960-61 prices)

Relevant Extract From: R.K. Sau, "Indian Economic Growth" *Economic & Political Weekly*, Annual, February, 1972, p. 371.

Having shown the very poor category of people we may also show other classes of people. Further classification may have some arbitrariness, but they help in analysis. Beside the bare minimum it is necessary for a household to spend some money on better quality of clothes, education, rituals, medical care etc. Hence those whose per capita annual income is between Rs. 401-600 may be considered as a category of poor people. Very poor (80.5%) and poor (5.0%) may be regarded as poorer sections. There are definitely certain households who are economically richer sections. Among them we may consider those between Rs. 601-1000 as rich (6.5%) and those above Rs.1000.00 as very rich (8.0%).

Organization of Agricultural Labour

There are three types of agricultural labourers. One is the employment of persons on yearly contract basis known as *chakri* (sometimes the word *noukri* is also used). There are persons who work in the fields of others on daily wages (*dinaguli*) and *bidiquli* (casual labour). The third type is called *guttige* which means a kind of contract for doing a particular fixed work. During harvests, especially, a group of people consisting of four to five persons may undertake *guttige* work, as remuneration may work out more if the contract is made properly. The daily wages for a man-day were Rs. 2.00 to 2.50 whereas women got Rs. 1.25 to 1.50 in 1973. During rush of work, however, wages may increase. For instance, when the present author was in the village in December 1974, the wages had been increased by about 50 to 30 per cent for men and women respectively due to the cane-cutting season. Weeding is a specialised work of women during rainy season but the wages are meagre. For a three hour weeding work, women get fifty paise. Many women belonging to landowning households also work on such occasions and earn extra money.

Agricultural labour as available during a normal year is given in Table 7.

It may be seen that employment in the field is available for about 6 & 1/2 months for men and five months for women. Some labourers were found to have a better expertise in certain agricultural operations like ploughing, and sowing, weeding etc., and they may get employment for longer period.

Farm Servants

The big and very big farmers employ farm servants on yearly contract basis. It is a full time job during day time and hence a farm servant would describe it as *chakri*. The payment varies from Rs. 300 to Rs. 500 to a farm servant with an additional terminal benefit of 32 local seers (about 70 kgs) of millet. During harvests, in case one worked at night shifts particularly during jaggery preparation, one is entitled for one maund of jaggery. No holidays are given. If one absented for any day, one has to work for additional days in lieu of such absence. The contracts for farm service are entered into either orally or by written agreement. Both the parties are free to terminate the contract of *chakri* any time after settling their accounts.

TABLE 7: Availability of labour work

Season	Agricultural operations	Work days		
		Man	Woman	
A. Summer				
April-May	Digging, harrowing, ploughing, manuring, levelling etc. (for *kharif* crop)	35	15	(mainly assisting men)
B. Rainy				
June-September	Ploughing, sowing, weeding etc.	50	40	(Sowing & Seeding)
October-November	Harvesting and preparing the land for Rabi. & sowing.	40	20	(Assisting in harvesting)
C. Winter				
December-March	Weeding. levelling, guarding, the crop harvesting etc.	75	70	(Weeding and assisting in harvesting)
Total		200	145	

At the time of my field-work I found that there were 18 farm servants. Usually, the landless or nearly landless take up *chakri*. Among them eight belonged to Harijan, four to Muslim, five to Kurubagond and one to Kumbar. *Chakri* is not regarded high when compared to the daily labour. In the former case, one is tied up for a fixed period and has no freedom, but in the other case, one worked for a specified time in a day. A farm servant, once in a while, has to hear abuses by their employers. Some may not like it. The farm servants working in the house of the village headman were unhappy because of the ill treatment and frequent abuses of the wife of the employer. Despite these difficulties there is some kind of security. For example, they may get some instant loans if required for any contingencies and against future adjustments of farm work. Therefore, some people would like to seek this type of job depending upon the financial difficulties of a person. It may be noted that usually people of higher and middle castes like the Brahman, Kabbaliga, and Lingayat do not go in for *chakri*.

Land Tenure

Those who have small quantities of land, say, two or three acres, ordinarily lease such land to others for cultivation on *char ane* (1/4th), *aath ane* (1/2th), *bara ane* (3/4th) share-cropping tenure. Some times a contract is made on the basis of a fixed yearly payment (*koulu*). Lands are leased on specific condition to vacate the possession whenever required by the owner of the land. Many a time, written agreements are made. It was observed that this system works out to the advantage of farmers who are either actual cultivators or get the work done through hired labour. Those who have more than five acres may need a few acres of additional land in order to make best use of the agricultural machinery. It was noted that most of the big and very big farmers maintained one or two pairs of bullocks[3] and arranged for cultivation of their own as well as tenure lands by employing hired labour and farm servants. Taking the share-cropping tenure data, it may be noted that out of 54 sample households, nearly 13 households having less than five acres had given their land to others for cultivation, and seven out of 14 having landless than five acres cultivated lands of other persons. This is indicative of an important fact that marginal farmers find their small land holding as uneconomic and non-viable and hence lease them to others and they take agricultural labour.

Small farmers having a pair of bullocks take the lands of others on share-cropping tenure. The tenure conditions vary according to the fertility of the soil. The share-cropper is known as the *palukar* and the employer is the *malik*(owner). These terms are used by the parties while referring to high caste people. There are cases of middle caste people like the Kurubagond who had taken lands of the Harijan, but in that case, the word *palukar* is avoided. Some of the farmers of Vithalgera have taken lands of others situated in the boundaries of other villages. Usually the cost of the agricultural operations and the yield are shared by the owner and the share-cropper. The land tax is given by the *malik*. The latter sees that in the land revenue records his name is retained as the owner as well as self cultivator.It is customary that owner of the land visits frequently his land given for share-cropping and at the time of the harvests, a member of the household keeps constant vigil so that the share-copper may not steal any grain or tell lies about the yield. In case of the absentee land-owner, the share-cropper is in an advantageous position as the former may not question the integrity in order to continue the sharecropping tenure.

Agricultural Innovation

The very big and big farmers generally use improved fertilizers like Urea, Super Phosphate and insecticides. In case of irrigated lands (there are a few acres of such land) fertilizers are required for crops like sugarcane, wheat, and hybrid maize. Such innovations to some extent trickle down to the small and marginal farmers who use insecticides for dry crops of pulses. Usually pulses are affected by pests and hence use of insecticides is in vogue. The marginal and small farmers cannot easily get fertilizers, insecticides etc., at the controlled rates as many do not have any contact by which they can get help. The bigger farmers use their contact to their advantage.

It was noted that as most of the land is dry, cultivation is done generally by the traditional method using local wooden ploughs and draught animals. With the supply of electricity in 1966,irrigation pump sets have been installed in the various wells. Altogether there were six pump sets in the village. Some of the small and marginal farmers were desirous of getting aid from cooperative banks which grant credit for digging wells and buying pump sets. Many are afraid of bearing the burden of expenditure on them which is quite high.

Land Reform

The Mysore Land Reforms Act has been passed recently (1974) with a view to putting ceiling on landholdings and redistribute excess lands, if any, to the scheduled castes and tribes, landless and other categories. According to the categories of land classification, the ceiling on dry areas having no assured sources of water from any government tanks and canals, lift irrigation system, etc., as specified in the Act (not to go into legal complexities) have to be taken as 54 acres. It is also possible that some provision to allot a few acres to any additional members in a family is made. If this were to be limit, there will not be a single case of a person holding lands over ceiling limit in the village, provided that those who are not in the village but who are personally cultivating their land in absentia are excluded. There are four such cases of the latter type. Two minor sons of a rich Kudu Vokkaliga are studying in Gulbarga in whose name there are lands. Two of the former Brahman village accountant's younger brothers have lands though they are away from the village doing other jobs. In my revisit in 1974, I was told of a land transaction wherein a rich man of the neighbouring village who has lands in Vithalgera had sold about 12 acres of land to a man who lives in a far off city, probably to avoid ceiling limit. In view of the legal complexities it is not sure if any land could come easily for redistribution, and even if it comes it is very meagre.[4]

Material Life Style and Consumption Pattern

The dwellings of the Harijan and Waddar are mostly small and thatched with zinc sheets. In many cases they are made of mud wells. Repairs are not made when needed, as they could hardly afford such repairs. Many of the dwellings of the Kabbaliga, Kurubagond, Panchal, Varik, and Muslim are also small but they are in good condition. The three very big farmers have specious well-built houses. Electricity is used by them for domestic purposes. The headman of the village (police *patil*) was thinking of rebuilding his old house for which he has stored necessary stones and expects to spend about Rs.10,000.

It may be observed that there are many household articles including jewellery which were inherited and gifted. Attempt to calculate the value may not give a correct picture because of their prestigious values attached to them. However, a cursory glance at the household articles shows that the majority of the Harijan, Waddar, and Muslim have very few articles of material possessions. The main reason for this was the extreme poverty. Another reason was that due to drought, many of them had sold away such articles like vessels, water pitcher, zinc sheets, gold and silver ornaments, etc. Only a few essential aluminium and earthen vessels are left with them. The contrast was quite evident in the case of the richer sections who possess large quantity of household articles worth thousands of rupees.

TABLE 8: Average monthly household expenditure on various items of different communities

Sl. No.	Occupations / Communities	Banajiga (Lingayat)	Brahmin	Christian Madaru	Dhor	Hindu Madaru	Holeya	Jangam (Lingayat)	Iliga	Kabbaliga	Kudu-Vokkaliga (Lingayat)	Kumbar	Kurubagond	Muslim	Panchal	Varik	Waddar
	1	2	3	4	5	6	7	8	9	10	11	12	13	14	15	16	17
1.	Rice	4.50	200.00[1]	1.50	—	4.56	3.90	8.16	1.25	19.85	72.00	3.75	6.07	4.21	4.50	5.25	8.75
2.	Millet	40.50	200.00[1]	63.33	—	27.25	56.75	95.66	83.00	86.85	300.00	64.00	94.68	63.66	54.50	44.75	74.66
3.	Liquor[3]	—	—	3.33	—	1.50	1.20	3.34[2]	—	1.00	—	0.25	1.15	0.16	—	—	5.00
4.	Misc.food articles	5.00	200.00	30.83	—	10.87	27.80	46.34	32.00	44.40	172.00	37.75	47.40	21.00	26.75	17.00	29.33
5.	Housing	2.00	75.00	1.00	—	2.12	6.00	3.12	5.00	4.10	17.00	2.50	2.10	1.33	2.50	1.75	0.83
6.	Education	1.00	210.00	—	—	2.50	7.20	6.00	—	4.00	117.00	—	8.70	0.50	9.00	5.25	—
7.	Medical	—	210.00	0.66	—	0.25	4.30	10.00	2.00	7.70	50.00	2.50	1.30	1.83	8.50	2.00	12.66
8.	Clothing	12.50	210.00	6.16	—	6.25	25.20	30.66	25.00	33.20	133.00	10.25	16.00	11.91	12.50	24.50	16.66
9.	Rituals[4]	—	—	0.33	—	—	—	12.50	—	2.60	—	1.00	28.30	—	4.00	1.25	8.33
10.	Conveyance	—	25.00	2.16	—	6.25	0.20	9.66	8.00	15.50	42.00	3.00	3.40	0.91	4.50	1.00	2.33
11.	Incidental	—	10.00	1.50	—	0.75	2.30	5.66	3.00	4.80	15.00	5.25	5.75	3.75	2.50	0.75	3.00

Note: 1. Information has exaggerated the expenditure.
2. The Lingayat Jangams are teetotaller and the persons included in the sample is an exception.
3. The data in this case was suppressed to a great extent resulting in underestimation.
4. Expenditure on marriage rituals is not included.

TABLE 9: Level of literacy among different communities

C MALE				FEMALE			
Classes and communities	Population	No. of literates	% age	Classes and Communities	Population	No. of literates	% age
I. No. literates and upto 10% literates (very low)				I. No. of literates & upto 10% literates Harijan			
1. Kumbar	19	—	—	(Christian Madaru)	30	—	—
2. Waddar	26	—	—	Kabbaliga	95	1	1.1
3. Harijan (Dhor)	2	—	—	Kumbar	17	—	—
4. Muslim	57	5	8.8	Jangam	25	2	8.0
5. Harijan (Holeya)	67	5	7.5	Harijan (Hindu Madaru)	31	—	—
II. Literacy 10-25% (Low)	38	8	21.1	Muslim	53	—	—
1. Harijan (Hindu Madaru)	136	28	20.6	Panchal	14	—	—
2. Kurubagond				Harijan (Dhor)	13	—	—
				Iliga	4	—	—
III. Literacy from 26-50% (high)							
1. Harijan (christian Madaru)	34	8	30.7				
2. Kabbaliga	85	28	32.9	Kurubagond	127	2	1.6
3. Jangam	16	7	43.8	Waddar	34	—	—
4. Kudu Vokkaliga	9	4	44.4	Harijan (Holeya)	49	—	—
5. Iliga	3	1	33.3	Kudu Vokkaliga	5	—	—
IV. Literacy above 50% (very high)				II. Literacy 10-25%			
1. Panchal	25	14	56.0	Brahmin	8	2	25.0
2. Brahmin	6	5	83.3	Varik	8	1	12.5
3. Banajiga	16	10	62.5	Banajiga	14	2	14.3
4. Varik	11	7	63.6	There are no 3rd & 4th Classes.			
Total	550	130	24.0	Total	527	10	1.9

Note: Literates are those who have studied or studying from first class in primary school upto college.

Food Expenditure Pattern

The staple food in the village is the millet (*jola*). The economically well-to-do household use rice in addition to the millet. Pulses, mainly the *togari* (dal) is taken. Poorer sections however, use a kind of pulse, *nenki*, a local variety. It is a cheap pulse and those who cannot afford to buy dal purchase *nenki*. In fact, *nenki* is given as fodder to cattle by the richer sections. Data on expenditure of 54 sample households were collected. For the purpose of monthly consumer expenditure the preceeding month was taken into consideration. For some articles, expenditure for a full year i.e., March 82 of February 1973 was taken. In the latter case the expenditure on each item was divided by 12 months so as to calculate average monthly expenditure. The 54 sample households were sorted out into various communities and average differential household expenditures on food, clothing, housing, education, medical, ritual, conveyance etc., are given in Table 7. The table reveals that the average monthly household expenditure for the communities like the Parijan, Kumbar, Iliga, Waddar, Varik, and Muslim are far less than for the communities like the Brahman, Kudu Vokkaliga, and Jangam. The Kudu Vokkaliga and Brahman particularly spent more on food, education, medicine and clothing compared to others and their decisive dominance is revealed here. There are, however, such communities like the Kabbaliga, Kurubagond, and Banajiga who fall in between these two broad categories of lower and higher expenditure pattern.

It is said that millet (*jola* or Maize) was considered inferior food. Poorer sections would say that they were living on *ambli* (gruel) to denote poor food. In fact, a Harijan elder told the present investigator that what their people ate everyday was gruel, a *saitan's* (devil) food, meaning unfit for general consumption. Rice, wheat, and sweet dishes are superior food. They are cooked on festival occasions and offered to deities. On Ugadi (new year's day) festival, although poorer sections cannot afford *holige* (sweet pudding) made of wheat, jaggery, and gram, unlike richer sections, they prepare *godi huggi* (sweetened wheat).

Vegetarian food is considered superior to the non-vegetarian food. Among the latter, beef and pork are treated as much inferior. A Harijan informant described his food containing beef was *galeeju uta* (a dirty meal), while a Waddar elder called his pork food as *kharab uta* (bad meal). Eating carcass of cattle is considered very much inferior. The Madaru lift the dead animals and even now they do it. It may be noted that about 15 years or so ago, many a Harijan belonging to the Madaru (both Hindu and Christian) stopped eating carcass. Some of the Christian among them began consuming pork, although they did not relish it. During the severe drought in 1973, almost all the Madaru ate carcass of animals which died in large number in the village. Consuming toddy and arrack is regarded as not good, although the Harijan and Waddar have them. Usually, the Waddar take toddy in plenty. Arrack is favourite of the Harijan. People, however, were reluctant to give information on consumption of beef, pork, and liquor. While, the Harijan, Waddar and other middle and lower castes took liquor, they considered it a bad habit, perhaps, mainly due to the influence of Veerasaivism which forbids people to consume liquor.

Indebtedness and Savings

Agriculturists are found tο take loans both in cash and kind and repaid the debt with interest. Before the sowing season commenced, loans in kind, usually groundnut seeds for Kharif sowing are taken and such a loan is repaid in kind with 50 per cent of the groundnut as interest. When calculated in terms of cash, the rate of interest is Rs. 2.00 per month for Rs. 100.00. Loans are also available for the farmers if they are members of any co-operative society. Sometimes *taccavi* loans and loans for buying bullocks etc., are granted by revenue authorities. But many do not go in for such official loans as they have to follow somebody of the village and spend some money for getting such a loan.

The data on indebtedness highlights the economic aspect. Many a time borrowing might not be a simple transaction. There could be multiple transactions. For instance, Shri Birgond of Kurubagond community had taken a loan of Rs. 300.00 worth groundnuts out of which he had given 1/4th quantity to Shri Sivappa. When the question of returning the loan came, Birgond turned to Sivappa who was reluctant to settle the accounts. Both had started quarreling on this count. Sivappa had given the groundnuts to a relative of his. The latter had not returned the loan and there was no immediate possibility of returning it due to his poverty conditions. Such cases occur and they cannot be explained in mere economic terms as they have bearing on caste and kinship. In view of the complex nature of borrowing, the quantitative data on indebtedness is not analysed here.

Caste Hierarchy

It has been already stated that there are marked boundaries for different communities especially the Harijan and Waddar. Traditionally these communities have not been ascribed equal statuses. Certain hierarchical order is conceived, although it is difficult to give the exact hierarchical rank to each group. Many of my informants stated that such criteria like tradition, food consumed, the occupation followed determine hierarchy of castes. For example, vegetarians are considered very high. The Brahman, Lingayat (Kundu Vokkaliga, Jangam, and Banajiga), Panchal and Varik are included in this category. But there is difference of opinion as to who is on the top whether a Brahman or a Lingayat Jangam. Both are regarded as having equal status by many. The Varik is a Lingayat Vegetarian caste and hence they are also included in the above category, although occupation of Barber is rated low. The Kabbaliga, Kurubagond, Kumbar, and Iliga who are meat eaters (sheep, goat, and fowl) but they have high status among the non-vegetarian castes. The Muslim are considered low as they are beef eaters. However, this does not come in the way of their free articulation with other high castes on equal terms. Members of the single household of the Harijan (Dhor) who take meat are regarded low because of the occupation of leather curing. The Dhor live near the Harijan settlement. They constitute a scheduled caste. The Harijans and Waddar are grouped as very low for their taking beef and pork. In broader frame of reference, the Brahman and Lingayat, and Panchal are considered as higher castes. The Kabbaliga, Kurubagond, Iliga are considered as middle castes and the Harijan and Waddar as lower castes. The Muslim's position is not clear, though they are considered low.

Social Interaction

In their articulation with other communities the Harijan and Waddar suffer from certain social disabilities. Previously, untouchability was said to be practised very rigorously. Prior to the merger of the area in the Indian Union, the Harijan were treated as untouchables. That was perhaps one of the reasons why one of the Harijan groups viz., the Holeya, co-operated with the Razakars. The very high and high castes used derogatory language like Holdea, Madiga, Wadda, etc. Till 1972, the land records maintained by the high caste village accountant showed that the names of the Harijan and Waddar as Sangya, Kamya, Mallya, Rudrya, Mergya, and so on. No other communities were addressed in this way. The records are now corrected with the honorific appa to their proper names as is done for many other communities. Boys of the higher castes use singular terms for the Harijan and Waddar. But they would cautiously use the same in the case of others like the Muslim, Kurubagond, Kumbar, etc. A Kurubagond boy take a Harijan class-mate to school on his bicycle. But this interaction is limited to youngsters only. Elders of high and middle castes shun to articulate with the Harijan and Waddar. During leisure time men engage in playing cards in different places like the village cafes, temple verandah, when all groups including the Muslim, would freely sit together, but the Harijan are usually not welcomed. In case they showed any interest and if they have money, they are also made to participate but they have to sit at some distance and play. No Waddar is associated with their plays as Waddar do not like to play with money stake.

The village cafe observes untouchability in respect of the Harijan. Separate glasses are kept for their use. Water to tea are poured from some distance in these separate glasses are to be cleaned by the user. Even educated Harijan cannot escape this discrimination. To cite an example, a Harijan S.S.L.C passed employee of the agricultural department was offered tea in a glass kept separately for the Harijan for which the former's colleague of the Kabbaliga caste could not help but accept caste norm.

The various social disabilities and social segregation suffered by the Harijan and Waddar may be summed up:

1. During meetings of the Panchayat, Co-operative Society, or informal gathering, the Harijan have to sit at some distance from all the other communities. The Waddar sit in the middle of the Harijan and other communities. During festival occasions, they have to sit separately and eat their food usually after the people of high and middle castes have taken their food.
2. During marriages, the Harijan are given white rice for

throwing on the bridal couple whereas consecrated *jola* are given to all others including the Muslim and Waddar.

3. At the time of the festival of *Nag Chauti* the village Barber does the job of frying *jola* and gram into *allu*. The Harijan and Waddar have to get their frying work done at last. In this, Waddar get preference.
4. The Village Barber does not shave the Harijan and Waddar. They help mutually for the job. Young people go to saloons in the nearby village.
5. Recently i.e. in 1974, the government granted house sites to the landless Harijan and others. The plan contained some sites of the Harijan along with other high castes and Muslim. The Panchayat Chairman was so upset that he was planning to get the arrangement of house sites changed.

Literacy

Literacy could be one of the determinants of weakness and 'dominance'. Those who are literate get some kind of prestige in villages. In the village it was observed that 130 men and 10 women had formal education at various levels. It was considered useful to calculate percentages of literates for each community separately and put them into the four different categories for the purpose of this analysis.

Those communities which had no literates and also literates upto 10 per cent may be considered as very low percentage of literacy. Those having 10-25 per cent as low, those with 26-50 per cent as high, and finally those above 50 per cent constituting as very high. With this specific categories the data given in Table 8 shows that the Harijan (Holeya and Dhor), Waddar, Kumbar and Muslim are very low. The low percentage is that of the Harijan (Hindu Madaru) and Kurubagond. The high category has the Kabbaliga, Jangam, Kudu Vokkaliga, Illiga, and Harijan (Christian Madaru). It may be noted that among the christian Harijan, the percentage of literacy is higher (31 per cent). This was mainly due to the influence and encouragement of Christian missionaries visiting the area. The very high percentage group consists of Brahman, Banajiga, Panchal. and Varik. Excepting three communities viz, Brahman, Banajiga, and Varik, all the others in respect of literacy of female population are within the group of very low only.

They are two families among the Harijan (Holeya), who were able to send their boys to High School. One boy had failed in S.S.L.C and later taken up a job at Gulbarga, although it was a menial job. The other boy had passed the First Year Pre-University and was continuing the education. Among the Christian Madaru, however, one boy has studied upto S.S.L.C and left the school. He was not interested in working as an agricultural labourer in his village. His parents were complaining that their boy has turned out to be a burden on their family. Some of the boys of the lower and middle castes who are belonging to the Kabbaliga, Kurubagond, and Muslim had continued their education, but their failure at the S.S.L.C and also drop-outs at the pre-S.S.L.C level had a disconcerting effect on the parents. Among the Brahman, almost all the boys who went to colleges at Gulbarga have completed their graduation. Excepting two, all have got government jobs. These two boys having passed recently have been trying for jobs. Among the Kudu Vokkaliga, one boy was able to pass the pre-university and he was trying to join either Medical or Agricultural Science courses. Among the Lingayat Banajiga one boy had failed at the S.S.L.C but has taken up cultivation.

Traditional Authority

The village administration in the erstwhile semifeudal structure, was carried on by three officers whose offices were hereditary. They were, the police *patil*, the *mali patil*, and the *kulkarni*. The first two looked after criminal and civil matters respectively of the village and the last one was responsible for land revenue collections. The office of the traditional *kulkarni* (village accountant) was abolished, and the government has appointed a village accountant (*telathi/kulkarni*) who took charge in 1972. He looks after the revenue collections and also he is the official secretary of the Village Panchayat.

Village Panchayat

The Village Panchayat has been functioning since 1961. Formerly, its headquarter was situated in the neighbouring village, as it is one of the members of the Group Panchayat. After the Panchayat elections in 1968, the Chairman was elected from Vithalgera. Since assuming the charge, the Chairman Shri C, arranged for shifting of the

Panchayat office to Vithalgera. This way very much resented by the people of the other member village and their people are not participating in any activities of the Village Panchayat. Among the 15 representatives 10 are from Vithalgera. Two are reserved for scheduled castes. Among the others, three are Lingayats (2 women), four are Kurubagond and one Kabbaliga. The Chairman of the Village Panchayat appeared to have some prejudice towards the other member village. The village accountant who has jurisdiction over the other member village has established a good rapport and he tried to bring rapprochement but failed. As a result of this situation collection of house taxes that village is becoming difficult and hence financially the Panchayat is in difficulty. Many times, due to lack of quorum meeting are not held. No improvement is seen even in the Chairman's village. Street lights are not provided, drainage are not made, repairs to school building are not carried out, no betterment committee for the school is organized, mid-day meal arrangement is not supervised etc. Thus, many of the functions have remained unattended. The Panchayat is helpless. Neither they have finances nor the co-operation of the villagers.

Emergence of Elites

It has been noticed that a few of the individuals from the economically and socially dominant group have emerged as the prominent rural elite. The case of Shri B, is of particular interest. Shri B, who was an ordinary Kabbaliga, by his clever maneuver came to have actual control over the offices of the Mali and Police Patil and became the village headman (*goudaru*).

The Case of the Village Headman

The office of the *mali patil* inherited by the previous incumbents daughter who belongs to the Kabbaliga caste, after her father's death. In such a case, any person nominated could officiate as a *gumasta* (clerk) and carry on the activities on her behalf. The woman has employed a person (Brahman) of the neighbouring village as a *gumasta*[5] who acts under the supervision of her husband. But the real *gumasta* is the husband of the woman, that is, B(*gourdaru*). B also got the office of the *police patil*. Formerly the office of the *police patil* was held hereditarily by a Kabbaliga, Shri S, and the latter was a close relative of B. But S was a drunkard and a diseased person. He was wooed by B's family by supplying drinks and sympathetically treating the disease. By these acts S became a member of B's family leaving his wife and children. Later he 'sold' away all his lands and also gifted the office of the *police patil* to B by stating that he had no legal heir to take possession of the lands and also the office of the *police patil*. B, thus, became a very powerful person both in terms of money and power. The aggrieved person, that is, the son of the former Police Patil, Shri X, fought for the legal heir of the office since 1952 in the revenue courts till 1968, but he could not win as no responsible person in the village could give witness in his support and to point out his identity. In private conversation many told me that the headman had perpetrated great injustice on the legal heir and had made X a pauper.

The village headman has held his position quite securely. Though not much educated, he has made efforts to learn various languages including Urdu and English by himself. Since he has more than 37 acres of land, he is economically well off. His wife is *goudti* (headman's wife) and has some influence over many of the poorer sections. A recent case illustrates this point. The headman's daughter attained puberty, and puberty rituals were held on the 16th day. Usually on that day the relatives fed the girl with a special feast. At that time the goudti's sister had arranged a feast. The venue was the headman's house. On that day the *goudti* and others took fancy to perform an entertainment programme. The *goudti* was given the role of Raja (King) with some others as ministers, and attendants. Most of the participants belonged to high and middle castes. Profuse praise was given by the audience which mainly constituted the Harijan and women of other communities. The Harijan (Madaru) provided the music. In appreciation of the programme those who had gathered started giving cash gifts and their names were loudly announced by an attendant to the Raja. Almost every Harijan and Muslim who went there paid a cash gift of one rupee each. Later all the persons were given the food.

The headman has some capacity to argue cases. By constant association with lawyers, perhaps, he has come to know about some law (*kanunu*) and atleast before the villagers he poses that he knew law. Hence people approach him for any matter requiring help of police, or Court. He is, therefore, known as *pairvikar* (follower or supporter). During the present investigator's stay in the village, he saw him moving with files of cases from the neighbouring villages. During revisit, he heard that two Kurubagond households were fighting among themselves for a piece of their ancestral land, and one of the parties had given their case to the headman as their *pairvikar.*

Other Elite

The headman was always supported by the former Brahman village accountant, Shri Z and late father of Z. The Brahman are referred to as Maharaja the kind. The former Brahman village accountant is economically very rich. Formerly, he was a link to the revenue officials and villagers. He has backing of the headman. Now that the office of the village accountant has gone to another person and also that he is not keeping good heath, he often remains in his son's house at Gulbarga. Many persons of the Kabbaliga and Kurubagond consult him on matters relating to agriculture, and share-cropping. The share-croppers and farm servants are still loyal to him and hence he is able to maneuver the agricultural operations very efficiently. Besides his own lands, he supervises the lands of his brothers also. This is possible mainly due to the strong support of the headman.

Since the dispute started over the issue of legal heir to the office of the police *patil,* two young Lingayat had emerged as persons fighting for justice. Both these persons C and V are not much educated. They belong to very high castes. Economically however their position was good previously, but now they are no well-to-do. Both these youths were then in Socialist Party. By 1970, both had come out of the Socialist Party. C had joined the undivided congress and later became an active worker of Congress(O). The other, that is, V became an active supporter of C.P.I. and has remained so. The former was elected as Chairman of the Village Panchayat and even now he is holding the office. Formerly he was a Director of the Primary Land Development Bank at Humnabad. Then he used to arrange loans from the bank to farmers and used to get commission for orders on pump sets from the pumpset dealers. He was defeated in 1971 elections of the Board of Directors and since then his strength is reduced. During election time in 1971 and 1972 C was contacted. He feels that even now he is a great force to reckon with. The other person V, is outspoken. He was once an influential person but which his certain habits like meat eating and drinking etc., (he belongs to Lingayat Jangam which is a strict vegetarian and teetotaller caste) he has lost confidence of the people. But the headman B wants to woo him and set him against the Panchayat Chairman. Both the former village accountant and the headman had managed to take loans for the Agricultural Co-operative Society and later allowed it to go defunct. Therefore, there was the need for its revival. So in 1972, many of the Marginal and Small Farmers met and revived the society and converted it as the Service Co-operative Society. This was possible due to interest of the Panchayat Chairman. The result was that many persons of the poorer sections (upto 2&1/2 acres of lands) got loans, fertilizers etc. Shri D belonging to the Kabbaliga caste was elected its President. He too, is not much educated. D has service as motto and during the drought he used to provide finances for bringing grains for distribution and do other work. This benefited people of poorer sections. He was still continuing as the President. Some persons do not want the Society to function. During revisit of the present author, D expressed his inability to continue in the office. He had stopped bringing grains as there was no funds. The village headman was indirectly discouraging the Society to function, by inciting some members (of poorer sections) against the President. Sometimes the Panchayat Chairman also did not co-operate. The latter was angry on the President as the latter had not given five kgs of sugar once and hence there were attempts to topple him from the Presidentship. The position of the emergence of elite among other communities was that there were no effective elite among the Harijans, Waddar, Kumbar, and Muslim. There are a few educated young men among the Harijan, Kabbaliga and Kurubagond as said earlier. Those who had studied up to S.S.L.C wanted to leave the village. The migration of educated persons to other places have only strengthened the hands of the Headman, Panchayat Chairman and he former village accountant.

Factions

The headman, as the leader of one faction has been in the forefront since 1950. His rival is the Panchayat Chairman. Supporters are there for both the factions. If the Panchayat Chairman did anything the headman opposed and vice-versa. When the School was opened the headman was against it. In this case, the headman B and the former village accountant, Z, did not want their village people were educated they would challenge their authority. They helped those who supported them. For instance, some six landless households including two Harijan, were made to grab two acres each of the government grazing land. But the Panchayat Chairman then had represented to the Government and saw that the land grabbers were evicted. Due to these factions the Poorer sections suffer as they are used by either parties for their own ends, thereby resulting in emergence of some dominant individuals, who may be belonging to minority caste groups.

Values and World View

The tutelary deity of the village is goddess Lakshmi. Prior to Independence, there used to be a big annual festival in honour of the deity. The main participants were the Kabbaliga and Harijan (Madaru). The households which did certain rituals had *inam* lands for this function. The festival was topped due to the political turmoil existing in the then Hyderabad territory. But recently, a small structure over the Lakshmi shrine has been built by the efforts of the headman. A Vithal shrine was established about ten years ago. A Hanuman temple is also existing. The previous school teacher (Lingayat) used to arrange Bhajan on every Saturday to which people of all communities attended except the Harijan and Waddar. The latter were not invited. On such occasions, some Muslim singers also participated in the Bhajan. In my revisit I noted that no such Bhajan were held on Saturdays as the teacher had left village on transfer.

In the Harijan (Holeya) and Waddar settlements, there are shrines of their village goddesses whom they worship on important festivals. The Harijan(Christian Madaru) would observe Christmas by organizing Bhajan. There are some Kannada songs in praise of Lord Christ which are sung in chorus. The Harijan (Madaru) attended to all functions of the villagers including the ritual observance by Muslims at *dargas*.

Conversion of Harijan(Madaru) to Christianity has been taking place in Bidar area since 30 years or so. A person from Chambol village near Bidar settled in this village about 30 years ago. He was mainly responsible for conversion of his affinal kin in this village. Though a few households have taken to Christianity, all the Harijan (Madaru) call themselves as Christian. When I asked them if they are all converted, people of 16 households told they have not. They worship Ambabai of Tuljapur (Maharashtra) and observe all the rituals of other communities in the village. The Christian among them, that is, nine households, however, claimed that they worship Christ, perform marriage and death rituals according to Christian customs. The attitude of the other communities is the same towards the converts. The Harijan (Holeya) group was influenced by Baba Saheb Ambedkar's teachings, but it has remained Hindu. Some of the Harijan leaders in the Humnabad area were Arya Samaji and this influence is seen to pervade. In the village, Bhajan are conducted by the Harijan (Holeya) youths during Ambedkar's Jayanti day.

Most of the people particularly of the poorer sections and lower castes believe in the theory of Dharma and Karma[6]. Usually it is said that those who did good work, humble service, did not tease others got reward in their next life and earned good and prosperous life. Those who were bad, behaved rudely, told lies, got punishment. Somewhat the same line of argument is made for attaining heaven and hell and so is the relation between *punya* and *papa*. There views are told by well-to-do and higher caste people. Thus traditional Hindu ethos were preached whenever opportunities came and Bhajan are sung in similar vein. This, perhaps helped maintain *status quo* and fatalism among the poorer sections for whom these ideologies made them to adjust to the miseries of life.

Identification of Weak and Dominant Sections

Considering various parameters of economic, social political, and religious angles, certain communities or households could be classified into decisively weak, weak, dominant and decisively dominant. Based on the various counts, distinctly we may identify the Harijan (all the four groups) and Waddar as decisively weak. Almost all the households fall in this category in terms of landholding, income, expenditure pattern, material possession, dwelling pattern, caste hierarchy, social segregation etc. The decisively dominant are the Brahman, Kudu Vokkaliga (one household), and Kabbaliga (one household). If any of the counts described above are considered, then the Muslim, Kumbar, Varik and Iliga are weak. In the case of the two numerically dominant communities and three numerically minority groups, there are varying degrees of dimensions which cannot be specifically categorised at the level of communities. These communities are the Kurubagond, Kabbaliga, Banajiga, Jangam, and Panchal. In the case of the Kabbaliga, one household crossed the threshold of dominance and became a decisively dominant. Among these communities, although there are some households who may be regarded as dominant sections, but there is a large section who are weak in terms of income, land holding and other criteria, although they are dominant with regard to socio-religious aspects.

The population which is covered in the decisively weak section works out to be nearly 30 per cent. Other 16 per cent are weak. In the village studied we find that 46 per cent are emerge as a clear category of weaker sections. They very poor, i.e., the decisively weak are referred to as *gor garib*. They are mostly drawn from the Harijan, Waddar, Muslim, Iliga, Kumbar, and Varik communities. There are also considerable population from among the middle castes like the Kurubagond and Kabbaliga nearly 39 per cent belong to the poorer sections solely from economic criteria.

Social Dynamics of the Dominant and Weak

With the abolition of the Zamindari system long ago, most of the land is controlled by the people belonging to high castes. The former Brahman village accountant and others like the *mali patil* and police *patil*, and some individuals from among the Lingayat and Kurubagond are in possession on major portion of land. The Harijan and service castes like the Panchal (Carpenter) Kumbar (Potter), and Varik (Barber) got *inam* lands for rendering service to the villagers. Fragmentation of landholding arose due to breaking up of joint families among the marginal and small landholders which resulted in smaller nonviable economic holdings.

There are some individuals who are economically, politically, and socially dominant. Since Independence, it was the village accountant and the headman who have retained their influence as leaders in the village and acquisition of more land helped them to become more powerful. Normally the Marginal and Small Farmers who were cultivating land of the Bigger Farmers on share-cropping tenure could not become protected or permanent tenants as required under law unless proper entries in the revenue records were made. It may be interesting to note that till 1972, the former village accountant did not divulge the records to many farmers and copies of the record of rights extracts were given by the former village accountant after lot of troubles. Marginal and Small Farmers were happy to receive *Patta* (records of rights of ownership of land) books in 1972 and 1973, when the newly appointed village accountant issued them. Earlier the former village accountant was supported by the headman. As has been described earlier, the late father of the Brahman village accountant had strongly supported the headman to win the case of the latter in getting the office of the police *patil*. From the records of the land transfers that have taken place since Independence up to 1972, it may be noted that the most beneficiaries in this respect were the families of the former village accountant, the headman, and some of their supporters. The headman, for example, who had inherited only six acres of ancestral property as his share when he got separated from his joint family was able to accumulate an additional land to the extent of 31 acres in due course and has already laid claim over nine acres of land of an absentee landowner. The former village accountant had brought 37 acres. A young widow of Kurubagond had purchased nine acres and it was alleged that this was due to her special favour shown to the former village accountant. There is a rich man of the Kudu Vokkaliga who is known as the *dhori* (lord). He was able to buy 11 acres. Most of the land bought belonged to absentee landlords belonging to Muslim, Lingayat and other communities. There were two other cases, in which one case is important. A Waddar who was tilling the land of an absentee landowner of the Harijan (Madaru) got land (about seven acres) as he had given his active support for many years to the headman. Previously it was not possible for the weaker sections to buy any land. But this situation has slightly changed because of taking charge of the newly appointed village accountant. In my revisit I learnt that a Harijan (Holeya) had bought three acres of land from a Kurubagond.

It is interesting to note the *modus operandi* of the dominant individuals. The former village accountant and the village headman act in collusion, and most of the people do not challenge their authority. The two most prominent opponents to them are socially and politically dominant, but they are economically decisively weak and hence they are not very effective in protesting against the actions of these two dominant individuals. But they too, have their own way of exploiting others and sphere of operation. We may also call them dominant individuals. One of them is the Panchayat Chairman. He has large number of supporters from among the Kurubagond. Although the village headman was not liked by many people of his own caste, but in terms of solidarity, they would take his side. For example, in the Panchayat elections (1968) the Kabbaliga supported the brother (Kabbaliga) of the headman who was elected. The lingayat and Kurubagond candidates were supported by the people of their respective castes. Muslims had supported the candidates of the Panchayat Chairman.

The former Agricultural Co-operative society was allowed to go defunct by the two influential dominant individuals. The Society was revived by the supporters of the weaker sections. But it was facing some difficulties in its proper functioning. The Panchayat was not functioning effectively and the Chairman was responsible for it. The former was always interested in making many promises, but ultimately was working to get some benefit for himself. Any outsider coming into the village has to face those dominant individuals for example, the school teacher got involved in the faction lead by the Panchayat Chairman being belonging to the same caste of the latter. The Brahmin pool secretary of the revived Cooperative Society aligned himself with the group of the former Brahmin village accountant and the headman. There have been dissensions among the factional groups. The result was that the institutions of school, cooperative society and the Panchayat were not functioning effectively and this obviously vitiated the interests of the weaker sections. If the cooperative society did not function, the Marginal and Small Farmers do not get credit, seeds, fertilizers etc.

As discussed earlier, the weaker sections consist mainly of the Harijan, the Waddars, the landless and marginal landholders of the Kurubagond, Muslim, the Kabbaliga and the service castes like the Carpenter potter and Barber. They constitute nearly 85 per cent, (decisively weak - 30%, weak - 16%, and economically weak - 39%). Since long these helpless people must have built in capacity to adapt to the conditions of object poverty, and social disabilities. The Harijan (Holeya) cooperated with the Muslim Razakars before the region merged with the Indian Union. Soon they had to face non-cooperation from the people of the high and middle castes. But many of them joined in supporting the village headman in his activities as they knew that it gave them strength. Even now they have been supporting him actively. There is only one case of exception. It is that of Shri S. The members of S's family have been associated with the *dhori* and have been working as farm servants and agricultural labourers since many years. Since the *dhori* has proved to be a benevolent employer and does not associate himself with the feuds of the village factions, this particular Harijan family was economically better that others. The Harijan (Madaru) are the village functionaries and musicians and they sweep the harvesting fields of the farmers at the time of harvest and get some grains. They have not tried to associate themselves with any faction group. Out of the two prominent Waddar who had supported the headman one of them has already got the benefit for it. Others were mostly semi-nomadic and they would go on their errand i.e., stone cutting work to other places for nearly four to six months in a year. They too aspire to have land and settle down permanently as their leader has done it has not been possible. Some of them who had earlier co-operated with the headman, have been seen giving their support to the Panchayat Chairman for the latter was promising to get them land. The Panchayat Chairman had got them a few pairs of he-buffaloes for their carts and also some zinc sheets for roofing in 1968-69.

The value and world view of weaker sections appear to be guided largely by the ideologies of *karma* and *dharma*. The exploitative mechanism of the dominant individuals *per se* are understood by them and they know that they cannot help themselves out of the social reality. These ideas help perpetuation of weakness as a way of life and does not augur well to bring socio-economic changes to alleviate their conditions. Some of the individuals from among the weaker sections too take advantage of their personal capabilities in taking best help from the dominant sections. The case of the Harijan (Madaru) musician is a pointer. The village headman always wanted an escort for him whenever he went out of the village, and also to carry his personal leather bag. The Madaru musician has himself volunteered to do the job on many occasions. Although he may not get much pecuniary benefit, he and members of his household feel a kind of special status. I observed that few of the weaker sections of the Kabbaliga were trying to be closer to the headman and the former Brahmin village accountant, and so was the case with some individuals of the Kurubagond and Muslim. The adaptive strategies of the weaker sections revealed an in-built structure where in life continued under conditions of poverty, misery, social segregation, less opportunity to get educated as well as become elite. While many of the weaker sections would aspire to come out of this sub-culture of poverty to use Oscar Lewis's (1968) concept but the question is where is the possibility for them to cross the threshold of this social reality in the *cultural matrix* of a small, rural society.

The weaker sections have more avenues for spending on such

items as rituals, liquor, etc. There is not much scope for earning any additional money unless some efforts are made. The weaker sections of different communities are not organised. In some of the states like Kerala and West Bengal political action has been used to change the agrarian hierarchy (Beteille, 1972) and to better the lot of agricultural workers. But nothing of the sort has happened in this area. Status quo situation, as existed some decades ago appears to continue in this village in the agrarian structure giving rather a static picture. In some of the taluks of the district, especially Bhalki and Aurad, it is said that agricultural labourers are voicing their grievances. The Humnabad taluka was once a *stronghold* of the previous undivided Socialist Party. Now also, it is in this area that a C.P.I. member represents the electorate. But the political base appears to be in favour of the Congress (O). Though they too swear in the socialism, organised activity in any great measure towards working for the welfare of the weaker of the weaker sections seems to be lacking.

It was observed that the economic conditions of the poorer sections could be improved if some industries are established. For instance, industries whose infrastructure could be localised that may give employment to large sections of the village people specially the weaker sections. This would force the dominant sections to agree for increasing wages, and regulate working hours etc. It is interesting to state the case of the Milk Chilling Plant opened in 1972, at a nearby big village. The milk collected in villages (more than 50 villages) are bought by the Co-operative Milk Diary, chilled and sent to Gulbarga. In Vithalgera, five poor Muslims had taken up the job of collecting milk and earned nearly Rupees five a day. There were about 25 households most of whom belonged to the 'weaker sections' who had begun selling milk to these vendors and were able to earn Rs.2.00 to 3.00 per day. This was an additional source of income. There is great demand for milk. The society was buying milk from villages and supplying milk to Bangalore in tankers. The Society has also proposals to put up a plant for making other milk products. Therefore, villagers can give attention to milk supply as an industrial raw material. Another example needs citation here. Some of Big Farmers in the area are growing sugarcane. Normally the sugarcane are crushed in the village for making jaggery. With the Cooperative Sugar Factory at Hallikhed starting its cane-crushing operation and some small scale Khandsari Sugar Factories operating, there was sudden demand for labourers for cutting sugarcane and transporting it to the factories. Due to these operations, labour was not available. Hence there was increase in wages, and the rise was to an extent of 50 per cent. Of course, the milk supply and sugarcane work are seasonal activities in this region where the land is dry and dependent upon rain. However, these two cases illustrate how small scale industrial efforts could better the economic conditions of the weaker sections.

To sum up the decisively weak and weak have been living in conditions of abject poverty and self degradation. Most of them are landless or nearly landless (marginal landholders). The means of production is controlled mostly by a few dominant individuals. The attempt by the latter to keep their hold over almost all activities in the village does not help the weaker sections. Therefore there is no possibility of any qualitative changes to occur soon in improving the socio-economic conditions of the weaker sections, especially those of the decisively weak. In case weaker sections could better their economic conditions there is possibility of ushering in socio-political changes. For that certain urgent steps are needed to gear up the processes of planning and implementation.

As said earlier, localised industries could generate good amount of employment potentiality to villagers. Land is scarce and hence pressure on it has to be eased. Creation of industries, and other measures alone may not help solve the vexed problems of the weaker sections. Although they are necessary, the weaker sections may need a certain kind of organizations at the village level to understand their difficulties and to fight against reactionary forces among the dominant sections, by political action, if required. The weaker sections cannot do it all by themselves in the social situation. Hence, exogenous (outside the village) sources could do it to give inner strength to the weaker sections who could organise themselves to combat perpetuation of weakness and to cross the threshold of weakness.

NOTES

1. The people of shepherd community in the area call themselves the Gond and few of them have got caste certificates to denote Gond, a Scheduled Tribe and also got jobs in government, against Scheduled Tribe reservation quota. In the village, however, they are known as shepherd.
2. "Anatomy of Poverty", *Indian Express News*, August 5, 1974.

3. During the severe drought in 1973, several farmers had to sell away some of there bullocks due to paucity of fodder. The situation has since improved. When I revisited the village in December 1974, 24 households had a pair of bullocks each. Three households of the Very Big Farmers had an additional pair each.
4. Parvathama, (1973) states that in Karnataka not mush surplus cultivable land might be available even after the government imposed ceiling limits, and explains that the problem of distribution of surplus land might seldom arise in rural areas.
5. It was observed that this Brahman boy used to accompany the headman carrying the gun of the headman whenever the latter went out of the village.
6. A Harijan Madaru sings a song on the Satya Harishchandra's story in which ideas of truth, justice, previous deeds etc. are highlighted.

REFERENCES

Beteille, Andre *Inequality and Social Change.* Oxford University Press, Delhi,1972

Dandekar V.M. & Rath Nilakantha "Poverty in India I and II. Dimensions and Trends & Policies and Programmes" I and II *Economic and Political Weekly.* Vol.6, 1&2 Nos, 1971.

Harp John & Hofley *Poverty in Canada*, Prentice Hall, John K. (ed). Canada, 1971.

Lewis, Oscar *LaVida : A Puerto Rican family in the Culture of poverty* San Juan and New York. New York : Vintage Books, 1968.

Parvathama C. "Land Reforms-Problems of redistribution of Surplus Land", - A note presented at the seminar on Land Reforms held at Mysore, January 22-23, Cyclostyled, 1973.

Sau, Ranjit "Indian Economic Growth", *Economic and Political Weekly* Vol. VIII. Annual Number, 1972.

Townsend, Peter *Concept of Poverty.* (Ed.) London, 1970.

23

PALAYASIVARAM : A VILLAGE IN TAMIL NADU

RAJALAKSHMI MISRA

In describing the original affluent society, Sahlins observed that the most primitive people of the world are not considered poverty stricken though their possessions are meagre. He defined poverty as a relationship between people and not between possession of material goods (1972 ; 37). According to official U.S. standard for 1970, a family of four was poor if its income was less than 3944 dollar a year and a fifth of the U.S. population were described as living in conditions of poverty. If judged by this standard, probably 99 per cent of India's population could be said to be living in poverty (Dantwala 1973:15). This suggests that there cannot be a single standard for measuring poverty. Townsend thus concludes, ". . . possession by individuals and families of relatively low resources does not automatically mean they are in poverty, but only if they are thereby unable to have the types of diets, participate in the activities and have the living conditions and amenities which are customary in that society" (1970: 42).

According to Dadabhai Naoroji India's poverty during the later half of nineteenth century was due to the enormous drain of the produce of the country to England (Dantwala 1973 : 4). Karl Marx attributed the poverty of India to the destruction of the entire framework of Indian society by the British with their steam engine and science and in their uprooting the union between agricultural and manufacturing industry in the country (Dantwala 1973:10/11). Now the process of draining out wealth has stopped and most of infrastructure destroyed by the British rule has been restored. Poverty, however, still persists. The present study intends to examine the intensity of poverty in rural India in order to understand the possible reasons for its perpetuation.

The paper is based on an intensive study of Palayasivaram, a village in Chingleput District of Tamil Nadu. This forms part of an all India study of rural poverty undertaken by the Anthropological Survey of India.

Field techniques

Before I selected Palayasivaram for the present study after I had visited a number of villages in Chingleput district. The village Palayasivaram satisfied all the characteristics of the village to be selected for this enquiry and it also appeared that the village was convenient for me for conducting the field work. However, during the first two months I could not find out an appropriate place for stay in the village. One of the major problems being, which will become more clear later, was that the settlement of Harijans was far removed from the main village. I being a Tamil Brahman knew very well that stay in the Harijan colony would completely severe my relationship with the rest of the villagers. I, for the first two months, stayed in Walajabad, 3 miles away and used to commute to the Harijan colony. After two months, however, when I shifted to the main village I had no difficulty to be identified as one like the local Brahmans. Women in particular addressed me by extending conventional kinship terms. The result of this was that my contact with the Harijan became limited, they could not call on me any more as could I visit them any time I choose. However whenever I went to the Harijan colony with my three year old child, his innocent movements and actions enlivened the atmosphere and made it easier for me to cross the caste barrier to some extent and collect relevant data.

In the Harijan colony, as well as in the main village, I was repeatedly questioned about the purpose of my enquiries. Whatsoever I explained did not seem to satisfy the people. While collecting data on landholdings and other wealth I requested the village *munsif* to send one of his *thalayaris* (tax-collectors) along with me to convince the villagers regarding my bonafides. With this arrangement the villagers appeared less skeptic but they did not necessarily give more accurate information.

The village land records with the *karnam* (village accountant) was not correct in all respects. There were cases of partition of landholdings without official knowledge. This was done to avoid payment of stamp duties. There were also cases of unrecorded land mortgage locally called *suddhabogvam* with special right to the creditor of cultivating the mortgaged lands till complete repayment of the loan. Thus, according to official records some may own land others being beneficiaries of the same. Similar phenomenon is observed with reference to lease arrangements. The Vaishnava temple in this village has about 150 acres of land for its maintenance. The lands are leased out to the villagers in various ways. But in several cases the actual tenant was not cultivating the land allotted as per the lease register. Details and extent of such anomalies cannot be fully known through quick surveys.

Regarding movable property, the reliability of available data appears more doubtful. Most of the Harijans and the impoverished in the main village mortgaged the few ornaments and metal vessels they had but villagers in general declared them as sold.

I had difficulty even in gathering census information. The head of one of the Harijan households was a P.W.D. Inspector who would not let me know the number of children being afraid of my evil eyes.

Returns of indebtedness were generally overstatements. In a few cases, people felt shy to admit any debt.

Regarding actual expenditure, the data was not very satisfactory either. Villagers do not buy things or spend money in a very planned way. As and when necessity arises,keeping their limited resources in mind, they spend normally without maintaining any detailed account, particularly of petty expenditures. Thus, the data given on the amount spent monthly or annually on clothes, education, medicine,food etc., are mere approximations.

In any intensive field-study the investigator becomes intimate only with a limited number of informants. Thus eliciting accurate information seems possible. But when such data are to be collected from the total universe the same degree of accuracy appears impossible.

Notwithstanding the problems stated above, my stay for six months in the field did help me to observe the village life fairly closely. After some period of stay I remained no more a stranger to the villagers. The intimacy between me and a few families laid the foundation for mutual confidence through whom I could get detailed and reliable data. Interlinkages between groups also gradually became clear to me.

Village life is rich and complex. The richness and complexity of the various issues gradually unravelled themselves before me as I continued my stay in the village. The mask which people wear cannot be retained all the time and everywhere. Sudden outbursts of emotions and quarrels, at times even in the middle of the nights, resulting in loud exchanges of choicest abuses, accusations and counter accusations gave me chances to know something that was latent or deliberately hidden from me by the village society. Following up of such cases presented to me a maze of information woven around issues, past actions, and present relations among different people.

Dynamics of social relationship

People of Palayasivaram belong to fifteen castes. Table 1 gives their population distribution by sex and respective traditional occupations. The settlement pattern of the village gives useful leads in understanding the social stratification in the village. The Brahmans, who were the dominant landlords of the village till recently lived in a centrally located street in the village. Other numerically dominant castes like Naicker and Mudaliar lived in their respective streets on either side of the Brahman street. The artisan and service castes lived at the fringe. The Parayans (who are now called Harijans by outsiders) lived in a separate settlement, about half a mile away from the main village. This settlement is still referred to as *cheri* by the the villagers but the outsiders and government officials call it colony. As there is hardly any vacant plot to construct a hut in the colony, the Harijans have started building their homes on the slopes of the adjacent hill.

Population growth among the Mudaliar and Naicker families has necessitated construction of new houses and thus they have been forced to live side by side on new streets, as there are no vacant plots on their respective original streets.

Most of the houses in the main village have wells some of whom dry up for a few days in summer. People then depend on the nearby river (Palar) and its irrigation canal for water supply. In the Harijan colony, there are two wells both of whom used to dry up during summer. The Harijans are not allowed to bath or draw water from the canal. Hence they had to depend only on the river water.

TABLE 1: Distribution of caste by traditional occupation number of households, and population

Sl. No.	Caste	Traditional occupation	No. of house-hold	Population		
				Male	Female	Total
1.	Harijan	Mainly agriculture	223	629	576	1205
2.	Naicker	Mainly agriculture	82	194	189	383
3.	Mudaliar	Weaving	30	94	96	190
4.	Brahman	Supervision of lands	13	23	23	46
5.	Akamudaya Mudaliar	Agriculture	6	14	20	34
6.	Kanakku Pillai	Keeping Accounts	5	15	14	29
7.	Naidu	Agriculture	8	14	15	29
8.	Ambattan	Cutting hair & playing pipe and drum	4	17	11	28
9.	Tambiran	Weaving	5	12	14	26
10.	Achari	Carpentry	4	11	11	22
11.	Pillai	Grazing cattle	4	8	12	20
12.	Vannan	Washing clothes	3	3	4	7
13.	Mann Wodder	Masonry	2	2	4	6
14.	Chettiar	Trading	1	3	2	5
15.	Kolamani Mudaliar	Priesthood	1	—	2	2
	Total		391	1039	993	2032

Members of all clean castes have the privilege of fetching water from the canal but they have to avoid the best spot reserved for the Brahman and select an area at the down stream for the purpose. Water touched by members of lower castes is unusable to the members of higher castes but water touched or used by members of upper castes is acceptable to others. When persons belonging to non-Brahman castes fetch water, then one placed higher in the caste hierarchy will have water from the upstream and the other from the down stream.

In 1969 and 1970 several other wells have been dug in the main village and in the Harijan colony by the Rural Welfare Committee and the Harijan Welfare Committee respectively. In the main village, pipe lines were laid and taps were installed at street corners by the Panchayat Union in 1971. Water pumped from wells by an electric motor is now available to the villagers every morning for an hour or two. Plan for supplying tap water in the Harijan colony has been drawn up and is awaiting execution.

In numerical strength the Harijan form the majority in the village. Out of the total population of 2032 in the village they constitute 1205. Naicker and Mudaliar are the next two numerous groups having 383 and 190 heads of people respectively. Though there are twelve other castes in the village none is represented by more than fifty people.

Distribution of income, landholding and literary by caste has been given in table 2. As groups, Kanakku Pillai and Mudaliar are economically well off. Ritually and socially, the Brahman and Kanakku Pillai occupy superior position. Among members of lower castes, some individually command respect on account of their accumulated wealth.

From the point of view of income, landholding, and education, the Harijan are the weakest and the Naicker are slightly above them. Other castes such as Kolamani Mudaliar and Ambattan are also weak but their number being small in the village it is difficult to say anything about the community as such. In the caste hierarchy, the Harijan are the lowest and referred to as untouchables. Locally the Harijan and Naicker are referred to as *Parayan* and *Pallan* which are now considered derogatory terms. They are economically impoverished, socially handicapped and suffer from the stigma of being unhygenic and unclean in their personal habits. A reference to Thurston about Parayan (Harijan) appears important.

"In a note on the Parayan, Sonnerat, writing in the 18th century says that they are prohibited from drawing water from the wells of other castes, but have wells of their own near their habitations round which they place the bones of animals, that they may be known and avoided. Parayan had to hold his hand before his mouth while talking to an Indian lest the latter may be contaminated with his breath and if he is met on the highway, he must turn on one side to let the other pass. If any Indian by accident touches a Parayan, he is obliged to purify himself in a bath. If the Parayan happens to see the utensils of caste people they break the utensils away. The Parayan eat beef, spit in their houses and even in their temples and while drinking they sip and thus are defiled with the spittle " (1909: Vol. 6: 77).

The style of address by the people reflects their hierarchical position in the village. One has to address a person belonging to higher caste with respect but the latter calls the former by name. The Harijans are called by their names by others whereas they have to address all others with respect.

The degree of refinement in language depends on the rank of the castes spoken to. When a Brahman or a member of any other caste talks to a member of lower caste the former does not use his language but uses the language of the lower group.

From the point of view of the villagers the hierarchy of the fifteen castes in the village can be shown as follows :

Brahman
Kanakkupillai
Mudaliar, Chettiar, Kolamani Mudaliar, Akamudaya Mudaliar, Tambiran, Naidu, Pillai, Mann Wodder
Achari
Naicker
Vannan, Ambattan
Harijan

Rules of commensality, purity and pollution, and untouchability correspond to the above order. One belonging to a lower caste does not enter the house belonging to a higher caste and vice versa. None among the clean caste population in the village has ever visited the Harijan colony. If a person of a lower caste has to convey any message or goods to a person of higher caste, he does so standing on the road. If the former is a rich person and not a Harijan, then he is offered seat on the outer verandah of the house of the higher caste man. Gestures of hospitality across caste in the form of offering a cup of coffee or any other drink were never observed.

Marriage is entirely an intra-caste business. Normally members of other castes, particularly those belonging to higher castes, never attend the marriage of the lower castes even when invited. During the present fieldwork, the richest man of the village, a Naicker, celebrated the marriage of this grand-daughter. Though he had invited all none but the Naickers attended the marriage. Some from the higher castes, had sent money as gifts to the bride.

The Harijans usually are never invited by the clean castes to the wedding feasts but are some times given some paddy and cash.

One of the ways a caste maintains its boundary is through endogamy. The religious activities are also organised caste-clusterwise, i.e., a group of castes arrange some religious fair in which each caste has its own role to perform. The Brahman maintain their superiority and remain a closed group. They disallow all processions-whether of marriage or of a deity-arranged by non-Brahmans to pass through their street. Avoidance of interaction with members of other castes is taught at the family level. In school though kids of all the castes including Harijans sit together in the same class, they hardly interact after the school hour. Children play on the streets of their respective castes and are not permitted to mix with children particularly belonging to lower castes. I observed children being beaten by their parents for the former's sitting on the streets of lower castes and watching games played by children belonging to lower castes.

Numerical strength and economic status do not seem to have brought any change in the socio-ritual hierarchy. Some individuals belonging to lower castes have been able to improve their economic conditions. As a result they enjoy only this much leeway now that the overall social situation is not as harsh on them as on their impoverished caste fellows :

> The intergroup relationship, between Harijan and the other weaker group namely Naicker, reveals a sharp cleavage who otherwise are close to one another. With reference to occupation, income and landholding, majority in both the groups are identical. Marriage is not an unbreakable tie among them. Elopement even after marriage is tolerated. Educationally both are backward. In spite of these common features and having been pushed to most oppressive conditions vis-a-vis the landowning higher caste people, there is no unity among them. The Harijan being untouchables, suffer from added disqualification and the Naicker maximally harp on the issue. The Naicker are the most vociferous in criticising the Harijan and spare no opportunity to emphasize that the Harijan are lowly caste and should have no claim for equal status with clean castes. Perhaps, the narrow social distance between the Harijan and the Naicker has made the latter over-conscious of their superiority. As a result, the two groups could seldom unite to fight for their common benefits such as higher wages and better economic conditions. The disunity among them helps the landowners to take full advantage of the situation (Mencher 1974).

Even within each of these two groups there is no unity. Petty matters like sex feuds and family quarrels become issues of major concern. There are reported cases of murders among both the

Naicker and Harijan due to internal conflicts. For instance, in a Naicker family there was a quarrel eight years ago over some women's making cowdung cakes on the threshing floor of their husband's brother. The quarrel started at night and before 12 O'clock one was killed on the spot and another had bad injuries on his face and hands in an attempted murder. In the Harijan colony, a girl was betrothed to a boy. Later on when the boy's brother-in-law went to her house to announce that for certain reasons the marriage had to be cancelled, he was instantly killed by the uncle of the girl. These divide the village society into innumerable inter caste and intra caste factions that inhabit economic and social development.

Social mobility

There is a conscious effort among almost all non-Brahman castes to raise their social status. The Harijans are no exception. They observe the following rules for gaining social status :

i) Adopt vegetarianism permanently as the Kanakku Pillais have done or to observe vegetarianism on certain occasions like new-moon days, Saturdays etc., which is done by most of the upper castes. One Harijan family has also adopted vegetarianism.
ii) Some Naicker and Harijan have given up eating beef.
iii) Observance of ancestor worship among lower castes including the Harijan. Two families among the Harijan observe ancestor worship.During my fieldwork, I witnessed one family observing that ritual at an expense of Rs. 150.00. A non-Brahman priest attended the ritual in the Harijan house and also in the houses of the lower castes, such as Naicker, Naidu, Pillai. Uncooked rice, pulses, vegetables, coconut, and cash were given to him. A new sari or dhoti was purchased according to the sex of the deceased and given to the nearest kin after the puja was performed. A vegetarian meal was cooked and eaten by the family that day.
iv) The practice of negotiated marriage is becoming popular among all caste including the Harijan, Previously marriage by elopement and bringing a wife home without any formal celebration or announcement was the accepted norm. Among the Harijans there were two such incidence during my stay in

the field but the concerned parties were very much ashamed about it. Now a days they prefer arranged marriages.

Deliberate attempt for gaining social status has brought about some changes, mostly at the individual level. As a group, only the Kanakku Pillai have succeeded in raising their social status to such an extent that even the Brahman eat food from them.

Elite and their role

One household of the Harijans, members of which are somewhat educated in comparison to others has adopted vegetarianism and the practice of offering ancestor worship and thus stands unique in the colony. The young men of that household and their friends from the colony wish that their community should soon be freed from the stigma of untouchability. They also aspire for better economic prosperity.

These youngsters have substantial control over economic resources. Some have good jobs. They work for the upliftment of their community. They feel that their community is not weak by itself. The machination of people of the higher castes has made their existence miserable. Their contention is that the Harijan should no more accept the office of *vettian*, the lowest position in the cadre of village officials. Out of the 223 Harijan households, there are eight that inherit the office of *vettian* for one year once in eight years. A *vettian* has to keep watch over the village fields, a service that earns him some grains from the farmers at the time of harvest. He also attends funerals and cremation ground (watching the corpse burn completely), removes carcasses and makes any announcement in the village as instructed by the village *munsif*. The enlightened Harijans do not appreciate this assignment but the *vettian* concerned does not mind it as this gives him some monetary gains. The former want that the Harijans should give up beef-eating but the Harijans in general do not want to give it up as they cannot afford to buy any other meat.

The majority of the Harijans feel that the enlightened ones have already built a sound future for themselves and are demanding sacrifices from the impoverished lot. The dire poverty condition of the large majority of the Harijans has left little hopes for any bright future. So they prefer to stick to their traditional life-style.

The enlightened few among Harijans are particular about

cleanliness. They have become vegetarians, and keep ordinary Harijans off their way. This alienates the mass from their leaders. The more the elite imitate the upper caste way of life the more becomes their relative distance.

Education

There are two schools in the village, one in the main hamlet having classes upto the eighth standard and the other in the Harijan colony, having classes upto the fifth standard. In the former students constitute the upper caste Hindu and the Harijans, the latter is attended exclusively by Harijan children. Children passing out from the eighth standard school go to Walajabad High School for further study. Nearest colleges are situated in Chingleput and Conjeevaram.

Only among the Brahman and Kanakku Pillai there are some graduates. All other castes put together, there is only handful of matriculates. Among the Pillai, Mann Wodder, and Kolamani Mudaliar there is a very high proportion of illiterates but as their numerical strength too small no generalization by caste seems valid. Among the Harijan and Naicker also the proportion of literacy is low.

Those who are educated above IXth or Xth standard aspire for white collar jobs. They consider it below their dignity to work as labourers. The literates include school going children and post-school adults. Adults of this category seldom used their education for deriving any benefits. At present many of them forgot how to read or write.

Economy

Agriculture is the main source of livelihood in the village. Traditionally the Harijan served as *padial* under the Brahman landlords. The *padi* service is a type of unwritten contract between the landlord and the agricultural labourer according to which the labourer has to work from sunrise to sunset and at times even beyond that hour. For this service he gets some ragi porridge in the morning, a meal consisting of rice and curry in the afternoon and about 75 kgs of paddy per month. In this arrangement, he is assured of his payments every months irrespective of whether agriculturally it is a peak or loan season. Marriage and funeral are occasions when

TABLE 2: Percentage distribution of households by income, landholding, and literacy

No. of households	caste, population		Percentage distribution of per capita/annual income (in Rs.)			Percentage distribution of per capita/landholding (in acres)			Percentage distribution of literacy (Standards)				
			< 360	< 500	> 500	Nil	< .6	> .6	Nil	I to VIII	IC & X	SSLC & PUC	B.A. & more
223	1205	Harijan	80	92	8	51	96.6	3.4	73	24	2.8	.2	—
82	383	Naicker	39	75	25	53	87.2	12.8	59.5	36.8	3.4	.3	—
3	7	Vannan	28	100	—	100	100	—	57	43	—	—	—
1	2	Kolamani Mudaliar	100	100	—	100	100	—	100	—	—	—	—
1	5	Chettiar	—	—	100	100	100	—	20	60	20.0	—	—
2	6	Mann Wodder	—	100	—	100	100	—	66.7	33.3	—	—	—
3	22	Achari	—	91	9	50	100	—	36.4	63.6	—	—	—
4	28	Ambattan	100	100	—	78.6	100	—	35.7	57.1	3.6	3.6	—
4	20	Pillai	20	30	20	60	100	—	85	15	—	—	—
6	34	Akamudaya	66	65	34	70.6	100	—	11.8	55.9	26.5	5.8	—
5	26	Tambiran	31	88	12	50	100	—	30.7	61.5	—	7.7	—
8	29	Naidu Mudaliar	38	52	48	48.3	89.7	10.3	44.8	41.4	13.8	—	—
30	190	Mudaliar	7	15	85	11.6	54.2	45.8	33.2	51	13.2	2.6	—
5	29	Kanakku Pillai	—	—	100	—	—	100	6.9	58.6	17.2	10.3	7
13	46	Brahman	—	30	70	26.1	80.4	19.6	6.5	43.5	13	32.2	4.4

people run short of money. A landlord then gives his *padial* interest free loan even without any security. But growing awareness among Harijans of their socio-ritual and economic deprivation has created a feeling of disfavour for the *padial* service. Now hardly 10 per cent of them are engaged as *padials* and this is the only type of permanent contract for labourer existent in the village.

The Harijans are mostly employed as daily wage labourers. In this term there is no obligation on either side. The landlord as well as the labourer can make his choice. During peak agricultural seasons like transplanting, weeding, and harvesting all Harijan men and women get employment as wage labourers. Sometimes labourers from outside the village are also employed. But during the lean period there is little demand for labour and as a result none among daily wage labourer remain engaged throughout the year.

Previously the Naicker worked only as agricultural labourers and never as a *padial*. At present there are three *padials* among them, and most of the others are daily wage earners. In 1973 a woman labourer was paid Rs. 1.50 per day and a man was paid Rs. 2.50 per day.

Details of monthly household budget in a Harijan or Naicker household indicates that about 87 per cent of their total expenditure is on food. Cereals alone cost them 67 per cent. Dantwala stated that between 60 per cent and 80 per cent of household expenditure of low income groups is spent on food (1973 :23). Thus, from the economic angle it may be advantageous for the Harijan to go in for *padial* service, particularly when the price of rice in Tamil Nadu has shot up from Rs. 1.50 per kg. in 1973 to Rs.3 per kg. in 1975. In spite of this advantage the majority of the Harijans have given up *padial* service as it is considered derogatory. As the rate of daily wage do not record any corresponding change with the fluctuation of price of food grains the real income of the Harijans has declined With population increase and unexpandable job situation their employment problems has further intensified.

Landowner - Tenant Relationship

In Palayasivaram, there are two types of tenancy. The first is known as *kuthagai*, according to which the tenant has to pay a fixed amount either in cash or kind (grains) to the landowner, irrespective of the quantum of yield. If the tenant does not pay it either due to failure of crops or some other reason, the dues are carried forward to the next year. Lands having irrigation facilities are given on *kuthagai* contract.

The second type is known as *vaaram*, according to which the tenant has to pay 50 per cent of the yield on the land. Lands irrigated by rains water are generally given on *vaaram* terms. As both the parties are interested in making maximum gain out of the contract they do not have very cordial relationship. The landlords suspect the tenants and the latter considers the former blood-suckers.

Land Reforms and Tenancy

The Tamil Nadu land reforms (fixation ceiling on land) Act 1962 (Act 58/61) has fixed the ceiling limit from 30 to 60 standard acres depending on the number of members in the family and certain other factors. In continuation of this, the Tamil Nadu land reforms (Reduction of ceiling on land) Act 1970 (Act 17/70) was added in 1970 limiting the ceiling from 30 to 15 standard acres. There were also other acts such as the Tamil Nadu Occupants of Kudiyiruppu (Conferment of ownership) Act (1971) and the Tamil Nadu Cultivating Tenants Protection Act, 1955 which were in favour of the tenants and labourers. Though no one has been directly affected by these acts in this village, they have made the landlords alert and hence no landlord wishes to give his lands on long term lease. He keeps on changing his tenants every year. This has created a feeling of insecurity among tenants. This and the increase of man per acre of land has made people rush for lands. As a result, land rents have enormously increased. The amount of rent has increased fourfold between 1971 and 1973. This leaves scope only for marginal profit of tenants. As most of the village lands depend on rain water the tenant not only lose marginal gain but become indebted in case of any drought.

Occupational Mobility

There had not been any significant change in the occupation of the different castes. Majority in each of the castes continue their traditional occupation.

Agriculture is still the main source of livelihood. In the cases of Vanna, Ambattan, and Achari the *jajmani* system, locally termed as *murai*, still persists. The barbers are adversely affected because the youngsters prefer to go to the saloons in the nearby town of Walajabad for hair-cut and they shave their beards themselves. Only the old men utilize services of barbers once or twice a week. The income or patronage extended to the barber has thus decreased. Due to availability of trained midwives and maternity hospitals in the rural areas services of the barber's wife at child-births are not utilised either. With two free meals and whatever remunerations they receive for playing musical instruments during auspicious occasions in Hindu homesteads they manage themselves. A barber boy matriculated two years back is yet to get a job.

The younger generation among the Achari have migrated to the nearby city and towns as there is a steady demand for their services in urban areas on better wages. In the newly developed areas also they continue to live on their traditional occupation. Other minority castes of Palayasivaram like Kolamani Mudaliar, Chettiar, Mann Wodder, Pillai, Akamudaya Mudaliar, Tambiran, and Naidu live on their respective traditional occupations. Partly because of non-availability of alternatives and partly due to hangover of traditional values and structure, they continue their traditional occupations. A few Akamudaya Mudaliar and Tambiran have, however, taken to teaching profession.

In the year 1942, when yarn price went up, the Mudaliar suddenly prospered and some of them turned out as substantial land-owners. Brahmans by then had started migrating to the urban areas selling out their land. About 50 per cent of the Mudaliar who could not take advantage of the situation continue their traditional occupation of weaving. Prosperous landowners are now interested in diversification of their investment and opening textile shops, flour mills, or wholesale trade of *lungis*.

The Kanakku Pillai are successful agriculturists. As the region is not rich in water supply, they have started growing casuarina trees and doing trade in groundnuts through which they could build fortunes. Their youngsters after graduation have secured well-paying white collar jobs in banks and offices.

Most of the previous Brahman landlords have either leased out or sold away their lands. Many of them now depend on white collar jobs. They still live in the village as the cost of living here is low but those who have some lands in the village and derive full benefits of them prefer to live in the village.

TABLE 3 Occupational distribution by caste

Sl. No.	Occupa-	Hari-jan	Naic-ker	Van-nan	Amba-ttan	Kola-mani Muda-liar	Che-ttiar der liar	Man-wod-Muda-	Ach-ari ran	Pil-lai pallai	Akamu-daya	Tam-bi-	Nai-du	Kana-kku	Brah-man	Muda-liar	Total
1	2	3	4	5	6	7	8	9	10	11	12	13	14	15	16	17	18
1.	Landlord	—	1	—	—	—	—	—	—	—	—	—	—	—	1	13	15
2.	Cultivator	40	29	—	—	—	—	—	—	1	—	—	3	—	—	1	74
3.	Cultivator & Agricul-tural labour	32	23	—	—	—	—	—	—	—	—	—	—	—	—	—	55
4.	Agricultural labour	206	23	—	—	—	—	—	—	—	—	—	—	—	—	—	229
5.	House keeping & Agricul-tural labour	191	59	—	—	—	—	—	—	2	—	—	2	—	—	1	225
6.	White collar job	27	5	—	—	—	—	—	—	—	2	1	2	3	10	6	56
7.	Traditional service	—	—	6	4	1	1	2	7	6	—	—	—	1	—	19	47
8.	Traders	3	10	—	—	—	—	—	—	—	1	—	1	—	—	4	19
9.	House keeping	92	57	—	8	—	1	2	7	5	8	8	8	7	13	40	256
10.	Studying	178	60	1	9	—	3	2	5	2	11	4	3	12	12	63	365
11.	Not enga-ged in any work	341	86	—	7	1	—	—	3	4	10	7	7	4	4	41	515
12.	Teacher	2	2	—	—	—	—	—	—	—	2	1	—	1	2	1	11
13.	Padi Service	39	3	—	—	—	—	—	—	—	—	—	—	—	—	—	42

(Contd.)

TABLE 3 (*Contd.*)

1	2	3	4	5	6	7	8	9	10	11	12	13	14	15	16	17	18
14.	Grazing cattle	28	7	—	—	—	—	—	—	—	—	—	—	—	—	—	35
15.	Thotta Kaval	2	—	—	—	—	—	—	—	—	—	—	—	—	—	—	2
16.	Rearing Duck	4	—	—	—	—	—	—	—	—	—	—	—	—	—	—	4
17.	Factory or Dock worker	7	1	—	—	—	—	—	—	—	—	—	—	—	—	—	8
18.	Tiffin Business	1	—	—	—	—	—	—	—	—	—	—	—	—	—	—	1
19.	Dhobi	2	—	—	—	—	—	—	—	—	—	—	—	—	—	—	2
20.	Jalli (stone) breaking	9	—	—	—	—	—	—	—	—	—	—	—	—	—	—	9
21.	Cook	—	—	—	—	—	—	—	—	—	—	—	—	—	2	—	2
22.	Weaving	—	7	—	—	—	—	—	—	—	—	5	—	—	—	—	12
23.	Priest	—	—	—	—	—	—	—	—	—	—	—	—	—	1	—	1
24.	Tailor	—	4	—	—	—	—	—	—	—	—	—	—	—	—	1	5
25.	Village Officer	1	—	—	—	—	—	—	—	—	—	—	—	3	1	1	6
26.	Carpentry	—	6	—	—	—	—	—	—	—	—	—	—	—	—	—	6
	Total	1205	383	7	23	2	5	6	22	20	34	26	29	29	46	190	2032

Among the Naicker and Harijan, the majority are agricultural labourers. Some of them, after retirement from military service have acquired lands and a few others have become tenant cultivators. Excepting three Harijan and a few Naicker, landholdings among them are meagre. They, however, carry on cultivation on own land as well as on others land.

Among the Harijans and the Naickers there are white collar job holders, traders, teachers, and dock workers. Some of the Naickers have taken to non-traditional occupations such as weaving, tailoring, and carpentry.

A large number of the Harijans and Naikers are not engaged in any work. If children below 15 years of age and old people above 60 years of age are discounted, the respective percentage of unengaged Harijan and Naicker becomes 55 and 42 per cent.

Access to economic innovations

Villagers having enough capital adopt agricultural innovations such improved variety of seeds, chemical fertilizers, pesticides and irrigation facilities. A few Brahman landowners, some Mudaliar, Kanakku Pillai, and a few Naickers have adopted these new practices. People having enough resources if fall short of money, banks and other agencies help them. The small landowners are unable to take advantage of modern innovations because they lack supporting funds and have minimum control over resources.

The canal from Palar used for irrigating fields had been maintained by the Brahman, Mudaliar, Kanakku Pillai, and Naicker since decades. The Harijans, some of whom have now become landowners are denied the privilege by members of other castes even if they offer their share of labour in maintenance of the canal.

A prosperous Harijan does not like improved variety of seeds because this rice when cooked in the form of rice or *idli* (a rice cake) does not come out tasty. Secondly, the straw they get is less and is insufficient for their cattle.

Poultry and fishing development programmes have not been successful among the poor and low caste groups. As both men and women among them go for work they have no time to maintain poultry which needs considerable care. Poultry itself can be taken up as a full time job. But to start one in large scale one requires both capital and some know-how. The poor and lower castes lack both. As there is no tank around and as the sea is far off the villagers have no fishing industry.

Sources of finance for agricultural production/distribution

Small farmers for meeting expenses of their agricultural operations borrow money from money-lenders as banks as also other governmental agencies demand adequate surety before granting loans. Private money-lenders often charge the interest in terms of grain 75 kgs of paddy per annum on Rs. 100. At the time of harvest they come and collect interest. Poor villagers having low income, borrow money to make good the deficit of family budget. Due to difficulties in getting loan from banks, they approach private money-lenders. If some ornaments (gold or silver) or vessels are mortgaged, the rate of interest comes down between 50 to 75 per cent per annum.

None among Harijans of Palayasivaram got credits from banks at Walajabad and Conjeevaram. A few substantial landowners due to their contact and influence had managed to get credits from the banks in time.

Assets and Income

Most of the houses had live-stock cows and/or bullocks. A few among Naickers and Harijans reared sheep, duck, and chicken.

Substantial landholders and all Brahmans had some gold ornaments and silver vessels. Most of the Naickers and Harijans also had ornaments but of little resale value. Ornaments they get at the time of marriage are mostly pawned out within a year or two. It may be stated here that exact assessment of wealth of villagers was not possible as the people did not like to divulge such information.

Accurate income of villagers could not be calculated either. A few villagers having regular jobs in office, factory, school, and the landowners could give exact information. In case those who get their wages partly in cash and partly in kind like the *padial*, the income has been calculated by converting kind to cash. People in business or trade could not state their exact income. In case of daily wage earners also there was considerable difficulty in working out income because of no record keeping and unsteady employment situation.

The following chart indicates monthly consumption requirement of a Harijan or Naicker family consisting of five members.

Item	Quantity required for a month	Approximate amount spent per month in rupees (1973)
1. Rice	$1^1/_2$ Madras measure per day @ Rs. 1.50 per M.M.	70
2. Ragi	1 Madras measure per day Re.1 per M.M	30
3. Pulses, spices & other provisions Oil	—	10
4. Oil	—	8
5. Vegetable & meat	—	12
6. Clothes	—	10
7. Miscellaneous (medicine, soap, betel) nut & leaves, liquor etc.	—	10
Total		150

Nearly 80 per cent of the Harijans and almost 58 per cent of the village population as a whole lived on income below Rs. 360.00 per head per year. According to Vagiswari's study of Harijan in Chingleput District, 80 per cent of Harijan had their income below Rs. 363.00 per annum. From the data on the landholdings in table 2, it is observed that 966 people (48 percent) in the village,irrespective of the caste,are landless and 844 (42 per cent) people have very small landholdings (less than 0.6 acre per head). Clubbing these two categories together 1810 persons or about 89 per cent of the village population are either landless or near landless. Detailed distribution of landholdings by caste and number of households is given in table 4.

As already indicated, the great majority of the Harijans and Naickers either have no land or very small landholdings. Only 3 per cent of Harijans and 13 per cent Naickers have more than 0.6 acre per head. Harijan households having more than 5 or 10 acres of land are large joint families with all married brother living together. Repeated failure of rains and poor irrigational facilities invite very few buyers of small plots of land. In their anxiety to become landowners for enhancing prestige the Harijans and Naickers go for such land even if their possession is uneconomic.

TABLE 4: Distribution of landholdings

Sl. No.	Caste	Total no. of house holds	No land	No.of households having Upto 3 acres of land	3-5 acres of land	5-10 acres of land	More than 10 acres
1	2	3	4	5	6	7	8
1.	Vannan	3	3	—	—	—	—
2.	Ambattan	4	3	1	—	—	—
3.	Kolamani Mudalliar	1	1	—	—	—	—
4.	Chettiar	1	1	—	—	—	—
5.	Mann Wodder	2	2	—	—	—	—
6.	Achari	4	2	2	—	—	—
7.	Pillai	4	2	2	—	—	—
8.	Akamudaya Mudaliar	6	4	2	—	—	—
9.	Tambiran	5	2	3	—	—	—
10.	Naidu	8	5	2	1	—	—
11.	Kanakku Pillai	5	—	—	—	4	1
12.	Brahman	13	7	3	2	—	1
13.	Mudaliar	30	6	11	3	5	5
14.	Naicker	82	46	27	3	4	2
15.	Harijan	223	141	75	3	3	1

Among fifteen castes in the villages the Chettiar, Mudaliar, Brahman, and Kanakku Pillai are economically well off. The Kannakku Pillai and the majority of the Mudaliar have substantial landholdings. The Kanakku Pillai derive good income both from lands as well as from white-collar jobs in which their young men are engaged. For the Mudaliar, land is the main source of income and quite a good number of them are substantial landowners. Trade provides sufficient income to the Chettiar. The Brahman due to their higher education have taken to white collar jobs which fetch them high and steady income.

Consumption pattern and material life style

Types of dwellings people live in indicate their economic status. Till recently, all the Harijan and Naicker lived in huts, with roofs thatched with straw. Some Brahmans, Mudaliars, and Carpenters lived in houses with tiled roofs. The remaining Brahmans lived in houses having terraced roofs while all others lived in huts. Recently some of the Naickers and Harijans also have improved their economic condition and started living in tile and terrace-roofed houses.

No houses in the village has attached latrines. Open lands at the back of the houses or fields, in and around the village are used for defecation. There are no scavengers but, pigs and dogs do the cleaning.

In the main hamlet each house has some open space at its back. In the Harijan colony there is very little open space and the streets are narrow. Though there are more than two hundred and twenty houses of Harijans, the area they have for residential purposes is much smaller than the area on which 167 houses of the upper castes are built. Every houses in the Harijan colony without exception had one or more persons suffering from some diseases whereas in the main hamlet such cases were few.

In the past when rice was available in plenty and at a fair price, for Harijans and Naickers its intake was a luxury. They would consume rice only on rare occasions. Ragi (millet) was and is their staple diet. Members of higher castes who are economically well off can only afford to eat rice regularly.

The Harijans and Naickers could rarely afford to celebrate festivals in their own homes. They had to satisfy themselves by observing festivals at their master's home. Now a few Naickers and Harijans celebrate festivals by buying new clothes, preparing good and special food in their respective households. A few also consume rice once a day.

Brahmans, Kanakku Pillais, and Mudaliars eat food rich in quality and variety. They have coffee and snacks (*idli, dosa, uppittu* etc.) every morning and rice with *sambar*, *rasam*, buttermilk, and vegetables twice a day. A Naicker has been able to accumulate wealth and is now the richest man in the village. He can well afford to eat good food but seldom does so. He prefers to save as much as possible and spends money only on essential items.

In the past, Harijans would not dare to wear shirts, foot wear, or a clean *lungi* in the presence of higher castes. Their women were not accustomed to use blouses. Now at least some of them use pants, clean *lungis*, blouses, and good silk saris. Gold ornaments are also used by a few atleast at the time of wedding celebrations.

Magico-religious life

There are many temples in the village three of whom devoted to Mariamman, one to Ganesha, and another to Sri Lakshmi Narasimha Swamy. Animal sacrifices are made in the Mariamman temples. In the past goats and fowls were sacrificed there. Now only fowls are sacrificed and that too occasionally. In all other temples offerings consist of coconuts, other fruits, and cooked food. The priest in the Sri Lakshmi Narasimha Swamy temple is a Vaishnava Brahman. In other temples non-Brahmans officiate as priests. Among weaker sections, Naickers though live in the main hamlet rarely attend temples. One of them, however, works as the watchman of the Sri Lakshmi Narasimha Swamy temple on a fixed monthly wage and some food. Brahmans and members of other higher castes like Kanakku, Pillai, Mudaliar attend temples, more or less regularly.

The deity of Kancheepuram temple is brought in a procession to the village once a year. This is considered a very important occasion for the villagers. Expenses of the day are contributed by the villagers in proportion to their landholdings. Harijans and Naickers were previously landless and no money used to be collected from them. Now, a few families among them own land and landowning Naikers contribute some money for the purpose. As the deity is not taken in procession to the Cheri where the Harijans live, no money is collected from them.

Local Ambattans play music daily in the temple of Shri Lakshmi Narasimha Swamy, a Kankku pillai is the temple accountant, three Brahmans (Iyengar) officiate as priests and one Iyengar cooks the *prasad* for offering to the deity. All receive nominal payments for their services. During the annual festivals when the deity is brought down from the hill to the main village in procession, service of Naickers are employed to carry on their shoulder the whole platform on which the deity and the Brahman priests are seated. For this service the Naickers receive a day's wage in cash. Harijans are permitted to come to the temple and see the deity once a year when the deity from Conjeevaram is also brought there.

The villagers do not observe any regular cycle of pilgrimage. One goes on pilgrimage according to individual needs and conveniences. Higher the caste position wider is the network of pilgrim centres. Two Brahmans have visited Banaras, Rameswara, Haridwar, and Tirupati, Among Mudaliars, some have gone to Tirupati while among Naikers and Harijan no one visited any pilgrim centre beyond 20 miles of the village. Festivals celebrated within a range of ten miles are attended by most of the villagers irrespective of their caste identity. The annual festivals in the Mariamman temple are considered great event for those belonging to the lower castes.

Though according to the Temple Entry Act of 1947, a Harijan has the right to enter any temple, he does not normally visit this temple. He does not visit even the other temples maintained by non-Brahmans. They mostly make offerings to Mariamman individually and none from the higher castes ordinarily attend that temple in the Cheri. Of late the popularity of the Marimman has impressed Brahmans some of whom have started attending this temple and making offerings.

Concepts like heaven-hell, virtue-sin, *karma, dharma*, are not usually understood by the Naickers and Harijans. The enlightened few among them have knowledge about these concepts but they interpret them as tools of higher castes to exploit them.

Conversion/change in faith

About half a dozen Harijans have embraced Christianity. All of them are educated and well employed. They hardly interact with fellow castemen or other co-villagers. Converts in general are, however, not considered unsuitable for matrimonial purposes.

Politics

In the past, Brahmans were politically dominating all over Tamil Nadu. Economic, ritual, and social gaps between the Brahmans and non-Brahmans in the villages were very wide. Only after 1940, nearly 50 per cent of the Maudiliars could build fortunes and buy large agricultural landholdings. As Brahmans being educated started migrating to cities and towns in search of white-collar jobs, the Kanakku Pillai in the village became prosperous and powerful. The office of the village Munsif (headman) created by the British in the 1816 (Gough : 1960;36) with police is still held by a Brahman. This office has become hereditary. In the year 1836, collection of revenue was added to his function and even now he has the legal authority to try cases of debt, theft, or other disputes involving not more than 50 rupees. Cases involving bigger amount are referred to the police station at Walajabad. The Karnam is the Kanakku Pillai and the Thalayaris are Naidus. The lowest post, Vettain, is held by a Harijan.

With the introduction of the Panchayat Raj in 1960, every district is divided into 3 or 4 blocks. Each block has a Panchayat union which is responsible for implementation of development programmes in villages within the jurisdiction. Every village in a block elects its own president and the presidents from among themselves elect the chairman of the block or Panchayat Union. These elections are conducted once in five years on the basis of adult franchise. Though the Naickers and Harijans are numerically dominant in the village, due to inter-group and inter-group conflicts among themselves they could not so far derive any benefit.

In the elections of the State Legislative Assembly and Parliament members of the lower castes agreed to vote for one party and did accordingly. The State Legislative Assembly member for this locality is a Harijan. He has not visited the village as yet.

Concluding Remarks

The whole framework of the society in this village is still based on caste principles as in the past, with only difference that the Brahmans who were dominant earlier in all spheres of activities are not in the same commanding position at present. There are less Brahmans in the village now and those who have remained there are indifferent in village affairs. Taking Tamil Nadu as a whole, consolidation of anti-Brahman forces and rise of middle range castes led to the decline of power of Brahmans. This shift, however, did not lead to any structural change in the society. In villages like Palayasivaram, instead of Brahmans, Kanakku Pillais or Mudaliars dominate the village scene. Naickers and Harijans are at the bottom as before.

There has been hardly any change in the means of production and in the distribution mechanism in the village. Due to lack of irrigational facilities modern agricultural innovations could not make much inroads. Traditional methods of cultivation are still largely in vogue. Traditional employer – employee relationships also continue to exist to a large extent. As in the past, landlords derive the maximum benefit out of the toil of poor labourers.

Leach remarks that the economic sufferings of the low castes are not entirely due to their position in the caste system i.e. not because they are low castes but because present conditions have turned them into an unemployed working class (1960: 6). Facts of Palayasivaram support this view.

Systematic education leads people to development and prosperity. But even a crash programme of education benefits only the second or third generation of the group of people among whom it is implemented, provided efforts to make it a success are not relaxed. Measures such as compulsory education atleast upto SSLC (matriculation) for all, co-operative farming among small landholders, credit facilities at lower rates of interest for all, opening of some industries in the rural areas to absorb the unemployed and thc under-employed may improve the economic and social lot of the weaker sections if these measures are undertaken earnestly, honestly, and sincerely.

REFERENCES

Dandekar, V.M. & Nilakantha Rath. Poverty in India, *Economic and Political Weekly*. Vol. VI, No.1, 1971.

Dantwala, M.L. *Poverty in India, Then & Now 1870-1970*. Macmillan Co. of India Ltd, 1973.

Leach, E.R. (ed.) *Aspects of Caste in South India, Ceylon & Northwest Pakistan*. Cambridge University Press, 1960.

Mencher, Joan P. The Caste System Upside Down, or the Not-so-Mysterious East, *Current Anthropology* Vol.15, No.4, 1974.

Peter, Townsend(ed.) *The Concept of Poverty*. Heinemann Educational Book Ltd., London. 1970.

Sahlins, Marshall. *Stone Age Economics*. Chicago, 1972.

Vagiswari, A. *Income-earning Trends & Social Status of the Harijan Community in Tamil Nadu*. Sangam Publishers, Madras, 1972.

24

ANJUMOORTHY : A VILLAGE IN NORTH KERALA

P.R.G. MATHUR

Introduction

Malabar had been, for many years, a subject of profound interest and has attracted many distinguished scholars, explorers, missionaries, investigators, and in recent times a number of social scientists. But no detailed study of the weaker sections inhabiting this region has been attempted with the exception of the studies of Iyer (1908), Thurston (1912), Logan (1912), and Aiyappan (1944). Several other social anthropologists have, however, attempted studies on the economic aspects of castes. These are Wiser (1936), Bailey (1958), Majumdar (1958), Epstein (1962), Gough (1960), Aiyappan (1965) and Beteille (1967) to mention a few.

Field Methods

The present study was conducted in Anjumoorthy, a village in Palghat District of North Kerala. This district was chosen for the present study for three reasons. First, Palghat is the granary of Kerala where the Cherumans and Iravas constitute the overwhelming majority of the agricultural population. Second, Palghat has been exposed to the process of economic and social changes slowly and steadily during the last fifty years, yet caste plays a crucial role in the life of the people not only in the economic but also in the social and ideological sphere. Third, the peasant movements in Palghat organised by different political parties, have changed the lot of the weaker sections of the population to an appreciable extent. Incidentally, the present author was born and brought up there and thus had an intimate knowledge of the entire district, particularly of the neighbourhood of Palghat.

The field work in Anjumoorthy was conducted between January and July, 1973. Field techniques used in the present study included interviews, participant observation, case studies, use of questionnaires, schedules, village revenue records, and the census data.

A major part of the data was collected through participant observations and case studies. The village had a large concentration of the weaker sections. I lived with the weaker sections of the people in the village during the major part of the field work in order to know them as one of them. I participated in all activities of the every day life of the weaker sections. I took part particularly in their economic, social, and religious activities. I dined with them particularly at marriages and ceremonies connected with life cycle rites. My close and sustained observation enabled me to understand the happenings in the lives of the weaker sections of society and study the manner in which social, cultural, and economic institutions work in an organized whole.

The method of interviewing people either individually or in groups has been employed for eliciting information. Life histories and other materials provided by elderly and particularly informative informants have been taken down verbatim. I had to contact a number of informants for the collection of quantitative case materials since information provided by one source or an individual sometimes sounded meaningless. For instance Kunjan, a Cheruṃan was an expert in economic and political affairs. But his knowledge of magic, religious rites, values, attitudes etc was limited. He was unwilling to reveal that he was an active worker of the Communist Party of India (Marxist). Vella, an aged headman, was an expert in mythologies, but his knowledge of genealogies was limited. Shaman Chami was superb in his speciality of occult, art, magic, mythology, and religion but his knowledge in economic and political affairs was very poor.

The method of participant observation has certain weaknesses. The most important draw back is that one cannot witness or participate in all sorts of functions. One can observe or participate a behaviour which is generally allowed to be observed. In order to compensate such loss I had to employ a number of informants for case studies. I laid emphasis on collection of cases of economic transactions, caste disputes, quarrels between peasants and agricultural labourers on the one hand and between the landlords and tenants on the other besides marriages, magical performances, rituals, etc. Sometimes several informants gave different accounts of the same case. The individuals who were physically present in such cases were generally interviewed for ascertaining the truth. Thus, accurate data about individual transactions were gathered. These were used for both qualitative and quantitative analysis.

Whenever I found a case study inadequate, individual informants were invited to my camp and served with food. I led discussions to the topics in which I was interested. Such informants gave information about private matters such as possession, savings, financial deals, debts, credits, sales, leases, besides their attitudes towards their leaders and national leaders. They also provided information on agrarian relations, land disputes, caste disputes and unrest among the agricultural labourers. I avoided generalisation and concentrated upon facts about which the informant himself had the first hand information. A large number of male and female informant were thus subjected to extensive interrogations. I used the general pattern of a questionnaire in order to observe comparative values in the interviews. Thus my queries were divided into informants' life history, economic, social, political and kinship relationships, technological skills and practices, attitudes, values, ideas, and beliefs.

I also interviewed a number of informants for recording genealogies. From each lineage the headman was interviewed. His information was checked and counter checked by one or two other informants belonging to the same lineage. While recording genealogies, I noted the individual names of genealogical relationships, the affiliations, the domicile, the name of villages from which or to which a girl was given in marriage, the age of the living and so on. The genealogies enabled me to obtain significant demographic material and abundant data on kinship and marriage. Furthermore, they helped me to check and counter check the accuracy and reliability of several informants.

Detailed mapping has been undertaken with the assistance of revenue officials and educated informants. Fields, both wet and dry, irrigated lands and tapioca and sugarcane lands, coconut gardens, the settlement pattern of the village, particularly the location of the houses of the weaker sections were mapped. The maps became an important source for analysing the economic organisation of the village.

There were some problems connected with the determination of the yield of both tapioca and rice. The estimates of their yields were made on the basis of my own observation and the information given by informants. The prices of the commodities prevalent at the time of field work were taken into consideration.

During the first week of my research, my main purpose was to establish rapport with the informants belonging to the weaker sections, particularly the Cherumans, the artisans and the Iravas. Accordingly the first week was devoted to informal talks with the Harijans, the Iravas, and other weaker sections of the population besides eliciting information on improvements they felt were needed, the kinds of improvements they considered more feasible, both on the family and caste basis, the history of past efforts of the Government etc. Afterwards I collected a sufficient amount of basic demographic data. Much of these materials were gathered on a household and family basis. As the villagers were not ready to reveal their assets, I collected the data on land holding from the head of the households. A census of the village was taken. After establishing rapport with the informants, I collected data from them on the pattern of land ownership, size of their holdings, the expenditure on cultivation, possession of animals, oxen, bullock carts, agricultural implements including tractor etc. Apart from the economic pursuits, data were also collected on the kinship system, lineage and family organization besides political affiliations, ideas, values, attitude, and beliefs. The account in all these spheres were related to the economy of the weaker sections and also to the changing pattern since Independence.

Anjumoorthy

Anjumoorthy is a multi-ethnic village located in the south west of Palghat District, Kerala. The village is 30 km. away from the district town and about 9 km. away from Alathur, the tahsil headquarters. Anjumoorthy occupies an area of 3215.89 acres, out of which 1157.75 acres are wet land and 1586.5 acres are unoccupied dry land. Homesteads occupy 118.57 acres and the *poramboke* (Government waste land) 126.76 acres and the rest are garden land. Out of a total of 1157.75 acres wet land, 836.17 acres are irrigated by Mangalam and Pthundi dams.

According to the 1901 Census the population of the village was

2878. In 1961 the population increased to 4671. According to my census of 1973, the population figure rose to 5625.

Communication

Anjumoorthy is served by three all weather roads through which buses ply connecting the village with the towns of Palghat and Trichur. One of the roads is a National Highway leading to Trivandrum, the capital of the State. The village is about 35 km. south west of the Olavakot Railway junction from where the villagers go to different places in India.

The village had little communication facilities before Independence. The present main road connecting Palghat and Trichur was built only in 1947. Now buses ply at an interval of 30 minutes. Most of the private buses are owned by the Irava and most of the trucks are owned by the Irava and Muslim. The village is connected to pilgrim centres like Guruvayur (90 km. from the village) and Palani (130 km. from the village) by road.

Previously the major means of transport of goods was bullock cart. Now-a-days trucks are used for transporting paddy to Palghat rice mills. There are two taxis in the village which are owned by two local Nair. There are about 20 taxis at Vadakkancherry, 2 km. away from the village, which are frequently hired by the rich Irava.

The villagers of Anjumoorthy do not constitute an isolated community. Some of the enterprising members of the Tamil Brahman and Nair communities have crossed the seven seas as far as America, Burma, Malaysia, and Singapore in search of employment. One of the Tamil Brahmans of the village holds a very senior post in Delhi. Though there is a high rate of literacy among the Brahman and Nair there is not a single person from the weaker sections like the Irava, Harijan, and other backward castes who holds a degree.

In the past the local traders supplied the necessities of life to the villagers and it was they who took frequent trips to Palghat. Now villagers themselves make daily trips there.

Well-to-do Brahman and Nair often go to Palghat for medical check up and performing pilgrimage to Sabarimala, Guruvayur and Palani. At present there is a great deal of traffic among the Irava and Nair to the courts at Palghat and Aluthur because of litigation with the implementation of the Land Reforms Acts passed by the Government of Kerala in 1969 and 1970. The development of transport and communication has facilitated the artisan castes like carpenters, blacksmiths, and goldsmiths to go to neighbouring places in Karnataka and Tamil Nadu in search of lucrative employment and return to the village on festive occasions.

Settlement Pattern

The settlement of the village is spread over a large area. There are independent households and also a cluster of houses. The independent households and clusters can easily be distinguished by caste. Houses of the people belonging to low castes and untouchables are located in certain pockets of the village away from the houses of the higher caste Hindu. Each house has its own compound and is enclosed by a fence made of bricks in case of rich people and bamboo for the poor. It may be pointed out that in former times the untouchable castes like the Irava, Kammala, and Harijan were not permitted to put fence of bamboo splits with inner parts exposed outside (*vellamalath velikettal*).

Houses in Anjumoorthy are rectangular in their ground plan, with their basement raised one or two feet above the ground level. The verandah in these houses are the distinguished feature of their architecture. A verandah or porch is indispensable during the summer months. Guests are received and entertained here. Men use the verandah for sleeping at night in summer that women seldom do. The entrance to the house is usually through a door opening from the verandah. There may be one or two doors of a house depending upon the financial position of the owner and its size. The roof is either tiled or thatched with palmyrah palm.

In early days the Irava, Cheruman, and other low castes were not permitted to tile their roof. They were not even allowed to use timber for making rafters, purlins, and trusses. Since Independence a number of them have built houses with tiled roofs and have used timber for various purposes. Houses belonging to the rich Tamil Brahman, Nair, and Irava contain costly and durable material and have also built storage chambers. Out-houses for shelter are occasionally constructed at the entrance to the courtyard. Every house has a courtyard. The yard is swept every day after applying an emulsion of cowdung once or twice a week. This is where important feasts and ceremonies both religious and secular are held. Milch cattle or draught animals are tethered to posts in annexes or on rear side of houses. Rich have built their cattle sheds away from their dwelling houses. The number of rooms in a house increases upto a certain extent along with the wealth of its owner. The untouchables have no more than one living room, one hearth, and a verandah. The rich Nair, Irava, and Tamil Brahman have separate rooms for storage, kitchen, sleeping, and sitting. The majority of the houses in the village belonging to the weaker sections have a single room which serves all purposes. A negligible percentage of the people, particularly the immigrant Christian, are living in rented houses.

The Tamil Brahman, Nair, and other higher castes have made their own arrangements for drawing drinking water from wells. The Cheruman and other polluting castes often fetch drinking water from the village wells, ponds, and tanks which are used for bathing, washing, and watering cattle. Now the rich Irava have their own wells. The village Panchayat and the Harijan Welfare Department have dug a few wells for the public which the Harijan also use. The Harijan colonies have been set up in the village by the Harijan Welfare Department.

The village is divided into three *taras*[1], viz., Thekke tara, Vadakke tara and Kizhakke tara (with 250, 374 and 330 households each). Each of them has a number of hamlets belonging to five to eight caste groups. Each caste is subdivided into several sub-castes or *jatis*. Traditionally each *tara* has its own local caste council for settling minor disputes. But serious cases were referred to the central council of the village. In olden times the Irava and artisan castes used to submit their disputes to the local Nair headman for adjudication. Now-a-days each caste manages its own affair.

Different castes living in three *tara* had prescribed functions to discharge at the time of annual temple festival managed by the Nair. Now the management of the village temple including the celebrations of the annual festival is vested with the Irava and Kammala.

Most of the shops and dwellings are located on either side of the main village roads. These have been built during the last three decades. The front portion of a house is used for running shops and backside for dwelling. The owners of these houses in most cases are the Muslim, Nair, and Irava.

Just off the main road, on the south west of the village lies the Thekke Gramam Road. On either side of this live the Tamil Brahman, Chozhadesa Vadama in their tile-roofed houses. Similarly the Vadakke Gramam road lies on the north west of the village, on either side of which live the Tamil Brahman (Chozhiyan). The eaves of these houses touch one another. Cattle sheds and gardens are behind the houses enclosed by fences. Two temples stand near the Thekke Gramam, one of which is dedicated to Siva and the other to Vishnu. Bathing ponds, exclusively meant for the use of the Brahman, are attached to these temples. The Brahman with their temples, bathing tanks, and caste shrines, thus occupy the south west corner of the village. The Vadakke Gramham have their Vishnu temple and an exclusive bathing pond.

There are only two Namputiri households in the village which are situated near the Anjumoorthy temple. There are three households belonging to the Ambhalvasi (temple servants) in Kizhakke tara but these are not far from the temple.

Eighty-five households belonging to the Nair are situated in the Vadakke *tara*, 50 in Kishakke tara and 43 in Thekke tara. No member belonging to the polluting castes like Irava, artisans and Harijan live near the house of Tamil Brahman and Nair. In each *tara* there is a *mannu* or *altara* (a raised platform at the foot of a baniyan tree near a temple dedicated to a Bagavathy). For instance, the Vadakke *tara mannu* is dedicated to the Cherumba Bagavathy whereas the Thekke *tara mannu* to the Managoti Bagavathi. The main village temple, Kizhekke tara mannu dedicated to the Managoti Bhagavathi is situated in Kizhekke tara. This temple was managed by the Nair. The village has another temple where Anjumoorthy (five deities Siva, Vishnu, Sasta, Ganapathy and Bagavathy) have been installed. This temple belongs to the Anjumoorthy Devaswam of which three Namputiri *illom* who owned 1200 acres of land in the village are the trustees but the management rests with the Nair who are the employees of the trust. The untouchable castes had restricted access to worship in the temples managed by the Brahman and Nair. The Namputiri priest attached to the temple lives near it.

The Irava who belong to various clans have their houses scattered in three *tara*. The Irava caste settlement is seldom called a *tara*. However, households belonging to a clan tend to congregate. The Irava were not formerly allowed to tile their houses and construct double storeyed houses. Only two Irava have double storeyed houses. It is therefore felt that they would invite the wrath of their village deities. Out of 300 Irava houses, 255 are thatched with Palmyrah leaves. Those who have their roofs tiled, have also their compounds demarcated by boundary walls. The Irava never had their own place of worship in the village. But they were under obligation to discharge certain prescribed rituals under the supervision of the local Nair during the temple festival.

There are forty households belonging to the Parava situated in Thekke *tara*. When the caste council of the Irava excommunicated some of its members for the violation of caste rules, the excommunicated persons found it very difficult to get spouses from the Irava. Consequently they were obliged to marry offsprings of excommunicated persons belonging to different castes. Since the group has been formed by members belonging to *pala jati* (different castes), it is called Palaver. The Paravar is thus a corrupt form of Palaver. Many of the Paravar are today tappers.

The settlement of the Kammal is called the Kammal *tara*. They consist of 54 households situated mainly in Thekke *tara*. Twenty six households belonging to two lineages of carpenters are huddled together on the eastern side of the Thekke *tara* Panchayat road. The blacksmiths have 14 households on the western side of the main road, near the village market. There are also six households belonging to the blacksmiths to the east of the main road, but opposite to Shree Krishna Saw Mill. Six households of the goldsmiths are found in the Nair Angadi (village bazar) to the south west of the main road in the Vadakke *tara*. The Kammala have rights of worship in the village shrines. They are obliged to discharge certain prescribed functions at the time of the temple festival. The Kaikkolar, who number 31 households, live in the Thekke *tara*. Their settlement is called the Kaikkola *tara*. They have their own temple dedicated to Mari Amma (deity of small pox).

The Vannans or washerman who have 15 households also live in the north of Thekke tara. The Vannan still performs his traditional duties. There is one family of the Kaniyan (astrologer) the members of which live near the Vadakke tara Govt.L.P.School. Twenty six households belonging to the Panan (barber-cum-musician) are situated south of Vadakke tara mannu. The Panan have their hair cutting saloons on the main village road at the Nair Angadi. They still discharge their traditional duties.

The Kumbara (potters) have their settlement in the Vadakke tara on the extreme north-west of the village. Their settlement is called Kumbara tara which consists of 14 households.

Twenty houses of the Vadukka (a Tamil immigrant caste) are scattered in all three *tara*. They are mainly cultivators and some of them run dairies.

The Veera Saiva (*pappad* maker) who have five households live in the east of the Nair Angadi. Ten houses belonging to the Naicker (Tamil immigrant masons) are situated in Vadakke tara to the west of the Anjumoorthy temple. There is a *Kavara tara* (settlement of the basket makers) with a total number of 10 households. Their houses are situated at the south-west of the Gandhi Smaraka Kendram Uttar Pradesh School. The two houses of the Chakkalian (leather worker) are situated near the Kizhakke tara Harijan Colony. There is only one house of the Thottiyan (engaged in piggery) which is situated at the north-west of Vadakke *tara*.

There are 25 Cheruman settlements in the village with a total number of 200 households. The settlement of the Cheruman is generally named after their homestead. However, the settlement of the Valluva Cheruman (a subcaste of the Cheruman) is known as the *Valla tara* and this consists of 26 households.

The Kanakka Cheruman who constitute the dominant element (164 households) in the Cheruman population live in different parts of the three *tara* at the periphery of the village. The houses of the Kuda Cheruman a sub-caste of the Kizhakke are near the Vishumala forest. It is interesting to point out here that among all the untouchables, the Kanakka Cheruman alone have their own shrines in honour of the Manangodi and the Cheruman Bagavathi. Apart from this, they have customary rights in the main Manangodi village temple.

Women belonging to the Irava, Cheruman, Kammala, and other lower castes were not permitted to cover their breasts about 35 years ago. Today young women among the Harijan put on blouses whereas the older ones do not cover their breasts. Irava maidens wear blouses while the elderly women either keep their breasts bare or throw a piece of cloth carelessly over the shoulders which may sometimes cover the chest. Elderly Nair women cover their breasts with a bodice, called *raoukka* in Malayalam while the younger ones wear brassiers and blouses over which they put on the sari. The men folk used to wear only a loin cloth and sported with the *kudimi* (tuft of hair worn or the front or back). Only a few Irava are found with *kudimi* in the Village. The Tamil Brahman wear *kudimi* even today. Almost all men comb their hair.

The Cheruman and other Harijan had to cut their hair by themselves in olden days. Now-a-days they go to the village saloons and have their hair cut. Young men in the village including the Harijan wear either a banian or a shirt while they are out. Some Cheruman youngsters wear shirts while they do agricultural operations. More children from the weaker sections of the population attend school these days and the news-papers are read daily by the villagers. Three decades ago newspaper was a rarity in the village. Today both Englich and Malayalam papers are read by the villagers.

The village has a upper primary and two lower primary schools. A high school at a distance of 5km. at Ayyakat caters to the needs of the students passing out from the local primary school.

Formerly the village had its own Panchayat. The Anjumoorthy Panchayat functioned independently until it was amalgamated with the present Vadakkanchery Panchayat. Thus, Anjumoorthy with two adjacent revenue villages at Vadakkancherry and Ayyakat has a common village Panchayat. The Panchayat office is at Vadakkan-cherry. The village office is also situated at Vadakkancherry.

Social Structure

The Namputiri Brahman in general occupy the top ladder of the Hindu caste hierarchy in Kerala. The two Namputiri families of Anjumoorthy do not enjoy that status as they are engaged as priests in the Anjumoorthy temple. They are not considered at par with the Namputiri of the rest of the State as they are immigrants from the Tulu *nadu* (South Kanara). They are no better than Potti and Embranthiri in the rest of the state. One of them has turned into a politician and is at present the D.C.C Secretary.

Below the Namputiri Brahman stand the Tamil Brahman. They belong to the Smarata sect. The Tamil Smarata of Anjumoorthy belong to the Vadama and Chozhiyan sections. The Vadama are segmented into Vadadesha Vadama and Chozhadesha Vadama of whom the latter is predominant. The Chozhiyan are divided into three endogamous groups, the Sadarana Chozhiyan, Mukkali Chozhiyan and Kozhakkan Chozhiyan. The Kozhakkan Chozhiyan are found in the village. Of the 24 Tamil Brahman households enumerated in the village in 1973, 13 are Chozhadesha Vadaman and all are Kozhakkan Chozhiyan. The former have their settlement in the Thekke Gramam (South Agraharam) while the latter in the Vadakke Gramam (North Agraharam). The Kozhakkan Chokhiyan officiate as priests at religious ceremonies. The Mukkali Chozhiyan are officiating priests at the Subrabraniya temple. The Sadarana Chozhiyan claim a superior status to the Mukkali Chozhiyan and Kozhakkan Chozhiyan. They are musicians and priests. The famous Karnatic Musician late Chembai Vaidyanatha Bagavatar belongs to Sadama Chozhiya. The Sadarna Chozhiyan are found in the Chembai and Mekkanakulam agraharam of Palghat District. The Chozhiyan have their tuft in the front whereas the Chozhadesa Vadama have it in the back. It is interesting to point out that the Kozhakkan Chozhiyyan are found only at the Vedakke Gramam of Anjumoorthy and Kodumthirapully village of Palghat District. The Kozhakkan Chozhiyan like the Namputiri follow the *Samaveda,* particularly the *Jaimini Sutra*. On the other hand the other two endogamous sub-divisions follow the *Rig* and *Yajur Veda.* The Vadama of Anjumoorthy follow the *Rig, Yajur* and *Sama Veda*.

Out of the 24 households of the Tamil Brahman, 20 own about 200 acres of land under the *Kanam*, *Janam*, and *Verumpatam* tenures. Some of them also own about 60 acres of land outside the village. A number of the Tamil Brahman are employed outside the village. Five Tamil Brahman have started cultivating their own lands. One of them is cultivating more than 60 acres of paddy fields. Many Tamil Brahman landlords are not getting their *pattom* (rent) for the past four years since the passing of the Kerala Land Reforms Act, 1969. Some of them are on the verge of starvation as they mainly depended on the *pattom* from their tenants for their livelihood.

Below the Brahman are the Ambalavasi (temple servants). They are divided into Varier (garland maker) and Marer (drummer). Below the Ambalavasi stand the Elayat, the priests of upper caste Nair. But the Elayat claim a superior social status than the Nair.

The Nair rank next to the Ambalavasi. They are the peasants and land owners (owner-cultivators). They are matrilineal and matrilocal. The Nair in the village are divided into Sudra, Charanath, Vattekkad, Pallichan, Athikurussi, Veluthedan, and Velakkathala segments. Hypergamous marriage is generally prevalent though no marriage between an upper caste Nair and Velakkathala Nair (Nair barber) or Veluthedan (Nair washerman) has so far taken place in the village. The division among the Nair is based on ranking attached to their traditional occupations such as agriculture, military service etc. For instance the Athikurussi Nair were ritual priests to the Nair community while the Pallichan were the palanquin bearers to the

Nair chieftains. Each social group is divided into several *tarawad* and *tavazhi*. The Athikurissi Nair still discharge their traditional ritual duties on the occasion of death and birth.

TABLE 1: Social Segmentation among the Brahman in Anjumoorthy and Ownership of Land

Category	Total No. of household	No. of house-hold owning	No. of persons
(1)	(2)	(3)	(4)
Tamil Speaking Smartha			
Chozhadesha Vadama	13	11	112
Kozhakkan Chozhiyan	11	9	65
Malayalam Speaking Smartha			
Namputiri Brahman	2		8
Total	26	20	185

One hundred and twenty five out of 178 Nair households have *verumpattam* (simple lease) and *kaman* (copy hold) tenures. Over 90 per cent of them cultivate land engaging Irava and Cheruman labourers. The Nair in the village formerly did not perform any manual operations connected with agriculture. A few Nair have started doing agricultural work in recent years with their own hands in their own fields as the labourers struck work in 1970 and 1971. Their *jenmi* (free holders) are the Namputiri, Kavalapara Moopil Nair (a Nair chieftain) Anjumoorthy temple devaswam (the trustees are three Namputiri families), Tiruvallamala Devaswam (trust under the former Cochin State) and the Cochin Devaswam (lands of the former Cochin State). Some of the Nair have sublet their land to Irava tenants. The majority of the Nair families have become owners of land they cultivated with the enactment of the Land Reforms Act of Kerala, 1969. There are three Nair families which hold Jenmam lands. Two of them are owner cultivators and one a non-cultivator. The latter is much affected by the implementation of the provisions of the said legal enactment. The Nair own more than 600 acres of land in the village. Only a few Nair own more than 600 acres of land in the village. Only a few Nair are working outside the village.

Below the Nair stand the Irava (toddy-tappers).Out of 300

households, 130 own about 300 acres of land in the village under the three tenures. Five Irava own only Jenmam lands varying from five to 30 acres. Twentyfive Irava own five to seven acres of land under the Kanam tenure and the remaining 100 Irava own lands below five acres on Verumpattam tenure.

It will be noticed from the above that 30 families make their livelihood from their land. They are economically better of. Out of 100 Irava who hold lands below 5 acres, 50 have to take up to agricultural labour as their secondary occupation. It may be mentioned that the Irava tenants in the village have applied to the land tribunal for getting ownership of lands. They have stopped payment of pattam to their landlords and intermediaries.

Seventy out of 300 Irava families depend on tapping toddy and agricultural labour. They have their own union called the Chethu Thozhilali Union. They have recently succeeded in getting enhanced prices for toddy, besides annual bonus. On the other hand 100 Irava families are engaged in farm labour. They are attached to the rich Tamil Brahman, Nair, and Irava. Agrarian movements started under the auspices of the Indian National Congress and the Communist Party of India (Marxist) have improved the lot of the Irava agricultural labourers who get higher wages today.

Ranking below the Irava are the Kaniya or village astrologers. A Kaniya is generally addressed by the title Panicker. Though lower in status, a Kaniya is generally respected by all for his knowledge of Sanskrit and astrology. The Kaniya claim today a superior social status than the Irava. Although they are landless in this village, they do not undertake any manual labour. The traditional duties of the caste are discharged by a Kaniyan who is in great demand in the village for his service such as prescribing auspicious time for movements for marriage and other ceremonies, causes of illness, prediction of future, etc. No marriage is settled among the Hindu in the village without matching the horoscopes of the partners. The Kaniyan is now paid mostly in cash. He has not stopped his personal call on the households of the peasants on the Vishnu festival day in April for supplying a copy of his forecast for the new year. The astrologer is consulted for the first ceremonial sowing and harvesting which are performed only after ascertaining the auspicious hours. There is only one Kaniya in the village.

Next to Kaniya stand the Kammala or the artisan. There are three artisan castes namely, goldsmiths, carpenters, and blacksmiths.

Although intermarriages among sub-castes of the Kammala is not generally allowed, there is interdining.

Among the artisan castes, the carpenters are numerically dominant in Anjumoorthy with 28 out of 54 households. Fifteen carpenters work for the past 10 to 15 years in the neighbouring district of the Nilgiri of Tamil Nadu. They pay their annual visit to the village at the time of temple festival which falls in the month of May every year. Only one carpenter holds three acres of Kanam land whereas the remaining carpenter families depend on their traditional calling for their living. The carpenters have recently formed their own union and once struck work for getting higher wages. Twelve blacksmiths work in Mysore and Coimbatore. The demand for the services of the Kamala, particularly those of carpenters, has gone up as a consequence of the improvement in the economic conditions of the Irava and Nair peasants. The peasants have built a number of houses with tiled roofs in recent years. The carpenters' wages have increased from Rs. 5.00 to Rs. 10.00 per day. The charge of blacksmiths has also shot up on account of the rise in demand for their services. Though the Kammala work for wages in any place, they do not forget to perform their traditional duties in the village.

The Kammala have produced one matriculate so far who is employed by the State Government. The womenfolk of the Kammala do not go for farm labour. In spite of the fact that the Kammala get higher wages, they have retained their traditional calling. They are a minority group numerically and as such are politically weak.

The Vaduka rank below the Irava. Out of 20 families, 10 own land ranging from two to five acres. The Vaduka is an immigrant caste. Some of them are running dairies.

There are 31 Kaikkola (weaver) families in the village and four of them own 2 to 5 acres of land. They speak Tamil. Next to the Kaikkola is the Veera Saiva (pappad Maker). They have the title of Gurukkal. Next to Veera Saiva is the Kumbaran (potter). Out of 14 Kumbara families four own land varying from one to three acres. Below the Veera Saiva stand the Vannan (weatherman for the upper polluting castes). There are 16 families of Vannan in this village. They have retained their traditional patron-client relationship. Out of 16 families two families own two acres of land each. They cultivate the land by employing agricultural labourers.

The Vannan used to wash clothes only for the Irava in the village. The Brahman and Nair used to get their clothes washed by the

Veluthedan (Nair washerman). Now-a-days the Vannan wash not only the clothes of the Irava but also those of the Brahman and Nair. The Vannan have, of late, started washing clothes of the Harijan which was not the case in former days. The Vannan even now supply a *mattu*, a piece of newly washed loin cloth, to the villagers (Nair and Irava) at the time of puberty, death, birth, marriage and for bathing just after the attack of small pox. Women at their first menstruation and child-birth use the *mattu* even today in order to purify themselves from ritual pollution. Similarly at the time of death all the mourners have to get the *mattu* before taking the purificatory bath. The *mattu* is necessary when a person takes his first and seventh bath immediately after an attack of small pox. Before Independence, the washermen were paid at the time of harvest and seasonal festivals in kind for their services. Now they are paid partly in kind and partly in cash.

Ritually ranking below the Vannana are Panan (barber-cum-musician). They act as messengers for the Irava. They have now opened their saloons in the village bazaar, where the Nair, Irava, and Harijan go in for their hair cut. Both the Panan men and women are proficient in folk songs, folk dances, and casting magical spells, especially, to save children from the effects of the evil eyes. They are also experts in making umbrella made of palm leaves for the use of farm labourers. They are attached to the peasant families and are obliged to supply the required number of palm leaf umbrellas to their patrons at the onset of monsoon. They also supply leaf plates to the Irava on ceremonial occasions. They even now are paid in kind during harvest seasons. The Panan are drummers. A few Panan today work as agricultural labourers under their Nair and Irava patrons. They are landless.

The Cheruman come next to the Pana. They are farm labourers attached to the Tamil Brahman, Nair, and the Irava. They were until recently tied labourers. During the time of author's field work in 1973 about 20 per cent of Cheruman labourers were found to be tied labourers in spite of the fight put up by the Karshaka Thozhilalai Union led by the C.P.I(M) and the Desiya Karshaka Thozhilalai Union led by the Indian National Congress for ameliorating their condition. Out of a total of 200 families, only one Kanakka Cheruman owns about five acres of land under *kanam* and *verumpattam* tenures and four Vella Cheruman held 2 acres each under *verumpattam* tenure. The Cheruman used to receive *alavu* a fixed measure of paddy, salt, and chillies from their masters. Once a Cheruman received the *alavi* from a particular patron he was obliged to work for a year under him. He could not normally seek employment without permission of his master. This unwritten contract was renewed every year, on the Vishnu day in April or on the Uchar day in March. This contract system was called *vishupidikkal* or *uchar pidikkal*. The Cheruman attached to the peasants were known as *janma cherumakkal*. They were given clothes at the time of the Onam festival.

Formerly a Cheruman was paid a pittance of paddy for his labour such as ploughing, harvesting, and digging. He was paid twenty fifth of the harvested yield as *pathembu* (harvesting wage). Now they have awakened and demand increased wages. Their wages have been increased consequent upon the direction of the Government and the agrarian movements led by the Indian National Congress and the C.P.I(M). A number of Cheruman agricultural labourers have been working for he construction of the national highway for the past three years. The commencement of the construction of the national highway in the village and in the adjoining areas has helped the Cheruman labourers to tide over their unemployment and financial difficulties. There is an increase in the circulation of money. This has also resulted in the severance of the traditional relationship between the Cheruman and their masters. During the construction of the national highway the Cheruman struck work and demanded higher wages. They, along with other labourers, also joined the National Highway Labour Union.

The Cheruman in this area are divided into four maximal endogamous sub-division, viz-Earyan or Kudan, Kanakkan, Valluvan, and Pulayan. The Kanakkan is segmented into minimal endogamous groups such as Patineshu Kanakkan and Ombatu Kanakkan. All these sub-divisions do not intermarry and there is no interdining. They have, in turn, their own hierarchical order: Erayan, Patineshu Kanakkan, Ombatu Kanakkan, Valluvan, and Pulayan. Pulayas of Malabar are categorised as a scheduled tribe, although they are one of the sub-castes of the Cheruman. They do not call themselves a tribe. The Erayan do not accept cooked food and water from the rest of the Cheruman. The Patineshu Kanakkan accept water and cooked food only from the Eraya. In olden times they never took food from the Ombatukar. Now-a-days the Ombatukar and Patinezhukar have started inter-marrying and inter-dining. However, the Kanakkan do not accept cooked food and water even today from the Valluvan and Pulayan. On the other hand, the Valluvan receive food and water from all other sub-divisions excepting the Pulayan. The Pulayan have been degraded as they remove the carcasses of cows and bulls (not dead buffaloes) and catch frogs. They eat beef but not the meat of buffaloes. While the Pulayan and Valluvan are matrilineal, the Eryan and Kanakkan are patrilineal.

TABLE 2: Social segmentation of the non-Brahman of Anjumoorthy and ownership of land

Category	Total No. of household	No. of house-hold owning	No. of persons
(1)	(2)	(3)	(4)
Ambalavasi (temple servants)			
Varier (garland maker)	1	—	3
Marar (drummer)	1	—	2
Elayat: Nair Group (cultivating castes)			
Sudra Nair	1	1	15
Charna Nair	34	29	242
Pallichan	100	68	450
Vettakad Nair	35	25	342
Athikurissi Nair	2	2	15
Veluthedan	1	—	6
Velakkathalavan	5	—	15
Irava :	300	130	1700/
Parava	40	1	238
Other cultivating communities :			
Henefee	62	14	329
Shafei	10	10	120
Vadukan	20	10	110
Artisan castes			
Tattan	6	—	45
Kollan	20	1	125
Asari	28	1	160
Kumbaran	14	4	65
Service castes:			
Kaniyan	1	—	10
Vannan	16	2	84
Panan	29	—	98
Kavara	10	2	47
Non-Malayalee castes :			
Kaikkolam	31	4	180
Naicker	10	1	58
Total	777	305	4459

In Anjumoorthy over 99 per cent of the Cheruman are

agricultural labourers. In view of the recent land legislation, they have become owners of their homestead. The overwhelming majority of the Cheruman are no longer the the *janma chrumakkal* in the village.

The solitary Thottiyan household in Anjumoorthy is engaged in its traditional occupation, piggery. They speak Telugu although they are settled in the village for several generations.

The Chakkalian are traditionally associated with leather work and beef eating. The Chakkalian of Anjumoorthy (two households) are engaged in their traditional occupation but their womenfolk work as agricultural labourer.

The Muslim are engaged in agricultural pursuits and retail trade. Out of a total of 72 households, 24 own land under different tenures varying from one to 12 acres.

TABLE 3: Social segmentation among the Harijan of Anjumoorthy and ownership of land

Category	Total No. of household	No. of house-hold owning	No. of land persons
(1)	(2)	(3)	(4)
Cheruman group:			
Kuda Cheruman	10	—	80
Kanakka Cheruman	164	1	648
Valluva Cheruman	26	4	219
Thottiyan	1	—	5
Chakkalian	2	—	7
Total	203	5	959

Castes in Anjumoorthy as any where else are organised into a hierarchical structure. Before Independence the Nair were decisively the dominant caste in Anjumoorthy as they had control over economic, political, social, and religious institutions. Since Independence, the Irava being numerically the dominant caste have become politically important. The land reforms initiated by the State Government and the activities of the labour Unions have awakened them. They have stopped paying rent to their Nair landlords. The traditional relationship between the landowner and tenants has been severed. However, the majority of the Irava and the Cheruman in the village are landless and as such still suffer from abject poverty, particularly during the agriculturally lean season. Thus, the artisan castes, service castes, and the Harijan and Irava are decisively the most weak sections in the village.

Economic organisation

The economy of the village is based primarily upon agriculture and hence the nature of the relationship is that of landlords, tenants and agricultural labourers. The relationship between the landlords (Nair, Irava, Namputiri, Tamil Brahman, etc.) and tenants (Nair and Irava) and agricultural labourer (Irava and Cheruman) today are governed by a number of legislations, political movements, and market forces, besides traditional norms and values. An important aspect of such relationship over the last three decades has been its continuously changing character. The recent changes in the class structure of Anjumoorthy can be understood only in the context of the state-wide peasant and political movements spearheaded by different political parties.

The organisation of agriculture in Anjumoorthy is such that most of the villagers, particularly the decisively weak sections of the populations such as the Harijan and Irava are in one way or other dependent on it for their livelihood. The arable land in Anjumoorthy is 2745-50 acres. This consists 1157.57 acres of wet and 1588.5 acres of unoccupied dry lands. Most of the wet land in the village is irrigated and is under paddy cultivation. Out of a total of 1157.75 acres of wet land, 836.17 acres have been brought under irrigation in 1959. Irrigation has increased the yield of agricultural crops. The demand for farm labour in Anjumoorthy has also gone up. The economy of the village has changed from one of subsistence to cash. Moreover, the irrigation has widened the gap between the upper class and middle class farmers on the one hand and those of the middle class farmers and the marginal farmers on the other. Irrigation has in fact strengthened the economic position of the Nair and Irava farmers. The agricultural labourers – the Irava and Cheruman – have now found it very difficult to assail the status of the former. Ultimately they have been forced to join the agricultural labour unions led by the Congress and the C.P.I.(M).

The process of production is organised in Anjumoorthy in such a manner that it involves the mutual co-operation of different sections of the villagers in accordance with their rights, duties, and obligations which are socially defined. The production process venerally creates cleavages and bonds between those who own land and those who do not. It is evident from the previous description that there is a marked difference between the big absentee landlords (Namputiri, Nair chieftains and Tamil Brahman)and the small-owner cultivators (Nair and Irava) who till the land with the help of their own labourers or that of their own family members. It has also been noticed from the foregoing pages that there is also a marked difference between small cultivators, tenant, and agricultural labourers.

The analysis of the relationship between different castes has to begin with a description of the principles of the land tenures. The nature of the tenures has undergone drastic changes, particularly during the last two decades. Land tenures in Malabar have a complex history and it is necessary to have some background of this in order to understand the agrarian relations obtaining today.

In olden times the threat of eviction and execution of eviction decrees was the major instrument by which many Irava families in Anjumoorthy were alienated from their lands. Even after passing of the Malabar Tenancy Act, 1929 eviction was a powerful weapon to extort more *pattam* and thus reduce the Irava peasantry to pauperism. Evictions were also directed against a number of intermediary tenants (Irava and poor Nair) in the drive of landlords (jemmi) against elimination of the *kanamadar* (intermediary). A large number of small Irava tenants were the worst victims. Even though several laws regarding land were enacted to give protection to tenants since 1952, there were several intermediary rights still to be abolished. But the Kerala Land Reforms (Tenancy) rules 1969, have given a final blow to the intermediary rights. This was possible because of an organised and strong peasant movement which was able to withstand the counter-pressure of the vested interests. All rights, title and interests of land owners and intermediaries in respect of holdings held by cultivating tenants entitled to fixity of tenure have been vested with Government on January 1, 1970 under the provisions of the Kerala Land Reforms (amendment) Act, 1969. But in Anjumoorthy the right of ownership has not been conferred on tenants so far, in a substantial number of cases due to apathy , if not active antipathy on the part of the Government officials who belong to the decisively dominant sections.

In Anjumoorthy the absentee landlords are Nair chieftains, and the temple trustees (trustees are Namputiri, Nair chieftains, and Tamil Brahman). These trusts own more than 50 per cent of the total land in the village. Land legislation since 1952, has progressively weakened the position of absentee landlords as well as non-cultivating land-owners. Thus, the old land owning castes of Namputiri Brahman, Nair, and Tamil Brahman have found themselves with their back to the wall. But it cannot be denied that a new land owning class from amongst the Irava of Palghat has also emerged in recent years. In 1970, the imposition of a ceiling of six to 20 acres of land gave final blow to the big land owners (Nair, Irava and, Tamil Brahman) of Palghat but not in Anjumoorthy. Not many were directly affected by the law, as almost all the estates in the village had been partitioned among the adult members of the family. It is often a matter of policy for a landowner to have title deeds entered even in the names of different members of his family. Sometimes the title deeds are registered in the names of distant kins - who may be living elsewhere. Thus, in Anjumoorthy the holdings of several individuals are managed, and administered by a person who does not have land in his name which is against the above prescribed ceilings. For instance, the biggest land owner residing in Anjumoorthy, a Tamil Brahman, has only five acres of land in his own name. Some of the land is recorded in his father's name, some in his several brother's name who are employed in Calcutta, Bombay, Delhi, and Washington and some even in the names of relations who are not members of his household. All this land (more than 70 acres), which nevertheless constitute a single unit for production purpose, is controlled and managed by a single individual who is also one of the legal heirs of the estate. A number of such cases have been noticed in the village. This has defeated the provision of ceilings in the Land Reforms Act, 1969. However, ceiling had a profound effect in altering the attitudes of investment among the land owners. It has been observed that no surplus land is likely to be made available for distribution among the landless poor when the provision relating to ceiling is implemented fully with great care, at least in Anjumoorthy.

Formerly, the number of owner-cultivators was confined to a few Nair. Today the picture is changing. Many Nair and Tamil Brahman have started cultivating their own land.

Thus we find that the ownership of Land is finally vested with three sections of the people.

1. A section of absentee landlords (temple trustees, Nair chieftains, Namputiri, and Tamil Brahman)
2. A section of non-cultivating land-owners residing in the village (Tamil Brahman and Nair)
3. Small holders, residents in the village (Nair, Irava, Muslim, Kaikkola, Vaduka etc.).

We may group the landlord-owners into two major divisions: rentiers and farmers. Rentiers are those who live on the *pattam* (rent) without contributing any manual labour to the agricultural operations. Farmers are those who contribute their labour either by physical participation in cultivation or by management. The rentiers in Anjumoorthy are the absentee land-lords and non-cultivating land-owners (Namputiri, Nair, and Tamil Brahman). On the other hand, the farmers are mainly the Nair and Irava.

The relationship between the rentiers and the farmers has been almost snapped. However, it has been observed that a number of Irava small farmers have paid their *pattam* to their landlords because they place value on personal relations and traditional norms. One of them has been cultivating the land attached to the Krishna temple of Tamil Brahman for the last 30 years. Although he was aware that the Government of Kerala had directed all farmers not to pay the contracted rent, he paid the *pattam* of 1972. He told me, "I do not want to earn the wrath of God. After all, I have been eating the food of God for the last 30 years. I do not want that the *puja* of the temple suffer on account of insufficient funds". It is however, reported that in 1974 all tenants in the village stopped payment of rent and applied in the Tribunal for ownership of land. It may be mentioned here that a number of Tamil Brahman widows are on the verge of starvation due to non-payment of rents by their tenants.

According to the existing land laws, a tenant needs to give 50 per cent of the contract which has been accepted as rent. He gets the ownership of the land by paying sixteen times the value of the fair rent in respect of the holding under his cultivation. The value can be paid in a lumpsum or in 16 instalments spread over 16 years. In Anjumoorthy, 120 Nair and 125 Irava families will be benefitted by this provision of the law.

The majority of the people who are engaged in agricultural operations are the landless Irava and Cheruman. They work on land owned by the Tamil Brahman, Nair, and Irave and thus constitute a link in the economic and social ties between different classes of people in the village. Most of the tenants (*Verumpattamdar*) are Nair and Irava. Most of the tenants having less than three acres land work as agricultural labourers.

The *kudiyan* (tenants) as a class, were the typical complement of the *janmi* (landlords). The general practice of the *janmi* was to let out their land to one or more Nair or Irava *kudiyan* who paid them a fixed quantity of grain at the end of the harvest. The *kudiyan* are required to meet the entire cost of production and only the land revenue is paid by the *janmi.* The relationship between the *janmi* and *kudiyan* was marked by cordiality and was more or less permanent. The recent land legislation has given a death blow to the ties between the *Janmi* and the *kudiyan* in Anjumoorthy.

There are two traditional systems for the lease of land, i.e., *kaman* and *verumpattam*. Both are prevalent in village. In the *kanam* system, the tenant (kanari or kanakkaran) gives a portion of the produce to the landlord (*jenmi*) and pay his tribute in kind every new year's day and at the succession of a new landlord. Most of the *kanari* in the village are Nair. Each Nair *kanari* household retains a portion of the land for cultivation by its agricultural surfeit, the Cheruman. The surfeits are attached to the plots on which they lived. Each *kanari* household gives portions of its land at a very higher rent to cultivating sub-tenants (*verumapattamdar*), who mostly are the Irava. Most of the *kanari* (copyholders) are non-cultivating tenants. They may be called the intermediaries between the *janmi* and the *verumpattamdar* – leaseholders. The *kanari* had to renew his tenure in every 12 years in former times by paying enhanced rent. This was known as *polichezhethu*.

The aim of the recent land legislation has been to make the tenants owners. The legislation has conferred fixity of tenure on the lessee and has taken away the right of the landlords and intermediaries to evict them for arrears of rent. Thus, it affords full protection to the tenants from eviction and fixes the fair rent by reducing the contract rent by 50 percent. A tenant is entitled to get ownership of the land which he cultivates by paying sixteen times the value of the fair rent. Some tenants are now richer than their landlords. This increased affluence among the peasant castes has shaken to a great extent the very foundation of the traditional social structure.

The Irava and Cheruman are the two agricultural labourer groups in Anjumoorthy. They differ in many ways from lessees or tenants. The striking difference between the agricultural labourers and tenants is that labourers get a very low wage. The agricultural labourers, particularly the Cheruman, were tied labourers until 1970. On the other hand, once a tenant acquired a lease he is assured of work and some fixed income. Until 1970, the Cheruman used to receive some fringe benefits from their masters. The majority of the Irava also work as permanent labourers but they do not receive fringe benefits. The agricultural workers were paid one-sixth of the crop they harvest. Their daily wages have increased by more than 50 percent.

The movements initiated by the Karshaka Thozhilali Union/ Agricultural Labourers' Union led by the Communist Party of India (Marxist) and the Congress-led Desiya Karshaka Thozhilali Union have severed the *patron-client* relationship that existed earlier. The agricultural labourers went on a strike under the instigation of the above two unions and observed *dharna* before the houses of landlord-peasants on a number of occasions in 1971-72 in order to press their demand for higher wages and security of employment. They have succeeded in getting their demands conceded. However, it has been observed that about 60 labourers in Anjumoorthy working under a Tamil Brahman landlord, are sympathisers of CPI(M), but have not participated in any strike so far. They wanted to retain their traditional relationship with their master to retain their master on the pretext that the latter had assured them employment throughout the year. It is interesting to note here that the Brahman landlord has not cared to increase the wages for harvesting and daily wages although most other landlords in the village have been forced to do so.

The State Government have passed the Kerala Karshaka Thozhilali Rules, 1974, a few months ago. This legislation had made provisions for the security of employment, provident fund, higher wages etc.

It is evident from the above that different classes of people are engaged in agricultural production. It is also seen from the foregoing pages that the ownership of land in the village vests mostly with absentee landlords. The relationship between different classes in production is not very cordial today as has been the case before the enactment of land legislations. Thus, changes in social and economic relationship have been brought about by political agencies, agrarian movements, and legislation besides external forces like irrigation and sophisticated marketing.

Agricultural labourers constitute more than half the total of the farm population in the village. They are very much class conscious and have started advocating class struggle. As is well known, these radical movements have met with success in Kerala. But the rising prices have both material and psychological effect on the agricultural labourers. Despite marginal increase in the money wages their financial conditions are declining as the prices are rapidly rising. Thus, the conditions of the agricultural labourers, the decisively weaker section of the population, have been aggravated in recent years due to the explosion in population and soaring prices coupled with unemployment and under employment.

During 1973-74, two land owners sold lands in the village but they were compelled to pay compensation to the labourers attached to their lands due to the timely intervention of the leaders of the agricultural labour unions led by the Indian National Congress as well as Communist party of India (Marxist).

There have been some radical political changes in Anjumoorthy as well. The members of the village Panchayat are elected on the basis of adult franchise. The majority of the members of the Panchayat are the Irava. A Cheruman is also a member of the Panchayat. The Panchayat election was fought on political issues. The villagers are politically conscious as there are office-holders of the Indian National Congress and the Communist parties in the village. The Irava and the Cheruman, as a result, play an effective role in the political life of the village.

The contribution of social, economic, and political factors have aroused expectations among the weaker sections, particularly the Irava and the Cheruman. Inequalities in the agrarian system, however, cannot be bridged unless and until the rise in price is timely checked (Beteille, 1974).

In the context of socio-economic changes, it is felt that the education may open a way for the weaker sections to come out from the enclosed society of the village to the wider world to create new attitudes and improving the traditional skills.

There are weaker sections of the population like the Irava, Cheruma, Kammala, and Muslim in the village of whom 70 per cent are normally illiterate. It has been observed that the educational attainments of a caste in the village depends to a large extent on its economic resources. Children between 10 and 14 belonging to the weaker sections (Irava, Cheruma, Kammala, Vadukka, Naicker, Kaikkola, etc.) are forced to discontinue studies because their services are required for earning a livelihood.

The weaker sections of the population have not been able to produce a graduate so far in this village. So long as the material support particularly the food is available for the Irava, they do not attach much importance to education.

Innovation

There are now 14 tractors in the village. Two of them are owned by a Tamil Brahman, two by the Muslim, three by the Irava and the remaining seven by the Nair. These have been obtained by paying a high price varying from Rs. 10,000.00 to Rs. 30,000.00. Some of these tractors have been purchased by taking loans from nationalised banks on the security of agricultural land. The number of tractors is not increasing as the villagers find that they require more financial support and frequent repairs. As a result, only the really well-to-do farmers having 15-60 acres have purchased tractors. Over 25 per cent of the landlord hire tractors by paying Rs. 20 to 25 per hour for ploughing. The tractors are mostly driven by the Irava and Cheruman of the village. The earliest innovator in this respect, a Tamil Brahman, has trained six Irava and six Cheruman in tractor driving. Four of them today work as tractor drivers outside the village.

Because of the growing independence of carpenters and blacksmiths and the higher wages demanded by the farm labourers the tenant cultivators (the Tamil Brahman, Muslim, Irava and Nair) who own substantial lands have been taking a great interest in labour saving devices.

Chemical fertilisers (urea and ammonium sulphate) are now used, besides cakes of groundnut and coconut. Prior to Independence, groundnut cake was considered a waste and chemical fertilisers were supposed to destroy the natural fertility of the soil. Fertilizers were generally obtained on credit from the local Service Co-operative Society which provides loans to its members against the security of crops. Forty to fifty per cent of the loan is given in fertilizer and the remainder in cash. Shareholders of the society get loans against the hypothecation of crops while non-members of the society have to buy fertilizers in open market at exorbitant prices.

The fee for a share is Rs. 5.25. The amount of loan advanced to a farmer depends upon the number of his shares in the society and the extent of the land he cultivates. However, the loan given to a shareholder is limited upto Rs. 3,000. Although the Service Co-operative Society is under obligation to meet demands of shareholders in respect of fertilizers, a number of them could not get fertilizers in 1972 and were forced to buy them in the open market at exorbitant prices. Better and high yielding varieties of seeds in large quantities are being stocked by the Department of Agriculture. Effective guidance has been given at least in Anjumoorthy concerning the sowing and harvesting of the seed, but a number of wealthy and able farmers are averse to adapt the innovation. The small holders have succeeded in the use of improved seeds. It cannot therefore, be said that the villagers have lagged behind in adapting innovations. It was thought to be a disgrace or a sign of poor management to borrow or buy seed in the past. The peasant takes special care in storing enough food to sustain his family and in preserving paddy seeds. When he buys the seed he has to make cash payment. He is very particular about the quality of seeds he buys. If a farmer gets a good crop by sowing improved seed, others buy seeds from him.

Since 1959, the village is irrigated by Mangalam and Pothundy dams. The advent of irrigation marks the turning point in Anjumoorthy's recent history.

Before the advent of irrigation, the majority of the peasants could not sow a second crop. Paddy, horsegram, blackgram, and cereals were cultivated before the advent of irrigation and villagers had more leisure but they had little cash. Only a few men drank toddy and *arrack* from illicit distillers and smoked cheap *bidi*. But today their number is on the increase. During the pre-irrigation days the weaker sections of the population could buy no more than a loin-cloth to cover their private parts. The villagers, particularly the Harijan and backward classes, seldom visited Palghat, not to speak of Alathur, the tahsil headquarters, about five kilometers away. The irrigation system has changed the face of Anjumoorthy. With it came new economic opportunities to the people of Anjumoorthy. Villagers, particularly, from the weaker sections, today wear shirts, use of which was restricted to the upper castes before Independence. Their womenfolk wear colourful blouses and clothes. Before Independence, women belonging to the weaker sections were prohibited to cover their breasts. Today they spend lavishly on dress during weddings and festivals. The menfolk from the weaker sections of the population pay frequent visits to Alathur, Vadakkancherry, and even to Palghat and frequent the coffee and liquor shops.

Drastic changes have occurred with the advent of irrigation; but all of them cannot be attributed to irrigation alone. There are other external economic stimuli operating at the same time such as food shortage and black marketing, growth of employment opportunities and the improved system of transport and communication facilities. All these stimuli and political forces have acted in unison upon the economy of Anjumoorthy and have brought about changes in the social structure of the village. Of the various economic stimuli affecting the village, irrigation and land reforms are the dominant, they made land more sustaining and cultivation more profitable. Sugarcane was not grown in the district but the establishment of a sugar mill at Chittur, has changed the situation. Sugar cane is grown by a Tamil Brahman and an Irava in Anjumoorthy and several farmers in the neighbouring villages.

The diet of the villagers has become less nutritious over the past 25 years. The staple food now is the rice. Milk and clarified butter are generally consumed only by the upper castes like Tamil Brahman, Namputiri Brahman and Nair. Today more food stuffs, mostly rice, are brought to Palghat, Alathur and Trichur from the village than was the case previously. Consumption of vegetables has increased among the weaker sections of the population. During the harvesting season when the ryots and agricultural labourers like the Irava and Cheruman have paddy in stock, they buy vegetables on cash payment. They even go to Vadakkancherry, the neighbouring village, where there is a market to buy dry fish. Tea and coffee are becoming popular among the weaker sections of the population. For instance, the menfolk from village invariably take coffee from local tan shops. It has also been observed that a number of Cheruman families have coffee without milk. Households of (over 500) the overwhelming majority of the weaker sections dispose of their rationed sugar every month to a CPI(M) leader at the rate of Rs. 1.29 per card. The CPI(M) leader, after he collects the rationed sugar, disposes it in black market at the rate of Rs. 4.00 per kilogram. It is gathered that some patrons of the Cheruman agricultural labourers give a loin cloth in return for their surrender of their rationed sugar throughout the year.

People belonging to the weaker sections eat meat, though often they cannot afford it. The Cheruman of the village formerly did not eat beef. Now-a-days a number of them take beef along with toddy. On certain week days, especially on Monday, Friday, and Saturday, vegetarianism is observed in honour of deities like Subramaniam, Bagavathi, and Lord Krishna (Guruvayurappan). The only one leather worker family in the village has stopped eating beef in recent years. They go to one pilgrimage at the Aiyappan Temple of Sabarimala every year. Consumption of dried fish and fresh fish getting popularised in the village. The Nair and Irava are now thinking of abandoning meat in order to raise their social status. Mill made coconut oil is used for the purpose of cooking. Cigarettes are smoked by a large number of villagers, besides *bidi* manufactured locally. The majority of the weaker sections drink liquor. A number of well-to-do Nair also consume liquor. There is a tendency among the Irava and Cheruman today to adopt food habits of the higher castes and abjure alcoholic drinks.

Conclusion

The economy of the Irava continues to depend wholly on agriculture, whereas that of the Nair being subjected to diversification led to closer integration with the regional economy.

We have seen that the rich peasants of Anjumoorthy were quick to adopt modern methods of cultivation and high yielding seeds particularly after the irrigation facilities reached the area. They do not lag behind in the mechanisation of farming and the use of chemical fertilizers. The mechanisation of farming and the availability of irrigation facilities improved the economic condition of rich and middle class farmer-peasants. The peasants could not get two crops before the advent of irrigation.

Many Nair have purchased land and constructed houses of their own. A few have bought taxis and tractors. A considerable number of them have taken up employment outside the village. A few of them have become owners of hotels in the village and the neighbourhood. Thus, the Nair of Anjumoorthy have improved their lot to a considerable extent. The interdependence between the Irava sub-tenants and the Nair tenants on the other hand diminished to a great extent resulting in the severance of the hereditary patron-client relationship Although the majority of the Irava do not have the control over the means of production, a few farmers among them have become very rich in recent years. Some of them own cars, tractors and taxis. The rice mill in the village is owned by the Irava.

There has been a perceptible change in economic opportunities, and traditional economic relations. The basic traditional structure, however, still persists, particularly among the weaker sections. For instance, the washermen, barber, and artisan castes even today discharge their traditional functions in the village. The introduction of chemical fertilizers, high yielding variety of seeds, and mechanisation of farming, coincided with the high demand for rice in other districts of Kerala. This attracted traders from South Kerala and Calicut to the village who were willing to buy rice in black market. The Nair and a few Irava got windfall gains from the sale of their stock of paddy. This changed the economy of the Irava to a limited extent from one of subsistence to cash.

The ties with the outside world did not affect the customary relations between the owner cultivators and agricultural labourers until 1970. The services of a large number of agricultural labourers were in great demand in the changed economic conditions. In fact, the Nair , Tamil Brahman, and Irava landlords were anxious to retain their labour forces, though several new Acts had been brought into force which compelled the villagers to raise the wages of labourers.

Social status in the village is still ranked in terms of land ownership and material possessions. Innovations like irrigation, mechanisation of farming, introduction of high yielding variety of seeds, and modern fertilisers have enhanced the economic capabilities. This did not mean that the hereditary position had been undermined by the time of passing of Land Reforms Act, 1970. Under the banner of the Unions organised by the Indian National Congress and C.P.I.(M), mass *satyagraha* and *dharna* were conducted in front of the houses of big farmers. Thus, the agricultural labourers awakened themselves and demanded higher wages. This resulted in decreasing the reliances on the Irava and Cheruman labourers for agricultural operations. Some of the rich farmers sought intervention from the High Court in 1971 and 1972 to restrain the agricultural labourers from resorting to strikes on the plea that their crops were liable to the damaged on account of illegal strikes. Thus, they were allowed by the Court to bring labourers from Tamil Nadu for harvest of crops under police protections. Such arrangement became impossible after the enactment of the Kerala Karshaka Thozhilali

Bill, 1975. The agricultural labourers prefer work on the farms to any other form of occupation. They have grown in an agricultural environment with personal relations maintained with the owners of land. The majority of the labourer suffer from grinding poverty, but they all nurse the hope that one day they too would become owners of land.

The Nair are no more the arbitrators in caste disputes among the untouchable castes including the Irava. The traditional political relationships between the Nair and Irava have been completely snapped. The villagers have already begun to understand that the leadership need not be hereditary. However, among the weaker sections of the population the indigenous caste panchayats still function. But they are today less effective as a council. In Anjumoorthy, the break in the traditional economic relationship between the land owner and tenants on the one hand and former and agricultural labourers on the other has led to a severance of ritual relations to some extent between the individual households involved. Since the agricultural labourers refused to accept the customary annual rewards since 1972 from their peasant masters, the latter refused to advance loans to the former at the time of marriage and life cycle rites. When the Irava were not allowed to sit in the same row where the Nair used to sit during the performance of the ritual celebrations they forcibly took up the management of the temple. This resulted finally in a caste conflict between the Irava and Nair. The annual temple festival in the village is now conducted under the leadership of the Irava.

The farmers of Anjumoorthy have their customary ritual relations with the functionaries of some selecteed castes. The barber and washermen continue to perform their traditional duties in their patrons' houses during life cycle rites. Though ritual still plays a vital role in the life cycle of the peasants and some castes play some roles, but economic roles of such castes are declining. During the whole stay in the village, the author did not see a single ceremony performed with the co-operation of all sections of the population. We have already seen how the conflicts between the Nair and Irava led to the non-participation of Nair in the temple festival. This had also led to the ritual conflict in the village, between the high and low castes.

NOTE

1. Any kind of raised foundation is called a *tara* (meaning neighbourhood). This is derived from the large earthen platform around a scared milk extracting tree (*alstonia* scholaris) located near temple dedicated to Bhagavathi. The village leaders assemble on this mound.

REFERENCES

Botoillo, Andre *Studies in Agrarian Social Structure*. Oxford University Press, Delhi, 1974.

———, *Caste, Class and Power*. Oxford University Press, Bombay, 1969.

Epstein, T.S. *Economic Development and Social Change in South India*. Manchester University Press, 1962.

Mathur, P.R.G. "Caste Council among the Namputiri Brahmans of Kerala", *The Eastern Anthropologist*. Vol.XXII, No.2, 1969.

———, "The Mappila Fisherfolk of Kerala. A study in Inter-relationship between Habitat, Technology, Economy, Society and Culture". Ph.D Thesis(in the press).

Misra, P.K. "Economic Development among the Jenu Kurumbas", *Man in India*. Vol.50, No.1, 1970.

Sinha, Surajit "Caste in India, its Essential Pattern of Socio-cultural Integration", Reprinted from symposium on *Caste and Race Comparative Approaches*. 1967.

Srinivas, M.N. *Social Change in Modern India*. Allied Publishers, Bombay, 1967.

CONCLUSION

Under the project "The Weaker Sections of the Indian population" 24 villages were selected for intensive survey (ranging from 3 to 6 months of fieldwork) in 16 states of India. The main objectives of these village studies were (1) to identify the weaker sections in terms of their access to the socio-political control institutions and control over land, (2) to find out the social disabilities suffered by the weaker sections and also the socio-cultural implications of their being weak, (3) to spell out socio-economic and political constraints, and (4) to find out why there has been only marginal improvement in the socio-economic condition of the weaker sections. As per the preamble attached to the research guideline of the project it was proposed to define the social situation of the decisively weak sections, particularly of those who have either no control or least control over local resources-economic, political, social and communicational.

These village studies covered 386 communities of which as many as 176 communities were identified as forming the weaker sections on account of their low access to the socio-political institutions and poor control over land and other resources. Analysis of descriptive material and computer analysis of quantitative information generated under this project suggests that these 176 communities either have no control or have least control over local resource – economic, political, social and communicational, in their respective villages. Our review also reveals that all of these 176 weak communities invariably belong to lower or lower-middle strata of caste hierarchy in their respective villages. Fortytwo communities among them are identified as Harijan or untouchables. In fact all of these Forty-two scheduled castes emerge as 'decisively weak' in terms of these five parameters such as access to land, literacy, socio-ritual status, participation in political institutions and use of communicational networks.

Though one of the major objectives of this project was to identify the weaker sections in terms of access to the socio-political institutions and control over the land, all researchers have invariably found it appropriate to explain the phenomenon of *weakness* broadly in terms of the socio-ritual stratification of the Indian rural society shaped by the *varna-jati* model. Almost all reports reveal that the caste system retains its over-powering influence on social situation. Thus these reports have distinctly shown that the caste differentiation and hierarchy fairly correspond with economic differentiation and socio-economic inequality. Review of the reports suggests that while in Haryana and Punjab the Harijan castes such as Chamar, Chuhra and Dhanak exclusively form the bulk of the weaker sections, no community could be identified as the Harijan or untouchable among the weaker sections in West Bengal and Tripura.

The following are the Harijan (untouchable) communities who have been identified as the decisively weak castes in different states covered under this project.

1. Andhra Pradesh	1. Baindla
	2. Mala
	3. Madiga
2. Assam	1. Hira
3. Bihar	1. Chamar
	2. Dhobi
	3. Dusadh
	4. Mahar
	5. Mehtar
	6. Pasi
4. Gujarat	1. Dhedha
5. Haryana	1. Chamar
	2. Chura/Chuhra
	3. Dhanak
6. Karnataka	1. Dhor
	2. Madaru
7. Kerala	1. Kaniyan
	2. Naicker
	3. Parvan
	4. Shafei
	5. Cheruman
	6. Irava
8. Madhya Pradesh	1. Dhanak
	2. Nona Chamar
	3. Ladiya

9. Maharashtra	1. Chambhar
	2. Ramozhi
	3. Mang
	4. Meher
10. Orissa	1. Gokha
	2. Hadi
11. Punjab	1. Chamar
	2. Chura/Chuhra
12. Rajasthan	1. Balai
13. Tamil Nadu	1. Parayan
	2. Naicker
14. Uttar Pradesh	1. Chamar
	2. Churot
	3. Pasi
	4. Kori
	5. Hela
	6. Dhobi

Indian society based on *varna-jati* model assigns the lowest position to those who are considered untouchables because of their impure calling. The Hindu concept of purity and pollution is so over-powering that everybody who practises the impure profession or otherwise, is subjected to the socio-ritual constraints.

The Harijan communities shown above are placed at the lowest strata of the caste hierarchy in their respective village and state. In many states they are referred to as 'untouchables'. They are not only economically impoverished and socially handicapped but also continue to suffer from the stigma of being unclean and unhygienic. The Harijans in some parts of India are prevented from drawing water from the wells of higher castes. The Harijans live in isolated settlements away from the main village settlements.

Absolute landlessness, meagre income, illiteracy, poor participation in political institutions and lowest socio-ritual status are the five main factors which place the untouchables in the decisively weak category among all the weaker communities covered under this project.

Considering the two most important factors of absolute landlessness and low socio-ritual status, the following forty communities in different states form the weakest segments of Indian population, other than the Harijan, as revealed through these reports.

1. Assam	Namsudra
2. Bihar	Turah, Dhanuk
3. Gujarat	Bhausar, Soni, Sutar
4. Karnataka	Iliga
5. Kerala	Panam, Thottiyan, Tattan
6. Orissa	Kharura, Kumbhar, Mali, Keot
7. Maharashtra	Khati, Wadhai, Bhuti, Mahali, Kosti, Beldar, Panhal
8. Tamil Nadu	Mannwodder, Varnam
9. Tripura	Mahisya Das
10. Uttar Pradesh	Barai, Jogi, Kahar, Gadaria, Dhuna, Aheria, Dhimar, Kumhar
11. West Bengal	Bauri, Barui, Badia, Charal, Dom, Dhopa, Hari,Suri

We have thus identified above the two categories of 'Weaker Sections' (Harijan and non-Harijan) mainly in terms of 'total landlessness' and 'low socio-ritual status' in caste hierarchy.

The stratification system of Hindu society is so all-pervasive that even the non-Hindu and tribals, who apparently fall outside the *Varna-jati* framework, have come to be accorded ascribed positions in the regional caste hierarchy. Thus the non-Hindu and tribals in these village studies are not treated as independent entities, outside the *jati*-based stratification system. The only exception in this regard is the Tripura village which has its feudal background and a strong tribal base in the Tripura village (old Agartala), studied under this project, where application of caste prescriptions appear less rigid. Basilardanga, a village from North Bengal, with a strong tribal base, approximates to the Tripura village in many respects.

The following list provides names of those communities (including tribals) who emerge as weak communities in their respective states, though not all of them occupy low ritual status and some members of these communities are even in possession of some amount of land.

Andhra Pradesh	Ausula, Aiyavaru, Bhata-Raju, Bogam, Chakali, Golla, Ganda, Kattika, Kuruva, Kummari, Komati, Kammari, Lingayat, Mangali, Muthirashi, Vod-deru, Vodala.
Bihar	Barhi, Kumhar, Momin, Nunia, Nauwa, Sundi, Teli

Gujarat	Dubla
Karnataka	Holeya, Kumbar, Kurubagond, Kabbaliga, Panchal, Varik, Waddar.
Kerala	Asari, Chakkaliyan, Kaikkolam, Kumbaran, Kavara, Kollan, Vannan, Vadukan.
Orissa	Guria, Patra, Barik, Sankhari, Tanti
Madhya Pradesh	Dhobi, Kuch Bondi, Kabir-Panth, Sonar
Rajasthan	Jogi, Rana
Tamil Nadu	Ambatten, Pallai, Tambiran.
Tripura	Dhopa, Jugi-Debnath, Kumbhar, Kaibarta, Malakar, Natya, Sunri, Tripuri
Uttar Pradesh	Bhuj, Dhobi, Khatik, Kalowar, Teli
West Bengal	Adhikari, Bagdi, Bhumij, Chick, Dule, Goala, Jele, Jolha, Kumhar, Keora, Karan, Kora-Mudi, Kolu, Mahali, Mahato, Mahishya, Napit, Pod, Rajbanshi, Santal, Sahis, Tanti.

Although much occupational mobility has taken place in rural India during post-Independence era, the Harijan and other lower caste people have invariably adopted the job of agricultural labour almost all over India by abandoning partially or totally their traditional occupations. Among the Harijan only the Chamar and some other communities have continued to pursue the occupation of leather-work to a lesser or greater degree. In fact these were the communities who were never dependent upon land for their livelihood even in pre-independence era. Hence land could not be regarded as a viable criterion for determining the weakness of a community. Land possession, however, remains a very important factor in helping us to determine the notions of dominance and weakness in rural India.

We may now discuss the total number of villages and communities studied under the project, distribution of weaker sections (Harijan and non-Harijan, identifying them as 'decisively weak' and 'weak' communities respectively), and the extent of landlessness and land-possession among the weaker sections in 16 states, with the help of the following table. We have divided these states into five zones in the table and the discussion that follows for convenience.

Zone/State	No. of villages studied	No. of communities studied	Identification of decisively weak and weak communities** — WEAKER SECTION: Non-Harijan	Harijan	Total	No. of landless communities	% of landless among non-Harijan	% of landless among the Harijan	% landless among the total weaker section
1 2	3	4	5	6	7	8	9	10	11
I. Eastern Zone									
1. Assam	1	6	1	1	2	0	—	—	—
2. Bihar	2	35	11	6	17	4	(2) 18.18	(2) 33.33	(4) 23.53
3. Orissa	1	15	10	2	12	4	(3) 30.00	(1) 50.00	(4) 33.33
4. Tripura	1	18	9	0	9	1	(1) 11.11	— —	(1) 11.11
5. West Bengal	4	56	30	0	30	8	(8) 26.67	—	(8) 26.67
II. Western Zone									
1. Gujarat	1	8	4	1	5	3	(3) 75.00	—	(3) 60.00
2. Maharashtra	3	50	8	4	12	9	(8) 100.00	(1) 25.00	(9) 75.00
3. Rajasthan	1	9	2	1	3	0	— —	—	—

(Contd.)

(*Contd.*)

1 2	3	4	5	6	7	8	9	10	11
III. Northern Zone									
1. Haryana	1	10	—	3	3	3	—	(3) 100.00	(3) 100.00
2. Punjab	1	8	—	2	2	2	—	(2) 100.00	(2) 100.00
3. Uttar Pradesh	3	67	13	6	19	8	(8) 61.54	0	(8) 42.11
IV. Southern Zone									
1. Andhra Pradesh	1	22	17	3	20	NA	—	—	
2. Karnataka	1	16	8	2	10	1	(1) 12.50	—	(1) 10.00
3. Kerala	1	33	11	6	17	5	(3) 27.27	(2) 33.33	(5) 29.41
4. Tamil Nadu	1	15	6	2	8	4	(3) 50.00	(1) 50.00	(4) 50.00
V. Central Zone									
1. Madhya Pradesh	1	18	4	3	7	NA	—	—	—
Total 16 (States)	24		134	42	176	52	29.85	28.57	29.55

N.B. Figures within parenthesis are numbers of communities within the state.

** Shri B Dey, Senior Statistician and Shri B.N. Sarkar, Anthropologist (P) have helped the author in preparation of this table.

This above table discloses that out of 176 weaker communities, 52 communities are absolutely landless (29.55%). It also reveals that most of the weaker sections in the states of Karnataka, Kerala, Tripura and Bihar possess some amount of land, while in Haryana and Punjab the weaker sections do not possess any land. With regard to land possession among the weaker communities there is no marked difference between the Harijan and non-Harijan communities. The fact, however, remains that the quality of land owned by the Harijan, whether in north India or south India, is invariably inferior.

Reports from Tamil Nadu, Kerala, Karnataka and Andhra Pradesh, roughly in that order, have suggested the process by which the Brahman have been displaced from their pre-eminent position by the land-owning middle range castes of the respective regions. These castes captured the prominent positions in the political arena. In Kerala, on the other hand, a good number of tenants belonging to lower castes have acquired land. Some individuals of the lower castes (Irava and Cheruman) also gained important positions in the political arena. Lower caste associations formed across villages helped them.

Anjumoorthy is a multi-caste village studied under this project in Palghat district of Kerala. Traditionally the castes in this village have been hierarchically organised but there has been some reshuffling of positions in terms of dominance. Before independence the Nayar exercised control over economic resources and controlled socio-political institutions. The situation dramatically changed after independence. The Irava, the most oppressed caste of the past, who have a numerical edge over others, have now gained political dominance, and their economic position has also changed owing to several land reform acts. The Irava who were once mostly tenants of the Nayar landowners do not pay any more rents to them. The traditional landowner-tenant relationship has thus broken down. On account of irrigation facilities the economy of the village has changed from subsistence to cash. The economic interests of the labourers are protected by the Kerala Krashak Tozhilali Act, 1974, according to which the agricultural labourers are to be provided security of job, higher wage and facilities such as the provident fund. The agrarian movement, political activities and legislation have brought about changes in social and economic relationships. There are unions of agricultural labourers. The Irava and Cheruman, two oppressed castes, now play an effective role in political life of the village. In fact, the political initiative in the village now rests with the Irava, who are not only larger in number but also have strong linkages outside the village.

Unlike south India, the phenomenon of weakness could be observed in most parts of north India in terms of the ascribed stratification model (Varna-Jati). Let us discuss Bihar situation. Bihar is represented by two village studies in this book. In Sikri, a south Bihar village, the untouchables are not allowed entry into village shrines. Political authority is under the control of the upper castes. There are two Rajput families in the village who have pucca buildings. They control trade and business of local products. One Bania family having not much land is also engaged in trade and business. They sell local products, maintain a grocery, liquor shop, and a fair price shop. The forefathers of these Rajput and Bania families were landlords and Zamindars and that Lala families were in the service of the rulers. These families try to maintain the dignity of their forefathers but today village people do not show much respect to them. They possess fire arms and one of the Rajput families occasionally employs wrestlers to scare the village people. In Hamidur, the north Bihar village, the upper castes are dominant in terms of landholding, literacy and political control, although they are weak in numerical strength. The Dusadh and Chamar, in spite of their numerical strength are weak on all counts such as land-holding, education etc., and they remain where they were in the past.

Most of the reports have shown that those who are placed low in caste hierarchy generally strive for attaining a higher status. The Harijans are no exception. While the process of gaining higher social status at the individual level, through the process of sanskritization, is more pronounced in most parts of rural India, the Kanakku Pillai community, as observed in the Tamil Nadu village under this study, have succeeded in raising their social status at group level, to such an extent that even the Brahman eat food provided by them.

The following steps were taken by the Harijans to raise their status in Polyasivaram, a Tamil Nadu village.

(i) Adopt vegetarianism permanently or observe vegetarianism on certain occasions such as new-moon days, Saturdays etc.
(ii) Give up eating beef.
(iii) Observance of ancestor worship among the Harijan and other lower castes.

(iv) Adoption of the practice of negotiated marriage. Previously marriage by elopement and bringing a wife home without any formal celebration was the accepted norm.

Social reform movements are reported among the following communities (Harijan, tribals and other weaker sections) in different states.

1. Assam	Hira
2. Bihar	Nunia, Turah
3. Gujarat	Dubla
4. Karnataka	Dhor
5. Kerala	Naicker, Marar
6. Maharashtra	Gond, Mang
7. Uttar Pradesh	Dhimar, Gadaria Lohar
8. West Bengal	Moira

In the Vidharbha region of Maharashtra the Mahar are numerically dominant who came to be enumerated as Bouddha in 1961 Census. The Neo-Buddhist movement initiated by Dr. Ambedkar and subsequently formation of the Republican Party of India gave the Mahar a new identity. They embraced *enmasse* Neo-Buddhism in 1956. By doing this they intended to eradicate social injustice and promote economic betterment. Eradication of mass illiteracy was yet another objective of these Mahars. Conversion of the Mahar to new faith did not give them the social status they aspired for. Some caste Hindus still consider the Neo-Buddha inferior.

The general picture that emerges out of these studies is that the gap between the affluent and weaker sections in villages was wide. In most villages those who needed the benefits the most could not utilise the development programmes to their full advantage. There were exceptions like the Irava of Kerala, the Bouddha of Maharashtra, the Ladiya of Madhya Pradesh and to some extent the Dubla of Gujarat who deviated significantly from the general ascribed stratification pattern and demonstrated resistance to the age-old *Varna-jati* based system and a capacity to improve their position and status.

N.K. DAS

LIST OF CONTRIBUTORS

Dr. Surajit Chandra Sinha
Former Director
Anthropological Survey of India
Udayachal, Shyambati
P.O. Shantiniketan, W.B. 731235.

Dr. K.S. Singh
Director General
Anthropological Survey of India
27, Jawaharlal Nehru Road
Calcutta-700016.

Dr. R.K. Bhattacharya
Acting Director
Anthropological Survey of India
27, Jawaharlal Nehru Road
Calcutta-700016.

Dr. N.K. Das
Anthropological Survey of India
27, Jawaharlal Nehru Road
Calcutta-700016.

Shri S.K. Mukherjee
Anthropological Survey of India
North Eastern Regional Centre
Lachumiere, Shillong.

Shri Bhabananda Mukherjee
Former Superintending Anthropologist (Cultural)
Anthropological Survey of India.

Shri Pranab Jyoti De
Anthropological Survey of India
North Western Regional Centre
192/1, Kaulagarh Road
Dehra Dun-248195.

Smt. Gopa Banerjee
Anthropological Survey of India
2, Ripon Street, Calcutta.

Smt. Chandrima Chaudhury
Anthropological Survey of India
Eastern Regional Centre
27, Jawaharlal Nehru Road
Calcutta-700016.

Dr. S.B. Chakraborty
Superintending Anthropologist (C)
Anthropological Survey of India
North Eastern Regional Centre
Lachumiere, Shillong.

Shri Sem Topno
Former Assistant Anthropologist (Cultural)
Anthropological Survey of India
Now Education Officer, U.G.C.
New Delhi-110002.

Shri Pijush Chaudhury
Anthropological Survey of India
Eastern Regional Centre
27, Jawaharlal Nehru Road
Calcutta-700016.

Shri A.P. Nandan
Anthropological Survey of India
27, Jawaharlal Nehru Road
Calcutta-700016.

Shri Sunil Mitra
Anthropological Survey of India
Western Regional Centre
16, Madhuban, Udaipur-313001.

Shri P.C. Hembram
Formerly of Anthropological Survey of India; now posted in All India Radio.

Dr. (Mrs.) Dipali G. Danda
Anthropological Survey of India
Central Regional Centre
11, Seminary Hills, Nagpur-6.

Dr. D.K. Samanta
Anthropological Survey of India
Western Regional Centre
16, Madhuban, Udaipur — 313001.

Late Shri N.N. Kundu
Former Assistant Anthropologist (Cultural)
Anthropological Survey of India
North Eastern Regional Centre
Lachumiere, Shillong;
Residence : 21/1 Ramgarh
Dakshineswar, Calcutta.

Shri Sadhan Sengupta
Anthropologist (C)
Anthropological Survey of India
North Eastern Regional Centre
Lachumiere, Shillong.

Shri Hasan Ali
Anthropologist (C)
Anthropological Survey of India
Southern Regional Centre
2963, Gokulam Road, Mysore-570002.

Shri Sukumar Banerjee
Former Superintending Anthropologist (Cultural)
Anthropological Survey of India
27, Jawaharlal Nehru Road
Calcutta-700016.

Shri S.P. Lala
Anthropologist (C)
Anthropological Survey of India
27, Jawaharlal Nehru Road
Calcutta-700016.

Dr. William Ekka
Anthropologist (C)
Ranchi Field Station
Anthropological Survey of India
C/o The Department of Tribal and Regional Languages
Ranchi University, Morabadi
Ranchi-834008.

Shri Bageshwar Singh
Anthropologist (C)
Anthropological Survey of India
Southern Regional Centre
2963, Gokulam Road, Mysore-570002.

Shri D.B. Mandal
Anthropologist (P)
Anthropological Survey of India
Eastern Regional Centre
27, Jawaharlal Nehru Road
Calcutta-700016.

Dr. Ashim Maitra
Anthropological Survey of India
27, Jawaharlal Nehru Road
Calcutta-700016.

Shri T.N. Pandit
Joint Director
Anthropological Survey of India
27, Jawaharlal Nehru Road
Calcutta-700016.

Dr. S.G. Morab
Former Superintending Anthropologist (Cultural)
Anthropological Survey of India;
Residence : L-18, Ist Stage
Kuvempunagar, Mysore-570023.

Mrs. Rajalakshmi Misra
Former Assistant Anthropologist (Cultural)
Anthropological Survey of India
Southern Regional Centre
2963, Gokulam Road, Mysore-570002;
Residence : 108, Ganesh Gunj
Nawaiah, Lucknow, U.P.

Dr. P.R.G. Mathur
Formerly of the Anthropological Survey of India, and former Director of KIRTAD.
Residence : P.O. Agraharam
Palghat-678571, Kerala.

INDEX